Avolution and Man

Jiayou Liew

Avolution and Man

© Jiayou Liew 2015

All rights reserved. No part of this publication may be reproduced, stored in a retrieval system or transmitted in any form or by any means, electronic, mechanical, photocopying or otherwise, without prior permission in writing from the copyright owners.

Library and Archives Canada Cataloguing in Publication

ISBN 978-1-77221-037-8

Printed and bound by York University Printing Services
Printed in Canada

Contents

Preface 7

Chapter I Symmetry I: the Coming into Being of Animals, or, the Coming into Being of Man 9

§ 1.1 Symmetry, or Harmony: the Coming into Being of Life 9

§ 1.2 The Coming into Being of Double Helical Symmetry: from RNA to DNA 10

§ 1.3 The Coming into Being of Sexual Symmetry: from Asexual Reproduction to Sexual Reproduction 13

§ 1.4 The Coming into Being of (Bilateral) Symmetry in Animals: the Primordial Explosion 16

§ 1.5 The Fulfillment or Realization of Symmetry: the Coming into Being of Man 103

Chapter II Symmetry II: the Coming into Being of Plants 109

§ 2.1 The Coming into Being of Bilateral Symmetry in Plants: the Devonian Explosion 109

§ 2.2 The Fusion of Bilateral Symmetry and Sexual Symmetry: the Coming into Being of Flowers 178

Chapter III Symmetry, Harmony, and Avolution 235

§ 3.1 Avolution, the Word, the Term, and its Meaning 235

§ 3.2.1 Symmetry in Plants 242

§ 3.2.2	The Ordovician Radiation	243
§ 3.2.3	The Primordial Explosion	244
§ 3.2.4	The Primordial Explosive Moment	245
§ 3.2.5	Symmetry and the World	245
§ 3.2.6	The Division between Radial Symmetry and Bilateral Symmetry	246
§ 3.2.7	The Journey of Life on Earth	248
§ 3.2.8	The Origin of Species	249
§ 3.2.9	Genetics and Complexity	250
§ 3.2.10	Comb Jellies	251
§ 3.3	Harmony, Science, and the World	252
§ 3.4.1	Symmetry and Physics	267
§ 3.4.2	The Fundamental Forces	267
§ 3.4.3	Energy, Space, and Symmetry	273
§ 3.4.4	Dark Energy, and the Cosmic Symmetry	275
§ 3.4.5	The Expansion of the Universe	278
§ 3.4.6	The Cosmic Symmetry, and the Cosmic Microwave Background	282
§ 3.4.7	The Big Bang, and the Cycles of Universe	287
§ 3.4.8	The Big Bang, the Big Split, and the Harmonic Being	289
§ 3.4.9	The Higgs Field	290
§ 3.4.10	$E = mc^2$	292
§ 3.4.11	Taijitu, the Diagram of the Supreme Ultimate	292
§ 3.4.12	The Ecliptic	294
§ 3.5	Symmetry, Harmony, and Development	294
§ 3.6	Symmetry, Harmony, and Avolution	355
§ 3.7	The Untitled	361

Chapter IV Humorality: as the Fulfillment of Symmetry or Realization of Harmony . 371

§ 4.1	Humorality, Anteanity	371
§ 4.2	The True	372

§ 4.3.1	The Good	403
§ 4.3.2	The Coming into Being of the Good	404
§ 4.3.3	The Common Good	406
§ 4.4	The Coming into Being of Meaning	407
§ 4.5.1	Heart	412
§ 4.5.2	Heart is the Way	417
§ 4.6	The Human Being and the Harmonic Being	418
§ 4.7	The True and Man	419
§ 4.8.1	The Humoral and the Animal	420
§ 4.8.2	The Animal	421
§ 4.9	Harmony and Man	422
§ 4.10	The Unfreedom of Symmetry	423
§ 4.11	Heart and Man	424
§ 4.12	The Two Faculties of Man: Feeling and Reason	424
§ 4.13	Humorality: as the Fulfillment of Symmetry or Realization of Harmony	479
§ 4.14	The Untitled	489

Chapter V The Way of Heaven 501

§ 5.1	The Structure of Truth	501
§ 5.2	The Structure of Being	512
§ 5.3.1	Symmetry, the Symmetries, and the Symmetric Powers	526
§ 5.3.2	The Nature of the Symmetries	528
§ 5.3.3	The Nature of the Symmetric Powers	536
§ 5.3.4	Morality, Beauty, Reason, and the Humorality of Man	545
§ 5.3.5	The Rational Truth, the Rational Being	552
§ 5.3.6	Heart, Feeling, Reason, and Mind	554
§ 5.4	The Tree of Symmetry	562
§ 5.5	The Being of Man	565
§ 5.6	Harmony and Avolution	568

§ 5.7　**What is the Way of Heaven?** 576
§ 5.8　**Heaven, Earth, and Man** 578
§ 5.9　天行健, 君子以自强不息 579
§ 5.10　**The Way of Heaven** 583

Preface

Considerable attention has been paid to the coming into being of animals and plants, in the sense that, through the discussion on the coming into being of animals and plants, it may be revealed, things may not be so simple or straightforward as we might have thought. Symmetry or harmony may have played a fundamental role in the coming into being or development of animals or plants. Human beings are animals. Symmetry or harmony may have played a fundamental role in the coming into being or development of human beings. In other words, the human existence may have to do, in a fundamental sense, it might be said, with symmetry or harmony.

Apart from the discussions concerning the human existence, other things are also discussed, in a way to illustrate the possible roles that symmetry or harmony may have played.

Jiayou Liew
Jul. 26, 2015
Toronto

Chapter I Symmetry I: the Coming into Being of Animals, or, the Coming into Being of Man

§ 1.1 Symmetry, or Harmony: the Coming into Being of Life

How did life happen? How did life come into being? How did life happen on earth? How did life come into being on earth? People have been concerned with the origin of life for a long time. To explain the origin of life, people have proposed a number of theories. Some suggest that, life might have come into being in a primordial "soup" of organic compounds. Such organic compounds might have appeared as a result of energy, such as sunlight, working in the atmosphere of the early earth. Life might come into being on earth eventually as organic compounds underwent a series of processes. Others propose that, life might have first appeared close to the deep sea vents, as such hydrothermal vents on the sea floor might have provided some favorable conditions for the coming into being of life. Still, some think that, the coming into being of life might have to do with the kind of things such as lightning or radiation.

Experiments seem to have demonstrated that, under some specific conditions, organic molecules or compounds may be formed from inorganic things. What does this mean? Does it mean that life may come into being through such kind of process? Not necessarily. Life is not just organic molecules. Life is not just organic compounds. Life is much more than organic molecules. Life is much more than organic compounds. It is a gigantic leap, from organic molecules to life. It is a gigantic leap, from organic compounds to life. What has made such a leap possible? What has made such a leap necessary? Who has the power to make such a leap possible? Who has the energy to support such a leap? Who has the energy to maintain such a leap? Who has the energy to sustain such a leap?

Is it a molecular process? Is it a physical process? Is it a chemical process? Is it an evolutionary process? Life is a magnificent thing. From inorganic things to life, it is a magnificent process. For such things to happen, something extraordinary might have happened. A molecular process might not have been enough. A physical process might not have been enough. A chemical process might not have been enough. An evolutionary process might not have been enough.

Given what we see in the coming into being or existence of plants or animals, it seems, it might be said, symmetry might have played a significant role in the coming into being of life. A molecular process might have participated in the coming into being of life, but such a process itself might not be enough. A physical process might have participated in the coming into being of life, but such a process itself might not be enough. A chemical process might have participated in the coming into being of life, but such a process itself might not be enough. An evolutionary process might have participated in the coming into being of life, but such a process itself, again, might not be enough. Symmetry might have been behind such processes. Symmetry might have been the power behind such processes. Symmetry might have been the energy behind such processes. That is, it might be said, the coming into being of life might have to do, first of all, with symmetry. It might have been, first of all, a symmetric process. It might have been, first of all, a harmonic process. It might have been, first of all, an avolutionary process.

Some may say that life might not have originated on earth. It is possible. It is possible that life might have come into being first in outer space, and was brought to earth by comets or meteorites. If that is the case, then it might be said, the symmetric development possibly behind the coming into being of life might have occurred outside of earth, that is, in outer space. And, it seems, certain findings may support the notion that life might have originated in outer space.

§ 1.2 The Coming into Being of Double Helical Symmetry: from RNA to DNA

Though both DNA, deoxyribonucleic acid, and RNA, ribonucleic acid, are essential to life, they are different in several ways. They play different roles. They fulfill different functions. They possess different structures. As we know, DNA has a double-stranded structure. Unlike DNA, RNA is usually found to have a single-stranded structure. This structural difference may be seen as significant, in the sense that it may

Symmetry I

determine how DNA and RNA are related, differently, to life, or to the development or existence of life.

While the presence of double helical symmetry may be observed in the double-stranded structure of DNA, such a sense of symmetry may not be seen in the single-stranded structure of RNA. In other words, it might be said, while DNA may exhibit a strong sense of symmetry, RNA may not. It is true that the single-stranded RNA may often be found to fold unto itself, but such folding may not be regarded as equivalent to a symmetric existence.

The double helical symmetric structure of DNA constitutes a stable, complex, and powerful framework. As a result, when it comes to the storage of genetic information, DNA may be much more efficient than RNA. It may store genetic information in a more stable way. It may store more genetic information. It may store more complex genetic information. It may store genetic information in a longer term. Such qualities associated with DNA may explain why it plays a fundamental role in the development or existence of life.

DNA provides the genetic information for the development or existence of life. RNA, through its various forms, works to make such development or existence of life possible. In other words, it might be said, while DNA may provide the guidelines, RNA may do the work. Such difference between DNA and RNA may be seen, in a sense, as having to do with their structural difference. The structural difference may enable them to play different roles, or to fulfill different functions.

That the structural difference can be so significant may be seen in that the structural difference between DNA and RNA constitutes a symmetric difference. A symmetric difference is not just a difference. It is a difference, in the most fundamental sense. A symmetric difference is not just a structural difference. It is a structural difference, in the most fundamental sense. With the coming into being of such a symmetric difference, some fundamental changes may occur, and some significant things may happen.

The coming into being of double helical symmetry in DNA constitutes a symmetric difference from RNA to DNA. With the coming into being of double helical symmetry, as we can see, two of the most important qualities associated with life may appear, that is, stability and complexity. Stability and complexity may be seen as two of the most important qualities or preconditions for complex life to emerge, to develop, to thrive, to prosper, or to flourish. Compared to

RNA, DNA is more stable. Compared to RNA, DNA is more complex. Compared to RNA, DNA means the genetic information with stability. Compared to RNA, DNA means the genetic information with complexity.

The way has been paved, for the emergence of complex life. The way has been paved, for the development of complex life. The way has been paved, for the thriving or flourishing of complex life. The coming into being of double helical symmetry may be seen as paving the way for the emergence of complex life. The coming into being of double helical symmetry may be seen as paving the way for the development of complex life. The coming into being of double helical symmetry may be seen as paving the way for life to thrive, to prosper, or to flourish.

Life on earth today has to do with DNA, RNA and proteins. It is possible that before the appearance of the current life, life might have been based on RNA. That is, it is possible that an RNA world might have existed prior to the emergence of the world of DNA, RNA and proteins. Then, one may ask, how did the world of DNA, RNA and proteins happen? That is, in a sense, one may ask, how did DNA come into being, in the world?

Some suggest, DNA might have come to this world as a mutation, that is, as a mutation of RNA. Was DNA a mutation? Was DNA a mutation of RNA? Was the coming into being of DNA a mutation? Was the coming into being of DNA a result from some damage to RNA? Was the coming into being of DNA a result from some failure happened to RNA? Was the coming into being of DNA a mistake? Was the coming into being of DNA an error? Was the coming into being of DNA an accident? Or, did DNA happen, in the world, by chance?

When we are unable to see into things, things may not be accidents. When we are unable to see into things, things may not happen by chance. When we are unable to understand things, things may not be mistakes. When we are unable to understand things, things may not be errors. Mutations may not be errors. Mutations may not be mistakes. Mutations may not be accidents. Mutations may not result from some damages. Mutations may not result from some failures. Mutations may not happen by chance. Something deep may be behind mutations. Something profound may be behind mutations. Something symmetric or harmonic may be behind mutations. Something avolutionary may be behind the happening or occurrence of mutations.

DNA may not be a mutation. DNA may not be a mutation of RNA. The coming into being of DNA may not be a mutation. The coming into being of DNA in the world may have to do with something deep, or profound. It may have to do with symmetry. It may have to do with the working or operation of symmetry. It may be a symmetric happening. It may be a symmetric occurrence. It may be a symmetric development. It may be the working of symmetry to provide a stable foundation so that complex life may appear. It may be the operation of symmetry to make it possible that life may develop further. That is, it might be said, it may be an avolutionary development of symmetry to pave the way for the eventual development of life. It is in such a sense that, it might be said, the coming into being of double helical symmetry may be understood. It is in such a sense that, it might be said, the significance of the coming into being of double helical symmetry in the world may be understood.

§ 1.3 The Coming into Being of Sexual Symmetry: from Asexual Reproduction to Sexual Reproduction

Why did sex happen? Why did sex happen, at all? Why did sexual reproduction happen? Why did sexual reproduction happen, at all? People have long pondered over the phenomenon of sex. The phenomenon of sex seems to be around us, and the phenomenon of sexual reproduction seems to be everywhere in the world, in plants, in animals, in humans. Why is it sex? Why does sex occur so often? Why does sexual reproduction play such a prominent role in life? It is found, once animals acquired sex, it would be very hard for them to lose that ability. And, sometimes, they would fight to their death to defend the right to live a sexual life. Why is sex so great? Why is sex so powerful? Why is sex so enduring? Why is the sexual attraction so strong?

Sexual reproduction may have appeared on earth about 1 billion years ago. It seems, it is a way of reproduction for most of the complex life forms such as plants or animals. To explain the origin of sex, people have proposed a number of theories, mostly in an evolutionary sense. Some suggest that, sexual reproduction may come into being to promote adaptation. Some suggest that, sexual reproduction may come into being to curb bad mutations. Some argue that, sexual reproduction may come into being to repair DNA damages. Underlying the evolutionary theories about sex is the notion that sexual reproduction may give rise to genetic variation, and genetic variation may contribute to the fitness or survival of offspring. Genetic variation may give rise to new genes. Genetic variation may enable organisms to better adapt to environment. Genetic variation may make organisms less vulnerable to parasites.

But, it seems, many counterarguments may be made, and numerous cases may be found in which things may not happen as the evolutionary theories have described. In order to make a cogent argument, different theories may have to be proposed, since, it seems, the proposed theories may only apply to certain organisms or species. It is true that, in many cases, sex brings evolutionary benefits to the development of organisms. But, it is found, in certain cases, evolution seems to be at odds with sex. It is true that, in many cases, sex contributes to the development of organisms. But, it seems, in certain circumstances, sex may lead to unfavorable consequences.

And, we cannot forget, after all, asexual reproduction may not be regarded as less efficient than sexual reproduction, in a certain sense, when it comes to reproduction. That is, in a sense, it might be said, asexual reproduction may be seen as more efficient than sexual reproduction, if we consider what may be involved in such a process. It takes two parents, male and female, to reproduce sexually. And, it is often the case that only females may give birth to the next generation. If it is asexual reproduction, it would be much simpler. Each member is capable of producing offspring, and there is no need to invest any energy in the development or maintenance of sexes. In other words, it seems, it might be said, sexual reproduction may be more costly, and asexual reproduction may be more efficient.

So, given all such things about sex, why did sex happen, at all? The evolutionary theories may explain the occurrence of sex, in an evolutionary sense, but, it seems, arguments may also be made against the happening of sex, in an evolutionary sense, as well. Is sex evolutionary? If sex is evolutionary, why are there so many problems associated with the explanations? The evolutionary benefits of sex may not necessarily necessitate the happening of sex. The benefits of sex may be remarkable. The disadvantages of sex may be equally apparent, as well.

Symmetry I

Apart from the happening of sex, one may ask, how is sex maintained? What binds males and females in sex? Where does such a binding force come from? What might be its source? What might be its origin? If sex is the result of pure evolution, then it seems, it is possible that, it may have been lost long time ago. After a considerably long period of time, the factors that contributed to the coming into being of sex might have lost their force, and other factors might come up and lead, eventually, to the loss of sex. If sex is the consequence coming out of a selective process, then it seems, sex may go away after a long period of time, only if that time is long enough. That is, if selection could give rise to sex, then it seems, it might be said, selection may also give up sex. That is, if sex could be selected, it seems, there is no reason to rule out that, sex could also be selected away.

Did sex go away? No, sex stays. Sex is still strong. Sex is still powerful. Sex is still binding. It is found, once animals acquired sex, very few of them had ever lost that ability. If sex is the result of an evolutionary or selective process, as people claim, it seems, we may have much difficulty to explain why it stays, why it stays so strong, why it stays so powerful, or why it stays so enduring.

Sex may not have to do with evolution. Sex may not have to do with selection. Sex may have to do with symmetry. Sex may have to do with harmony. Sex may have to do with avolution. The binding force of sex may have to do with symmetry. It may be the binding force of symmetry. It may be the binding power of symmetry. It may be the binding force of sexual symmetry. It may be the binding power of sexual symmetry. Sex may have to do, first of all, with sexual symmetry. Sex may have to do, first of all, with the fulfillment or realization of sexual symmetry. Sex may have to do, first of all, with the fulfillment or realization of sexual symmetry in nature. Sex may have to do, first of all, with the fulfillment or realization of sexual symmetry in the world.

The endurance of sex may be seen as the endurance of symmetry. The endurance of sexual reproduction may be seen as the endurance of sexual symmetry. Sex may not be maintained by evolution. Sex may not be maintained by selection. Sex may be maintained by symmetry. Sex may be maintained by harmony. Sexual reproduction may not be maintained by evolution. Sexual reproduction may not be maintained by selection. Sexual reproduction may be maintained by symmetry. Sexual reproduction may be maintained by harmony. The maintenance of sex may not be an evolutionary process. The maintenance of sexual reproduction may not be a selective process. The maintenance of sex may be a symmetric process. The maintenance of sexual reproduction may be a harmonic process. The maintenance of sex or sexual reproduction may be an avolutionary process.

So what is sex? It may be the fulfillment of symmetry in life. It may be the realization of harmony in nature. What is sexual reproduction? It may be the fulfillment of sexual symmetry in life. It may be the realization of sexual harmony in nature. Sex, in its essence, it might be said, may not be about evolution. Sex, in its essence, it might be said, may not be about selection. Sex, in its essence, may be about symmetry. Sex, in its essence, may be about harmony. Sex, in its essence, may be about avolution. It is through a symmetric process that sex may come into being. It is through a harmonic process that sex may appear. It is through an avolutionary process that sexual reproduction may come to this world. It is through an avolutionary process that sexual reproduction may be maintained or sustained, in the world.

§ 1.4 The Coming into Being of (Bilateral) Symmetry in Animals: the Primordial Explosion

The Primordial Explosion refers to the emergence or coming into being of animals for the first time, in a relatively rapid pace, on earth. Thus, it roughly covers both the Ediacaran and the Cambrian. The life forms called animals may be seen as first coming into being in the Ediacaran, around 600 million years ago, and rapidly diversifying and radiating in what is called the Cambrian explosion. Most of the modern animals can be traced back to the organisms appearing in the Cambrian. That is, it is found, the origin of nearly all living animals may be traced back to the geologic period called the Cambrian. It is in the Cambrian, it seems, fossilized organisms, with remarkable and tremendous diversity, appeared on earth. Such an event is usually called the Cambrian explosion. The Cambrian explosion might have happened from around 530 to 520 million years ago. During such a short period of time, geologically speaking, the ancestors of most living animals emerged or came into being on earth.

Symmetry I

The Cambrian explosion is usually believed to have happened in a quite short period of time, about 10 million years, from around 530 to 520 million years ago. Certainly, as people often say, geologically speaking, it was a very short period of time. Was it *really* a short period of time, if considered in other terms, in other senses, or on other scales? When we say that, it was a short period of time, what we are really thinking in our mind is the evolutionary development, and we are using the evolutionary standards to measure such a period. What about if such a period was not evolutionary at all, or, if evolution had merely constituted part of what happened in such a period, or, if evolution had just played a minor role to what happened in such a period? 10 million years may be short in the evolutionary terms, but it may not be that short in the symmetric terms. 10 million years may be short in the evolutionary sense, but it may not be that short in the harmonic sense. 10 million years may be short on the evolutionary scale, but it may not be that short on the avolutionary scale. The geological or evolutionary consideration of such a period is about to mean a gradual, slow, continuous, and incremental development or process. Is the symmetric development gradual, in the beginning? Maybe not. Is the harmonic growth slow, at the start? Maybe not. Is the avolutionary process continuous and incremental, in the initial stage? Maybe not. The symmetric development of the Cambrian organisms might be a burst, in the beginning. The harmonic growth of the Cambrian life forms might be a widespread radiation, at the start. The avolutionary coming into being of the Cambrian animals might be truly an explosion, in the initial stage.

10 million years might not be enough for evolution to work to bring the Cambrian organisms into the world, but it might be enough for symmetry to shape the animal body plans such that the new organisms might emerge in the Cambrian. 10 million years might not be enough for the natural selection to select the fittest to appear in the Cambrian, but it might be enough for harmony to mould the animal body structures such that the fresh life forms might arise in such a period. 10 million years might be too short for evolution to give rise to a widespread biological diversification, but it might prove to be not that short if an avolutionary process was being involved. The natural selection might be slow; the symmetric or harmonic selection might be fast, in the beginning, or at the start. The evolutionary process might be gradual or incremental; the avolutionary development, on the other

hand, in the initial stage, might be rapid, sudden, swift, or explosive. The 10 million years that saw the sudden appearance of the Cambrian animals might be a period in which avolution played the major role in bringing forth things, while evolution might only have played a minor part, in such a process. In other words, during such a period, it might be said, it was symmetry or harmony that had worked to give rise to things, and the symmetric workings or harmonic operations may be seen as what defined or characterized such a short and yet remarkable, significant, and magnificent period.

Certainly, the remarkably short and far-reaching period in which the Cambrian organisms suddenly appeared constitutes an enormous difficulty by itself for us, as it is so remote from us now and it would be difficult for us to get into the developmental details of such a period. That is, the very nature of the shortness of such a period seems to make it almost impossible for us to examine the actual developmental processes of such a period. Certainly, this does not necessarily mean that we should be looking for in such a period some kind of developmental patterns or some kind of developmental stages. No, we are not looking for such kind of things, in such a period, it must be said, as, it seems, the fossil record thus far does not appear to indicate or support the possible existence of such patterns or stages in such a period. In other words, what makes such a period remarkable is the fact that, apart from the brevity or shortness of such a period, there seemed to be no apparent developmental processes being involved in such a period. The shortness of such a remote period makes it difficult for us to examine the actual development of things. The seeming lack of developmental processes, or the absence of the kind of developmental patterns or stages, during such a time, appears to make our examination or investigation of such a period harder or more difficult. What to do with such a period? How to look into such a period? How to make sense of such a period? How to examine it? How to investigate it? How to understand it? In what way? In what sense? Or, in what manner?

The symmetric development may be quite different from the evolutionary development. The development of harmony may be quite different from the natural selection. The avolutionary process may be quite different from the evolutionary process. The movement of symmetry may be what defined the Cambrian. The movement of harmony may be what established the Cambrian period. The movement of symmetry or harmony may be what was truly underlying the

Symmetry I

developmental process in the Cambrian. That is, the remarkable shortness of the period experiencing the sudden Cambrian emergence may be seen as related, in a sense, to the movement of symmetry, or, the lack of apparent developmental process in such a period may be seen as being associated, in a sense, with the movement of harmony. That is, it might be said, it might be the movement of symmetry that had rendered such a period short, remarkably short, and it might be the movement of harmony that had turned such a time into a period without apparent developmental process, or without apparent developmental patterns or stages, that is, without the kind of things that might be interpreted by the human eyes or senses as development. In other words, to understand or grasp such a remarkable short period, the movement of symmetry or harmony may be what we should be looking for, and the movement of symmetry or harmony may be the process that we should focus on, to examine, to investigate, or, in a sense, to analyze.

It might not be easy to examine the development of symmetry. It might not be easy to investigate the development of harmony. It might not be easy to examine the movement of symmetry. It might not be easy to investigate the movement of harmony. It might not be easy to find, to discover, or to reveal the workings or operations of symmetry or harmony in nature. They are usually deep. They are usually profound. They are usually far-reaching. They are everywhere, and everywhere they are behind things. They may be plain, but they are not easy to be found. They may be visible, but they are not easy to be seen. They may be simple, but they are not easy to be understood. To find them, we need sharp eyes, or more than sharp eyes. To see them, we need keen senses, or more than keen senses. To understand them, we need all our human intellect, intelligence, wit, or wisdom.

The symmetric workings or harmonic operations in the Cambrian may be observed, in a sense, if we take a close look at how the Cambrian organisms had come into being. That is, the possible symmetric workings or harmonic operations behind the coming into being of the Cambrian organisms may be tracked down, in a sense, if we examine, carefully, what happened in the Cambrian, or what happened before the Cambrian. If we search carefully into the Cambrian and the preceding Precambrian period called the Ediacaran, it seems, things might not have appeared so suddenly at all. People often talk about the Cambrian explosion, as if it might be the only explosion that saw the appearance of the earliest animals. That might not be the case. The coming into being of the earliest animals might have undergone several stages, several phases, several periods, or several explosions. That is, the movement of symmetry or harmony giving rise, finally, to the appearance of the animals we know today might not have followed a straightforward course. Such a course might have been a process punctuated with a number of stages, phases, periods or explosions. In other words, the symmetric or harmonic movement leading to the coming into being of the Cambrian organisms might not have been so simple or clear-cut as we may think.

The Ediacaran period is the geological period just before the Cambrian, lasting from about 630 to 540 million years ago. The first Ediacaran organisms seemed to have emerged around 600 million years ago. It is found, just like the Cambrian, the Ediacaran might also have been marked with a kind of biological explosion of its own, called sometimes the Avalon explosion, in which the organisms during such a period seemed to have proliferated on a tremendous scale. The Avalon explosion might have occurred around 580 million years ago, about 40 million years before the Cambrian. Given the complex multicellular Ediacaran organisms found in the fossil record, it seems, it might be said, it was probably during the Avalon explosion that the Ediacaran organisms proliferated, radiated and diversified, and eventually left their unprecedented and sometimes perplexing traces in the fossils.

From their first appearance around 600 million years ago, the Ediacaran organisms developed and finally, it appears, about 580 million years ago, they entered a new stage and began their rapid proliferation and diversification. That is, it seems, it took about 20 million years for the Ediacaran organisms to prepare for themselves, to develop, to grow, to ripen, so that they might have blossomed, after about 580 million years ago, into the kind of rich and diverse biological community known for the first time on earth. The coming into being of the Ediacaran organisms heralded a new era for the development of life on earth, as such organisms stood for the earliest appearance of the complex multicellular life forms called animals on this planet. From that time on, our planet earth was no longer occupied only by the kind of things such as the single-celled or simple multicellular organisms. Life on earth began to multiply. Life on earth began to proliferate. Life on earth began to radiate. Life on earth began to diversify. Life on earth began to blossom. Life on earth began to explode. A new and

Symmetry I

magnificent chapter of the great drama known as the life on earth had started.

Multicellular life forms might have appeared on earth more than 1 billion years ago, but prior to the coming into being of the Ediacaran organisms, such multicellular life forms might only possess or exhibit a sense of simple or limited complexity. It was the appearance of the Ediacaran organisms that signaled the coming into being of the true complex multicellular life forms on earth. And we can see, as the true complex multicellular life forms appearing on earth around 600 million years ago, the Ediacaran organisms represented the emergence or coming into being of the kind of new life forms on this planet that we eventually call, animals.

The earth was probably formed 4.6 billion years ago. The simple cells appeared around 3.6 billion years ago. The earth welcomed the coming into being of the complex cells about 2 billion years ago. The development of the simple multicellular organisms on earth might have happened more than 1 billion years ago. The coming into being of the complex multicellular animals on this planet might have occurred around 600 million years ago. From the simple cells to the complex cells, it was complexity on the increase. From the simple multicellularity to the complex multicellularity, it was complexity in a developmental process. The development of the simple cells, it seems, gave rise to the complex cells. The development of the simple multicellularity, it appears, led to the coming into being of the complex multicellularity. It was a developmental process. It was a process in which complexity increased, strengthened, and improved. And, it was a process in which the kind of new life forms called animals gradually came into being. From the simple cells to the complex cells to the simple multicellular organisms to the complex multicellular animals, it was a remarkable process defined or characterized by the continuously increasing complexity of life. From the simple cells to the complex cells to the simple multicellular organisms to the complex multicellular animals, it was an extraordinary journey of life that saw the eventual arrival of the magnificent life forms called animals on this planet.

Why should the simple cells appear on earth? Why should the complex cells come into being? Why should the simple multicellular organisms develop? Why should the complex multicellular animals emerge? Why should the complex cells come into being after the appearance of the simple cells? Why should the simple multicellularity develop after the coming into being of the cells? Why should the complex multicellularity emerge after the development of the simple multicellularity? Why was there no stop to the development of cells? Why was there no stop to the development of multicellularity? Why was there no stop to the development of complexity? Why was there no stop to the emergence of new life forms? Why was there no stop to the journey of life? Why, after all, should the life forms called animals appear and come into being, on earth, at all?

What was behind all these things? What was behind all these phenomena? What was behind the eventual development of cells? What was behind the eventual development of multicellularity? What was behind the eventual development of complexity? What was behind the eventual development of life? Was it just evolution? Was it merely natural selection? Evolution may not fully explain the development of complexity, as complexity may not necessarily mean the developmental advantages. Natural selection may not fully explain the appearance of the complex cells, as the simple cells may fit well and survive well, even to this day. Evolution may not fully explain the emergence of the complex multicellular organisms, as the simple multicellular organisms may fit well and survive well, even at the moment. Natural selection may not fully explain the development of life, as the journey of life on earth seems to be defined or characterized by such extraordinary events as the Avalon explosion or Cambrian explosion.

Evolution may only explain one of the many possibilities. Natural selection may only account for one of the many possible outcomes. Evolution may have only looked into one of the possible developmental processes. Natural selection may have only investigated one of the many possible results. Many other possible processes may have been overlooked. Many other possible results or outcomes may have been ignored. Many other possible paths may have been bypassed. Evolution may have only shed light on the kind of things that it is, by chance, capable of. Natural selection may have only made sense of what it could, coincidentally. What about all the other possibilities? What about all the other possible results? What about all the other possible outcomes? What about all the other possible paths? Should they be explained? Should they be accounted for? Should they be made sense of? Or, should they be excluded? Or, should they be ruled out? Can you overlook all the other possibilities? Can you ignore all the other

Symmetry I

possible results or consequences? Can you bypass all the other possible paths or processes?

Is it possible that evolution has just been designed in such a manner that it could explain certain things, in a seemingly scientific sense, and at the same time brushing aside all the other things possibly essential? Is it the case that natural selection has just been formulated in such a way that it could make sense of certain things, in a seemingly rational manner, and at the same time dismissing all the other things possibly fundamental? Is it possible that evolution has been designed to explain certain things, but such things do not necessarily represent the most essential or fundamental aspects of nature? Is it the case that natural selection has been formulated to account for certain things, but such things do not necessarily stand for the most crucial, primary, or intrinsic things existing in the world?

Is it possible that evolution just overlooks all the other possibilities, since it cannot explain them? Is it the case that natural selection merely ignores all the other possible results or consequences, since it cannot grasp them? Is it possible that evolution just pays no attention to all the other possible processes, since it cannot understand them? Is it the case that natural selection merely bypasses all the other possible developmental paths, since it can in no way make sense of them? That is, in other words, is it possible that evolution may have just looked at part of the picture, a small part of the picture, that is called life? That is, is it the case that natural selection may have merely shed light on part of the workings or operations, or a small part of the workings or operations, that have paved the way for the coming into being or development of life?

To only explain one possibility is not science. To be science, it has to tell us, why the other possibilities are not possible. To only explain one consequence is not science. To be science, it has to tell us, why the other possible results or outcomes cannot materialize. To only make sense of one process is not science. To be science, it has to tell us, why the other possible processes may not happen. To only grasp one developmental path is not science. To be science, it has to point out, why the other possible developmental paths are not real. What is science? What defines science? What makes science science? What does science tell us? Science usually tells us that things would not develop otherwise. Science usually tells us that certain things may not materialize. Science usually tells us that certain things will not happen.

Avolution and Man

Science usually tells us that certain things are not real. That is, it might be said, science is, in a sense, to rule out the other possibilities. Science is to point out, the other outcomes or results may not come about. Science is to tell us, the other processes or paths may not happen or materialize.

But, it seems, the Cambrian explosion did happen. And it appears, the Avalon explosion occurred, most likely, as well. The complex cells came into being, even though, it seems, the simple cells survived well. The complex multicellular organisms emerged, even though, it appears, the simple multicellular organisms lived well. The Ediacaran organisms came on the scene, after all, even though, it seems, there were no signs for their appearance at such a time. The Cambrian life forms proliferated, radiated, and diversified, on a massive and unprecedented scale, even though, it appears, neither evolution nor natural selection could explain or make sense of such a remarkable and extraordinary phenomenon.

It is possible that, the complex cells might not have to come into being, given that the simple cells seemed to have survived well. Then why did they have to come into being? Can evolution *fully* explain this? It seems, it may not. It is possible that, the complex multicellular organisms might not have to emerge, given that the simple multicellular organisms appeared to have lived well. Then why did they have to emerge? Can natural selection *fully* explain this? It appears, it may not. It is possible that, the Ediacaran organisms might not have to come on the scene, given that, it seems, nothing existed prior to the Ediacaran would indicate such an occurrence. Then why did they have to come on the scene at such a time? Can evolution *fully* explain this? It seems, it may not. It is possible that, the Cambrian explosion might not have to happen, given that, it appears, the world was already inhabited by numerous life forms such as the Ediacaran organisms. Then why did it have to happen? Can natural selection *fully* explain this? It appears, it may not. It is possible that, there might not have to be a continuous and sustained developmental process, in a general sense, from the simple cells to the complex cells to the simple multicellular organisms to the complex multicellular animals. But there was indeed such a developmental process. Why? Why did it have to happen? What had driven such a process? What had sustained such a process? Can evolution *fully* explain this? It seems, it may not. It is possible that, there might not have to be a developmental process defined by a steady increase of complexity or characterized by a constant growth of sophistication in the life forms, in a general sense. But it seems, there was indeed such a developmental process. Why? Why did such a process have to happen? What had driven such a process? What had supported and maintained such a process? Can natural selection *fully* explain this? It appears, it may not. And, as we have known, while the simple cells appeared around 3.6 billion years ago, the complex multicellular animals emerged about 600 million years ago as the first Ediacaran life forms. This means, from the simple cells to the complex cells to the simple multicellular organisms to the complex multicellular animals, the continuous and sustained development took almost about 3 billion years. And, we have also known, such a long period of time, about 3 billion years, had seen a steady increase of complexity or a constant growth of sophistication in the life forms. So, we may have to ask, what had actually sustained such a continuous development in such a long period of time, about 3 billion years? What had actually made such a steady increase of complexity possible in about 3 billion years? What had actually brought about such a constant growth of life sophistication, in about 3 billion years? Who could sustain a development in about 3 billion years? Who could provide a steady increase in about 3 billion years? Who could generate a constant growth in about 3 billion years? What things could? What kind of things could? What kind of things could be capable of? What kind of things could be really capable of, at all?

Is evolution science? Is natural selection science? If they cannot explain all these things, how could they be called science? If they cannot rule out all the other possibilities, how could they be regarded as science? If they only pick up one of the many possible developmental processes or paths, how could they be seen as following a scientific or rational approach? If they only try to account for or make sense of one of the many possible results or outcomes, how could they be treated as science in a real or proper sense? They may just be a concoction made to suit what is found. They may just be a human formulation worked out to describe what is unknown. They may tell some truth, but the real truth may have slipped away. They may reveal certain things, but the things behind such things may be beyond their reach. They may only account for part of what is found. They may only shed light on part of what is unknown.

Avolution and Man

What are the things behind things? What constitutes the real truth? What leads to what we find? What are underlying truly, in a sense, the unknown? To look for the kind of things behind the coming into being of the simple or complex cells, we may have to turn to symmetry or harmony. To seek the reasons for the appearance of the simple or complex multicellular organisms, we may have to look to symmetry or harmony. To search into the eventual emergence of the Ediacaran or Cambrian life forms, we may have to look deep into symmetry or harmony. To search into the kind of things leading to a steady increase of life complexity, in about 3 billion years, we may have to look deep into symmetry or harmony. To search into the kind of things giving rise to a constant growth of life sophistication, in about 3 billion years, we may have to look deep into symmetry or harmony. To search into the kind of things sustaining a development of about 3 billion years, from the simple cells to the complex cells to the simple multicellular organisms to the complex multicellular animals, we may have to look deep into the workings or operations of symmetry or harmony. Symmetry or harmony may be what behind things. It may not be evolution. Symmetry or harmony may be what constitutes the real truth. It may not be natural selection. Symmetry or harmony may lead to what we find in the world. It may not be evolution. Symmetry or harmony may be what truly underlying, in a sense, the unknown. It may not be natural selection.

The coming into being of the Ediacaran organisms may reveal, in a sense, the workings or operations of symmetry or harmony in such a period. The first Ediacaran organisms, as the earliest complex multicellular life forms called animals on earth, appeared around 600 million years ago. What does such an event mean? What does such an event mean to the development of life? What does such an event mean to our understanding about the development of life on earth? What does such an event tell us? What does such an event tell about life? What does such an event tell about the development of life on earth? It was a remarkable event. It was an extraordinary occurrence. It was a magnificent happening. It was the beginning of a new era. It was the beginning of a new era for life. It was the beginning of a new era for the development of life on earth. The Ediacaran organisms came on the scene; the complex multicellular life forms called animals came into being. The Ediacaran organisms came on the scene; the ancestors of the life forms called animals as we know today appeared. The Ediacaran

Symmetry I

organisms came on the scene; the animal life on earth began. It was the beginning of the animal life on earth. It was the beginning of the animal life thriving or flourishing on earth. It was the beginning of the animal life booming or blooming on earth. It was the beginning of the development of symmetry or harmony entering a new stage or phase. It was the beginning of the movement of symmetry or harmony approaching a new threshold or a fresh level. That is, it was the beginning of the development of symmetry or harmony giving rise to new life forms. That is, it was the beginning of the movement of symmetry or harmony bringing the new complex life forms called animals into the world.

The appearance of the Ediacaran organisms marked the beginning of the animal life on earth. The coming into being of the Ediacaran organisms signified a new stage or phase in the development of symmetry or harmony on earth. That is, it might be said, the emergence of the Ediacaran organisms may be seen as representing the movement of symmetry or harmony, on earth, at a new level. The symmetric or harmonic movement, at a new level, in the Ediacaran, may be seen in the coming into being of both radial symmetry and bilateral symmetry in the complex multicellular Ediacaran organisms.

With a close look at the Ediacaran fossils, we can find, the organisms existing in this period appeared to possess a number of different body plans, such as, tubular forms, disk-like forms, segmented forms, or frond-like forms. The tubular body forms and disk-like body forms may be seen as demonstrating a sense of radial symmetry in the organisms. The presence of a sense of bilateral symmetry, on the other hand, may be observed in the body plans of the organisms bearing the segmented forms, frond-like forms, or with some organisms, some disk-like forms. While the organisms with frond-like forms may be seen as demonstrating, in a vivid sense, the presence of a sense of bilateral symmetry, bilateral symmetry may also be observed in the organisms with segmented body forms. With regard to some of the disk-like body forms, even though they may demonstrate the existence of a sense of radial symmetry in a fairly perfect way, they may be found to display, at the same time, a sense of bilateral symmetry, if we take a close look.

That is, it might be said, both radial symmetry and bilateral symmetry may be seen as having appeared in the body plans of the organisms coming into being in the Ediacaran period. The coming into being of both radial symmetry and bilateral symmetry in the Ediacaran organisms made such a period, in a sense, just as significant, essential, and important as the Cambrian, in that, it might be said, it was through the development in these two periods that the animal life came into being, developed, and eventually flourished on earth. The Ediacaran heralded the coming into being of the Cambrian. The Ediacaran prepared for the coming into being of the Cambrian. The Ediacaran paved the way for the coming into being of the Cambrian. The Cambrian followed the Ediacaran. The Cambrian succeeded the Ediacaran. It was a continuous process. It was a continuous development. It was a continuous movement.

Radial symmetry may be observed in the Ediacaran organisms such as Arkarua, Yorgia, or Cloudina. Bilateral symmetry, on the other hand, may be found in the Ediacaran organisms such as Charnia, Dickinsonia, Kimberella, Onega, Parvancorina, or Spriggina. While radial symmetry and bilateral symmetry may be observed in these organisms, a sense of mixture or combination of radial symmetry and bilateral symmetry may also be seen in some of these Ediacaran organisms, such as, in Yorgia, Dickinsonia, or Charnia. The coming into being or appearance of radial symmetry, bilateral symmetry, and the combination of radial symmetry and bilateral symmetry in the Ediacaran organisms truly makes the Ediacaran, it might be said, an age of symmetric burgeoning or multiplication. It is in such a sense that, it might be aid, the Ediacaran may be seen as an age of symmetry, or, an age of harmony.

Arkarua is an organism existed in the Ediacaran period. Its body plan is defined or characterized by a sense of pentamerous radial symmetry, as its disk-like upper surface is usually divided, radially, into five parts. Such a kind of body structure may remind us of the later marine animals such as starfish. And indeed, even though the relationship of Arkarua with other organisms, either contemporary or later, may not be easily explained, some people have suggested that it may be regarded as the earliest echinoderm appearing on earth. Certainly, it is found, there are some differences between Arkarua and the later echinoderms, as some features found in the latter appeared to be absent in the former. This, in a sense, may not be surprising, as Arkarua, coming into being as possibly the first organism leading to the eventual emergence of the later echinoderms, might not have possessed all the echinoderm features. In other words, what is remarkable and significant here is that, both Arkarua and the later echinoderms seemed

Symmetry I

to have shared one fundamental feature in their body plans, the presence or existence of the pentamerous radial symmetry. It is the coming into being of the pentamerous radial symmetry that distinguished the appearance of Arkarua. It is the presence of the pentamerous radial symmetry that bridged the gap between Arkarua and the later echinoderms. It is the existence of the pentamerous radial symmetry that linked the coming into being of Arkarua in the Ediacaran with the emergence of the possibly first real echinoderms during the Cambrian. That is, what Arkarua signifies is that, the development of things might have continued from the Ediacaran period to the Cambrian period. That is, what Arkarua means is that, the movement of symmetry might not have been disrupted, and symmetry might have developed, moved, or progressed continuously, and successfully, from the Ediacaran to the Cambrian. Symmetry developed; organisms came on the scene in the Ediacaran. Symmetry moved; Arkarua came into being. Symmetry progressed; the Cambrian came after the Ediacaran. Symmetry developed; the Cambrian organisms appeared. Symmetry moved; the real echinoderms emerged, finally, in the Cambrian.

Yorgia is an Ediacaran organism with a disk-like body form. It is an interesting early organism in that, it seems, both radial symmetry and bilateral symmetry may be observed in its body plan. The front of the body is broad, appearing to form something like a head. The rest of the body is segmented, in a quite regular and balanced manner. Together with the front, the whole body demonstrates a fairly strong sense of radial symmetry. With such a sense of radial symmetry, we can also perceive, at the same time, the presence of a sense of bilateral symmetry in the body structure. But, unlike the way radial symmetry is being expressed, bilateral symmetry appears to have manifested itself in this organism in some unique and curious manners. First, it appears, the segments of the two body parts, left and right, are not arranged in a strictly bilateral manner. That is, the segments appear to be arranged in a manner that may be called glide symmetry or glide reflection symmetry, as they face each other in the two body parts not in a direct way but alternately. This pattern of segment arrangement may also be observed in other Ediacaran organisms, as glide symmetry may be seen as one of the features defining the appearance of symmetry in the Ediacaran. On the other hand, while the segment arrangement conveys a sense of the presence of bilateral symmetry, though only in a pattern of glide symmetry, this organism may exhibit a sense of asymmetry with the front segment of the right body part somehow growing continuously into the left. This may make this Ediacaran organism look asymmetric. In other words, it is interesting to notice that, Yorgia may be seen as the Ediacaran organism exhibiting a sense of radial symmetry, a sense of bilateral symmetry, and a sense of asymmetry at the same time and in the same body plan.

How to understand this? How to understand this phenomenon? Why was Yorgia so peculiar in possessing or expressing such various senses of symmetry? What was behind its possession of such senses of symmetry? What was behind its expression of such senses of symmetry? To understand Yorgia, we may have to first understand the nature of the Ediacaran. To understand Yorgia, we may have to first understand how, why and through what process the Ediacaran had come into being. It might be the case that, Yorgia, as the Ediacaran organism, represented, embodied, or illustrated, in a sense, the coming into being, development, or movement of symmetry or harmony in such a particular period. When symmetry first arose in the complex multicellular life forms called animals in the Ediacaran, it is possible that such symmetry might not have to appear in the perfect forms. In other words, it is possible that, while there were symmetric forms appearing in the organisms, some asymmetric features might also exist in the body structures of the same organisms. Such may be seen in Yorgia. While symmetry was being expressed, radially, and bilaterally in a sense of glide symmetry, the presence of asymmetry may also be observed as the body seemed to have demonstrated a sense of unbalanced structure. On the other hand, it might be said, as symmetry strived to fulfill or realize itself in or through the Ediacaran organisms such as Yorgia, for the first time in a complex multicellular fashion, it is possible that, all the symmetric forms might appear, and even the asymmetric elements might also be present as well. This may, in a sense, explain what we see in Yorgia. It might be the first coming into being of symmetry in the complex multicellular life forms that had led Yorgia to possess at the same time all the senses of both symmetry and asymmetry. It might be the initial emergence of symmetry in the complex multicellular life forms that had led Yorgia to emerge with both radial symmetry and bilateral symmetry. It was the beginning of symmetry in the complex multicellular life forms called animals. It was the beginning of symmetry to express or manifest itself in the complex multicellular life forms called animals. It was the beginning of symmetry to fulfill or realize itself in the complex multicellular life forms called animals. It was the beginning of symmetry to lead the complex multicellular life forms called animals to emerge. It was the beginning of symmetry to lead the complex multicellular life forms called animals to come on the scene. It was the beginning of symmetry to lead the complex multicellular life forms called animals to come to this world.

Radial symmetry may also be witnessed in the Ediacaran organism named Cloudina. It is an organism whose body plan is distinguished by a series of small tubes or cones. Such small tubes or cones appear to form a tubular structure, with each emerging from the one below. Such a tubular body structure may be regarded as one of the main characteristics of this organism. The presence of radial symmetry may be seen in such a tubular structure or in the cones connecting with each other. Cloudina is an interesting Ediacaran organism in several respects, even though its relationship to other organisms may be hard to figure out. Its small tubes or cones are mineralized shells, and thus it may be regarded as one of the earliest organisms capable of mineralization for their own existence. Some people have suggested that, Cloudina may be related to polychaete worms, or bristle worms, given that it appears to have a tubular body structure and the fact that it seems, certain holes can be found in the fossils that might have been left by the attacking predators. On the other hand, some people may disagree with this and point out that, this Ediacaran organism may better be regarded as something linked with cnidarians such as corals, as some of its fossils seem to indicate a lifestyle of asexual reproduction.

Given that Cloudina seems to possess mineralized body shells, it is likely that it may not be closely related to polychaete worms, and it may have a better relationship with the cnidarians such as corals. It should not be taken as a surprise if such a relationship is really to exist, as they share one important and fundamental feature in their body plans, the presence or existence of radial symmetry. The possible continuation of radial symmetry from Cloudina to the cnidarians such as corals may be seen in that corals are made up of polyps, and polyps are usually radially symmetric. Polyps are the little animals forming a coral head. They are genetically identical, usually possessing a central mouth opening covered with a circle of tentacles. The body plan of polyps demonstrates the presence of radial symmetry, as such a symmetric presence may also be observed in Cloudina. On the other hand, if the close relationship between Cloudina and polychaete worms is to stand, then given the fact that worms are usually bilaterally symmetric animals, it is possible that, the Ediacaran organism Cloudina might have possessed bilateral symmetry in its body plan, in some way or in some form. But this may have to be proved through further studies.

As the organism whose fossils had been first identified as coming from the Precambrian period, Charnia represents the coming into being or existence of the Ediacaran life forms in a number of ways. It is an organism possessing a frond-like body structure, with the segmented branching body parts aligned along the central line from both sides. It might have lived on the sea floor by absorbing the nutrients in the water. Given the frond-like body form it exhibits, it might be the case that this Ediacaran organism may be related to the kind of later life forms such as sea pens, a group of marine cnidarians living on the sea floor. Certainly, it might be said, the most distinctive feature of this organism is its frond-like body form, as shared, to a certain extent, by some of the later sea pens. This frond-like body structure can also be observed in other Ediacaran organisms such as Rangea. These organisms are usually distinguished by their frond-like body plan and it may be found, they might have thrived in certain locations during the Ediacaran. So, we may have to ask, why should such Ediacaran organisms have to develop or possess such a kind of body plan or structure? To look into this, it may be of some help if we do some research on the coming into being of plants in the Devonian. Among the earliest plants appearing in the Devonian, it may be found, the frond-like body plan or structure had played a major role. That is, the fossil record from the Devonian appears to tell us that, the leaves of many plants coming into being in the Devonian actually possessed a frond-like form or structure. Why, then, should the plants have to possess a kind of frond-like body form or structure when they first came to this world, in the Devonian? If the plants emerged, for the first time, in the Devonian, with their frond-like leaf structure, why should the Precambrian animals, such as Charnia or Rangea, have to emerge, for the first time, in the Ediacaran, with their frond-like body plan? In other words, if the earliest animals came to this world with bilateral symmetry, in a frond-like manner, why should the earliest plants also

Symmetry I

have to come to this world with bilateral symmetry, in a similar frond-like manner? Was symmetry behind the coming into being of the earliest animals, just as it was behind the coming into being of the earliest plants? Was symmetry behind the coming into being of the earliest plants, just as it was equally behind the coming into being of the earliest animals? That is, was symmetry, that is, bilateral symmetry in this case, underlying the coming into being of both animals and plants, in their earliest forms or during their earliest stages? The earliest appearance or coming into being of frond-like body plan in both animals and plants may indicate that symmetry, that is, bilateral symmetry, might develop or move readily, or with less effort, in a sense, in a frond-like fashion or manner. That may be, in a sense, what behind the appearance of the frond-like body plan in the earliest animals such as Charnia or Rangea, or in many of the earliest plants.

While the bilateral frond-like body plan may indicate, to a certain extent, a sense of relationship between Charnia and the later life forms such as sea pens, it is necessary for us to bear in mind that sea pens are cnidarians whose body structures often exhibit a sense of radial symmetry. Such a sense of radial symmetry may be demonstrated through the structures of polyps. With regard to Rangea, it might be said, the fossil record seems to indicate that it was radially symmetric. So, what might be the presence of radial symmetry in Charnia, if the relationship we are talking about is going to really exist? The presence of radial symmetry may be seen in Charnia in that, the fossils seem to show, the segmented Charnia body parts arranged on the two sides appear to be raised and exhibit a sense of roundness in structure. This may indicate that such body parts might have been radially symmetric, in some sense, with their round forms or shapes. As to the relationship between Charnia and the later life forms such as sea pens, some people have denied its existence, based on the research on their different growth patterns. It is found, Charnia and sea pens might have followed different growth patterns, as their developments might be initiated either from the top or from the base. Could this difference in growth patterns constitute something pointing to the nonexistence of a relationship between Charnia and the kind of life forms such as sea pens? It may not necessarily be such a case, as, it might be said, the bilaterally symmetric body plan shared by them may constitute something more fundamental or more essential in their individualized existence. That is, it is possible that, the different growth patterns might be a later development arising from certain circumstances. In other words, it might be said, such a difference in growth patterns may not necessarily constitute something that would rule out, completely, the possibility that a relationship may exist between Charnia and the kind of later life forms such as sea pens.

As an Ediacaran organism, Dickinsonia may be seen as the Precambrian life form that has expressed or demonstrated bilateral symmetry in a remarkable sense. The possible feeding traces left by Dickinsonia may tell us that, it was able to move and thus likely an early animal living in the Ediacaran period. The Dickinsonia body forms can be found in several types, such as, round, oval, or very elongated. But no matter what forms their bodies may take, it seems, they all express or demonstrate a clear and strong sense of bilateral symmetry, with the segments in the two sides of their bodies arranged in the manner of glide reflection symmetry. Glide reflection symmetry, though not bilateral symmetry in a strict sense, may be regarded as a sense of the realization of bilateral symmetry in that, such a sense of bilateral symmetry may be seen as coming into being from symmetry fulfilling or realizing itself in a process. That is to say, glide reflection symmetry may be seen, in a sense, as bilateral symmetry in movement, in development, or, with movement, with development.

Life is not, in a sense, the mathematical. Life is, in a sense, the movement or development of the mathematical. Life is, in a sense, the fulfillment or realization of the mathematical. Life is, in a sense, the movement or development of the mathematical in the life forms. Life is, in a sense, the fulfillment or realization of the mathematical in or through the life forms. Glide reflection symmetry in life may be seen as symmetry moving or developing in life. Glide reflection symmetry in life may be seen as symmetry fulfilling or realizing itself in life. That is, glide reflection symmetry in life may be seen as the movement or development of bilateral symmetry in life. That is, glide reflection symmetry in life may be seen as the fulfillment or realization of bilateral symmetry in life. It is in such a sense that, it might be said, the glide reflection symmetry found in the kind of Ediacaran organisms such as Dickinsonia may be seen as the movement or development of bilateral symmetry in the Precambrian life forms, or, regarded as the fulfillment or realization of bilateral symmetry in the Precambrian animal life.

Symmetry I

And indeed, as we can see, the Ediacaran organisms such as Dickinsonia do possess a bilaterally symmetric body plan and exhibit a clear and strong sense of the presence or existence of bilateral symmetry. On the other hand, the different body forms possessed by the different species of Dickinsonia may be seen as indicating, in a sense, a sense of development on the part of Dickinsonia itself. And we can almost feel, or perceive, it might be said, a sense of transitional or transformational development being exhibited or manifested by such different body shapes or forms. Both radial symmetry and bilateral symmetry may be found in this Ediacaran organism. While radial symmetry may be observed in the species with round or oval shapes, the very elongated members may be regarded as mostly demonstrating the coming into being of bilateral symmetry in this early life form. The coexistence of such different body forms in Dickinsonia, or, the coexistence of both radial symmetry and bilateral symmetry in its body plan, may indicate that a transitional or transformational development, in a sense, might have happened in the coming into being of this Ediacaran organism. When symmetry worked to give rise to this early organism, it might be said, it might have experimented with different body shapes or forms, such as, in this case, from the round, the oval, to the very elongated. In other words, we may have to remember, this may be the first time when symmetry exploded to give rise to the earliest animal life forms. It was in such an explosion that the earliest animal life forms came into being. It was in such an explosion that the earliest animal life forms came to this world. It was in such an explosive process that, it might be said, the Ediacaran organisms like Dickinsonia emerged. And it may not be very surprising, in a sense, that, several body plans might have come into being, seemingly, at the same time, in the same organism. This may be what happened to Dickinsonia. It might have been a happening in an explosive period. It might have been a happening in an explosive operation. It might have been a happening in an explosive process. The different body shapes or forms of Dickinsonia might be part of such an explosive event. The different body shapes or forms of Dickinsonia might have appeared in such an explosive operation. The different body plans of Dickinsonia might have come into being during such an explosive process. From the round to the oval to the very elongated, the body plans of Dickinsonia appeared to represent or stand for, in a sense, a sense of transitional or transformational development in the body structure. If such a sense of development did exist, it might be said, it was a development shaped, conditioned, or made possible by such an explosive symmetric process.

There has been some difficulty in determining Dickinsonia's relationship with other organisms, though it resembles in structure other Ediacaran organisms such as Yorgia. People have suggested that, Dickinsonia may be related to the kind of early animals such as placozoans. Like sponges or jellyfish, placozoans, as some of the simplest organisms on earth, are among the earliest animals appearing on this planet. The relationship between Dickinsonia and placozoans may be established by analyzing the ways they shared to sustain themselves. It appears, they all absorbed nutrients through the underside of their bodies.

Kimberella is an Ediacaran animal living on the sea floor. Some traces can be seen in the fossils left by the burrowing Kimberella, as such organism might have tried to survive the possible sandy currents in the sea. The surprisingly good conditions in which the Kimberella fossils were preserved had made it possible that, this organism may be the first bilaterally symmetric animal that had undergone a relatively detailed scientific investigation. It is usually thought that, Kimberella was a mollusk-like organism living in the Ediacaran. While the body plan of Kimberella may resemble, to a certain extent, that of mollusks, it has to be pointed out, some of its features may not always be compatible with that of mollusks. As an early organism coming into being in the Ediacaran, it may be understandable that some of its features may not necessarily be the same as exemplified by the later organisms. But overall, it might be said, this organism may be regarded, in a sense, as an early animal that had possessed some sense of development or enjoyed some developmental advantages. It is found that, it was an animal that developed through sexual reproduction. And it is observed, in the body of Kimberella, there existed several types of muscles, and some of them may be seen as fairly developed. It may be the case that, these muscles were responsible for making this early organism able to move on the Ediacaran sea floor.

It is significant to note that, it appears, there is no fossil evidence for the existence of radial symmetry in the body plan of Kimberella, and the only symmetry present in its body structure is the bilateral symmetry. In other words, it might be said, Kimberella might have been one of the earliest animals that had developed to such an extent that, whose body plans had come to possess a full and complete sense

Symmetry I

of bilateral symmetry. This is significant in the sense that, among the Ediacaran organisms, apart from the ones exhibiting a full and complete sense of radial symmetry and the ones exhibiting a sense of mixture or combination of radial symmetry and bilateral symmetry, those possessing a full and complete sense of bilateral symmetry may be regarded as the kind of organisms that had reached, in a sense, a sense of advanced development. This may be said in that, there exists an essential and fundamental difference between radial symmetry and bilateral symmetry, and the coming into being or existence of such different symmetries in the body plans may mean that, such organisms may come to possess or demonstrate some different properties, capacities, or characteristics. The Ediacaran organisms exhibiting a full and complete sense of radial symmetry may be seen as the ones such as Arkarua, Cloudina, or Tribrachidium. The Ediacaran organisms exhibiting a sense of mixture or combination of radial symmetry and bilateral symmetry may be seen as the ones such as Yorgia, Dickinsonia, or to a certain extent, Charnia. The Ediacaran organisms possessing a full and complete sense of bilateral symmetry may be seen as the ones such as Kimberella, Parvancorina, or Spriggina. Certainly, as we can see, these organisms did seem to have possessed different symmetric body plans, and it appears, they did seem to have exhibited or demonstrated, in some senses, different properties, capacities, or characteristics. Such differences may be seen, to a certain extent, in these organisms in their mobility, in their internal body structures, or in their physical closeness to the modern animals.

The fossils of Kimberella are usually found together with that of Yorgia, Dickinsonia, and Tribrachidium. That is to say, it seems, they might have existed together in the Ediacaran seas. Tribrachidium may be seen as the Ediacaran organism possessing a full and complete sense of radial symmetry. Yorgia and Dickinsonia may be seen as the Ediacaran organisms bearing a sense of mixture or combination of radial symmetry and bilateral symmetry. Kimberella may be regarded as the Ediacaran organism demonstrating a full and complete sense of bilateral symmetry. Thus, from the coexistence of these Ediacaran organisms, it might be said, all the three types of symmetry, that is, radial symmetry, bilateral symmetry and the combination of radial symmetry and bilateral symmetry, might have come into being and appeared in the Ediacaran. Was it the case that they came into being in the Ediacaran at the same time? Was it the case that radial symmetry might have come into being first? Was it the case that, bilateral symmetry, or the combination of radial symmetry and bilateral symmetry, might have come into being later, after radial symmetry? Or, was it the case that, bilateral symmetry, or the combination of radial symmetry and bilateral symmetry, might have come into being before the appearance of radial symmetry? Or, was it simply the case that, all these three types of symmetry had come into being, all at once, all at the same time, in the Ediacaran, that is, it would be almost nonsensical or of little meaning if we attempt to talk about the timing of their happenings as they had happened so closely with each other, either in time or in the nature of their occurrences? If so, then, how could we talk about something like a sense of advanced development, with regard to the kind of Ediacaran organisms possessing a full and complete sense of bilateral symmetry?

We may be able to witness the advantages enjoyed by the animals possessing bilateral symmetry, but it may be difficult for us to see or look into the kind of things such as a sense of advanced development that might have been associated with the kind of organisms possessing a full and complete sense of bilateral symmetry in the Ediacaran. Why? It is the development not in an ordinary sense. It was the symmetric development. It was the symmetric process. It was the symmetric radiation. It was the symmetric diversification. It was the symmetric explosion. It was not an ordinary event. It was not an ordinary happening. It was not an ordinary coming into being. It was not an evolutionary development. It was not an evolutionary process. It was not development through natural selection. It was not evolution by natural selection. It was not natural selection. It was not evolution. It was symmetry. It was harmony. It was avolution. It was symmetric movement. It was harmonic development. It was an avolutionary process. Evolution might have played some role, in some way, in some sense, or in some manner, but it was avolution that had defined or characterized such a process. Natural selection might have contributed to such a process, in some sense, in some way, in some manner, or to some extent, but it was symmetry or harmony that had initiated, guided, conditioned, or determined such a process. The Ediacaran may thus be seen as a period of symmetric movement or development, a period of symmetric burgeoning or multiplication, a period of symmetric outburst or eruption, or, a period of harmonic surge or boom. It was the bang of symmetry. It was the bang of harmony. It was the bang with which the

Symmetry I

fresh life forms called animals were to come into this world. It was the bang that opened a new age for the life on earth.

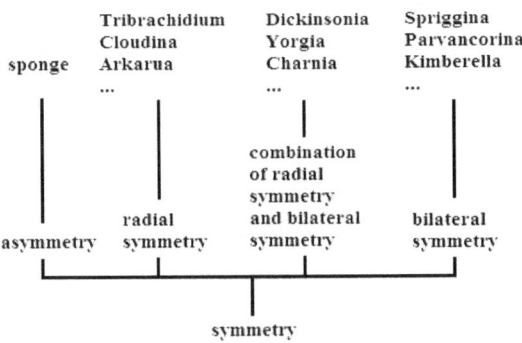

Figure 1.1   The Ediacaran Symmetric Explosion

It is in such a sense that we may be able to understand the Ediacaran. As it was a period of symmetric movement or development, it was possible that there might have been some sense of development associated with the coming into being of the various symmetries in such a period, such as, radial symmetry, bilateral symmetry, or the combination of radial symmetry and bilateral symmetry. And, as it was a period of symmetric outburst or eruption, it was possible that, it might be difficult for us to see or look into the kind of development that might have been associated with the coming into being of the various symmetric body plans in such a period. Such things might have happened so fast, or in such an innate or intrinsic manner that we may only be able to get a glimpse of what might be in the final stage. On the other hand, the symmetric outburst or eruption, characteristic of such a period, may mean that, the symmetries might have appeared or come into being in such a period not necessarily in the kind of ways we may think of. They might have appeared at the same time. They might have appeared one after the other. Radial symmetry might have appeared first. Bilateral symmetry, or the combination of radial symmetry and bilateral symmetry, might have appeared before the coming into being of radial symmetry. It was a symmetric radiation. It was a symmetric diversification. It was not necessarily following a straightforward process, such as, from simplicity to complexity. Compared to bilateral symmetry, radial symmetry may be simpler, in some sense. But that is to our human perception. That may not necessarily be the case, to symmetry or harmony. Compared to radial symmetry, bilateral symmetry may be more complex, in some way. But that is to our human understanding. That may not necessarily be the case, to symmetry or harmony. To symmetry or harmony, radial symmetry, bilateral symmetry, or the combination of radial symmetry and bilateral symmetry, may just be the symmetric movements or harmonic developments that have to be fulfilled or realized in nature, or, in plants or animals. There might be some senses of difference associated with such different symmetries, but such differences may not necessarily mean or constitute the kind of things such as simplicity or complexity as we understand them.

The appearance of Kimberella in the Ediacaran is important, in that, with its appearance, the animal body plan possessing or demonstrating bilateral symmetry had finally come into being, and the possible development or the possible developmental advantages associated with such a kind of body plan may be seen, observed, and investigated. This is important, in the sense that, the coming into being or appearance of the bilaterally symmetric animal body plan may be seen as what truly made the Ediacaran an age of symmetric explosion, or an age of harmonic boom. While both the radially symmetric body plan and the bilaterally symmetric body plan may be seen as the fulfillment or realization of symmetry in the animal life forms in the Ediacaran, one cannot overlook or ignore the enormous or even fundamental difference between such two symmetric body plans. Such difference may be seen, in a sense, or to a certain extent, in some senses of relatively "advanced" existence of Kimberella, such as, in its use of sexual reproduction, in its possession of mobility, or in its growth of muscles for movement. It is in such a sense that, it might be said, it may not be surprising that such an early organism may be related to the later animals such as mollusks.

Unlike the radially symmetric animals such as cnidarians, ctenophores or echinoderms, which live mostly in the sea, mollusks can be found in the sea, in the fresh water, or on the dry land. Except for a few examples such as the freshwater jelly or freshwater hydra, most cnidarians such as jellyfish, sea anemones, sea pens or corals live in the sea. Ctenophores or comb jellies also live in the sea. Echinoderms, such

Symmetry I

as starfish, sea urchins or sea cucumbers, are the animals with pentamerous radial symmetry. They do not live in the fresh water or on the dry land. They can only be found in the sea. Why, one may ask, should these radially symmetric animals exist mostly in the sea? That is, one may ask, in a sense, why should animals like mollusks be the kind of animals that are able to live not just in the sea, but also in the fresh water or on the dry land? What has given animals like mollusks such ability? What has given animals like mollusks such capacity? What has given animals like mollusks such a potential? In other words, what has limited, in a sense, the radially symmetric animals? What has confined them, mostly, to the sea? What has prevented them from spreading into the fresh water or onto the dry land? What has made them unable to develop such abilities, such capacities, or such potentials? That is, what has blocked the possible developments of the radially symmetric animals, as such developments may be seen as having been achieved or experienced by the kind of animals such as mollusks?

Mollusks are usually bilaterally symmetric animals. One of the characteristics that distinguish them from the radially symmetric animals is the nervous system that they may possess. Such a nervous system usually consists of nerve cords and ganglia. It works better than a simple nerve net, often found in the radially symmetric animals. It is bilateral symmetry that distinguishes mollusks from the radially symmetric animals. It is bilateral symmetry that enables mollusks to possess a nervous system that is much more powerful than a simple nerve net. It is bilateral symmetry that enables mollusks to develop the kind of abilities, the kind of capacities, or the kind of potentials, so that they may spread, eventually, from the sea, into the fresh water, or onto the dry land. The radially symmetric animals cannot do this. The radially symmetric animals cannot fulfill this. The radially symmetric animals cannot realize this. They could not spread from the sea to the fresh water or dry land, on a large scale. They are limited. They could not advance as other animals might. They are constrained. They could not develop the kind of abilities, the kind of capacities, or the kind of potentials so that they might leave the sea and colonize the fresh water or land. They are blocked. It is radial symmetry that has limited them. It is radial symmetry that has constrained them. It is radial symmetry that has blocked them.

Symmetry regulates the development of animals. Symmetry guides the development of animals. Symmetry conditions the development of animals. Symmetry controls the development of animals. Symmetry determines the development of animals. Symmetry means the existence of animals. Symmetry means the ways of the existence of animals. Symmetry means the symmetric body plans of animals. Symmetry means, with the different symmetric body plans, different ways of existence will come into being for animals. Radial symmetry means a way of existence for animals, through its fulfillment or realization in the body plans of these animals. Bilateral symmetry, on the other hand, means a different way of existence for animals, through its fulfillment or realization in the body plans of such animals.

Animals like mollusks are the organisms fulfilling or realizing bilateral symmetry, and thus they may live in the sea, in the fresh water, or on the land. The radially symmetric animals are the organisms fulfilling or realizing radial symmetry, and thus they may be constrained, restricted, or limited in the ways of their existence. The difference between radial symmetry and bilateral symmetry may thus be seen. The difference between the radially symmetric body plans and the bilaterally symmetric body plans may thus be seen. The difference between the radially symmetric animals and the bilaterally symmetric animals may thus be seen. They represent the different symmetries. They represent the different body plans. They represent the different life forms. They represent the different abilities. They represent the different capacities. They represent the different potentials. They represent the power of radial symmetry. They represent the power of bilateral symmetry. They represent the different powers of the different fulfillments or realizations of symmetry in nature, or in the world. It is in such a sense that, it might be said, the coming into being or appearance of the kind of bilaterally symmetric organisms like Kimberella in the Ediacaran was significant, remarkable, full of meaning, and full of hope, for the life on earth.

People are sometimes concerned with the appearance of Kimberella in the Ediacaran, as they focus on the Cambrian explosion. It is understandable. Animals with bilateral symmetry are sometimes divided into protostomes and deuterostomes. One of the differences between them may be seen in the embryonic development, in that, while the mouth appears first in protostomes, the mouth is formed in a later stage in deuterostomes. Even though both protostomes and

Symmetry I

deuterostomes are animals of bilateral symmetry, a number of differences may exist between them, either in their body structures or in their developments. If Kimberella was related to mollusks, given its resemblance to them, then it is possible that it might have belonged to the protostomes. If this is the case, then it means that, the protostomes might have diverged from the deuterostomes prior to the happening of the Cambrian explosion. This certainly may pose a problem for the Cambrian explosion. On the other hand, after all, Kimberella is usually taken as an Ediacaran organism exhibiting or demonstrating bilateral symmetry. Then, this means that, simply, the separation between radial symmetry and bilateral symmetry in animals might have happened well before the coming into being of the Cambrian explosion. What do all these mean? They may mean that, if such things were the case, then, the Cambrian explosion might not have been so fundamental, primary, significant, or remarkable as people might have thought.

The protostomes might have diverged from the deuterostomes in the Ediacaran, prior to the appearance of Kimberella. The separation of the radially symmetric body plan from the bilaterally symmetric body plan in animals might have occurred in the Ediacaran, before the coming into being of Kimberella. Symmetry might have moved, in the Ediacaran, prior to the Cambrian. Symmetry might have developed, in the Ediacaran, prior to the Cambrian. Symmetry might have progressed, in the Ediacaran, well before the Cambrian. The movement of symmetry may not just be seen in the Cambrian; it may be seen in the Ediacaran. The development of symmetry may not just be observed in the Cambrian; it may be observed in the Ediacaran. The progress of symmetry may not just be what characterized the Cambrian; it might also have characterized the Ediacaran. The explosion of symmetry may not just be what defined the Cambrian; it might also have defined the Ediacaran. Animals came into being in the Ediacaran. Animals came into being in the Cambrian. Animals came into being in the Ediacaran explosion. Animals came into being in the Cambrian explosion. Animals came into being after the primordial explosive moment. Animals came into being in the primordial explosion. Symmetry moved, from the primordial explosive moment. Symmetry moved, the primordial explosion was under way. Symmetry moved, animals came to this world. Symmetry moved, new life appeared on this planet.

People often talk about the difference between the Ediacaran and the Cambrian, as if little linkage could be found to connect these two periods. The separation of these two periods may not be that big, and the disconnection may not be that strong. In other words, what we have witnessed may just be a surface, and certain things underlying these two periods might connect them in some vital, intrinsic and fundamental ways. The continuation from the Ediacaran to the Cambrian may be seen, in a sense, in many ways. Even though there exists some difficulty in pinpointing, conclusively, the continuous developments occurring in the Ediacaran and Cambrian, given, in a certain sense, the explosive or experimental nature of the symmetric movement in such two periods, it seems, it is still possible for us to see or perceive, overall, a sense of development from one period to the other. That is, it might be said, the Ediacaran might be connected with the Cambrian, as the Ediacaran organisms might be connected with the Cambrian organisms. The Ediacaran organisms like Onega might be linked, in some sense, or to some extent, with some Cambrian arthropods, like Skania. Skania was an arthropod from the middle Cambrian. Onega was an Ediacaran organism resembling, to some extent, Dickinsonia. It is often found in the same locations where other Ediacaran organisms may be discovered, such as Yorgia, Dickinsonia, Kimberella, or Parvancorina. The continuation, or a sense of development from the Ediacaran to the Cambrian may also be seen or observed in the possible connections between the kind of Ediacaran organisms such as Parvancorina or Spriggina and the Cambrian trilobites.

The name of Parvancorina comes from the Latin words meaning small anchor. Such a name may fairly describe the shape of this Ediacaran organism, which possessed a bilaterally symmetric body plan resembling, to a certain extent, a small anchor. The raised ridges found in the fossils of Parvancorina seem to have divided the body in a fashion similar to what may be found in the Cambrian arthropods, such as Skania or the trilobites. Though certain questions remain with regard to the possible different ways of life enjoyed by Parvancorina and the Cambrian arthropods, given the strong symmetric or structural similarity, it may still be reasonable to say that, Parvancorina may be seen as an arthropod-like organism living in the Ediacaran and possibly related, in an intrinsic or fundamental way, to the Cambrian arthropods such as the trilobites.

The difficulty in determining the true relationships of the Ediacaran organisms may be seen, fairly clearly, in the case of Spriggina.

Symmetry I

Spriggina has been thought, at various times or by various people, to be a segmented worm, a frond-like creature, or an early arthropod. Why should there be such a kind of confusion with regard to its classification? Why should there be such a kind of uncertainty when it comes to the Ediacaran organisms? Why should it be the case that we may find so many possible relationships for almost every organism coming into being in such a period? The answer may lie nowhere but in the possibility that this was an age of symmetric explosion. It was the explosion of symmetry. It was the explosion of harmony. It was the symmetric proliferation. It was the symmetric radiation. It was the symmetric diversification. Symmetry emerged. Symmetry appeared. Symmetry came into being. Symmetry came on the scene. Symmetry multiplied. Symmetry surged. Symmetry boomed. Symmetry blossomed. Thus, we see, different symmetries might have appeared in the organisms. Thus, we see, different symmetries might have emerged in the animals. Thus, we see, different symmetries might have come into being in the new life forms. Thus, we see, different symmetries might have appeared in a single organism. Thus, we see, different symmetries might have emerged in one animal. Thus, we see, different symmetries might have come into being in an individual life form. The multiple symmetric appearance in a single organism might thus connect such an organism with other organisms. The multiple symmetric emergence in one animal might thus link such an animal with other animals. The multiple symmetric coming into being in an individual life form might thus relate such a life form to other life forms. It was the symmetric connection. It was the symmetric linkage. It was the symmetric relationship. It was the symmetric connection coming into being as a result of the symmetric radiation. It was the symmetric linkage originating from the symmetric diversification. It was the symmetric relationship arising out of the symmetric explosion. It was the symmetric connection expressing the coming into being of organisms from symmetry. It was the symmetric linkage showing the symmetric origin of animals. It was the symmetric relationship revealing the true source of the new life forms.

That is to say, the kind of confusion or uncertainty usually associated with the classification of the Ediacaran organisms may be seen, in a sense, as originating from the very nature of such an age. It was the explosive time of symmetry. Symmetry exploded. Symmetry diversified in various organisms. Symmetry surged in various animals.

The diversification of symmetry in organisms may mean that, such organisms might have shared certain things, certain features, or certain characteristics, no matter how different they might be, in some sense, or to some extent. The radiation of symmetry in animals may mean that, different animals might have been related, no matter how dissimilar they might look, in some sense, or to some extent, with each other. This may mean that, it may be difficult for us to pinpoint the exact relationships when it comes to the Ediacaran organisms. While they may look related to some organisms, they may be associated, at the same time, with other life forms. While they may share some features with some organisms, they may possess, at the same time, certain characteristics that may be found in other animals. It is symmetry that may be seen as behind this. It is the symmetric explosion that may be seen as behind this. It is the symmetric explosion, in a preliminary stage, that may be seen as behind this. Such may be the case with Spriggina, as we know, it has been classified either as a segmented worm, a frond-like creature, or an early arthropod.

The Ediacaran symmetric explosion may be seen as the first step in the long process of the movement of symmetry in the animal life. As such, it may only be regarded, in a sense, as a preliminary stage. In this preliminary stage, it might be said, things might have happened, in a sense, with a tentative or experimental nature. That is to say, the movement of symmetry in this stage might not have been so regular, straightforward, smooth, or in a sense, streamlined. It was just the beginning. It was just the start. It was just the beginning of creation. It was just the first step towards the birth of the new life forms called animals. The process was not yet fixed. The process was not yet established. There might be convolutions. There might be confusions. There might be explorations. There might be experiments. There might be hesitations. There might be uncertainties. Symmetry might have moved with explorations. Symmetry might have developed with experiments. Symmetry might have advanced or surged with uncertainties. Symmetry might have appeared in animals, but only in the first step. Symmetry might have emerged in the animal life forms, but only in a preliminary or preparatory stage.

It is in such a sense that, it might be said, there might exist a sense of ambiguity or obscurity when it comes to the appearance of organisms in the Ediacaran. And it is also in such a sense that, it might be said, the confusion or uncertainty associated with the Ediacaran

Symmetry I

organisms or their relationships, discussed above, may be understood. As the preliminary or preparatory stage, while the Ediacaran symmetric explosion led or gave rise to the coming into being of the new life forms called animals, it might have left certain works undone or unfinished. It might take the later stages, or the later periods, to fully accomplish such works. This may be seen with the Cambrian. As we know, it is in the Cambrian that the ancestors of most current animal life forms may be found. The Ediacaran explosion might have laid down the symmetric foundation, and the Cambrian explosion might have continued the symmetric development, based on such a foundation. In other words, in an intrinsic, fundamental, or symmetric sense, the Ediacaran may not be separated from the Cambrian, or, the Cambrian may not be severed from the Ediacaran. The Cambrian was not an isolated period. The Cambrian was not an isolated phenomenon. It built on the Ediacaran. It followed the Ediacaran. It succeeded the Ediacaran. It inherited the Ediacaran. It continued the Ediacaran. They were the same process. They were the same movement. They were the same development. They constituted, together, the movement of symmetry. They embodied, together, the development of harmony. Together, they gave rise to the coming into being of animals. Together, they brought new and fresh life forms into this world.

While the exploratory or experimental nature of the Ediacaran may be seen, in a sense, in the possible absence of ancestors for the modern animals, we cannot overlook or ignore, at the same time, the signs pointing to a sense of continuation or a sense of development from the Ediacaran to the Cambrian. In other words, as a preliminary or preparatory stage, many aspects of what the Ediacaran established or prepared may not be seen or observed today, but this may not mean that such a period was not important. No. It was important. It was of the utmost importance or significance, in a sense, for the life on earth, or, for the development of life on earth. The Ediacaran organisms might have mostly disappeared at the end of such a period, but what such a period established or prepared might have constituted the backbone of life, or the backbone of the existence of life, and continued to this day. The disappearance of the Ediacaran organisms may just be one aspect of the Ediacaran development, and such a thing may not lead us to such a position that we are no longer able to notice or look into the kind of possibly significant or vital things happening in such a period. Many things happened in such a period, and many significant and vital things had happened in such a period. The disappearance of the Ediacaran organisms might just be the surface; what gave rise to the appearance of the Ediacaran organisms might have remained. That is, the Ediacaran organisms might have gone extinct, but what underlying their coming into being or existence in the first place, might have lived on, and strong. The specific shapes of the Ediacaran organisms might have disappeared, but the Ediacaran blueprints might have been taken over by the Cambrian. The individual forms of the Ediacaran animals might have vanished, but the Ediacaran symmetric essence might have been inherited, cherished, or continued by the Cambrian. It is in such a sense that many things in the Ediacaran may be understood. It is in such a sense that many things in the Cambrian may be understood. And it is in such a sense that, it might be said, both the Ediacaran and the Cambrian may be understood.

People sometimes try to rule out the possible relationship of Spriggina with arthropods, based in part on the fact that, it seems, what it possessed is not the true bilateral symmetry, but merely glide symmetry. When people do this, it seems, they have forgotten that, this was the Ediacaran age, and things had just started to happen. When things develop in their initial stages, they may look like differently from what they may become later on, though the fundamentals may largely stay the same. The Ediacaran organisms might have developed glide symmetry, instead of bilateral symmetry, as symmetry might have just begun its movement in the animal life. As we have discussed above, glide symmetry, or glide reflection symmetry, may be seen, in a sense, as bilateral symmetry in movement or with development. When symmetry moved in the initial stages, it might easily take the form of glide symmetry, instead of bilateral symmetry. The later developments might transform glide symmetry into bilateral symmetry, or, it might be the case that glide symmetry might stay the same, as a form of expression of symmetry, in or among things. The possession of glide symmetry by Spriggina may thus be seen, in a sense, as a thing not that alien or strange to the Ediacaran. Actually, it seems, many of the organisms coming into being in the Ediacaran appeared to have developed or possessed glide symmetry. This may indicate, in a sense, the organisms might have just emerged, and only developed in their initial stages.

The real significance of Spriggina may lie in that, as a segmented organism, it may be regarded as one of the Ediacaran animals that had

Symmetry I

developed or possessed a head-like body structure, with possibly eyes, antennas, and a mouth. This is truly significant, as a head, with eyes, mouth, or possibly antennas, might have emerged or appeared in the Ediacaran, for the first time, in the history of the animal life on earth. We all know the importance of head to the existence of animals on earth. As such, the appearance or coming into being of head in animals may be regarded as one of the most significant steps in the long development of the animal life on this planet. The appearance of the Spriggina head, possibly with eyes, mouth or antennas, may thus be regarded, in a sense, as one of the most important things happened in the Ediacaran. Marywadea may be the other organism of this period possessing a similar head structure. Together they seem to suggest, a new life might have appeared on earth, a life with head, with eyes, with mouth, or with antennas. It was a new animal life, and as we know, such a kind of animal life had continued, from that point, well to this day.

So, who could claim that the Ediacaran is not important? Who could claim that such a period is irrelevant? Who could claim that, to study the origins of animals, one may only focus on the Cambrian, or one may only pay attention to the Cambrian? Or, is it only the Cambrian that matters? Or, is it only in the Cambrian that the earliest forms of the current animal life may be found? It is true that most of the organisms in the Ediacaran might have disappeared at the end of such a period, but how to explain the appearance of the kind of Cambrian animals such as the trilobites, resembling the organisms like Spriggina, with their heads or eyes appearing from the very beginning? How to explain their sudden appearance in the Cambrian? How to explain the appearance of their heads? How to explain the appearance of their eyes? Was there a relationship between the Ediacaran and the Cambrian? Was there a relationship between the Ediacaran organisms and the Cambrian animals? Was something arranged for the coming into being of the Cambrian? Was the way prepared for the Cambrian to happen? Who had laid down the groundwork? Who had prepared the way?

The fossils of the Ediacaran organisms such as Spriggina or Marywadea seem to indicate the appearance or coming into being of the head, that is, the animal head, possibly with eyes, mouth, or antennas, in the Ediacaran. The head is not just an ordinary animal body part. It usually has eyes, mouth, or some other fairly developed

Avolution and Man

organs. It often functions as a body part controlling or coordinating other body parts. Thus, the head may not be treated, in a certain sense, as an ordinary body part, and the appearance or coming into being of the head may not be seen as something that is insignificant or usual. How did the head appear in such a period? How did the head come into being in such an early age? How did the head come into being, at all, in the first place? And we cannot forget, the Ediacaran may be seen as the time when the animal life first emerged and the fresh life forms called animals had just started to make their appearance on this planet. And, it was exactly in such a time, it seems, the head came into being. How did the head come into being, in the beginning? How did the head come into being, from the start? How did the head come into being, in a sense, in the very beginning of the animal life? How did the head come into being, in a sense, from the very start of the animal existence on earth? How? How? Why? Why? What does it tell us? What does it point to us? What does it demonstrate? What does it reveal? What does it reveal about life? What does it reveal about the existence of life? What does it reveal about the coming into being of life? What does it reveal about the life on earth? What is behind it? What is underlying it? What makes it possible? What makes it necessary?

The symmetric movement or development may be seen as the only explanation when it comes to the appearance or coming into being of the animal head in the Ediacaran. The coming into being of the head in the Ediacaran may not be taken as an evolutionary development, as such a sense of development may not be observed, encountered, or perceived. There might have been a sense of development, with regard to the appearance or coming into being of the head in the Ediacaran, but such a sense of development might have been so unusual that it may only be regarded, to our human perception or understanding, as innate, intrinsic, or, symmetric. Such a sense of symmetric development, leading to the coming into being of the head, may be seen as a sense of development that was deep, innate, or intrinsic, and which may not be seen, observed, or perceived by us, due to the symmetric speed, the symmetric intricacy, or the symmetric profundity fulfilled or realized in such a process. That is, such a symmetric development might have been accomplished with such a symmetric speed, with such a symmetric intricacy, or with such a symmetric profundity that we the human beings may only be left with the choice to meet or encounter the appearance, the coming into being, or the existence of the head.

Symmetry I

The coming into being of the head in the Ediacaran may not be regarded as something incidental or trivial. It was the movement of symmetry. It was the result or consequence of the movement of symmetry. More specifically, it might be said, it was the movement of bilateral symmetry, or, it was the result or consequence of the movement of bilateral symmetry. In other words, in a sense, it might be said, it was the bilateral symmetry fulfilled or realized in the animal life in the Ediacaran that may be seen as behind, ultimately, the appearance or coming into being of the head. Bilateral symmetry moved in the animal life in the Ediacaran. Bilateral symmetry developed in the animal life in the Ediacaran. Bilateral symmetry had moved or developed in such a way, that is, in such an innate way, in such an intrinsic way, in such a deep way, or, in such a symmetric way, that, the head eventually came into being in animals. It was the movement of bilateral symmetry in the Ediacaran that led the bilaterally symmetric organisms like Spriggina to develop or possess a head. And at the same time, it might be said, the coming into being of the head in the animals like Spriggina may be seen as representing or embodying, in a sense, the true or final fulfillment or realization of bilateral symmetry, in the Ediacaran.

Bilateral symmetry is different from radial symmetry. And in a sense, it might be said, such a difference may be so big that, it seems, while the bilaterally symmetric animals may develop a centralized nervous system, the radially symmetric animals may only develop or possess a simple nerve net. A simple nerve net is not a centralized nervous system, and thus it usually lacks the kind of capacity, the kind of power, or the kind of potential that may be seen in a centralized nervous system. This may be seen, in a sense, in that, the radially symmetric animals are usually found to be without a well-developed head structure, as such a head structure, with eyes, mouth or other organs may need the support of a nervous system much more powerful than a simple nerve net. Cnidarians, ctenophores, and echinoderms may be seen as among the radially symmetric animals. Cnidarians, such as jellyfish, sea anemones, sea pens, corals, or hydras, usually lack a well-developed head structure. Just like them, ctenophores or comb jellies possess a simple nerve net only and thus no well-developed head structure may be found in them. As the animals with pentamerous radial symmetry, echinoderms such as starfish, sea urchins, sea cucumbers, or sand dollars may not be expected to develop a centralized nervous system, and indeed they seem to only possess a simple nerve net.

Some might question the classification of echinoderms here as the radially symmetric animals, by pointing to the fact that, it seems, these animals may express or demonstrate bilateral symmetry in the larval stage. This may be true. But, when we talk about the presence of symmetry in animals, what we are mostly concerned with is usually what such a presence of symmetry means to the existence of such animals. That is to say, when we talk about the symmetric animals, what we are focusing on is usually to what extent a symmetric presence may dominate or define the existence of animals. A dominant or defining form of symmetry may thus be what we are mainly looking for in animals. For the echinoderms, even though bilateral symmetry may be expressed or demonstrated in the larval stage, but, it might be said, it is radial symmetry that may be seen as the form of symmetry dominating or defining their existence. Such may be seen in a number of ways. Though echinoderms constitute one of the largest groups of living species, they nevertheless demonstrate conspicuously a lack of ability to live in or adapt to the environments other than the sea, such as in the freshwater or on land. Such limitations may be seen as coming from their radially symmetric existence, as such a sense of inability may not be observed in other bilaterally symmetric animals. And, as we know, just like other radially symmetric animals, echinoderms seem to have only developed or possessed a simple nerve net. As the animals with only a simple nerve net, certainly, it may be expected, no well-developed head structure may be found in them. It is in such a sense that, it might be said, the dominant or defining form of symmetry in echinoderms may be seen as radial symmetry, and they may thus be classified as the radially symmetric animals, even though there might be some sense of presence of bilateral symmetry in their existence.

The lack of a centralized nervous system or a well-developed head structure in the radially symmetric animals reveals, in a sense, the capacity, the power, or the potential of bilateral symmetry. It is in such a sense that we talk about the coming into being of the head, and it is in such a sense that, it might be said, we may contemplate or look into the meaning or significance of the appearance of the kind of animals like Spriggina in the Ediacaran. Bilateral symmetry may be seen as what behind the appearance of the kind animals like Spriggina. The movement of bilateral symmetry may be seen as what behind the

Symmetry I

appearance or development of the head in the kind of animals like Spriggina. The innate or intrinsic movement of symmetry may be beyond, in a sense, our human perception or understanding. But we may sense, in a sense, the power of symmetry, as such a power might have driven the early organisms to develop a body structure as intricate, complex, or exquisite as the head, with possibly eyes, mouth, or antennas, or, limited some other organisms so that they might have been unable to develop such kind of things. The power of symmetry may be seen in the appearance or coming into being of the early animals. The power of symmetry may be seen in the coming into being of the kind of intricacy or complexity appearing in the early animals. The power of symmetry may be seen in the speed with which the early animals appeared or came into being. The intricacy appearing in the early animals may be seen as the symmetric intricacy. The complexity coming into being in the early animals may be seen as the symmetric profundity. The speed with which the early animals came into being may be seen as the symmetric speed. It was with such symmetric intricacy, symmetric profundity, or symmetric speed that the early animals emerged. It was with such symmetric intricacy, symmetric profundity, or symmetric speed that the Ediacaran explosion occurred. Symmetry was so powerful that, it seems, new life came into this world in an explosion. That is, it might be said, symmetry may be seen as so deep, so intricate, so sharp, so profound, or so powerful that, it seems, any development might be within its reach, easily, in a sense.

This may be what happened in the Ediacaran. Symmetry moved, with the symmetric speed. Symmetry developed, with the symmetric intricacy. Symmetry surged, with the symmetric profundity. Symmetry exploded, with the symmetric power. This may be why we see the appearance or coming into being of the animal head in the Ediacaran. This may be how the animal head appeared or came into being in such a period. This may be why the head appeared or came into being, in a sense, in the very beginning of the animal life. This may be how the head appeared or came into being, in a sense, from the very start of the animal existence on earth. The appearance or coming into being of the kind of Ediacaran organisms like Spriggina illustrated or demonstrated the power, profundity or speed of symmetry, and it is in such a sense that, it might be said, the existence of the kind of Ediacaran organisms like Spriggina defined such a period as an age of symmetric explosion.

The Ediacaran explosion laid the symmetric foundation for the Cambrian. The appearance of the Ediacaran organisms prepared the way for the coming into being of the Cambrian animals. It may be time now for us to take a good look at the animals coming into being in the Cambrian. And let us first pay our attention to the trilobites. Trilobites are some of the earliest arthropods coming into being in the Cambrian. The appearance of trilobites in the Cambrian may have raised, it might be said, a number of questions, some of them quite fundamental, about the Cambrian explosion. One of the surprising things about the trilobites may be their remarkable diversity and wide distribution, it seems, from the very beginning. The fossil record seems to indicate that, from the very time when trilobites were first preserved, they were already spread out and quite diverse. So, where did this trilobite diversity come from, from the very beginning? Or, how was such trilobite distribution realized, at the very start of their appearance? How to explain such trilobite phenomena? How to explain the trilobite existence before their appearance? Was it the case that the trilobites or their forerunners had existed and developed prior to their appearance in the fossil record, that is, prior to their appearance in the Cambrian? If no such existence or development had happened, how should we explain what we have witnessed in the fossil record?

Trilobites were among the dominant life forms in the Cambrian. And, it seems, they had left a vast amount of fossils, compared to other organisms, on which we may conduct a relatively thorough investigation. Thus, it is fitting that we may here focus on them in order to look into the possible developments or happenings occurred in the Cambrian. The study of trilobites appears to reveal that, trilobites in their early developmental stages were not always preserved in the fossils, possibly due to the fact that they had not undergone the process of calcification or mineralization. And, it appears, even the earliest trilobites had possessed their body plans from the beginning, just like other trilobites. That is, it seems, it is hard for us to see from where such early trilobites might have acquired their body plans, or through what kind of stages they might have reached their developments. The lack of developmental or transitional stages raises serious questions about the appearance of the early trilobites in the Cambrian, as their appearance seems to be, in a sense, inexplicable. They seemed to have appeared, suddenly, from nowhere. No organisms may be treated as their ancestors, through some transitional stages. No organisms may be

Symmetry I

linked to them, as their forerunners, in a developmental sense, as no such developments may be found. So, where did the early trilobites come from? Where was their beginning? What might be their source? From where had they started their developments? And, how did they get their trilobite body plans? Where did such trilobite body plans come from? From nowhere? How were they formed? How did they come into being? How did they emerge? How did they appear? Was it the case that, no body plans may be regarded as the forerunners of such body plans? Was it the case that, no developments may be linked to their appearance? Was it the case that, no transitional processes may be seen in their eventual coming into being?

Some might say that, the fossil record may not have truly revealed the developmental history of trilobites, as such a record may have only reflected the existence or development of the kind of trilobites with mineralized exoskeletons. It is true that the fossils may have only recorded the mineralized trilobites, but how about the non-mineralized trilobites, if they indeed had existed or developed? Soft-bodied organisms had left their traces in the fossils. If non-mineralized trilobites had indeed existed, it should be the case that they might have left some records in the fossils. And, given the relatively big amount of fossils left by the trilobites, it seems, such a chance may be even higher than we think. Thus, it appears, the argument that the fossil record may not have truly reflected the history of trilobites may not have been made, in a sense, on a firm ground. But, we do see, as the fossil record seems to have reflected, trilobites appeared to have emerged suddenly in the Cambrian, and no organisms may be treated as their forerunners or ancestors, in a conclusive way.

While the fossil record seems to point to a sudden appearance of trilobites, other studies may suggest, quite strongly, that trilobites might have indeed existed and developed prior to their appearance in the Cambrian. Geologists have suggested, a supercontinent named Pannotia might have existed from about 600 million years ago to about 550 million years ago. The evidence related to this supercontinent may lead us to conclude, it is reasonable to say that, there might be some form of trilobite existence or development before the Cambrian. The examination of the different groups of early trilobites seems to suggest, the breakup of Pannotia might have affected the development of trilobites. While some features common in trilobites may be seen as originating from before the breakup, trilobites appeared to have developed, after the breakup, into different groups defined by their association with the different landmasses formed following the breakup. That is to say, it seems, different trilobite features or characteristics might have come into being, in different groups, as a result of the breakup of Pannotia.

The earliest trilobites might have come into being around 530 million years ago. The breakup of the supercontinent Pannotia might have happened around 550 million years ago. That is to say, the breakup of Pannotia might have occurred about 20 million years before the first appearance of trilobites in the Cambrian. What does all this mean? It may mean that, before the breakup of Pannotia, there might have been some sense of existence or development for the trilobites. It may mean that, the existence or development of the trilobites might have happened much earlier than their appearance in the fossil record. It may mean that, the trilobites might have existed or developed, in some sense, in some way, or in some manner, long before the Cambrian.

So, what is the Cambrian explosion? Was it a real explosion? Was it not? Or was it? If it was truly an explosion, how and why should the trilobites be supposed to have some sense of existence or development prior to their appearance in the Cambrian? If it was not an explosion, then, how should we explain or account for the apparently sudden appearance of the animals like the trilobites in such a period? What is wrong here? What have we missed? What has been overlooked by us? What has been ignored by us? What has been forgotten by us? Have we forgotten something fundamental? Have we overlooked or ignored something essential? Have we missed something innate, inherent, or intrinsic?

Apart from the things discussed so far about the trilobites, another aspect of the trilobite existence may also raise some significant or profound questions about the Cambrian explosion. That is the presence of eyes in the trilobites. It is found, from the very beginning, trilobites had possessed highly developed compound eyes. Such compound eyes were usually made up of many lenses, with the upper level reaching sometimes up to thousands. The trilobite lenses were formed with a mineral substance called calcite. Calcite is a stable form of calcium carbonate. It can be found in rocks or in the shells of marine animals. Calcite can be transparent if it is pure. The transparency of the calcite crystals was thus utilized by the trilobites to develop their lenses.

Symmetry I

Certainly the kind of lenses made of calcite might not be able to change focus by changing their shapes. That is, they might not be the kind of flexible lenses often found in other animal eyes, such as in the human eyes. This limitation may be seen as being compensated, to a certain extent, through a well-structured arrangement in the lenses that seemed to have effectively enhanced the optical functioning of such lenses.

To find calcite in the shells of marine animals is one thing, it seems, but to find it in the eyes of trilobites, and as the major constituent, appears to be quite another. Eyes are not shells. Eyes are exquisite. Eyes are delicate. Eyes are intricate. Eyes are subtle. Eyes are complex. Eyes are profound. Eyes are beautiful. Shells are not. Shells are not as complex. Shells are not as intricate. Shells are not as exquisite. Shells are not as delicate. Shells are not as subtle. Shells are not as profound. Shells are not as beautiful. Eyes are a complex and exquisite organ, that may involve a highly developed nervous system. Shells are not. Shells may not necessarily involve a highly developed nervous system. Shells may come into being; eyes may not. Shells may appear; eyes may not. For the eyes to appear, a highly developed nervous system may have to come into being in the first place. For the eyes to emerge, a well-developed head structure may have to be ready, in a sense, in advance.

That is to say, if the trilobites had indeed possessed their complex compound eyes from the very beginning, while appearing for the first time in the Cambrian, then, given the complexity and exquisiteness of eyes, it seems, such eyes might have been developed prior to the Cambrian. And, given all of this, it might be said, it is highly probable that, a highly developed trilobite-like nervous system might have come into being before the Cambrian, and a well-developed trilobite-like head structure might have appeared prior to such a period. This certainly constitutes a major problem for the Cambrian explosion. If eyes had come into being before the Cambrian, then the Cambrian explosion may not be seen as a real explosion, as eyes constituted some of the most complex, subtle and profound organs in the animal life. If the highly developed nervous system had emerged before the Cambrian, then the Cambrian explosion may not be regarded as a real explosion, as the nervous system functioned as the foundation of the animal existence. If the well-developed animal head structure had appeared before the Cambrian, then the Cambrian explosion may not be treated as a real explosion, as the appearance of the animal head may be considered, in a sense, the most significant step in the development of animal life on earth.

It may be difficult to pinpoint the existence of the nervous system in the Precambrian or Cambrian animals, by finding the direct evidence, as the soft body parts, especially something like the brain, might not have been easily preserved. Apart from the nervous system, it seems, we may have encountered the kind of organisms or animals possessing a well-developed head structure and eyes. We have discussed the kind of Ediacaran organisms, such as Spriggina, that might have developed or possessed a head structure, possibly with eyes, mouth or antennas. The appearance of the organisms like Spriggina in the Ediacaran may tell us something about the coming into being, or development, of the kind of animal body structures, such as the head or eyes, in the Precambrian. In other words, the appearance of the Ediacaran organisms like Spriggina may be seen as representing or signifying the coming into being of the animal head or eyes in the Precambrian. As we have discussed, it seems, trilobites may be associated with the kind of Ediacaran organisms like Spriggina in a number of ways, either in their body plans, in their head structures, or in their possession of the eyes, mouth or antennas. Such similarities, underpinned by the symmetric or harmonic body structure, may constitute, in a certain sense, the developmental continuation in the animal life from the Precambrian to the Cambrian.

The appearance of the organisms like Spriggina in the Ediacaran may be seen as the possible appearance of the animals with a well-developed head structure in the Precambrian. The emergence of the organisms like Spriggina in the Ediacaran may be regarded as the possible emergence of the animals with eyes in the Precambrian. The coming into being of the organisms like Spriggina in the Ediacaran may be considered as the possible coming into being of the animals with a highly developed nervous system in the Precambrian, as both the head and eyes had to be supported by a highly developed nervous system. In other words, if we are looking for the signs of the appearance of the animal head, eyes, or the highly developed nervous system in animals, before the Cambrian, we may have to look into the kind of Ediacaran organisms like Spriggina.

The study of trilobites seems to have revealed to us many things about the coming into being or development of the early animal life on earth. Trilobites seemed to have been quite diverse and widely

Symmetry I

distributed from the very beginning. They appeared to have already possessed their body plans when they first emerged in the Cambrian. Different trilobite groups existed, and the differences seem to point to a Precambrian origin for trilobites. Trilobites possessed highly developed compound eyes from the beginning, and as such, it is reasonable to infer that, some Precambrian animals might have existed or developed prior to the Cambrian explosion, possibly with eyes, a well-developed head structure, and a highly developed nervous system.

Thus, the appearance of trilobites in the Cambrian seems to lead us to the possible existence or development of the kind of Precambrian animals that might have possessed the trilobite-like features, that is, the kind of features that might have supported or sustained an animal life with head, eyes, or a nervous system. Otherwise, it seems, we cannot explain why, from the beginning in the Cambrian, trilobites should have enjoyed the level of their diversity or distribution, possessed their body plans, developed into different groups, or had their complex compound eyes. But, what might be such Precambrian animals? What animals might be seen or regarded as such Precambrian animals? What organisms might be treated as such Precambrian animals? Where did they live? When did they live? How did they live? In what sense did they live? In what ways did they live? In what manners did they exist, at all? And, how were they related to the Cambrian? How were they related to the Cambrian explosion? How were they related to the animal life coming into being in the Cambrian? How were they related to the animals appearing in what is called the Cambrian explosion?

To understand the Precambrian organisms, we may have to look at the microbial mats, as the existence of the Precambrian organisms was largely associated with them. A microbial mat is a layered colony of microorganisms, such as bacteria. It may be found on the surface of something, such as, on the surface of the sea floor. The microbial mats on the sea floor might have played a significant role in the coming into being or appearance of the early animal life on earth. Microbial mats were among the first life forms appearing on earth. With the appearance of the photosynthesizing bacteria, microbial mats gradually became the vibrant ecosystems in which life thrived. The microbial colonization of the sea floor constituted the biological foundation upon which the new life forms, such as the animals, the complex multicellular organisms, might eventually appear. And we see, indeed, such complex multicellular organisms emerged in the Ediacaran, as the life forms surviving on the microbial mats.

The Ediacaran organisms may be seen, in a sense, as the mat organisms, in that, the existence of such organisms may be seen as closely associated with the microbial mats. On the one hand, few Ediacaran organisms may be found to have existed without being related to the microbial mats. And on the other hand, it seems, no matter how the organisms had existed, with regard to the microbial mats, either anchored in them, embedded in them, burrowing just under them, or living on them, they had been highly dependent on them. Microbial mats were their home. Microbial mats were their base. Microbial mats were their world. That is, in a word, it might be said, they could hardly survive without the microbial mats. And indeed as we can see, with the destruction of the microbial mats, the foundation for the existence of the Ediacaran organisms collapsed.

The limited ability to move may be seen, in a sense, as at the heart of the dependence of the Ediacaran organisms on the microbial mats. But the early Cambrian saw a marked increase of animal burrowing, in terms of both quantity and complexity, which may not be seen as having happened in the previous period. This change in animal burrowing, proving to be quite crucial for the early animal development, is usually called the Cambrian substrate revolution. Before the happening of the Cambrian substrate revolution, animals usually lived on the microbial mats or burrowed just under them, with limited ability of movement. The microbial mats on the sea floor separated the water from the substrate. That is, the existence of the microbial mats meant that, the substrate would have been a world of its own, with its specific conditions and with the kind of microorganisms capable of living there.

The occurrence of the Cambrian substrate revolution may be seen as the animals with increased capability for movement flexing their muscles and expanding their lives. Now, it seems, not only were they able to burrow in or under the microbial mats, they were also capable of burrowing, deeply, into the sediment. The sediment had been largely undisturbed by the animals, but now it was being dug, tunneled, or loosened constantly by the burrowing animals. As a result, the microbial mats were largely destroyed, and water and oxygen came into the upper layers of the sediment. This transformed the upper layers of

Symmetry I

the sea floor into a place where animals might live, hiding for protection, digging for food, or building a home for rest.

The trace fossils from the Ediacaran appear to indicate that, the burrows made by the organisms in such a period were usually horizontal and simple. Such simple horizontal burrows were made, in the sense that, the early organisms were only the kind of life forms with a limited ability of movement. And as the lives of these organisms were closely associated with the microbial mats, the burrows made by them might have been just under the mats. But now, with their increased ability for movement, the organisms would dig deep, wide, and with some unprecedented sophistication or complexity.

Thus the coming of the Cambrian may be seen as being represented by a number of significant changes occurred in the animal life at the time, such as, the disappearance of the Ediacaran organisms, the appearance of the complex animal burrowing behaviors, or the Cambrian substrate revolution. With the arrival of the Cambrian, it seems, the animal burrowing behaviors began to diversify and multiply. New patterns and forms appeared, and among these fresh patterns or forms were the vertical burrows exhibiting a certain sense of complexity or sophistication. The first appearance of the complex animal burrowing behavior patterns is thus taken to signal the beginning of the Cambrian, and as such, it represents the end of the Ediacaran period. The trace fossil bearing such a kind of burrowing pattern is called Treptichnus pedum. This kind of trace fossil appears to indicate that, the organisms had made a series of vertical burrows in a rather regular and sophisticated way. The complexity and regularity, evident in such burrows, seem to have not been observed in the earlier time, that is, in the Ediacaran. In other words, the organisms at this time appeared to have developed or possessed some more advanced capabilities, which may not be seen in the Ediacaran life forms, and they could live their lives with some unprecedented complex and sophisticated behaviors. Certainly, given the complex and fresh behavior patterns exhibited by such organisms, it might be said, they were different from the Ediacaran life forms.

Such organisms might be likely the kind of life forms related, in some way or to some extent, to the priapulid worms, as the burrows made by such worms may be seen as similar to what may be found in Treptichnus pedum. Fortunately, some priapulid-like worms might have existed in the Cambrian. Ottoia might be an early priapulid worm living in the early or middle Cambrian. It was a worm with bilateral symmetry, though a sense of radial symmetry might be observed in its front body parts. As a predator, Ottoia might have burrowed in the substrate, to find protection from other predators, or to prey on other organisms. It is found, Ottoia might be one of the most common organisms active during the early or middle Cambrian. Its existence may tell us that, the Cambrian substrate revolution was well under way in the early or middle Cambrian, fresh life forms with new behaviors and higher abilities emerged, and the animal life might have changed considerably with the progress of the substrate revolution.

Though the burrows from the Ediacaran period are found to be mostly horizontal and simple, they nevertheless may carry significant meaning for the early development of animal life on earth. Their existence may indicate, in a certain sense, that, the organisms that had left such trace fossils were necessarily moving organisms, and that, such moving organisms were likely the kind of early animals possessing their heads. Movement may be seen as what defines the animal species, and the appearance of the moving organisms may be regarded as what signaled the true beginning of the animal life on earth. It is in such a sense that, it might be said, the Ediacaran burrows, while simple and horizontal, may be regarded as the evidence that the animal life might have indeed started on earth, in the Ediacaran.

We have discussed the coming into being of the animal head and its meaning for the early development of the animal life. The head constituted one of the most crucial and sophisticated animal body parts. Its development may be seen as a measure of the animal development. Its coming into being may be seen as the true beginning of the animal life. Its appearance may be seen as the true rise of animals. The head is usually formed with eyes, mouth, a nervous system, or some other sensory organs such as antennas. We have seen that, such a kind of head structure might have appeared in the Ediacaran, in the organisms like Spriggina. The presence of the Ediacaran burrows may in another way tell us that, the animal head might have indeed appeared in such a period, as the head, or its coming into being, may be seen as being involved with the animal movement, or the coming into being of the animal movement, in some intricate, complex, or profound ways.

The horizontal nature of the Ediacaran burrows may not be seen, in a sense, as simple, as such a nature might have reflected the true process of the coming into being of the animal head, or the animal

Symmetry I

movement, in the early development of the animal life. To move, an organism likely needed to sense. Thus, some kind of sensory organs might have to come into being. To move, an organism likely needed to make sense of direction. Thus, some kind of apparatus for this purpose might have to appear. To move, an organism likely needed to balance itself or to coordinate all its actions. Thus, some kind of control center like a nervous system might have to emerge. That is, in other words, movement, or the appearance of movement, might have led or contributed, in a sense, to the coming into being of the animal head.

Moving toward one direction might have led the organisms to develop their sensitive organs, in a concentrated manner, in the front parts. This may explain, in a sense, the appearance of the head, a body part containing some of the most important and sensitive organs in an animal. In the initial development of the animal life, the head might not have been developed to such an extent that it could support or handle the kind of complex animal activities we see later, and certainly, the other aspects of the animal existence at this stage might also be unable to sustain such kind of activities. This may be seen in that, the organisms at this stage might only be able to make the simple and horizontal burrows. The simple and horizontal burrows may thus be seen as an indication that the life forms that had left such traces might be the emerging organisms, with their body structures that might have just come into being. Such may be corroborated, to some extent, by the fossil findings. The fossil record seems to reveal, the development of the head structures of the organisms like Spriggina may only be seen as in the initial stage, with eyes, mouth, or antennas merely in their very preliminary forms.

On the other hand, it might be said, the appearance of movement in the animal life may not be seen as so simple, and the coming into being of the animal head may not be seen as so straightforward. That is, something deep, something complex, something subtle, something powerful, or something profound might have been involved. The appearance of movement in the animal life was not something simple or ordinary. It may be seen as a gigantic leap forward in the development of life on earth. It meant not one thing. It meant many things. It meant many things at the same time. It meant the coming into being of many things at the same time. It meant the appearance of many things at the same time. It meant the emergence of many things at the same time. In other words, the appearance of the animal movement meant that, while the complex multicellular organisms called animals grew with the kind of bodies vastly different from the other life forms, such as, microorganisms, they had to develop the corresponding mechanisms or processes, and certainly, above all, they had to develop or possess the kind of body organs responsible for their movements, such as, muscles, antennas, eyes, or a nervous system. When all these things came into being or appeared at the same time, it seems, it might not have been something simple, straightforward, or ordinary. And, it appears, these things might have indeed come into being or emerged in a very short period of time, in the Ediacaran or Cambrian.

The evolutionary theory seems to be in no position to provide an explanation for the coming into being or appearance of these things. Apart from the coming into being or appearance of these things, the actual realization of these things seems to be also beyond, in a sense, the evolutionary explanation. The head was a structure formed out of bilateral symmetry. It was so symmetric that, one may ask, why should it be formed in bilateral symmetry, or how was it formed in such a symmetric way? The eyes were the sharp, delicate and subtle body organs. They were exquisite, beautiful, and profound. Were they made? Or were they created? How were they made? How were they created? Who had made them? Who had created them? Who had the power to make them? Who had the power to create them? Who had the capacity to make them? Who had the potential to create them? Was it evolution? Was it natural selection? An evolutionary process might not have been so fast. An evolutionary process might not have been so powerful. An evolutionary process might not have been so perfect. An evolutionary process might not have been so exquisite. An evolutionary process might not have been so beautiful. An evolutionary process might not have been so profound. It was not evolution. It was not natural selection. It was symmetry. Symmetry is fast. Symmetry is powerful. Symmetry is perfect. Symmetry is exquisite. Symmetry is beautiful. Symmetry is profound.

While the appearance of movement might have led to the coming into being of the animal heads, movement may also be seen as having played a significant role in the coming into being of the bilaterally symmetric animal body plans. The Ediacaran burrows were likely made horizontally, and this means that, the early animal movement may be seen as being characterized by the horizontal movement. On the one hand, the horizontal movement may be seen as representing the initial

Symmetry I

development of the animal movement. On the other hand, the horizontal movement may be regarded as having initiated, in a sense, the appearance of bilateral symmetry in the animal body structures.

In a horizontal movement toward one direction, it might be better for an organism to possess a two-sided body structure. In such a structure, each side of the body might balance the other, and together they might constitute the whole organism. The bilaterally symmetric body plans might thus become the most convenient or economically favorable body structures for the moving animals. Certainly, it might be said, the coming into being or appearance of the bilaterally symmetric body plans in animals might not have been so simple or straightforward, in a sense. Such a process might have involved symmetry in some subtle, deep, delicate or profound ways. For example, the radially symmetric animals might also have made some horizontal movements in their early developments, but apparently they had not developed or acquired the kind of bilaterally symmetric body structures in a full sense. That is to say, the coming into being or appearance of the bilaterally symmetric animal body plans might have to do, in a sense, fundamentally, with the fulfillment or realization of symmetry in nature, in that, symmetry might have moved, developed, or strived, to fulfill or realize itself in nature not only in the radially symmetric manner but also in the bilaterally symmetric fashion. And it might be said, it was in such a process of symmetric fulfillment or realization that the early horizontal animal movement might be seen as having played its role. The horizontal movement might have triggered the development of the bilaterally symmetric animal body plans in the sense that, on the one hand, the coming into being of bilateral symmetry in the animal life may not be seen as a direct result or consequence of any movement, as the symmetric existence might have to do more with symmetry than anything else; and on the other hand, while symmetry worked to pave the way for the appearance of movement in the animal life, it might have fulfilled or realized itself in the animal life in bilateral symmetry through the early animal horizontal movement. Thus we see, the heads appeared, with the bilaterally symmetric animals. And thus we see, the horizontal movement appeared, likely with the emergence of the early bilaterally symmetric organisms, such as Spriggina.

The time period immediately prior to or after the start of the Cambrian may be of some special significance, in that, some clues may be found in such a period about the Cambrian substrate revolution or the Cambrian explosion. The early animal mineralization may be seen as one of the characteristics defining such a period. The small shelly fauna or small shelly fossils (SSF) refer to the mineralized fossils of various organisms living primarily from the late Ediacaran to the early Cambrian. These organisms could be either small or large, with the small ones like Cloudina and the larger ones like some mollusks, echinoderms, or some arthropod-like organisms. Among other things, it might be said, the SSF period saw the disappearance of the last Ediacaran organisms, the rise of the complex burrowing animals, the start of the Cambrian substrate revolution, the appearance of the first arthropods, the emergence of trilobites and echinoderms, and certainly, above all, the occurrence of the Cambrian explosion. Thus, the SSF period may be seen as representing an important and critical time in the development of the early animal life on earth.

People have provided a number of explanations to the appearance of animal mineralization. Some take it as a result of climate change. Some think that the early animals had mineralized for stronger or larger bodies. Some suggest, mineralization might be a way of adaptation, on the part of the early animals, to the chemical changes in the seas at the time. It seems, the beginning of the SSF appearance might have coincided, roughly, with the earliest animal burrowing. That means, the SSFs might have appeared as a way for the organisms to protect themselves from the potential predators. In other words, the SSF appearance might mean that the competition between predator and prey might have already begun, as early as in the late Ediacaran, and such an arms race might have led, in a sense, to the appearance of both animal mineralization and animal burrowing.

The SSFs from the late Ediacaran appear to point to some early organisms possibly related to sponges, cnidarians, or some worm-like life forms. Cloudina and Namacalathus may be seen as among the important SSFs from the late Ediacaran. The mineralized fossils of these two organisms are often to be found in the same places. Namacalathus was an organism with a cup-like structure attached to the bottom of the sea. The mineralized tubular fossils are often found either in the late Ediacaran or in the early Cambrian. The Cambrian SSFs may indicate that some new life forms might have emerged, as some organisms seemed to have developed scale-like mineralized body structures. While many of the SSFs have been identified with the early mollusks, early echinoderms, or some early worm-like or arthropod-like organisms, many of them are still not clearly understood. In most cases only small pieces or fragments are found, and this means, the full understanding of the SSFs may not be easily achieved unless more discoveries, especially the complete fossils, are made.

The time range of the SSFs may be of special importance, in that, it seems, they may have represented a continuous development, in a certain sense, from the late Ediacaran to the early Cambrian, and well into the so-called Cambrian explosion. As such, it might be said, the SSFs might have something special to say about the Cambrian explosion. The boundary between the Ediacaran and the Cambrian fell in this time range. The Cambrian substrate revolution fell in this time range. The Cambrian explosion fell in this time range. Thus, it seems, if we want to search into the transition from the Ediacaran to the Cambrian or into the big events occurred in the Cambrian, such as the Cambrian substrate revolution or the Cambrian explosion, we may have to take a good look at the SSFs or their developments.

Researches seem to reveal that, the SSFs may be linked to the different stages in the development of the early organisms, and it appears, that, the earlier the SSFs were, the more primitive developmental stages they might represent. As the earliest SSFs appeared in the late Ediacaran, and this means, the later SSFs found in the early Cambrian may be traced back to their precursors in the late Ediacaran. This is important, in the sense that, a sense of continuous development, from the late Ediacaran to the early Cambrian, may be observed in or among the SSFs.

At the same time, it may have to be said, while a sense of continuous or orderly development may be observed in or among the SSFs, it does not necessarily mean that, all the organisms appearing in the late Ediacaran or early Cambrian might have experienced such a kind of development. It might not be such a case. While some organisms, represented by the SSFs, might have indeed experienced such a kind of development, others might have undergone a very different process. That is to say, while the SSFs point to a sense of continuous development among the early organisms from the late Ediacaran to the early Cambrian, their existence may not necessarily rule out the possible developments other than the evolutionary during such periods. In other words, the continuous development might just stand as one of the many aspects of a process defined by both evolution and avolution, as the evolutionary and the avolutionary combined to give rise to a great age called the Primordial Explosion.

Now, it seems, it may be reasonable to say that, the coming of the Cambrian may be seen as being represented or signified by two significant events happening at such a time, that is, the Cambrian substrate revolution and the appearance of the SSFs. The Cambrian substrate revolution may be seen as the dramatic increase of animal movement at such a time. The SSFs may be seen as the appearance of the early animal mineralization. These two events, the increase of animal movement and the appearance of animal mineralization, may be seen, in a sense, as lying at the heart of possible explanations to the coming of the Cambrian, or to the coming into being of the Cambrian explosion. The dramatic increase of animal movement in the early Cambrian may be observed in that, now animals appeared to be capable of burrowing with both depth and sophistication. They began to move below the microbial mats and burrowed into the sediment, with depths and patterns unknown before. The animal mineralization, on the other hand, may be witnessed in the large amount of SSFs discovered around the world.

What did the increase of animal movement mean? What did the animal mineralization mean? What did the increase of animal movement mean to the Cambrian? What did the appearance of animal mineralization mean to the coming of the Cambrian? Why did the increase of animal movement happen? Why did the animal mineralization appear? Why did the Cambrian substrate revolution happen? Why did the SSFs come into being? How did the Cambrian substrate revolution happen? How was the animal mobility enhanced? Where did such animal mobility come from? Where did such enhancement in animal mobility come from? What was behind the Cambrian substrate revolution? What was behind the increase of animal movement? What was behind the enhancement in animal mobility at such a time? How did the SSFs come into being? How did the animal mineralization happen? Where did the SSFs come from? Where did the animal mineralization come from? What was really behind the coming into being of the SSFs? What was really behind the appearance of the early animal mineralization?

Movement may be seen as the essence of the Cambrian substrate revolution. Movement may be seen as at the core of the Cambrian substrate revolution. Movement may be seen as the real meaning of the

Symmetry I

Cambrian substrate revolution. Movement is the essence of the animal being. Movement is the essence of the animal life. The coming into being of movement in the animal life led to the coming into being of the first animal life forms, the Ediacaran organisms. But, as the first animal life forms, the Ediacaran organisms were only endowed with a very limited or minimal sense of mobility. That is, they might be able to move, but their movements were usually short, limited, confined, or even hardly to be observed. That may explain, in a sense, why people sometimes even question the classification of the Ediacaran organisms as animals. It was only with the coming of the Cambrian that, it seems, the animal mobility was enhanced significantly and the organisms began to exhibit or demonstrate their animal features in some clear or unmistakable manners. Thus, it might be said, the increase of animal movement, around the start of the Cambrian, might not be something simple. It might have to do, in a sense, or to some extent, with the kind of things fundamental or essential to life, that is, to the animal life.

Mineralization is not a simple matter. The animal mineralization is not a simple matter. The early animal mineralization was not a simple matter. The animal mineralization in the late Ediacaran or early Cambrian was not a simple matter. The power to mineralize was not simple. The capacity to mineralize was not simple. The potential to mineralize was not simple. For the organisms to be able to mineralize, something beyond mineralization might have to be in place. For the organisms to be capable of mineralization, something higher than mineralization might have to come into being. For the organisms to possess the potential to mineralize, something more powerful or more profound than mineralization might have to exist in them. And, as we all know, prior to this time, there had never been such a thing on earth as the animal mineralization. It was never seen before. It had never happened before. It was new. It was creation. It was the creation in nature. It was the creation of nature. It was the creation in the world. It was the creation of the world. It was the creation in a relatively short period of time. It was the creation in a rather rapid, sudden, or explosive manner. It meant something. It meant something quite unusual. It meant something deep, fundamental, essential, profound, and powerful.

Some might suggest that, the increase of animal movement or the appearance of animal mineralization, around the start of the Cambrian, might have happened as a result of an evolutionary process. Such an evolutionary process may be generally called an arms race between predator and prey. The increase of animal movement might have only reflected the harsh reality that the organisms at the time had to develop the kind of surviving skills or capabilities so that they might burrow deep into the sediment to avoid predators. And the appearance of the animal mineralization might only mean that, the organisms had by that time found some effective ways to arm themselves, so that they might be able to live in the same environments with the potential predators.

Is this kind of explanation plausible? To be honest, it may have to be said, it is plausible. And it seems, one cannot rule out, no matter what, such a possibility that such a process might have indeed happened at such a time, in some sense, in some way, or to some extent. But, if we think more and look deeper into what had really occurred at such a time, we may find, such an evolutionary explanation may not be truly convincing after all.

If such an evolutionary process had indeed happened, then, with the evolutionary progresses in mobility or mineralization, the organisms at such a time should be able to advance, equally in an evolutionary sense, in other aspects of their existence. That is to say, if they had evolved the kind of skills or capabilities to make complex burrows or to mineralize, it should be expected that, they might have also evolved or developed the other kinds of skills or capabilities so that they might eventually survive. The evolutionary development is usually a gradual process, with natural selection working its way in an incremental manner. Changes may come, but relatively slow. While such an evolutionary process is usually gradual or relatively slow, it gives time to the organisms to develop the kind of traits or features so that they may successfully adapt to the changes or environment. That means, in an evolutionary process, while some species may disappear, it is usually not the case that all species will go extinct. In other words, if the organisms prior to the Cambrian had really experienced an evolutionary process in their developments, then most likely it would not be the case that almost all of them would disappear or become extinct.

But, as we all know, the organisms prior to the start of the Cambrian, that is, the Ediacaran organisms, had undergone a mass extinction. If such organisms had indeed evolved at such a time, their evolutionary developments should have enabled them to weather or survive the possible changes or transformations occurring in their

Symmetry I

environments. Yes, it was their burrowing activities that might have changed their environments, the microbial mats. But such burrowing behaviors were supposed to be evolutionary in nature. If such burrowing behaviors were evolutionary, that is, an evolutionary process was going on with such organisms, then, with the changing conditions of the environments, the organisms should have evolved or developed the kind of adaptive traits or features to deal with such changes. If the complex burrowing behaviors could be evolved, if the animal mineralization could be evolved, then it should be the case that, such adaptive traits or features could also be evolved or developed. But, we cannot find such adaptive traits or features, and we cannot find the supposed adaptation by the Ediacaran organisms, in an evolutionary process, to the changing environments, that is, to the changing microbial mats.

What does this mean? It may mean that such an evolutionary process, as suggested by some people, might not have happened. It may mean that, even if a sense of evolutionary process had happened, it might not have happened in such a way or in such a manner as some people might have imagined. That is to say, what had really occurred around the start of the Cambrian appears to tell us that, even if evolution had played a role in the development of the organisms at such a time, it might not have played the major role. If evolution had played the major role, if evolution constituted the driving force behind the development of the organisms, it might not have been the case that the organisms at such a time would eventually experience a mass extinction. So, around the start of the Cambrian, what had truly happened? What had really occurred? What was truly behind such happenings? What was really behind such occurrences? Who had played the major role, in the existence of the organisms at such a time? Who had constituted the driving force behind their developments? What was behind the mass extinction? What was behind the coming of the Cambrian? What was, really, the meaning of the Cambrian?

Was it evolution? No. It seems, it was not truly evolution. Was it evolutionary? No. It seems, it was not really evolutionary. It was symmetry. It was the symmetric development. It was the symmetric movement. Symmetry played the major role. Symmetry constituted the driving force behind the development of the organisms at such a time. It is in such a sense that we may come to understand the significant increase of animal movement or the appearance of animal mineralization around such a time. The increase of animal movement at such a time may be seen as the symmetric movement fulfilled in the animal movement. The animal mineralization around such a time may be seen as the symmetric development realized in the animal mineralization. Such symmetric fulfillment or realization, in the early animal life, might not be simple. It might have involved both evolution and avolution. The fulfillment of animal movement had to do with many things, such as, among other things, muscles, sensors, or a nervous system. Thus the significant increase of animal movement in the early animal life might mean that all these aspects of the animal existence might have to be improved or enhanced, in a sense, significantly. In other words, such increase or enhancement in animal movement might not mean some minor changes to the animal life. Rather, some significant changes might have occurred to the early animal life. Evolution might have participated in the development of the organisms at the time, but an evolutionary process alone might not be able to give rise to such significant changes. The symmetric power might be behind the coming into being of such significant changes. The symmetric potential might be behind the emergence of such significant changes. The symmetric speed might be behind the appearance of such significant changes. That is, such significant changes might have to do with symmetry, with the movement or development of symmetry, in the early animal life. In the same sense, the early animal mineralization may be seen as a complex occurrence. While the presence of an evolutionary process may be witnessed, an avolutionary process might be underlying the appearance or development of the early animal mineralization, in that, such early animal mineralization might have to do, first and foremost, with the capacity, the potential, or the power to mineralize, and such capacity, potential or power might have to do, in the early animal life, largely, with symmetry, or with the fulfillment or realization of symmetry.

The coming of the Cambrian may thus be seen as standing for a double process, both avolutionary and evolutionary, in the development of the early animal life on earth. An avolutionary process usually refers to a developmental process that includes what is called an evolutionary process, that is, a process initiated, supported or sustained by natural selection. But here we may have to single out, as we have done sometimes before, the evolutionary process, in order to have a clearer or more detailed picture of the coming into being of the animals at such

Symmetry I

a time, and let the avolutionary process just refer to the symmetric movement or development during such a period. In such a sense, it might be said, both the avolutionary process and the evolutionary process may be seen as dynamic or robust in working to give rise to what are known as the Cambrian animals. The ability of movement may be seen as one of the key features of the animal life, and in a sense, it might be said, it constitutes the foundation of the animal existence. Without the ability of movement, things, or organisms, may have to largely rely on other things for their existence. Once the ability of movement is acquired, organisms may expand their activities and exist with some improved or enhanced lifestyles. And certainly, it might be said, with the coming into being of the ability of movement, or with the increased ability of movement, the Cambrian animals had thrived and flourished, and lived lives richer or more abundant than their Ediacaran predecessors.

Just as the coming of the Cambrian may be regarded as a process involving both evolution and avolution, the occurrence of the Cambrian substrate revolution may be understood in a similar manner. The Cambrian substrate revolution was behind the transition from the Ediacaran to the Cambrian. To understand the Cambrian, we have to understand the Cambrian substrate revolution. To understand the transition from the Ediacaran to the Cambrian, we have to understand the Cambrian substrate revolution. The Cambrian substrate revolution led to the destruction of the microbial mats, and the disappearance of the microbial mats may be seen as behind both the mass extinction experienced by the Ediacaran organisms and the "gradual" emergence of the Cambrian animals. The coming into being of the Cambrian animals was gradual in the sense that, a sense of evolutionary process might have been involved and such a sense of gradual process may be seen, in a sense, in that the Cambrian explosion did not happen immediately after the start of the Cambrian, and it only happened after some time, around 10 million years, in the later half of the early Cambrian.

The Cambrian began with the Cambrian substrate revolution, around 540 million years ago. The Cambrian explosion is usually believed to have happened from about 530 to 520 million years ago. Thus, it seems, there was an interval between the start of the Cambrian substrate revolution and the Cambrian explosion. This lapse of time, about 10 million years, may explain the considerable effects of the

Cambrian substrate revolution on the development of the early animal life. The Ediacaran organisms were basically mat organisms. Their Ediacaran modes of existence depended on the existence of the microbial mats. When the microbial mats were dissolved, due to the Cambrian substrate revolution, their Ediacaran modes of existence would disintegrate accordingly. That means, when the Cambrian substrate revolution came, or when the Cambrian substrate revolution was under way, if the Ediacaran organisms wanted to survive, they had to strive for some very different modes of existence. Unlike the Ediacaran modes of existence, such modes of existence would certainly distance the organisms from the microbial mats, or rather, detach the organisms from the microbial mats. In other words, these modes of existence might mean that the organisms might have to strive for their survival in the kind of ways that they might live or exist in a world devoid of microbial mats. These modes of existence might have emerged in the early animal life, as a result or consequence of the Cambrian substrate revolution or the disappearance of the microbial mats.

Was it possible that some Ediacaran organisms might have strived for such modes of existence? It was possible. After all, the organisms strived to survive, at least in an evolutionary sense. Was it possible that some of such modes of existence might have been successfully achieved? It should be possible, and it seems, we have no reason to believe otherwise. The fossils from such a period, such as the SSFs, seem to indicate that an evolutionary process was going on, to some extent, with the organisms from the late Ediacaran to the early Cambrian, as some of such fossils may be traced back, in a certain sense, to their earlier predecessors, even to the ones from the late Ediacaran. That is to say, it seems, there is no reason to believe that the modes of existence that we are talking about here might not be achieved, at least for some organisms, in an evolutionary sense, or through an evolutionary process.

Now it was the Cambrian. The Cambrian came. It was no longer the Ediacaran. The Ediacaran passed. The Ediacaran modes of existence were outdated now. The Cambrian modes of existence came into being. The Cambrian modes of existence emerged. The Cambrian modes of existence appeared. The Cambrian substrate revolution led to the destruction of the microbial mats. The Cambrian substrate revolution led to the disappearance of the Ediacaran modes of

Symmetry I

existence. The Cambrian substrate revolution led to the coming into being of the Cambrian modes of existence. What were the Cambrian modes of existence? What were they? What did they mean? What did they mean to life? What did they mean to the animal life? They meant that, the Cambrian life forms, different from the Ediacaran ones, might come into being, in their Cambrian shapes or forms. They meant that, the Cambrian organisms, unlike the Ediacaran organisms, might emerge, with their Cambrian features or characteristics. They meant that, the Cambrian animals, distinct from the Ediacaran animals, might appear, and live or survive in their Cambrian modes of existence.

The disappearance of the microbial mats meant a dramatic change for the organisms living, existing, or surviving during such a period. They could no longer live in, above, or under the mats. They now were forced to exist without the mats. That is to say, they now were forced to live or survive in the wide, deep and open seas. What did this mean? It meant a lot. It meant a lot to the organisms. It meant, the world of the organisms was greatly expanded. It meant, the organisms now had to deal with an environment immensely different from the microbial mats. It meant, the organisms were now free to explore a new and vast world, to go up, to swim afar, or to burrow deep down. It meant challenges. It meant freedom. It meant opportunities. It meant, it seems, the stage had been set for the animals to develop, to thrive, or to flourish, so that the animal life might eventually become what we see today.

This may be why we see the coming of the Cambrian. This may be why we see the coming into being of the Cambrian animals. This may be why we see the happening of the Cambrian explosion. The need to adapt to a vastly different environment, the need to face the challenges, the need to compete with the other organisms, the opportunity to make use of their new-found freedom, the opportunity to take advantage of the greatly expanded world… all these factors might have combined to influence the Cambrian life forms in such a way that they eventually developed into the kind of Cambrian animals as we know them. It was an evolutionary process. It was an evolutionary development. It was an evolutionary process roughly from the start of the Cambrian to the end of the Cambrian explosion. It was an evolutionary development taking about 20 million years, from around 540 to 520 million years ago.

Certainly, when we talk about an evolutionary process in the development of the Cambrian animals, it may not mean that, the development of the Cambrian life forms should be viewed solely in such a sense. No. The actual happening might be much, much more complex, subtle, or profound. That is to say, just like the development of the Ediacaran organisms, the development of the Cambrian animals might have also involved both evolution and avolution. This may be discussed in several aspects. First, the mass extinction experienced by the Ediacaran organisms was not a simple or light matter, in that, many of the later life forms might have to undergo a process of re-emergence, re-appearance, or it might be said, re-creation, even if some Ediacaran organisms might have remained, survived, and continued their development into the Cambrian. The re-emergence, re-appearance or re-creation of such life forms might not be simply evolutionary in nature, and an avolutionary process might have played its essential or fundamental role. Secondly, even the evolutionary process may not be regarded as so evolutionary, in that, on the one hand, such a process during the early Cambrian was, in a sense, so sudden, rapid, or explosive that it may not be seen as bearing the characteristic evolutionary qualities; and on the other hand, given such sudden, rapid or explosive nature exhibited by such a developmental process, the avolutionary might have worked or operated, side by side, with the evolutionary, in such a process, since otherwise, it seems, things may not be explained. And thirdly, apart from the kind of Cambrian life forms that may be traced back, in some sense, or to some extent, to their possible Ediacaran predecessors, there were many animals existing in the Cambrian may not be easily related to the Ediacaran organisms, and this means, in a sense, that, the evolutionary development might not be the sole development in such a period, and an avolutionary process might have happened and the avolutionary development might be ultimately behind the appearance of such animals.

This kind of development, both evolutionary and avolutionary in nature, might be behind the appearance of the animals in the Cambrian. The Cambrian explosion happened from around 530 to 520 million years ago, lasting for about 10 million years. The Cambrian started, as we know, from about 540 million years ago. This period, from the start of the Cambrian to the beginning of the Cambrian explosion, may be seen, in a sense, as holding the key to the Cambrian explosion. It was from about 540 to 530 million years ago, about 10 million years. During this period of about 10 million years, the animal life on earth underwent a remarkable process, from the disappearance of the

Symmetry I

Ediacaran organisms to the explosion of the Cambrian animals. The disappearance of the Ediacaran organisms was due to the substrate revolution, as we know, as the substrate revolution caused the microbial mats to disintegrate. But, what was the cause of the Cambrian explosion? From the disappearance of the Ediacaran organisms to the beginning of the Cambrian explosion, it was only about 10 million years. It was short, very short, in geological terms. Why, after so short a period of time, would the animal life re-emerge on earth? Why, after so short a period of time, would the animal life re-appear on this planet? Why, after so short a period of time, would the animal life enter a stage of rapid or explosive development? How, after so short a period of time, would the animal life be able to re-emerge on earth? How, after so short a period of time, would the animal life be able to re-appear on this planet? How, after so short a period of time, would it be possible that the animal life would radiate, diversify, or explode?

Was it possible that, there might be some Ediacaran "seeds" that had survived the mass extinction experienced by most of the Ediacaran organisms? Was it possible that, such Ediacaran seeds might have grown in the Cambrian and developed into the Cambrian life forms? Was it possible that, the development of such Ediacaran seeds in the early Cambrian might have caused, in part, the happening of the Cambrian explosion? Was it possible that, the development of such Ediacaran seeds in the early Cambrian might have constituted part of the Cambrian explosion? It seems, all of these might be possible. And it seems, this may explain, in a way, after such a short period of time, why or how the animal life re-appeared on earth, or why or how the animal life exploded in the Cambrian explosion.

As we have discussed before, the mineralized fossils such as the SSFs appear to indicate an evolutionary process going on with the organisms from the late Ediacaran to the early Cambrian. In other words, it might be said, it was possible for some of the Ediacaran organisms, the Ediacaran seeds, to survive the mass extinction and continue their development into the Cambrian. But, once such seeds entered the Cambrian, they might have to face a vastly different environment. It was no longer the microbial mats. It was the wide, deep, and open seas. The seeds could no longer find the mats, with which their parents might be very familiar. That means, unlike their parents, the seeds might have to adjust themselves, to modify, to change, to rearrange or reorganize themselves in such ways that they might be able to adapt to the new environment. Such a process might not be easy, given the limited development of the early animal life in the late Ediacaran or early Cambrian. But, no matter how hard or difficult it might be, it seems, the seeds might have to undergo such a process. They might have to modify themselves. They might have to change themselves in some ways. They might have to rearrange their body forms. They might have to reorganize their lifestyles. They might have to adopt new modes of existence. In a word, such an adaptive process might prove highly challenging or demanding for the seeds, and in fact, such a process might be so tough, arduous, challenging or demanding that the seeds might have to undergo a process of complete transformation, ranging from the changes in their lifestyles to the modifications in their body plans.

The disappearance of the microbial mats was a dramatic change, and subsequently the wide, deep and open seas becoming the new environment might have been even more shocking to the early animal life. After all, the early organisms were only in the earliest stages of animal life. They were limited, very limited, in all the ways. They might be able to move, but in a very confined manner. They might be able to develop, but in a very limited sense. They might be able to survive, but only in some very primitive ways. Thus, it might be said, the disappearance of the microbial mats and the sudden appearance of the vast seas as the living environment might have constituted both tremendous challenges and unprecedented opportunities for the early animal life forms. The limited state of existence of the early organisms may mean that, such challenges or opportunities might lead to some significant changes in them. We cannot forget, this was only in the earliest stages of animal life, and the animal life at this time had not been fully developed in many aspects. The animal body structures had not been fully developed. The animal body plans had not been fully established. The animal lifestyles had not been fully fixed. The organisms were still emerging. The animals were still in the process of becoming or growing into the animals. In other words, the animal life at this time may only be seen as in its early formative stage of development. What does this mean? It may mean that, such challenges or opportunities that we are talking about here might work or operate to give rise to some real or significant changes to the animal life, at least, in an evolutionary sense. That is to say, while some of the seeds might have continued their developments in the early Cambrian, in a sense,

Symmetry I

some new life forms might appear, and some new organisms might emerge. This may be, in a sense, what we see in the early Cambrian, as some new animals emerging with characteristics or features unseen before in the Ediacaran organisms.

This may have explained, in a sense, why there existed an interval between the start of the Cambrian substrate revolution and the actual happening of the Cambrian explosion. The Cambrian substrate revolution opened a new age that is called the Cambrian, and with the coming of the Cambrian, the early animal life had to face a new environment. It took time. It took time for the early animal life to adjust itself. It took time for the early animal life to adapt to the new environment. It took time for the early animal life to modify itself, to change itself, to remodel or reshape itself so that it might live or survive in such a new environment. For the Ediacaran seeds, this was almost like, they had to start from scratch, again. They had to re-develop themselves. They had to reorganize their lives. They had to re-adapt to the new environment that was certainly not the microbial mats. What might be the result? What might be the consequence? The result might be that, some new organisms might have emerged, with new characteristics or features, and we call them the Cambrian animals. The consequence might be that, it took some time for such animals to emerge, to come into being, or to appear on this earth, and it was only after about 10 million years that such animals entered a period of rapid development. In other words, the time period between the start of the Cambrian and the happening of the Cambrian explosion may be explained, in a sense, in that it took time for the Ediacaran seeds to re-adapt to the new environment and re-develop into the Cambrian animals.

There was, certainly, a sense of evolutionary process going on with the seeds, as they strived to adapt to the new environment in order to live or survive. Should such a sense of development be the sole development for the seeds? It might not be the case. If the evolutionary development was the sole process for the seeds, it seems, we might not be able to explain how such seeds had developed into the full Cambrian animals in such a short period of time, in an evolutionary sense, starting from scratch. 10 million years was a short period of time, for new species to come into being. That is, it seems, it might not be enough for the Ediacaran seeds to fully develop into the Cambrian animals. So, what else had happened here? That is, what else had happened in the early Cambrian, leading to the appearance or coming into being of the Cambrian animals? It might be said, symmetry might have participated in such a process. Symmetry might have supplied the power. Symmetry might have provided the potential. Symmetry might have delivered the speed. It was through the symmetric power that the new animal body structures might have come into being, in such a short period of time. It was through the symmetric potential that the new animal shapes or forms might have appeared, in such a short period of time. It was with the symmetric speed that the new animal body plans might have emerged, in such a short period of time. And such may be seen in that, it was by this time that, generally speaking, the animals began to exhibit, manifest, or embody symmetry in some clear, obvious, definite or unmistakable ways.

In the same sense, it might be said, the actual happening of the Cambrian explosion might have involved both evolution and avolution. While both evolution and avolution might be seen in the possible development of the Ediacaran seeds from the start of the Cambrian to the beginning of the Cambrian explosion, such a kind of developmental process might also be seen in the Cambrian explosion. That is to say, the Cambrian explosion might not be solely an evolutionary process. Certainly, it might be said, an evolutionary process might have played its role in the coming into being or appearance of the animals during the Cambrian explosion. Such an evolutionary process might be responsible, in some sense, or to some extent, for the eventual appearance or emergence of the kind of animal body structures, the kind of animal shapes or forms, or the kind of animal body plans in the Cambrian explosion. But, the coming into being or appearance of such animal body structures, such animal shapes or forms or such animal body plans in the Cambrian explosion might be something more complex, subtle or profound. Or, it might be said, the coming into being or appearance of the new animal life forms in the Cambrian explosion might have to do with something more powerful, robust, strong, or mighty. An evolutionary process might not be that powerful. An evolutionary process might not be that robust. An evolutionary process might not be that strong. That is, natural selection might not be that mighty. That is, natural selection might not be that speedy.

If the evolutionary process were the only process happening in the Cambrian explosion, the Cambrian explosion might not have been so rapid, sudden or explosive. If the evolutionary process were the only

Symmetry I

process happening in the Cambrian explosion, the animals found in the Cambrian explosion might not have developed so fast or so unexpectedly. If the evolutionary process were the only process happening in the Cambrian explosion, the animal life during the Cambrian explosion might not have radiated or diversified on such a large scale, in such a short period of time. The Cambrian explosion happened in about 10 million years. It was during that 10 million years that, it seems, the ancestors of most of the currently living animal species appeared and came into being. It was a significant event. It was a significant event happening in a short period of time. A similar event, with similar scale or magnitude, had never been seen thereafter, in the long history of animal development on earth. It seems, the evolutionary process might have operated, in some sense, or to some extent, during such a period, but the major work might have been done by or through the avolutionary process. That is, it might be said, during the Cambrian explosion, the animal development might be mostly an avolutionary development, the animal radiation might be mostly an avolutionary radiation, and the animal diversification might be mostly an avolutionary diversification.

An avolutionary process might also be seen in the coming into being or appearance of the kind of animals possibly unrelated to the Ediacaran organisms. That is to say, apart from the kind of animals possibly originating from the Ediacaran seeds, there were other animals in the early Cambrian whose coming into being or appearance might have to do, largely, with the movement or development of symmetry. Some of such animals might have come into being before the Cambrian explosion. Some of them might have emerged during the Cambrian explosion. It may be hard to explain their appearance in an evolutionary sense, in that, unlike those coming into being from the Ediacaran seeds, their origins might not be easily discerned. Was it possible that their origins might have lain outside an evolutionary process, ultimately? It seems, it might be possible, as we have seen before, an evolutionary process might not have necessarily underlain the coming into being or appearance of the Ediacaran organisms. The symmetric explosion might have been underlying the coming into being of the Ediacaran organisms. The symmetric explosion might have been equally behind the appearance of such animals in the early Cambrian.

Thus the early Cambrian might have witnessed the workings or operations of both evolution and avolution. On the one hand, the evolutionary process might have played its part in the coming into being of the Cambrian animals. On the other hand, it might be the case that, while an evolutionary process developed the animal life in the Cambrian, it might have functioned, at some time, or at some point, as something triggering the movement or development of symmetry, in such a way, or in such a sense that the symmetric power might have been released or fulfilled in the animal life forms, or in the fulfillment or realization of the animal life forms. That is, it might be said, in a sense, it was through an evolutionary process that an avolutionary process might have been initiated or in a sense, accomplished, and symmetry might have thus fulfilled or realized itself in the animal life forms. At the same time, while an evolutionary process might have played its part, it alone may not be seen as responsible for the emergence or coming into being of the new animal life forms, as their appearance or emergence might have to do, largely, with the symmetric power or potential that might have been released or fulfilled in an avolutionary process. Thus, during the early Cambrian, it might be said, in a sense, it was through an avolutionary process that an evolutionary process might have been realized, or brought to fruition, in some speedy or rapid manners.

So, what was the true meaning of the Cambrian explosion? It was the combination of evolution and avolution. It was the union of evolution and avolution. It was the fusion of evolution and avolution. It was evolution in avolution. It was avolution in evolution. It was the fruition of evolution in avolution. It was the fruition of evolution through avolution. It was the fulfillment of avolution in evolution. It was the realization of avolution through evolution. It was the working-together of evolution and avolution. It was the co-operation of evolution and avolution. It was natural selection working with symmetry. It was symmetry operating through natural selection. It was the coming into being of the animal life. It was the formation of the animal life. It was the establishment of the animal life. Evolution worked. Natural selection selected. Avolution progressed. Symmetry harmonized. Symmetry fulfilled or realized itself, in the animal life, on earth.

Now, it seems, we may be able to answer the questions that have been raised with regard to the appearance of trilobites in the Cambrian. We have asked a number of questions about trilobites, such as, among other things, about the appearance of their head structures, about the coming into being of their eyes, or about their possession of a relatively advanced nervous system. It seems, all the studies on trilobites appear to point to the possibility that, as the Cambrian animals, they might have begun their developments well before the Cambrian. This might be true. Some of the Ediacaran seeds might have been among the ancestors of trilobites, and their Ediacaran developments might have constituted the foundation for the developments of trilobites in the Cambrian. In other words, the trilobite developments in the Cambrian may be regarded, in a sense, as a continuation from the Ediacaran to the Cambrian. Trilobites in the Cambrian might have inherited certain fundamental things from the Ediacaran organisms, through the seeds, though such Ediacaran organisms may not be known or called as the trilobites. Among the fundamental things inherited by trilobites from the Ediacaran organisms might be the bilaterally symmetric body plans, the head structures, the eyes, or the trilobite nervous system. At the same time, it may have to be said, such fundamental features or body structures might not have been well developed in the Ediacaran, and trilobites might have only inherited the blueprints of them and continued their developments in the Cambrian. This might be, in a sense, how trilobites appeared in the Cambrian. This might be, in a sense, how the trilobite heads emerged in the Cambrian. This might be, in a sense, how the trilobite eyes came into being in the Cambrian. This might be, in a sense, how the trilobite nervous system was formed, again, in the Cambrian. As we can understand, it might be said, the existence of other Cambrian animals, with similar circumstances, may be explained in a similar manner.

The Cambrian thus may be regarded, in a sense, as the continuation of the Ediacaran. The Ediacaran and the Cambrian constituted, together, the Primordial explosion, in which the fundamental animal body plans emerged or came into being, and the animal life on earth finally took its basic shapes or forms. The Ediacaran was different from the Cambrian in a number of ways, and certainly one of the most important differences might be the happening of the Cambrian substrate revolution. As the cause of the disappearance of many Ediacaran organisms, the substrate revolution might have eventually led to the appearance of the Cambrian animals, in a certain sense, by drastically changing the environment. Thus the Cambrian animals might be different from the Ediacaran organisms in some ways. But, as we have discussed, there might be a sense of continuation from the Ediacaran to the Cambrian, as the animal life might have kept its development, continuously, from the Ediacaran to the Cambrian, at least in some cases or in some ways, in both evolutionary and avolutionary senses. That is to say, while the Ediacaran and the Cambrian might be different in a number of ways, they nevertheless might have constituted a whole process that saw the eventual appearance or coming into being of the animal life on earth that we may still witness today. This may be the meaning of the Primordial explosion. The animal life did not come into being in one explosion. It took two explosions, the Ediacaran explosion and the Cambrian explosion. The animal life emerged in the Ediacaran, but the subsequent development met with some drastic changes, and it was such drastic changes that, in a sense, ushered in the Cambrian. The developmental process of the early animal life thus encompassed both the Ediacaran and the Cambrian. These two periods were equally important. These two periods were equally necessary and indispensable. They complemented each other. They were internally or intrinsically connected. Together, they gave rise to the animal life. Together, they brought the animal life into this world. This is the Primordial explosion. This is the meaning of the Primordial explosion.

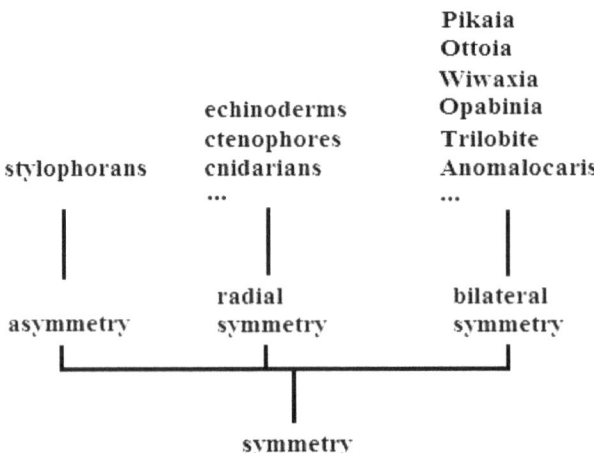

Figure 1.2   The Cambrian Symmetric Explosion

Compared to the Ediacaran organisms, the Cambrian animals appear to have demonstrated prominent features of symmetry, either in

Symmetry I

a radially symmetric sense, or in a bilaterally symmetric way. Such may be understood in the sense that, the Ediacaran development might have paved the way for the development of animals in the Cambrian. The Ediacaran prepared for the Cambrian. The Ediacaran laid the foundation for the Cambrian. The animals in the Cambrian might thus be able to develop the kind of features that may not be seen in the organisms living in the Ediacaran.

This may explain, in a sense, the possible differences between the Ediacaran symmetric explosion and the Cambrian symmetric explosion. One of such possible differences may have to do with what is called the combination of radial symmetry and bilateral symmetry. We have seen, a group of organisms living in the Ediacaran might have exhibited a sense of combination of radial symmetry and bilateral symmetry. That is, it might be said, both radial symmetry and bilateral symmetry may be seen as being present in such organisms. But, that phenomenon might not be so prominent or salient in the Cambrian. After the Ediacaran development, animals in the Cambrian might be able to develop, it might be said, in such a way that symmetry might achieve its dominance, either radially or bilaterally. That is, animals in the Cambrian might develop in such a way that they might be able to demonstrate, more clearly, their radially symmetric features or their bilaterally symmetric structures. The Cambrian symmetric explosion may be regarded, in such a sense, as having to do with the asymmetric animals, radially symmetric animals, and bilaterally symmetric animals.

Some organisms classified as stylophorans may have appeared in the Cambrian, and may be regarded as the asymmetric animals, in that they may demonstrate neither radial symmetry no bilateral symmetry. Cnidarians, ctenophores, and echinoderms may be seen as the radially symmetric animals appearing in the Cambrian. It seems, while some cnidarians may have come into being before the Cambrian, some cnidarians may have appeared in the Cambrian. Fossils seem to suggest, ctenophores may have appeared in the Cambrian. And, echinoderms may have appeared in the early Cambrian.

Bilateral symmetry may be found in the Cambrian animals such as Anomalocaris, Opabinia, Wiwaxia, Ottoia, or Pikaia. Bilateral symmetry may be seen in Anomalocaris, in its two big eyes, in its two arms, or in its bilaterally symmetric body structure. Bilateral symmetry may be observed in Opabinia, though it may possess some unusual features. Bilateral symmetry may be observed in the arrangement of the five eyes on its head, or in its bilaterally symmetric body plan. Bilateral symmetry may be observed in Wiwaxia, in the two rows of spines on its back, or in its body structure. Ottoia may be seen as an early priapulid worm living in the early or middle Cambrian. It may be a worm with bilateral symmetry, though a sense of radial symmetry may be observed in its front body parts. It is included in the bilaterally symmetric animals, in a sense that it possesses a nervous system featuring a sizeable and substantial nerve cord. Bilateral symmetry may be seen in Pikaia, in its two tentacles, in the structure of its head, or in the muscles on the two sides of its body.

It has to be said, the fulfillment or realization of symmetry in the early animal development might not be that simple, clear, linear, or straightforward. That is, the actual fulfillment or realization of symmetry in the early animal life might have been rather complex, intricate, convoluted, or in a sense, ambiguous. Such complexity, intricacy or ambiguity may be seen, in a sense, in the coming into being or appearance of a number of early life forms.

Homalozoans were a group of early organisms that may be seen as asymmetric. Among this group of early organisms might have been the stylophorans. Stylophorans were a group of early life forms that had been regarded by some people as the early echinoderms. The Cambrian organisms like mitrates may be seen as belonging to this group. The early stylophorans were usually asymmetric, but later on some of such organisms seemed to have developed some features that might have to do with either radial symmetry or bilateral symmetry.

That is to say, it seems, while radial symmetry or bilateral symmetry may not be seen as present in the early asymmetric stylophorans, some of such organisms might have developed, later on, with certain features that might have to do with either radial symmetry or bilateral symmetry. What happened, then? What happened to such organisms? What happened to symmetry? What happened to the fulfillment or realization of symmetry in the animal life?

Should the stylophorans be regarded as the early echinoderms? That is, should the stylophorans be treated as the early life forms possibly leading to the radially symmetric organisms? Or, should the stylophorans be regarded as the kind of early animal life forms that might have to do with bilateral symmetry? It appears, asymmetry, radial symmetry, and bilateral symmetry seemed to have somehow converged in the organisms like stylophorans, and it may be difficult for us to see clearly what form of symmetry was really operating in such organisms, what form of symmetry was working in such organisms, or what form of symmetry might have been dominating their development or existence.

Such intricate or ambiguous presence of symmetry might have reflected, in a sense, it might be said, the burst of symmetry in the beginning of the animal life, or the explosion of symmetry in the early development of animals, in that, all symmetries, including asymmetry, radial symmetry and bilateral symmetry, might have strived, or struggled, to fulfill or realize themselves in the animal life. They might have burst at once. They might have surged together. They might have exploded at about the same time.

A complex, intricate, convoluted, or ambiguous presence of symmetry might thus be observed in some of the early animal life forms. At the same time, it seems, it might have to be said, though the organisms' body plans might have come into being as a result or consequence of the symmetric surge or explosion, but that does not necessarily mean that, such body plans were the kind of favorable ones. That is, it might be said, later on, some of them might have gradually disappeared, possibly due to the disadvantages that might be associated with them, such as, the kind of disadvantages related to their unusual or irregular body shapes or forms. Such may be seen in that, some of such organisms might have gone extinct, and some of them might have continued their development and possibly became the ancestors of some organisms today.

It may have to be said, the presence of symmetry may sometimes be found, in a sense, in some sponge species. Some sponge species, like barrel sponge, might demonstrate through the body structure a sense of radial symmetry, though not in a clear or well-defined manner. Glass sponges are a group of sponges likely with a kind of cup-like body appearance. With such a kind of body appearance, a sense of radial symmetry may be seen as being expressed or demonstrated, to some extent, in the glass sponges.

The sponges expressing or exhibiting, to some extent, a sense of radial symmetry may not be only observed today. The kind of sponges with some sense of radial symmetry may also be observed, in a sense, among the early animal life forms. The archaeocyathans were some sponge-like organisms living in the Cambrian. They were the reef-building organisms and some of them possessed cup-like body forms. For those possessing such body forms, it seems, their conical body structures appeared to express or demonstrate a sense of radial symmetry.

Three things may be said about the kind of sponges with some sense of radial symmetry. First, it might be said, unlike the kind of radial symmetry fulfilled or realized in the radially symmetric animals such as cnidarians or echinoderms, the kind of radial symmetry seen in the sponges may not be regarded as the well or fully developed radial symmetry. That may be the reason, in a certain sense, why the sponges, such as the barrel sponge or glass sponges, have not developed or possessed a kind of nervous system like a simple nerve net, even though some sense of radial symmetry may be observed in them.

Secondly, it may be important to note that, only radial symmetry, but not bilateral symmetry, may be seen in the sponges. That is significant. That is significant, in the sense that, radial symmetry may mean, in a sense, or to some extent, limitations. But that is not the case with bilateral symmetry. when it comes to bilateral symmetry, it seems, things might be different and it might be a different matter, as we all have seen, in many cases, the power of bilateral symmetry and what capacities or potentials it might bring into things.

Thirdly, it is interesting to see that, both asymmetry and radial symmetry appear to have been expressed or demonstrated in the kind of sponges we discuss here, and yet, such a symmetric presence may only be regarded as representing or standing for a state of radial symmetry not well or fully developed. That is to say, even radial symmetry may be seen as being fulfilled or realized, to some extent, with asymmetry, in such sponges, it may not be regarded as having been fulfilled or realized to such an extent that it may dominate or govern the existence of such sponges. On the contrary, it seems, it is asymmetry that dominates or governs the existence of such sponges, as their asymmetric existence may be seen as being represented or embodied by their lack of nervous system. The radially symmetric animals usually possess a simple nerve net as their nervous system, but such a net may not be found in sponges. In other words, even a sense of radial symmetry may be observed, to some extent, in some sponges, sponges generally may be regarded or treated as the asymmetric animals.

It appears, sponges may not be regarded, in some cases, as completely asymmetrical. While some sponges exist with asymmetry,

Symmetry I

others may live with a sense of symmetry, though vaguely, to some extent. A sense of the combination of asymmetry and radial symmetry may be seen in the sponges. A sense of the combination of radial symmetry and bilateral symmetry may be seen in the kind of life forms such as the echinoderms. Nature is deep. Nature is complex. Nature is intricate. Such may be seen as the depth of symmetry. Such may be seen as the profundity of harmony. Such may be seen as the intricacy of nature. Such may be seen as the complexity of the world.

According to the fossils, it seems, strange forms or body plans may be found in the Cambrian or Precambrian organisms. That is, it seems, some of the Cambrian or Precambrian organisms might have developed with some kind of body shapes or forms that may be regarded as being strange or bizarre by some people today. Such strange forms or body plans found in the organisms existing in the Cambrian or in the Precambrian may be seen, in a sense, as the transitional forms or body plans, in that, the explosion of symmetry might have given rise to such forms or body plans, and with the development of symmetry, new forms or body plans might emerge to facilitate the further development of the organisms.

People may think that the Ediacaran organisms like Tribrachidium are strange and the Cambrian animals like Anomalocaris or Opabinia are bizarre. The strangeness of Tribrachidium may be seen in its unique body form. The fossils seem to indicate that it might be an organism of radial symmetry, with three curved lobes encircling such an organism in a somewhat spiral manner. The strangeness of Anomalocaris may be seen in its body form, in its head structure, in its two big eyes, or in the two long arms in front of its head. The strangeness of Opabinia may be seen in its feeding apparatus, in the position of its mouth, or in the arrangement of its five eyes on its head.

The most important thing about the strange forms or body plans possessed by the Cambrian or Precambrian organisms may be that, such strange forms or body plans appeared to share one significant feature, the presence of symmetry, that is, the presence of radial symmetry or bilateral symmetry. The presence of symmetry may be seen as the most important thing, when it comes to the Cambrian or Precambrian organisms, in that, the coming into being of symmetry may be seen as behind, ultimately, the coming into being of the Cambrian or Precambrian organisms. It was the coming into being of radial symmetry or bilateral symmetry that might have led to the coming into being of such organisms. It was the coming into being of radial symmetry or bilateral symmetry that might have guided such organisms to emerge, to develop. It was the coming into being of radial symmetry or bilateral symmetry that might have driven such organisms to continue their development, in a sense, until new forms or body plans emerged, it might be said, in some later periods.

Are they strange? Are they bizarre? No. They are not strange. No. They are not bizarre. They are symmetric. They are harmonic. They are beautiful. Are they weird? No. They are not. They are wonderful. Are they strange? No. They are not. They are splendid. They are beautiful, in a symmetric way. They are beautiful, in a harmonic sense. They are wonderful, if considered as a symmetric happening. They are splendid, if considered as a harmonic occurrence.

It was the burst of symmetry. It was the burst of harmony. It was symmetry bursting into the world with remarkable forms. It was harmony bursting into the world with unprecedented plans. The strange forms were the blossoms of symmetry. The strange body plans were the blossoms of harmony. They represented the movement of symmetry. They represented the development of harmony. They represented the workings of symmetry in the animal life. They stood for the operations of harmony in animals. They represented the first fulfillment of symmetry in the animal life. They stood for the first realization of harmony in animals.

The strange forms were the harbinger of a new era in which symmetry might work or operate to give rise to new life forms. The strange body plans were the sign that a new era for life had come, on earth. They represented a fresh movement of symmetry on earth. They embodied a fresh development of harmony on this planet. Their meaning may never be overstated. Their significance may never be overvalued. They are meaningful. They are significant. They are meaningful, in the symmetric sense. They are meaningful, in the harmonic way. They are significant, symmetrically. They are significant, harmonically. Symmetry demonstrated itself. Symmetry demonstrated its power. Harmony displayed itself. Harmony displayed its power. Symmetry demonstrated itself or its power in the animal life. Harmony displayed itself or its power in animals.

To be honest, I am so amazed by the balanced, symmetric and harmonious forms or body plans found in some of the Cambrian or Precambrian organisms, even though they may be regarded by some people as being strange or bizarre. They were so nicely balanced. They were so symmetric. They were so harmonic. They were so refined. They were so exquisite. They were so beautiful. Sometimes, I just wonder, they had come into being some 500 million years ago!

They were regular. They were balanced. They were symmetric. They were harmonic. They were harmonious. They were pleasing. They were beautiful. Was beauty coming into being? Had beauty come into being? Was fresh beauty appearing on earth? Had fresh beauty appeared on earth? Beauty appeared. Beauty appeared on earth. Fresh beauty appeared on earth. Fresh beauty appeared on earth; fresh life forms appeared on earth. Beauty appeared; existence came into being. Beauty appeared; the Cambrian or Precambrian organisms came into being. Beauty came into being; the Cambrian or Precambrian organisms appeared. Beauty appeared; existence appeared. Beauty came into being; existence came into being. Beauty was existence; existence was beauty. Beauty is existence; existence is beauty. Beauty means existence. Existence means beauty.

Why did the Ediacaran or Cambrian organisms appear? Because, beauty appeared. Why did the Ediacaran or Cambrian organisms emerge? Because, beauty emerged. Why did the Ediacaran or Cambrian organisms come into being? Because, beauty came into being. Why did the Ediacaran or Cambrian organisms develop? Because, in a sense, symmetry developed. Why did the Ediacaran or Cambrian organisms move? Because, in a sense, symmetry moved. Why did the Ediacaran or Cambrian organisms progress? Because, in a sense, it might be said, symmetry or harmony had progressed. It was the development of symmetry that might have led to the development of the animal life forms in the Ediacaran or Cambrian. It was the movement of symmetry that might have led to the movement of the animal life forms in the Ediacaran or Cambrian. It was the progress of harmony that might have led to the progress of the complex multicellular life forms in the Ediacaran or Cambrian. That is, in other words, it might be said, it was the appearance of beauty that might have led to the appearance of the Ediacaran or Cambrian organisms. It was the coming into being of beauty that might have paved the way for the coming into being of the Ediacaran or Cambrian organisms. It was the coming into being of beauty that might have brought the Ediacaran or Cambrian organisms, finally, into the world.

The coming into being or appearance of both radial symmetry and bilateral symmetry in the complex multicellular animal life forms during the Ediacaran constituted, truly, a significant, spectacular, momentous, and magnificent event in the history of life on earth. Its importance may never be overstated, and its meaning may never be, in a sense, exhausted. Why should both radial symmetry and bilateral symmetry appear in the complex multicellular organisms at this time? Why should the complex multicellular organisms appear with both radial symmetry and bilateral symmetry at this moment? Why should the complex multicellular organisms and symmetry, both radial and bilateral, emerge, together, at this point? Why was it not the case that, the complex multicellular Ediacaran organisms emerged, but without their radially or bilaterally symmetric body plans? Why was it not the case that, symmetry emerged, both radially and bilaterally, but no organisms with complex multicellularity would have come into being, at this time? Was it the case that the coming into being of symmetry, both radial and bilateral, led to the coming into being of the complex multicellular organisms in the Ediacaran? Or, was it the case that, the coming into being of the complex multicellular Ediacaran organisms actually fulfilled or realized the development or movement of symmetry, both radial and bilateral? Or, was it the case that, it was the development or movement of symmetry that had given rise to the appearance of the Ediacaran organisms, in an integration, union or fusion of symmetry and complex multicellularity?

The appearance or coming into being of symmetry, both radial and bilateral, in the Ediacaran organisms may not be seen or regarded as coincidental. No. It was not coincidental. It was of the utmost importance. It was of the utmost significance. When symmetry was absent, both radially and bilaterally, it seems, no life forms with complex multicellularity had ever come into being. When the development or movement of symmetry had not reached such a stage or level that both radial symmetry and bilateral symmetry might be fulfilled or realized, it appears, the life forms on earth existed, at most, only with simple multicellularity. It was the coming into being of the fulfillment or realization of symmetry, both radial and bilateral, that had ushered in a new era for the development of life on earth. That is, it was the fulfillment or realization of symmetry that may be seen as behind the coming into being of the Ediacaran organisms. It was the fulfillment of symmetry that may be seen as behind the fulfillment of

Symmetry I

the Ediacaran body plans. It was the realization of symmetry that may be seen as behind the realization of the Ediacaran life forms. That is, it was the development or movement of symmetry or harmony that may be seen as behind the coming into being of the Ediacaran age.

The presence of the Ediacaran burrows may suggest, in a sense, that, the race between predator and prey might have already begun, as early as in the Ediacaran. Some organisms might have to burrow to hide from their predators. An arms race between predator and prey might thus have started among some of the Ediacaran organisms. In a sense, it might be said, this might have been a subtle, intricate, or profound process, in that, what happened in such a process might have triggered a symmetric development, a development that may be seen as behind, in a sense, or to some extent, the coming into being of the movement in the animal life. The development of movement in the animal life, or the development of the ability of movement in animals might not be a simple matter. The animal movement involved a number of things, such as, head, body, legs, muscles, or above all, in a sense, the nervous system. For such things to happen, it seems, an arms race might not be necessarily adequate or sufficient, that is, it might be said, a symmetric development may be seen as necessary. While an arms race might not be enough, it might work to trigger, in a sense, a symmetric development, such that, such things might eventually come into being. And, as we can see, it appears, at around the end of the Ediacaran, or at around the start of the Cambrian, movement seemed to have exploded in the animal life.

Just like Cloudina, Sinotubulites was an organism showing early animal mineralization. These two early organisms are often found in the same locations. Sinotubulites possessed a tube-like body structure, very similar to that of Cloudina. The interesting thing about these two shelly organisms is that, while some mineralized shells of Cloudina bear holes possibly made by predators, no such holes are found in Sinotubulites shells. And, it appears, the holes in the Cloudina shells were made by predators in a quite selective way, with the bigger holes in the larger shells. With all these facts in mind, we seem to be able to say that, first, an arms race between predator and prey might have been under way in the late Ediacaran, in a sense, represented by the appearance of the animal mineralized shells; and secondly, a process of speciation might have possibly happened, in a sense, as Sinotubulites

Avolution and Man

might have developed in such a way that it became an organism capable of avoiding certain predatory attacks.

People sometimes take what we are discussing here as the possible causes of the Cambrian explosion. This may not be true. The arms race between predator and prey happens, it seems, all the time. It did not happen solely in such a time. It happens, it seems, all the way along the process with which the animal life develops on earth. If the arms race during such a time led to the Cambrian explosion, then, why had it not led to some other explosions in the past? It seems, if the arms race really worked that way, then the long development of the animal life on earth might have provided enough time for it to cause at least several other explosions to happen. But, we only see once, and it only happened in the Cambrian.

Should this mean that no arms race between predator and prey had happened in such a time? The answer may be that, a sense of arms race between predator and prey might have indeed happened, and such an arms race might have led to the appearance of the early animal mineralization. But, at the same time, it may have to be pointed out, such a sense of arms race might not be the kind of arms race we understand in the evolutionary sense. That is to say, such a sense of arms race might not mean the kind of developmental process in which natural selection would play the major or full role. No. It might not be that way. Natural selection might have indeed played some role, but it might not have played its role in such a way that the early animal mineralization might thus come into being, as a result. The early animal mineralization might come into being and natural selection might have operated in some sense, but natural selection, alone or by itself, might not have the power, the speed, or the capacity to make such a thing as the early animal mineralization to happen. That is, some other things, some other more fundamental, more profound, or more powerful things might have to participate in such a process. In other words, the arms race that we are discussing here, with regard to the Cambrian explosion, might not have to do so much with the evolutionary process, and it might have to do more with an avolutionary process, in which, apart from natural selection, symmetry might have worked its way to fulfill or realize itself in the early animal life, with its symmetric speed, through, in a sense, the animal mineralization. The early animal mineralization, or the early arms race between predator and prey, may thus be seen as a developmental process involving, in a sense, or to

Symmetry I

some extent, both natural selection and symmetry. Symmetry may be seen as having played the major role, in the sense that it provided the kind of things such as the symmetric power, the symmetric speed, or the symmetric potentials so that the early organisms might develop themselves as they did in the Ediacaran or Cambrian. Natural selection, or in such a selective sense, the arms race between predator and prey, may be seen, in a sense, apart from the possible evolutionary process, as having triggered or activated the symmetric movement. Symmetry, once triggered or activated by natural selection or the arms race, might advance in the early animal life with its full power and speed, in such a way, or in such a sense that natural selection might be achieved and the arms race might be suitably handled or managed. This may be what ultimately behind the appearance of the early animal life forms. This may be what ultimately behind the appearance of the early animal mineralization.

The speciation of the early animal life might be true, in a sense, or to a certain extent. Two things may be said here, with regard to such a process. First, it might not have happened completely in an evolutionary sense. Secondly, its implications on the Cambrian explosion might not be that big or decisive as some people suggest. The process of speciation, in an evolutionary sense, usually takes a long period of time to accomplish, and the kind of speciation, possibly happening in the late Ediacaran or early Cambrian, represented by the coming into being of the kind of early organisms like Sinotubulites, might not demonstrate, in a full sense, the characteristics of a real process of speciation. For one thing, we cannot see or find such a process. Yes, we see or witness the possible results of such a process. Yes, we can infer from the fossil findings that something like speciation might have happened. Yes, we can see the similarities and differences of the organisms, such as in Cloudina and Sinotubulites. Yes, it seems, we may come to the conclusion that a process of speciation might have occurred among the early animal life forms in the early times. But, where is the process? Where was it? Where could we see the process? Where could we find such a process? Where could it happen? What might be the stages? What constituted the developmental steps? What fossils point to such stages? What fossils represent such steps? It seems, no, we cannot find such fossils, and we cannot find such stages or steps. It may be possible for us to see or find the kind of fossils revealing the developmental processes for later organisms, but for the early organisms like Cloudina or Sinotubulites, it seems, it may be a very difficult task.

What does this mean? It may mean that, such a process might not actually exist. It may mean that, such a process might not have happened, in reality, that is, in the human reality, that is, in the human sense. That is, it may mean that, if such a process had indeed happened, it might have happened in a way deeper or more profound than the human sense. That is, it may mean that, if such a process had indeed happened, it might have happened in an innate or intrinsic way. That is, it might be said, the possible process of speciation in the early animal life might be a process dominated, defined, sustained, or driven, in a sense, by symmetry. The symmetric movement may be seen as ultimately behind such a process. The symmetric development may be seen as ultimately underlying such a process. That is, the symmetric burst, the symmetric surge, or the symmetric explosion may be seen as what constituted, in a dominant or fundamental sense, such a process. The process of speciation in the early animal life might not be, fully, an evolutionary process, in that, an evolutionary process might not be able to give rise to the early organisms like Cloudina or Sinotubulites in the ways we have seen. In other words, a sense of evolutionary process might have indeed happened, to a certain extent, but for the early organisms like Cloudina or Sinotubulites to appear as they had, it seems, some other things, fundamental, powerful, profound, or speedy might have to take part in such a process. That is to say, the coming into being of the early organisms, or the possible process of speciation among the early life forms, might be a complex, intricate, and subtle process involving both evolution and avolution. The evolutionary forces leading to speciation might have been joined by the avolutionary forces. The avolutionary forces might have been stimulated or helped by the evolutionary forces. Evolution might have merged with avolution. Avolution might have been united with evolution. It was complex. It was intricate. It was subtle. It was delicate. It was deep. It was profound. It was powerful. It was mighty. It was the union from which the early organisms might have emerged. It was the fusion through which the process of speciation among the early life forms might have been accomplished. And it is in such a sense that, it might be said, the possible process of speciation among the early organisms like Cloudina or Sinotubulites may thus be seen as not that

Symmetry I

fundamentally important or decisive, when it comes to the possible causes of the Cambrian explosion.

When it comes to biology or life, it seems, people like to talk about the genes. What are genes? Do genes play the major role in life? To what extent do genes play the major role in life? Do genes determine life? To what extent do genes determine life? Do genes determine the development of life? To what extent do genes determine the development of life? Do genes determine the development of animals? To what extent do genes determine the development of animals?

What may be behind genes? What may be behind the coming into being or existence of genes? What may be behind the workings or operations of genes? Why should genes come into being? Why should genes come to exist? What makes genes to come into being? What makes the coming into being of genes necessary? What makes the existence of genes possible? Why should genes work or operate in the ways that are observed? What makes genes to work or operate in the ways that are found?

People sometimes may think that, once they find the genes and discover the workings or operations of the genes, they may be able to understand the development of various life forms and eventually reveal the secrets of life. This may not be true. Finding the genes may not necessarily mean that we have reached the source of life. Discovering the workings or operations of the genes may not necessarily mean that the secrets of life are going to be revealed, in such a way. Genetics may reveal some of the processes or mechanisms associated with life, but it may not be able to reach the real cause or the real source of life.

Genes may just be the effect, but not the cause. The workings or operations of genes may just be the effect, but not the cause. The cause may lie much deeper. The cause may exist in a much more profound way. To take genes as the cause may be to overlook the real cause. To take genes as what design the various life forms may be to ignore the real source. To take genes as what determine the development of the various life forms may be to overlook the real cause, or the real source behind the things.

Some might say that, the Cambrian explosion might be caused by the random mutations of some of the key genes, such as the Hox genes. Researches seem to tell us that, for various animals, such genes, like the Hox genes, seem to only function after the coming into being of the body plans. What does this mean? It may mean that, the random mutations of the genes, such as the Hox genes, may not be able to explain the speedy and sudden appearance of the incredibly diversified animal body plans or forms in the Cambrian.

On the other hand, the random mutation explanation may also have other difficulties in explaining the kind of events such as the Cambrian explosion. When the genetic mutations happen, they could happen at any time. They could happen in the Cambrian. They could happen in all the other periods after the Cambrian. But, what we see is that, it might be said, the animals have generally maintained their body plans or structures, ever since their first appearance in the Cambrian. Why was it the case that no random mutations occurred to change the animal body plans or structures, in such a long period of time after the Cambrian? Why was it possible? Why was it such a case?

For new organisms to arise, for new structures to emerge, for new body plans or forms to appear, new genetic information must have been there to form the basic building blocks. But, where was the genetic information before the arrival of the various organisms in the Cambrian? What might be such genetic information? What might constitute such genetic information? How could such genetic information come into being? What might be the source of such genetic information? What might be the origin of such genetic information? What might be the root of such genetic information? What might be the fountainhead of such genetic information? Or, what might be the beginning of such genetic information? The enormous amount of genetic information necessary for the emergence of the various Cambrian organisms may be seen as coming into being with symmetry or harmony working its way during the Precambrian or Cambrian to fulfill or realize itself, in the sense that, it was the symmetric proliferation or harmonic radiation that, with the preparation made in the Precambrian or Cambrian, had enhanced, refined, or enriched the whole Cambrian genetic pool. In other words, the Cambrian genetic explosion may be seen as a symmetric proliferation or harmonic radiation, as symmetry strove to fulfill itself or harmony worked to bring itself to fruition in such a period. The genetic potential, preconditioned or predetermined by symmetry or harmony, signified by the appearance of the symmetric body plans or forms in such a period, exploded at this time, as symmetry or harmony led or drove such a process for their own completion or fruition. Thus, the genetic proliferation of the Cambrian may be seen as the symmetric completion

Symmetry I

of such a period, and the genetic radiation of the Cambrian may be regarded as the harmonic fruition at such a time. The real process of the genetic proliferation or radiation during the Cambrian may not be easy to understand, as such was a process led, supported, guided, preconditioned, predetermined, sustained, or maintained by symmetry, or harmony. It is in such a sense that, it might be said, we may not be able to truly understand, that is, in the scientific sense, the remarkable phenomenon of the rapid genetic proliferation or radiation in the Cambrian. We may understand part of the phenomenon, as we are capable of doing certain genetic researches or studies. But, when it comes to the symmetric workings or harmonic operations that might have been involved in such a phenomenon, we may be at a loss if we only focus on the rational or scientific sides of things.

The rapid genetic proliferation of the Cambrian was a symmetric proliferation. The rapid genetic radiation of the Cambrian was a harmonic radiation. The genetic explosion of the Cambrian was a symmetric or harmonic explosion. It was a symmetric process. It was a harmonic happening. It was a symmetric event. It was a harmonic phenomenon. It was the genetic information enhanced rapidly by symmetry. It was the genetic materials refined in a speedy manner by harmony. It was the genetic pool enriched quickly and suddenly through a symmetric or harmonic process. It was the genes increased unexpectedly through the symmetric workings or harmonic operations. The genetic was intertwined with the symmetric. The genetic was combined with the harmonic. Symmetry fused with genes. Harmony merged into the body plans or forms. Genes proliferated, as a result of the both genetic and symmetric process. The genetic information exploded, as a result of the both genetic and harmonic explosion. It was the genetic and symmetric development. It was the genetic and harmonic enhancement. It was the refinement through the fusion of genes and symmetry. It was the enrichment achieved through the integration or union of genes with harmony. The focus on the genetic researches or studies may not fully reveal the nature of such a process. To fully understand or grasp such a process, not only do we have to engage in the kind of related genetic researches or studies, we may also have to pay attention, carefully, to the symmetric workings or harmonic operations.

What gives rise to the genetic similarity observed in life? What gives rise to the genetic similarity found in the world? It is symmetry. It is harmony. It is symmetry that gives rise to the genetic similarity observed in life. It is harmony that gives rise to the genetic similarity found in the world. The genetic similarity observed in life may be seen as the workings or operations of symmetry in guiding the formation of the various life forms. The genetic similarity found in the world may be seen as the fulfillment or realization of harmony in the world, in the various life forms.

Geneticists may like to point to their discoveries about the workings or operations of the genes, in claiming that it is the genes that play the major role in determining the patterns or formats of animals, such as, the nervous system, the circulatory system, the sensory system, or their bilateral body plans. It is the bilateral symmetry that determines the bilateral body plans. It is the bilateral symmetry that leads, in a sense, to the coming into being or existence of the genes that may be responsible, in a sense, or to some extent, for the formation of the bilateral body plans or the kind of structures or systems found in animals. It is not the genes that determine the patterns or formats of animals. It is the bilateral symmetry that determines the patterns or formats of animals. It is symmetry that determines the patterns or formats of animals. It is not the genes. It is the bilateral symmetry. It is not genes. It is symmetry.

The genetic similarity existing in animals may lead us to engage in the kind of activities, such as, to find the ancestor of all animals, including the human beings. Does the genetic similarity really mean that, a single ancestor might have existed in the early times that may be regarded as the forebear to all the animals we know today? This may not necessarily be the case. There might be ancestors. There might be forebears. But it may not necessarily be the case that there might be a single ancestor or forebear that might have led to the coming into being of all the animals we know today. The ancestor is symmetry. The forebear is harmony. The ancestor is the coming into being of symmetry. The forebear is the coming into being of harmony. The ancestor is the explosion of symmetry. The forebear is the explosion of harmony. The ancestor is symmetry bursting with the various products. The forebear is harmony bursting with the numerous results. Thus, what we see is that, there might be various organisms coming, at the same time, on the scene. Thus, what we observe is that, there might be numerous organisms, with numerous shapes or forms, some of them even unfamiliar or strange, appearing suddenly in the world. The

Symmetry I

ancestors came on the scene, even though possibly not a single one, as the result of the coming into being or bursting of symmetry. The forebears appeared, even though probably varied and numerous, as the consequence of the coming into being or bursting of harmony. The coming into being or bursting of symmetry might not have only produced one single organism. The coming into being or bursting of harmony might not have only given rise to one single creature that may be regarded as *the* ancestor to all animals. The ancestor might be many. The forebear might be varied and numerous. This may be seen as one of the significant characteristics that have defined the great ages such as the Precambrian period called the Ediacaran, or the Cambrian.

Given the avolutionary nature of the early animal development, it seems, it may not be surprising that, the findings in the fossil record sometimes have forced scientists or researchers to come to such a conclusion that, the real tree of life might be a tree-like form turned upside down, that is, with a wide base at the bottom while the tree itself grows somewhat narrower upwards. Certainly, the traditional Darwinian evolutionary theory cannot explain such a phenomenon, and yet those researchers cannot deceive themselves into believing that the occurrence or development of life is just like the story told by the traditional theories. They see in the fossils that, it seems, many different organisms appeared suddenly at the same time. And they witness in the fossil record that the remarkable diversity arose, it seems, from the very beginning. Was it evolution? Was it gradual development from one ancestor? Was it new biological forms emerging from the previous ones? It seems, it might be said, probably not. It was new biological forms emerging together at the same time. It was the development of many new biological forms at the same time. It was the coming into being of the remarkable biological diversity from the very beginning. It was the burst of symmetry. It was the burst of harmony. It was the explosion of symmetry. It was the explosion of harmony. It was life emerging from symmetry. It was the tree of life growing from symmetry. The tree of life began not with one ancestor, but with symmetry. The tree of life began not with a single forebear, but with harmony. It was symmetry that gave rise to the tree of life. It was harmony that fulfilled or realized the tree of life, and made it grow.

The evolutionary theory usually takes the development of life as a branching tree, but when it comes to the Cambrian explosion, it seems, it was not a branching tree at all. It was not a branching tree; it was the branching of symmetry. It was not a branching tree; it was the branching of harmony. It was the branching symmetry giving rise to various forms. It was the branching harmony giving birth to numerous organisms. It was the various forms sprouting from symmetry. It was the numerous organisms arising from harmony. Such forms had not sprouted from a branching tree; they had sprouted from symmetry. Such organisms had not arisen from a branching tree; they had arisen from harmony. It was not an evolutionary branching. It was a symmetric branching. It was a harmonic branching. It was not an evolutionary radiation. It was a symmetric radiation. It was a harmonic radiation. It was not an evolutionary explosion. It was a symmetric explosion. It was a harmonic explosion.

Some biologists, including Darwin, may think that, not enough fossils have been found, as the organism existing in the Precambrian periods might be too small or their bodies might be too soft to be preserved perfectly in the fossils. Researches seem to tell us that, in some areas, it seems, soft body tissues from the Cambrian or Precambrian periods could be preserved perfectly in the fossils. This means, if the organisms had indeed existed, they could be preserved and might be found today.

Trilobites were among the most common organisms in the Cambrian. The complexity of the trilobites may be seen in their eyes. The coming into being of the trilobite eyes, and the sudden appearance of the Cambrian organisms like trilobites may prove a significant explanatory difficulty for the Darwinian evolutionary theory. And indeed, Darwin was right in seeing that the Cambrian explosion may constitute one of the biggest challenges to his theory of evolution.

The Ediacaran and the Cambrian are the remarkable and significant geological periods distinguished by the coming into being of both radial symmetry and bilateral symmetry in the complex multicellular organisms. While we see the coming into being of such organisms in such remarkable periods, we may also have to see the complexity, subtlety, and depth possibly associated with such a coming into being. That is, in a sense, it might be said, if we want to understand the occurrence or development of the early animal life on earth, we may have to see into the complexity, subtlety, and depth possibly associated with the coming into being of radial symmetry and bilateral symmetry in the Ediacaran and Cambrian organisms.

Symmetry I

§ 1.5 The Fulfillment or Realization of Symmetry: the Coming into Being of Man

The early animals might have appeared on earth about 600 million years ago. Mammals might have come into being about 200 million years ago. The appearance of primates might have happened about 60 million years ago. Great apes might have lived on earth about 20 million years ago. The rise of the genus *Homo* might have happened about 2.5 million years ago. The human species, *Homo sapiens*, might have emerged about 500,000 years ago. Modern humans, *Homo sapiens sapiens*, might have appeared about 200,000 years ago. With the coming into being of modern humans, it seems, the way had been paved for human beings to develop into what they are today.

From the appearance of animals to the coming into being of man on earth was a long process. It was a long process that had seen numerous changes, developments, or great leaps forward, such as, from living in the water to colonizing the land, from fish to amphibians, from amphibians to reptiles, from reptiles to mammals, from mammals to primates, or from primates to humans. While an evolutionary process may be seen in such changes, developments or great leaps forward, an avolutionary process may also be seen in them, in that, symmetry may be seen as behind, in an avolutionary sense, the happening or occurrence of such changes, developments or great leaps forward.

Amphibians might have appeared in the Devonian, about 370 million years ago. They might have come into being from the lobe-finned fish, as such fish might have possessed the body structures suitable for developing a possible land life. The appearance of amphibians in the Devonian may be seen as an indication of the land colonization by animals. The Devonian was a period that had seen a rapid development or diversification of plants on the land. In other words, it seems, this period might have been the time when the land was colonized actively by both animals and plants.

The colonization of land by both animals and plants might bode well for the development of animals and plants. a favorable ecosystem might come into being as a result, and such a system might support well the further development of animals and plants. The seeds of plants might be spread through the various animal activities on land. The seeds or leaves of plants might be good food for animals, providing the necessary nutrition for them. The vegetation might provide a living environment for animals. The activities of animals, in their turn, might facilitate the development of plants. It was a co-developmental process for animals and plants. It was beneficial to both of them.

Amphibians developed. Reptiles emerged. Reptiles developed. Mammals appeared. The appearance of mammals on earth may be seen as one of the major events in the developmental history of life on earth. Mammals usually feed their young with milk produced by the mammary glands. This way of feeding may mean that a close relationship may come into being between the parents and the young, especially between the female mammals and their offspring. Feelings may grow as the mammal parents nurse their young with the precious and nutritious food produced by their own bodies. Close and intimate feelings may arise, as the parents and the young are devoted to each other, keep bodily contacts, and live together. A bond may thus be established between the parents and the young, as the young develop and the parents take care of them.

In such a sense, it might be said, the mammal life might lead to the coming into being or strengthening of feelings. The intensity of feelings might be boosted. The content of feelings might be enriched. The complexity of feelings might be enhanced. The depth of feelings might be increased. With the increase of feelings, in terms of intensity, content, complexity or depth, it seems, it might be said, the mammal life might mean a transition of feelings, from the early, physical, primitive, or animal feelings to the kind of feelings with intensity, content, complexity or depth. That is, it seems, it might be said, with the increase of feelings, in terms of intensity, content, complexity or depth, the mammal life might mean the coming into being or emergence of the mammal feelings.

The animal feelings may be seen as constituting the animorality of animals. The mammal feelings may be seen as constituting the mammorality of mammals. The primate feelings may be seen as constituting the primorality of primates. The human feelings may be seen as constituting the humorality of human beings. The steady increase of feelings may be seen as behind the process from the animal feelings to the mammal feelings to the primate feelings to the human feelings. That is, it seems, it might be said, a steady increase of feelings, in terms of intensity, content, complexity or depth, may be seen as behind the process from animorality to mammorality to primorality to humorality.

Symmetry I

With the development from animals to mammals to primates to humans, feelings might have been enriched, intensified, and refined. With the development from animals to mammals to primates to humans, the width of feelings might have been widened, the breadth of feelings might have been expanded, and the depth of feelings might have been increased. The human feelings are the feelings with intensity, content and complexity. The human feelings are the feelings with width, breadth or depth. The human feelings are the humoral feelings.

From animals to mammals to primates to humans, it might have been a process of the increase of feelings, in terms of intensity, content and complexity. From animals to mammals to primates to humans, it might have been a process of the increase of feelings, in terms of width, breadth or depth. From animorality to mammorality to primorality to humorality, it might have been a process of the coming into being of the humoral feelings. From animorality to mammorality to primorality to humorality, it might have been a process of the humoralization of feelings. From animorality to mammorality to primorality to humorality, it might have been a process of the coming into being of the humoral man.

The humoral feelings came into being in a process from animals to mammals to primates to humans. The humoral feelings came into being in a process in which feelings might have been gradually enriched, intensified, and refined. The humoral feelings came into being in a process in which feelings might have been gradually developed with width, breadth or depth. The humoral man came into being, in a process from animals to mammals to primates to humans. The humoral man came into being, in a process from animorality to mammorality to primorality to humorality. It was a process of the humoralization of feelings. It was a process of the humoralization of man. It was a process of the coming into being of man.

What was behind the development of animal feelings into the humoral feelings of man? What was behind the humoralization of feelings? What was behind the humoralization of man? What was behind the process from animals to mammals to primates to humans? What was behind the process from animorality to mammorality to primorality to humorality? What was behind the process of humoralization that might have given rise to the coming into being of humorality? What was behind the process of humoralization that might have given rise to the coming into being of man? It might be said, it might be the bilateral symmetry. Bilateral symmetry might have been behind the development of animal feelings into the humoral feelings. Bilateral symmetry might have been behind the process from animals to mammals to primates to humans. Bilateral symmetry might have been behind the process from animorality to mammorality to primorality to humorality.

Bilateral symmetry may be seen as behind the coming into being of the centralized nervous system. Unlike the radially symmetric animals that only possess simple nerve nets, the bilaterally symmetric animals usually possess centralized nervous systems. Simple nerve nets are different from the centralized nervous systems. Simple nerve nets are not as powerful as the centralized nervous systems. Organisms with simple nerve nets may do certain things, but they may not be able to act, behave, or live as the organisms with the centralized nervous systems. That is to say, while simple nerve nets may enable organisms to live with their activities or functions, such activities or functions may be regarded as being performed in a simple or rudimentary manner. In other words, it might be said, organisms with simple nerve nets may not be able to live or exist in a complex or highly complex way.

The centralized nervous systems are usually more complex than simple nerve nets. The centralized nervous systems are the systems possessing powerful nerve centers that may process information or coordinate activities in a highly efficient way. That means, organisms with the centralized nervous systems may be able to live or exist in the kind of ways that may not be seen in the organisms with simple nerve nets. And, it seems, the limitations seen in simple nerve nets may not be observed in the centralized nervous systems. Unlike simple nerve nets, it seems, the centralized nervous systems may develop into the kind of systems with remarkable complexity, sophistication and power. Such may be observed in animals, mammals, primates or humans, as they may demonstrate the kind of behaviors, the kind of functions, or the kind of lifestyles that may exhibit complexity, sophistication or depth. In such a sense, it might be said, the development of the centralized nervous system may be seen as behind the development from animals to mammals to primates to humans. With the development of the centralized nervous system, organisms may be able to perform more and more complex activities. With the development of the centralized nervous system, organisms may be able to develop more

Symmetry I

and more sophisticated functions. With the development of the centralized nervous system, it seems, organisms may be able to live or exist eventually in some complex, rich, or sophisticated lives.

The development of the centralized nervous system may be seen, in such a sense, as behind the development of feelings. With the development of the centralized nervous system, feelings might have been gradually enriched, intensified, and refined. With the development of the centralized nervous system, feelings might have been gradually developed with width, breadth or depth. That is, with the development of the centralized nervous system, feelings might have gradually come into being with intensity, content and complexity. That is, with the development of the centralized nervous system, feelings might have gradually come into being with width, breadth or depth.

The development of the centralized nervous system may thus be seen as playing a significant role in the development from animals to mammals to primates to humans. The development of the centralized nervous system may thus be seen as vital to the process from animorality to mammorality to primorality to humorality. With the development of the centralized nervous system, it might be said, it might have been made possible that a process might occur, from animals to mammals to primates to humans. With the development of the centralized nervous system, it might be said, it might have been made possible that a process might happen, from animorality to mammorality to primorality to humorality.

Bilateral symmetry may thus be seen as behind the development of feelings. Bilateral symmetry may thus be seen as behind the coming into being of the feelings with intensity, content and complexity. Bilateral symmetry may thus be seen as behind the coming into being of the feelings with width, breadth or depth. Bilateral symmetry may thus be seen as behind the development of animal feelings into the humoral feelings. Bilateral symmetry may thus be seen as behind the humoralization of feelings. Bilateral symmetry may thus be seen as behind the humoralization of man. Bilateral symmetry may thus be seen as behind the coming into being of the humorality of man. Bilateral symmetry may thus be seen as behind the coming into being of man.

Certainly, it might be said, bilateral symmetry may be seen as behind the coming into being of the vertebrate body structures. Bilateral symmetry may be seen as behind the coming into being of the

Avolution and Man

centralized nervous system. Bilateral symmetry may be seen as behind the coming into being of the centralized nervous system of vertebrates. Bilateral symmetry may be seen as behind the coming into being of vertebrates. The centralized nervous system of vertebrates may be seen as a powerful system, as we know, well developed, and well protected. In vertebrates, the brain is the center of the nervous system, is enclosed in the head, and is well protected by the skull. In vertebrates, the spinal cord mainly connects the brain with the body, is enclosed in the vertebral column, and is well protected by the vertebral column. Thus, as we can see, the centralized nervous system of vertebrates may be seen as being well developed and protected in vertebrates.

Human beings are vertebrates. Human beings possess the vertebrate body structures. Human beings possess the centralized nervous systems of vertebrates. Vertebrates have to do with bilateral symmetry. The vertebrate body structures have to do with bilateral symmetry. The centralized nervous systems of vertebrates have to do with bilateral symmetry. The human nervous system has to do with bilateral symmetry. The human body has to do with bilateral symmetry. The human being has to do with bilateral symmetry. The coming into being of man has to do with bilateral symmetry.

Man is the fulfillment of bilateral symmetry. Man is the realization of bilateral symmetry. Man is the fulfillment or realization of bilateral symmetry in animals. Man is the fulfillment or realization of bilateral symmetry in the animal forms. Man is the fulfillment or realization of bilateral symmetry in life, or through life. Man is the fulfillment or realization of bilateral symmetry in the human life, or through the human life. Man is the fulfillment or realization of double helical symmetry. Man is the fulfillment or realization of sexual symmetry. Man is the fulfillment or realization of bilateral symmetry. Man is the fulfillment of symmetry. Man is the realization of symmetry. Man is the fulfillment or realization of symmetry in animals. Man is the fulfillment or realization of symmetry in the animal forms. Man is the fulfillment or realization of symmetry in life, or through life. Man is the fulfillment or realization of symmetry in the human life, or through the human life.

Chapter II Symmetry II: the Coming into Being of Plants

§ 2.1 The Coming into Being of Bilateral Symmetry in Plants: the Devonian Explosion

The earliest plants may have appeared on earth in the Silurian period, after developing from some groups of green algae. The moving of plants onto the dry land from the waters may be seen as one of the major events in the history of life on earth, as the colonization of the land by plants paved the way for a whole new ecosystem, together with animals, to gradually take its shape on this planet. Certainly, this process, the movement of plants onto the dry land from the waters, may be a delicate and complex one which may have involved a number of factors, such as, atmospheric, climatic, oceanic, geological, environmental, or evolutionary. As this discussion is mainly concerned with the Devonian explosion, we focus our attention on the developmental phase of plants in which they may be seen as having developed into the kind of plants forming the forests near the end of the Devonian, in a rather rapid and robust manner, from the early simple, primitive, and small plant organisms.

The study of the early leaves may have shown that it may be difficult to tell exactly how the early leaves had actually come into being. One reason for this may be the fact that the fossil record is far from complete. As such, the full story of the earliest coming into being of leaves may elude us, in a sense, at least, it seems, for now. From the fossil record, we may come to several suggestions with regard to the early appearance of leaves. One possibility is that the early leaves might have come into being from the enations. That is, the earliest leaf-like structures might have emerged in plants from the scaly, spiny projections on the plant stems, called enations, as they usually did not possess vascular tissue present in the true leaves. These tiny or small outgrowths covered the stems of plants, as often can be found in the early plant fossils. It appears, in the earliest stage of the development of plants, the scaly and spiny enations grew out of the stems, without developing a vascular connection with them. After some time, that is, after a period of time when these enations came into being and acquired their existence in plants, their internal structures might have begun to change, in the sense that, some kind of vascular tissue came to be gradually formed within them. The growth or coming into being of vascular tissue in the enations found in the early plants may be seen as one of the major steps in the development, or, in a sense, evolution, of the early plant leaves. This development might have been driven, in a sense, by the photosynthetic process, as the plants grew more and more relying on the energy provided through such a process, and as the leaf-like enation structures gradually took a bigger role in such a process. In this sense, it might be said, the growth or coming into being of vascular tissue in the enations may be seen as an evolutionary development for the early plants. That is, combined with other factors, the photosynthetic process, among other things, might have prompted or triggered the growth of vascular tissue in the enations. The coming into being of vascular tissue in enations thus, in a sense, heralded a new stage in the development of leaves, as the true leaves started to appear on the land surface of this planet.

The fossil record shows, some of the earliest land plants in the Silurian and early Devonian did not have leaves or roots. Aglaophyton, a pre-vascular plant from the early Devonian Rhynie chert, had no roots. Rhynia, a vascular plant also from the Rhynie chert, possessed neither roots nor leaves. The Zosterophylls, a group of plants from the late Silurian to Devonian, possessed only enations without vascular tissue. The enation-like structures might be found on the stems of Asteroxylon, a group of early Devonian plants, and a sense of vascular trace might also be found under the base of each of such enation-like structures. But these enation-like structures had not yet developed to such an extent that a vascular thread was to be formed within them. Thus, these structures may only be seen as enations, but not leaves, or not microphyll leaves.

The enation-like structures might be seen as having developed, in the kind of early plants such as Drepanophycus or Baragwanathia, into the kind of small and simple leaves, called microphylls, the kind of simple leaves usually containing a single vascular thread within them. The microphyll leaves of Drepanophycus, from the early to late Devonian, often grew on the stems in a spiral or random way. The microphyll leaves of Baragwanathia, from the late Silurian to early Devonian, often grew spirally on the stems. Thus, as the kind of leaves containing vascular tissue, the microphyll leaves of the early plants like

Symmetry II

Drepanophycus or Baragwanathia may be seen as the kind of first true leaves emerging in the plant kingdom, or on the land surface of the earth.

It is suggested by some paleontologists and paleobotanists that, the coming into being of the earliest true leaves may also be seen as the result or consequence of several processes happening with the early plant branching systems, called planation, webbing, and fusion. The process of planation means that some of the branching systems of the early plants might have grown in such a way that a planar structure eventually came out. The process of webbing may be seen as the development of the early plant branching systems giving rise to some kind of weblike structure between or among the branches. The process of fusion may be seen as the kind of process in which the weblike structures eventually formed, by fusing their different parts, the kind of thin and flat leaf structures we see today.

Thus, it might be said, it seems, it was through such developmental processes of the early plant branching systems that the early true leaves might have, in a sense, come into being. The development of the early plant branching systems into the true leaves may be regarded, in a sense, as the increasingly more sophisticated or complex plant response to the photosynthetic process, the lifeline for the plants except the root systems. Needless to say, in the actual transformation of the early plant branching systems into the leaves, there might be a number of factors involved, apart from photosynthesis. But, as the primary plant organs for photosynthesis, it may be reasonable to say that, with regard to the leaves, the photosynthetic process may constitute one of the major factors in their early emergence or coming into being. As such, it seems, the process of the gradual formation of the early leaves may be explained, in a sense, with regard to the kind of processes such as planation, webbing, or fusion.

Before the appearance or coming into being of the early true leaves, the early plants might only be able to rely on their stems, or the kind of non-vascular enations on the stems, for the photosynthetic process. Clearly, after the appearance of the planar structure of the branching systems, it was becoming possible that the emerging leaves might be able to spread and catch more and more light. This might constitute a selective process as the plant photosynthetic mechanism developed further as the time went on. The webbing of the branching systems might have begun as the planation process leading gradually to the closer and tighter connection of the branches or the outgrowths on the branches. With the closer and tighter connection of the branching systems coming into being, such closely connected branching systems might eventually grow into the kind of fused or integrated leaflike structures, as such a kind of structure might be able to enhance or improve the efficiency or capacity of the photosynthetic process for the plants.

The branching activity of the early plants may be seen as having started with the forking or bifurcating of the plant stems. This may be seen in the development of a number of early plants. In the plant fossils from the late Silurian or early Devonian, one may find, the branches of plants during these periods often forked or bifurcated, that is, a branch often ended up with a fork-like shape, or dividing in a dichotomous fashion. The Zosterophylls, a group of plants growing during the late Silurian to Devonian, had branches forking or bifurcating profusely. The pre-vascular plant Aglaophyton, from the early Devonian, had fork-shaped stems that grew with sporangia at the top. The stems of Asteroxylon, a group of plants from the early Devonian, might also be found to have branches dividing in a dichotomous fashion. The stems of both Drepanophycus and Baragwanathia are found to bifurcate in some cases.

Psilophyton is a group of vascular plants growing in the early or middle Devonian. This group of early plants possessed neither leaves nor true roots. One of the characteristics of Psilophyton is the profusion exhibited by its leafless bifurcating stems. Such a characteristic bifurcating profusion can be seen in some species of Psilophyton, such as Psilophyton dawsonii. With regard to this species, it can be found, not only did the branches bifurcate profusely, the branching units that usually produced sporangia also forked in a dichotomous fashion.

The forking or bifurcating of the early plant stems or branches may thus be regarded, in a sense, as the earliest stages in the development or coming into being of the true plant leaves. Initially, the stems or branches might just have forked or bifurcated, in a way taking such a dichotomous fashion as their growth pattern. Such a growth pattern might have, over time, combined with the branching planation process, driven, in a sense, by the photosynthetic process, to eventually give rise to the kind of things such as overlapping or webbing of the branching systems. Again, over time, with the photosynthetic process at the core of the forces behind the development of things, such overlapping or webbing of the branching systems might eventually develop into the kind of flattened laminar structure of the leaves. While forking or bifurcating may be seen as representing, in a sense, the first stages in the development of the branching systems of plants, the branching activities of the early plants might not have been confined to just forking or bifurcating. It is found, the stems or branches of the early plants might trifurcate, or even five-furcate. This may not be surprising in the sense that, with their continuing development, with their leaf structures playing a more and more robust role in providing energy through the photosynthetic process, the early plants became more and more complex, either in their root systems, in their internal structures, or in their leaf patterns or plans.

The true plant leaves came into being. Either from the enationlike structures or from such branching processes as planation, webbing or fusion, the appearance or coming into being of the true plant leaves during the Devonian period marked a significant transformation in the history of plants, as the early plants developed from the simple leafless and rootless organisms into the kind of leafy true plants with roots. The appearance of the leaf organs in the plants, and the coming into being or formation of the leaf patterns or structures may prove to be, in a sense, of the utmost importance to the plant development. The consequences, originating from such a transformation, are far-reaching, and may still be felt today. Prior to the coming into being of the true leaves, the organisms called plants were usually without roots or leaves, small, short, and most likely close to the ground. After the leaves appeared, the plants are usually found to have developed roots, tall, high above the ground, and sturdy. Actually, after the leaves coming into being, the plants had developed so well, so rapidly, or, in a sense, so explosively, that, widespread shrubs and trees can be seen to have flourished in the middle Devonian, and forests can be found to have been formed in the late Devonian.

With the coming into being of the true plant leaves, the leaf patterns or structures gradually appeared. This may be seen in the fossil record from the middle or late Devonian. Trimerophytes, including the kind of early plants such as Psilophyton, were a group of vascular plants growing in the early or middle Devonian. This is the group of early plants that is usually regarded as what eventually had given rise to the later ferns and seed plants. The aneurophytaleans were a group of early plants from the middle Devonian, forming the order of

Aneurophytales. These early plants are also called progymnosperms, meaning that they might have been the ancestors to the later gymnosperms, the kind of plants with naked seeds. The progymnosperms reproduced like the ferns, through bearing spores. They might have developed from the early plants like the trimerophytes, such as Psilophyton.

It is found that, among the aneurophytaleans, Aneurophyton appeared to have grown the kind of leaves with some sense of frond-like structures, which may be seen as distinct from the previous plant organ patterns or structures. The aneurophytaleans, as the progymnosperms, might have eventually given rise, in the late Devonian, to the pteridosperms, the seed ferns, such as the Lyginopteridales. The seed ferns, called pteridosperms, may be seen as the first plants to have born true seeds. The seed ferns were not ferns, as ferns reproduced, unlike the seed ferns, through spores. The reason that such early seed-bearing plants are called seed ferns is that, they shared with the true ferns in one significant aspect, the frond-like leaves.

Thus, it appears, the early simple plants like the trimerophytes, such as Psilophyton, might have given rise to the kind of early plants called progymnosperms, such as the aneurophytaleans. And, over time, the aneurophytaleans might have, in their turn, given rise to the seed ferns, such as the Lyginopteridales, in the late Devonian. The late Devonian thus saw the coming into being of the seed-bearing plants, with leaves possessing the frond-like structures. The trimerophytes such as Psilophyton, growing in the early or middle Devonian, had neither leaves nor roots. The aneurophytaleans, the progymnosperms from the middle or late Devonian, appeared to have begun growing the kind of frond-like leaves. And, eventually, we see, the seed ferns appeared in the late Devonian, with their fern-like leaves.

It seems, it may have to be said, the coming into being of the true early plant leaves might have been a process that is much more complex, subtle, and convoluted than what has been discussed here, given that the fossil record from such early times is usually sparse and incomplete, and the details are often missing. Nevertheless, it appears, by the late Devonian, we do witness an intensified and robust development in the various plant leaves.

From the non-existence in the late Silurian or early Devonian to the abundance in the late Devonian, the plant leaves had undergone a

Symmetry II

remarkable process of development and transformation during the Devonian. The result of such a process can be seen vividly in the appearance of various well-developed plant leaves by the end of the Devonian. The seed ferns had frond-like leaves. The aneurophytaleans in the late Devonian are also found to have such kind of leaves. A group of early spore-bearing plants called Wattieza, probably the earliest trees, from the middle Devonian, are found to have grown fronds. Large frond-like leaves are also found to have grown on the late Devonian trees such as Archaeopteris. And, around the end of the Devonian, the real ferns appeared, certainly, with their true fronds.

The remarkable and robust development of the plant leaves during the Devonian may be seen as one of the major characteristics defining the development of plants in such a period. It is impressive in the sense that, in the beginning, what is called plants were basically simple, tiny and primitive organisms without roots, leaves, or vascular systems, but at the end of such a period, the plants came to exist as the kind of complex organisms that possessed vascular systems, roots, and leaves, and they could even grow into the large and tall trees and form the forests.

What had happened? What had happened with the plants? What had happened with the plant leaves? What had made the plants to transform in such a dramatic way? What had made the plants to grow into the kind of complex life forms, from the previous simple, tiny, and primitive organisms? What had made the plants to grow with vascular systems, roots, and leaves? What had been behind the fundamental change from the non-vascular, rootless and leafless existence to the existence with vascular systems, roots and leaves? What had been behind the coming into being of vascular systems? What had been behind the coming into being of roots? What had been behind the coming into being of leaves? Was it evolution? Was it just evolution? Was it merely evolution? Could evolution explain the dramatic development or transformation of plants during the Devonian? Could evolution alone explain such a dramatic phenomenon? Could evolution alone explain such a dramatic explosion?

The frond-like leaves can be found in many cases in the early fossil record. And indeed, as we can see from the above discussion, the frond-like appearance seemed to have dominated, in a sense, the leaf patterns or structures in the Devonian. One of the important features of the frond-like leaves is, certainly, the expression or demonstration of bilateral symmetry, expressed or demonstrated through the whole leaf, or leaflets. The fern-like leaves of the seed ferns exhibited bilateral symmetry, either through the whole leaves or through the small leaflets. The large frond-like leaves of the late Devonian trees such as Archaeopteris also exhibited bilateral symmetry, through the whole leaves or the small leaflets. The pinnate leaves of the ferns demonstrated bilateral symmetry, as both the whole leaf structure and the small leaflet structure may be regarded, in the same sense, as bilaterally symmetric.

    One may ask, why is it the case that the well-developed plant leaves found in the Devonian were mostly frond-like? Why is it the case that the plant leaves had not developed into other kind of forms or shapes, in such an early period? It seems, two things may be said in this regard. First, it is possible, and in a sense, highly possible, that, the plants in the Devonian might have developed the kind of leaves with the kind of forms or shapes other than the mere frond-like, but, such kind of leaves may not be easily discovered or observed in the sense that, either they were only in their earliest developmental stages, or the fossil record may be too sparse, incomplete, or lacking the necessary details. On the other hand, the predominantly frond-like pattern or structure of the plant leaves in the Devonian may be explained in the sense that, this was the coming into being of bilateral symmetry in plants, and such a coming into being of bilateral symmetry in plants might have taken, in its first or initial stages, predominantly, the frond-like pattern or structure. The reason may be hard for us to know, eventually, as to why in the initial stages the bilateral symmetry in plants had to be expressed or realized predominantly through the frond-like patterns or structures. We may observe the frond-like patterns or structures commonly found in the early fossil record. We may witness the gradual development or transformation of the frond-like leaves during the Devonian. But, the reason lying behind the coming into being of such frond-like leaves may be beyond, it might be said, our rational examination or investigation, in the sense that, such a coming into being may not be regarded as the coming into being of some ordinary things. It was the coming into being of symmetry. It was the coming into being of bilateral symmetry. It was the coming into being of symmetry in plants. It was the coming into being of bilateral symmetry in plants.

Symmetry II

The coming into being of bilateral symmetry in plants in the Devonian may be regarded as one of the most significant, important, and fundamental developments ever occurred on the planet earth. Its significance may only be matched, in a sense, by the coming into being of bilateral symmetry in animals, that is, by the Cambrian explosion. The coming into being of bilateral symmetry in animals in the Cambrian established the foundation for the development and diversification of animals. In the same sense, the coming into being of bilateral symmetry in plants in the Devonian may be regarded as what had established the foundation for the development and diversification of plants. This may be the meaning of the coming into being of bilateral symmetry in plants in the Devonian. This may be the meaning of the coming into being of the frond-like leaves in the Devonian. This may be the meaning of the growing of the various frond-like leaves by the plants in the Devonian, such as, by the seed ferns, by the aneurophytaleans, by the ferns, by the middle Devonian plants called Wattieza, or, by the late Devonian trees such as Archaeopteris.

The appearance of the frond-like leaves in the Devonian was not just the appearance of leaves; it was the appearance of symmetry. The appearance of the frond-like leaves in the Devonian was not merely the appearance of leaves; it was the appearance of bilateral symmetry. Thus, it might be said, the process of the coming into being of the frond-like leaves in the Devonian may be regarded as the process of the coming into being of symmetry in plants in the Devonian; or, it might be said, the process of the coming into being of the frond-like leaves in the Devonian may be regarded, in a sense, as the very process of the coming into being of bilateral symmetry in plants in the Devonian.

People sometimes ask, why is it the case that the development of the complex plant leaves had taken such a long time, given that plants seemed to have begun colonizing the land from the late Silurian or early Devonian, and the well-developed leaves only appeared substantially in the late Devonian? Indeed, it seems, the plant leaves appeared to have developed, gradually, in a sense, during the whole Devonian, from their basic non-existence in the beginning to their relative abundance near the end of such a period. The Devonian began around 410 million years ago and drew to its end around 360 million years ago. So, it seems, it took about 50 million years for the plants in the Devonian to develop the kind of complex and well-formed leaves with symmetry, that is, in the case of the frond-like leaves, with bilateral symmetry. The appearance of the symmetrically formed leaves in the Devonian may be seen as the appearance of symmetry in plants in such a period. The coming into being of the bilaterally symmetric leaves in the Devonian may be seen as the coming into being of bilateral symmetry in plants during such a time. In other words, to talk about the appearance of the plant leaves in the Devonian is, in a sense, to talk about the appearance of symmetry in plants; or, to talk about the coming into being of the bilaterally symmetric leaves in the Devonian is, in a sense, to talk about the coming into being of bilateral symmetry in plants. Thus, the appearance of symmetry in plants may be seen, in a sense, as taking about the whole time of the Devonian. Or, it might be said, the coming into being of bilateral symmetry in plants may be regarded, in a sense, as taking about 50 million years, in the Devonian.

It was not just the appearance of leaves; it was the appearance of symmetry in leaves. It was not merely the coming into being of plant leaves; it was the coming into being of bilateral symmetry in plants. It was the appearance of symmetry. It was the coming into being of bilateral symmetry. It was the appearance of symmetry in the plant kingdom. It was the coming into being of bilateral symmetry in the plant world. It was symmetry expressing itself in leaves. It was bilateral symmetry demonstrating itself in plants. It was symmetry fulfilling itself through the leaves. It was bilateral symmetry realizing itself through the plants. It was symmetry expressing itself in the plant kingdom. It was bilateral symmetry demonstrating itself in the plant world. It was symmetry fulfilling itself as the leaves. It was bilateral symmetry realizing itself as the plants. It was symmetry fulfilling itself as the leaves developed. It was bilateral symmetry realizing itself as the plants grew. It was symmetry expressing itself as the plant kingdom unfolded. It was bilateral symmetry demonstrating itself as the plant world spread out. It was not just the development of leaves; it was the development of symmetry. It was not merely the development of plants; it was the development of bilateral symmetry. It was not just the development of leaves; it was the development of leaves in the sense of symmetric fulfillment. It was not merely the development of plants; it was the development of plants in a way of the realization of bilateral symmetry. Thus, the development of leaves in the Devonian may not be seen as a simple process; it may be regarded as a process of the fulfillment of symmetry in the world. That is, the development of plants in the Devonian may not be seen, simply, as an ordinary happening or occurrence; it may be regarded, in the end, that is, intrinsically or fundamentally, as the realization of bilateral symmetry in the world, on the earth, in the plant way, in the plant manner, or, in the plant sense. This may be seen as the process behind the appearance of the symmetric leaves in the Devonian. This may be seen as the process behind the development of plants in the Devonian. And, this may be seen, in a sense, as the reason why the leaves in the Devonian had to take such a long time to fully develop, or, why the plants in the Devonian had to take such a long time to develop their leaves.

Some might notice a difference between the Devonian explosion and Cambrian explosion in the sense that, it appears, the former might have taken a much longer time than the latter to fully develop the kind of patterns or structures that would determine the later developments. In the Cambrian, it seems, the speed was really remarkable, as some have suggested, it merely took the animals about 10 million years to develop their various body plans or structures. But when it comes to the Devonian, it appears, the plants had to take, in a sense, about 50 million years to fully develop their complex leaves. That may be seen as a quite big difference, as it constitutes almost five times more time. Such a difference may be explained, in a sense, on the ground that, what happened in the Cambrian was an animal event, or an animal process, while what happened in the Devonian was a plant phenomenon, or a plant process. As a plant process is usually slower, in a sense, than an animal process, such a difference might have been reflected in the ways through which the vital bodily patterns or structures were developed, either in the Cambrian or in the Devonian. That may be the reason, in a sense, why we see the different developmental paces in the Cambrian and Devonian.

The kind of relatively slower pace of development observed in the Devonian may also be seen in the coming into being or formation of plant leaves, in the sense that, we have seen, the leaf patterns or structures found in such a period were predominantly frond-like. That is to say, in other words, the development or coming into being of the plant leaves in the Devonian might have undergone a gradual process in which the leaves had not yet diversified to such an extent that other patterns or forms could have emerged extensively by the end of the Devonian. That may be one of the reasons why we witness mostly frond-like leaves in the early fossil record from the Devonian. And, indeed, it appears, as people have found, the various complex plant leaves seemed to have developed from the late Devonian to early Carboniferous, and continued their diversification and development well into the Carboniferous. Thus, it is not surprising that, while there was a remarkable and robust development in the plant leaves in the Devonian, from the basic non-existence to their abundance, it is in the Carboniferous that we see the widespread diversification or development of the leaf patterns or structures. The diversification or development of the leaf patterns or structures well into the Carboniferous may not be seen as something that diminishes the significance or meaning of the Devonian, or, of the Devonian explosion, in the sense that, the most crucial, fundamental, and significant aspect of what happened in the Devonian may be seen as the coming into being of symmetry, or bilateral symmetry, in plants. That is, what makes the Devonian significant is the transformation of symmetry or bilateral symmetry into the plants, or, rather, the construction, organization, or growth of symmetry or bilateral symmetry in the plants. It is such development of symmetry in the plants in such a period that laid the foundation for the later diversification or development of plants. And it is such realization of symmetry in the plants in such a period that heralded a new age for the earth, or, for the world.

Some have suggested that the development of the complex plant leaves in the Devonian might be related, in some sense, to the rapid decline of the atmospheric CO_2 during such a period. This may not be too farfetched, in the sense that, the eventual appearance or coming into being of the plant leaves in the Devonian might have been caused, or triggered, in some sense, in some way, or in some manner, by several factors, and among such factors might be the rapid decline of the atmospheric CO_2. In other words, the development of the complex plant leaves in the Devonian may not be regarded as a simple or straightforward process, in the sense that, such a process might have actually involved certain things that may not be easily discerned or observed. Symmetry is subtle. Symmetry is delicate. Symmetry is exquisite. Symmetry is deep. Symmetry is profound. The coming into being of symmetry is a subtle process. The appearance of symmetry is a delicate phenomenon. The emergence of symmetry is an exquisite event. The fulfillment of symmetry is a deep undertaking. The realization of symmetry is a profound happening. Such subtlety, delicacy or exquisiteness, with regard to symmetry or the coming into

Symmetry II

being of symmetry, may be seen in that, the coming into being of the symmetric plant leaves in the Devonian may be regarded, ultimately, in a sense, as the result or consequence of a worldly, or universal, harmonic happening or process, involving not just the kind of plant or animal things, but all the other things as well. And it is in such a sense that, it might be said, the very depth or profundity of symmetry fulfilled or realized in the Devonian plants may be seen, ultimately, in a sense, as coming or originating from such a worldly or universal harmonic happening, or process.

The plant leaves are not just leaves; they are the carriers of symmetry. The plant leaves are not just leaves; they are the bearers of bilateral symmetry. The plant leaves are not merely leaves; they are the fulfillers of symmetry. The plant leaves are not merely leaves; they are the realizers of bilateral symmetry. They are the expressers of symmetry. They are the demonstrators of bilateral symmetry. They are the way of the world through which symmetry is fulfilled. They are the way of the world through which bilateral symmetry is realized. They are the way of the world through which the plant kingdom appears. They are the way of the world through which the plant world emerges. That is to say, to understand the plant world is, in a sense, to understand the leaves. To understand the appearance of the plant world is, in a sense, to understand the appearance of leaves. To understand the coming into being of the plant world is, in a sense, to understand the coming into being of leaves. Symmetry is behind the leaves. Symmetry is behind the appearance of leaves. Symmetry is behind the coming into being of leaves. Symmetry is behind the plants. Symmetry is behind the appearance of the plant world. Symmetry is behind the coming into being of the plant kingdom.

Was it just a coincidence that, with the appearance of the symmetric leaves, the plants developed rapidly in the Devonian? Was it just a coincidence that, with the coming into being of the symmetric leaves, the plants developed with their advanced root systems? Was it just a coincidence that, with symmetry appearing in plants, the plants developed their complex leaves with such delicate and sophisticated structures or mechanisms as the stomatal regulation? Was it just a coincidence that, with symmetry coming into being in the leaves, the plant leaves gradually became the primary location for photosynthesis in plants? Was it just a coincidence that, with the appearance of the symmetric leaves, it seems, the plants developed seeds? Should all these things be deemed as coincidences? Should all these things be deemed as evolutionary developments? Should the appearance of leaves in the Devonian be deemed as an evolutionary process, purely, in which, just like other plant organs or parts, the leaves simply evolved, along with other parts or organs, together with the whole plants? Should the roots and leaves be treated in the same way? Should the coming into being of the complex leaves with delicate and sophisticated structures or mechanisms, such as the stomatal control, be treated in the same way as the development of other plant organs or parts, such as stems or roots? Should it be deemed a purely evolutionary process that the complex symmetric leaves developed eventually into the primary photosynthetic organs in plants and assumed the major role of providing energy for plants? Should the appearance of seeds be seen as an evolutionary process of its own, possessing little innate or intrinsic connection with the coming into being of the symmetric leaves?

Or, is it reasonable that, the leaves should be treated in a different way? That is, is it reasonable that, the appearance or coming into being of the symmetric leaves in the Devonian be treated in the ways other than the mere evolutionary? Should the leaves be distinguished, in a sense, from the other plant organs or parts? Should the leaves be regarded as the organs of plants expressing or demonstrating symmetry? Should the leaves be treated as the organs of plants fulfilling or realizing symmetry? Should the leaves be treated as the representation or manifestation of symmetry in plants? That is, should the symmetric leaves be seen as what represented the source of symmetry? Should the symmetric leaves be seen as what manifested the force of symmetry? Should the symmetric leaves be seen as what embodied the power of symmetry? That is, in other words, should the symmetric leaves be regarded, in a sense, as what represented the source of the development of plants in the Devonian? That is, should the symmetric leaves be regarded, in a sense, as what represented the force driving the development of plants in the Devonian? That is, should the symmetric leaves be regarded, in a sense, as what represented the power, eventually, behind the development of the plants in such a remarkable period? It was the symmetric source. It was the symmetric force. It was the symmetric power. It was the inner source. It was the innate force. It was the intrinsic power. It was the inner source from which the plants might have developed. It was the innate force that might have driven the development of plants in the Devonian. It was the intrinsic power that might have been behind the rapid development or diversification of plants in such a remarkable and significant period.

As the important organs to plants, the true roots are different from the other organs of plants such as stems in that, they possess a different kind of internal structure, and they usually develop with different growth patterns. That is to say, though some of the early plants may be found to have some kind of root-like structures, they may not necessarily be regarded as the plants possessing the true roots, as such root-like structures might not have shared the same characteristics seen in the true roots. Roots are important to plants as they act as the source of water, minerals and other nutrients necessary for the maintenance and growth of plants. The fossil record appears to show that, in the Devonian, the root systems of the early plants developed gradually, becoming more and more visible, and sinking deeper and deeper into the soil. As the true roots developed, the early plants were able to grow taller and faster, and that may constitute, in a sense, one of the factors leading to the widespread growth of shrubs and trees in the middle Devonian and formation of forests in the late Devonian.

The development of the root systems of the early plants may not be seen, to a certain extent, as an isolated phenomenon, in the sense that, such a development might have been associated, in an innate or intrinsic way, with the appearance or coming into being, or development, of symmetry in plants. That is to say, the coming into being or development of the root organs in plants may be better regarded as a part, or an integral part, of the development of plants as a whole. That is, while the coming into being or development of symmetry in plants may be seen as what had been lying, in a sense, behind the development of plants in the Devonian, the development of the root organs in plants may also be seen as having been driven, or prompted, in some sense, to some extent, by or through such a coming into being or development of symmetry. In other words, the coming into being or development of the roots may not be regarded as purely an evolutionary process. The eventual formation of the internal structures of the roots might not have been a process of its own, and such a process might have something to do with the coming into being or development of symmetry in plants. The force, or energy, or power, that was behind the various activities of the roots, such as sinking deeper and deeper into the soil, may not be seen as coming or originating merely from the roots themselves. Such force, or energy, or power, might have been the kind of things that ultimately came or originated, in some sense, in some way, or in some manner, from the coming into being or development of symmetry in plants, or, simply, from the pure being or existence of symmetry in plants.

Certainly, as some might suggest, there was, to a certain extent, a sense of evolution going on in the process of the coming into being or development of the plant roots. The development of the leaves might have enabled the plants to further develop their roots. And in the same sense, the development of the roots might have enabled the plants to have more resources to further develop their leaves. Such a sense of coevolution should not be ruled out in the sense that, the roots and leaves together formed the whole plants, and as parts or organs of the same plants, the roots and leaves were closely related and they could influence or affect each other in an intrinsic or intimate manner. But, could such a sense of coevolution explain, adequately, the development of the roots, or the leaves, in the Devonian? It seems, it might not, given that, from their rootless and leafless existence in the late Silurian or early Devonian to their abundance in forming the large forests during the late Devonian, the organisms called plants had truly undergone a process of rapid and tremendous transformation. Such a rapid process of significant transformation, on the part of plants, may not be easily explained, either in the sense of the root evolution, or in the sense of the leaves evolving along with the other organs or parts of the plants. A sense of root evolution, to a certain extent existed, may not be able to explain, adequately, the relatively rapid and significant emergence of the roots from their non-existence to their complex and sophisticated systems supporting, supplying, and maintaining the tall and large trees near the end of the Devonian. In the same sense, a sense of leaf evolution, that is, in the evolutionary sense, though again, to a certain extent existed, may not be seen as capable of accounting for, adequately and sufficiently, either the pace of the root development, or the pace of the development of plants as a whole, in the Devonian.

When we talk about the appearance of leaves or the development of plants in the Devonian, we have to be very careful not to make the kind of mistakes that things may be taken or understood with simplistic approaches. In other words, it might be said, the appearance of leaves or the development of plants in the Devonian might be the kind of happenings or occurrences that had involved the kind of processes both innate and external, or, both intrinsic and extrinsic. The kind of innate or intrinsic processes involved might be the kind of processes constituted, or in a sense, underlain, guided, or conditioned by the coming into being or presence of symmetry. The kind of external or extrinsic processes involved might be the kind of processes that might have to do with the outside world, such as the changing states of the environment. Both the innate and external processes are important to our understanding of the coming into being of leaves or the development of plants in the Devonian. That is, it might be said, we can not overlook or ignore either of them if we want to acquire a full understanding of the things happened in such a period. The innate or intrinsic processes were innate, intrinsic, and fundamental in the sense that, it might be said, it was them that had established the foundations, or conditions, or, provided the potentials or capacities, for the leaves or plants to develop in such an early period. In other words, it might be said, it was those processes that had made, in a fundamental sense, the development of leaves or plants in the Devonian possible. Without such processes, there might have been only organisms called plants without leaves or roots. Without such processes, there might have been only organisms called plants close to the ground, tiny, small, weak, and primitive. Without such innate or intrinsic processes, it might be said, there might have been no big and tall trees, and no forests to form the landscapes on earth in the late Devonian.

Such innate or intrinsic processes may be seen as what constituted the most fundamental aspects of things happened in the Devonian. And it is in such a sense that, it might be said, the external or extrinsic processes happened in such a period should be viewed, examined, and understood. When people talk about the possible connection between the appearance of leaves or the development of plants in the Devonian with the concurrent environmental changes, such as the rapid decline of the atmospheric CO_2, it is important to note, while such external or extrinsic processes should be taken into consideration, fully and completely, they nevertheless should not be taken, deemed, or understood as contributing to the development of leaves or plants in the same way, in the same sense, or in the same manner, as the innate or intrinsic processes. That is, while the external or extrinsic processes might have contributed to the appearance of leaves or the development of plants in the Devonian, they might have done so in different ways, or in different senses, from the innate or intrinsic processes.

Take again the example of the decline of atmospheric CO_2. It is observed that there was a dramatic increase of stomata in the leaves during the Devonian. The increasing appearance of stomata in the leaves might be related to the rapid decline of atmospheric CO_2 in the Devonian. That is, in a certain sense, the rapid decline of atmospheric CO_2 might have contributed to the development of leaves in the Devonian. But, does this mean that, the appearance or coming into being of the leaves in the Devonian could be explained by such a rapid decline? Not necessarily. The rapid decline of atmospheric CO_2 may provide some answer, but it may not provide all the answer. That is, it may constitute an explanation, in a sense, to the appearance or development of leaves in the Devonian, but it may only tell, by itself, one side of the story. The mechanisms surrounding the stomatal control or regulation in the leaves may be seen as sophisticated, as the stoma complex had to constantly respond to the changing states of the outside world, as well as the interior states of the leaves. Such kind of monitoring-regulating mechanisms, or processes, may not be seen as the kind of things that could be easily achieved. In other words, it might be said, it might have taken a lot of resources for the plant leaves to develop such kind of highly complex and sophisticated structures or mechanisms in such an early time as the Devonian. The decline of atmospheric CO_2 in the Devonian may be seen as constituting, in a sense, a part of such resources. But, it might be said, it might not have constituted all the resources, or even the most fundamental resources. That is, though the decline of atmospheric CO_2 might have been among the factors leading to the increasing appearance of stomata in the leaves, such a decline may not be deemed, or understood, to a certain extent, as among the kind of things giving rise, adequately and sufficiently, to the appearance or coming into being of the kind of things such as stomata themselves.

As a plant organ, leaves usually exhibit remarkable structural complexity, consisting mainly of three different parts, the epidermis, the mesophyll, and the vascular system. The epidermis is the surface layer of the leaves, on which the stomatal openings can be found. The mesophyll is the middle layer of the leaves, functioning as the primary site of photosynthesis. The vascular system is the veins of leaves, responsible for transporting water and sugar that are involved in the photosynthetic process. As the primary site in plants for photosynthesis, it is not surprising that the mesophyll usually possesses a complex structure of its own. There are often two different layers in the mesophyll, the palisade mesophyll and spongy mesophyll. The cells in the palisade mesophyll are usually responsible for most of the photosynthetic activities happening in the leaves. The highly specialized vascular system, the veins, indispensible for the photosynthetic process, can be found in the spongy mesophyll. Apart from such parts or structures, leaves are also often found to have tiny hairs. Overall, even though normally existing as the thin and flat organ of plants, leaves demonstrate remarkable complexity either in their structures or in their functioning mechanisms.

The complexity of the leaf structures and mechanisms should not be underestimated, in the sense that, it was those structures and mechanisms that had enabled the leaves to exist as some of the most highly organized and sophisticated parts or organs of plants. Such a kind of complexity stood even more prominently, and significantly, given that it had emerged or come into being in such an early time as the Devonian. In a sense, it might be said, it might have been exactly such a kind of complexity that had eventually enabled the leaves to exist, or to function, as the primary site of photosynthesis in plants. The process of photosynthesis is vital to plants, as such a process converts light energy into the biochemical energy necessary for the maintenance and growth of plants. Photosynthesis happened much earlier in the history of life prior to its appearance in plants. Such a process can be found to have been performed by many of the early organisms such as algae and bacteria. Though there is a sense of similarity existing between the different photosynthetic processes happening in algae, bacteria, and plants, certainly, the photosynthetic process in plants may be seen as standing out in the sense that, such a process is being performed primarily in or by the leaves. The leaves thus have to be equipped with the necessary structures and mechanisms to deal with the various biochemical processes involved in the photosynthetic process. How were the leaves equipped with such structures and mechanisms in the Devonian? How were the leaves able to afford such structures and mechanisms in such an early period? How were the leaves transformed in such a time? How were the leaves grown in the Devonian, so that they could develop the necessary structures and mechanisms? How were the leaves developed in such a period, so that they would grow in such a way, in such a sense, or in such a manner that they performed the process of photosynthesis? What had given them the power? What had given them the force? What had given them the energy? What had given them the ability? What had given them the capacity? What had given them the potential?

Could the mere evolution give them such a power? Could the mere natural selection give them such a force? Could the mere evolutionary process provide them with such energy? Could the mere selective pressure make them to develop such ability? Could the mere evolutionary process produce such capacity? Could the mere process of natural selection give rise to such potential? That is, could the mere evolution enable the leaves to develop the kind of necessary structures and mechanisms, relatively rapidly, in the Devonian? Could the mere natural selection enable the leaves to transform, relatively rapidly, into the primary organs of photosynthesis in plants, in the Devonian? Could the kind of things such as the decline of atmospheric CO_2 explain, fully, the relatively rapid emergence of photosynthetic phenomenon in the leaves? Could the kind of things such as the decline of atmospheric CO_2 explain, fully and sufficiently, the relatively rapid development of leaves, and plants, in such a great period? The possibility of the leaves developing the kind of photosynthetic structures and mechanisms in the Devonian may not be seen as originating, ultimately, from the mere evolutionary process or the process of natural selection, though such a process might have existed to a certain extent, in the sense that, such a process may not be deemed or regarded as capable of, by or through itself, providing, supplying, or equipping the leaves with such a kind of ability, capacity, or potential. In other words, the complexity of the leaves in the Devonian may not be seen as originating, in a sense, ultimately, from the mere evolution or natural selection, though again, such an evolutionary or selective process might have made some contributions to some extent. The complexity of the leaves in the Devonian may be seen as coming or originating, ultimately, from the innate or intrinsic processes happening or occurring in such a period, that is, it might be said, in a sense, from the kind of processes concerning the coming into being or development of symmetry in the leaves. It was the coming into being of symmetry that had, in a sense, given the leaves the power to develop their structures. It was the coming into being of symmetry that had, in a sense, given the leaves the force to develop their mechanisms. It was the coming into being of symmetry that had, in a sense, given the leaves the energy to develop their body plans. That is, it was the development of symmetry in the leaves that had, in a sense, enabled the leaves to acquire their photosynthetic ability. That is, it was the development of symmetry in the leaves that had, in a sense, made it possible that the leaves gradually possessed the capacity for photosynthesis. That is, it was the development of symmetry in the leaves in the Devonian that had, in a sense, ultimately, provided the leaves with the potential to grow eventually into the primary site of photosynthesis in plants. It is in such a sense that, it might be said, the appearance or coming into being of the symmetric leaves in the Devonian may be seen as representing, in an intrinsic and fundamental sense, a gigantic leap forward in the development of plants, as the leaves, becoming gradually the primary organs of photosynthesis, drove or propelled the development of plants in their symmetric, potent, and powerful ways.

As the fossil record tells us, the early organisms called plants reproduced through spores. The reproductive systems of the heterosporic plant organisms may be seen, in a sense, as a transitional way to the development of seeds, with their megasporangia containing single viable megaspore individually. The true seeds may be seen as first appearing with the coming into being of the seed ferns. The seed ferns first appeared in the late Devonian, probably developing from the kind of earlier plants such as the aneurophytaleans, the so-called progymnosperms. The progymnosperms reproduced like most of the early plants, through bearing spores. Their ancestral groups might be the early plants like the trimerophytes, such as Psilophyton. The spores of Psilophyton are found to have been produced by the sporangia that were usually grown at the end of the branches. Thus, it appears, before the coming into being of the seed ferns, the early plants reproduced themselves through the mechanism of spores. The coming into being of the seed ferns thus represented a new era in the development of plants, as the seeds replaced the spores as the way of reproduction for the newly emerged plants.

Seeds are different from spores in many ways, such as, in their sizes, in the ways of their dispersal, in the kind of environments suitable for their germination, or in the kind of energy needed for their developments. The most significant difference that distinguishes seeds from spores may be the kind of complexity that can be found in seeds. Seeds usually possess a level of complexity, especially in terms of their internal structures and mechanisms, that can hardly be seen in spores. Seeds usually possess an embryo, the food for the embryo, and the seed coat. While no embryo can be found in spores, seeds usually contain an embryo in themselves. Apart from the embryo, seeds also usually possess in themselves a certain amount of food stored for the embryo. Such storage of food may prove crucial for the initial stages of development of the embryo, as the self-supplied nutrients may help the developing embryo fend off the possible harsh environmental conditions. Spores usually do not have such a reserve of food within themselves, and thus the initial stages of their development may prove to be more challenging. In other words, the more complex and, in a sense, advanced internal structures and mechanisms found in seeds may help the seed plants to better survive and reproduce themselves. Such an advantage, afforded by the coming into being of seeds, may be seen in the fact that the land surface of the earth is relatively dominated by the seed plants.

From spores to seeds, it was a great advance in the development of plants. It was the coming into being of a new level of plant complexity. It was the appearance of a new stage of plant development. It was a mighty advance that would have far-reaching consequences for the plant kingdom. As a significant step in the development of plants, how could the seeds come into being in the late Devonian? What had made it possible for the seeds to appear? What had made it possible for the seed plants to emerge in such an early period? What had prepared the Devonian plants to develop such structures? What had enabled the Devonian plants to develop such mechanisms? Where did the seed complexity, ultimately, come from? Where did the seed energy, ultimately, come from? Where did the seed power, ultimately, come from? Where did the seed capacity, ultimately, come from? Where did the seed potential, ultimately, come from? Did it come from what is called evolution? Did it come from what is called the natural selection? Did it merely come from such an evolutionary process? Did it merely come from such a process of natural selection? Did it merely come from such a selective process? Did it merely come from such a kind of selective pressure? That is, in other words, could evolution, or natural selection, or selective pressure, or whatever mechanisms associated with them, explain, fully, the coming into being or appearance of seeds in the Devonian?

Symmetry II

The coming into being or appearance of seeds in the Devonian is such a significant and far-reaching phenomenon that we still feel and witness its consequences even today. The Devonian is a period more than 360 million years ago. After such 360 million long years, we still live today with the seed plants in this world. And we survive, thrive, and prosper together with them. Is such a phenomenon something that could be easily explained? Is such a phenomenon something that could be easily explained by what is called evolution? Is such a phenomenon something that could be easily explained by the natural selection? Is such a phenomenon something that could be easily explained by or through the kind of things such as the workings of selective pressure on plants? Probably not. It may not be the kind of things that can be easily explained by an evolutionary process. It may not be the kind of things that can be easily explained by the natural selection. It may not be the kind of things that can be easily explained through the so-called selective pressure. It was not selective. It was symmetric. It was not selection. It was symmetrization. It was harmonization. It was not a process of selection. It was a process of symmetrization. It was a process of harmonization. It was not an evolutionary process. It was a symmetric process. It was a harmonic process. That is, it might be said, more than the mere evolution, it was the coming into being of symmetry or harmony. That is, it might be said, more than the mere natural selection, it was the fulfillment of symmetry, it was the realization of harmony. That is, it might be said, more than the workings of selective pressure, it was the expression, demonstration, or manifestation of symmetry, or harmony, in the world. It was evolution underlain by symmetry. It was natural selection conditioned by harmony. It was the workings of selective pressure guided by the coming into being or presence of symmetry, or of harmony. That is, it might be said, it was symmetry that may be seen as ultimately behind the development of plants in the Devonian. It was symmetry that may be seen, in a sense, as driving the development of plants. It was symmetry that may be seen, in a sense, as driving the development of leaves. It was symmetry that may be seen, in a sense, as driving the development of seeds. That is, it might be said, the coming into being of plant complexity in the Devonian may be seen, in a sense, as originating ultimately from symmetry. It was the coming into being of symmetry that had given rise, in a sense, to the leaf complexity. It was the coming into being of symmetry that had given rise, in a sense, to the seed complexity. It is in such a sense that, it might be said, the eventual appearance of seed plants in the Devonian may be seen as related, closely, to the appearance of symmetry in plants in such a period.

The coming into being or appearance of symmetry in the Devonian plants may be seen as being exhibited in many ways. We have talked about the forking or bifurcating of the early plant branches. The forking or bifurcating of the early plant branches or stems, such as branching in a dichotomous fashion, may be seen, in a sense, as a possible indication of the coming into being of bilateral symmetry in the early plants. Such a dichotomous branching pattern can often be observed in the early plants from the late Silurian or early Devonian. That may indicate, in a sense, that the first appearance or coming into being of bilateral symmetry in plants might have happened in such early periods.

It is also observed that, forking or bifurcation may not be the only phenomenon, as the three-forked or five-forked patterns may sometimes be found in the early plants. As the complex leaves developed, it is found that, some three-forked or five-forked leaves might have grown on the late Devonian plants. The appearance of the three-forked or five-forked leaves in the late Devonian plants may indicate that, as the overall conditions for the growth of plants improved, the leaves continued their development with complexity. Some might question the appearance of the three-forked or five-forked leaves, in the sense that such appearance might have constituted something distinct or away from the coming into being of bilateral symmetry. This may not be necessarily the case. Even though such leaves might have exhibited their three-forked or five-forked patterns, such leaf plans should not be taken as strictly non-bilateral, as the overall leaf shapes or forms may still be treated as expressing or possessing the bilateral symmetry. In other words, the appearance of the three-forked or five-forked leaves may not be seen as constituting the kind of things against the coming into being of bilateral symmetry in the Devonian. Rather, such appearance may only point to the possibility that the plant leaves had truly developed with their complexity as time went by.

The early signs of the coming into being of symmetry, or harmony, in plants may also be found, in a sense, in the ways of how the microphyll leaves were grown in the early plants. We may find a growth pattern for the microphyll leaves in the early plants that may be

Symmetry II

called helical or spiral. In such a helical fashion, the microphyll leaves usually grew spirally on the stems. This phenomenon can be observed in the kind of early plants such as Baragwanathia, a group of plants growing in the period roughly from the late Silurian to early Devonian, or Drepanophycus, a group of plants from the early to late Devonian. In each of these early plants, one may find, the microphyll leaves might have grown on the stems in a helical or spiral fashion. The microphyll leaves of Baragwanathia usually grew on the stems in a helical or spiral way. The microphyll leaves of Drepanophycus grew on the stems often in two ways, either spirally or randomly.

The spiral pattern may also be seen in the form of the sporangia of the early Devonian pre-vascular plant Aglaophyton. Runcaria is a middle Devonian plant. One of the interesting things about this plant is that, the megasporangium found on its stems may be seen as exhibiting radial symmetry. The helical or spiral patterns, found either in the growing ways of the microphyll leaves or in the forms of sporangia, may be seen as representing, or standing for, in a sense, the happening or occurrence of symmetry, or harmony, in the early plants. The radial symmetry exhibited by the Runcaria megasporangium may be seen as implying that, radial symmetry might have appeared or come into being in plants as early as the middle Devonian.

The coming into being of bilateral symmetry in the Devonian plants may be seen vividly in the emerging leaf plans or structures of the frond-like leaves of the late Devonian plants called Archaeopteris, a group of primitive tree-like plants extinct after the early Carboniferous. With regard to Archaeopteris, it can be found in the fossil record, there were several types of leaves emerging in the late Devonian. Such different types of leaves might have possibly belonged to different species in this group. Even though certain differences or distinctions may be found to have existed between or among the different types of leaves, such leaves may be seen as possessing or sharing an emerging leaf plan: a kind of frond-like pattern. It is in such a frond-like pattern that, we can witness, strongly, the presence of the bilaterally symmetric existence in these early plants, or, in these Devonian trees.

Both radial symmetry and bilateral symmetry may thus be seen as having emerged in the Devonian plants. They might have come into being in the leaves. They might have come into being in the sporangia. They might have come into being in the forking branches. They might have come into being in the ways of the leaves growing on the stems.

Apart from all these phenomena we have observed, it is possible that there might be other kinds of happening or occurrence that might have to do with the coming into being of symmetry in plants in the Devonian, but about which we may not be in a position to have any detailed knowledge, given that the fossil record is so incomplete and the time period is so remotely distant from us now. Nevertheless, from what we have witnessed and observed, it seems, it is reasonable to come to the conclusion that symmetry, that is, both radial symmetry and bilateral symmetry, indeed had appeared or come into being in plants in the Devonian. With the coming into being of radial symmetry and bilateral symmetry in the Devonian plants, the development of plants in the Devonian may thus be regarded, in a sense, as representing or standing for a process of development of symmetry, in that, on the one hand, it was through the development of plants that symmetry, in a sense, had fulfilled or realized itself, and on the other hand, it was the fulfillment or realization of symmetry that had, in a sense, propelled, driven, or powered the development of plants, or, provided the foundation for such a development in the Devonian.

At this point, it seems, we may have to address the issue of symmetry in plants, in the sense that, sometimes, people may object to the notion that there exists symmetry, exactly, in plants. People often point to the fact that, it appears, the plant leaves are not really symmetric, in the sense that, upon a close examination, the plant leaves are often found to have two halves not exactly the same. That is, it is often found, the two halves of leaves are usually different, in some sense, in some way, or in some manner, from each other, that is, not exactly the mirror image of each other, either in their vein patterns or in their exact shapes or forms. It is true indeed. As we often observe in the other aspects of nature, what happens in nature may rarely be regarded as exactly mathematical. The mathematical may be a little bit different, in some sense, from the natural. In other words, when the mathematical is translated into the natural, or, rather, when the mathematical is fulfilled or realized in the natural, there might be some senses of variation coming into being, either in the forms, in the shapes, in the structures, or in the patterns. Such variations, nevertheless, may not be seen, in a sense, as constituting some kind of fundamental differences separating the mathematical from the natural. Rather, such variations may be regarded, in a sense, as the necessary steps, or developments in nature, in the process of the transformation of the mathematical into the natural, or, in the process of the fulfillment or realization of the mathematical in the natural.

This may be seen in what happens with regard to the leaves or plants. Let us first discuss what happens with the leaves. People objecting to the notion of symmetric leaves may likely point to the fact that the veins in the two sides of the leaves are usually not the same, with the vein patterns often appearing differently in the two sides. That is, it is often the case that, instead of expressing a sense of straight and exact bilateral symmetry, the veins in the two sides of the leaves demonstrate a sense of what is called glide symmetry. The veins with glide symmetry often appear in the two leaf sides alternately, giving the impression that, it seems, they are not bilaterally symmetric at all. This seems to be a quite common phenomenon in the structures of leaves. Often, we can witness, there exists some sense of bilateral symmetry in the leaf veins, and then, a sense of glide symmetry may appear, and blend in with the existing bilateral symmetry. The result is often that, either a sense of mixture of glide symmetry and bilateral symmetry coming into being, or a sense of strong glide symmetry appearing for some leaves. As to the exact bilateral symmetry, it might be said, it may be difficult to find, strictly speaking. Why should it be such a case, with the leaf veins? Why should it be such a case that the leaf veins do not often show a clear sense of bilateral symmetry, given that the overall shapes or forms of the two leaf sides usually express or demonstrate a sense of strong bilateral symmetry? In other words, why should the glide symmetry come into being? Why should the glide symmetry come to exist in the leaves? Why should the glide symmetry feature so prominently in the leaf vein patterns?

I think, this may have to do, in a sense, with the development of things. The glide symmetry does not just appear in the leaf veins. If we observe closely, we can find, the existence of glide symmetry can also be found in some pinnate leaves, as the leaflets in these pinnate leaves appear alternately on the leaf stems. The pinnate leaves often exhibit bilateral symmetry, with their leaflets arranged in a bilaterally symmetric way on the leaf stems. But, at the same time, it appears, it may not be an uncommon phenomenon that the arrangement of leaflets in some pinnate leaves may express a sense of glide symmetry.

Symmetry may be seen as what, ultimately, behind the development of plants. Symmetry may be seen as what, ultimately, behind the development of leaves. In such a sense, it might be said, symmetry may be expressed in the development of leaves or plants; or, the development of leaves or plants may necessarily be expressed, in a sense, in the appearance or coming into being of symmetry. Bilateral symmetry may thus be seen in the existence of plants, such as, in the shapes or forms of leaves, in the vein patterns of leaves, or in the ways of leaves appearing on the stems. While bilateral symmetry may be observed in the development of leaves and plants, the development of leaves and plants may reflect, in some sense, in some way, or in some manner, the appearance or coming into being, or development of bilateral symmetry. That is, the existence of bilateral symmetry in leaves or plants may not be just a sense of bilaterally symmetric existence. Such a sense of symmetric existence may, in some sense, in some way, in some manner, or to some extent, be expressed, reflected, or transformed, in the growth or development of leaves or plants. In other words, such a sense of symmetric existence may ultimately be transformed, realized, actualized, or physicalized, in some cases, in the leaves or plants, into or as the symmetric existence of growth or development. Such may be seen, in a sense, as the coming into being or appearance of what is called glide symmetry. That is to say, glide symmetry may not be regarded as different or distinct, fundamentally, from bilateral symmetry, in the sense that, glide symmetry may have come into being through a process of growth or development, such as in the leaves or plants, from bilateral symmetry. That is, rather than a clearly different kind of symmetry, glide symmetry may be regarded, or treated, as a sense of bilateral symmetry in growth or development, or, as a sense of bilateral symmetry with growth or development.

This may, in a sense, be observed in the leaf patterns found in some of the pinnate leaves. With regard to these pinnate leaves, one can find, with a good look, that, the closer to the tips of the pinnate leaves, the shorter intervals there might be between the alternating leaflets. It may be difficult, in a sense, to find the perfectly arranged leaflets with exact bilateral symmetry, even close to the leaf tips, but, it seems, the closer to the tips, the more likely it appears that the arrangement of leaflets resembles a sense of bilateral symmetry. On the other hand, when it comes to the lower part of the pinnate leaves, one can find, the intervals between the alternating leaflets look much bigger. Actually, the intervals usually become bigger and bigger as we look down further along the leaf stems. In other words, it appears, the glide symmetry present in such pinnate leaves seems to grow or develop as the leaves

Symmetry II

themselves grow or develop. This may tell us, that, glide symmetry in leaves or plants may not be seen or regarded as an isolated phenomenon, detached from all the other aspects of leaves or plants, and separated from the processes of their growth or development. That is, such a phenomenon may tell us that, the presence of glide symmetry in leaves or plants may have to do, in some sense, or to some extent, with the growth or development of leaves or plants.

The closer to the start of growth, it seems, the more glide symmetry may resemble bilateral symmetry. The closer to the initial stages of development, it seems, the more glide symmetry may approximate bilateral symmetry. As the growth appears, it seems, glide symmetry may also grow. As the development comes into being, it seems, glide symmetry may also develop further and further. Thus, it seems, glide symmetry may be seen, in a sense, as a form of bilateral symmetry growing, or a form of bilateral symmetry developing, along with the growth or development of things. In other words, glide symmetry may not be seen or regarded as something fundamentally different from bilateral symmetry; rather, it may be seen or regarded as a form of bilateral symmetry in growth or development, or, a form of bilateral symmetry with growth or development. This may be seen, in a sense, as the appearance or coming into being of glide symmetry in leaves or plants. With the appearance of glide symmetry, bilateral symmetry may no longer be seen, in a sense, as something static; it may, in a sense, grow. With the coming into being of glide symmetry, bilateral symmetry may no longer be regarded, in a sense, as something unmoving; it may, in a sense, develop.

What does this tell us? It may tell us that, when symmetry is realized in nature, symmetry may live in nature. That is, when symmetry is fulfilled in nature, symmetry may manifest itself in nature as something living, moving, growing, or developing. Symmetry may not be lifeless. Symmetry may be alive. Symmetry may be living. Symmetry may not be motionless. Symmetry may move. Symmetry may grow. Symmetry may develop. Nature has life; symmetry in nature may also have life. Life is alive; symmetry in life may also be alive. Symmetry is in nature, inherent, vital. Symmetry is in life, intrinsic, fundamental. Nature grows; symmetry may also grow. Nature develops; symmetry may also develop. Life lives; symmetry may also live. Life moves; symmetry may also move. It is in such a sense that, it might be said, it may not be surprising that, we may witness the living or movement of symmetry in life, or the growth or development of symmetry in nature. Symmetry is part of nature. Symmetry is part of life. Symmetry is an essential part of nature. Symmetry is a fundamental part of life. The living or movement of symmetry may thus be seen, in a sense, as inherent in life. The growth or development of symmetry may thus be regarded, in a sense, as an integral part of nature.

It is in such a sense that, it might be said, the seemingly imperfect leaf plans or structures may be understood. That is, the appearance of glide symmetry seen sometimes in the leaf vein patterns may not be regarded, in a straightforward manner, as an indication of the existence of non-bilateral symmetry in leaves. Such an appearance may, rather, be regarded, in a sense, as the coming into being of a form of bilateral symmetry in growth or with development. That is to say, while the leaves may be seen as the kind of life forms with growth or development, the symmetry existing in such leaves may be regarded as partaking, at the same time, in some sense, in some way, or in some manner, in such leaf growth or development. The seemingly imperfect leaves may thus still be seen, in a certain sense, as expressing or possessing the sense of bilateral symmetry, even though there might be some sense of existence of glide symmetry in their leaf vein patterns.

The growth or development of symmetry may also be seen, in a sense, in other aspects of the plant life. We have discussed above the appearance or coming into being of what is called helical or spiral patterns in the early plants. The helical or spiral patterns can be witnessed in the early plants in several ways, such as, in the ways through which the emerging leaves were arranged on the stems or branches, or, in the forms of the sporangia growing on the early plants. The microphyll leaves of the early Devonian plants called Baragwanathia usually grew on the stems in a helical or spiral way. The microphyll leaves of the Devonian plants called Drepanophycus also grew, sometimes, on the stems in a helical or spiral fashion. The helical or spiral patterns may also be seen in the forms of the sporangia grown by the early Devonian plants called Aglaophyton, as, it appears, such sporangia might release the spores through their spiral openings.

How to understand the helical or spiral patterns appearing in the early plants? I think, they may be understood, in a sense, in a similar manner with the appearance or coming into being of glide symmetry in plants. That is, it might be said, the appearance or coming into being of

Symmetry II

helical or spiral patterns in the early plants may be seen, in a sense, as the appearance or coming into being of some senses of symmetry in the early plants. Glide symmetry may be seen, in a sense, as a sense of bilateral symmetry in growth or with development. The helical or spiral patterns may be seen, in a similar sense, as a sense of radial symmetry in growth or with development. In other words, while glide symmetry may be seen as expressing, or representing, in a sense, a sense of bilateral symmetry in growth or development, the helical or spiral patterns may be regarded, in a similar sense, as expressing or representing, in a sense, the growth or development of radial symmetry in nature, or in life. That is, while bilateral symmetry may be seen as a sense of symmetry growing or developing, sometimes, or in some cases, in nature or life, radial symmetry may be treated in a similar way. The living or movement of symmetry in life may not be confined to bilateral symmetry; radial symmetry may also be living in life. The growth or development of symmetry in nature may not be limited to bilateral symmetry; radial symmetry in nature may also demonstrate or manifest itself, in some cases, or in some senses, with growth or development.

As we all know, the helical or spiral patterns can be found in things other than plants, such as in some animals. We often encounter land snails with shells formed in the helical or spiral patterns. Apart from the land snails, there are many species of shell animals living in the seas or waters. The helical or spiral patterns can be found frequently in the shells of these animals. It has to be said, the animal shells may not be the only things in nature that demonstrate the helical or spiral patterns. The horns grown by some animals may also be seen as possessing the helical or spiral patterns. It seems, either in the case of plants or in the case of animals, the helical or spiral patterns exhibited may be seen as sharing certain characteristics that distinguish them from the other forms of existence found in nature. That is to say, in a sense, it might be said, with regard to the helical or spiral patterns, found either in plants or in animals, it appears, the closer to the beginning of growth or development, the more such helical or spiral patterns may resemble, or approximate, a sense of radial symmetry. With the coming into being of growth or development, it appears, such helical or spiral patterns also grow or develop, in a sense, at the same time. In other words, the growth or development of the helical or spiral patterns found in nature, that is, in plants or animals, may be seen as expressing or representing, in a sense, a sense of growth or development of radial symmetry in nature, that is, in plants or animals. It is in such a sense that, it might be said, the helical or spiral patterns found in nature may be seen, in a sense, as a sense of radial symmetry growing or developing in nature. That is, the helical or spiral patterns found in nature may be regarded, in their natural senses, as a sense of radial symmetry in growth, or with development. It is symmetry realized in nature. It is symmetry realized in plants or animals. It is symmetry growing, or developing, in nature. It is symmetry growing, or developing, in plants or animals. It is symmetry fulfilling itself. It is symmetry fulfilling itself in nature. It is symmetry fulfilling itself in plants or animals. It is radial symmetry growing, in a sense, in nature. It is radial symmetry developing, in a sense, in plants or animals. It is radial symmetry realizing or fulfilling itself, in a sense, in the helical or spiral patterns, in nature, or in plants or animals.

People have observed such a phenomenon in nature for a long time, and they have discovered that, the helical or spiral patterns found in nature, either in plants or in animals, may be expressed in a mathematical form called the Fibonacci sequence, or Fibonacci numbers, or Fibonacci series. Such a mathematical form may be seen as what illustrates, mathematically, the helical or spiral patterns when they are realized in nature, that is, in the plants or animals. This may not be very surprising in the sense that, the helical or spiral patterns found in nature may be seen as a sense of symmetry realized in nature, in plants or animals, through a process of growth or development. The fact that the helical or spiral patterns can be expressed in a mathematical form may tell us that, when symmetry is realized in nature, such a symmetric realization may be expressed in a mathematical way, and, when symmetry is realized in a process of growth or development, such symmetric growth or development may also be expressed, in some sense, mathematically. The symmetric is closely related to the mathematical. The mathematical is closely associated, in a sense, with the symmetric. The realization of the symmetric in nature may be seen, in a sense, as the realization of the mathematical in nature. The realization of the mathematical in nature may be seen, in a sense, as the realization of the symmetric in nature. The symmetric is intrinsic; the mathematical is fundamental. The symmetric is innate; the mathematical is essential. The symmetric is physical; the mathematical is theoretical. The symmetric is natural; the mathematical is nonmaterial. The symmetric is mathematical; the mathematical is natural. Through a process of growth, the symmetric is realized in the helical or spiral patterns; through a process of growth, the symmetric is realized in the mathematical. Through a process of development, the mathematical is realized in the symmetric; through a process of development, the symmetric is realized in a mathematical series. The symmetric is realized in the mathematical. The mathematical is realized in the symmetric. The symmetric is realized as the mathematical in nature; the mathematical is realized as the symmetric in the plants or animals.

The growth or development of symmetry may thus be seen, in a sense, as an innate or inherent feature of nature. Apart from the growth or development of symmetry, we may have to discuss what may be called the diversity of symmetry, as, it appears, we may witness its existence abundantly in nature. The diversity of symmetry may be seen as the symmetric variations found in nature, associated with either plants or animals. The diversity of symmetry may be seen as what happens when symmetry is realized or fulfilled in nature, in the sense that, such a symmetric realization or fulfillment may be achieved, while symmetry is being maintained, with or through different or diverse shapes, forms, structures, plans, or patterns. Such may be seen in a number of ways in nature. We have discussed the vein patterns in leaves, and talked about the glide symmetry, as a sense of bilateral symmetry in growth or development. Apart from the glide symmetry found in the leaf vein patterns, we may observe other kinds of symmetric vein patterns in leaves. The pinnate veins demonstrate bilateral symmetry with the veins in the two sides facing each other. The arcuate veins also demonstrate a sense of bilateral symmetry, though with the veins in the two sides curving towards the leaf tips, usually along the leaf margins. The dichotomous veins express a sense of bilateral symmetry by forking in a symmetric way. The parallel veins are often found in the leaves of grasses, and they possess a sense of bilateral symmetry with the veins in the two sides typically paralleling with each other along the axes of leaves. The palmate veins usually show a sense of bilateral symmetry, just like the palmate leaves. The peltate leaves are usually rounded leaves with stalks attached near the center. While a sense of bilateral symmetry may be seen as often emerging from the rounded leaf shapes or forms, the veins of the peltate leaves may be regarded as often exhibiting a sense of radial symmetry. Thus, it appears, a number of symmetric forms, plans, or structures may be seen as existing in the various leaf vein patterns. Apart from the glide symmetry, bilateral symmetry may be expressed in the leaf vein patterns through the pinnate, arcuate, dichotomous, parallel, or palmate veins. Radial symmetry may be demonstrated through the veins of the peltate leaves. Symmetry may thus be seen as being fulfilled or realized in the leaf vein patterns in its diverse forms, plans, or structures. Such may be seen as the diversity of symmetry realized or fulfilled in the leaf veins.

The diversity of symmetry may also be observed, vividly, in the numerous shapes or forms possessed by the leaves. Leaves usually exhibit a sense of bilateral symmetry, even though different leaves may possess different shapes or forms. Many leaves have pointed tips. Some leaves may possess very long pointed tips, while others may only have short tips, or even small spiny ones. Even though such leaves may only share a pointed form of leaf tips in various degrees, through their different leaf plans or structures, they generally express or demonstrate a sense of bilateral symmetry, with the two sides of leaves mirroring each other approximately. There are plenty of shapes that can be found with the leaves, such as, oval-shaped, heart-shaped, diamond-shaped, fan-shaped, wedge-shaped, kidney-shaped, spoon-shaped, spear-shaped, narrowly shaped, triangularly shaped, truncate, elongate, lanceolate, pinnate, palmate, rounded, or circular. One can observe these leaves, and one can find, it might be said, there is usually a sense of bilateral symmetry emerging out of these leaves, no matter what kind of shapes they might actually possess. In other words, it might be said, these leaves express or demonstrate a sense of bilateral symmetry through their varied or different leaf shapes or forms.

The sickle-shaped leaves may also be seen as possessing a sense of bilateral symmetry, though such a sense of bilateral symmetry may be expressed or demonstrated with some well curved forms. Take for example the mature leaves of some eucalyptus plants, also known sometimes as gum trees. The mature leaves of these trees may be found to possess the sickle-like shapes, though the leaves in the earlier stages may be oval-shaped. Look at the mature sickle-shaped leaves. One may find, there is a sense of bilateral symmetry emerging out of the leaves, as the two sides of the leaves arranged around the central veins often in a harmonious manner. It is true that the central veins are sometimes curved, but along these curved veins the two leaf sides are still usually arranged in a balanced, unified, and harmonious way. It is from such a sense of balanced, unified, and harmonious existence of the two leaf sides along the central veins that, it might be said, a sense of symmetry comes out. That is, it might be said, even among the sickle-shaped leaves, a sense of bilateral symmetry may still be seen as being present, expressing or demonstrating itself through the well curved leaf plans or structures.

The well curved leaf shapes or forms of the sickle-shaped leaves may be seen, in a sense, as representing another aspect of the harmonious existence of the leaves, apart from their bilaterally symmetric existence. That is to say, in the sickle-shaped leaves, symmetry may be seen as being expressed or fulfilled in two ways, that is, in the bilaterally symmetric way and in the harmoniously curved forms. While the bilaterally symmetric shapes may be seen as representing one aspect of the symmetric existence of the leaves, the harmoniously curved forms may be seen as standing for another aspect of the symmetric existence of the leaves. Symmetry is no longer plain; symmetry develops. Symmetry is no longer simple; symmetry diversifies, in a harmonious way, or in a delightful and pleasing manner. Bilateral symmetry no longer stands alone; it is combined with other harmonious forms. Bilateral symmetry no longer exists in its plain or straight forms; it develops, it moves, it progresses, it diversifies, and, it develops harmoniously, it moves gracefully, it progresses in a delightful manner, it diversifies in a pleasing fashion. Symmetry develops and moves with balance and harmony. Bilateral symmetry moves and diversifies with unity, grace, and beauty. It is in such a sense that, it might be said, while the sickle-shaped leaves maintain their bilaterally symmetric existence as the leaves, they represent, in a sense, the development, movement, progress, or diversification of symmetry in the leaves.

The diversity of symmetry, and the harmony, unity, grace, or beauty coming with it, may thus be seen, in a sense, in the sickle-shaped leaves. Actually, such a sense of diversity of symmetry may not be observed only in the obviously sickle-shaped leaves. Many leaves can be found to have pointed tips, and such pointed tips are often to be found with a certain sense of curved shapes or forms. Such curved leaf tips may be seen, in a sense, as representing or standing for the same kind of development, movement, progress, or diversification of symmetry that may be observed in the obviously sickle-shaped leaves, though to a lesser extent or with smaller scales. We can see the curved leaf tips. They often bend or turn gracefully. Their curved shapes or forms usually manifest a sense of delicacy, unity, and harmony. It is delightful to see how they are shaped or formed in such delicate, minute, and wonderful ways. It is beauty, certainly, in a sense, to exist in such shapes or forms as the leaves. It is in such a sense that, it might be said, the curved leaf tips may be seen as some of the examples in nature in which symmetry diversifies, or, the diversity of symmetry is expressed, demonstrated, or fulfilled, realized.

There is a type of leaves that may be generally described as lobed. Such kind of leaves can be found in a number of shapes or forms. Some are with deep and wide divisions between the lobes. Some may only have small or shallow divisions. Some of such leaves may possess a kind of lobing patterns that almost resemble the pinnate leaves, while others may have clearly defined lobes looking like the palmate leaves. Such a type of leaves may be seen as expressing or possessing a sense of bilateral symmetry, even though they may vary considerably in their lobed leaf patterns or plans.

The pinnate leaves can be found in several types. The bipinnate leaves have a double pinnate pattern, with the leaflets also pinnate. The bipinnate leaves may be found growing in plants such as some young locust trees. The tripinnate leaves have a triple pinnate pattern, with the leaflets bipinnate. The tripinnate leaves may be seen in the trees called malunggay, or Moringa oleifera, in a scientific manner. The pinnate leaves may also be divided into two groups based on whether they have one or two leaflets at the leaf tips. The pinnate leaves may be seen, in a sense, as truly demonstrating a sense of bilateral symmetry. As the leaflets are usually bilaterally symmetric, the simple or regular pinnate leaves may thus be seen as expressing a sense of bilateral symmetry in a double manner. As such, while the bipinnate leaves may be seen as expressing a sense of bilateral symmetry in a triple way, the tripinnate leaves may be regarded as demonstrating a sense of bilateral symmetry in a fourfold manner. It is truly impressive that bilateral symmetry, or symmetry, may be expressed or demonstrated in leaves, that is, in plants, that is, in nature, in such a dramatic and magnificent way.

This may be seen, in a sense, as a wonderful example of the diversity of symmetry realized or fulfilled in nature. While bilateral symmetry may be expressed by the individual leaflets, the simple or regular pinnate leaves show a second sense of bilateral symmetry as a

Symmetry II

whole. The bipinnate leaves, more than the simple or regular pinnate leaves, express a third sense of bilateral symmetry through their symmetric arrangement of the double bilateral symmetry existing already in their leaflets. The tripinnate leaves, in a similar manner, demonstrate the fourth sense of bilateral symmetry through a complex arrangement of the triple bilateral symmetry existing already in their leaflets. It is clearly, in a sense, an expression of complexity. It is also clearly, in a sense, an expression of the progress of complexity. It is an expression of symmetric complexity. It is an expression of symmetric complexity in progress. It is the progress of complexity expressed in the leaves. It is the progress of symmetry exemplified in the more and more complex leaf patterns or plans. It is symmetry, in a sense, moving deeper and deeper into the being of things. It is symmetry, in a sense, manifesting itself more and more intricately in the existence of things. It is symmetry, in a sense, progressing or diversifying with the coming into being of complex and symmetric leaves. From the single symmetry to the double symmetry to the triple symmetry to the fourfold symmetry, symmetry moves, symmetry progresses, symmetry diversifies. Symmetry lives in symmetry. Symmetry gives rise to symmetry. Symmetry lives side by side with symmetry. Symmetry gives rise to the complex and symmetric leaves by multiplying symmetry. Symmetry gives rise to the complex and symmetric leaves by diversifying itself.

The symmetric progress or symmetric diversification may also be seen, in a sense, in that, it appears, even the rounded or circular leaves may exhibit a sense of bilateral symmetry. Such rounded or circular leaf shapes or forms may give an impression of roundedness or circularity in the first place, but upon a close and careful examination, one may find, such leaves may also be viewed, after all, as possessing a sense of bilateral symmetry. Such may be seen in the peltate leaves, as such leaves often exhibit a sense of bilateral symmetry with their rounded or circular leaf plans or structures being able to be divided into two mirroring parts. It is interesting to see that, even the rounded or circular leaves may express or demonstrate a sense of bilateral symmetry. On the one hand, this may indicate that, in a sense, the existence of bilateral symmetry is usually strong or robust in the leaves, or, it might be said, vital or essential to the existence of leaves. The rounded or circular leaf shapes or forms may be seen, in a sense, as representing a sense of radial symmetry coming into being or existing in the leaves. Radial symmetry may not be always observed in the leaves, as we have seen, but, in this case, it seems, radial symmetry comes into being in the leaves and bilateral symmetry appears to emerge out of the existence of radial symmetry. The coming into being of bilateral symmetry, in a sense, out of radial symmetry may be seen, in a sense, as an indication of the power, strength, potential, or energy of bilateral symmetry with regard to the leaves. While radial symmetry may not be always observed in the leaves, bilateral symmetry seems to be often present in the various leaf plans or structures. And it may even be found in the leaves that express or demonstrate, primarily, in a sense, a sense of existence of radial symmetry. It is in such a sense that, it might be said, the power, strength, potential, or energy of bilateral symmetry may be closely related, in an intrinsic way, to the life, vitality, existence, or energy of leaves. On the other hand, the emergence of bilateral symmetry, in a sense, out of radial symmetry may tell us that, bilateral symmetry and radial symmetry may exist in the same leaves, and together they constitute the symmetric being or existence of such leaves. The symmetric diversification may be seen in this case, in the sense that, it seems, bilateral symmetry may come into being in the radially symmetric shapes, and radial symmetry may exist in the bilaterally symmetric structures. The diversification of symmetry may thus be seen, in a sense, as being represented by the coming into being, or co-existence, of both radial symmetry and bilateral symmetry in the same leaves.

While radial symmetry, unlike bilateral symmetry, may not always be observed in the individual leaves, some plants may come to possess a very strong sense of radial symmetry by forming such a sense of radially symmetric existence through their usually bilaterally symmetric leaves. There are plants whose leaves may grow in a circular pattern that is usually called rosette. The plants showing the rosette form can be quite common, such as, cabbages, dandelions, or some succulent plants like agaves. Before the cabbage heads are formed, the cabbage leaves usually grow in a rosette. Such a pattern often gives rise to an impression that the cabbages grow in a radially symmetric fashion. Dandelions are a family of common plants with entire or lobed leaves. Their leaves usually form a rosette by growing tightly together close to the ground. It is easy to see that, such a rosette form manifests a sense of radially symmetric existence. As a family of succulent plants, agaves often exhibit a sense of radial symmetry with their thick, fleshy and bilaterally symmetric leaves usually arranged in a rosette form. Thus, it seems, while the cabbage leaves, the dandelion leaves, and the agave leaves may all be seen as bilaterally symmetric, they all give rise to a strong sense of radially symmetric existence through their collective growth patterns or structures.

While symmetry, that is, both radial symmetry and bilateral symmetry, may be fulfilled or realized in such common plants as cabbages or dandelions, sometimes, it may be expressed or demonstrated in plants, that is, in nature, in some quite unusual ways. The whorled leaves are the kind of leaves that grow around the stem, and at each node they usually form a delightful circle. The whorled leaves may be seen as giving rise to a sense of radial symmetry by growing in such a circular manner around the stem at each node. While the whorled leaves exhibit a sense of radial symmetry through their circular growth patterns, it has to be noted, they are usually bilaterally symmetric leaves, except the kind of leaves grown by the plants such as horsetails. There is a kind of leaves that may be called the perfoliate leaves, as such leaves appear to be pierced by the stems on which they are growing. The perfoliate leaves may be observed in the plants such as large-flowered bellworts or perfoliate bellworts. One can see, it is usually the case that, the perfoliate leaves are bilaterally symmetric leaves, though they may appear growing on the stems in some unusual ways. The perfoliate leaves of Claytonia perfoliata, or miner's lettuce, are the leaves that grow on some long stalks. When the time comes, small flowers may grow above these leaves. These perfoliate leaves may appear circular in shape, but they are formed through two leaves coming together with the stalks at the center. And we can see, the basal leaves of this plant are usually heart-shaped and bilaterally symmetric.

The pinnate leaves of some locust trees are interesting, in the sense that, it seems, sometimes, both the pinnate leaves and bipinnate leaves may grow on the same young branches. The old branches usually produce pinnate leaves, but if one pays attention to the young shoots, one may discover something quite interesting. On the greener, tender, young, and new shoots, one may find, some bipinnate leaves may appear, along with the pinnate leaves. This is an interesting phenomenon, in the sense that, such bipinnate leaves seem to only appear on the young and tender branches, but not the old ones. And, they can exist side by side with the pinnate leaves on the same young and tender branches. The pinnate leaves may grow on either old branches or new shoots, but the appearance of bipinnate leaves on the new shoots may indicate something distinct or different. Why should the bipinnate leaves appear only on the new shoots? Why is it the case that the bipinnate leaves only grow on the young, tender, and new shoots? Why is it the case that the bipinnate leaves are not so often found on the old branches? Is it possible that the pinnateness of leaves may be related to the tenderness or youngness of the locust shoots? Is it possible that the pinnateness of leaves may be related to the strength, vigor, energy, or vitality of the locust branches? That is, is it possible that symmetry may be related, in a significant sense, to the strength, vigor, energy, or vitality of plants? That is, is it possible that symmetry may be associated, closely, with the newness or creation of nature?

We have seen, while the pinnate leaves express a sense of double bilateral symmetry, the bipinnate leaves may be regarded as representing a sense of triple bilateral symmetry. That is to say, in a sense, the bipinnate leaves may be seen as representing a sense of movement or progress of symmetry, from the single or double bilateral symmetry to the triple bilateral symmetry. In other words, the coming into being of the bipinnate leaves on the young, tender and new locust shoots may not be seen, in a sense, as something ordinary or insignificant. It is the coming into being of symmetry. It is the movement of symmetry. It is the progress of symmetry. It is the creation of symmetry. That is, it might be said, it is the coming into being of symmetry in the new branches; it is the movement of symmetry in the young shoots; it is the progress of symmetry in the tender plants; it is the creation of symmetry in the new life forms. This may explain, in a sense, why the bipinnate leaves only appear on the young, tender, and new locust shoots. The coming into being of symmetry is related to the strength or energy of plants. The movement of symmetry is related to the vigor or vitality of leaves. The progress of symmetry is associated with the tenderness or youngness of branches. The creation of symmetry is linked with the creation of new life forms in nature. It is in such a sense that, it might be said, the coming into being or appearance of bipinnate leaves on the young, tender, and new locust branches may tell us that, in a sense, symmetry is closely related to the development of life, symmetry is closely related to the strength or vigor of growth, and symmetry is closely linked with the power and vitality of life.

Symmetry II

The power of symmetry may also be seen in the trees called malunggay, or in their scientific name, Moringa oleifera. The malunggay trees grow tripinnate leaves. The tripinnate leaves are the complex leaves with a triple pinnate pattern, with the leaflets bipinnate. We have seen, the tripinnate leaves may be seen as representing a sense of fourfold bilateral symmetry, as the single and individual leaflets themselves may be seen as bilaterally symmetric. In other words, the malunggay trees are the kind of plants that possess a remarkable sense of symmetry. Look at the miraculous leaves of this tree. One may be amazed by the complex and symmetric patterns or structures expressed or exhibited by the leaves. It is not single bilateral symmetry. It is not double bilateral symmetry. It is not triple bilateral symmetry. It is the fourfold bilateral symmetry! What a remarkable sense of coming into being of symmetry! What a remarkable sense of existence of symmetry in the trees!

The malunggay trees are often called by the people familiar with them as the magic tree, or the miracle vegetable, as such plants offer considerable benefits, either nutritional or medicinal, to humans. A malunggay tree can be used in many ways. It can be used as food. It can be used as medicine. The malunggay leaves are a good source of vitamins and minerals. They are usually cooked just like other vegetables such as spinach. The roots and seeds may be used as seasoning. The flowers may be eaten like fresh vegetables. The malunggay trees may also be used to treat a number of health problems. They may be used as herbal medicine to lower blood pressure or to treat malnutrition. The leaves may be used to cure bleeding or internal inflammation. The pods or seeds may be used to treat joint pains or arthritis. And it is said, this plant may also be useful in treating other health problems such as diabetes or tumor.

It is indeed a magic tree. It is indeed a miracle vegetable. As a plant, it can offer so many benefits to the humans. As a tree, it can be so useful to the human life. It is magical in the sense that, it appears, all parts of the tree can be used. It is a miracle in the sense that, it seems, this is not an ordinary tree; it is a tree with amazing and marvelous powers and effects. Why is a malunggay tree so useful? Whay is a malunggay tree so beneficial? Why is a malunggay tree so amazing, miraculous, and powerful? A malunggay tree is not an ordinary tree; it is a tree with fourfold bilateral symmetry. A malunggay tree is not an ordinary tree; it is a tree in which symmetry has moved or progressed to an extraordinary extent. A malunggay tree is not an ordinary tree; it is a tree that has fulfilled or realized symmetry in a remarkable and significant sense. This may, in a sense, explain why a malunggay tree is so useful and beneficial. And this may, in a sense, explain why a malunggay tree is so amazing, miraculous, and powerful. Symmetry may be seen as behind the uses or benefits of this tree. Symmetry may be seen as behind the magic or miracle of this tree. The coming into being or existence of the fourfold symmetry in this tree may be seen as what constitutes, in the end, the power or miraculous effects of this tree.

Symmetry is power. Symmetry is the power behind things. Symmetry is the power behind plants. Symmetry is the power behind the branches. Symmetry is the power behind the leaves. Symmetry is the power behind the bilaterally symmetric leaves. Symmetry is the power behind the pinnate leaves. Symmetry is the power behind the bipinnate leaves appearing on the young, tender, and new locust shoots. Symmetry is the power behind the malunggay leaves exhibiting the extraordinary patterns or structures. It is power to give rise to symmetry. It is power to give rise to bilateral symmetry. It is power to give rise to double bilateral symmetry. It is power to give rise to triple bilateral symmetry. It is power to give rise to the fourfold bilateral symmetry. That is, in a sense, it is power to be plants; it is power to be branches giving rise to new shoots; it is power to be new shoots giving rise to pinnate or bipinnate leaves; and it is power to be the trees possessing the tripinnate leaves. That is, in a sense, it might be said, it is power to live as plants with symmetry. It is power to live as plants giving rise to symmetry. It is power to exist as branches with bilateral symmetry; it is power to exist as branches giving rise to bilateral symmetry. It is power to exist as trees with the fourfold symmetry; it is power to exist as trees giving rise to the fourfold symmetry. That is, in a sense, it might be said, it is power to exist as the bilaterally symmetric leaves; it is power to exist as the pinnate leaves giving rise to double bilateral symmetry; it is power to exist as the bipinnate leaves giving rise to triple bilateral symmetry; and it is power to exist as the tripinnate leaves giving rise to the fourfold bilateral symmetry. Symmetry exists in power; power exists in symmetry. It is symmetry that, in a sense, gives plants the power to grow the bilaterally symmetric leaves or the pinnate, bipinnate, or tripinnate leaves. It is the bilaterally symmetric leaves or the pinnate, bipinnate, or tripinnate

Symmetry II

leaves that fulfill or realize symmetry in plants. That is, in a sense, it might be said, symmetry gives rise to plants; plants fulfill or realize symmetry. It is through the power of symmetry that the pinnate, bipinnate, or tripinnate leaves come into being. It is through the power of the pinnate, bipinnate, or tripinnate leaves that symmetry appears. It is through the plants that the power of symmetry is expressed. It is through symmetry that the existence of plants is realized. It is through the young, tender, and new shoots that the power of symmetry is exhibited. It is through the fourfold symmetry that the malunggay trees come to exist in this world. Symmetry exists in the vigor of growth; the vigor of growth exists in symmetry. Symmetry exists in the vitality of life; the vitality of life exists in symmetry. Symmetry exists in the energy of leaves; the energy of leaves exists in symmetry. Symmetry exists in the power of plants; the power of plants exists in symmetry. Symmetry exists in the creation of nature; the creation of nature exists in symmetry. Symmetry exists in the world; the world exists in symmetry. Symmetry gives rise to plants; symmetry exists in plants. Plants give rise to symmetry; plants exist in symmetry. The power of symmetry is expressed in plants. The power of plants is expressed in the symmetry fulfilled in the young, tender, and new locust shoots or realized in the miraculous malunggay leaves.

Certainly there may be other plants that may grow in the kind of patterns or structures expressing or demonstrating some significant and remarkable senses of symmetry. Just like cabbages, dandelions, agaves, the locust shoots, or the malunggay trees, their existence may only tell us that, symmetry, that is, both radial symmetry and bilateral symmetry, may be seen, in a sense, as a common feature of nature, and such a symmetric existence may be regarded, in a sense, as constituting the symmetric being or existence of the world. The power of symmetry may thus be seen in the existence of plants in a number of ways. It may be seen in the coming into being or existence of the various leaf vein patterns. It may be seen in the numerous symmetric shapes or forms that leaves possess. It may be seen in the coming into being of symmetry, either radial symmetry or bilateral symmetry, in the cabbages, dandelions, or agaves. It may be seen in the appearance of bipinnate leaves on the young locust shoots. It may be seen in the tripinnate leaves grown by the malunggay trees. It is the power of symmetry exhibited in the plants. It is the movement of symmetry expressed in the plants. It is the progress of symmetry accomplished in the plants. It is the diversity of symmetry manifested, fulfilled, or realized in the plants. Symmetry may thus be seen, in a sense, as vital or essential to the plants, and the diversity of symmetry may thus be regarded, in a sense, as an inherent or integral part of the existence of plant life forms in the world.

Some might ask, when you talk about the diversity of symmetry, are you talking about something like the diversity of nature, or are you just confusing the two diversities? It is a good question, as it may prompt us to look deeper into the relationship between symmetry and nature. What are plants? Plants are the realization of symmetry. Plants are the realization of symmetry in the plant forms. What are animals? Animals are the realization of symmetry. Animals are the realization of symmetry in the animal forms. What is life? Life is the realization of symmetry. Life is the realization of symmetry in the life forms. What is nature? Nature is the realization of symmetry. Nature is the realization of harmony. Nature is the realization of symmetry in the natural forms. Nature is the realization of harmony in the natural ways. In such a sense, it might be said, in a sense, symmetry is nature, or, nature is symmetry; or, harmony is nature, or, nature is harmony. That is, it might be said, in a sense, symmetry is the source of nature, symmetry is the origin of nature, symmetry is the fountainhead of nature, symmetry is the root of nature. Nature comes from symmetry. Nature comes from harmony. Nature comes from the way of heaven. Nature comes from heaven. Heaven is the source of all things. Heaven is the source of plants. Heaven is the source of animals. Heaven is the source of nature. Symmetry is the way of heaven. Symmetry is the way of heaven realized in plants. Symmetry is the way of heaven fulfilled in animals. Symmetry is the way of heaven realized or fulfilled in nature.

Thus, to talk about nature is, in a sense, to talk about symmetry. That is, to talk about nature is, in a fundamental sense, to talk about the workings or operations of symmetry in nature. The workings or operations of symmetry in nature may be seen as the innate or intrinsic activities of nature, while, it might be said, the appearances of nature may be seen, in a sense, as the outward expressions or manifestations of such innate or intrinsic activities, that may be observed by us, from time to time, such as, the existence of plants, or, the existence of animals. In other words, the innate or intrinsic activities of symmetry in nature may be regarded, in a sense, as what truly constitutes the

Symmetry II

foundation or source of nature. It is in such a sense that the diversity of symmetry may be understood in nature.

That is, while the diversity of symmetry may be seen as part of the diversity of nature, it may be regarded, in a fundamental sense, as what constitutes the very essence or foundation of the diversity of nature; in the sense that, it might be said, nature comes, ultimately, in a sense, from symmetry, or, it might be said, it is symmetry that has given rise, in an intrinsic and fundamental sense, to nature. The diversity of symmetry may thus be seen, in such a sense, as the backbone of the diversity of nature. In other words, it is the diversity of symmetry that may be seen, in a sense, as laying or preparing the foundation for the diversity of nature to come out, to appear, to emerge, to increase, to develop, or to multiply. The diversity of symmetry may be seen as the innate or intrinsic diversity of the world; the diversity of nature may be seen as the outward or apparent diversity of the world. The diversity of symmetry may be seen as the inner diversification of the world; the diversity of nature may be seen as the realization of such an inner diversification of the world in nature. That is, what the diversity of symmetry represents may be seen as an intrinsic process, that is, the symmetric process, fulfilling or realizing itself in the world, and nature, that is, in such a sense, the diversity of nature, may be seen, in a sense, as the result or consequence of the realization of such an innate, intrinsic, fundamental, and profound process.

The diversification of symmetry may thus be seen, in a sense, as one of the most profound and fundamental things happening in the world. How does symmetry diversify? Why does symmetry diversify? What may be the process of the diversification of symmetry? What may be the process of the movement of symmetry? What may be the process of the development of symmetry? What may be the process of the progress of symmetry? It may be hard for us to look into the inner workings or operations of symmetry in the world, as reason may not be up to such a task by itself. That is, in order for us to look into the inner or intrinsic activities of symmetry in nature, we may have to, first, in a sense, look at some of the more apparent, outward, or perceptible phenomena of nature, in the sense that, in such a way, we may be able to come to comprehend or grasp some of the inner or intrinsic secrets of symmetry in nature, or in the world.

As, in a sense, the source of the diversity of nature, the diversity of symmetry may be observed in nature in a number of ways. As we have discussed above, the diversity of radial symmetry may be observed in plants in several aspects. Runcaria is a middle Devonian plant. The Runcaria megasporangium may be seen as possessing a sense of radial symmetry. The helical or spiral patterns found in the growing ways of the microphyll leaves in the early plants may be seen as representing, in a sense, the happening or development of radial symmetry in the early plants. The presence of radial symmetry may be seen in the circular or peltate leaves. Apart from the individual leaves, the presence of radial symmetry may also be observed in the patterns or structures formed collectively by the plant leaves. The plants such as cabbages, dandelions and agaves grow with the radially symmetric forms called rosette. The whorled leaves are the kind of leaves growing with a sense of radial symmetry by forming a circle around the stem at each node. This may be seen in a number of plants. The leaves of horsetails may be seen as the whorled leaves, though they may not be seen as the kind of leaves with bilateral symmetry. Thus, it seems, radial symmetry may be observed in plants in a number of ways, in the shapes of sporangia, in the growing patterns of leaves on the stems, in the shapes or forms of individual leaves, in the rosette growing structures, or in the patterns formed by the whorled leaves. That is, it seems, radial symmetry may be observed in plants in various ways, in various manners, or in various senses, either in the sporangium shapes, in the leaf shapes, in the growing patterns of leaves on the stems, or in the growing structures of the whole plants. It is radial symmetry expressed in plants. It is radial symmetry expressed in plants in various aspects. It is radial symmetry fulfilled in plants. It is radial symmetry fulfilled in plants in the appropriate manners, in the appropriate senses, or in the appropriate parts. It is the diversity of radial symmetry exhibited in plants. It is the diversity of radial symmetry manifested in plants. It is the diversity of radial symmetry realized in plants. It is the diversity of radial symmetry realized in plants in different manners, in different senses, or through different plant parts. It is radial symmetry diversifying itself in plants. It is radial symmetry fulfilling or realizing itself, in various ways, in various manners, or in various senses, in the plant life forms.

    The diversity of bilateral symmetry may be seen as being expressed or demonstrated, more strikingly, in a sense, in plants. The numerous shapes or forms possessed by the usually bilaterally symmetric leaves, discussed above, such as, oval-shaped, heart-shaped, diamond-shaped, fan-shaped, and so on, may remind us how powerfully bilateral symmetry has diversified itself, in a sense, in the plant kingdom. The diversification of bilateral symmetry may be seen in the early plants in the forking or bifurcating of the early plant branches or stems, or in the coming into being or appearance of the frond-like leaves in the Devonian. With the development or diversification of plants, bilateral symmetry developed, or diversified. Or, it might be said, with the development or diversification of bilateral symmetry, plants developed, or diversified. This may be the reason why we can now witness so much diversity of bilateral symmetry in plants. Plants no longer just grow the kind of frond-like leaves. They can grow so many different kinds of leaves now that, it seems, bilateral symmetry has indeed diversified itself well, at least in this regard, in the plant life forms.

The diversity of bilateral symmetry can be seen in the leaf shapes. The diversity of bilateral symmetry can be seen in the leaf vein patterns. The diversity of bilateral symmetry can be seen in the curved leaf tips or sickle-shaped leaves. The diversity of bilateral symmetry can be seen in the lobed leaves. The diversity of bilateral symmetry can be seen in the circular or peltate leaves. The diversity of bilateral symmetry can be seen in the whorled or perfoliate leaves. The diversity of bilateral symmetry can be seen in the pinnate leaves. The diversity of bilateral symmetry can be seen in the bipinnate leaves on the young locust shoots. The diversity of bilateral symmetry can be seen in the tripinnate leaves growing on the malunggay trees. The diversity of bilateral symmetry can be observed so well in plants. Bilateral symmetry fulfils itself. Bilateral symmetry realizes itself. Bilateral symmetry fulfils itself in plants. Bilateral symmetry realizes itself in nature. Bilateral symmetry fulfils itself in plants in so many shapes or forms that the plant kingdom is a kingdom of richness and abundance. Bilateral symmetry realizes itself in nature in so many ways that, it appears, nature becomes a world of vitality, color, splendor, and magnificence.

People sometimes try to explain the diversity of symmetry, and in such a sense, the diversity of nature, in a manner that, it seems, the evolutionary or selective process may be seen as playing the major role. Such an evolutionary approach may account for certain things observed in nature, but it may not be able to explain all the things happening in nature, and more importantly, and fundamentally, it may not be able to make sense of what truly constitutes the foundation or source of things in nature. That is to say, in order to truly understand or comprehend what really happens in nature, we may need to go beyond the mere evolutionary or selective approach, in the sense that, while such an evolutionary or selective approach may enable us to comprehend or grasp certain things or certain aspects of nature, we have to keep in our mind that what happens in nature may be well beyond the reach of such an evolutionary, selective, or rational approach.

A number of factors may be cited as what contribute to the eventual coming into being of the various shapes or forms possessed by the plant leaves. People may say that, due to the winds, high trees usually do not grow large leaves, as large leaves may not be able to sustain themselves long in the winds. The plants in the cold regions may grow pointed leaves, so that ice or snow may be shed timely. The plants with dense leaves may grow the kind of narrowly shaped leaves, so that all the leaves may be able to catch the sunlight for photosynthesis. The development of leaves may also be shaped by the animals. The animals may eat the leaves of some plants, and over time, such plants may develop the kind of leaves with certain traits, such as hairs or little spines, to turn the animals away and protect themselves. That is, it seems, when it comes to the coming into being or formation of the plant leaves, a number of factors may have to be taken into consideration and may be seen as playing their roles, in certain senses, or to a certain extent. Such factors may have to do with the environment, climate, temperature, winds, or the kind of ecosystem in which the plants live.

Should such explanations be treated as valid, with regard to the coming into being or formation of the plant leaves? I think, yes, they should be treated as valid, and they may be seen as revealing, indeed, in a certain sense, or to a certain extent, what may be behind the eventual coming into being or appearance of the plant leaves. While the symmetric or harmonic process may be seen as what lays or prepares the foundation for the development of leaves, this does not necessarily mean that the evolutionary or selective process may be excluded from the developmental processes of the plant leaves. The evolutionary or selective process may well work its way in giving rise to the specific leaf shapes or forms. The various factors, such as environmental, climatic, ecological, or geological, may contribute to the development of leaves by defining or establishing the conditions or constraints under which the leaves may have to grow, exist, or develop. In other words, the evolutionary or selective process may work its way in the eventual

Symmetry II

coming into being or formation of the leaves by providing some of the advantages with which the plants may be able to better survive in their environments. The wind factor may lead the high trees to develop the kind of small or narrow leaves. The cold temperature may lead the plants to develop the kind of leaves with pointed tips, so that the leaves may not be easily frozen as ice or snow may fall down from their surfaces readily. The narrowly shaped leaves may give the plants a photosynthetic advantage, as the sunlight may reach all the leaves. The co-existence of plants and animals may lead the plants to develop certain traits in themselves, including in their leaves, in the sense that, while the plants benefit from such a situation, they may be able to shield themselves from the possible harm or damage coming from the animals.

That is to say, the coming into being or appearance of the various leaf shapes or forms may be explained, in a sense, by or through the evolutionary or selective process. The evolutionary advantages acquired through the formation of the specific leaf shapes or structures may enable the plants to better cope with the various forces or conditions present in the environments in which they live. With such advantages coming into being through the evolutionary process, the plants may thrive, prosper, and flourish. The process of natural selection may thus be seen as possibly playing a significant role in the eventual coming into being or appearance of the various leaf shapes, forms, or structures. This may be seen, in a sense, as a scientific or rational explanation, in the sense that, as the selective pressure is taken into consideration, the plants appear to strive for their better survival through the specific formation or structuring of their leaves. This is how we see the coming into being of the different leaves. The small leaves may better cope with the winds. The narrow leaves may better facilitate the photosynthetic process. The pointed leaves may enable the plants to endure the cold weather or temperature. The leaves with other specific traits or features may help the plants to deal with certain situations or circumstances found in the environment. It seems a quite good explanation. It seems rational. It seems scientific. And it seems, all of us can understand and comprehend it.

Is this really a good explanation? To answer this question, we may have to take a good look at all the leaves. Not just the small leaves. Not just the narrow leaves. Not just the pointed leaves. Not just the kind of leaves that may be easily explained by or through the evolutionary or selective process. The small leaves can be found to have many kinds, such as, oval-shaped, heart-shaped, diamond-shaped, or fan-shaped. The narrow leaves can be found to possess many shapes, such as, wedge-shaped, spoon-shaped, spear-shaped, elongate, or lanceolate. The pointed leaves can be found to have many forms, apart from the pointed leaf tips, such as, needle-shaped, sickle-shaped, heart-shaped, diamond-shaped, triangularly shaped, pinnate, or palmate. And, leaves can also be found to have other kinds of shapes or forms, apart from the shapes or forms mentioned now, such as, kidney-shaped, truncate, circular, peltate, lobed, bipinnate, or tripinnate.

Given that, it seems, leaves can possess so many different kinds of shapes and grow with so many different types of forms, we may have to ask, can the explanations discussed right now, that is, the kind of evolutionary explanations, really explain the true coming into being or appearance of the plant leaves? The small leaves are not just small; they can have many different shapes. The narrow leaves are not just narrow; with their narrowness, they can exhibit many different types of forms. The pointed leaves are not just pointed; with their pointed leaf tips, they can express or demonstrate so many different leaf plans or structures. That is, it might be said, so much variety or diversity exists with regard to the leaf plans or structures that, it seems, it may not be adequate or sufficient to only explain the coming into being or appearance of the small, narrow, or pointed leaves, or the kind of leaves that may be explained in a similar manner or approach.

The small leaves may be explained as a result of an evolutionary process to cope with the winds, but how about the various shapes that the small leaves may possess? The narrow leaves may be explained as the consequence of a selective process to maximize the use of sunlight by the plants, but how about the different forms that the narrow leaves may have? The pointed leaves may be seen as an evolutionary development of the leaves to quickly shed snow or ice, but how about the other kinds of leaf plans or structures that may be found with the pointed leaves? How do you explain the leaves that are oval-shaped, heart-shaped, diamond-shaped, or fan-shaped, apart from their smallness? Why do such leaves have to possess such different shapes? Why is it not the case that they just share one shape? Why is it not the case that the small leaves are just small, that is, without showing such a variety of shapes? Why do the leaves have to be oval-shaped? Where does such a shape come from, apart from the possible smallness? Why

Symmetry II

do the leaves have to be heart-shaped? Where does such a shape come from, apart from the possible smallness? Why do the leaves have to be diamond-shaped? Where does such a shape come from, apart from the possible smallness? Why do the leaves have to be fan-shaped? Where does such a shape come from, apart from the possible smallness?

The same questions can be asked with regard to the other leaves, such as the narrow or pointed leaves. How do you explain the leaves that are wedge-shaped, spoon-shaped, spear-shaped, elongate, or lanceolate, apart from their possible narrowness? How do you explain the leaves that are needle-shaped, sickle-shaped, triangularly shaped, pinnate, or palmate, apart from their pointedness? And, how do you explain the kind of leaves that are kidney-shaped, truncate, circular, peltate, lobed, bipinnate, or tripinnate? Why do the leaves have to be wedge-shaped, spoon-shaped, spear-shaped, elongate, or lanceolate? Where do such shapes come from? Why do the leaves have to be needle-shaped, sickle-shaped, triangularly shaped, pinnate, or palmate? Where do such forms come from? Why do the leaves have to be kidney-shaped, truncate, circular, peltate, lobed, bipinnate, or tripinnate? Where do such leaf plans or structures come from?

Why do leaves, after all, have to grow with so many different shapes? Why do leaves, after all, have to possess so many different forms? Why do leaves, after all, have to express or demonstrate such a variety of leaf plans or structures? From where have so many different shapes come? From where have so many different forms originated? From where have such a variety of leaf plans or structures emerged, or arisen? What is the source? What is the origin? What is the beginning? What is the fountainhead? What is the true root? What is the real process? What are the operations behind such a variety of leaf shapes? What are the workings behind such a variety of leaf forms? What are the real processes behind such a great diversity of leaf plans or structures?

Should we ask so many questions? Should we ask so many whys? Should we ask so many wheres? Should we ask so many whats? Yes. We should. The human understanding should not stop at the end of reason. The human understanding of the world should not stop when reason fails to reach further. Beyond reason, there may be a vast realm, in which, man lives, the world exists, and the universe operates. Reason may only understand what it can understand. Reason may only comprehend what it is capable of comprehending. Reason may only reach what it is able to reach. Reason may only be able to understand part of man. Reason may only be able to comprehend part of the world. Reason may only be able to reach part of the universe. To take the parts of man that reason understands as man is to limit the human understanding of man, that is, in a sense, to limit man. To take the sections of the world that reason comprehends as the world itself is to narrow the human understanding of the world, that is, in a sense, to narrow the world. To treat the portions or aspects of the universe that reason is able to reach as the universe itself is to restrict the human understanding of the universe, that is, in a sense, to restrict the universe. Man may be vastly bigger or richer than the parts that can be understood by reason. The world may be significantly more intricate or complex than the sections that can be comprehended by reason. The universe may be immensely deeper or more profound than the portions or aspects that may be reached or grasped by or through reason. Apart from the parts that reason understands, man may have other rich and important life. Apart from the sections that reason comprehends, the world may exist in other vital and essential ways. Apart from the portions or aspects that may be reached or grasped by or through reason, the universe may be found to operate in other deep or profound fashions.

    The evolutionary or selective approach may explain the coming into being of the small leaves by pointing to the wind factor, but how could it explain the coming into being of the different shapes of the small leaves, such as, possibly, oval-shaped, heart-shaped, diamond-shaped, or fan-shaped? Certainly, it seems, involving the wind factor or something like it may not easily explain the coming into being of such different shapes. The evolutionary or selective approach may explain the coming into being of the narrow leaves by pointing to the photosynthetic process, but how could it explain the coming into being of the various forms that the narrow leaves may exhibit, such as, possibly, wedge-shaped, spoon-shaped, spear-shaped, elongate, or lanceolate? Certainly, it seems, involving the photosynthetic process or something like it may not easily explain the coming into being of such different forms. The evolutionary or selective approach may explain the coming into being of the pointed leaves by pointing to the possible evolutionary benefits that such a leaf structure may bring, but, how could such an approach explain the appearance of the different leaf plans or structures that often can be found with the pointed leaves, such as, needle-shaped, sickle-shaped, heart-shaped, diamond-shaped, triangularly shaped, pinnate, or palmate? Could such an approach explain the appearance of these leaves by pointing to some sense of or some kind of evolutionary or selective advantage? What is, possibly, the evolutionary advantage of the needle-shaped or sickle-shaped leaves? What is, possibly, the evolutionary advantage of the heart-shaped or diamond-shaped leaves? If it were the case that certain evolutionary advantage may be associated with the needle-shaped or sickle-shaped leaves, why would the heart-shaped or diamond-shaped leaves have to come into being? If it were the case that certain evolutionary advantage may be associated with the heart-shaped or diamond-shaped leaves, why would the needle-shaped or sickle-shaped leaves have to appear? What is, possibly, the selective advantage of the triangularly shaped leaves? What is, possibly, the selective advantage of the pinnate leaves? What is, possibly, the selective advantage of the palmate leaves? If it were the case that the triangularly shaped leaves have some selective advantage, why would the pinnate or palmate leaves have to come into being? If it were the case that the pinnate or palmate leaves have some selective advantage, why would the triangularly shaped leaves have to appear? If it were the case that the pinnate leaves have some selective edge, why would the palmate leaves have to come into being? If it were the case that some selective edge may be found with the palmate leaves, why would the leaves have to be pinnate?

It seems, the similar kind of questions may be asked, in a sense, with regard to all the other leaves. If it were the case that the oval-shaped, fan-shaped, wedge-shaped or spoon-shaped leaves have some evolutionary advantage, why would it have been the case that many leaves are spear-shaped, elongate, or lanceolate? If it were the case that some evolutionary advantage may be found with the leaves that are spear-shaped, elongate, or lanceolate, then, why would it have been the case that the leaves are also to be found oval-shaped, fan-shaped, wedge-shaped, or spoon-shaped? If it were the case that some selective advantage may be found with the leaves that are needle-shaped, sickle-shaped, heart-shaped, diamond-shaped, triangularly shaped, or palmate, why would the leaves also have to be kidney-shaped, truncate, circular, peltate, lobed, bipinnate, or tripinnate? If it were the case that the kidney-shaped, truncate, circular, peltate, lobed, bipinnate, or tripinnate leaves have some specific evolutionary advantages due to their individual shapes or forms, why would it have been the case that so many leaves are found to be needle-shaped, sickle-shaped, heart-shaped, diamond-shaped, triangularly shaped, or palmate? Why? Why? What may be the reason? How do you explain such a phenomenon?

Certainly, this discussion does not mean that, no evolutionary or selective advantages should be seen in the coming into being or appearance of the various leaf shapes or forms that we are discussing now. It is only meant to point out that, it seems, when it comes to the coming into being or appearance of the various leaf shapes or forms, the evolutionary or selective explanations may amount to, in a sense, or to a certain extent, a self-defeating approach. How do you explain the appearance of the needle-shaped or sickle-shaped leaves, after all? How do you explain the coming into being of the heart-shaped or diamond-shaped leaves, after all? How do you account for the appearance of the triangularly shaped leaves, eventually? How do you account for the coming into being of the pinnate or palmate leaves, in the end? Why should the leaves have to be oval-shaped, heart-shaped, diamond-shaped, or fan-shaped, while the others are wedge-shaped, spoon-shaped, spear-shaped, elongate, or lanceolate? Why should the leaves have to be needle-shaped, sickle-shaped, triangularly shaped, pinnate, or palmate, while the others are kidney-shaped, truncate, circular, peltate, lobed, bipinnate, or tripinnate? Could the evolutionary or selective approach really explain the appearance of all these different leaves? Could the evolutionary or selective process really account for the coming into being of all these different forms? Could the theory of evolution or natural selection really provide the answer for the coming into being or appearance of such a great diversity of leaf plans or structures in nature?

Why should the curved leaves come into being, with their pleasing harmonic forms, apart from the other leaves? Why should the lobed leaves appear, with their varied leaf plans, apart from the other leaves? Why should the rounded or circular leaves have to come into being, with bilateral symmetry existing in a radially symmetric structure, apart from the other leaves? Why should the pinnate leaves have to appear, with their double bilateral symmetry, apart from the other leaves? Why should the bipinnate leaves have to appear on the young locust shoots? Why should the malunggay trees have to grow their tripinnate leaves? It seems, the appearance or coming into being of such a great diversity of leaf plans or structures in nature may not be easily explained by the

Symmetry II

mere evolutionary or selective process. Undoubtedly, it has to be said, the appearance of certain traits or features of leaves may be explained by or through such a process, that is, in a certain sense, or to a certain extent. The fact, or possibility that certain traits or features of leaves may be explained by or through the evolutionary or selective process may not necessarily mean that, such a process may be taken as what is able to account for all the coming into being or appearance of leaves. While the kind of traits or features such as smallness, narrowness, or pointedness, or the kind of things like them, may be easily explained by or through the evolutionary or selective process, other things associated with the leaves may not be so readily explained away in such a manner, or through such an approach. If the development of leaves were only associated with the evolutionary or selective process, then, it appears, it might not have been the case that the leaves should have developed into so many shapes or forms, or into so many plans or structures. That is to say, in a sense, it seems, the evolutionary or selective process may give rise to a number of leaf plans or structures, but such a process itself, alone, may not be seen as what is behind the appearance or coming into being of such a great diversity of leaf plans or structures in nature. First, it seems, if some leaf plans or structures possess certain evolutionary or selective advantages, then the evolutionary process or selective pressure may tend to sustain or maintain such leaf plans or structures, and thus, in a sense, limit the appearance or coming into being of other leaf plans or structures. In other words, from an evolutionary or selective point of view, it might be said, a certain sense of variety may be found with the leaf plans or structures, but such a great diversity may not be what is required with the leaf shapes or forms. That is, in a sense, simply, it may not be necessary or inevitable. Secondly, as we have said, the evolutionary or selective approach may give rise, in a sense, to self-contradiction, as such explanations may refute each other between or among themselves.

So, how to understand the appearance of the various leaf shapes or forms in plants? How to understand the coming into being of such a great diversity of leaf plans or structures in nature? What may be the reason? What may be the source? What may be the origin? That is, what may be truly behind such a great phenomenon in nature? Leaves are not just leaves. Leaves are the carriers of symmetry. Leaves are the demonstrators of harmony. Leaves are the realization of symmetry. Leaves are the realization of symmetry through the leaves. Leaves are the realization of symmetry in the plants. Leaves are the fulfillment of harmony. Leaves are the fulfillment of harmony in the plants. Leaves are the fulfillment of harmony in nature. So, to understand the appearance of the various leaves, we have to pay attention, enough attention, to the symmetric being of leaves. That is, to fully comprehend the eventual coming into being of the various leaf plans or structures in nature, we have to see into the harmonic existence of the leaves, that is, the harmonic existence of the various leaf plans or structures. Does this mean that, the evolutionary or selective process is not important? No. It is important. It is important in the sense that, in a sense, or to a certain extent, such a process reveals the possible evolutionary or selective, though not symmetric or harmonic, development of leaves. That is to say, in an evolutionary or selective sense, the evolutionary or selective process explains the possible development of leaves caused, brought about, or conditioned, by a range of factors, such as, environmental, climatic, ecological, or geological. While the symmetric or harmonic being of leaves may have to do, in a fundamental sense, or to a great extent, with the intrinsic existence of leaves, the evolutionary development of leaves may not be dismissed or overlooked in any way, as such development may be seen as constituting the survival of leaves in their environments. It is in such a sense that, it might be said, the evolutionary or selective approach may help us understand the development of leaves, as the leaves, or the plants, adapt to their environments, cope with the selective pressure, and strive to thrive and prosper.

On the other hand, the evolutionary or selective process may be seen as playing a role, in a sense, in the coming into being or emergence of the symmetric or harmonic existence of the leaves. The symmetric or harmonic existence of the leaves may develop in a sense that such existence may contribute to the survival or well-being of the leaves, or of the plants. As the leaves or plants adapt to the environment for their better survival, such adaptation may be featured, in a sense, or to a certain extent, in the overall symmetric or harmonic existence of the leaves. That is, the symmetric or harmonic leaves may develop in such a way that their symmetric or harmonic development may benefit, eventually, the survival of the leaves or plants in the environment. That is to say, to enhance the survival in the environment, for the symmetric or harmonic leaves, the symmetric or harmonic development may have to integrate itself with the evolutionary or selective process, in the

Symmetry II

sense that, while the symmetric or harmonic development is attained, the aim for a better survival by coping suitably with the selective pressure may also be achieved. That is, for the leaves or plants to survive and prosper, it seems, both the symmetric or harmonic development and the evolutionary or selective process may have to participate in the overall development of the leaves or plants, that is, in a sense, in the coming into being or appearance of the various leaf plans or structures. The symmetric or harmonic development may lay the foundation; the evolutionary or selective process may shape the structure. The symmetric or harmonic development may define the evolutionary or selective process; the evolutionary or selective process may trigger the symmetric or harmonic development.

That is, in a sense, it might be said, when it comes to the development of the leaves or plants, the symmetric or harmonic development may guide or determine the evolutionary or selective process, and the evolutionary or selective process may influence or affect the symmetric or harmonic development. That is, it might be said, these two processes interact, in a sense, on each other, and they work together, in a sense, in their intrinsic and innate ways, to give rise to the various leaf plans or structures found in nature. The development of leaves or plants may thus be seen, in a sense, as involving both the symmetric or harmonic development and the evolutionary or selective process. The coming into being or appearance of the various leaf plans or structures in plants may thus be regarded, in a sense, as the result or consequence of such two processes working together in nature. The evolutionary or selective process may enable the leaves or plants to survive and develop in the environment, while the symmetric or harmonic development of the leaves may provide the intrinsic support or underpinning. The symmetric or harmonic existence of the leaves may have to do, in a fundamental sense, with the symmetric or harmonic development of the leaves, while the evolutionary or selective process may participate in such a development in such a way that the various manifestations of such symmetric or harmonic existence may be fulfilled or realized. The evolutionary or selective process alone may not be able to account for the coming into being of the symmetric or harmonic existence of leaves. The symmetric or harmonic development of leaves itself may not explain, in a sense, all the manifestations of leaves, such as all the leaf plans or structures found in nature.

The great diversity of leaf plans or structures in nature may thus be seen as what leads us, in a sense, to the coexistence of the symmetric or harmonic development and the evolutionary or selective process, or, in a sense, to the interaction of such two processes. Leaves are often found to possess, as we know, different traits or features. While such traits or features may be regarded, in a sense, or to a certain extent, as coming out from an evolutionary or selective process, such traits or features may eventually manifest themselves in the symmetric or harmonic existence of the leaves. That may be the reason, in a sense, why we witness so many different leaf plans or structures in the plants, while the leaves themselves maintain, in a general sense, their symmetric or harmonic existence. In other words, the coming into being or appearance of the various leaf plans or structures in nature may not be regarded, solely, as the result or consequence of the evolutionary or selective process. The evolutionary or selective process may have worked, in a sense, in the coming into being of the various leaf plans or structures, but such a process may only be seen as working with the conditions set out or defined by the symmetric or harmonic development of leaves. The symmetric or harmonic existence of leaves may be seen as what constitutes the foundation of the leaves. The evolutionary or selective process may be regarded as what works on such a foundation. The symmetric or harmonic development of leaves may be seen as what defines the leaves. The evolutionary or selective process may be regarded as what participates in such a leaf development, so that a great diversity of leaf plans or structures may eventually come to this world.

The symmetric or harmonic existence of leaves may thus be seen as having to do, in a sense, or to a certain extent, with the evolutionary or selective process of leaves. While the leaves or plants strive to secure their evolutionary survival, the leaves themselves may develop in their symmetric or harmonic ways. As the leaves grow symmetrically, or harmonically, they may also have to develop in such a way that they may be able to cope with the selective pressure and survive better. The symmetric or harmonic development of leaves may thus be seen, in a sense, as not purely a symmetric or harmonic development, as such a development may involve, to a certain extent, the evolutionary or selective process. In other words, the symmetric or harmonic existence of leaves may not be regarded, in a sense, as purely the result or consequence of the symmetric or harmonic development of leaves. The symmetric or harmonic development may have laid the foundation for the leaves, but when it comes to the overall development of leaves, the evolutionary or selective process may have to be taken into the consideration, in a sense, or to a certain extent, as the leaves or plants themselves may have to adapt to the environment for their survival. It is in such a sense that the symmetric or harmonic existence of leaves may be understood, and it is in such a sense that the great diversity of leaf plans or structures in nature may be understood.

The diversity of leaves may thus be understood in such a manner. The diversity of symmetry in leaves may thus be understood in such a way. The diversity of symmetry in leaves may be seen as representing or reflecting the diversification of symmetry in the leaves, or in the plants. The diversification of symmetry in the leaves or plants may be seen as an innate or intrinsic process, in the sense that, symmetry diversifies itself, apart from the evolutionary or selective process, in such a way, or to such an extent that the symmetrization or harmonization of the world may be seen as being well fulfilled or realized in the plant kingdom. The diversification of symmetry in the leaves or plants may be seen as an intricate or complex process, in the sense that, while the symmetric or harmonic development of leaves may be regarded as what constitutes the essential or fundamental process through which the diversification of symmetry is being fulfilled or realized in the leaves or plants, such a development or process may have to be integrated with the evolutionary or selective process, in such a way, or to such an extent that the leaves or plants may eventually survive in the environment and grow or develop better. The diversification of symmetry in the leaves or plants may be seen as a deep or profound process, in the sense that, as such a process fulfils or realizes symmetry in nature, that is, in the leaves or plants, a great diversity of leaf plans or structures come to this world, and, while such a great diversity of leaf plans or structures present the world with variety, colorfulness, and beauty, such a sense of great diversification may constitute the very foundation of the survival of the world, that is, the survival of the plant world.

The diversification of symmetry in the leaves or plants may be seen, in such a sense, as one of the most essential or fundamental aspects of the plant world. It is what, in a fundamental sense, gives rise to the plant world. It is what makes the plant world diverse. It is what makes the plant world rich. It is what makes the plant world abundant.

It is what makes the plant world splendid. It is what makes the plant world magnificent. It is what makes the plant world beautiful. It is a process in which symmetry fulfils or realizes itself in the plants. It is a process in which the plants fulfill or realize themselves in symmetry. It is a process involving both the symmetric or harmonic development and, in a sense, or to a certain extent, the evolutionary or selective process. It is a process that may be seen as behind the coming into being of the leaves or plants. It is a process that may be seen as behind the coming into being of the various leaf shapes or forms. It is a process that may be seen as behind the appearance of the various leaf plans or structures. Symmetry diversifies itself, so that the various leaf shapes or forms come into being. Symmetry diversifies itself, so that the various leaf plans or structures are exhibited or expressed. Symmetry diversifies itself, with the participation of the evolutionary or selective process, such that the plant leaves come into being, and develop, and the plants survive, thrive, and prosper.

The mere selective process may not be able to explain the coming into being of the various leaf shapes or forms. Evolution alone may not be able to explain the great diversity of leaf plans or structures in nature. It is not just the selective process. It is not just evolution. It is the symmetric development. It is the harmonic process. It is the symmetric development integrated with the selective process. It is the harmonic process fused with the evolutionary development. It is symmetry combined with selection. It is harmony united with evolution. It is avolution. It is avolution, in the sense that, while symmetry or harmony develops, in a sense, the evolutionary process is fulfilled. It is avolution, in the sense that, as the selective pressure is being dealt with suitably, the symmetric or harmonic development is realized, in a sense, at the same time.

It is avolution that may be seen as behind the great diversity of leaf plans or structures in nature. The avolutionary development may be seen as what, eventually, gives rise to the various leaf shapes or forms. The avolutionary process may be seen as what, in the end, leads to the coming into being or appearance of the various leaf plans or structures. The great diversification of symmetry in the leaves or plants is an avolutionary process. The great diversification of symmetry in the leaves or plants is an avolutionary development happening in the plant world. It is the avolutionary diversification. It is the avolutionary development. It is the avolutionary fulfillment. It is the avolutionary

Symmetry II

realization. It is symmetry fulfilled or realized in the plant world through an avolutionary process. It is the plant world fulfilled or realized in symmetry in an avolutionary way.

Evolution may be easy to understand; avolution may be not. Evolution may be compatible with reason; avolution may be not. Evolution may be easily understood in a rational way; avolution may not be so readily. Evolution may only reveal the kind of things that we can observe, but it may overlook the kind of things deep down in nature. Evolution may only explain the kind of things that are apparent or visible, but it may fail to take notice of the kind of things innate, intrinsic, or inherent. Evolution may only explain the kind of things that can be explained readily in its own way, but it may have bypassed the kind of things more intricate or complex. Evolution may only explain the kind of things having to do with the outside or external world, but it may have ignored the kind of things arising or originating from within. Evolution may be able to reveal some mechanisms in nature, but it may not be able to touch the deeper secrets of the world. Evolution may be able to account for some of the phenomena we observe, but it may not be able to explain the kind of things innate, intrinsic, or inherent in nature. Evolution may explain the survival of plants, but it may not be able to explain the intrinsic being of plants. Evolution may account for the apparent existence of nature, but it may not be able to account for the intrinsic existence of the world. Evolution may be a shortcut, as it may have bypassed the deeper or more profound things. Evolution may be an easier way, as it may have paid no attention to the intrinsic or innate being of things. Evolution may have followed reason, but it may not have followed nature. Evolution may have satisfied reason, but it may not have satisfied the way of the world.

Apart from the small, narrow, and pointed leaves, there are many other leaves. That is, when it comes to the leaves, it may not be just an evolutionary coming into being. Apart from the small, narrow, and pointed leaves, there are the curved leaves, lobed leaves, rounded or circular leaves, pinnate leaves, bipinnate leaves, or tripinnate leaves. That is, when it comes to the leaves, it may not be just a happening responding merely to the selective pressure. If it were merely an evolutionary coming into being, why should the leaves come into being with so many different shapes or forms, such as, oval-shaped, heart-shaped, diamond-shaped, fan-shaped, wedge-shaped, spoon-shaped, spear-shaped, elongate, or lanceolate? If it were merely a happening responding only to the selective pressure, why should the leaves appear with so many different leaf plans or structures, such as, needle-shaped, sickle-shaped, triangularly shaped, kidney-shaped, truncate, circular, peltate, lobed, palmate, pinnate, bipinnate, or tripinnate? If it were merely an evolutionary process, why should the bipinnate leaves appear on the young locust shoots? If it were merely a selective matter, why should the tripinnate leaves grow on the malunggay trees? Why should the curved leaves, lobed leaves, circular leaves, palmate leaves, or pinnate leaves happen at all? Why should the bipinnate leaves appear? Why should the tripinnate leaves come into being in the world?

It is not merely evolutionary. It is not merely selective. It is symmetry. It is harmony. It is the movement of symmetry. It is the progress of harmony. It is the fulfillment of symmetry. It is the realization of harmony. It is the diversification of symmetry in the leaves. It is the realization of harmony in the plants. It is the diversification of symmetry in the leaves, with, in a sense, the participation of the evolutionary process. It is the realization of harmony in the plants, in unity, in a sense, with the selective process. Symmetry diversifies itself, in an avolutionary process, so that the various leaf shapes or forms may come into being. Harmony realizes itself, in an avolutionary way, so that the various leaf plans or structures may be fulfilled or realized in the world. It is the avolutionary diversification of symmetry that may be seen as what explains the coming into being or appearance of the various leaf plans or structures in plants. It is the avolutionary realization of harmony that may be seen as what ultimately behind the great diversity of leaves found in nature, or in the world.

Nature is beyond the evolutionary. Nature is more than the evolutionary. Nature is beyond the selective. Nature is more than the selective. Nature is beyond the rational. Nature is more than the rational. Nature is life. Nature is plants. Nature is animals. Nature is symmetry. Nature is harmony. Nature is symmetry expressed or demonstrated in plants or animals. Nature is harmony fulfilled or realized in plants or animals. Nature is an avolutionary process. Nature is an avolutionary coming into being. Nature is an avolutionary coming into being of plants or animals involving, in a sense, both symmetric and selective processes. Nature is an avolutionary coming into being of plants or animals involving, to a certain extent, both harmonic and evolutionary activities. Nature is the avolutionary fulfillment of

Symmetry II

symmetry. Nature is the avolutionary realization of harmony. Nature is the avolutionary fulfillment of symmetry in plants, or through plants. Nature is the avolutionary realization of harmony in animals, or through animals.

As the great diversity of leaf plans or structures may be seen as the result or consequence of the avolutionary development of the leaves or plants, such may explain, in a sense, the phenomenon that the earliest leaves are often found to be mostly frond-like. We have discussed this phenomenon before, and it seems, the fossil record from the Devonian appears to show that the leaves from that period are likely to be frond-like. This may be explained, in a sense, in that, the development of the earliest leaves or plants may be seen as an avolutionary process; that is, in the sense that, the earliest leaves or plants may be seen as the result or consequence of the two processes operating or working together, in a sense, in the Devonian. The symmetric or harmonic development of the leaves or plants may be seen as constituting one of the processes. The evolutionary or selective development of the leaves or plants may be seen, in a sense, as the other. These two processes, or in a sense, the interaction or integration of these two processes may be seen as what defined or determined the growth or development of the leaves or plants in the Devonian. The Devonian may be seen as the period in which symmetry came into being in the leaves or harmony realized itself in the plants, but it may not be seen as a period in which symmetry or harmony might have developed in such a way or to such an extent that the diversification of symmetry might be well displayed or the realization of harmony might be diversely demonstrated. The Devonian may be seen as a time when the evolutionary or selective process began working its way in the development of the leaves or plants, but it may not be regarded as a time when the evolutionary or selective process might have worked or proceeded in such a way or to such an extent that the various leaf plans or structures might come into being, as a result or consequence of such a process. That is to say, the Devonian might see the coming into being of symmetry in the leaves or the realization of harmony in the plants, but it might not experience the kind of large-scale diversification of symmetry in the leaves or diverse realization of harmony in the plants, as such, as we know, may be seen as what characterizes the later development of leaves or plants. And, it might be said, when the evolutionary or selective process works, it usually takes time. That is to say, in other words, when the leaves or plants evolved in the Devonian, they might have developed in such a way or to such an extent that, only a limited variety of leaf plans or structures might have come into being by the end of the Devonian. In a similar sense, it might be said, during such a period, symmetry might have developed, or harmony might have progressed, in such a way, or to such an extent that, only a limited range of diversification of symmetry or realization of harmony might have been fulfilled. That may be the reason, in a sense, why we often witness the appearance of the usually frond-like leaves in the Devonian. The lack of diversity in the leaf shapes or forms in the Devonian may be seen as the result or consequence of the initial avolutionary development of leaves or plants. As the leaves or plants avolved and continued their development, harmony might advance, symmetry might further diversify itself, and new leaf plans or structures might come into being. That may be what we see in the following geologic periods after the Devonian, such as, in the Carboniferous, as the great diversity of leaves, or in such a sense, of plants, gradually came into being on the surface of this planet.

The avolutionary coming into being of leaves or plants may be seen as what behind one of the most significant phenomena observed in the plant world, that is, the seemingly unchanging nature of the leaf plans or structures. The frond-like leaves coming into being in the Devonian may be observed today, without, it seems, much difference, even after some 360 million years. The leaves of some Carboniferous plants preserved in the fossil record may be seen in today's world, even after some 300 million years. The flowering plants appeared in the early Cretaceous, and by the middle Cretaceous, around 100 million years ago, they had diversified to such an extent that a great diversity may be found in the fossil record. With the process of diversification well under way, it is not surprising that, the late Cretaceous saw the appearance of plants that may be regarded as the ancestors of many modern trees, such as, among others, oaks, figs, maples, or magnolias. People have witnessed the generally unchanging nature of the leaf plans or structures for a long time, and naturally, they might wonder why it is so, what may be the reason, or what may lie behind such a phenomenon.

The seemingly unchanging nature of the leaf plans or structures is no small matter, as the leaves appear to have kept their same shapes or forms unchanged, in a general sense, for a very long time, for millions of years, for tens of millions of years, or for hundreds of millions of

Symmetry II

years. For something to remain the same for millions of years, for tens of millions of years, or for hundreds of millions of years, something extraordinary or quite unusual must have happened. What happened to the leaves? What happened to the plants? What happened to the plant world? What happened to the leaf shapes or forms? What happened to the leaf plans or structures? What happened to the development of leaves? What happened to the development of plants? If the leaves remain the same in their shapes or forms for millions of years, for tens of millions of years, or for hundreds of millions of years, what kind of development might they have undergone? If the plants possess their leaves generally unchanged in the leaf plans or structures for millions of years, for tens of millions of years, or for hundreds of millions of years, what kind of development might that be? How to explain such a kind of development? How to account for such a kind of development? How to interpret such a kind of development? Is it evolution? Is it selection? Is it evolutionary? Is it selective?

Seeing that the leaves seem to have possessed their shapes or forms unchanged for millions of years, for tens of millions of years, or for hundreds of millions of years, some have suggested that, it was not evolution. Evolution seems to be incapable of explaining such a phenomenon. Evolution seems to be unable to account for such a phenomenon. In the same sense, it seems, natural selection cannot explain such a kind of development. In the same sense, it appears, natural selection may not be able to account for such a kind of development.

Yes, it was not evolution. Yes, it was not selection. Yes, it was not an evolutionary development. Yes, it was not a selective process. It was avolution. It was an avolutionary development. It was an avolutionary process. It was the avolutionary coming into being. It was not the world of evolution; it was the world of avolution. It was not the world of natural selection; it was the world of symmetrization or harmonization. It was not just the world of evolution; it was the world of avolution. It was not just the world of natural selection; it was also the world of symmetrization or harmonization. It was the world of selection combined with symmetrization. It was the world of evolution united with harmonization. It was the world of selection underlain by symmetry. It was the world of evolution guided, supported, or conditioned by or through symmetry, or harmony.

Avolution and Man

In a sense, the Devonian explosion may better be seen as a period of the coming into being of symmetry in plants, rather than just the coming into being of bilateral symmetry in the plant life, in that, while the bilateral symmetry might have been expressed or realized in the coming into being of the bilaterally symmetric plants, the radial symmetry might also have been, at the same time, expressed or fulfilled in nature through the coming into being of the radially symmetric plants. Though, it seems, the leaf fossil evidence may point to the possibility that bilateral symmetry might have been the predominant form taken by the plants during the Devonian, mainly through their leaf plans or structures, it may not be ruled out, it was possible that some plants might have come into being at the time that might have possessed or demonstrated the kind of radially symmetric forms, in some way, in some sense, or in some manner. Such plants may stand as the ancestors to the radially symmetric plants emerged later, such as the conifers.

Going out in a winter day, one may quickly notice, the kind of plants called conifers stand distinct from the other plants, such as grasses, bushes, or trees. While the other plants usually stay in a dormant state in the winter and lose their green colors, conifers like pines or firs are still green, and have their existences maintained outwardly like in other seasons, though, certainly, with some internal changes or adaptations. It has to be said, there are other evergreen plants growing even in the winter, and some of them possessing bilaterally symmetric leaves, but, it seems, they are mostly shrubs or bushes, but not trees.

In a sense, it might be said, this should constitute a very big difference between the conifers and other plants. What has made the conifers so different from the other plants? What is behind such differences? As we know, unlike the other plants, conifers usually have needle-like leaves, and produce no flowers. They are seed-bearing plants, but their seeds are usually contained in their scaly cones, which are certainly not the same as the flowers. One may also witness the conical shapes formed by some of the conifers such as firs. Sometimes, the shapes of the plants are so streamlined that, it seems, they do express or demonstrate, in nature, a remarkable sense of radial symmetry.

The differences associated with the kind of plants like conifers may have to do, in a sense, with the difference between radial symmetry and

Symmetry II

bilateral symmetry, or, it might be said, with the limitations of radial symmetry. The limitations of radial symmetry may also be observed, in a sense, in the fact that, it seems, the plants like the conifers have not diversified in such a manner that their diversity or types of species can match that of the other kinds of plants, such as, the bilaterally symmetric flowering plants.

It seems, it may have to be said, the leaves of some plants among the conifers do, in some sense, express or demonstrate a kind of bilateral symmetry, with some sense or form of bilaterally symmetric leaf plans or structures visible to the human eyes. And, it appears, it is likely the case that, the scales of the conifer cones often display a sense of bilateral symmetry, with the scale structures often arranged in a way or manner that something may be regarded as bilaterally symmetric. Certainly such conifer scales are usually hard and woody, unlike the soft tissues of leaves. But, it may have to be said, in a sense, or to some extent, it seems, they do express or possess a sense of bilateral symmetry.

That is to say, while the overall shapes or forms of conifer cones exhibit a sense of radial symmetry, the cone scales may be seen as often demonstrating a sense of bilateral symmetry. The cones may be compared, in a sense, to the flowers, though such cones may be seen as having not developed into the real flowers, due, in a sense, it might be said, to the limitations of radial symmetry. The cone scales may be compared, in a sense, to the flower petals. While the flower petals may be seen as coming from the leaves, it seems, the same thing may not be said about the cone scales. The sense of bilateral symmetry exhibited by the conifer leaves or the cone scales may not be overlooked, ignored or dismissed. Such a sense of the presence of bilateral symmetry may indicate that, a sense of bilateral symmetry may indeed exist in the kind of plants like the conifers.

One can go out and witness these things. Should we call the plants like the conifers, as such, the bilaterally symmetric plants? Even with such a kind of presence of bilateral symmetry, I still want to call the plants like the conifers the radially symmetric plants. The reason is that, first, as with the most cases with regard to the conifers, their characteristic leaf plans or structures are needle-like. That is, even with some sense of presence of bilateral symmetry, either in their leaves or cone scales, such a sense of bilateral symmetry may not be seen as well pronounced or fully developed. In other words, with the plants like the conifers, it might be said, the dominant form of symmetry is the radial symmetry, expressed or demonstrated through their needle-like leaves or their radially symmetric cones. Secondly, as we all know, the plants like the conifers usually produce cones, but not flowers. Thirdly, it might be said, bilateral symmetry may be seen as closely related to the coming into being or growth of flowers, but such a connection may not be seen as existing with regard to the radial symmetry.

At this point, it may have to be said, even the flowering plants, which are called the bilaterally symmetric plants for their bilaterally symmetric leaves and production of flowers, usually demonstrate a certain sense of radial symmetry. Such a sense of radial symmetry can often be observed in the radial arrangement of the flower petals or stamens around the axis of the flowers. Even with such a presence of radial symmetry, we may still call the flowering plants the bilaterally symmetric plants to emphasize that, first, the dominant form of symmetry demonstrated by the flowering plants may be seen as bilateral, as expressed through the leaves or petal forms or structures, and, secondly, a close relationship may exist between bilateral symmetry and the production or growth of flowers.

Some researches may reveal, it seems, there may be a parallel development between the flowering plants and other non-flowering seed-bearing plants, such as conifers. This may not be very surprising, if we take into consideration the different kinds of symmetry being involved. That is to say, the radial symmetry manifested by the non-flowering seed-bearing conifers is certainly different from the bilateral symmetry expressed in the flowering plants. Such a symmetric difference, as big as from radial to bilateral, may, in a certain sense, explain the separate developmental routes ultimately taken by the non-flowering seed plants like conifers and flowering plants.

Some might attribute the symmetric patterns or structures of plants, either radial or bilateral, to some kind of genetic mutations happening early on in the development of plants. Is it possible? Is it true? If the genetic mutations could bring the symmetric patterns or structures of plants into the world, how could you rule out that, the genetic mutations might cause such symmetric patterns or structures of plants to disappear? If it is possible that some genetic mutations might give rise to the symmetric patterns or structures in plants, why is it not possible that some genetic mutations might lead to their disappearance? If mutations could cause the symmetric patterns or structures to appear

Symmetry II

in plants, in an equal sense, it might be said, mutations might work to undo the symmetric patterns or structures in plants. That is, it is equally possible that, some genetic mutations might occur and cause the plants to eventually lose, it might be said, their symmetric patterns or structures. But, such symmetric patterns or structures of plants seem to have lasted to this day. How is it possible? How have they been maintained? How have they been supported? How have they been sustained? Where are the genetic mutations? Why is it the case that they did not happen? Why is it possible? How is it possible?

We like to be close to the grasses. We often notice their long and narrow leaves. If we examine carefully, we may find, there is usually a central vein, among the parallel veins, in the grass leaves, often more visible on the underside. A form of bilateral symmetry may be expressed or demonstrated by the grass leaves. In a sense, it might be said, grasses have developed in a rather sophisticated way, in that, it seems, they are mostly leaves. As their bodies are mostly leaves, they may be able to take advantage, fully, in a sense, of the benefits afforded by the bilateral symmetry, that is, in their case, afforded by their usually bilaterally symmetric leaves. In such a sense, there is no wonder that, it is found, grasses are among the most recently developed plants on earth, and stand as some of the most efficient and successful plant species occupying and colonizing the land surface of this planet.

The colonization of the land surface of earth by the early plant organisms might have happened in the late Silurian or early Devonian, about 410 million years ago. The well developed complex plant leaves might have appeared in the late Devonian, on a widespread scale, around 360 million years ago. From the colonization of the land by the earliest plant organisms to the appearance of the well developed complex leaves, it was about 50 million years. During such a period of about 50 million years, that is, the time roughly spanning the Devonian, we see, plants had undergone a remarkable process of tremendous transformation, from the simple, primitive, leafless and rootless organisms in the beginning, to the tall, large, sturdy, and leafy plants with true roots. It is such a remarkable, significant, and in a sense, mighty transformation that has distinguished the Devonian from all the other periods in the history of plants. The Devonian thus occupies a special place in the development of the plant life on earth.

Seeing the relatively rapid development of plants in such a period, witnessing the relatively fast diversification of plant life forms during such a time, people, including many paleontologists and paleobotanists, would undoubtedly ask, where did this period come from? Where did the Devonian energy come from? Where did the Devonian strength come from? Where did the Devonian power come from? Where did the Devonian capacity come from? Where did the Devonian complexity come from? Where did the Devonian potential come from? That is, after all, where did the Devonian explosion come from? What does it mean? What does it signify? What does it indicate? What does it represent? What does it point to? What does it imply? What does it stand for? Or, what does it tell us?

It may tell us that symmetry is powerful. It may tell us that symmetry is innate in plants. It may tell us that symmetry is intrinsic in plants. It may tell us that symmetry is behind the coming into being of plants. Symmetry fulfilled or realized itself in the Devonian; the plant life came into being. The plant life came into being in the Devonian; symmetry fulfilled or realized itself. The Devonian explosion represents the appearance of symmetry in the plant life. The Devonian explosion represents the appearance of the plant life in symmetry. The Devonian explosion represents the coming into being of symmetry in the plant life. The Devonian explosion represents the coming into being of the plant life in symmetry. The Devonian explosion represents the movement of symmetry in the plant life. The Devonian explosion represents the development of the plant life in symmetry. The Devonian explosion represents the fulfillment or realization of symmetry in the plant life. The Devonian explosion represents the fulfillment or realization of the plant life in symmetry.

§ 2.2 The Fusion of Bilateral Symmetry and Sexual Symmetry: the Coming into Being of Flowers

Let us, now, turn our attention to the flowers, or, to the coming into being of flowers.

The fossil record suggests that flowering plants might have first appeared in the early Cretaceous period, about 130 million years ago, and by the middle Cretaceous, about 100 million years ago, the diversification of flowering plants had developed in such a rapid and massive manner that widespread and numerous flowering plants may be seen as having come into being for the first time on this planet.

Symmetry II

Flowering plants are seed-bearing plants, and are distinguished from other seed-bearing plants, certainly, on the basis that they produce flowers, and fruits. Fruits, in biological terms, are usually the growth of the plant female reproductive organs after fertilization for the protection and dispersal of seeds. Flowers function as the reproductive organs for the flowering plants. It seems, for the majority of the flowering plants, one may often find, both male and female reproductive organs may be contained in the flowers. In some other flowering plants, it may be the case that, only male or female reproductive organs may be found in the flowers.

People usually dismiss flowers as the mere reproductive or sexual organs of plants that possess little meaning other than that they have evolved through an evolutionary process to facilitate the plant sexual reproduction. Certainly, as we have seen, as the reproductive or sexual organs, flowers do provide the flowering plants with some evolutionary advantages, such as, the genetic variation or diversity, or the possibility for DNA damage repair. But, apart from the fact that flowers act as the reproductive or sexual organs of flowering plants, we can also see, they represent or stand for a sense of beauty. That is, *they are beautiful*. They are usually so beautiful that, it seems, the workings or endeavors of human beings could hardly match their true beauty. So, is it possible that, when we look at the flowers, we should ask some questions that may be related to beauty? That is, is it possible that, when we look into the flowers, it may be necessary for us to ask certain questions that may not be confined to the fact that they are mere reproductive or sexual organs, just like the other kinds of reproductive or sexual organs found in other species, such as in animals?

The other kinds of reproductive or sexual organs, such as in animals, usually do not demonstrate, express, or display a sense of beauty. But flowers do. And they usually demonstrate, express, or display, exceptionally, a sense of beauty. What is behind such a sense of beauty? What is possibly underlying such a sense of beauty? What is possibly existing, in flowers, intrinsically, so that what is called flowers should come into being? What is possibly existing, in flowers, innately or inherently, so that the beauty called flowers should be demonstrated, expressed, displayed, fulfilled, or realized?

Flowers are not just the reproductive or sexual parts of plants; they are also the beautiful parts of plants. Flowers are not just the parts of plants that accomplish the sexual reproduction; they are also the parts

Avolution and Man

of plants that give rise to beauty. The function of flowers, as the reproductive or sexual organs, may thus be seen, in a sense, as being fused with the existence of beauty; or, it might be said, beauty may be seen, in a sense, as being fused with the function of sexual reproduction, in or through the flowers. Nature has thus, in a sense, given rise to a natural function called sexual reproduction through beauty. Or, it might be said, nature has thus, in a sense, given rise to beauty through a natural function, or working, or operation that is called sexual reproduction. Thus, when we look at the flowers, while we are conscious of the reproductive function they are playing, we are also attracted by their beauty. And, needless to say, while we appreciate their tender and delicate beauty, we should not fail to take notice, what a wonderful way nature has provided for the accomplishment of the reproduction of plants.

In other words, it might be said, when we look into the workings or operations of flowers, we may have to look into all the things associated with both sexual reproduction and beauty. That is, in other words, when we look into the coming into being of flowers, we may have to look into all the aspects of flowers that may have to do with both the coming into being of plant sexual reproduction and the coming into being of flower beauty. To look only into the coming into being of plant sexual reproduction may not be able to fully explain the coming into being of flowers. To look only into the possible workings or operations of flowers as the mere sexual reproductive organs may not be able to fully expose all the secrets behind the coming into being of flowers. Flowers are not just related to the sexual reproduction; they are also related to the plant beauty. Flowers are not just associated with the sexual reproduction; they are also associated with the beauty of the world. The coming into being of plant sexual reproduction certainly constitutes an important part of the coming into being of flowers, but it may not constitute all the things about flowers. The appearance of sexual reproductive organs in plants certainly stands as some of the most significant meanings for the existence of flowers, but it may not represent all the meanings when it comes to the eventual coming into being of flowers. The sexual reproduction may be just one of the floral functions. The sexual reproductive organs may be just one of the floral appearances. The other floral function may be the representation, or, realization, or, fulfillment, in a floral way, of the beautiful. The other

Symmetry II

floral appearance may be the appearance, or, expression, or, manifestation, in a floral manner, of beauty.

To look at the flowers is to look at both beauty and reproductive organs. To look at the flowers is to look at both expression of beauty and function of reproduction. That is, to look into the flowers is to look into both beauty and reproduction. That is, to look into the coming into being of flowers is to look into both the coming into being of reproduction and the coming into being of beauty.

What is beauty? Beauty is meaning. Beauty is the significant meaning. Wherever beauty exists, meaning exists. Wherever beauty exists, the significant meaning exists. Wherever there is beauty, there is meaning. Wherever there is beauty, there is the significant meaning. Flowers represent beauty; there is meaning behind the flowers. Flowers demonstrate beauty; there is meaning in the flowers. Flowers express beauty; meaning exists in the world. Flowers stand for beauty; meaning exists in nature. To look into the flowers is to reveal the meaning in the flowers. To look into the flowers is to reveal the meaning behind the flowers. To look into the flowers is to reveal the significant meaning existing in nature. To look into the flowers is to reveal the significant meaning existing in the world. That is, to see beauty is to see the flowers; to see the meaning of beauty is to see the meaning of the flowers. That is, to see the meaning of the flowers is to see how, why or when the flowers came into being, were formed, or were positioned in the lives of plants.

Flowers usually possess four different parts, including sepals, petals, stamens and carpels, though such may not always be the case with all flowers. Stamens are the male reproductive organs of flowers. Carpels are the female reproductive organs of flowers. It has to be said, on the one hand, some flowers may possess a number of carpels while others may only have one carpel; and on the other hand, some flowers may possess several carpels growing together individually while others may have multiple carpels fused into a single female organ.

Sepals are usually the small leaf-like structures growing closely under the petals. They protect the flowers in their initial stages, and may help to hold the petals in place later on. Petals are perhaps the most visible parts of flowers, as their beautiful forms or colors may instantly attract our attention. They are usually arranged in a circular manner around the reproductive organs of flowers, the stamens and carpels. As the male reproductive organs of flowers, stamens usually have two parts, the filaments and anthers. The filaments are the thin stalks supporting the anthers. Anthers are usually the two-lobed structures responsible for producing pollen. Carpels, as the female reproductive organs, are usually the innermost part of flowers, surrounded by the stamens.

Usually three parts may be found in a carpel, the ovary, the style, and the stigma. The ovary is the lower big part where ovules are produced and fertilized by the pollen grains. The style is the stalk part where pollen grains may penetrate and find their way to the ovary. The stigma is the part atop the style, and its function is mainly to collect pollen. Pollen is what produces the male sperm cells. The process of pollination is the transfer of pollen from the male reproductive organs to the female reproductive organs, that is, in the case of flowers, from the stamens to the carpels, that is, from the anther to the stigma. When deposited on the stigma, pollen grains will grow what are called pollen tubes through the style. The pollen tubes will extend into the ovary and it is through such tubes that the sperm cells will reach the ovules in the ovary and fertilize them.

The actual process of fertilization in the ovary is often a rather complex one, as such a process usually gives rise to the seeds containing both endosperm and embryo. It is called a process of double fertilization, referring to the fact that two parts are usually generated in the seeds through such a process. The embryo may develop later into the plant. The endosperm is the stored food for the future developing embryo. Thus, through the process of double fertilization, the ovules will develop into the seeds by joining the sperm cells, and the ovary will develop into the fruit that contains such seeds and may serve as the protection for such seeds and contribute to their future dispersal.

For most of the flowering plants, it seems, flowers usually possess both stamens and carpels. And this means that, both male and female reproductive organs usually can be found in flowers. Certainly, this should not be taken as the case with all flowers. Some flowers may possess only stamens or only productive stamens, and such flowers may be seen, in a general sense, as the male flowers. Some flowers may have only carpels or only productive carpels, and such flowers may be taken, in a general sense, as the female ones.

This may only be regarded as a general description of flowers, as when it comes to the individual flowers, great varieties or variations may be encountered, either in the flower structures, in the flower

Symmetry II

patterns, in the flower functions or mechanisms, or in the complexities being involved. That is to say, on the one hand, symmetry may be seen as having fulfilled or realized itself in nature in some of the most tender, delicate, exquisite or beautiful ways we can imagine in the world, as we can witness in the flowers; and on the other hand, it seems, we should not fail to take notice that, the fulfillment or realization of symmetry in flowers may not be a simple or straightforward process and may have involved certain things deep, subtle, complex, or even powerful. In other words, the appearance of flowers may not be simply treated as an ordinary thing. It is the appearance of beauty. It is the appearance of beauty in plants. It is the appearance of beauty in the plant reproductive organs. It is the emergence of the plant reproductive organs. It is the emergence of the plant reproductive organs in beauty. It is the appearance of beauty in sex. It is the emergence of sex in beauty. It is the union of beauty with sex. It is the fusion of sex with beauty. It is the union of symmetry with sex. It is the fusion of sex with symmetry. It is the fulfillment of symmetry in sex. It is the realization of sex in symmetry. It is the fulfillment of symmetry in nature. It is the realization of nature in symmetry.

The depth or complexity involved in the appearance of flowering plants may be seen in the coming into being of flowers. The sepals are usually small and green, not as prominent as the petals, and they are often regarded as the reduced or modified leaves. The petals may be seen as having developed from the leaves, though they are often softer, colored, or with some pleasing shapes or forms. Stamens may also be seen as coming from the leaves. This may be seen in a number of senses. Some molecular or genetic studies seem to indicate that, the different flower parts may have been the result of certain genetic processes, and it is through one of such processes that, for example, the stamens and carpels may have been differentiated from each other. Certain things observed in nature may also point to the possibility that the flower parts may be closely related. It is observed, in some flowers, the anthers may be found on the margins of some leaf-like stamens. While this may indicate a sense of closeness between stamens and leaves, the canna flowers may reveal a deep relationship between stamens and petals, as, in a sense, both of them may have originated from the leaves. The bright and beautiful flowers of cannas are special, in the sense that, their "petals" are actually not the petals, and they are in fact the modified stamens that have taken, in a sense, the place of petals. While the petal-like stamens are usually big and beautifully colored, the real petals are small or hardly to be noticed. It is interesting to witness in nature such a dramatic transformation in flowers. It demonstrates, in a sense, the potential of symmetry when it fulfils or realizes itself in nature, that is, in flowers. The connection between stamens and petals may be seen in such a case. The connection between stamens and leaves may also be seen in the structures of anthers, in that, the two-lobed structures of anthers may stand, in a sense, as an indication of the eventual coming into being of stamens from the bilaterally symmetric leaves.

Just like stamens, it seems, carpels may have also developed from leaves. The ovule-bearing leaves or some ovule-producing leaf-like structures may be the origin of carpels. Such ovule-bearing leaves or leaf-like structures may have developed, over time, into the kind of structures or forms in which ovules may be enclosed. The enclosed state may mean a sense of protection for ovules, as they may develop or exist away from the outside forces. This enclosed state is only found in flowering plants, the angiosperms, as ovules are usually contained in carpels. It is a different case with the gymnosperms, as their ovules are often found on the surface or margins of their fertile leaves. The intrinsic closeness of carpels with leaves may also be observed in some primitive flowering plants, in that, it seems, their carpels indeed appear to look like leaves, to some extent.

It is interesting to see that, it seems, flowers, the most crucial or sophisticated organs of plants, in a certain sense, may have developed from leaves. Given the fact that leaves may be regarded as the bearers of symmetry in plants, it is not surprising that the origins of flowers may be found in them. It is in leaves that symmetry is fulfilled. It is in leaves that the bilateral symmetry is realized. It is in leaves that symmetry is fulfilled in nature. It is in leaves that the bilateral symmetry is realized in the plant world. The leaves represent the fulfillment of symmetry. The leaves stand for the realization of harmony. They represent the power of symmetry. They represent the potential of symmetry. They represent the capacity of symmetry. They stand for the power of bilateral symmetry. They stand for the potential of bilateral symmetry. They stand for the capacity of bilateral symmetry. They embody the power of bilateral symmetry. They embody the potential of bilateral symmetry. They embody the capacity of bilateral symmetry. They are the power. They are the potential. They are the capacity. That is why flowers came from them. That is why flowers developed from them. That is why they gave rise to flowers. That is why we find the closeness or connection between them and the different parts of flowers. And that is why, it might be said, flowers appeared, emerged, or came into being in the Cretaceous.

Look at the carpels. We would be amazed by their complex structures or mechanisms. Their stigmas have to develop the kind of structures or mechanisms to capture pollen. They have to differentiate the pollen coming from different flowers, and only accept that from the same species. And it is found, certain mechanisms exist in flowering plants to prevent self-fertilization. Such mechanisms are important in the sense that they lead to the increase of genetic diversity in flowering plants, and thus contribute to the development of flowering plants. As we have known, fertilization in flowers usually involves the stigma, the style and the ovary. In other words, just like playing their roles in the process of fertilization, the stigma, the style and the ovary may all participate in the process to prevent self-fertilization. And this means, the stigma, the style and the ovary may all develop the kind of mechanisms necessary for such a purpose.

While the carpels work with such complex structures or mechanisms, we cannot forget, they exist, at the same time, with beauty, or simply, in beauty. Together with stamens, petals and sepals, they constitute the beautiful existence that is called the flowers. Look at the stamens. While they give rise to pollen, the source of the male sperm cells, they are so delicate and subtle. Look at the sepals. Staying in the background, they provide a wonderful comparison to the beautiful petals. Look at the petals. They are so tender, so soft, so brightly colored, or so gracefully shaped or formed. They are the carriers of beauty. They are the bearers of beauty. They are the embodiments of beauty. They are beauty themselves.

While seeds grow in the carpels, pollen is produced by the stamens. While the petals exhibit the beauty of flowers, the sepals work to protect or support them. It is unity. It is harmony. It is cooperation. It is beauty. It is seeds growing out of the harmonic cooperation. It is beauty coming out of the harmonic existence. It is life coming out of harmony. It is life growing out of beauty. It is life existing in harmony. It is life existing in beauty. It is life growing in harmony. It is life developing in beauty. It is the unity of life with beauty. It is the union of life with beauty. It is the fusion of life with beauty.

Again, we cannot forget, it is the leaves that might have given rise to flowers. Why should flowers have to come from the leaves? Why should the leaves have to develop into flowers? Why should flowers have to develop their parts, the sepals, the petals, the stamens and the carpels, from the leaves? Why should the leaves have to develop into the sepals, the petals, the stamens, and the carpels? Why should flowers have to develop their complex structures or mechanisms, from the leaves? Why should the leaves have to develop into such complex structures, or such complex mechanisms? Why is it the case that the leaves should be able to develop into flowers? Why is it the case that the leaves should be able to develop into the sepals, the petals, the stamens, or the carpels? Why is it the case that the leaves should be able to develop into such complex structures or mechanisms?

Why is it not the case that conifers have flowers? Why is it not the case that flowers are also found with conifers? Why is it not the case that the leaves of conifers may also develop into the sepals, the petals, the stamens, or the carpels? Why is it not the case that the leaves of conifers may also be able to develop into flowers? Why, should the presence of bilateral symmetry be so prominent in the flowering plants? Why, should the presence of bilateral symmetry be so prominent in the appearance of flowers? Why, should bilateral symmetry be associated with the flowering plants? Why, should bilateral symmetry be so closely related to the existence of flowers?

Conifers may be regarded as the radially symmetric plants, mostly in the sense that bilateral symmetry may not be seen as being well or fully developed in them and they may only produce cones, instead of flowers. But, why is it the case that flowers may not be found with the radially symmetric plants? Why is it the case that the radially symmetric plants may not be able to produce flowers? Why is it the case that bilateral symmetry may be the foundation of flowering? Why is it the case that bilateral symmetry may be the basis for the coming into being of flowering plants? That is, why is it the case that the bilaterally symmetric leaves should be the origin of flowers? Why is it the case that the bilaterally symmetric leaves should determine or define the existence of the flowering plants? Why is it the case that the different parts of flowers, the sepals, the petals, the stamens, and the carpels, have to develop from the bilaterally symmetric leaves? Why is

Symmetry II

it the case that they have to develop, in the first place? Why is it the case that flowers have to happen, in the beginning? Why is it the case that flowers have to appear, emerge, or come into being, at all?

Could evolution explain all these? Maybe not. Evolution may explain certain things, but it may not explain all these things. It may explain some processes, but it may not be able to explain all the processes. It may be able to explain certain mechanisms, but it may not be able to explain all the mechanisms behind the appearance of flowers, or the coming into being of the flowering plants. To explain the appearance of flowers, we need to look deeper than evolution. To explain the coming into being of the flowering plants, we need to see beyond evolution, or, the mere natural selection.

Flowers are the seeds of life. Flowers are the beginning of life. Flowers are the source of life. Flowers are the root of life. Flowers are the author of life. That is why flowers are so connected with symmetry. That is why flowers are so linked with symmetry. That is why flowers are so associated with the leaves. Symmetry is the beginning of life. Symmetry is the source of life. Symmetry is the root of life. Symmetry is the author of life. Leaves are the representatives of symmetry in plants. Leaves are the carriers of symmetry in plants. Leaves are the bearers of symmetry in plants. Leaves are the fulfillers or realizers of symmetry in the plant world. That is why flowers came or emerged from the leaves. It was symmetry fulfilling or realizing itself in flowers, through the leaves. It was symmetry fulfilling or realizing itself in the flowering plants, through the leaves. It was symmetry fulfilling or realizing itself in the plant world, through the leaves. It was symmetry fulfilling or realizing itself in nature, through the leaves. Leaves are the bridge between symmetry and flowers. Leaves are the bridge between symmetry and flowering plants. Leaves are the bridge between symmetry and the plant world. Leaves are the bridge between symmetry and nature.

It was not something easy for leaves to transform themselves into carpels. It was not something simple for leaves to change themselves into stamens. It was not something easy for leaves to become sepals. It was not something simple for leaves to grow into the tender, soft, delicate, exquisite, colored, or beautiful petals. It was not something easy for leaves to transform themselves into the female reproductive parts of flowers. It was not something simple for leaves to change themselves into the male reproductive parts of flowers. It was not

Avolution and Man

something easy for leaves to become the protection for the reproductive parts of flowers. It was not something simple for leaves to grow into the kind of existence fused with both beauty and sexual reproduction. It was the coming into being of beauty with sexual reproduction. It was the emergence of sexual reproduction with beauty. It was the coming into being of the fusion of beauty and sexual reproduction in plants. It was the emergence of the fusion of sexual reproduction and beauty in flowers. It was the fusion of beauty and sexual reproduction in flowers, through the leaves. It was the fusion of beauty and sexual reproduction in the flowering plants, through the leaves. It was the fusion of beauty and sexual reproduction in the plant world, through the leaves, that is, through the bilaterally symmetric leaves. It was the fusion of beauty and sexual reproduction in nature, through the leaves, that is, through the leaves of bilateral symmetry.

It was the fusion of sexual symmetry with bilateral symmetry. It was the fusion of bilateral symmetry with sexual symmetry. It was sexual symmetry coming into being in bilateral symmetry, through the bilaterally symmetric leaves. It was bilateral symmetry fulfilled or realized in sexual symmetry, through the bilaterally symmetric leaves. It was the sexual organs of plants called flowers coming into being from bilateral symmetry, through the bilaterally symmetric leaves. It was the sexual organs of plants called flowers coming into being through bilateral symmetry, that is, through the bilaterally symmetric leaves. Sexual symmetry thus appeared in flowers. Sexual symmetry thus emerged in the flowering plants. Sexual symmetry was thus fulfilled or realized in the plant world, through the bilaterally symmetric leaves. Sexual symmetry was thus fulfilled or realized in nature, in the plant way, through the bilaterally symmetric leaves.

Sexual symmetry is one of the most powerful fulfillments or realizations of symmetry in nature. Sexual symmetry is one of the most powerful expressions of symmetry in nature. Sexual symmetry is one of the most powerful indications of symmetry working or operating in nature. The power of sexual symmetry may be seen in its extraordinary endurance with animals. The power of sexual symmetry may be seen in its extraordinary endurance with plants. The power of sexual symmetry may be seen in its extraordinary force affecting the humans. The power of sexual symmetry may be seen in animals, in that, the competition for sex may lead to stronger or better species. The power of sexual symmetry may be seen in plants, in that, it may lead to the increase of

Symmetry II

genetic diversity in the plant world. the power of sexual symmetry may be seen in flowers, in that, it might be said, it is sexual symmetry that may be seen as ultimately behind the coming into being of flowers, in combination with bilateral symmetry, and as a result or consequence, the protective sepals grew, the graceful petals appeared, and the delicate stamens or complex carpels emerged, all from the bilaterally symmetric leaves.

That is, both sexual symmetry and bilateral symmetry may be seen as behind the coming into being of flowers. It was them that led the plants to develop into the flowering plants. It was them that led the leaves to develop into the flowers. It was them that led the leaves to develop into the protective sepals, the delicate stamens, the complex carpels, or the tender, soft, brightly colored and beautiful petals. It was beauty coming into being from sexual symmetry and bilateral symmetry. It was sexual reproduction coming into being from sexual symmetry and bilateral symmetry. It was the fusion of beauty and sex coming into being from the fusion of sexual symmetry and bilateral symmetry. It was the union of beauty and sex coming into being from the union of sexual symmetry and bilateral symmetry. It was the integration of beauty and sex coming into being from the integration of sexual symmetry and bilateral symmetry. It was beauty bloomed in sex. It was sex realized in beauty. It was beauty flourished in sex, through the fusion of sexual symmetry and bilateral symmetry. It was sex thrived in beauty, through the union of sexual symmetry and bilateral symmetry. It was beauty and sex coming into being, together, in plants, through the cooperation of sexual symmetry and bilateral symmetry. It was sex and beauty appearing in the world, hand in hand, in the plant way, through the working together of sexual symmetry and bilateral symmetry.

It was power. It was the power of sexual symmetry. It was the power of bilateral symmetry. It was the power of sexual symmetry combined with the power of bilateral symmetry. It was the power of sexual symmetry united with the power of bilateral symmetry. It was the power of sexual symmetry fused with the power of bilateral symmetry. It was the great powers of sexual symmetry and bilateral symmetry expressed in beauty. It was the great powers of sexual symmetry and bilateral symmetry manifested in sex. It was the great powers of sexual symmetry and bilateral symmetry demonstrated in flowers, in the flowering plants, or in the plant world. It was the great powers of sexual symmetry and bilateral symmetry fulfilled or realized in nature, in the plant way, in the plant sense, or in the plant manner.

It was power. It was the great power. It was potential. It was the great potential. It was capacity. It was the magnificent capacity. It was the symmetric power. It was the symmetric potential. It was the symmetric capacity. It was the great symmetric power. It was the great symmetric potential. It was the magnificent symmetric capacity. It was the great power of symmetry exhibited. It was the great potential of symmetry expressed. It was the magnificent capacity of symmetry demonstrated. It was the great power of symmetry exploded in the Cretaceous. It was the great potential of symmetry achieved in the Cretaceous. It was the magnificent capacity of symmetry expressed, manifested, or demonstrated in the plant way, in the plant world, in the flowering plants, in flowers, during the great age called, the Cretaceous.

Beauty thus came into being, in flowers, as the fusion of sexual symmetry and bilateral symmetry. Sex thus came into being, in plants, as the fusion of sexual symmetry and bilateral symmetry. Flowers thus came into being, in the world, as the fusion of bilateral symmetry and sexual symmetry.

When it comes to the appearance or development of flowering plants, it seems, the possible coevolution between flowering plants and animal or insect pollinators is often cited as one of the major causes. People usually like to take the appearance of flowering plants and the dramatic diversification of pollinating animals or insects as the typical example of coevolution exemplified in nature. This may not be completely true. Certainly, there is no doubt that, there might be a sense of coevolution going on between flowering plants and the pollinating animals or insects, during or after the first appearance of flowering plants. But, the problem is, or the question is, is it really the case that it was this so-called "coevolution" that had led to the rapid appearance or development of flowering plants?

Is it possible that this coevolution explanation might be just a shortcut? Is it possible that people have just seen the surface? Is it possible that people come to this explanation because it is handy and they cannot see deeper? Is it possible that this coevolution explanation might have bypassed or overlooked certain things profound, intrinsic, essential, or fundamental? What was truly behind the sudden appearance or dramatic development of flowering plants? What was truly behind the rapid diversification of pollinating animals or insects? Were they the same thing? Were they caused by the same thing? Were they all attributed to the same thing, the same phenomenon, the so-called "coevolution"?

The earliest seed-bearing plants might have appeared on earth in the late Devonian. Such early seed plants usually produced ovules, the female reproductive eggs of seed plants. At this stage, it seems, the seed plants had not yet developed to such an extent that they might bear cones or fruits. But, the fossil evidence appears to indicate that the process of pollination might have already begun among the seed plants. Runcaria, a middle Devonian plant, is found to have grown certain structures for wind pollination. Even though this plant may not be regarded fully as a seed plant, it nevertheless appeared to have engaged in some form of wind pollination. In other words, it is possible that seed plants coming into being after Runcaria might be able to develop to such an extent that they engaged in some forms of pollination of their own.

Insects might have appeared on earth as early as the Silurian period, as some developed insect fossils may have been discovered from the early Devonian Rhynie chert, a rich fossil deposit from about 400 million years ago. Certain features possessed by such insect fossils from this deposit may also suggest, it is possible that the insect wings might have started to develop early on from that point. Even if insects had first appeared in the early Devonian, that would constitute a very early time period for the insect development, especially for our discussion here about the insect pollination between insects and seed plants.

We are all familiar with insect pollination, happening between insects and seed plants. With the existence of insects in the early Devonian and the appearance of seed plants in the late Devonian, it may be imagined that, after the late Devonian, some forms of insect pollination might have gradually developed between the insects and seed plants. Such a case should be possible, given that, on the one hand, we see the possible pollination occurring in the middle Devonian; and on the other hand, we have all witnessed how widespread insect pollination had been among insects and seed plants during the long history of their developments. The Devonian ends about 360 million years ago. That means, after about 360 million years ago, it is possible that insect pollination might have occurred, in some way, in some sense, or in some manner, between some insects and some seed plants.

Gymnosperms, the plants with naked seeds, might have first appeared in the late Carboniferous, about 300 million years ago. It is found, some early gymnosperm species might have engaged in some forms of pollination, likely with some insects, during the Triassic period and the Jurassic period. The early scorpionflies might be one of such insects. As the early insects, the scorpionflies developed a kind of special proboscis-like mouth structure for feeding on the liquid produced by the plants. By drinking the liquid, they might have pollinated such early gymnosperms at the same time. The possible insect pollination associated with the early gymnosperms and scorpionflies may tell us that, the phenomenon called animal or insect pollination might have appeared long before the coming into being of the "coevolution" of insects and flowering plants.

The fossil record seems to tell us that, beetles and flies had been among the early insect pollinators in the long history of plants. Researches show that, beetles might have first appeared in the late Carboniferous, about 300 million years ago. The fossils of beetles have been found from the Permian period. After the Permian-Triassic extinction event, happening about 250 million years ago, it is found, many new beetle species appeared in the Triassic period. And the fossil record also indicates, beetles continued their developments well into the Jurassic. Flies might have first appeared in the Middle Triassic. Their developments might have been quick and fast, as by the Late Triassic they are found to have been well developed and diversified. Such rapid developments may also be observed in the Jurassic period.

What do all these discussions tell us? They tell us that, prior to the Cretaceous, that is, prior to the coming into being of flowering plants, animal or insect pollination had already been a phenomenon associated with seed plants. The early gymnosperms might have engaged in animal or insect pollination with the kind of early insects like scorpionflies. Beetles appeared in the late Carboniferous, and after their coming into being, they might have acted as the early insect pollinators. Flies appeared in the Triassic, and after their emergence, they too might have functioned, in some way, or to some extent, as the early insect pollinators. What does all this mean? It may mean that, in a word, if coevolution between animals or insects and seed plants had really functioned as the mechanism behind the appearance or coming into being of flowering plants, then, it is likely that, flowering plants would have appeared or come into being long before the Cretaceous.

As insects are found in the early Devonian and seed plants appeared in the late Devonian, insect pollination might thus be possible after the late Devonian. This means, if the "coevolution" was really behind the appearance of flowering plants, then it should be possible that flowering plants might have appeared sometime after the late Devonian. As we know, that is not the case, and flowering plants only appeared in the Cretaceous, after more than 200 million years. Gymnosperms appeared in the late Carboniferous, and certainly insects should have existed during such a time. We have seen, the early gymnosperms indeed might have engaged in insect pollination with some early insects, such as the scorpionflies, long before the Cretaceous. Did flowering plants appear, as a result of the "coevolution" of insects and seed plants, sometime after the late Carboniferous and before the Cretaceous? No. As we know, that was not really the case.

Ever since their first appearance in the late Carboniferous, the fossil record seems to have shown, beetles had maintained a relatively robust development. They are found in the Permian. And after the Permian-Triassic mass extinction, it seems, they regained their development in the Triassic and many new species appeared for the first time during such a period. The Jurassic, the period immediately preceding the Cretaceous, proved to be a remarkable time of diversification and development for beetles, as many new species appeared and the old groups increased and developed significantly. Just like the beetles, it seems, ever since their appearance in the middle Triassic, flies had also undergone a process of relatively robust development either during the Triassic or in the Jurassic. They can be found to have developed rapidly during the late Triassic, and they can be observed to have developed in a robust manner in the early Jurassic.

The relatively rapid developments of insects like beetles or flies during the Triassic and the Jurassic may in a sense raise some questions about the coevolution explanation. Were they rapid developments for beetles, during the Triassic, or during the Jurassic? Were they rapid developments for flies, during the Triassic, or during the Jurassic? Were they the early insect pollinators, the beetles or flies? If so, why is it not the case that flowering plants appeared during such periods? It seems, judged from the fossil record, both beetles and flies might have diversified or developed dramatically during the Triassic or Jurassic. Such rapid developments or diversifications, happening among the early insect pollinators like beetles or flies, might indicate, in a sense, or to some extent, the possible occurrence of some coevolutionary processes, if indeed the coevolution explanation really works. In other words, when we observe the kind of rapid developments or diversifications of beetles and flies in the Triassic or Jurassic, according to the coevolution explanation, we should be looking for the signs of possible coevolution happening between such early insect pollinators and seed plants. That is, if such early insect pollinators had undergone some processes of rapid development or diversification, it was likely that the seed plants might also have undergone some similar processes. That is, in other words, it was hopeful that, flowering plants might appear, or come into being, at the same time.

Certainly, flowering plants did not appear or come into being in the Triassic or Jurassic. They only emerged in the Cretaceous. From the first appearance of seed plants in the late Devonian, it seems, according to the coevolution explanation, there should be many opportunities for flowering plants to appear, prior to the Cretaceous. But, they did not. They did not appear in the late Devonian. They did not appear in the late Carboniferous, when gymnosperms appeared and possible insect pollination occurred. They did not appear, as a result of the possible insect pollination between the early gymnosperms and insects like scorpionflies. They did not appear in the Permian, when both gymnosperms and insects developed well. They did not appear in the Triassic, when the early insect pollinators like beetles or flies showed rapid developments. They did not appear in the Jurassic, even though some remarkable insect diversifications may be observed.

Was it coevolution? Or, was it, simply, evolution? If it were coevolution, it seems, flowering plants would have appeared, long, long ago, before the Cretaceous. If it were evolution, it seems, flowering plants might have really undergone some processes of coevolution, as the rapid developments or diversifications of the early animal or insect pollinators might have prepared, in a sense, or to a certain extent, the conditions for the happening of such processes. But, as we know, such things might not have happened. What happened is that, flowering plants occurred, and only occurred, in the Cretaceous. Why, should flowering plants occur in the Cretaceous? Why, should flowering plants appear in the Cretaceous? To see into the happening of flowering plants in the Cretaceous, we may need to see beyond the Cretaceous. To look into the appearance of flowering plants in the Cretaceous, we may need to look beyond the mere phenomenon of animal or insect pollination.

We cannot focus only on the Cretaceous. We have to see all the development of seed plants, from the late Devonian, to the late Carboniferous, to the Permian, to the Triassic, to the Jurassic. We cannot focus only on the animal or insect pollination occurring in the Cretaceous. We have to see the animal or insect pollination through all the periods, from the late Devonian, to the late Carboniferous, to the Permian, to the Triassic, to the Jurassic. Seed plants had an extremely long developmental history prior to the appearance of flowering plants, from the late Devonian, about 360 million years ago, to the early Cretaceous, about 140 million years ago. It was more than 200 million years. It was a long time. it was a significant time period, even in geological terms. What does this mean? It means that it was significant. It means that something significant was happening. It means that the appearance of flowering plants was significant, and it was not simple. If it were simple, it would not have taken so long for such a thing to happen. It was not simple. It was significant. It was not a simple event. It was a significant event. The mere animal or insect pollination may not explain its happening. The mere animal or insect pollination may not be able to explain its occurrence. Pollination as a mechanism may not possess the necessary power. Pollination as a mechanism may not possess the necessary potential. Pollination as a mechanism may not possess the necessary capacity. It was a great power underpinning the emergence of flowering plants. It was a significant potential underlying the coming into being of flowering plants. It was a magnificent capacity behind the appearance of flowering plants. It might not be coevolution. It might not be evolution. It might not be the animal or insect pollination. It might not be pollination, at all.

The long period of time before the Cretaceous was significant for the appearance of flowering plants, and for the explanation of the appearance of flowering plants. We have seen, plant pollination possibly occurred even before the appearance of seed plants, as certain features of the middle Devonian plant Runcaria may indicate. And, we have seen, insects might have first appeared in the early Devonian. In other words, it might be said, insect pollination might have been possible between the early insects and seed plants after the first appearance of seed plants in the late Devonian. What does this mean? It means that, the history of insect pollination with seed plants might have been just as long as the history of seed plants. How long was it? It was more than 200 million years, before the Cretaceous, or, prior to the appearance of flowering plants. If seed plants had existed for such a long time, why had flowering plants not appeared earlier? If coevolution could lead to the appearance of flowering plants, if plant pollination with insects had been possibly happening for so long, if rapid insect developments or diversifications have been observed during the long period of time when both insects and seed plants existed on this planet, from the late Devonian to the early Cretaceous, why had flowering plants not appeared earlier?

Why did it take so long, more than 200 million years, for seed plants to develop into flowering plants? Why did it take so long for "coevolution" to work? Why did it take so long for the animal or insect pollination to lead to the appearance of flowering plants? Why did it take so long for pollination to operate so that flowering plants might come to this world? Why, after all, did flowering plants have to wait for so long to appear, to emerge, or to come into being on earth? Many things had happened during such a long period of time. And we have seen, during such a long period of time, rapid developments or diversifications have been observed among the early animal or insect pollinators. If animal or insect pollination could lead to the coevolution of early pollinators and seed plants, it seems, prior to the Cretaceous, such "coevolution" should have occurred for a number of times. But, have we seen such "coevolutions," in the long period of time prior to the Cretaceous? Where were such "coevolutions"? Where were they? Why cannot we see them? Why cannot we find them? In other words, if animal or insect pollination could lead to the "coevolution" of early pollinators and seed plants, it seems, it might be said, prior to the Cretaceous, flowering plants would have appeared for a number of times, during the long history of seed plants, and during the long history of plant pollination with insects.

The appearance of flowering plants in the Cretaceous might not have been the result of some "coevolution," or "coevolutions." It might not have been the result of some interactions between seed plants and animal or insect pollinators. It might not have been the result of some kind of mutualistic existence happening between seed plants and animal or insect pollinators. Such coevolutions might not possess the power to give rise to flowering plants. Such interactions might not

Symmetry II

possess the potential to sustain the coming into being of flowering plants. Such kind of mutualistic existence might not possess the capacity to support the appearance of flowering plants. The appearance of flowering plants in the Cretaceous may be seen as the result of the symmetric explosion occurring in the Cretaceous. It may be seen as the movement of symmetry in plants in the Cretaceous. It may be seen as the movement of bilateral symmetry in plants in the Cretaceous. It may be seen as the movement of sexual symmetry in plants in the Cretaceous. It may be seen as the fusion of bilateral symmetry and sexual symmetry in plants in the Cretaceous. It may be seen as the fulfillment of bilateral symmetry in plants, in a floral fashion, in the Cretaceous. It may be seen as the fulfillment of sexual symmetry in plants, in a floral sense, in the Cretaceous. It may be seen as the realization of symmetry in plants, in a floral way, in the Cretaceous.

In a sense, it might be said, the possible coevolutions, interactions, or mutualisms occurring between seed plants and animal or insect pollinators may only be regarded as the external forces, processes, or mechanisms, when it comes to the happening of flowering plants. That is, in other words, when we look into the appearance of flowering plants, we may have to look into the kind of things that may not be just external. That is, we may have to look into the kind of things that may be innate, intrinsic, or inherent. The possible plant-pollinator coevolutions might be so external that they might not have the innate power to support the appearance of flowering plants. The possible plant-pollinator interactions might be so external that they might not have the intrinsic mechanisms to lead seed plants to develop into flowering plants. The possible plant-pollinator mutualisms might be so external that they might not possess the necessary inherent forces to bring the phenomenon of flowering into this world. Flowering, as a magnificent, outstanding and spectacular phenomenon in the plant world, in nature, may not be regarded, in a sense, as something merely coming from the external or outward things. That is, flowering, as a magnificent phenomenon of nature, may be regarded as something coming into being from the internal processes or mechanisms of things. That is, flowering, as an outstanding and spectacular phenomenon of the plant world, may be regarded as something coming into being as a result of the internal processes or mechanisms of plants. That is, more than anything else, flowering might be a phenomenon appearing, emerging, or coming into being from within the seed plants. It might be a realization of the innate being of plants, in a floral way. It might be a fulfillment of the intrinsic existence of plants, in a floral sense. It might be an expression, manifestation, or demonstration of the inherent plant lives, in a floral manner. The innate being of plants might be what was behind the appearance of flowering plants. The intrinsic existence of plants might be what was underlying the emergence of flowering plants. The inherent plant lives might be what constituted the real or true foundation of the coming into being of flowering plants, in the Cretaceous.

The appearance of flowering in plants might have revealed, in a sense, the real or true existence of plants, that is, the fundamental or essential existence of plants, that is, the innate, intrinsic or inherent being of plants. For flowering to happen, for it to appear, for it to come into being in the world, something fundamental, something essential, or something primordial might be needed. That is, it might be said, something innate, something intrinsic, or something inherent might have to be there in the first place. The possible coevolutions might not be that innate. The possible interactions might not be that intrinsic. The possible mutualisms might not be that inherent. That is, the possible coevolutions, interactions or mutualisms might not carry with them the innate power, the intrinsic potential, or the inherent capacity indispensable or necessary for the phenomenon of flowering to appear in the Cretaceous.

Such innate power might have determined the happening of flowering. Such intrinsic potential might have established the emergence of flowering. Such inherent capacity might have sustained the coming into being of flowering. It is in such a sense that, it might be said, flowering, as a phenomenon, might have to do, first of all, with the innate, intrinsic, or inherent being of plants. And it is in such a sense that, it might be said, flowering, as a phenomenon, might not have resulted from the external plant activities, such as, some coevolutions, some interactions, or some mutualisms. To see flowering is to see the innate being of flowering plants. To see flowering is to see the intrinsic existence of flowering plants. To see flowering is to see the inherent lives of flowering plants in the world. That is, to look at flowering is to look at the innate being of plants. That is, to look at flowering is to look at the intrinsic existence of plants. That is, to look into flowering is to look into the inherent lives of plants on earth.

Symmetry II

The innate, intrinsic or inherent nature of flowering may also be seen, in a sense, in the extraordinary endurance of such a phenomenon in the plant world, in nature. Ever since their appearance in the early Cretaceous, about 130 million years ago, flowering plants have thrived, prospered and flourished well to this day. They are the dominant forms in the plant world. And it seems, their thriving or prosperous existence on this planet will not end soon. Who has given them such a power? Who has given them such a potential? Who has given them such an extraordinary capacity? Who has sustained their development, in such a long period of time? Who has supported their existence, during the 130 million years? Who has maintained their varied, colored, beautiful and magnificent plant lives, ever since the early Cretaceous?

Was it some coevolutions? Was it some interactions? Was it some mutualisms? It seems, all these things might not be up to such a task, such an undertaking, or such a gigantic endeavor. They might have participated, in some sense, in some way, in some manner, or to some extent, in the development of flowering plants, ever since the early Cretaceous, but they may not be seen as carrying with them the kind of power, potential or capacity to make such a development of flowering plants possible. They might have contributed, in some sense, in some way, in some manner, or to some extent, to the existence of flowering plants, ever since the early Cretaceous, but they may not be regarded as possessing the necessary power, potential or capacity to sustain, support or maintain such a kind of existence for flowering plants.

If flowering plants were the result of some coevolutions, interactions or mutualisms between seed plants and animal or insect pollinators, it might be said, it was likely that, they would not have lasted to this day, given that, in a sense, plants, animals or insects came and went, it seems, all the time. that is, it was likely that, all such coevolutions, interactions or mutualisms might not have the kind of lasting force or enduring effect to secure, to bind, or to hold flowering in place as a plant phenomenon all the time ever since the early Cretaceous. In other words, the phenomenon of flowering might not have been the result or consequence of some coevolutions, some interactions, or some mutualisms, since, otherwise, it seems, such a phenomenon might not have survived to this day. That is, if some coevolutions, interactions or mutualisms were ultimately behind the phenomenon of flowering, it might be said, it was likely that, flowering might have disappeared long ago, given the extraordinarily long period of time after its appearance. The kind of things such as coevolutions, interactions or mutualisms may be regarded as only working or operating in a limited sense in that they might not be able to sustain, support, or maintain the phenomenon of flowering all the way from its appearance to this day. They might have participated in the development or existence of flowering plants, but they might not have played the major role in the phenomenon of flowering. They might have contributed to the development or existence of flowering plants, but they might not have worked or operated in such a way, in such a manner, or in such a fashion that flowering as a plant phenomenon would thus come into being and endure to this day. For flowering plants to develop all the way to this day, it seems, something more was needed. For flowering plants to exist all the time to this day, it seems, something deeper was required. For flowering as a phenomenon to endure all the time in the plant world, in nature, to this day, it seems, something more profound was necessary. That is, something more powerful was needed, something more enduring was required, and something more magnificent was necessary.

    Only symmetry might have such power. Only symmetry might have such potential. Only symmetry might have such capacity. Only symmetry might have such innate power. Only symmetry might have such intrinsic potential. Only symmetry might have such inherent capacity. Only symmetry might be able to give rise to flowering plants. Only symmetry might be able to support the coming into being of flowering plants. Only symmetry might be able to sustain the appearance of flowering plants. Only symmetry might be able to support the development of flowering plants. Only symmetry might be able to sustain the development of flowering plants. Only symmetry might be able to maintain the development of flowering plants. Only symmetry might be able to sustain the existence of flowering plants. Only symmetry might be able to support the existence of flowering plants. Only symmetry might be able to maintain the existence of flowering plants. Only symmetry might have the innate power to sustain the development or existence of flowering plants after their appearance. Only symmetry might have the intrinsic potential to support the development or existence of flowering plants ever since the early Cretaceous. Only symmetry might have the inherent capacity to maintain the development or existence of flowering plants to this day.

Symmetry II

Symmetry is lasting. Symmetry is enduring. Symmetry is powerful. Symmetry is magnificent. It was symmetry. It was the work of symmetry. It was the operation of symmetry. It was the movement of symmetry. It was the development of symmetry. It was bilateral symmetry. It was sexual symmetry. It was the development of bilateral symmetry. It was the development of sexual symmetry. It was the fusion of bilateral symmetry and sexual symmetry. It was the fusion of the development of bilateral symmetry and the development of sexual symmetry. It was the fulfillment of bilateral symmetry. It was the fulfillment of sexual symmetry. It was the fusion of the fulfillments of bilateral symmetry and sexual symmetry. It was the fusion of bilateral symmetry and sexual symmetry in flowers. It was the fusion of the developments of bilateral symmetry and sexual symmetry in flowering plants. It was the realization of bilateral symmetry and sexual symmetry, together, in the plant world.

Symmetry was behind the appearance of plants. Symmetry was behind the appearance of flowers. Symmetry was behind the appearance of flowering plants. Symmetry was behind the appearance of the plant world. It was symmetry that had given rise to flowers. It was symmetry that had given rise to plants. It was symmetry that had given rise to flowering plants. It was the symmetric explosion. It was the symmetric explosion in the Cretaceous. It was the bilateral symmetric explosion. It was the sexual symmetric explosion. It was the bilateral symmetric explosion in the Cretaceous. It was the sexual symmetric explosion in the Cretaceous. It was the explosion of bilateral symmetry and sexual symmetry, together, in the Cretaceous. It was the symmetric explosion fulfilled or realized in both bilateral and sexual ways. It was the symmetric explosion fulfilled or realized in both bilateral and sexual senses. It was the symmetric explosion fulfilled or realized in flowers, in flowering plants, in the plant world, in nature, in the Cretaceous. It is in such a sense that, it might be said, when people talk about the appearance of flowering plants as a result or consequence of some coevolutions, interactions or mutualisms between plants and animals or insects, it may be the case that they may have simply taken the effect as the cause and generalize it as the mechanism or process behind the appearance or coming into being of flowering plants. That is, it may be the case that people may have taken a peripheral phenomenon as the main thing and generalize it as something applying to all. That is, in other words, it may be the case that people may have just taken the easier road and failed to look into the deeper things underneath the surface.

Does this mean that the kind of things such as coevolution or mutualism should be deemed as meaningless or useless? No. They are not useless. They are meaningful. And they are important in our understanding of the evolutionary development of things, that is, in this case, of plants, of flowering plants, of flowers, or of some animal or insect pollinators. The animal or insect pollinators of flowering plants can be bees, wasps, flies, moths, beetles, ants, birds, or bats. Among these animal or insect pollinators, bees may be regarded as the most prominent ones. Bees belong to an insect order that also includes wasps, ants, and sawflies. It is generally believed that, like ants, bees might have developed from wasps. And as such, both bees and ants may be regarded as some special kinds of wasps that had developed their own features or characteristics. Now people usually think that bees might have first appeared in the early Cretaceous, probably as a result of the coevolution with flowering plants.

The beginning of the insect order that includes wasps, bees, ants and sawflies might lie in the early or middle Triassic, with some members of sawflies might have emerged first. Some people have suggested, wasps might have appeared in the middle Triassic, about 240 million years ago. If that is the case, then, given that bees might have developed from wasps, the notion of coevolution of bees and flowering plants might be called into question. If wasps had appeared so early, in the Triassic, why had bees not come into being, before the Cretaceous? It is found that wasps could be pollinators with gymnosperms. If the coevolution between pollinators and plants was true, then it is likely that bees might appear much earlier than the Cretaceous. Some processes of pollination between wasps and gymnosperms might have been going on from the middle Triassic to the beginning of the Cretaceous. That was a long period of time, lasting about 100 million years. That period of time should be enough, in a sense, for the pollination between wasps and gymnosperms to lead to the appearance of both bees and flowering plants, according to the theory of coevolution. But it seems, neither bees nor flowering plants appeared during such a period of time.

It is believed that ants might have first appeared in the middle Cretaceous, roughly about the time when bees emerged. Various studies seem to indicate that ants are closely related to wasps and bees,

Symmetry II

and it might be the case that both ants and bees might have developed from their wasp or wasp-like ancestors, during the Cretaceous. It seems, just like bees, ants appeared to have also undergone a process of rapid development or diversification after the appearance of flowering plants. This may be seen as an interesting phenomenon. And this phenomenon may tell something about the ants, bees, or in a sense, about the appearance or coming into being of flowering plants. As we have said, ants and bees are closely related insects. Then, one may ask, were they also closely related in their appearances in the Cretaceous, as it seems, they all radiated or diversified after the appearance of flowering plants? How did ants emerge, from their wasp-like ancestors, in the Cretaceous? How did bees emerge, from their wasp ancestors, in the Cretaceous? How did ants radiate or diversify, after the appearance of flowering plants? How did bees radiate or diversify, after the appearance of flowering plants? Had they radiated or diversified in the same way, in the same sense, or in the same manner? Had they radiated or diversified by following the same processes or through the same mechanisms? What do such radiations say about the ants? What do such diversifications say about the bees? What do such radiations or diversifications say about the appearance or coming into being of flowering plants?

It seems, ants may also act in some cases as the pollinators. That is, they may engage in insect pollination with some flowering plants. But, in most cases, it seems, they may not be seen as the efficient or effective pollinators of flowers. That is to say, in a general sense, unlike bees, ants may not be regarded as the major pollinators of flowering plants. It is in such a sense that, it might be said, ants might not have played a prominent role in the coming into being or development of flowering plants. And, in the same sense, it might be said, the possible ant pollination with some flowering plants might not have played a decisive or major role in the coming into being or development of ants. In other words, pollination might not have played a prominent role in the coming into being or development of either ants or flowering plants. Ants are the insects closely related to bees. They emerged at about the same time, during the Cretaceous. They all radiated or diversified after the appearance of flowering plants. They had much in common, it seems, with regard to the happening of flowering plants. But, if ant pollination did not have much to do with the coming into being or development of either ants or flowering plants, in a general sense, why should bee pollination be so closely associated with the appearance or development of either bees or flowering plants? Why? Why should bee pollination be treated as so crucial, while ant pollination might only have minimal effects, in a general sense? Why should bee pollination be taken as the process or mechanism behind the appearance or development of both bees and flowering plants? What was the reason? What was the cause? What was the intrinsic reason? What was the intrinsic cause? What was the intrinsic reason that bees were fundamentally different from ants? What was the intrinsic cause that made the bee pollination, but not the ant pollination, to give rise to the appearance or development of both insect pollinators and flowering plants?

If the appearance or development of ants was not closely related to the acts of pollination, how should the appearance or development of bees be so fundamentally linked with pollination? If the appearance or development of flowering plants was not closely associated with ant pollination, in a general sense, how should they be linked, in a decisive way, to bee pollination? If ant pollination had not played a decisive role in the coming into being or development of flowering plants, bee pollination might be expected as having functioned in a similar way, more or less, though it may not be ruled out that it might contribute, in some sense, or to some extent, to the coming into being or development of flowering plants. That is to say, in a word, to assign such fundamentally different roles to ants and bees seems to contradict, in a sense, the fact that they are the insects intimately and closely related.

A sense of disconnection between insect pollination and the appearance of flowering plants may be seen in a fossil possibly related to an early fig wasp. Fig trees have enjoyed a unique pollination relationship with fig wasps, and such a kind of relationship has led people to believe that fig wasps and fig trees have coevolved in a rather intimate manner ever since their appearance. But, it seems, this fossil may cast some doubt on such an idea, as fig trees might have only appeared tens of millions of years after the appearance of this possible early fig wasp. If fig trees and fig wasps had coevolved intimately, why should this fig wasp appear so early and fig trees come on the scene so late? It is certainly possible that this early fig wasp might have acted as a pollinator with some fig-like plants, but we still see the possibility that the appearance of fig trees might not have been so closely associated with the existence of fig wasps. That is to say, the presence of fig wasps might not necessarily mean the existence of fig trees, and the plant-pollinator mutualism between fig trees and fig wasps might not have been so fundamental or essential to either fig trees or fig wasps, as we might have believed.

The disconnection between pollination and the appearance of flowering plants may also be seen in a possibility that bees might have appeared before the Cretaceous. Such a possibility may be revealed by some trace fossils discovered, such as bee nests. Some bee nests may be found from the late Triassic, together with some wasp cocoons. Similarity can be observed between such early bee nests and the constructions of some modern bee species. And, it appears, pollen may be contained in such bee nests, implying that such early bees might have acted as the early pollinators of plants. If these nests are confirmed to be the ones left by the real bees living in the Triassic, then the theory of coevolution of bees and flowering plants may, in a sense, fall apart. If bees lived in the Triassic and acted as the pollinators, why had flowering plants not appeared during that time? Was the appearance of flowers not the result of the coevolution of bees and flowering plants? Was the development of flowering plants not a part of the mutualistic existence of bees and flowering plants? Were flowering plants not brought about by bees? Were bees not brought about by flowering plants? Who brought bees into being? Who gave rise to bees? Who brought flowering plants into being? Who gave rise to flowering plants? Who caused flowers to appear, to emerge, to come into being, only in the Cretaceous?

It seems, things did not develop in the kind of ways we imagined. It was not necessary that bees had to depend on flowering plants. It was not necessary that flowering plants had to depend on bees. The appearance or development of bees might not be tied to flowering plants. The appearance or development of flowering plants might not have to be linked with the appearance or development of bees. Pollination might have been, after all, not that important or crucial, either to bees or flowering plants. The reason for the appearance or development of bees might lie somewhere else. The cause for the appearance or development of flowering plants might be something other than the insect pollination. In other words, it might be the case that, we might have mistaken the results or consequences as the cause, in a sense, when we state that bees and flowering plants coevolved.

Avolution and Man

Then, how should we understand the development of bees or flowering plants in the Cretaceous, as it seems, both of them appeared to have radiated or diversified tremendously during such a period? It may have to do, in a sense, with our understanding of the appearance of things and the development of things. The appearance of things may be vastly different, in a sense, from the development of things. The appearance of things is the beginning of things. It is coming into being. It is initiation. It is creation. It is foundation. It is establishment. The development of things, on the other hand, may be blessed by the fact that certain things may have already been established, given that things have appeared, emerged, or come into being in the first place. That is to say, there might be a big difference between the appearance of things and the development of things, in that, certain things may have to be established in the appearance of things and such established things may work to support, maintain, sustain, or condition the development of things.

The appearance of bees might be one thing. The development of bees might be another thing. The appearance of flowering plants might be one thing. The development of flowering plants might be another thing. They might be very different from each other. The appearance of bees might be very different from the development of bees, either in the mechanisms, in the processes, or in the kind of things underlying them. The appearance of flowering plants might be very different from the development of flowering plants, again, in the mechanisms, in the processes, or in the kind of things underpinning them. That is, to understand the appearance or development of bees, we may have to look into different things. In the same sense, to understand the appearance or development of flowering plants, we may have to search into the kind of things that may not be necessarily of the same nature.

The appearance of bees might have been the result of a combined developmental process of some wasps, both avolutionary and evolutionary, in which the avolutionary movement might be seen as having played the major role, in that, it provided the necessary power, potential or capacity for such wasps to develop into the kind of insects that we eventually call bees. In the process of the appearance of bees, apart from the major role played by the avolutionary development, the evolutionary development might have also operated in a sense that, the possible insect pollination between the wasp ancestors and plants, or flowering plants, might have helped to lead such wasps to develop the kind of features or characteristics seen in bees. That is, while the avolutionary development might have laid the foundation for the appearance of bees, the evolutionary development, such as that associated with pollination, might have contributed to such a process of appearance, such as, by triggering or activating the avolutionary development to fulfill or realize some evolutionary aims or purposes. In other words, the process of the appearance of bees may be seen as a process of co-operation of the avolutionary development and evolutionary development. As the appearance of bees was the coming into being of bees, the avolutionary development might have played the more prominent role. It was with this co-operation, or fusion, of the avolutionary development and evolutionary development that, it might be said, bees came into being.

The development of bees might be closely related to the appearance or development of flowering plants. This may be, in a sense, different from the appearance of bees, as the evolutionary development might have played a more prominent role. The Cretaceous saw the dramatic radiation or diversification of both bees and flowering plants. Such radiations or diversifications may be seen as the developments of both bees and flowering plants after their appearances. Thus, the processes or mechanisms involved might have been somewhat different.

Bees are usually considered as the most efficient or effective pollinators of flowers. They appeared to have developed some specific traits for pollinating the flowering plants. They came from wasps, but their bodies appeared to have undergone some specific transformations to enhance their ability for pollination. Their behaviors might have also changed in certain ways for such a purpose. How did bees become the most efficient or effective pollinators? How did bees succeed in transforming their body structures? How did bees finally attain their specific bee features? That is, how did bees become bees, in the end? The appearance of bees might not mean necessarily the development of bees. The development of bees might have to do, in a sense, with the kind of things other than what had given rise to the appearance of bees. In this case, given what happened in the Cretaceous, it might be said, the development of bees might have to do, in a remarkable sense, with the appearance of flowering plants.

The appearance of flowering plants might have proved a crucial moment for the development of bees. With their appearance, flowering plants provided bees with unprecedented food sources or rewards. Prior to the appearance of flowering plants, though bees might have been equipped with their bee-like traits aimed for pollination, they might not be able to employ them in a large scale. Now with the appearance of flowering plants, all things seemed to be possible. Flowers, full of nectar and pollen, were sweet and tasty. The food sources were rich and delicious. The rewards were unprecedented. Bees, as the pollinators, could now enjoy a life unthinkable before. They could obtain high-quality nutrients easily. They could spread pollen readily with their bee features. They could pollinate flowers in some vast or massive scales. Bees began to thrive. And at the same time, it seems, flowering plants began to flourish, as well.

Bees might thus develop. Bees might thus be able to develop. The appearance of flowering plants might thus enable bees to fully realize their bee potentials. That may be why bees came into being. That may be why bees developed. That may be why bees became bees as we know them today. The appearance of flowering plants made it possible that bees could develop as the bees, to fulfill themselves, to realize themselves, to develop into the kind of efficient or effective insect pollinators of flowers. It was a process of evolution. It was an evolutionary process in the sense that, with their emergence, bees developed, or rather, achieved or fulfilled their bee traits in a coevolutionary developmental process with flowering plants.

While bees thrived and developed into the kind of specialized insect pollinators, we have seen, flowering plants might have flourished at about the same time. The development of insect pollinators made it possible for flowering plants to spread their pollen more widely and quickly. Thus, with the development of insect pollinators, flowering plants developed as well. It was a coevolutionary process. The more insect pollinators developed, it seems, the more flowering plants might develop. The more flowering plants developed, it seems, the more insect pollinators might develop. Thus, the radiation of insect pollinators might lead to the radiation of flowering plants. And in the same sense, the radiation of flowering plants might lead to the radiation of insect pollinators. This may be what we see in the Cretaceous. The development, radiation or diversification of insect pollinators like bees might have contributed greatly to the development, radiation or diversification of flowering plants. And the development, radiation or diversification of flowering plants, in the same sense, might have

Symmetry II

contributed greatly to the development, radiation or diversification of insect pollinators, such as bees.

The appearances of bees and flowering plants might not have shared the same source. Nevertheless, their developments might have converged. The appearances of flowering plants and bees might not have shared the same cause, but it seems, they all radiated or diversified in the Cretaceous. A developmental process, both avolutionary and evolutionary, might have given rise to bees, and the insect pollinators called bees might have found the most favorable evolutionary conditions in the Cretaceous, in flowering plants, and thus they developed, radiated, and diversified. A developmental process, both avolutionary and evolutionary, might have brought flowering plants into this world, and it seems, they might have benefited greatly from the presence or existence of insect pollinators like bees. While the appearances of both bees and flowering plants may be regarded, in a sense, as mainly avolutionary, their developments in the Cretaceous may be seen as evolutionary, though the avolutionary developments might still constitute the foundation. They were evolutionary in the sense that, both bees and flowering plants seemed to have benefited from their mutualistic existence and as a result they thrived and flourished. Such a sense of coevolution may be seen as what characterizes the developments of bees and flowering plants in the Cretaceous. Certainly, when we talk about coevolution in the Cretaceous, we should not forget that, the appearances of both bees and flowering plants might not be completely evolutionary, or even coevolutionary, and that, throughout all the processes, the avolutionary developments might have functioned, always, as the foundation.

When we say here that the appearance of flowering plants might have to do with a developmental process, both avolutionary and evolutionary, it means that, in a sense, the insect pollination, such as by bees, might have played a role in the coming into being or emergence of flowering plants in the Cretaceous. Though such an appearance may be regarded, mainly, as an avolutionary movement or development in plants, it may not be ruled out that some evolutionary processes such as insect pollination might have also been involved. That is to say, the insect pollination, such as by bees, might have operated in plants, during the Cretaceous, in such a way, in such a sense, or to such an extent that the avolutionary movement or development might thus start to give rise to flowers in plants, in a way or in a manner to fulfill or satisfy some evolutionary purposes. Such evolutionary purposes might be achieved or satisfied in plants, in the form of flowers, through a process of coming together or co-operation of the avolutionary movement and evolutionary development. That is, flowers appeared in the Cretaceous, in an evolutionary sense, so that flowering plants might benefit from insect pollination, such as by bees, develop better, and thrive and prosper. The evolutionary development might have worked to set the avolutionary development in motion, and the avolutionary development might have worked to realize or fulfill such evolutionary purposes.

But, when we talk about insect pollination in such a sense, with regard to the appearance of flowering plants, we have to be very careful, in that, as we have seen, animal or insect pollination was not a fresh thing by that time. Ever since the coming into being of insects and the appearance of seed plants, it seems, some forms or some kinds of insect pollination might have happened between insects and seed plants. In other words, insect pollination as a phenomenon happening between insects and seed plants might have had a long history prior to the Cretaceous. If pollination by the insects like bees could lead to the appearance of flowering plants, why had flowering plants not appeared before the Cretaceous, as it seems, insect pollination might have happened long before the Cretaceous? If pollination by bees could lead to the appearance of flowering plants in the Cretaceous, then it should be possible that pollination by other kinds of insects, such as beetles, flies, or wasps, might lead to the coming into being or emergence of flowering plants, well before the Cretaceous. We have discussed the long history of insect pollination between seed plants and the kind of insects like beetles or flies, prior to the Cretaceous. And we know, some wasps might have acted as the early pollinators. So, why had flowering plants not appeared before the Cretaceous? Why did they have to appear in the Cretaceous? Was it attributed to the pollination by bees? Should it be attributed to the pollination by bees? Or, was there something else that might have constituted the root? Was there something else that might have constituted the real cause?

Even if pollination by the insects like bees played a role in the appearance of flowering plants in the Cretaceous, such a process might not be regarded wholly as an evolutionary one, as we have discussed above. That is, such a process might have involved developments both avolutionary and evolutionary. That is, such a process might be one in

Symmetry II

which the avolutionary fulfilled itself by realizing the evolutionary and the evolutionary realized itself, in a sense, by uniting with the avolutionary.

When people see that, bees are so specially structured or enhanced for the purpose of pollination, they usually come to believe that the appearance of such specialized flower pollinators might be behind the dramatic development of flowering plants. In other words, they believe, the appearance of the kind of insects like bees might have been the driving force behind the radiation or diversification of flowering plants during the Cretaceous. This may only reveal part of the picture. The appearance of the insects like bees might have indeed contributed to the dramatic development of flowering plants during such a period, but such insect appearance might not have functioned as the only force, or as the fundamental driving force, behind the radiation or diversification of flowering plants. The appearance or development of the insect pollinators like bees might have constituted an evolutionary development for the development of flowering plants. For such an evolutionary development to work or operate for the development of flowering plants, it had to be supported, sustained, guided or conditioned by the avolutionary developments happening either in the insect pollinators like bees or in flowering plants. That is, it might be the case that, after the appearance of flowering plants, the appearance or development of the insect pollinators like bees might have driven, in an evolutionary sense, the development of flowering plants, based on the avolutionary developments of both insect pollinators like bees and flowering plants. thus, it might be said, the appearance or development of the insect pollinators like bees may be regarded as behind the dramatic development of flowering plants in the Cretaceous, but only in an evolutionary sense, and that, it was the avolutionary developments that may be seen as the ultimate fundamental driving force behind the developments of flowering plants and the insect pollinators like bees.

Out of a developmental process, both avolutionary and evolutionary, flowering plants might have come into being. After the appearance of flowering plants, the coevolutionary developments of flowering plants and the insect pollinators like bees were possible only in the sense that the avolutionary existences provided the power, potential or capacity for both flowering plants and the insect pollinators like bees to develop as they did. Without such avolutionary power, without such avolutionary potential, without such avolutionary capacity, it might be said, both flowering plants and the insect pollinators like bees might not be able to respond to natural selection, to adapt, to face the evolutionary pressure, and to develop accordingly, or to thrive and flourish, that is, in an evolutionary sense. That is, it might be said, it was the avolutionary existences that might have constituted the source or origin of the developments of both flowering plants and the insect pollinators like bees, and it was the avolutionary developments that might have constituted the real driving force behind the radiations or diversifications of flowering plants and the insect pollinators like bees in the Cretaceous.

The appearance and development of flowering plants in the Cretaceous was a significant and far-reaching event and may stand as one of the most complex, subtle, deep and profound developments in the long history of life on earth. To understand such a phenomenon, we may have to look beyond the mere animal or insect pollination, evolution, or coevolution. To understand such a phenomenon, we may have to search into the kind of things not just evolutionary, but avolutionary. That is, such a phenomenon may better be regarded as a process or development involving both avolution and evolution. That is, it may better be regarded, in a sense, as a fusion or union of avolution and evolution. It was through both avolution and evolution that flowering plants might have appeared. And it was through both avolution and evolution that flowering plants might have developed. It was avolution in evolution. It was evolution in avolution. It was avolution through evolution. It was evolution through avolution. It was avolution induced, initiated, or helped by evolution. It was evolution supported, sustained, guided, or conditioned by avolution. That is, when it comes to the appearance or development of flowering plants in the Cretaceous, it might be said, the evolutionary development may be seen as having functioned, in a sense, as the inducement, while the avolutionary development may be regarded as having acted as the foundation.

The avolutionary nature of the Cretaceous may thus be seen in that, it might be said, two forces might have worked or operated during the Cretaceous to give rise to flowering plants. One was the evolutionary force. The other was the avolutionary force. While the evolutionary force may be seen as working on an upper level, the avolutionary force may be seen as operating on a deeper level. The avolutionary force was deeper in the sense that it came from symmetry. It represented

Symmetry II

symmetry. It represented symmetry in plants. It represented the symmetric movement in plants. It embodied symmetry. It embodied symmetry in plants. It embodied the symmetric development in plants. It represented the power of symmetry. It represented the potential of symmetry. It represented the capacity of symmetry. It was powerful. It was potent. It was mighty. It was deep. It was profound. With this power, flowers came into being. With this power, flowering plants developed. With this power, flowering plants evolved. With this power, flowering plants avolved. With this power, flowering plants radiated or diversified in the Cretaceous. This may be the meaning of flowers appearing in the Cretaceous. This may be the meaning of flowering plants developing in the Cretaceous. This may be the meaning of flowering plants radiating or diversifying in the Cretaceous. This may be the meaning of the beautiful, magnificent and great age that is called, the Cretaceous.

With this understanding, we may be able to comprehend the kind of things such as coevolution between animals or insects and flowering plants. And with this understanding, we may be able to see into the possible workings or operations behind the phenomenon of flowering. Flowers are the sexual organs of flowering plants. To enhance their sexual attraction, flowers developed wonderful forms or shapes, beautiful colors, sweet tastes, or strong smells. How did flowers develop their beautiful shapes or forms? How did flowers develop their bright colors? How did flowers develop their strong smells? How did flowers grow with the sweet nectar? People might say that, to attract pollinators. Yes, it might be true, in a sense, that is, it seems, in an evolutionary sense. We may still ask, how should it be the case that flowers were able to develop such wonderful traits? How did they get the power? How did they get the potential? How did they get the capacity? Who gave them the power? Who gave them the potential? Who gave them the capacity? The fossil record indicates that, seed plants, such as gymnosperms, had a long history of pollination, with some early animal or insect pollinators, before the appearance of flowering plants. why, then, one may ask, had the early seed plants not developed the floral traits, as they might also have to attract pollinators? Why, then, one may ask, had the early gymnosperms not developed their flowers, as they might have to attract pollinators as well? And why, even today, are gymnosperms not growing with flowers?

It seems, to attract pollinators may not be a very good explanation for the appearance or development of flowers in plants. If it were true completely, then it seems, flowers would have appeared or developed in plants a long time ago before the Cretaceous. It may be true that, to attract pollinators might have played a certain role in the appearance or development of flowers in plants, but it may not explain all the things involved in such a great phenomenon. In other words, it might be said, apart from the possible roles played by the evolutionary mechanisms such as to attract pollinators, some other roles, some other mechanisms, or some other processes might have also participated in the appearance or development of flowers in plants. Otherwise, it seems, we may not be able to explain all the things observed with regard to such a phenomenon. What might be the other roles? What might be the other mechanisms? What might be the other processes? It might be said, they might have to do with symmetry, with harmony, with the movement of symmetry, or with the development of harmony.

Symmetry might have been behind the appearance or development of flowers in plants, apart from the evolutionary mechanisms or processes such as attracting pollinators. The symmetric movement or development might have been underlying the appearance or development of flowers in plants, apart from the coevolutionary existences between flowering plants and animal or insect pollinators. This may be seen, in a sense, in that the phenomenon of flowering may not be found in gymnosperms. Gymnosperms may be regarded as the seed plants of radial symmetry, in that, the presence of radial symmetry in them dominates their plant lives in such a way, in such a sense, in such a manner, or to such an extent that they may only produce the kind of things like cones, instead of flowers. Though a sense of bilateral symmetry may be observed, sometimes, in gymnosperms, such as in the shapes or forms of their leaves or in the structures of their woody cone scales, real or true flowers may not be found in them. That is to say, with regard to gymnosperms, radial symmetry may be seen as having the dominant presence, while bilateral symmetry may be expressed, to some extent, in them. It is this symmetric difference that separates gymnosperms from flowering plants. The radially symmetric existence of gymnosperms preconditions them to produce the kind of things like cones. The bilaterally symmetric existence of flowering plants enables them to give rise to flowers.

Symmetry II

It was this bilaterally symmetric existence that had been underlying the appearance or development of flowers in plants. It was this bilaterally symmetric movement that may be seen as behind the appearance or development of flowers in plants. It was this bilaterally symmetric development that may be seen as the driving force behind the appearance or development of flowers in plants during the Cretaceous. It was the movement of bilateral symmetry in plants. It was the development of bilateral symmetry in plants. It was the fulfillment of bilateral symmetry in plants. It was the realization of bilateral symmetry in the plant world, in a floral way, in a floral sense, in a floral manner, or in a floral fashion. It is this symmetric movement in the Cretaceous that is called flowers. It is this symmetric development in the Cretaceous that is called flowers. It is this symmetric fulfillment in the Cretaceous that is called flowers. It is this symmetric realization in the Cretaceous that is called, flowers.

Such a sense of symmetric fulfillment or realization may also be seen in that, the extraordinary power, potential or capacity of sexual symmetry may be seen as having been expressed, demonstrated, embodied, or fulfilled, realized in the sexual organs of plants called flowers. The evolutionary mechanisms or processes such as attracting pollinators might have contributed to the appearance or development of the floral traits in flowering plants, but for such floral traits to successfully appear or develop, some other things might have to participate in the processes and lay the foundation. It is in such a sense that the power, potential or capacity of sexual symmetry may be observed. The appearance or development of the kind of floral traits, such as the wonderful shapes or forms, beautiful colors, sweet tastes or strong smells, might not have been possible, in a sense, without the participation or contribution by sexual symmetry. That is to say, it might be said, sexual symmetry might have provided, in a sense, the power, the potential, or the capacity for flowering plants to develop their various wonderful floral traits. The appearance or development of the wonderful floral shapes or forms may be an indication that sexual symmetry was powerful, and its fulfillment or realization in plants might mean the coming into being or appearance of some lovely or graceful shapes or forms, as fulfilled or realized in the sepals, petals, stamens, or carpels, or in the overall structures. The appearance or development of the sweet tastes or strong smells in flowers may be seen, in a sense, as a result of the workings or operations of sexual symmetry, in that, sexual symmetry brought power, strength or energy to flowering plants, and consequently they were able to eventually develop the sweet tastes or strong smells so that they might, for example, successfully attract pollinators to accomplish the various processes of pollination. In other words, the sweet tastes or strong smells might be the means through which sexual symmetry reached its goals, or fulfilled or realized itself in plants, and as such they may testify, in a sense, to the power, potential or capacity of sexual symmetry, or to the movement or development of sexual symmetry in plants. The power of sexual symmetry may also be seen in the appearance or development of beautiful or bright colors in flowers. We all know how beautiful flowers might be. The beautiful colors can be seen in the sepals, in the petals, in the stamens, or in the carpels. Why should such beautiful colors appear or develop in flowers? To attract pollinators might only constitute one of the aspects of such a phenomenon. The other aspect might have to do with sexual symmetry. It might be sexual symmetry that had provided the ability for flowers to develop the beautiful colors. It might be sexual symmetry that had driven flowers to develop the beautiful colors. It might be sexual symmetry that had made it possible for flowers to develop the beautiful colors. It might be sexual symmetry that had made it necessary for the beautiful colors to appear in flowers, so that it might reach its goals, it might achieve its purposes, it might fulfill or realize itself, or so that it might demonstrate its power, it might exhibit its potential, it might display its capacity, or so that the plant kingdom might be interesting, nature might be attractive, and the world might be lovely, beautiful, and magnificent.

It was the workings or operations of bilateral symmetry. It was the workings or operations of sexual symmetry. It was the workings or operations of the evolutionary mechanisms or processes such as attracting pollinators. It was the workings or operations of both symmetry and evolution. It was the workings or operations of both avolution and evolution. This may be why we see wonderful shapes or forms in flowers. This may be why we see beautiful colors in flowers. This may be why we, or the animal or insect pollinators, can find sweet tastes or strong smells in flowers. This may be why we find the pleasing sepals. This may be why we find the tender and delicate stamens or carpels. This may be why we see the gorgeous and beautiful

Symmetry II

petals. This may be why we can live, today, in a world so lovely, so beautiful, and so magnificent on earth.

When we talk about the kind of coevolutionary or mutualistic phenomena such as animal or insect pollination, we may come to a realization that, after all, it seems, pollination between plants and animal or insect pollinators might not have to be, necessarily, through flowers. That is to say, it seems, it might not be necessary that flowers had to come into being so that plants might get pollinated. To attract pollinators, plants might develop or employ means other than flowering, such as, by tastes, by smells or scents, by some peculiar shapes or forms, or by some characteristic colors. In other words, flowers, as the expression or embodiment of beauty, might not have to come into being, necessarily. So why was it the case that flowers had to come into being? Why was it the case that beauty had to appear?

Tastes could attract pollinators. Smells or scents could attract pollinators. The peculiar shapes or forms could guide the pollinators. The characteristic colors could direct the pollinators. Coevolution could lead the plants to develop the tastes that the pollinators might enjoy. Coevolution could lead the plants to develop the smells or scents that the pollinators might like. Coevolution could lead the plants to develop the peculiar shapes or forms to guide the pollinators. Coevolution could lead the plants to develop the characteristic colors to direct the pollinators. In other words, coevolution might lead the plants to develop the various means, such as tastes, smells or scents, peculiar shapes or forms, or characteristic colors, so that the processes of pollination between plants and animal or insect pollinators might be smoothly and effectively accomplished. With these means, with the successful pollinating processes, the plants might thus develop, thrive or flourish.

But, such means might not necessarily mean the coming into being or existence of flowers in plants. Tastes might not have to be linked to flowers. Smells or scents might not have to be associated with flowers. The peculiar shapes or forms might not have to possess a harmonic appearance, and thus might not have to mean the coming into being of flowers or beauty. The characteristic colors might not have to present a sense of harmony, and thus might not have to mean the existence of flowers or beauty in plants. So, what might be the reason for flowers to come into being in plants? What might be the reason for beauty to appear in the plant world? That is, what might be the meaning of the coming into being of flowers in plants? What might be the meaning of the appearance of floral beauty in the world?

Did it mean the power of beauty? Did it mean the power of beauty in plants? Did it mean the power of beauty in the world? Did it mean the power of symmetry? Did it mean the power of harmony? Did it mean the power of symmetry in plants? Did it mean the power of harmony in the world? Did it mean that the power of symmetry had to be expressed? Did it mean that the power of harmony had to be demonstrated? Did it mean that the power of symmetry had to be fulfilled in plants? Did it mean that the power of harmony had to be realized in the world? Did the fulfillment of symmetry in plants mean the coming into being of flowers in plants? Did the realization of harmony in the world mean the appearance of floral beauty in the world?

The appearance or existence of flowers might mean that, apart from the other things possibly associated with pollination, it might be said, animal or insect pollinators might be attracted by beauty. That is to say, in other words, beauty might be attractive to animals. Beauty might be perceived by animals. Beauty might be felt by animals. Beauty might be recognized by animals. Beauty might be received by animals. Did it mean that, while beauty existed in plants, it also existed in animals? Did it mean that, while beauty appeared in plants, it also appeared in animals? Did it mean that, while beauty was intrinsic in plants, it was also intrinsic in animals? Did it mean that, beauty was so intrinsic in animals that they could feel, perceive, receive, recognize or experience it? That is, it might be said, the appearance or existence of flowers might mean that, as the pollinators, animals might be able to "appreciate" or experience beauty, in some way, in some sense, or in some manner, like their human relatives, the human beings. This may not be very surprising, as both animal pollinators and human beings may be regarded as the fulfillment or realization of symmetry in the animal kingdom. Symmetry might have fulfilled or realized itself in animals in such a way that animals were intrinsically close to their own symmetric coming into being, and they could develop a sense of perception or feeling of the symmetric or harmonic existence. That is, animals might develop a sense of perception or feeling of beauty. The appearance or development of flowers in plants in the Cretaceous might be such a case that, beauty appeared in plants, and at the same time, it was being, in a sense, perceived, received, recognized, felt or

Symmetry II

experienced by the animal or insect pollinators. That might be why, in a sense, the pollinators were attracted to the flowers. That might be how, in a sense, the processes of pollination had been accomplished. And that might be why or how, in a sense, the flowers came into being.

Thus, when we walk in the wild and joyfully appreciate the beauty of flowers, we may not say to ourselves that, it is good that we come, otherwise such beauty of nature may not be seen or appreciated. No. That might not be the case. Even if we had not come, such beauty of nature might still be seen, perceived, felt, experienced, or "appreciated," in some sense, in some way, in some manner, or to some extent. Animals other than us might also develop a sense of feeling or perception of beauty. They might have done so with flowers for a long time, as the pollinators, possibly ever since the appearance of flowering plants. Thus it might be said, flowers may not just blossom for us. They blossom for the world. They blossom for the animals. They blossom for the human beings. They blossom for themselves. They blossom for the development of plants. They blossom for the continuation of animals. They blossom for the fulfillment or realization of symmetry. They blossom for the harmonic existence of the world. Beauty means existence. Existence means beauty. Human beings are part of the existence of the world. Plants are part of the existence of the world. Animals are part of the existence of the world. Beauty is in the existence of human beings. Beauty is in the existence of plants. Beauty is in the existence of animals. Beauty is in the existence of all. Existence is in beauty. Beauty is in existence.

When we talk about beauty, with regard to the appearance or development of flowers in plants, some might say that such might not always be the case. People may point to the phenomena that, it seems, beauty might not be well expressed or demonstrated in the wind-pollinated flowers, or in the self-pollinated flowers. It is true that, it might be said, it is usually the case that the most lovely, beautiful, or conspicuous flowers are animal or insect-pollinated, and the wind-pollinated or self-pollinated flowers are often small, inconspicuous, and may sometimes lack petals or sepals altogether. So, how to understand such phenomena? How to understand the notion that symmetry was behind the coming into being of flowers, and the coming into being of flowers represented or embodied the coming into being of beauty in the world? That is, how to understand such a notion that the movement or development of symmetry may be seen as behind the appearance of flowers in plants, that is, behind the appearance of beauty in the plant world?

The wind-pollinated flowers may be found in grasses or some wind-pollinated trees. Compared to the animal or insect-pollinated flowers, the wind-pollinated flowers appear to be indeed small, less colored, and less conspicuous. Their petals or sepals may be missing, in many cases. The self-pollinated flowers are often, similarly, not as noticeable or beautiful as the animal or insect-pollinated flowers. So, what is the beauty of flowers? Where is the beauty of flowers? We may say that the flowers pollinated by the insects like bees are beautiful, but how could we say that the flowers of some grasses are also beautiful? How beautiful are such grass flowers? In what ways or in what senses should we say that such grass flowers are beautiful? How beautiful are the flowers of some wind-pollinated trees? In what ways or in what senses should we say that such flowers are also beautiful? And, how beautiful are the self-pollinated flowers? In what ways or in what senses should such flowers be compared to the animal or insect-pollinated flowers?

Why should it be the case that the animal or insect-pollinated flowers are usually brightly colored, attractive, or beautiful and the wind-pollinated or self-pollinated flowers are often conspicuously less so? The explanation is usually like, the animal or insect-pollinated flowers developed their floral features or traits to attract the animal or insect pollinators. But no such need may exist for the wind-pollinated or self-pollinated flowers, and thus the conspicuous floral features or traits may not be developed in them. That may be why the wind-pollinated or self-pollinated flowers may be found, sometimes, as not that brightly colored, attractive or beautiful. If this is true, could we say that beauty, as being represented or embodied by the lovely or beautiful flowers, may be seen as coming into being from the mutualism or coevolution between flowering plants and animal or insect pollinators?

So beauty came into being, because of the mutualism or coevolution between flowering plants and animal or insect pollinators? Where was symmetry? Where were the workings or operations of symmetry? Where were the movements or developments of symmetry? Was symmetry behind the appearance of flowers? Was symmetry behind the development of flowers? Was symmetry behind the appearance of beauty? Was symmetry behind the development of beauty? Was beauty the movement or development of symmetry? Was

Symmetry II

beauty the fulfillment or realization of symmetry? So, why should it be the case that beauty may not be found, in a sense, sometimes, in the wind-pollinated or self-pollinated flowers, while symmetry may be seen as being equally behind them?

I think, such may be understood in that, while the beauty of the animal or insect-pollinated flowers may be seen as largely coming into being from the mutualistic or coevolutionary developments of flowering plants with animal or insect pollinators, it was symmetry that may be seen as underlying or behind the appearance, development, or existence of all flowers, the animal or insect-pollinated flowers, the wind-pollinated flowers, and the self-pollinated flowers. In other words, it might be said, it might be true that coevolution or evolution may be seen as behind, largely, the coming into being of the beauty in the animal or insect-pollinated flowers, but the power, potential or capacity to develop such beauty may be seen as coming from symmetry. Without the avolutionary power, potential or capacity, coevolution or evolution, no matter in what forms, might not be able to give rise to the beauty appeared or developed in the animal or insect-pollinated flowers. In such a sense, it might be said, symmetry might have worked or operated, equally, in the animal or insect-pollinated flowers, wind-pollinated flowers, and self-pollinated flowers.

The beauty of the animal or insect-pollinated flowers may reveal, in a sense, the significance or meaning of the existence of animals. Animals, like plants, that is, like the flowering plants themselves, are the fulfillment or realization of symmetry in the world, that is, in nature. It should not be very surprising that the appearance or development of flowering plants was closely associated with the development or existence of animals, as they were closely related to each other, after all, through symmetry. It was symmetry that provided the power, potential, or capacity for animals to come into being. It was symmetry that provided the power, potential, or capacity for plants to appear. It was symmetry that provided the power, potential, or capacity for the flowering plants to emerge. It was symmetry that, it seems, provided the power, potential, or capacity for the flowering plants to develop, together, that is, closely, with the animals. Thus, it seems, the appearance or development of the animal or insect-pollinated flowers in the flowering plants may be seen or regarded, in a sense, as an occurrence happening, in a fundamental or essential way, out of the innate, intrinsic, or inherent workings or operations of symmetry. That is to say, in other words, the appearance or development of the animal or insect-pollinated flowers in the flowering plants may be seen or regarded, in a fundamental or essential sense, as a form of symmetric occurrence or happening. It was a form of symmetric movement. It was a form of symmetric appearance. It was a form of symmetric development. It was a form of symmetric creation. It was a form of symmetric progress. It was a form of symmetric fulfillment. It was a form of symmetric realization. It was a form of symmetric appearance or development through the coevolution of plants and animals. It was a form of symmetric creation or progress through the co-development of plants and animals. It was a form of symmetric fulfillment or realization through the coexistence of plants and animals.

Thus, on the surface, it might be said, the beauty of the animal or insect-pollinated flowers or the appearance or development of such flowers in the flowering plants may be seen, in a sense, as resulting from the coevolution of the flowering plants and their animal or insect pollinators, but deep down, it was symmetry that may be seen as what worked or operated behind things. It was the symmetric fulfillment or realization through the interaction or cooperation of the plant symmetric realization and animal symmetric realization. It was beauty coming into being from plants and animals. It was beauty coming into being from the interaction or cooperation of the plant beings and animal beings. It was beauty coming into being from the coexistence of the plant world and animal world. It was beauty coming into being through symmetry working in both plants and animals. It was beauty coming into being through symmetry working in both plant beings and animal beings. It was beauty coming into being through symmetry operating in both the plant world and animal world. It is in such a sense that, it might be said, the beauty of flowers may be seen as the symmetric fusion of plants and animals, the symmetric fusion of the plant existence and animal existence. That is, it might be said, the beauty of flowers may be seen as the symmetric fusion of the plant symmetry and animal symmetry, the symmetric fusion of the plant world and animal world. That is, it might be said, the beauty of flowers may be seen as the symmetric fulfillment or realization in plants through the symmetric fusion of the plant world and the animal world.

The symmetric union of plants and animals may be seen as behind the beauty of flowers. The symmetric union of the plant symmetry and animal symmetry may be seen as what behind the appearance or

Symmetry II

development of the lovely, beautiful, and magnificent flowers. While such flowers were usually bright, attractive, and conspicuous, the wind-pollinated or self-pollinated flowers had their places too, in the plant world. They might bring with them certain advantages. They might work well, in their own ways, for the pollination of plants. Their beauty might be modest, compared to the conspicuous beauty of other flowers, but they equally fulfilled the floral purposes for plant reproduction. With their modest beauty, they represented, in their own modest ways, the movement or development of symmetry in plants. With their modest beauty, they stood for, through their own modest manners, the fulfillment or realization of symmetry in the plant world. Their beauty might be modest, but they bore the same meaning for plants. Their beauty might be modest, but they carried the same significance for the plant world. If beauty is everywhere conspicuous, then no beauty might be conspicuous, and no beauty might be found in the end. Their modest beauty might be an integral part of the plant world, as it constituted, together with the beauty of other flowers, the diverse presence of beauty in plants. That is, it might be said, the wind-pollinated or self-pollinated flowers may be seen as representing or reflecting, in a sense, the variation or diversity of the fulfillment or realization of symmetry in plants, that is, in the plant world.

On the other hand, it might be said, the appearance or development of floral beauty in plants may be seen, in a sense, as a harmonic phenomenon. It was harmonic in the sense that, animal or insect pollinators may be seen as coming into being, in a sense, that is, in a harmonic sense, for flowering plants, and flowering plants may be seen as coming into being, in a sense, that is, in a harmonic sense, for animal or insect pollinators. It was harmonic in the sense that, it was symmetry or harmony that worked or operated behind all the things, behind the appearance or development of animal or insect pollinators, behind the appearance or development of flowering plants, and behind the appearance or development of the animal or insect-pollinated flowers. Even if bees did not come into being, it seems, symmetry or harmony might work to give rise to some other insects so that flowering plants might be pollinated efficiently and effectively. Even if bees did not act as the pollinators, it seems, symmetry or harmony might operate in such a way, in such a sense, in such a manner, or to such an extent that some other animals or insects might take over that role and act as the efficient or effective pollinating agents. In other words, it seems that, in a sense, it might be said, insects like bees appeared for flowering plants and flowering plants developed for insects like bees. Flowers thus came into being. Plants thus bloomed and blossomed. The world thus became lovely, beautiful, and magnificent.

Who could say that, it was not lovely? Who could say that, it was not beautiful? Who could say that, it was not magnificent? Who could say that, it was not harmonic? Who could say that, it was not harmonious? Who could say that, it was not arranged by symmetry or harmony? Who could say that, it was not designed by symmetry or harmony? Who could say that, it was not created by symmetry or harmony? Was it not the beauty of the world? Was it not the harmony of the world? Was it not the harmonic existence of the world? Was it not the harmonization of the world? Was it not the harmonic existence of plants and animals? Was it not the harmonic existence of nature? Was it not a world of symmetry? Was it not a world of harmony? Was it not a world created, after all, by symmetry? Was it not a world created, after all, by harmony?

A number of hypotheses have been proposed with regard to the appearance or development of seed plants. One of them is the anthophyte hypothesis. The anthophyte hypothesis is concerned with a group of gymnosperms called gnetophytes. Gnetophytes are usually classified as gymnosperms, along with conifers, cycads, and ginkgo. As the members of gymnosperms, gnetophytes may be seen as occupying a special place, in that, while they have their gymnosperm characteristics, they also share certain features with angiosperms. One of the shared features is the possession of the flower-like reproductive structures. Another shared feature is the presence of vessels in plants, a water conducting system mostly found in angiosperms. Based on such shared features and other similarities, the anthophyte hypothesis suggests that gnetophytes and angiosperms may be closely related to each other, and they may have constituted the sister groups in the appearance or development of seed plants.

Is it necessarily the case that gnetophytes and angiosperms are to constitute the sister groups, even if they share certain features or traits, such as the possession of flower-like structures or presence of vessels? It seems, that might not necessarily be the case. The molecular or genetic researches appear to have indicated that gnetophytes and angiosperms may not be actually related to each other closely, and their shared features like flower-like structures or vessels may have been

Symmetry II

developed separately in their own ways. With such findings, people now seem to have agreed that the anthophyte hypothesis may not have truly reflected what happens in plants. This should not be taken as a surprise. Gnetophytes, as the gymnosperms, may be seen as the plants of radial symmetry. They are different, symmetrically, from the angiosperms, which may be seen as the plants of bilateral symmetry. The symmetric difference defines their different existences and determines, in a fundamental sense, the different ways of their appearances or developments.

It is in such a sense that, it might be said, when it comes to the origin of angiosperms or flowering plants, we may have to look to the kind of early plants of bilateral symmetry to find the answer. That is, it is likely the case that, the beginning of angiosperms or flowering plants may not lie in the gymnosperms like gnetophytes, but in the kind of early plants that might be bilaterally symmetric, dominantly, in their nature. Gymnosperms may be seen as the plants of radial symmetry in a dominant sense and flowering plants may be seen as the plants of bilateral symmetry in a dominant sense. But, the problem is, how to determine an early plant that was bilaterally symmetric dominantly? We have seen that, the presence of bilateral symmetry may be found in gymnosperms, such as, in the cone scales of conifers, in the pinnate leaves of cycads, in the leaves of some gnetophytes, or in the often two-lobed and fan-shaped leaves of the ginkgo. It seems, it might be said, the only way to determine completely whether an early plant was bilaterally symmetric in a dominant sense is to see whether it produced flowers. But, this is exactly what we want to find out. We want to find out whether an early plant was bilaterally symmetric in a dominant sense so that it may be treated as the possible ancestor of flowering plants. How to decide whether an early plant was bilaterally symmetric in a dominant sense? How to know that an early plant was not bilaterally symmetric in a dominant sense? While angiosperms often exhibit the presence of radial symmetry, such as in their floral structures, gymnosperms appear to have also possessed, to a certain extent, a sense of bilateral symmetry. That is, it appears to be often the case that, radial symmetry may be observed in flowering plants, the plants of bilateral symmetry in a dominant sense, and bilateral symmetry may be found in gymnosperms, the plants of radial symmetry in a dominant sense. Thus, it seems, the complexity, subtlety, intricacy or profundity of the fulfillment or realization of symmetry in plants makes it almost impossible to decide whether an early plant was bilaterally symmetric in a dominant sense, unless we observe the production of flowers.

This may make it very difficult for us to determine the possible ancestors of flowering plants. It is likely the case that the ancestors of flowering plants should be bilaterally symmetric in a dominant sense. But, given the complex and subtle fulfillment or realization of both radial symmetry and bilateral symmetry in seed plants, that is, in both gymnosperms and angiosperms, it appears, it would be immensely challenging if we want to determine whether an early plant was bilaterally symmetric in a dominant sense. The possible ancestors of flowering plants might be among the early seed plants existing prior to the Cretaceous. Gigantopterids were a group of extinct seed plants living roughly around 250 million years ago, in the late Permian. They are sometimes taken to be the possible ancestors of flowering plants. It appears, they possessed a number of features that may be found in flowering plants. They had leaves showing bilateral symmetry. Such leaves may be found to be very similar to the ones that we now see in flowering plants, with reticulate venation. They contained vessels, a water conducting structure found in flowering plants. The presence of oleanane-related chemical compounds has been also found in them, and such chemical compounds are often discovered in flowering plants. Based on such shared features or similarities, some people suggest that this group of early seed plants might be the ancestral plants leading to the appearance of flowering plants.

But, it seems, this may not be completely certain. The bilaterally symmetric leaves may also be found in the gymnosperms like gnetophytes or ginkgo. A similar vessel structure may also be found in gnetophytes. And, even the oleanane-related chemical compounds may also be found to be present in other plants such as ferns. Even gigantopterids were indeed the early seed plants ancestral to the flowering plants appearing in the Cretaceous, we may still have to face the task of looking for the possible ancestors of flowering plants. They were only the seed plants living in the late Permian. What might be the possible ancestral plants living in the Triassic? What might be the possible ancestral plants living in the Jurassic? Where are they? Where are their fossils? It seems, the search for the ancestors of flowering plants may be far from over.

Symmetry II

And in a sense, it might be said, before we set out looking for the possible ancestors of flowering plants, we may have to first understand how flowering plants came into being. The symmetric coming into being of flowering plants in the Cretaceous may mean that, the search for their ancestors may not be easy. If it were completely an evolutionary process, then it might be the case that we would discover some developmental stages or steps along the way. Such developmental stages or steps might constitute the foundation upon which we may proceed with our search in a systematic manner. But, the avolutionary coming into being of flowering plants in the Cretaceous may mean that we might be unable to proceed in such a manner.

Suppose, we are presented with two plants, one the ancestor of flowering plants, and the other not, could we tell the difference and point out the real ancestor, definitely? Not necessarily, it seems. We have already discussed the extraordinary complexity or subtlety involved in the symmetric fulfillment or realization in plants, that is, in both gymnosperms and angiosperms. The complex and subtle fulfillment or realization of both radial symmetry and bilateral symmetry in both gymnosperms and angiosperms means that it would be, it might be said, extremely difficult if we want to find out which plants may give rise to flowers, before we know the production of flowers.

Such difficulty may have to do, in a sense, that is, in a fundamental or essential sense, with the symmetric coming into being of flowering plants. The avolutionary coming into being of flowering plants in the Cretaceous might mean the innate or intrinsic coming into being of extraordinary complexity, intricacy or subtlety in seed plants. Such an innate or intrinsic coming into being might mean that the appearance of extraordinary complexity, intricacy or subtlety in seed plants, related to the happening of flowering plants, might occur in some extraordinary ways. That is, the avolutionary coming into being of flowering plants in the Cretaceous might have happened in such a way that the transition from non-flowering plants to flowering plants might be an innate or intrinsic process. Such an innate or intrinsic process might be so complex, deep or subtle that it might be beyond, in a sense, our rational or analytic examination. And, such an innate or intrinsic process might be so rapid, sudden, unexpected or explosive that it might be simply, in a sense, or to a certain extent, invisible or unperceivable to us. Thus, the difficulty that we face in our search for the ancestors of flowering plants may be seen as the difficulty associated with the possible movements or developments of symmetry. It is the difficulty coming from symmetry. It is the difficulty coming from the symmetric explosion. It is the difficulty coming from the symmetric emergence of flowers. It is the difficulty reflecting, in a sense, how the world truly came into being.

Some people have tried to establish the relationship of some plants with flowering plants by citing the common presence of the oleanane-related chemical compounds. We may have to be careful, as this might not be a very reliable approach, and such chemical compounds may also be found in non-flowering plants, such as ferns. And in a sense, it might be said, we may also have to be careful in employing the molecular or genetic analyses to define the relationships of plants. The workings or operations of symmetry in plants may be so subtle, complex, or deep that the existence of plants may not be easily scrutinized either molecularly or genetically. Some people have suggested, based on the genetic information, that gnetophytes may be treated as the sister group to all other seed plants including angiosperms. Given the dominance of different symmetries in gnetophytes and angiosperms, it seems, it might be said, such might not be the case.

Gymnosperms are the plants with naked seeds, while angiosperms are the plants with enclosed seeds. Such a difference in the seed condition may be seen as representing or standing for the different presences of symmetry in plants, in that, while radial symmetry may be seen as being dominant in gymnosperms, angiosperms may be regarded as the plants of bilateral symmetry. Radial symmetry may be seen as possessing such a dominant presence in gymnosperms that the seeds of these plants may only develop through the kind of reproductive structures like cones. What happens in angiosperms may be a different story. The presence of bilateral symmetry in angiosperms may be so dominant that these plants are able to develop the kind of reproductive structures like flowers and their seeds may thus be able to develop in an enclosed condition. Certainly, it has to be said, accompanying such floral reproductive structures are some more complex or sophisticated reproductive processes or mechanisms, and such reproductive processes or mechanisms may only be found in angiosperms. In other words, it might be said, the different symmetric presences may have defined or determined the different plants and the different plants,

Symmetry II

gymnosperms and angiosperms, may have represented, stood for, or embodied the different fulfillments or realizations of symmetry in the plant world.

In terms of diversity or abundance, as we can observe, angiosperms far surpass gymnosperms generally. The overwhelmingly dominant presence of angiosperms over gymnosperms on earth may be regarded, in a sense, as the dominance of bilateral symmetry over radial symmetry, in that, compared to bilateral symmetry, radial symmetry may have brought with itself certain limitations and such limitations may have functioned to restrict or restrain, in a sense, or to a certain extent, the development of the radially symmetric plants. The development of gymnosperms may thus have to do, largely, with their radially symmetric existence. Such may be behind the fact that they usually do not develop or produce flowers. And such may be behind the phenomenon that they are usually less diverse or abundant than angiosperms. Such a sense of dominance of bilateral symmetry over radial symmetry may also be observed in the animal kingdom. It is generally the case that the bilaterally symmetric animals are usually more diverse or abundant than the radially symmetric animals, either in the waters or on the dry land. Such may have to do, fundamentally, and ultimately, it might be said, with the symmetric difference between radial symmetry and bilateral symmetry.

We often talk about beauty when we discuss the appearance or development of flowering plants. Does this mean that beauty may only be found in the flowering plants? Not necessarily. While beauty may be found in the flowering plants, beauty may also be observed in the non-flowering plants, such as in the gymnosperms. Conifers, cycads and ginkgo are the gymnosperms. They may be beautiful in their own ways. We may perceive beauty in the pines, cypresses or firs. They are tall. They stand upright. Even in the cold winter or in the snow, they are still there, tall, upright, evergreen, and unchanging. They have the beauty of endurance, strength, and longevity. We may find beauty in the cycads. They are unfailingly symmetrical. They are enduring. They are beautiful. We may also find a sense of unique beauty in the ginkgo. It is large. It is long-living. And as a living fossil, it still thrives with colors and magnificent forms today.

Should the flowering plants be seen as being more beautiful than the gymnosperms like conifers, cycads or ginkgo? Not necessarily. The beauty of flowering plants may be regarded, in a sense, as the beauty coming from bilateral symmetry, or simply, as the beauty of bilateral symmetry. The beauty of gymnosperms like conifers, cycads or ginkgo may be regarded, in a sense, as the beauty coming from radial symmetry, or simply, as the beauty of radial symmetry. They are different beauties. They originate from different sources. They come from different origins. They represent different symmetries. They stand for different harmonies. They embody the different fulfillments or realizations of symmetry in the world. Flowers may be tender; gymnosperms like conifers, cycads or ginkgo are enduring. Flowers may be delicate; gymnosperms like conifers, cycads or ginkgo are strong. Flowers may be colorful; gymnosperms like conifers, cycads or ginkgo are magnificent. Should the flowering plants be regarded as being more beautiful than the gymnosperms? Not necessarily, it appears. They may have expressed the different beauties. They may have manifested the different beauties. They may have embodied the different fulfillments or realizations of symmetry in plants. That is, they may have embodied the different symmetric beauties in plants, the beauty of radial symmetry and the beauty of bilateral symmetry. Should the beauty of radial symmetry be seen as being more beautiful than the beauty of bilateral symmetry? Or, should the beauty of bilateral symmetry be treated as being more beautiful than the beauty of radial symmetry? Not necessarily, it seems. They are the different symmetric beauties. They represent the different symmetric qualities or characteristics. They stand for the diverse fulfillments or realizations of symmetry in the world. They are all beautiful. They are all significant. They constitute, together, the beauty of symmetry in the plant world. They constitute, together, the beauty of the world.

Such a sense of beauty may also be observed in the animal world. Should we say that the bilaterally symmetric animals are necessarily more beautiful than the radially symmetric animals? Not necessarily. It appears, the radially symmetric animals are beautiful too. Cnidarians like jellyfish or corals are beautiful. Ctenophores are beautiful. Echinoderms like starfish are beautiful too. How can one say that the bilaterally symmetric animals are more beautiful than the radially symmetric animals? Who is more beautiful than the jellyfish or corals? Who is more beautiful than the ctenophores? Who is more beautiful than the starfish? The animals of radial symmetry may be just as beautiful as the animals of bilateral symmetry. Just like plants in the plant world, animals represent or stand for the different fulfillments or realizations of symmetry in the animal kingdom. They express the different symmetric beauties through their animal existences. They embody the different symmetric beauties through their animal existences. The animals of radial symmetry may manifest the beauty of radial symmetry. The animals of bilateral symmetry may demonstrate the beauty of bilateral symmetry. They are all the beauties of symmetry. They are all the beauties coming from symmetry. They are all the beauties representing or reflecting the fulfillment or realization of symmetry in the animal kingdom. They are all beautiful. They are all significant. They constitute, together, the beauty of symmetry in the animal kingdom. They constitute, together, the beauty of the world.

It may have to be noted, though flowering plants are generally the bilaterally symmetric plants, the presence of bilateral symmetry in plants may not necessarily mean the production or coming into being of flowers. Ferns are the plants with bilaterally symmetric fronds, but as we know, they only have spores and no flowers. The presence of bilateral symmetry may be observed in the cone scales of conifers, and a sense of bilateral symmetry may also be observed in the leaves of some conifers. But, we all know, conifers usually do not produce flowers. Cycads usually possess large pinnate leaves that exhibit bilateral symmetry. They produce cones, but not flowers. Though cycads are very similar in their appearances to palms, they are not flowering plants. Palms also often have pinnate leaves. But, unlike the cycads, palms are flowering plants, and they produce flowers and fruits. Some gnetophytes may also have bilaterally symmetric leaves, but they produce cones, not the real flowers. Two-lobed and fan-shaped leaves may be observed in the ginkgo, and only cones may be produced.

I found, at one time, an ornamental flowering plant, whose name I know not, with markedly non-bilaterally symmetric leaves. It has small- or middle-sized flowers, with different colors such as white or yellowish, but growing leaves that are not clearly bilaterally symmetric. The leaves are usually broad and roundish, with the central veins slanting towards one side of the leaves with pointed tips. They are visibly not bilaterally symmetric, unlike the body plans or structures of other flowering plant leaves. The flowers of this plant stand also differently from other flowers in the sense that, they exhibit a sense of double bilateral symmetry. The petals of these flowers are usually roundish, with tender colors, and bilaterally symmetric. Apart from the bilaterally symmetric shape, the petals are usually, remarkable in this sense, grown too in an arrangement of bilateral symmetry around the floral axis, with two petals existing in opposite direction in each whorl. This sense of double bilateral symmetry really amazed me, as I had never witnessed such a kind of existence of bilateral symmetry in flowers before. As I looked at these flowers, I was wondering, this strengthened version of existence of bilateral symmetry might be seen, in a sense, as a compensation for the loss of bilateral symmetry in the leaves, as the lack of bilateral symmetry in the leaves may be regarded as a sense of weakening or loss of bilateral symmetry overall for the plant. That is, in such a way, it might be said, the bilateral symmetry for such a flowering plant may be seen as being maintained, sustained, or kept, in a sense, or to a certain extent. That is, in such a way, such a flowering plant may be able to continue to exist, to survive, to prosper, and to blossom, as the flowering plant, as the plant bearing the beautiful, tender, and lovely flowers. The non-bilaterally symmetric leaves of this plant, it might be said, may have appeared as a result of some genetic mutation, artificial intervention, or some other factors.

While the Cretaceous symmetric explosion may be seen as what gave rise to the flowering plants, the beginning of such a symmetric explosion might lie much earlier than the Cretaceous. In other words, the way might have been prepared much earlier for such a symmetric explosion to happen in the Cretaceous. This may be seen in some molecular or genetic studies. Such studies seem to indicate that, some genetic processes might have happened prior to the Cretaceous, and consequently, certain genetic changes might have come into being, in the Jurassic period. Such genetic changes in plants in the Jurassic might have constituted the necessary steps that led to the occurrence of the symmetric explosion in the Cretaceous. That is to say, the symmetric movement leading to the Cretaceous symmetric explosion might have started well before the Cretaceous, and some genetic marks might have been left as a result in the plants.

Flowers usually demonstrate both radial symmetry and bilateral symmetry in their varied and beautiful ways. Bilateral symmetry may be observed in the sepals, petals, or in the usually two-lobed anther structures of stamens. Radial symmetry may be found in the radial arrangements of sepals, petals, or stamens around the central floral axis, or the carpels. Radial symmetry may also be seen in the shapes of the ovary. Through their diverse and varied ways, flowers embody beauty in the plant world, in nature. Can any language fully describe the

Symmetry II

beauty of flowers? Can anyone on earth create the beauty of flowers? Can technology produce the beauty of flowers? Can science give rise to the beauty of flowers? It seems, the answer might be, no. No language might fully describe the beauty of flowers. No person might artificially create the beauty of flowers. No technology might technically produce the beauty of flowers. No science might scientifically give rise to the beauty of flowers. The beauty of flowers is beyond language. The beauty of flowers is beyond the artificial human endeavor. The beauty of flowers is beyond technology. The beauty of flowers is beyond science.

Beauty is not reason. Beauty is not about reason. Beauty is not about rationality. Beauty is about something deeper. Beauty is about something richer. Beauty is about something profound. Beauty is about something infinite. Beauty is about something innate. Beauty is about something intrinsic. Beauty is about something so innately deep that reason may not be able to reach. Beauty is about something so intrinsically rich that science may not be able to fully grasp. Beauty is about something so profoundly touching that reason may not be able to describe. Beauty is about something so infinitely exquisite that science may not be able to demonstrate or explain. Beauty is beyond reason. Beauty is beyond science. Beauty is beyond language. No language could fully describe beauty, as beauty comes from within. No science could fully explain beauty, as beauty is innate. No reason could fully reach beauty, as beauty is intrinsic. That is, in a sense, it might be said, to fully explain beauty, we may have to go beyond reason or science. That is, in a sense, it might be said, to fully explain the beauty of flowers, we may have to go beyond the mere evolutionary explanations.

Beauty represents symmetry. Beauty stands for harmony. Beauty fulfils symmetry. Beauty realizes harmony. The depth of beauty comes from the depth of symmetry. The depth of beauty comes from the depth of harmony. The richness of beauty comes from the richness of symmetry. The richness of beauty comes from the richness of harmony. The profundity of beauty comes from the profundity of symmetry. The profundity of beauty comes from the profundity of harmony. With the appearance of beauty, flowering plants came into being. With the appearance of flowering plants, beauty came into being. With the appearance of flowering plants, the age of beauty arrived. The Cretaceous thus arrived as a great age. It was beautiful. It was significant. It was mighty. It was magnificent. It was an age of the coming into being of beauty. It was an age of the appearance of beauty. It was an age of the emergence of beauty. It was an age in which the plant world bloomed. It was an age in which symmetry moved or developed. It was an age in which symmetry exploded, to give rise to a beautiful world on earth.

The rapid and sudden appearance of flowering plants in the Cretaceous, very much like the appearance of animals in the Ediacaran or Cambrian, or the appearance of plants in the Devonian, with few, if any, developmental steps or stages observed, may constitute an enormous challenge to the human mind. And indeed, it seems, the rapid and sudden appearance of widespread flowering plants on earth, in a relatively short period of time, has puzzled scientists and researchers for a long time. Even Darwin was enormously concerned with such a phenomenon, and called it an "abominable mystery." Is it really an abominable mystery? No. It is not an abominable mystery. It is not abominable; it is adorable. It is not abominable; it is beautiful. It is not abominable; it is magnificent. It is an adorable mystery. It is a beautiful mystery. It is a magnificent mystery. It is an adorable mystery that expressed the power of symmetry. It is a beautiful mystery that led to the flowering of plants. It is a magnificent mystery that gave rise to the beauty of the world. It is adorable, as it is symmetric. It is beautiful, as it is harmonic. It is magnificent, as it stands for the mighty and magnificent fulfillment or realization of symmetry in plants, in flowering plants, in the plant world, in the animal world, in nature, on the planet earth.

Chapter III Symmetry, Harmony, and Avolution

§ 3.1 Avolution, the Word, the Term, and its Meaning

There are several reasons that I came to form the word or term, avolution.

Evolution, as a term, it seems, may no longer be used. Even when we talk about the kind of developmental processes of things, such as plants or animals, with which the term evolution may be applied, it seems, such evolutionary processes may still be, or necessarily, in a certain sense, regarded as being supported, maintained, sustained, or conditioned, guided, in some sense, in some way, or in some manner, by or through the symmetric or harmonic existence deeply and inherently present in such things.

We may use the term harmonic evolution to describe or discuss what is said above, that is, evolution being supported, maintained, sustained, or conditioned, guided by the symmetric or harmonic existence. But, it seems, the term harmonic evolution is very inconvenient, and confusing. Thus, after a period of reluctance and hesitation, I thought I had to find a new word or term to express or indicate the exact meaning of what may be seen in the awkward term harmonic evolution.

It proved to be quite difficult to form the right word. At first, I tried harvolution or harvolve. Then I tried havolution or havolve. Then I tried arvolution or arvolve. Then I tried harmolution or harmolve. But, it seems, the kind of words like harvolution or harvolve may have to do with half or halve, and the kind of words like harmolution or harmolve may have to do with the word harm. That is not good. Other possible choices may be the kind of words like syvolution or syvolve, symolution or symolve, or, hevolution or hevolve. It seems, they are not good too. After a period of unsuccessful attempts, I found, it seems, it is almost impossible to form the right word with the Latin or Greek roots. So, in the end, I decided not to follow the conventional ways to form the new word or term.

Avolution and Man

I have to say, more than anything else, I am attracted, in a sense, to the symmetric or harmonic presence in Avolution. The symmetric or harmonic presence is powerful in nature, in plants, in animals. Now, it seems, I find it, in a sense, in Avolution. This "Av" or "AV" appears to me the almost perfect symbol for symmetry or harmony, or, the coming into being, unbelievably, of the symmetric or harmonic existence in a word.

The first two letters, Av or AV, may be seen as representing a strong symmetric pattern or harmonic arrangement. That is to say, in a sense, it might be said, in such a word, there appears a strong sense of symmetry or harmony. That is exactly what I am looking for when I try to form such a word or term. The symmetric appearance may represent the symmetric being of things. The harmonic pattern or arrangement may stand for the harmonic existence of things. Even the "-" in the first letter "A" may be seen as symbolizing, in a sense, the fundamental symmetric or harmonic existence deeply, innately, or intrinsically present in the things of the world.

The first letter "a" in avolution or avolve may be seen in a number of similarly formed words, such as agree, accord, accustom, accompany, accumulate, arise, await, awake, avail, avoid, avouch, or avow. Agree, to be at -gre, that is, to be at will; accord, to be at -cord; accustom, to be in the custom of; accompany, to be the company of; accumulate, to cumulate; arise, to rise; await, to wait; awake, to wake; avail, to be of -vail; avoid, to void; avouch, to vouch; avow, to vow. Thus, in such a pattern of the formation of the words, it seems, the word that is to be formed as avolve may just mean that, simply, to -volve, that is, to roll, to proceed, to move, to grow, or, to develop.

And, it seems, the part a- in these words appears to indicate or imply a kind of force that makes the related things happen, such as, to agree, to accord, to accustom, to accompany, to accumulate, to arise, to await, to awake, to avail, to avoid, to avouch, or to avow. What may be the case with the word avolve? What makes something to avolve? What makes to avolve happen? What may be behind something avolving? What may be the force behind the avolving? It may have to do with symmetry. It may have to do with harmony. It may have to do with the symmetric or harmonic existence of things. Thus, it might be said, the word avolve may be seen as indicating or implying, through its very formation, in a sense, the intrinsic symmetric or harmonic being of things.

Symmetry, harmony and Avolution

-count	recount	account
-cord	record	accord
-ward	reward	award
-venge	revenge	avenge
-vert	revert	avert
-volve	revolve	avolve

From the root -count, we have the words recount and account. From the root -cord, we have the words record and accord. From the root -ward, we have the words reward and award. From the root -venge, we have the words revenge and avenge. From the root -vert, we have the words revert and avert. Thus, it seems, from the root -volve, while we have the word revolve, we may have the word avolve.

The roots like -vert and -volve are, in a sense, close in their meanings, as both implying a sense of turning, among other things. It is interesting to see the words formed from the -vert and -volve. While we have the word convert, we have the word convolve. While we have the word invert, we have the word involve. Thus, it seems, it might be said, it may not be that too far-fetched to have the word avolve, while we have the word avert.

While evolution may be pronounced [ˌevəˈluːʃən], avolution may be pronounced [ˌævəˈluːʃən]. Avolution may be seen, in such a sense, as possessing a fuller meaning, as *a* pronounced [æ], rather than just the [e], as *e* is pronounced. [e] may be seen as only half of [æ]. In such a sense, evolution may be seen as only indicating or implying half of the meaning of avolution. As [æ] is fuller than the mere [e], avolution may be seen as indicating or implying a fuller or more complete meaning than evolution. Evolution may only indicate or imply the evolutionary or selective process, but not the symmetric or harmonic process. Thus, in a sense, half of the processes that nature has gone through may not have been reflected in evolution.

Evolution may be only part of the meaning; avolution may be the full meaning. Evolution may be only part of the process; avolution may be the full process. Evolution may be only part of the development; avolution may be the full development. Evolution may be only part of the movement; avolution may be the full movement. Evolution may be only part of the progress; avolution may be the full progress. Evolution may be only about part of nature; avolution may be about the full nature. Evolution may be only about part of the world; avolution may be about the full, complete, and whole world.

In the word evolution, *e* may be seen as the key letter or key part of the word, signifying or indicating the meaning of such a word. By changing *e* into *a*, or, by changing [e] into [æ], it seems, avolution may be seen as containing in itself the meaning of evolution, apart from the other meanings that evolution may not be able to indicate or imply. The symmetric or harmonic pattern seems to disappear with the lower case avolution. This may be seen, in a sense, in that, symmetry or harmony may appear to stop working or operating in some of the developmental processes of things. Nevertheless, just as "av" comes from "Av" or "AV" and will be transformed eventually into them, symmetry or harmony, while hidden from us, may still work or operate in the background, in some fundamental ways.

"A" as a vowel is before "E" in the alphabet. Avolution may be seen, in a sense, as a word, or in its meaning, as being prior to the word Evolution, which, in turn, may be seen as corresponding to the fact that, in the development of things, the harmonic may be seen as being prior to the evolutionary. The symmetric or harmonic existence is so innate, intrinsic, fundamental, primary, or primordial that it may be befitting that the first and foremost letter A in the alphabet should be part of the word and lead in the formation of the word. It is the A-volution. It is not the B-volution. It is not the C-volution. It is not the D-volution. And it is not the E-volution, that is, Evolution, or evolution. It is the A-volution, that is, Avolution, or, avolution. Thus, while the word Avolution or avolution indicates or signifies the volutionary process in the development of things, it may also be seen, at the same time, as representing or expressing the innate or intrinsic primary nature of the symmetric or harmonic development of things, or the symmetric or harmonic existence of things. Such an innate or intrinsic primary nature is exactly the kind of things in my mind when I set out to find the right word or term for the developmental process of things that is called the harmonic evolution.

The avolutionary process may be seen as a fuller or more complete process than the evolutionary process. It is not just evolution; it is avolution. It is not just evolutionary; it is avolutionary. It is not merely an evolutionary process; it is an avolutionary process. It is not just evolution for the grasses; it is avolution for the grasses. It is not just evolution for the leaves; it is avolution for the leaves. It is not just

Symmetry, harmony and Avolution

evolution for the flowers; it is avolution for the flowers. It is not merely evolution for plants; it is avolution for plants. It is not merely evolution for animals; it is avolution for animals. The mere evolution may not give rise to the grasses, to the leaves, or to the flowers. The mere evolution may not give rise to the plants, or, to the animals. It takes more than evolution. It takes more than the evolutionary process. It takes more than the selective process. It takes more than the natural selection. It takes what is called the avolutionary process. It takes what is called, avolution.

Avolution is, relatively speaking, a simple word. Other choices may not be that plain or simple. This may mean that it may be accepted relatively easily and it may be convenient for people to use it. It is to express, signify or indicate both the harmonic and the evolutionary that this word comes into being. It is for the reason that evolution may no longer be able to reveal or describe the whole development or existence of the things in the world that this word is formed. Certainly, this is not the way that new words or terms are to be formed, as they are usually constructed by using the Latin or Greek roots.

When reason cannot capture all the meanings of the world, feeling may have to come forward. When the rational way may not be sufficient to grasp all the aspects of the world, the harmonic way may have to come to the fore. Our consideration with the word avolution may have to do with feeling. The sense of symmetry or harmony found in this word may have to do with feeling. Feeling may lead us to the harmonic way. Feeling may lead us to the deep or profound existence of the world. The pictorial language may have to do with feeling. The pictorial language may connect us with the harmonic way. The pictorial language may connect us with the deep or profound existence of the world.

Language may come from reason. Language may come from feeling. Language may have to do with reason. Language may have to do with feeling. The language associated with reason may lead us to the rational being of the world. The language associated with feeling may lead us to the harmonic being of the world. The language associated with reason may reflect or represent the rational being of the world. The language associated with feeling may reflect or represent the harmonic being of the world.

The coming into being of different languages may reflect the different perceptions of the world. Different languages may have their own advantages. Different languages may be equipped to better capture the different meanings of the world. Different languages may enable us to better grasp the different aspects of the world. Together, they may lead us to see deeper into life. Together, they may enable us to reach a better understanding of the existence of man. Together, they may enable us to have a fuller or more complete grasp of the world, or the universe.

The appearance or use of the word or term avolution should not affect the use or application of the term gevolution, in the sense that, gevolution as a word comes, ultimately, from the character *gai*, or, ge, and -volution. That is, the coming into being or formation of the term gevolution may be seen as having little to do with the change from evolution to avolution. On the other hand, it might be said, the appearance or use of avolution may, in a sense, highlight the sense that what gevolution leads is the deharmonization or desymmetrization of the avolutionary development of man.

The harmonic evolution is not just evolutionary; it may also involve the symmetric or harmonic. The harmonic evolution is not just harmonic; it may also involve the evolutionary. That is the reason why I think that both the harmonic and the evolutionary should be expressed in the new word or term. Once avolution is treated as expressing, indicating, or signifying what is called the harmonic evolution, then it may be seen as representing or standing for the two processes coexisting in the development of things, that is, the harmonic process and the evolutionary process. The harmonic process in the development of things may be called the symmetric or harmonic development of things, that is, the kind of development of things leading, or giving rise to the kind of symmetric or harmonic being or existence of things. The evolutionary process in the development of things may be called the selective or evolutionary development of things, since evolution proceeds, usually, through the means of natural selection, as Darwin has rightly pointed out.

So, what is avolution? First, avolution may be seen as the symmetric or harmonic coming into being of things, such as animals or plants. Secondly, avolution may be seen as the development of things, such as animals or plants, defined, preconditioned, supported, underlain, or guided by symmetry or harmony, and the evolutionary development may be seen as part of such a development that may be understood or comprehended by us through reason, that is, rationally.

Symmetry, harmony and Avolution

The coming into being of animals or plants may be seen as a symmetric or harmonic event, or as a symmetric or harmonic explosion. It is the symmetric or harmonic coming into being of animals or plants. It is the avolutionary coming into being of animals or plants, as such a coming into being may be seen as being defined, conditioned, dominated, or determined by symmetry or harmony.

After the coming into being or appearance, the development of things such as animals or plants may still be seen as avolutionary, that is, not just or merely evolutionary, in the sense that, such a development may still be seen as being defined, conditioned, supported, sustained, or guided by symmetry or harmony. The symmetric or harmonic process may not be so obvious or apparent, but symmetry or harmony may work or operate in the background, with no less force. That is, while the symmetric or harmonic process may not be so easily observed, that is, readily subject to the examination or investigation of reason, nevertheless, the workings or operations of symmetry or harmony should not be overlooked when we try to look into the development of things. In other words, even when we examine or investigate the evolutionary or selective process of things, we should not forget that, symmetry or harmony may work or operate in the background.

From evolution to avolution, in a sense, it might be said, it is from the scientific way to the symmetric way. From evolution to avolution, in a sense, it might be said, it is from the rational way to the harmonic way. It is a great leap forward. We may see deeper into things. We may see deeper into nature. We may see deeper into the world. We may see deeper into the universe. We may be brought closer to the beginning of things. We may be brought closer to the origin of nature. We may be brought closer to the source of the world. We may be brought closer to the fountainhead of the universe.

While evolution may lead us to the scientific understanding of things, avolution may lead us to the symmetric understanding of things. While evolution may reveal the rational being of things, avolution may reveal the harmonic being of things. Nature may not just follow the scientific way. The world may not just follow the scientific way. The universe may not just follow the scientific way. Nature may not just follow the rational way. The world may not just follow the rational way. The universe may not just follow the rational way. The symmetric way may be behind things. The symmetric way may be behind nature.

The harmonic way may be behind the world. The harmonic way may be behind the universe.

That is, while evolution may tell us to follow the scientific way, avolution may tell us that the scientific way may not be the adequate way. That is, while evolution may tell us to follow the rational way, avolution may point to us that, the rational way may not be the sufficient way. The symmetric way may be deeper. The harmonic way may be more profound. The scientific way may not be the only way of things. The scientific way may not be the only way of nature. The rational way may not be the only way of the world. The rational way may not be the only way of the universe.

At the same time, it has to be noted, the discussion of avolution should not be interpreted as meaning that, the theory of evolution is wrong, or outdated. No. The theory of evolution should not be treated as such. In an evolutionary sense, that is, in a selective sense, the theory of evolution is still right, and we still need such a theory to explain the various evolutionary phenomena of things. Our human quest into the unknown may lead us to see deeper and deeper into things, into the depths of nature, or into the secrets of the world. This may have happened before in our history. Is the Newtonian physics wrong, after the discovery of the theory of relativity? Not necessarily. The Newtonian physics has not been treated as invalid or wrong. It is still counted as one of the foundations underlying our understanding of the world.

And, it may have to be pointed out, evolution may still be used, in a strict sense, to refer to the development of things initiated, supported, maintained, or sustained by natural selection. In some cases, or in some situations, this may prove to be useful, and necessary.

§ 3.2.1 Symmetry in Plants

The presence in nature of the trimerous radial symmetry may be seen in a group of flowering plants which only have one embryonic leaf in their seeds. Such a group of flowering plants are distinguished from other flowering plants that usually have two embryonic leaves in their seeds. While this group of flowering plants may possess only one embryonic leaf in their seeds, their flowers usually exhibit a characteristic feature that may be called trimerous radial symmetry, such as, with three petals growing regularly in each whorl. This may be seen in the beautifully colored daylily flowers or in the gracefully colored or shaped flowers of the lady tulips. If one comes close to the daylily flowers or the lady tulip flowers, one can see, the trimerous radial symmetry is brightly exhibited. Three petals grow in each whorl. Each layer of petals are formed harmoniously upon the previous one. Together, all the petals, with the stamens, form a beautiful and harmonious existence that is called the flowers.

The trimerous radial symmetry of flowers can also be observed in a group of flowering plants including, among others, magnolia, avocado, and cinnamon. Upon close examination, one may find, the petals of the flowers, such as on a magnolia tree, are in threes. That is, such flowers usually have three, six, or nine petals, with three petals growing in each whorl. The existence of the tetramerous radial symmetry can be seen in the white correa flowers, whose four petals and four stamens, as we can see, usually form a floral structure that stands almost as a perfect representation of such a form of symmetry. The jade plant flowers may be seen as the floral examples that bear the pentamerous radial symmetry. Even though normally they are small flowers, with white or pinkish colors, they nevertheless demonstrate a remarkable form of pentamerous radial symmetry, with their five petals and five stamens symmetrically and harmoniously arranged together with the sepals.

The existence of radial symmetry, such as the trimerous, tetramerous, and pentamerous radial symmetries, in nature, in the structures and forms of flowers, is truly remarkable, in the sense that, on the one hand, it may reflect the avolutionary process in which flowers finally come into being, with symmetry playing an important and indispensable role in such a process; and on the other hand, it might be said, it may demonstrate the close, or innate or intrinsic relationship between, or rather, in a sense, the co-existence of beauty and symmetry. Flowers thus come into being. Flowers thus demonstrate beauty. Flowers thus exist with symmetry.

§ 3.2.2 The Ordovician Radiation

The Cambrian explosion may be seen as being followed by the Ordovician radiation in the sense that, with the structural, or rather, symmetric, foundation having been laid in the Cambrian, the various animal life forms in the Ordovician were now able to expand, either in sizes, in types, in lifestyles, or in adaptive sophistication, to respond to the localized survival pressures, or to reach new environmental niches.

Thus, what we see is that, after the Cambrian explosion and Ordovician radiation, the Paleozoic animal life forms were well establish and they continued thereafter their development, until we see the reptiles dominating the lands, birds developing from the dinosaurs, and the first mammals coming into being in the Mesozoic era.

As the Ordovician radiation was different, in a sense, from the Cambrian explosion, in terms of mechanisms or processes, some different explanations from the Cambrian explosion may be required, in the sense that, the local or regional mechanisms or processes might have played a significant role in driving or shaping the emergence of the new families, new species, or new groups of animals.

§ 3.2.3 The Primordial Explosion

Symmetry emerged in the animal life forms in the Primordial Explosion. Symmetry came into being in the animal life forms in the Primordial Explosion. The Primordial Explosion was a period of time when symmetry fulfilled or realized itself in the animal life forms. The Primordial Explosion was a symmetric explosion. The Primordial Explosion was a harmonic explosion.

The Ediacaran explosion may be seen as having happened from about 580 million years ago to about 540 million years ago. The Cambrian explosion happened in an extremely short period of time, in the geological sense, about 10 million years, from around 530 million years ago to about 520 million years ago. So in a stricter sense, the Primordial Explosion may refer to the period of time of about 60 million years, from around 580 million years ago to about 520 million years ago. During such a period of time, it might be said, two waves of symmetric surge might have happened, or two waves of symmetric explosion might have occurred. In other words, it might be said, in a relatively rapid pace, during a relatively short period of time, the life forms called animals emerged or came into being for the first time on earth.

§ 3.2.4 The Primordial Explosive Moment

The primordial explosive moment refers to the moment when, around 600 million years ago, it seems, the animal life first appeared on earth. It is a significant moment. It is a decisive moment. It is a far-reaching moment. It is a watershed in the history of life on earth. It represents the movement of symmetry to bring the animal life into being on earth. It signifies the appearance of the new life forms called animals on this planet. Its far-reaching consequences may be seen in the Ediacaran explosion, in the Cambrian explosion, or even in the human emergence around 2 million years ago with the rise of the genus *Homo*.

§ 3.2.5 Symmetry and the World

Symmetry is behind plants. Symmetry is behind animals. Symmetry is behind flowers. Symmetry is behind man. Symmetry is behind the plant world. Symmetry is behind the animal world. Symmetry is behind the world. Flowers are the flowers of symmetry, in a plant way. Human beings are the flowers of symmetry, in a human way. Flowers are the flowers of the plant world. Human beings are the flowers of the animal world. They are all flowers. They are all flowers of symmetry. They are all flowers of the world. They are all fulfillments or realizations of symmetry. They are all fulfillments or realizations of symmetry in the world. They are all fulfillments or realizations of symmetry in the world, though in different ways, in different senses, in different manners, or in different fashions. To see flowers is to see symmetry. To see man is to see symmetry. To see plants is to see symmetry. To see animals is to see symmetry. To see the world is to see symmetry. To look into plants is to look into symmetry. To look into animals is to look into symmetry. To look into flowers is to look into symmetry. To look into man is to look into symmetry. To look into the world is to look into symmetry.

§ 3.2.6 The Division between Radial Symmetry and Bilateral Symmetry

Cnidarians, ctenophores and echinoderms mostly live in the sea. That is, it seems, it might be said, the radially symmetric animals are mostly confined to living in the sea, except for a few species such as the freshwater jelly or freshwater hydra. The similar things may be seen in the radially symmetric plants. The radially symmetric plants, such as conifers, like pines or firs, are without flowers. They appear to stay all the same, it seems, in all the seasons, or in all the environments. Certainly, some things or changes may happen in them. Or, some mechanisms may operate and some processes may be triggered, in them, as a reaction to the changing seasons or environments. But, in a general sense, it seems, it might be said, a lack of ability to react to the changing seasons or environments may be observed in them. Such an inability, if it could be said as such, may be seen as being reflected, in a sense, that is, in a symmetric sense, in the radially symmetric animals, as they are generally unable to spread into the freshwater or onto the dry land.

Bilateral symmetry may be seen as behind the Ediacaran explosion, the Cambrian explosion, the Devonian explosion, the Cretaceous explosion, and the appearance of the human beings. Animals with bilateral symmetry have flourished. The bilaterally symmetric animals, such as fish, insects, birds, mammals, primates, or humans, have dominated the surface of the earth. Plants with bilateral symmetry have thrived, too. The flowering plants, as we know, react to the changing seasons or environments in some remarkable ways, and, they grow the beautiful flowers. Flowering plants are the bilaterally symmetric plants. Humans are the bilaterally symmetric animals. Bilateral symmetry gives rise to the flowers. Bilateral symmetry gives rise to the humans. Bilateral symmetry gives rise to the beauty and magnificence of the world.

On the other hand, it may have to be noticed, the division between radial symmetry and bilateral symmetry may not always be so obvious and clear-cut. Radial symmetry may be present in the bilaterally symmetric animals or plants. Bilateral symmetry may be found in the radially symmetric plants or animals. In other words, it might be said, when it comes to the actual division of radial symmetry and bilateral symmetry in or among plants or animals, it might be said, such a

Symmetry, harmony and Avolution

division may only be reached in an approximate or general sense. That is to say, in most cases, we may have to look for, in plants or animals, the dominant or defining form of symmetry, if we really want to decide whether a plant or an animal is radially symmetric or bilaterally symmetric.

Among echinoderms are some animals called brittle stars. Some brittle stars are found to possess the kind of bodies covered with crystal lenses. Such lenses may function as a light-detecting system, which may not be often found in other radially symmetric animals. Why should such brittle stars develop such a system? Why should such echinoderms be able to possess such a system? Given the difference between radial symmetry and bilateral symmetry, it might be said, the presence of bilateral symmetry in the existence of echinoderms may explain, in a sense, the appearance of such a kind of visual system in the echinoderms.

People sometimes think that the flowering plants, the angiosperms, might have originated from the gymnosperms, as such a thinking may seem to be compatible with the developmental models of things, in that, the gymnosperms appear to be more primitive and the angiosperms appear to be more developed, in some sense. This may not be true. The angiosperms and gymnosperms such as conifers are different plants. They come from different symmetries. They originate from different symmetries. They are the fulfillment or realization of different symmetries. The angiosperms may be seen as mainly the fulfillment or realization of bilateral symmetry in the plant world. The gymnosperms, especially the conifers, may be regarded as mainly the fulfillment or realization of radial symmetry in the plant kingdom. They represent the different symmetric fulfillments or realizations in nature. It is in such a sense that, it might be said, there might not be such a kind of developmental process from one to the other. In other words, it may not be the case that the angiosperms might have originated from the gymnosperms. And it seems, this may be revealed by some molecular or genetic studies, as such studies seem to indicate that the angiosperms and the gymnosperms may be actually two groups of plants quite different from each other.

Such a kind of misunderstanding may also happen with regard to animals. People sometimes think that, sponges appear to be primitive, in a sense, and thus other animals such as cnidarians, ctenophores or echinoderms might have originated from sponges. Or, as cnidarians, ctenophores or echinoderms appear to be primitive, the other animals more advanced, such as worms, birds, mammals, or even humans, might have come into being from them. No. They are different things. They are different animals. They are the different fulfillments or realizations of symmetry in nature. Sponges generally represent the realization of asymmetry. Animals like cnidarians, ctenophores or echinoderms mainly represent the realization of radial symmetry. The other animals more advanced, such as worms, birds, mammals or humans, may be regarded as the fulfillment or realization of bilateral symmetry. That is, they represent the different symmetries. They embody the different symmetries. They have different symmetric sources. They have different symmetric origins. It may not be the case that there might be some developmental processes from one group to the other. Animals like cnidarians, ctenophores or echinoderms might not have developed from sponges. In the same sense, animals like worms, birds, mammals or humans might not have developed from cnidarians, ctenophores, or echinoderms, or even from sponges. They are the different symmetric animals. They are the different symmetric embodiments. Together, they constitute the symmetric fulfillment or realization in the animal world.

§ 3.2.7 The Journey of Life on Earth

The journey of life on earth has been truly amazing. It may have been punctuated by a number of explosive moments. It may have been characterized by a number of explosive periods, phases, or stages.

The movement of symmetry on the planet earth may be seen in such a journey. The movement of harmony on the planet earth may be seen in such a journey. The movement of symmetry may be seen in such surging moments. The movement of harmony may be seen in such surging periods, phases, or stages.

The coming into being of the double helical symmetry may stand as the explosive or surging moment for the appearance of DNA.

The coming into being of the sexual symmetry may stand as the explosive or surging moment for the emergence of sexual reproduction.

The Ediacaran explosion and the Cambrian explosion may stand as the explosive or surging periods, phases or stages in which animals came into being, and in which both radial symmetry and bilateral symmetry might have fulfilled or realized themselves in or through the animal life.

The Devonian explosion may stand as the explosive or surging period, phase or stage in which plants came into being, and in which symmetry might have fulfilled or realized itself in or through the plant life.

The Cretaceous explosion may stand as the explosive or surging period, phase or stage in which the flowering plants came into being, and in which both bilateral symmetry and sexual symmetry might have fulfilled or realized themselves in or through the flowering plants.

The rise of the genus *Homo* about 2.5 million years ago on earth may stand as the explosive or surging moment for the appearance of the human species, or for the fulfillment or realization of symmetry in the human species.

The journey of life on earth may be seen as the journey of symmetry on earth. The journey of life on earth may be seen as the journey of harmony on earth. The movement of life on earth may be seen as the movement of symmetry on earth. The development of life on earth may be seen as the development of harmony on earth. Symmetry moves; life emerges. Harmony progresses; life develops. Symmetry fulfils itself on earth; life thrives on earth. Harmony realizes itself on earth; life prospers and flourishes in the world.

§ 3.2.8 The Origin of Species

As the simplest animals, sponges may be among the earliest organisms that appeared on earth. Are sponges possibly our ancient ancestors? Probably not. Sponges are the asymmetric organisms, and we are the bilaterally symmetric animals. As such, it is likely that they are not our ancestors. Do sponges and the human beings share certain things? Certainly, it might be said, they should share, to a certain extent, the basic building blocks of life with us.

Cnidarians such as jellyfish or sea anemones may be among the first animals that possessed a simple nervous system. Are they possibly our early ancestors? Probably not. Cnidarians such as jellyfish or sea anemones are the radially symmetric organisms, and we are the animals with bilateral symmetry. As such, it is likely that they are not our ancestors, though we may have shared certain things with them, such as, an ability to possess a kind of nervous system.

Comb jellies may be among the earliest animals that developed on earth. Are they possibly the ancestors of all animals on earth, including us? Probably not. Ctenophores like comb jellies are mostly radially symmetric organisms, and we are the animals demonstrating unequivocally bilateral symmetry. As such, it is likely that they are not the ancestors of all animals including us. Certainly, it might be said, we share some things with them, like the capabilities to move or to control the body.

What is the origin of species? Symmetry is the origin of species. Harmony is the origin of species. The way of heaven is the origin of species. Heaven is the origin of species.

§ 3.2.9 Genetics and Complexity

Genetic researches seem to have shown that, the workings or operations of genes are much more complex than people thought. People may think that, they may find or reveal all the secrets of genes by sequencing or identifying them. That may not be really the case. The complexity of the workings or operations of genes may be vastly beyond any people's expectations. Such as, people may think that, complexity may mean the quantity of genes. That is, people may think, the more complex an organism is, the more genes it may possess. That may not be the case, after all. More complexity may not necessarily mean more genes. Complexity may not come from the quantity of genes. Complexity may come from the possibility that the same genes may perform vastly different functions.

Why are the workings or operations of genes so complex? Why is this genetic complexity? Where does it come from? What does it mean? DNA means the double helical symmetry. The double helical symmetry means DNA. DNA means the genetic symmetry. The genetic symmetry means DNA. The genetic complexity may come from the genetic symmetry. The genetic complexity may mean the genetic symmetry. The genetic complexity may represent the genetic symmetry. The genetic complexity may stand for the genetic symmetry. It may mean the power of the genetic symmetry. It may represent the depth of the genetic symmetry. It may stand for the potential of the genetic symmetry. It may be the symmetric power. It may be the symmetric depth. It may be the symmetric potential. It may be the symmetric complexity.

The genetic complexity, coming from the symmetric complexity, may be beyond the full and complete grasp of reason. In a sense, it might be said, this may stand as a safeguard against the possible harm coming from man, or the possible destruction caused by man. Man could do anything. Man could wreak any havoc. Man could destroy anything valuable. Man could destroy anything meaningful. Man could destroy anything beautiful. If reason could reach all the information of DNA, if reason could reach all the secrets of nature, if reason could comprehend all the mechanisms of the world, if reason could grasp all the potentials of man, DNA would have been manipulated at will, nature would have been ripped apart, the world would have been broken into pieces, and man would not have survived long.

§ 3.2.10 Comb Jellies

Some genetic studies seem to suggest that, comb jellies might have appeared before the simpler sponges. Is it a problem? Not necessarily. The coming into being of the early animals might have been a symmetric or harmonic coming into being, not an evolutionary coming into being. That is, the coming into being of the early animals might have been a symmetric or harmonic event, not an evolutionary event. That is, the coming into being of the early animals might have to do with a symmetric or harmonic explosion, but not an evolutionary explosion. That is, the coming into being of the early animals might have to do with an avolutionary process, but not an evolutionary process.

Symmetries might have come into being together. Symmetries might have appeared side by side. Symmetries might have exploded at about the same time. Symmetries might have existed together with asymmetry. Symmetries might have come into being prior to the coming into being of asymmetry. Symmetries might have come into being after the coming into being of asymmetry. Radial symmetry might have appeared prior to the appearance of asymmetry. Radial symmetry might have appeared prior to the appearance of bilateral symmetry. In the same sense, bilateral symmetry might have appeared prior to the appearance of asymmetry or radial symmetry. Sponges may have to do with asymmetry. Comb jellies may have to do with radial symmetry. As the radially symmetric animals, it is possible that, comb jellies might have come into being or appeared before the asymmetric sponges.

People sometimes suggest that, sponges may be the ancestors of animals, including humans. Or, if the evidence indicates that comb jellies may have appeared before sponges, then comb jellies may be the oldest ancestors of animals, including humans. Is it true? Not necessarily. Comb jellies may not be the ancestors of all animals. They may be the ancestors of the kind of radially symmetric animals now classified as ctenophores, or to a certain extent, possibly, some cnidarians. Humans and many other animals are bilaterally symmetric animals. Comb jellies are the animals that may be seen as mainly having to do with radial symmetry. They are different. They are different animals. They are different animals, symmetrically.

§ 3.3 Harmony, Science, and the World

Man, as a form of existence, may be seen as just one form of existence among so many forms of existence in this world. As we can see or witness, around us are rocks, rivers, mountains, trees, flowers, grasses, clouds, stars, and so many kinds of animals. They all exist in this world, along with us. And together, we constitute the world in which we are living. Where do they come from? What may be their origin? From where do they and we humans originate? Why, after all, is it the case that there is something rather than nothing? We humans have developed from the early life forms. The early life forms came into being in a suitable environment on earth. The earth, like other planets in the solar system, was formed out of a mass of dust and gas in the solar system. The sun, like many other stars, is thought to have been formed out of a mass of gas called molecular cloud. The molecular clouds are mostly gases coming into being through the formation or combination of the particles, which, in their own turn, came into being as a result of the conversion of energy shortly after the Big Bang. Science has made great strides in the sense that so many phenomena, especially in the field of physical cosmology, have been explained in a rational and fairly convincing way. This is indeed a great achievement of mankind. Science indeed enables us to explore into the world and the universe, and provides us with the explanations and answers that our human minds are so eagerly looking for. Having been greatly impressed by the achievements of the modern science, we human beings nevertheless should not stop our thinking, or searching. We may ask more questions. We may raise more issues. We may inquire into things deeper and beyond. And we may call attention to the kind of things that may not necessarily be easily explained by or through science. What exactly was the energy at the initial stage of the Big Bang? From where did it come? Why did it come? Why should it come? Why is it not the case that there was no energy at all at the initial point? Why should the energy convert? Why should the energy not stay the same, as energy, even after the Big Bang? Why should the energy be converted into the particles? Why should the energy not be converted into other forms of existence, other than particles, as it appears, the chances or possibilities are just as unlimited or endless? Why should the energy be converted into something that could make certain things to come out, at all? Why should the energy be converted into the kind of things that could make gases or clouds? Who made the conversion? What made the conversion possible, or inevitable? In what sense? In what way? Or, through what kind of manner?

After the masses of gases or clouds came into being, theories such as the nebular hypothesis tell us that, due to gravitation, the density of the gases or clouds would increase, and as a result, the gases or clouds would eventually coalesce into what is now known as the planets or stars. The sun then came into being. The solar system then came into being. The earth then came into being. The environment for the happening of life was thus prepared and taking its shape. At this point, one may ask, as one should, even after the coming into being of the gases or clouds, why should they have to "coalesce" into the planets or stars? Why should they not stay the same, and remain the same? Why should they have to change? Why should they have to develop? What might be behind such development? What might be underlying such development? What might be beyond such development, in the end? Why should the planets or stars have to come into being? Why should the planets or stars have to be formed, at all, in the first place? People may say, that, theories such as the nebular hypothesis have already told us, and explained it, it was gravity. It was the gravitational force that led the gases or clouds to eventually form the planets or stars. It is a rational and scientific explanation, indeed. But, one may ask, why was it such a case? Why was it the gravity? Why was it gravity at all? Why was it not the case that there was no such thing as gravity, at all, no existence of gravity, and no force of gravity? Why was it not otherwise? Why was it not the opposite of gravity? Why was it not the opposite of the gravitational force? Why was it the case that the gravitational force had to work here? Why was it not a repelling force? Why was it a force holding things together, rather than driving things away? While the gravity came into the picture, it appears, the opposite of the gravity might hold the same chance. While the gravitational force came into play, it seems, the opposite of the gravitational force might deserve a similar role. But, why not? Why? Was it an accident? Was it by chance? Was it coincidence? Coincidence with what? By chance in what sense? An accident in what kind of way? Or, was it fate? Was it destiny? Was it something beyond? Was it something that is beyond our human conception? Was it something that is beyond our human comprehension? That is, was it something that is beyond our human understanding, that is, our human scientific understanding?

The gravity came into play, and the solar system came into being, the earth came into being. Once the earth was formed, life began to arise. The earth would see the coming into being, gradually, that is, step by step, or stage after stage, of plants, of fish, of amphibians, of reptiles, of mammals, of primates, of the early humans, or, of the modern humans. Certainly, as we all know, just like the scientific theories such as the nebular hypothesis illustrating in a fairly convincing way the formation or coming into being of the stars or planets, scientific achievements in the fields such as biology, chemistry, physics, physiology, or neuroscience provide us with the explanations or answers concerning the existence or development of the various life forms on earth. With regard to plants, it is revealed, it is the plant hormones that regulate, within the plant bodies, the life cycles of plants, such as, the shaping of the leaves, the formation of the flowers, the timing of the ripening of the fruits, or, the growth or development of the plant tissues. The plant hormones are produced by the plant cells. They constitute one of the most vital parts of plants, without which, it seems, plants may not grow into the plants as we know, and they may in no way exist, along with us, in this world, as plants. When it comes to the highly developed life forms on earth, the humans, we are told, the neurons are the basic units working to form the nervous system of a human being. The nervous system of a human being functions as the neurons, the nerve cells, transmit information through electrical and chemical signals within the body. Thus, through the electrical and chemical workings of the neurons, a human being is able to live or exist as a human being in the world, to interact with the environment, to control his or her movements, to respond to the stimuli, and to manage in a suitable way his or her behaviors or actions. Certainly, as one may expect, the working mechanisms of the neurons in a nervous system may be delicate and complex. It is only through the modern scientific advances that the intricate structures and complex workings of the neurons are revealed and disclosed to us.

Science has helped us improve our understanding about the ways or workings of the world. We now may see into the workings and functioning of the planets. We now may see into the living mechanisms of animals. We now may see into the inner structures or complexities of the human beings. We now know how plants exist. We now know how animals survive. We now know how the human beings live their lives, through a highly complex and integrated nervous system that had come into being after a long process of development. Science has indeed presented us with a picture, about various life forms and about the world. It is indeed a scientific and rational picture, in the sense that the details of such a picture are well investigated, well proved, and well corroborated by or through experiences or scientific researches. Is this the only and whole picture? To a scientist, or to a person inclined to science or reason, it seems, it is. It is the only picture. It is the whole picture. Otherwise, what other kinds of picture could we get? It is a great achievement. It is achieved through the efforts and hard works of so many people. It embodies the human spirits to explore into the unknown. It stands as a great testimony to the human struggle to look into the secrets of the world. Should we celebrate? Yes, we should. Should we be proud of ourselves? Yes, we should. Should we ask more questions? Yes, we should, too. Our achievements should not make us unable to ask more questions. Our achievements should not make us unable to look into ourselves, or to question ourselves. To question ourselves. To examine the things we have done. To look into the ways that we have come through. These are the kind of things that we should do. These are the kind of things that we human beings should not be afraid of. As we have seen above, there are still questions, and it seems, a lot of questions, that may remain unanswered, even though science may have made great strides and so many things may have been revealed or explained to us in a fairly convincing way, that is, scientifically. We may raise issues with the models of the Big Bang concerning the initial energy. We may raise issues with the nebular hypothesis concerning gravity. Certainly, we may ask more questions about the plant hormones, and we may also ask more questions about the neurons in a nervous system.

The scientific explanations tell us that the plant hormones are produced by the cells, within the plant bodies. Once they are produced, they function to regulate the plant lives. But, one may ask, why should the plant hormones be produced or formed, in the plant bodies, in the first place? Why? People might point to some explanations to tell us how the plant hormones are formed, secreted, or produced within the plant bodies, such as, through what kind of mechanisms, what kind of organs or tissues of the plants may be involved, or, how delicate or complex such processes might be. But, it seems, all these scientific explanations may only explain "how" the plant hormones are produced or formed in the plant bodies. They do not tell us, in any way, why the plant hormones should be produced in the plant bodies in the first place, at all. People may say, if the plant hormones were not produced within the plant bodies, then no plants would have existed as plants in this world. This may not be a good answer or explanation, as it tries to use the consequences to justify the possible causes. It seems, the existence of a world without plants may be perfectly ok, or possible, as we can imagine, that is, insofar as we can see, that is, insofar as we engage in this discussion at this point. That is, it seems, a world without plants is possible. So, why should the plant hormones be produced or formed in the first place? Why should the plant hormones come into being, at all? Is it the case that, the plant hormones are formed or produced, so that plants could exist? Is it the case that, the plant hormones are formed or produced, so that the world could exist with plants? Is it the case that, the plant hormones come into being, so that the world could support other life forms, and such life forms might develop further, and further?

Certainly, it seems, science has only explained to us the processes in which the plant hormones are formed or produced, and it does not provide us with the kind of explanations as to why the plant hormones should be formed or produced, that is, come into being, in the first place. But, "why" is what we are concerned. We are not satisfied just with the kind of answers concerning the processes of their coming into being. We are not satisfied just with the kind of answers concerning the "how". We want to ask "why". We want to know "why". We want the kind of answers that may address the "why". Then, why should the plant hormones come into being, in the first place, at all? Certainly, the same kind of questions may be asked with regard to the neurons or the nervous system. Why, after all, should the neurons come into being? Why, after all, should the nervous system come into being? The plant hormones are vital to plants. The neurons are vital to the nervous system. The nervous system is vital to the human beings, and to animals. So, why should such vital things be formed or produced in the first place? Why should such vital things come into being in this world, at all? Is there anything behind the eventual coming into being of such vital things, apart from the kind of processes associated with their formation or production? Is there anything behind the eventual coming into being of such vital things, apart from the kind of scientific explanations given to us? What is really behind the coming into being of the plant hormones, apart from the kind of processes associated with their formation or production? What is really behind the workings or mechanisms of the plant hormones, apart from the kind of things that we are told? What is really behind the coming into being of the neurons, apart from the kind of processes in which they are described to have come into being? What is really behind the workings or mechanisms of the neurons, apart from the kind of things that we are told? What is really behind the coming into being of the nervous system, apart from the kind of processes in which it is described to have been formed? What is really behind the workings or mechanisms of the nervous system, apart from the kind of things that are scientifically revealed to us?

People might say, no, there is nothing more. The scientific explanations or revelations are all what it takes, that is, the processes, the workings, or the mechanisms revealed by science are the only things of the world, when it comes to the coming into being or operations of such things like the plant hormones, the neurons, or, the nervous system. One should not look beyond science, as it is otherwise irrational. One should not believe in the things that are outside of science, as they are not reasoned, and thus they should be deemed as indefensible or groundless. Yes, we should respect science, as it has provided us with so much proved knowledge and understanding about the world. Yes, we should believe in science, as it has helped us improve our living conditions and has enabled us to live a better life. But, it seems, the world is not just about science, or, it seems, science may not be all of the world. There are many things that may lie outside of science. There are many things that may not be simply explained by science. There are many things that, it seems, may not be reached by or through science. A flower is beautiful. But, it seems, such a phenomenon cannot be simply explained by or through science. It is a humoral sense of man. We love the scene of a sunset. But, it seems, such a love cannot be simply explained by or through science. It is an antean harmony felt by we human beings. A mother's love of a child is beautiful. But, it seems, such a human love cannot be simply explained by or through science. It is a beauty coming out of, or displaying, or demonstrating, the humoral man. We have certain moral senses. But, it seems, they cannot be explained, or reached, by or through reason alone. The world is more than science. The world is beyond science. The world is more than reason. The world is beyond reason. The world is beyond reason to reach. The world is more than science could explain. We have to ask the whys. We have to continue our search. We have to explore further. We have to look into the things that may lie outside of the reach of reason or science. Otherwise, we are not the complete human beings. Otherwise, we are not the human beings in a complete sense. Otherwise, we cannot live as the human beings in a full way. Otherwise, we cannot fulfill ourselves as the human beings as the human beings should, that is, as they are expected, that is, as they are supposed to, that is, in a sense, as they are realized for.

 Is it the case that, while the beauty of a flower cannot be simply explained by or through science, there might be something behind the coming into being of the initial energy that may not be simply explained by or through science? Is it the case that, while the beauty of a sunset cannot be simply explained by or through science, there might be something behind the coming into being of the gravity amid the molecular clouds or between stars that may not be simply explained by or through science? Is it the case that, while the beauty of a mother's love of a child cannot be simply explained by or through science, there might be something behind the coming into being or the workings or mechanisms of the plant hormones that may not be simply explained by or through science? Is it the case that, while the moral senses of man cannot be simply explained, or reached, by or through science alone, there might be something behind the coming into being or the workings or mechanisms of the neurons, or of the nervous system, that may not be simply explained, or reached, by or through science alone? It seems, the world is so rich that, we should not confine our human mind to such an extent that anything outside of science should be pushed aside and disregarded. It appears, the world is so expansive that we human beings should look beyond the limited reason and into the kind of things that may lie at a level deeper or broader than science.

That is to say, the world may be richer than science; the world may be broader than reason. That is to say, the meaning of the world may be deeper than science; the meaning of the world may be deeper than reason. Science is great, but, it may not encompass all the meaning of the world. Science is great, but, it may not reveal all the secrets of man. Science is great, but, it may not reveal all the secrets of the world. To grasp fully the meaning of the world, we may have to go beyond science. To grasp fully the meaning of man, we may have to go beyond reason. To understand fully the secrets of the world, we may have to look beyond science. To understand fully the secrets of man, we may have to look beyond reason. Reason is limited. Science is limited. Reason is very limited when it comes to man. Is science very limited, when it comes to the world?

If one is to deny, categorically, the kind of things raised above that may be associated with the initial energy, the gravity, the plant hormones, the neurons, or the nervous system, then one of the logical conclusions may be that: the world may have come into being by chance, or, as an accident. Is it true that, the world comes into being by chance? Is it true that, the world comes into being as an accident? It seems, it may not be an accident, in the sense that, as we look around, it appears, as we can witness, all the things, such as fish, plants, animals, or humans, exist, side by side, with each other, and in a sense, depend on each other. It seems, it may not be by chance, in the sense that, it seems, meaning may be seen in this world, and meaning may be displayed or demonstrated in this world in many ways. The world has meaning. And some of the fundamental meanings of the world may be seen in the coming into being of man. Human beings are born, it might be said, with an inner affinity with truth, in the sense that, their humoral senses or instincts may be seen as closely related to or associated with truth, or, the coming into being of truth. The affinity or closeness between human beings and truth may be seen in their coming into being, and may also be seen in their lives. Human beings live with truth. Human beings live with meaning. The life of man develops with truth. The life of man develops with meaning. Meaning is in truth; meaning is in man. Meaning is reflected in truth; meaning is reflected in man. Meaning is demonstrated through truth; meaning is demonstrated through man. Meaning is in man through truth; meaning is in truth through man. Meaning is reflected in man through truth; meaning is reflected in truth through man. Meaning is demonstrated in man through truth; meaning is demonstrated in truth through man. Man comes into being, and truth comes to have meaning. Truth and man come together, meaning thus has meaning, and the world thus, in a sense, comes into being.

It seems, it is possible for the existence of a world without human beings, as we all know, there was a period of time on earth before the appearance of the human beings. So, why should such a world come into being, with the intelligent human beings? What might be behind the coming into being of such a world? Is there anything behind the things of such a world? Is there anything underlying the existence of the things in such a world? Even without the human beings, it seems, the world was full of significance. Before the coming of the human beings, the earth saw the existence of all kinds of things, animate or inanimate, such as, rocks, mountains, rivers, clouds, fish, plants, and the various animals. Rocks, mountains, rivers, and clouds formed an environment in which fish, plants and other various animals lived, survived, and thrived. Without such a favorable environment, it seems, all the life forms such as fish, plants and animals might not be able to survive, or even, came into being, at all. Among all the life forms, it seems, they depended, in a sense, on each other. They lived side by side. They survived together. They thrived together. It was a world of co-existence. It was a world of co-development. It was a world of dynamic development. It was a world of vitality. It was a world that would give rise to, eventually, the coming into being of man. Then man came into being, as an animal, as part of this world. As an animal, man could exist just like the other animals, alongside the rocks, mountains, rivers, clouds, fish, plants, and the other animals. As part of this world, man could live his life, thriving and prospering, as the human being, fulfilling and realizing himself, through his human endeavors or undertakings, such as, studying the various life forms like fish or plants, exploring the natural world, or appreciating the beauty of the mountains, rivers, or clouds.

Animals survive on the nutrients obtained from plants or other animals. Clouds are formed, and rains fall from the sky. The earth or soil is moistened, and plants grow. Fish swim in the rivers. Rocks form the mountains. Plants and animals arise and thrive on this planet. We human beings exist in this world, depending on the existence of all of these things, rocks, mountains, rivers, clouds, fish, plants, and the animals. Without them, it seems, we cannot survive. Without them, it seems, we may not live. Without them, it seems, we may not thrive. Without them, it seems, we may not exist as the human beings, as we know, or as we imagine. It is a world for us. It is a world prepared for us. It is a world from which we come. It is a world in which we may find ourselves. It is a world that may enable us to fulfill and realize ourselves as the human beings.

Things in this world are existing, it seems, in a sense, with harmony. Without rocks or soil, there might have been no mountains or plains. Without mountains or plains, there might have been no places for plants or animals to survive or thrive. Without clouds, there might have been no rains. Without rains, there might have been no rivers or waters. Without rivers or waters, there might have been no fish or other life forms. Without the various life forms, there might have been no plants or animals in this world. Without plants or animals, there might have been no human beings. Without the human beings, it seems, insofar as we know, in a sense, then, there might have been no beings to recognize or witness the meaning or significance of the world.

It seems, it might be said, the world is in a unity, the world is in a harmony. The world exists with unity. The world exists in harmony. Man comes into being, as an animal, as part of the world. Man comes into being, as part of the unity, as part of the harmony. Man comes into being, as part of the significance of the word, as part of the meaning of the world. From animals, man appears, with highly developed characteristics or qualities. From animals, man emerges, as a way to witness his own coming into being, and the coming into being of the world. From animals, man arises, as a way to witness the significance of his own being, and the significance of the being of the world.

From the harmony of the world, man comes into being. From the unity of the world, man emerges. If the world were not existing in harmony, it seems, it might disintegrate. If the world were not existing with unity, it seems, it might fall apart. If harmony did not exist among the things in the world, it seems, rocks might not be there, mountains might not stand, rivers might not flow, clouds might not be high in the sky, fish might disappear, plants might stop to grow, animals might not survive, and the human beings might wither, be lost, and eventually, cease to exist. If unity could not be found among the things in the world, it seems, nothing could last long, all the things could be in conflict, and life would be short, nasty and brutal. If there were no meaning in the world, then, life would be hopeless, existence would be empty, living would be of no value, and man would be nothing.

What is behind the beauty of a flower? What is behind the beauty of a sunset? What is behind the beauty of a mother's love of a child? What is behind the moral senses of man? It might be said, it is harmony. It is harmony that may be seen as behind the beauty of a flower. It is harmony that may be seen as behind the beauty of a sunset. It is harmony that may be seen as behind the beauty of a mother's love of a child. It is harmony that may be seen as behind the coming into being of man. It is harmony that may be seen as behind the moral senses of man.

It is harmony. It is harmony that may be seen as behind all these things. What is behind rocks? What is behind mountains? What is behind rivers? What is behind clouds? What is behind fish? What is behind plants? What is behind animals? It might be said, it is harmony. It is harmony that may be seen, in a sense, as behind the existence of rocks. It is harmony that may be seen, in a sense, as behind the existence of mountains. It is harmony that may be seen, in a sense, as behind the existence of rivers. It is harmony that may be seen, in a sense, as behind the existence of clouds. It is harmony that may be seen, in a sense, as behind the existence of fish. It is harmony that may be seen, in a sense, as behind the existence of plants. It is harmony that may be seen, in a sense, as behind the existence of animals. It is harmony that may be seen, in a sense, as behind the existence of the world. It is harmony that may be seen, in a sense, as behind the world. It is harmony that may be seen, in a sense, as having to do with the existence of the world. It is harmony that may be seen, in a sense, as having to do with the existence of rocks, mountains, rivers, clouds, fish, plants, animals, or the human beings. It is harmony that may be seen, in a sense, as having to do with the existence of all these things. It is harmony that may be seen, in a sense, as having to do with their co-existence. It is harmony that may be seen, in a sense, as having to do with the unity among them. It is harmony that may be seen, in a sense, as having to do with the unity of the world.

Harmony gives rise to things. Harmony gives rise to the coming into being of things. It was through harmony, it might be said, the initial energy came into being, from a previous state. It was through harmony, it might be said, the gravity came into being, so that stars or planets might be formed. It was through harmony, it might be said, the plant hormones came into being, so that plants might exist and grow. It was through harmony, it might be said, the neurons came into being, so that the nervous system might be formed. It was through harmony, it might be said, the nervous system came into being, so that the human beings might emerge, dwell in this world, and recognize or witness its meaning or significance.

What is harmony? Harmony is a sense of coming into being; harmony is a sense of passing away. Harmony is a sense of coming together; harmony is a sense of going away. Harmony is a sense of coming together, such that things may be formed; harmony is a sense of going away, such that conditions may be prepared. Harmony is the way. Harmony is the way of the world. Harmony is the way of things coming together. Harmony is the way of things coming into being. Harmony is the way of things passing away. Harmony is the way of things drawing to a close. Harmony is what driving things to come together. Harmony is what leading things to come into being. Harmony is what guiding things to an end. Harmony is what directing things to a close. Harmony is the force. Harmony is the power. Harmony is the potential. Harmony is the inner essence. Harmony is the vitality. Harmony is the dynamic. Harmony is the mechanism. Harmony is the process. Harmony is in the world. Harmony is in all things. In harmony, man comes into being. In harmony, man finds himself. In harmony, the world comes together. In harmony, the world celebrates itself, that is, fulfils or realizes itself. When harmony is realized, man is realized. When man is realized, harmony is realized. When the world is realized, harmony fulfils itself. When harmony fulfils itself, the world comes into being.

Can we reach harmony? Can we reach harmony through reason? It seems, no, we cannot. We may feel it. We may feel its presence. We may feel its existence. We may feel, in a sense, its workings or operations. We may feel, in a sense, its workings in flowers, in trees, in grasses. We may feel, in a sense, its presence behind rocks, mountains, rivers, or clouds. We may feel, in a sense, its existence in rains falling from the sky, in crops growing up and strong, in plants multiplying and spreading, in fish swimming in the rivers, or in animals roaming the land, robust and free. We may feel it in the subtle operations of the plant hormones, in the delicate workings of the neurons, or in the complex mechanisms of the nervous system. We may feel it in the beauty of a flower, in the beauty of a sunset, or in the beauty of a mother's love of a child. We may feel it among stars, among planets, or among the heavenly bodies high above us. It is a sense. It is a feeling. It is a sense about the world. It is a feeling about the world. It is a sense from the world. It is a feeling coming out of the world. It is a sense that something is behind the things around us. It is a feeling that something is underlying the things of the world, as, otherwise, it seems, things should not be the way they are, or, the world might not have come into being in the first place, at all. It is a sense of human recognition, in the sense that, the world comes into being with something, in some sense, in some way, or in some manner. It is a sense of human awareness, in the sense that, it seems, things are related to reach other, in some sense, in some way, or in some manner, and it seems, they come into being together, exist together, or fulfill or realize themselves, in a sense, together. It is a sense of human self-recognition or self-awareness, in the sense that, the human beings understand, they are just part of the world, along with them are so many things, marvelous and wonderful, such as, rocks, mountains, rivers, clouds, fish, plants, or animals, and without their presence, it seems, the human beings simply could not exist or survive. It is a human feeling about the world, in the sense that, there are so many possibilities, there are so many possible directions, and yet, as we know, the world is what it is and things are what they are. It is a human feeling, about the things in the world, in the sense that, there are so many choices for things to occur otherwise, there are so many opportunities for things to develop in other directions, and yet, as we know, the world is not in the other kinds of shapes or forms, and things have not come with the other kinds of structures, arrangements, or even, meanings. Out of so many possibilities, the world as we know emerges. Out of so many directions, things as we know come into being. A human sense, it seems, thus emerges, with the emergence of the world. A human feeling, it seems, thus comes into being, with the coming into being of the things of the world.

Symmetry, harmony and Avolution

Harmony may be seen in the flowering of a flower. Harmony may be seen in the rocks, mountains, rivers, clouds, and the setting sun coming together to display the beauty of a sunset. Harmony may be seen in a mother's love of a child, revealing the fulfillment of the humoral feelings of man. Harmony may be seen in the harmonious existence of stars and planets, forming the marvelous and wonderful spheres in the sky. Harmony may be seen in the realization of the humoral man as a moral man. Harmony may be seen in the growth or development of things in the world. Harmony may be seen in the growing of crops or plants following the rains. Harmony may be seen in the forming of a new planet system deep in the space. Harmony may be seen in the mating or breeding of animals. Harmony may be seen in the ripening of fruits. Harmony may be seen in the development or flourishing of a human civilization. Harmony may be seen in the falling of leaves. Harmony may be seen in the withering of a flower. Harmony may be seen in the aging of a human being. Harmony may be seen in the dying out of a star or planet. Things exist in this world. Things come and go in this world. Harmony may be seen in the existence of things. Harmony may be seen in the development of things. Harmony may be seen in the progress of things. Harmony may be seen in the regress of things. The advance of science may have provided us with explanations or answers to the various phenomena of the world, but, it seems, there are still a lot of things that may defy a scientific explanation, and may lie outside of the sphere of science. Science may explain certain things, but it seems, there are still other things that even science may prove to be unable to provide any explanation or answer, in the end. The limits of reason may mean the limits of science. The limits of reason may mean the limits of the scientific understanding of the world. The world is rich. The world is expansive. The world is abundant. The world is deep. The world is profound. The world is splendid. The world is magnificent.

Apart from reason, we may need our feeling to access such a world. Apart from reason, we may need our feeling to feel or perceive such a world. Apart from reason, we may need our feeling to delve into such a world and discover its true workings or operations. Reason has accomplished certain things, and indeed, some great things. But, while reason has led us to accomplish some great things, it may be the case that, it may stand in the way of our full grasp of the other aspects of ourselves, as well as of the world. That is to say, apart from reason, we may need our feeling. When reason falls short, it may be our feeling that may lead us to the deeper secrets or mysteries of the world. When reason falls short, it may be our feeling that may guide us to the deeper secrets or mysteries of ourselves. The harmonic existence of things may not be explained through a rational approach, in the sense that, the harmonic existence of things may be beyond the scientific tests or experimental demonstrations. But, this should not become the ground for us to rule out, completely, the presence of the harmonic existence of things. The harmonic existence of things and the scientific explanations of things may not be seen as necessarily excluding each other, in the sense that, they may be seen as coming from different levels. The scientific existence of things, explained by or through science, may be seen as coming from a rational level, in the sense that, it is understood by the human beings through a rational way. The harmonic existence of things may be seen, on the other hand, as coming from a level higher, or deeper, in the sense that, such an existence of things may reveal to us certain things that may lie beyond our human scientific understanding or comprehension.

If the rational way were the only way of the world, it seems, the world would not have been so colorful. If the rational way were the only way of the world, it seems, the world would not have been so rich. If the rational way were the only way of the world, it seems, the world would not have been so full of meaning or significance. Science may have to do with just one way of things, among a number of ways. Science may only reveal things at one level, while at levels deeper or beyond, things may be out of the reach of science. That is to say, while science may tell us about some processes or mechanisms of things, it may not be able to reveal the inner or deeper harmonic existence of things, and it might be said, it is the inner or deeper harmonic existence of things that may be seen as behind, or underlying, such processes or mechanisms of things. The inner harmonic existence of things may not be rational or scientific, but it may mean the deeper existence of things in the world, and it may enable us, eventually, to have a fuller, richer, or more meaningful existence on earth, as the human beings.

§ 3.4.1 Symmetry and Physics

There is an intrinsic correspondence between symmetry and conservation laws. Such as, the law of conservation of energy is corresponding to the symmetry in time, that is, the temporal symmetry; the law of conservation of momentum is corresponding to the symmetry in space, that is, the spatial symmetry. In a sense, it might be said, symmetry plays an important role, or rather, finds its significant and fundamental place in the modern theoretical physics, especially, in a sense, in particle physics. In particle physics, it is found that symmetry may hold the key to solving, consistently, a number of intricate and complex theoretical problems. Apart from the theoretical problems, it seems, the properties of particles may be seen as being closely related to the kind of symmetries with which they are associated.

From the development of the modern theoretical physics, we see that, symmetry has become one of the focal points that attract the attention of modern physicists, and, one of the central concepts or frameworks that may enable them to construct some meaningful models or theories that may lead them, hopefully, to the deep secrets of the universe. In such a sense, it might be said, through the research of the modern physicists, it may be revealed, symmetry exists innately or intrinsically in the world, and may be seen as lying at the very foundation of the structure of things.

§ 3.4.2 The Fundamental Forces

The gravitational force, the electromagnetic force, the strong nuclear force and the weak nuclear force are usually seen as the four fundamental forces of nature. Is it the case that only four fundamental forces exist in nature? How about the other forces that we may observe in nature? How about the sexual force? Is it not fundamental? Why not? The sexual symmetry may be seen as behind the sexual force. As such, the sexual force may be regarded as a fundamental force, as symmetry may be seen as constituting the essence of things.

How about the electric force? How about the magnetic force? The electric symmetry may be seen as behind the electric force. The magnetic symmetry may be seen as behind the magnetic force. As such, the electric force and the magnetic force may be regarded as the fundamental forces, as symmetry may be seen as distinguishing them from each other and from the other forces. The electromagnetic force may have to do with the fusion of the electric symmetry and the magnetic symmetry. That is, a fusion of symmetry may be seen as behind the electromagnetic force. It is in such a sense that, it might be said, the electromagnetic force may be regarded as a fundamental force.

What about the other forces that we may find in the world? What about the humoral forces that we may often find in the human life, such as, the moral force, the aesthetic force, or the logical force? What about the moral force? What about the aesthetic force? What about the logical force? Are they not fundamental? The aesthetic force may be seen in how we may be moved by beauty, or in how we may be attracted to beauty. The logical force may be seen in how mighty truth may be, or in how powerfully reason may work.

The moral force may be seen in how people sacrifice themselves for their faiths, or for others. For their faiths, people may have to face torture, or even execution. For others, people may have to endure hardship or suffering, or death. But, do these people show that they are cowards? No. No one can conquer them. No power can make them submit. They will endure torture. They will endure hardship. They will endure suffering. They will endure humiliation. Even when they face death, they will not hesitate. Even when they face execution, they will not lower their heads. Where do they get their strength? Where do they get their courage? Where do they get their power? It is the moral power. It is the moral force. It is the humoral power. It is the humoral force. It is the moral power of man. It is the moral force of man. It is the humoral power in man. It is the humoral force in man. It is the humoral power exhibited in the human species. It is the moral force demonstrated in mankind.

The moral symmetry may be seen as behind the moral force. The aesthetic symmetry may be seen as behind the aesthetic force. The logical symmetry may be seen as behind the logical force. Thus, it seems, different symmetries may be seen as behind these different humoral forces. In such a sense, it might be said, these humoral forces may be seen as the fundamental forces. And, we cannot forget, the bilateral symmetry may be seen as behind the coming into being and existence of man. In other words, it might be said, the bilateral symmetry may be seen as behind ultimately the humoral forces found in man. In such a sense, again, it might be said, the humoral forces may be regarded as the fundamental forces.

Apart from the humoral forces, we may find what may be called the physical forces in the world. It seems, we live with the physical forces all the time in the world. The physical forces exist in animals, such that animals may move, grow, or behave in some specific ways. The physical forces exist in plants, such that plants may grow, move, or function in some specific ways. The movement of plants may be seen in their growth, in the extension of their roots or branches, or in the activities occurring in their body parts such as leaves.

Symmetry is behind animals. Symmetry is behind plants. The radial symmetry is behind the radially symmetric animals or plants, such as jellyfish or conifers. That is, the radial symmetry may be seen as behind the physical forces found in the radially symmetric animals or plants. In such a sense, it might be said, the physical forces found in the radially symmetric animals or plants may be regarded as the fundamental forces. The bilateral symmetry is behind the bilaterally symmetric animals or plants, such as worms, birds, humans, or flowering plants. That is, the bilateral symmetry may be seen as behind the physical forces found in the bilaterally symmetric animals or plants. In such a sense, it might be said, the physical forces found in the bilaterally symmetric animals or plants may be regarded as the fundamental forces.

Thus, it seems, apart from the four fundamental forces usually discussed in physics, other forces in nature may also be regarded as fundamental. They are fundamental in the sense that they may have to do with symmetry. That is, their coming into being or existence may have to do with symmetry. While the four fundamental forces discussed in physics may play certain roles in their coming into being or existence, nevertheless, it seems, their coming into being or existence may not be separated from symmetry, or from the working or operation of symmetry. In other words, symmetry may be seen as constituting, in a sense, the foundation of their coming into being or existence. It is in such a sense that, it might be said, such forces may be regarded as the fundamental forces in nature.

Now let us focus, for a while, on the fundamental forces studied in physics. The sexual symmetry may be seen as behind the sexual force. The electric symmetry may be seen as behind the electric force. The magnetic symmetry may be seen as behind the magnetic force. The fusion of the electric symmetry and the magnetic symmetry may be seen as behind the electromagnetic force. Is it possible that a gravitational symmetry is behind the gravitational force? Is it possible that a strong nuclear symmetry is behind the strong nuclear force? Is it possible that a weak nuclear symmetry is behind the weak nuclear force? Otherwise, how could these forces come into being? Otherwise, how could these forces maintain or sustain themselves? It seems, symmetry is usually behind the various forces found in the world. Is it the case that symmetry may also be found behind the gravitational force, the strong nuclear force, or the weak nuclear force? Or, is it the case that some kind of fusion of symmetry may also be found behind some of such forces?

The electric force may be seen in Coulomb's experiment to measure the forces between two charged balls. The electric force may be seen in the various electrostatic phenomena in which the effects of the electric force may be witnessed. While the magnetic force may be associated with electric currents, it may be seen as having to do with the magnetic poles. That is, it might be said, as a fundamental and independent force, the magnetic force may be seen as having to do, in a fundamental sense, with the magnetic symmetry. The magnetic force may be observed between the magnetic poles. That is, the magnetic force may be seen in the forces existing between magnets, such as attraction or repulsion between them.

The electric force has to do with the electric symmetry. The magnetic force has to do with the magnetic symmetry. Thus, it might be said, the electric force and the magnetic force may be seen as the different forces, symmetrically. They have to do with different symmetries. They exist in different symmetries. They work or operate with different symmetries. They reflect or demonstrate different symmetries. They fulfill or realize different symmetries. It is in such a sense that, it might be said, they may be regarded as the fundamental forces in nature.

While they may be different symmetrically, they may be found to be fused together, in a symmetric way, as well. That is, the fusion of the electric symmetry and the magnetic symmetry may be seen as behind the electromagnetic force. The electromagnetic force may be seen as representing a fusion of the electric symmetry and the magnetic symmetry. And the interrelatedness of the electric and the magnetic in electromagnetism may thus be seen as reflecting such a sense of symmetric fusion.

According to the Big Bang theory, all the fundamental forces might have been fused together in the beginning of the universe. After the Planck epoch, the earliest period of the universe, from 0 to about 10^{-43} seconds, the gravitational force first separated from the other forces. After the grand unification epoch, from about 10^{-43} to 10^{-36} seconds after the Big Bang, the strong nuclear force separated from the fusion of forces. After the electroweak epoch, from about 10^{-36} to 10^{-12} seconds after the Big Bang, the weak nuclear force separated from the fusion of forces. Now, all the four fundamental forces, gravitational, electromagnetic, strong and weak, emerged separately in the universe, and the fusion of forces, as we know, had to do with the electromagnetic force.

Is it possible that the separation of the fundamental forces from the fusion of forces might have been a process of the creation of symmetry? Is it possible that the separation of the gravitational force from the fusion of forces might have been the creation of the gravitational symmetry? Is it possible that the separation of the strong nuclear force from the fusion of forces might have been the creation of the strong nuclear symmetry? Is it possible that the separation of the weak nuclear force from the fusion of forces might have been the creation of the weak nuclear symmetry? And, is it possible that, the electric force and the magnetic force might have separated from the electromagnetic force sometime after the emergence of the electromagnetic force, though the latter might have remained as a fundamental force separately in nature?

If that is the case, then the separation of the fundamental forces in the early universe might have been the creation of the symmetries behind such forces. In other words, it might be said, the fusion of forces in the early universe might be seen, in a sense, as the fusion of symmetries, and the separation of forces at such a stage might be seen, in a sense, as the separation of symmetries. It might have been the separation of symmetries. It might have been the creation of symmetries. It might have been the creation of the symmetries behind the forces. In such a sense, the Big Bang might be seen indeed as the creation of symmetries.

While the symmetries behind such fundamental forces might have been created early in the universe, other symmetries might have come into being later on along the development of the universe. We see the double helical symmetry behind DNA. We see the sexual symmetry behind sex. We see the radial symmetry behind the radially symmetric animals or plants. We see the bilateral symmetry behind the bilaterally symmetric animals or plants. We see other forms of symmetry in the world as well. While these symmetries might not have come into being in the early universe, nevertheless, it seems, all symmetries appear to have constituted the foundation of things in the universe.

That the gravitational force may be a symmetric force, just like the electric force, may be seen, in a sense, in that they follow the same inverse-square laws. The gravitational force follows Newton's law of universal gravitation, $F = G(m_1 m_2 / r^2)$, where F is the force, G is the gravitational constant, m_1 and m_2 are the two masses, and r is the distance between the masses. The electric force follows Coulomb's law, $F = k_e(q_1 q_2 / r^2)$, where F is the force, k_e is Coulomb's constant, q_1 and q_2 are the two charges, and r is the distance between the charges. One will quickly notice the extraordinary similarity between the gravitational force and the electric force. Why are the behaviors of these two forces so similar? Why do they exhibit the same patterns? Why do they follow the same laws? What might be the connection between them? What might be the internal linkage between them? Is it possible that symmetry may be the connection? Is it possible that symmetry may be the internal linkage? Is it the symmetric connection? Is it the symmetric linkage? Is it the symmetric similarity? That is, is it possible that it is symmetry underlying the similarity between them? That is, is it the case that the gravitational force may be a symmetric force, like the electric force?

The sexual symmetry means the sexual opposites, male and female. The electric symmetry means the electric opposites, positive charge and negative charge. The magnetic symmetry means the magnetic opposites, north pole and south pole. A gravitational symmetry may mean the gravitational opposites. A strong nuclear symmetry may mean the strong nuclear opposites. A weak nuclear symmetry may mean the weak nuclear opposites. What may be the gravitational opposites? Are they matter and antimatter? Or are they matter and dark matter?

Is it possible that antimatter and dark matter may be related? Antimatter and matter annihilate with each other, and a certain form of energy such as light may be released as a result. It seems, no such observation is made with regard to dark matter and matter. People thus think that dark matter is not antimatter. Positive charges and negative charges may be seen as annihilating each other, and they exist together in the world. The opposite magnetic poles may be seen as annihilating each other, and they exist together in the world as well. Cut a bar magnet, and we may find, new north and south poles may appear. The mystery of nature may be deep. The mystery of symmetry may be profound.

Symmetry may have its own ways. Symmetry may have its own ways to maintain the world. Symmetry may have its own ways to maintain the world such that matter, antimatter or dark matter may exist together in the world. We may have to keep in mind the presence of symmetry. We may have to keep in mind the power of symmetry. It seems, more matter may exist in the world than antimatter. It is called the asymmetry of matter and antimatter. If dark matter is somehow associated with antimatter, then it seems, in a sense, it might be said, such asymmetry may not be that asymmetrical.

The collision of dark matter particles may produce ordinary matter particles and antimatter particles, such as electrons, protons, antiprotons, positrons, or antielectrons. The collision of ordinary matter particles may produce antimatter particles, such as antiprotons, antielectrons, or positrons. What do these things mean? They may mean that, the relationship between matter, antimatter and dark matter may be much more complex or profound than we may think or anticipate. We can only observe directly the ordinary matter, and ordinary matter may only constitute a very small fraction of the universe. What does this mean? It may mean that, we are far from knowing or understanding the real nature of dark matter. The nature of dark matter may be vastly different from the nature of the ordinary matter that we experience or observe.

§ 3.4.3 Energy, Space, and Symmetry

The sexual force comes into being from the sexual symmetry. The electric force comes into being from the electric symmetry. The magnetic force comes into being from the magnetic symmetry. The sexual energy comes into being from the sexual symmetry. The electric energy comes into being from the electric symmetry. The magnetic energy comes into being from the magnetic symmetry. The sexual symmetry is behind the sexual force. The electric symmetry is behind the electric force. The magnetic symmetry is behind the magnetic force. The sexual symmetry is behind the sexual energy. The electric symmetry is behind the electric energy. The magnetic symmetry is behind the magnetic energy.

Energy has to do with field. The sexual energy is in the sexual field. The electric energy is in the electric field. The magnetic energy is in the magnetic field. Field has to do with space. The sexual field is the sexual space coming into being from the sexual symmetry. The electric field is the electric space coming into being from the electric symmetry. The magnetic field is the magnetic space coming into being from the magnetic symmetry. Symmetry is behind field. The sexual symmetry is behind the sexual field. The electric symmetry is behind the electric field. The magnetic symmetry is behind the magnetic field. Symmetry is behind space. The sexual symmetry is behind the sexual space. The electric symmetry is behind the electric space. The magnetic symmetry is behind the magnetic space.

Field is not just field; field has to do with symmetry. The sexual field has to do with the sexual symmetry. The electric field has to do with the electric symmetry. The magnetic field has to do with the magnetic symmetry. Space is not just space; space has to do with symmetry. The sexual space has to do with the sexual symmetry. The electric space has to do with the electric symmetry. The magnetic space has to do with the magnetic symmetry. Energy is not just energy; energy has to do with symmetry. The sexual symmetry is behind the sexual energy. The electric symmetry is behind the electric energy. The magnetic symmetry is behind the magnetic energy.

Symmetry is behind field. Symmetry is behind energy. Symmetry is behind space. Symmetry is behind the field in which energy may be found. Symmetry is behind the space in which field may be found. Symmetry is behind the space in which energy may be found. To understand the sexual field, we have to understand the sexual symmetry. To understand the electric field, we have to understand the electric symmetry. To understand the magnetic field, we have to understand the magnetic symmetry. To understand the sexual energy, we have to understand the sexual symmetry. To understand the electric energy, we have to understand the electric symmetry. To understand the magnetic energy, we have to understand the magnetic symmetry.

Symmetry, harmony and Avolution

To understand the sexual space, we have to understand the sexual symmetry. To understand the electric space, we have to understand the electric symmetry. To understand the magnetic space, we have to understand the magnetic symmetry. To understand the field with energy, we have to understand the symmetry behind the field. To understand the space with field, we have to understand the symmetry behind the space. To understand the space with energy, we have to understand the symmetry behind the space.

§ 3.4.4 Dark Energy, and the Cosmic Symmetry

To explain the accelerated expansion of the universe, physicists come up with a notion of energy present in all space, called dark energy. Dark energy is seen as the energy behind the accelerated expansion of the universe. People have tried to find out what dark energy might be. One explanation for dark energy is that it has to do with space, that is, with empty space.

The notion that empty space is not empty and may possess its own energy may be seen as originating from Einstein. Einstein was among the physicists who believe that empty space is not empty. In order to make his field equations of general relativity work, Einstein introduced the notion of the energy of empty space, in the form of the cosmological constant. Empty space is not empty. Empty space is not nothing. Empty space can acquire energy. Empty space can possess its own energy. Empty space can produce energy. It is a property of space. It is a property of space itself.

Dark energy may thus be seen as the energy of space, or, the energy of empty space. This energy-of-space, that is, the kind of energy possessed or produced by empty space, appears to be able to account for the accelerated expansion of the universe. Since it is the energy of space itself, it may accompany space all the time. When there is space, there is energy. Where there is space, there is energy. Space means energy. More space means more energy. And certainly, it might be said, less space means less energy. Thus, it may be expected, the expansion of the early universe might not be so accelerated, as less space of the early universe might mean less energy. With the continuous expansion of the universe, more energy may be created in the universe as more space may come into being. As a result, the

Avolution and Man

universe may expand in an accelerating fashion today, as more and more energy may come into existence in the universe.

Observations and measurements appear to point to such a cosmic phenomenon that empty space is filled with energy and this energy may have driven the accelerating expansion of the universe. The notion of the energy of space or the energy of empty space appears to be able to account for such a cosmic phenomenon, that is, the accelerating expansion of the universe. Yes, it seems, such an explanation may explain the phenomenon. But, we may have to ask, is this explanation right? That is, is such an explanation the actual case, when it comes to the expansion of the universe? That is, is it the case that empty space can acquire energy, or, empty space can possess energy, or, empty space can produce energy? Even if empty space is filled with energy, is it the case that such energy is created by empty space? Is it the case that such energy is produced by empty space? Is it the case that such energy has to do, fundamentally, essentially, or in the end, with empty space?

Empty space appears not empty. Empty space appears to possess energy. Why is it the case that empty space is not empty? Why is it the case that empty space has energy? Why is it the case that empty space possesses energy? That is, why is it the case that energy exists in empty space? Is it a property of space? Is it a property of empty space? Is it a property of space itself? Is it a property of empty space itself?

We have seen that energy exists in space, in some of the interesting phenomena of the world. Such as, we see energy existing in a space related to sex. Such as, we see energy existing in a space related to electricity. Such as, we see energy existing in a space related to magnetism. Why is it the case that energy exists in a space related to sex? It is the sexual space. It is the sexual energy. It comes from the sexual symmetry. It fulfils or realizes the sexual symmetry. Why is it the case that energy exists in a space related to electricity? It is the electric space. It is the electric energy. It comes from the electric symmetry. It fulfils or realizes the electric symmetry. Why is it the case that energy exists in a space related to magnetism? It is the magnetic space. It is the magnetic energy. It comes from the magnetic symmetry. It fulfils or realizes the magnetic symmetry.

Symmetry is behind the sexual energy. Symmetry is behind the electric energy. Symmetry is behind the magnetic energy. Symmetry is behind the sexual space. Symmetry is behind the electric space. Symmetry is behind the magnetic space. Symmetry is behind space.

Symmetry, harmony and Avolution

Symmetry is behind energy. Symmetry is behind the space with energy. Symmetry is behind the energy in space. It is in such a sense that, it might be said, the cosmic phenomenon that empty space is filled with energy and such energy may have driven the accelerating expansion of the universe may not be so simple. Symmetry may be behind such a cosmic phenomenon. Symmetry may be behind such a cosmic space. Symmetry may be behind such a cosmic energy. Symmetry may be behind such a cosmic expansion. The cosmic symmetry may be behind the cosmic energy filling the cosmic space. The cosmic symmetry may be behind the cosmic energy driving the accelerating expansion of the universe.

Thus, empty space is not empty, because it is not empty space. It is not the empty space; it is the space of symmetry. It is not the empty space; it is the symmetric space. It is not the empty space; it is the space of cosmic symmetry. It is the space supported by the cosmic symmetry. It is the space maintained by the cosmic symmetry. It is the space sustained by the cosmic symmetry. It is the space conditioned by the cosmic symmetry. That may be why empty space may acquire energy. That may be why empty space may possess energy. That may be why empty space may be filled with energy. It may not be the energy of space; it may be the energy of symmetry. It may not be the energy of empty space; it may be the energy of the cosmic symmetry. It may not be the energy created by space; it may be the energy created by symmetry. It may not be the energy produced by empty space; it may be the energy produced by the cosmic symmetry. It may not be the energy coming into being from space or empty space; it may be the energy coming into being from symmetry or the cosmic symmetry.

The energy field of symmetry fills the space of symmetry. The sexual energy field fills the space of the sexual symmetry. The electric energy field fills the space of the electric symmetry. The magnetic energy field fills the space of the magnetic symmetry. Energy may thus be found in space. Energy may thus be found in empty space. Space may thus be found with energy. Empty space may thus be found with energy. It is in such a sense that, it might be said, we may be able to understand what is called dark energy. Dark energy may not be seen as the energy of space. Dark energy may be seen as the energy of symmetry. Dark energy may not be seen as the energy of empty space. Dark energy may be seen as the energy of the cosmic symmetry. Dark energy may not be seen as the energy coming from space or empty space. Dark energy may be seen as the energy coming from symmetry or the cosmic symmetry. That is, it might be said, dark energy may not be seen as a property of space. That is, it might be said, dark energy may be seen as a property of symmetry, or, a property of the cosmic symmetry.

§ 3.4.5 The Expansion of the Universe

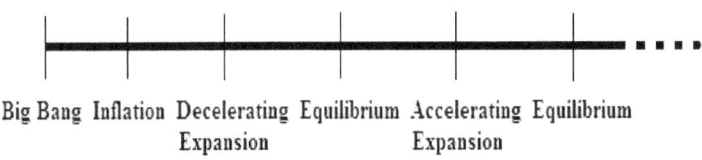

Big Bang Inflation Decelerating Equilibrium Accelerating Equilibrium
                     Expansion   Expansion

Figure 3.1   **The Expansion of the Universe**

The Big Bang theory is currently accepted by most physicists, as it tells us about the general development of the universe. The Big Bang marked the beginning of the universe. After the Big Bang, it is believed, the universe was initially formed in a period of explosive expansion in which the universe expanded rapidly in an extremely short period of time. This period is usually called the cosmic inflation. The inflation happened in a small fraction of the first second after the Big Bang. Given the astronomical formation of the universe in such an extremely short period of time, the expansion of the universe during the inflation period must have been spectacular and dramatic. Such an expansion may be seen as being driven by the energy released in the Big Bang. After the inflation, the universe continued to expand, though the expansion was no longer that explosive. This may be understood in the sense that, the gravitational force of matter in the universe might cause the universe to contract, resulting in a slowing down of its expansion.

Observations and measurements appear to suggest indeed that, after the inflation, the expansion of the universe decelerated. The decelerating expansion of the universe might have lasted until about 5 billion years ago, that is, when the universe was about 9 billion years old. After that time, it seems, a big change happened to the universe. Instead of continuing its decelerating expansion, the universe appeared to have reversed its course and expanded in an accelerated fashion. How to understand such a phenomenon? Was it dark energy? How to understand the working or operation of dark energy?

We have discussed that dark energy may be seen as the energy coming from the cosmic symmetry. That is, it may be the case that, a cosmic symmetry may be behind dark energy. Dark energy may be seen as the energy coming from such a symmetry, like the sexual energy coming from the sexual symmetry, the electric energy coming from the electric symmetry, or the magnetic energy coming from the magnetic symmetry. In such a sense, dark energy may be called dark symmetric energy or dark cosmic energy.

The gravitational attractive force may be seen as causing the decelerating expansion of the universe. For the universe to reverse its course and expand in an accelerating fashion, it seems, a repulsive force might have been in place and cause such an effect. In other words, it seems, unlike the gravitational attractive force, dark symmetric energy or dark cosmic energy may be of a repulsive nature, causing things to move outward from each other. The repulsive effect can be seen in the electric energy or the magnetic energy. When the electric charges are of the same sign, they repel each other. When the magnetic poles are of the same type, they push each other away. The repulsive effect of dark symmetric energy or dark cosmic energy may be understood in a similar manner. That is, it might be the case that, just like other cases in which likes repel, the cosmic symmetry behind dark energy might have come into being in such a way that dark symmetric energy or dark cosmic energy would cause the universe to expand, but not contract.

The decelerating expansion of the universe after the inflation may thus be understood in the sense that, during such a period, the gravitational attractive force was stronger than the repulsive dark symmetric energy. As the gravitational attractive force dominated the situation, the universe expanded in a decelerated fashion continuously. But, as we know, the gravitational force is inversely proportional to the square of the distance between objects. In other words, this may mean that, the gravitational attractive force might be weakened further and further as the universe continued its expansion. This may explain the coming into being of a state of equilibrium in the development of the universe after its decelerating expansion. As the gravitational attractive force was weakened further and further, a state of equilibrium might be eventually reached when it was balanced by dark symmetric energy, that is, its attractive effect might be balanced by the repulsive effect of dark symmetric energy. This state of equilibrium might have occurred, according to the observations and measurements, before or around about 5 billion years ago, that is, when the universe was about 9 billion years old.

Such a state of equilibrium might not be sustained forever, as the continuous expansion of the universe might mean the continuous weakening of the gravitational attractive force. That is to say, eventually, the repulsive dark symmetric energy might get the upper hand and dominate the situation. What does this mean? It may mean that, after a period of equilibrium, the universe might expand in an accelerated fashion, as the universe was dominated by the repulsive dark symmetric energy. And, we cannot forget, the more the universe expands, the less the gravitational attractive force may become, and this may inevitably lead to the increasing domination of dark symmetric energy in the universe. What does this mean? It may mean that, the expansion of the universe may have to accelerate. This may be what we have observed now.

We are living in a time when the expansion of the universe is accelerating. Could this situation last forever? To answer this question, we may have to look into the nature of dark symmetric energy. Dark symmetric energy may cause a repulsive effect in the universe, like what may be demonstrated by the electric charges of the same sign or the magnetic poles of the same type. If that is the case, then, it might be expected, dark symmetric energy may decrease as the distance between objects increases. The same things happen with the electric charges or the magnetic poles. The repulsive forces decrease as the distances between the electric charges or the magnetic poles increase. In other words, it might be the case that, dark symmetric energy may also decrease with the expansion of the universe.

Symmetry, harmony and Avolution

The gravitational attractive force decreases as the universe expands. Now it seems, dark symmetric energy may also decrease, if the universe expands. Then, how to understand the situations related to the decelerating expansion, the equilibrium or the accelerating expansion of the universe? It is possible that, though both gravitational force and dark symmetric energy decrease with the expansion of the universe, they may decrease at different speeds. In other words, it might be the case that, as the universe expands, dark symmetric energy may decrease more slowly than the gravitational attractive force. In the early universe, the gravitational attractive force was strong, and its domination led to the decelerating expansion of the universe. As it decreased more quickly than dark symmetric energy, a state of equilibrium might be eventually achieved when they balanced each other. After the equilibrium, the gravitational attractive force might continue to decrease more quickly than dark symmetric energy, and this might have led to the accelerated expansion of the universe.

If it is the case that dark symmetric energy may also decrease with the expansion of the universe, then the accelerating expansion of the universe may not be sustained forever. The more the universe expands, the less dark symmetric energy may become. That is, with the expansion of the universe, the energy driving such an accelerating expansion may become less and less. A time may thus come when such an accelerating expansion of the universe may not be sustained, and as a result, another state of equilibrium may be reached in which the universe expands, but no longer in an accelerated or decelerated fashion.

It is also possible that, dark symmetric energy and the gravitational attractive force may work or operate at different scales. We know that forces may work or operate at different scales, such as, while the gravitational force may work at an astronomical scale, the strong nuclear force may only operate at the subatomic level. In other words, it is possible that, dark symmetric energy and the gravitational attractive force may work or operate in their own ways, that is, their effects may only be felt at different scales or when the universe expands to certain stages. This may also explain the development of the universe, such as the coming into being of the decelerating expansion, the equilibrium or the accelerating expansion of the universe. In the early universe, the gravitational attractive force was strong, and thus the universe expanded in a decelerated fashion. With the expansion of the universe, dark symmetric energy might increase, and this might lead to a state of equilibrium in which the repulsive dark symmetric energy and the gravitational attractive force might balance each other. After the equilibrium, dark symmetric energy might continue to work, and drive the universe to expand, in an accelerated fashion. But, the continuous expansion of the universe might mean that dark symmetric energy may have to decrease eventually as the universe expands. This might lead to another state of equilibrium in which the universe expands, but neither in an accelerated fashion nor in a decelerated way.

Certainly, it might be said, other possibilities are likely, when it come to the expansion of the universe. Given that so much is unknown to us, it may be hard for us to decide which might be the right case. Some might ask, what might happen to the universe later on, such as, what might happen to the universe after the second equilibrium. Again, given that so much is unknown to us, it might be said, it may be hard to tell.

§ 3.4.6 The Cosmic Symmetry, and the Cosmic Microwave Background

Symmetry appears to fulfill or realize itself in varied ways. The cosmic symmetry may fulfill or realize itself in several ways, that is, we may find its fulfillment or realization in a number of forms. One of the fulfillments or realizations of the cosmic symmetry may be seen in the form of dark energy. That is, given the varied ways of the fulfillment or realization of symmetry in the world, it might be said, it is possible that the cosmic symmetry may be found in several forms. The cosmic symmetry behind dark energy may be only one of the cosmic symmetries fulfilled or realized in the universe, and it is possible that other cosmic symmetries may exist in the universe as well.

The existence of the cosmic symmetry in the universe may be seen, in a sense, in the cosmic microwave background (CMB). The cosmic microwave background is the radiation coming into being about 380,000 years after the Big Bang. As the oldest light in the universe, the cosmic microwave background is a background glow that may be found in the deep sky. Small fluctuations of temperature may be observed in the cosmic microwave background. Many efforts had been made to observe or measure the CMB. The Wilkinson Microwave Anisotropy Probe (WMAP) and the Planck space mission were among them. WMAP was launched earlier than the Planck mission. The Planck mission could observe or measure with more precision.

Through such efforts, we are now able to know better about the CMB. While we know better about the CMB, it seems, a number of unexpected things may be discovered, at the same time. It is found, among other things, the CMB demonstrates considerable unexpected features or characteristics. Distinctive anisotropies may be found. Unusual distributions may be discovered. Unexpected alignments may be observed. Such unexpected things discovered about the CMB appear to have really surprised some people and they strive to argue for their nonexistence. Some dismiss them as the observational errors. Some dismiss them as the possible misinterpretations. And some may simply call them evil.

Among the unexpected things found about the CMB is an alignment that may have to do with the ecliptic. The ecliptic is the path of the sun in the sky seen from the earth. In other words, the ecliptic is in the same plane with the orbit of the earth around the sun. As planets in the solar system circle the sun in almost the same plane, the ecliptic thus stands as a significant feature of the solar system. The CMB appears to be somehow aligned structurally with the ecliptic plane of the solar system.

The temperature fluctuations of the CMB may reveal its alignment. The temperature fluctuations of the CMB are supposed to be randomly distributed. That is, they should be found evenly across the universe. But, it seems, that may not be the case. It is discovered, the temperature fluctuations may be different in the two halves of the universe. That is, it seems, the temperature fluctuations in one half of the universe may be more significant than in the other. And it appears, this pattern may be aligned, in a sense, with the ecliptic plane of the solar system.

The possible ecliptic alignment of the CMB puzzles people, and some call it the axis of evil. Such things observed about the CMB are unexpected, as they are inconsistent with the current models or theories about the universe. Why should the temperature fluctuations of the CMB differ in the two halves of the universe? Why should the temperature fluctuations of the CMB correspond to the two halves of the universe? Why should the temperature fluctuations of the CMB not be distributed randomly or evenly in the universe? Why should the

CMB be found to be aligned with the ecliptic plane of the solar system? Why should the CMB be aligned structurally with the ecliptic plane? Why should the ecliptic plane be aligned with the CMB? Why should the solar system be aligned with the CMB? Why should the ecliptic alignment come into being, in the first place? Why? Why?

Who is responsible for such unexpected things? Who is responsible for such unusual distributions? Who is responsible for such unexpected alignments? Who is responsible for such arrangements? Who is responsible for such patterns? It seems, such unexpected things might have been found not just once. They might have been observed several times by the different missions. The pattern of the temperature fluctuations of the CMB might have been seen by both WMAP and the Planck mission. The ecliptic alignment of the CMB might have been observed by both WMAP and the Planck mission. That is, it seems, the so-called axis of evil might have been found by both WMAP and the Planck mission. The Planck mission could observe or measure with more precision than WMAP, and yet, it seems, they might have found the same or similar things.

Is it the case that symmetry may be behind all such things? Is it the case that the cosmic symmetry may be behind all such unexpected features or characteristics? Is it the case that the cosmic symmetry may be behind the temperature fluctuations of the CMB? Is it the case that the cosmic symmetry may be behind the alignment of the temperature fluctuations of the CMB? Is it the case that the cosmic symmetry may be behind the ecliptic alignment of the CMB? Is it the case that the cosmic symmetry may be behind the so-called axis of evil?

Is the universe evil? Is the alignment of the universe evil? Is the alignment of the CMB evil? Is the alignment of the solar system evil? Is the alignment of the ecliptic evil? It may not be evil. It may be symmetry. It may not be evil. It may be the cosmic symmetry. It may not be evil. It may be harmony. It may not be evil. It may be the cosmic harmony. It may not be the axis of evil. It may be the axis of symmetry. It may not be the axis of evil. It may be the axis of harmony. It may not be the axis of evil. It may be the axis of the cosmic symmetry. It may not be the axis of evil. It may be the axis of the cosmic harmony. It may not be the axis of evil. It may be the cosmic axis of symmetry. It may not be the axis of evil. It may be the cosmic axis of harmony.

The unexpected things observed about the universe may have to do with symmetry. The unexpected things observed about the CMB may

Symmetry, harmony and Avolution

have to do with symmetry. The unexpected things observed about the ecliptic may have to do with symmetry. Symmetry may be behind such unexpected things. Symmetry may be behind such unexpected distributions. Symmetry may be behind such unexpected alignments. Symmetry may be behind such unexpected features or characteristics of the universe. When reason cannot understand, things may not be called evil. When reason cannot grasp, things may not be called evil. When reason cannot reach, things may not be called evil. The rational may not be the fundamental. The analytical may not be the essential. The fundamental may have to do with the symmetric. The essential may have to do with the harmonic. The symmetric may be the fundamental underlying the rational. The harmonic may be the essential underlying the analytical. The symmetric may be behind the rational. The harmonic may be behind the analytical.

When people discuss the origin of stars or galaxies, they often talk about a disk-like cloud of gas and dust. It may be true that stars or galaxies, such as the solar system, might have come into being from the kind of things such as a disk-like cloud of gas and dust. Why should it be disk-like? Why should it be a disk? How was such a disk formed? How was such a disk formed in the first place? What might be behind such a disk? What might be behind the coming into being of such a disk? Who might affect the shape of such a disk? Who might determine the direction of such a disk?

People may say that, the gravitational force might cause the cloud of gas and dust to contract, and such contraction might make the cloud to rotate faster and faster. This increasing rotation might lead the cloud to eventually take the shape of a flat disk. This may be true, to a certain extent. That is, we may ask, was the gravitational force the only factor in shaping the coming into being of the disk? Is it possible that, apart from the gravitational force, other forces or factors might also work and participate in the formation of such a disk?

The coming into being of the disk might not be so simple. Other forces or factors might also take part in its formation. That is to say, it might be said, the disk might not be formed so randomly. It might have its shape. It might have its direction. And all such things might possibly have to do, in some sense, or to some extent, with the forces or factors other than the gravitational force.

The cosmic symmetry might also participate in the formation of the disk. The cosmic symmetry might also be behind the coming into being of its shape. The cosmic symmetry might also be behind the coming into being of its direction. The cosmic symmetric force might also work in forming the shape of the disk. The cosmic symmetric energy might also operate in determining the direction of the disk. The cosmic symmetric energy field might also be seen in the eventual coming into being of the disk, either in its shape or in its direction.

The ecliptic alignment may thus be seen as significant, in the sense that, it may reveal the direction of the solar system, or, it might be said, the direction of the cosmos. It may be seen as the symmetric direction of the solar system. It may be seen as the symmetric direction of the cosmos. It may be seen as the direction of the solar system or the cosmos under the influence of the cosmic symmetry. It may be seen as the direction of the cosmic symmetry. It may be seen as the symmetric direction. It may be seen as the solar direction. It may be seen as the cosmic direction. In such a sense, it might be said, it is a significant direction. It is vital. It is mighty.

People may say, you may only see the direction of the solar system, what about the direction of other star systems? What about the direction of other galaxies? Or, what about the direction of the Milky Way? It is found, the galactic plane of the Milky Way is not in the same plane with the ecliptic, and may be inclined to the ecliptic by about 60 degrees. That is a high inclination, it may have to be said. So, one may ask, what is the big deal even if an alignment may be found in the CMB with the ecliptic?

If an alignment with the ecliptic may be found in the CMB, then, it seems, no such alignment may be found with the galactic plane of the Milky Way. In other words, even if an alignment with the ecliptic exists, it seems, no such alignment may exist with the Milky Way. So, what is the big deal even if the ecliptic alignment may be found in the CMB? It may not mean something remarkable or significant. It may be just a random distribution of directions in the universe.

Compared to the Milky Way, the solar system is just a tiny part. Then, how to understand the existence of the ecliptic alignment found in the CMB? To answer this question, we may have to see some facts about the Milky Way. It is estimated that, billions of galaxies may exist in the universe, and the Milky Way may be just one of them. While the solar system may be a tiny part of the Milky Way, it seems, it may have to be said, the Milky Way itself may be, in an equal sense, a tiny part of the universe. In such a sense, it might be said, what happens in the

Symmetry, harmony and Avolution

Milky Way may not necessarily be related to what happens in the solar system. That is, in a cosmic sense, it might be said, what happens in the solar system may not necessarily have to do, or to be associated, with what happens in the Milky Way.

An alignment with the Milky Way may not exist in the CMB, but that does not necessarily mean that an alignment with the solar system in the CMB may not exist. Equally, it might be said, an alignment with the solar system in the CMB may not necessarily mean the existence of an alignment with the Milky Way in the CMB. In other words, it might be said, the lack of an alignment with the Milky Way in the CMB may not necessarily mean that an alignment with the solar system in the CMB may be a random occurrence. Or, while an alignment may not be found in the CMB with the Milky Way, but that does not necessarily mean that an alignment in the CMB with the ecliptic may be meaningless.

It is in such a sense that, it might be said, the ecliptic alignment found in the CMB may not be readily dismissed. Such an alignment may possess some meaning, and such an alignment may possess some significant meaning. What, after all, may be the meaning of the ecliptic alignment? It may be the meaning of symmetry. It may be the meaning of the universe. It may be the meaning of the cosmos. The ecliptic alignment may thus be seen as significant. It may reveal the symmetric existence of the universe. It may reveal the symmetric structure of the cosmos. It may reveal the symmetry behind the universe. It may reveal the cosmic symmetry behind the cosmos. It may reveal the way of symmetry. It may reveal the way of symmetry in the universe. It may reveal the way of the cosmos. It may reveal the way of the planets. It may reveal the way of the cosmic symmetry. It may reveal the way of the cosmic harmony. It may reveal the way of heaven.

§ 3.4.7 The Big Bang, and the Cycles of Universe

The coming into being of our universe may be seen as the coming into being of symmetry in our universe. That is, the Big Bang may be seen as the big bang of symmetry. The Big Bang may be seen as the big creation of symmetry. It may be seen as the beginning of symmetry. It may be seen as the birth of symmetry. It may be seen as the birth of the universe. The coming into being of symmetry may be seen in that symmetry may be seen as underlying the existence of various things of the world, or in that symmetry may be seen as behind the various forces in the world, such as, the electric force, the magnetic force, the electromagnetic force, or, the gravitational force, the strong nuclear force, the weak nuclear force, or, the sexual force, the humoral force, or, the moral force, the aesthetic force, the logical force. It is in such a sense that, it might be said, it may be the case that symmetry came into being in the universe after the Big Bang.

Figure 3.2   The Cycles of Universe

Universes may come and go in cycles. How about our universe? How did our universe come? How will our universe end? How does the end/creation dictate or establish the universes? What kind of end might have preceded our universe? Our universe might have come into being after the Big Bang. Then, what kind of end might have preceded the Big Bang that gave rise to our universe? It may be hard to answer. It is possible that, in the previous universe, symmetry might have played the fundamental role, just like in our universe, and the end of symmetry of such a universe might have led to the Big Bang. It is also possible that, the previous universe might be fundamentally different from ours, to the point that we may not be able to comprehend or understand it in any way, as we may have no experience whatsoever with such a kind of universe. If that is the case, then we may not be able to know the end of such a universe.

The end of universe may produce energy. If the universe before ours was like ours, then the end of such a universe might mean the split of symmetry. The energy produced at the end of such a universe might be the energy released through the split of symmetry. This energy might be the energy behind the Big Bang. If the universe before ours was fundamentally different from ours, its end might produce energy in a way that we may not be able to know. If that is the case, then this unknown energy might be behind the Big Bang.

As symmetry may be seen as constituting the essence of our universe, the end of our universe may possibly be a split of symmetry. That is, the development or movement of our universe may eventually end up in a split of its symmetric existence. That is, the end of our universe may be the eventual split of symmetry that constitutes the foundation of the existence of things in the world. It may be the end of symmetry. It may be the split of symmetry. It may be the end of the world. The Big Bang may mean the creation of the universe. The creation of the universe may mean the creation of symmetry. The end of the universe may mean the end of symmetry. The end of symmetry may mean the split of symmetry. The life of the universe may reflect the life of symmetry, from its birth to its end, that is, to its split. From the Big Bang, our universe may come. In the Big Split, our universe may come to its end. From the Big Bang to the Big Split, that may be the life of our universe.

What may happen, after the end of our universe? It is possible that a universe may be created in which symmetry may play the fundamental role. Is such a universe like ours? Not necessarily. Things in such a universe may be vastly different from what we may find in our universe, given that, it seems, infinite possibilities may be associated with symmetry, or with the creation of symmetry. It is also possible that a universe may be created that may have nothing to do with symmetry. If that is the case, then it might be said, such a universe may be well beyond our imagination or understanding.

§ 3.4.8 The Big Bang, the Big Split, and the Harmonic Being

As symmetry may be seen as constituting the essence of our universe, the harmonic being may be seen as the fundamental or essential being of our universe. The Big Bang may be seen as the creation of symmetry in our universe. As such, the Big Bang may be seen as a harmonic event. As a harmonic event, it may not be understood through reason. That is to say, though the things in the universe that the Big Bang had given rise to may be understood through reason, the Big Bang itself may not be understood in a rational way, that is, through reason. This may be seen, in a sense, in that the cosmological theories may explain the things happened sometime after the Big Bang, but they may be unable to explain the Big Bang itself.

In a similar sense, that is, in a harmonic sense, the Big Split may be understood. The end of our universe may be seen as the end of symmetry in our universe, that is, as the eventual big split of symmetry as we know it. As such, the Big Split may be seen as a harmonic event. As a harmonic event, we may not be able to understand it in a rational way, that is, through reason. In other words, the end of our universe may be seen as a harmonic event, and we may not be able to understand it through our reason, that is, rationally.

§ 3.4.9 The Higgs Field

Another case in which empty space is not taken by physicists as empty but with energy is the so-called Higgs field. The Higgs field is thought to be an energy field that gives particles mass. Again, it seems, empty space is not empty. And again, it seems, empty space is thought as being filled with energy. How to understand this? That is, how to understand the Higgs field?

We have discussed dark energy, and the cosmic symmetry or the cosmic energy field possibly associated with it. Is the Higgs field a cosmic field? Is the Higgs field a cosmic energy field? It seems, the Higgs field may be seen as an energy field present everywhere in the universe. In such a sense, it might be said, the Higgs field may be regarded as a cosmic field, or, a cosmic energy field. At the same time, as we all know, the Higgs field gives particles mass. In other words, it might be said, the Higgs field may be seen as an energy field working at the quantum or particle level. In such a sense, the Higgs field may be regarded as an energy field at the quantum or particle level.

As a cosmic energy field, the Higgs field may be seen as being associated with a cosmic symmetry, a symmetry that may provide the energy in such a cosmic field. As an energy field at the quantum or particle level, the Higgs field may be seen as being associated with a symmetry at such a level, that is, a symmetry that may provide the energy in such a field at the quantum or particle level. Thus, it might be the case that, the Higgs field may be an energy field involving not just one symmetry, but possibly several ones. One symmetry may have to do with the cosmic energy field, providing the cosmic energy. Another symmetry may have to do with the energy field at the quantum or particle level, providing the energy at such a level.

We know the electromagnetic force. We know the electromagnetic field. And we know the phenomenon called electromagnetism. What is electromagnetism? Electromagnetism is about electricity and magnetism. It is about the electric force and the magnetic force. It is about the electric field and the magnetic field. It is about the electric symmetry and the magnetic symmetry. That is, it might be said, electromagnetism is about not just one symmetry. It is about two symmetries. It is about both the electric symmetry and the magnetic symmetry. It is about the combination of the electric symmetry and the magnetic symmetry. It is about the fusion of the electric symmetry and the magnetic symmetry. It is about the amalgamation of the electric symmetry and the magnetic symmetry.

The electromagnetic field may thus be seen as an energy field involving two symmetries, the electric symmetry and the magnetic symmetry. It might be the case that, the Higgs field may be understood in a similar manner. That is, the Higgs field may be understood as involving the fusion or combination of several symmetries, just like the electromagnetic field. The symmetry at the cosmic level may have to do with the energy at the cosmic level. The symmetry at the quantum or particle level may have to do with the energy at the quantum or particle level. As the cosmic level is so vastly different from the quantum or particle level, the symmetries at these two levels may be different, and may work or operate in their different ways.

Seeing that both dark energy and the Higgs field are associated with empty space, people may ask, are they related? It may be hard to say. On the one hand, they may all have to do with the cosmic symmetry. In such a sense, it might be the case that, they may be related, or possibly closely related. On the other hand, given that symmetry may fulfill or realize itself in varied ways, the cosmic symmetry discussed here may take several forms. That is, the cosmic symmetry associated with dark energy may be different from the cosmic symmetry associated with the Higgs field. In other words, it is possible that dark energy and the Higgs field may not be related.

§ 3.4.10 $E = mc^2$

If symmetry is behind forces, if symmetry is behind powers, if symmetry is behind energy, then, one may ask, how to understand the formula $E = mc^2$? If one is familiar with the various laws or theories in physics, one may know that symmetry often plays a significant role in physics. That is to say, an intrinsic relationship may often be found between symmetry and the physical properties of things. We all know the conservation laws. The conservation laws may be seen as having to do with symmetry. The law of conservation of energy is corresponding to the symmetry in time, that is, the temporal symmetry. The law of conservation of momentum is corresponding to the symmetry in space, that is, the spatial symmetry. In other words, it might be said, the conservation laws may be seen as having to do, in a fundamental sense, with the symmetries of space and time. $E = mc^2$ may be understood in the same sense. As a formula, what it reveals may be observed, in a sense, in the vast amounts of energy released through nuclear reactions. But, to understand it, we may have to consider the symmetries of space and time. Just like other laws in physics, $E = mc^2$ has to do with the symmetries of space and time. It is in such a sense that, it might be said, we may be able to understand it.

§ 3.4.11 Taijitu, the Diagram of the Supreme Ultimate

The taijitu represents the ancient Chinese understanding about the existence of things, or, the coming into being of things. It is about yin and yang. It is about the symmetric or harmonic existence of yin and yang. Taiji is the Supreme Ultimate that gives rise to yin and yang. Yin and yang together, through their interaction, give rise to the things in the world. Yin and yang are usually depicted in the taijitu by dividing the circle into two halves, with different colors indicating the yin area and the yang area. Two large dots are often found in the taijitu, with a yin dot in the yang area and a yang dot in the yin area. These two dots represent the interconnection of yin and yang, and indicate that they may give rise to each other.

Symmetry, harmony and Avolution

Yin and yang may be seen as the symmetric opposites. As the symmetric opposites, they form the symmetries of the world. As the symmetries of the world, they constitute the foundation of things in the world. We see the symmetric opposites in the double helical symmetry underlying DNA. We see the symmetric opposites in the sexual symmetry underlying sex. We see the symmetric opposites in the electric symmetry underlying electricity. We see the symmetric opposites in the magnetic symmetry underlying magnetism. We may see the symmetric opposites in other forms of symmetry in the world that may constitute the foundation of things of the world.

Yin and yang represent symmetry. Yin and yang stand for symmetry. Yin and yang constitute symmetry. Yin and yang constitute the symmetric or harmonic foundation of the world. Yin and yang constitute the symmetric or harmonic existence of the world. When I saw the all-sky map of the cosmic microwave background obtained by the Planck mission, to be honest, I remembered the taijitu. They are so alike, even to the point that the dots may be found. The pattern of the taijitu seems to be reflected in the Planck map. The Planck map shows that the sky appears to be divided into two areas, in a symmetric sense. The radiation is not evenly distributed, and it appears to be stronger in the southern half of the sky. And, a large cold spot is observed in the southern half of the sky as well.

Such unexpected things had been observed by WMAP, an operation before the Planck mission. People have tried to explain such things. Some people have proposed that such things, such as the cold spot, may have been caused by the existence of other universes. And, it is suggested, we may have to look for a cold spot in the northern half of the sky.

How to understand such unexpected things observed? How to understand the cold spot? It seems, the cold spot appears in the southern half of the sky, and the southern half of the sky has stronger radiation. Is it possible that, the yin dot/spot appears in the yang area, like in the taijitu? Yin usually indicates cold, and yang usually signifies hot. That is, is it possible that, the Planck map may have reflected the taijitu?

If that is the case, then, it seems, a hot spot, instead of a cold one, may be looked for in the northern half of the sky. The yang dot/spot may appear in the yin area of the sky. And, it seems, it might be said, a hot spot might have been indeed observed in the northern half of the sky by WMAP, and an alignment with the ecliptic plane might have been also found at the same time. Such cold and hot spots may indicate that the universe is in a symmetric or harmonic existence, and such an existence may involve the interaction of yin and yang, or, the interaction of the two halves of the cosmos.

§ 3.4.12 The Ecliptic

The ecliptic has captured the imagination of human beings for a long time. People looked at it. People studied it. People meditated on it. People tried to grasp its meaning or existence.

It is said, when stars appear on the ecliptic, it would be auspicious. Isn't it auspicious? It seems, yes, it is auspicious. Plants are on the ecliptic. Flowers are on the ecliptic. Animals are on the ecliptic. Humans are on the ecliptic. Life is on the ecliptic. Nature is on the ecliptic. The world is on the ecliptic. Isn't it auspicious? Yes, it seems, it is auspicious. It is auspicious, earthly. It is auspicious, worldly. It is auspicious, cosmically. It is auspicious, heavenly.

§ 3.5 Symmetry, Harmony, and Development

People sometimes think, or believe that, the coming into being of things may be largely due to the mutation of things; in the sense that, as no supernatural being should be thought to be responsible for the coming into being or creation of things, thus, the coming into being or creation of things may be best attributed, in a reasonable evolutionary sense, to the mutation of things. Otherwise, it seems, one may ask, how could things be created, or, come into being? In a sense, it might be said, on the surface, such an explanation may sound reasonable, sensible, or even scientific. But, given that, we have seen, reason may not necessarily be able to reach the kind of things such as man, or the humoral senses of man, one may ask, is it really the case that things come into being as a result of some kind or form of mutation happening in the developmental processes of things, and thus, the coming into being of things may be seen or regarded, in a certain sense, or to a certain extent, as somewhat or somehow accidental, unpredictable, or, by chance? Certainly, from a scientific point of view, it might be said, there is some truth in such an explanation, as, it seems, if we want to give a convincing description of the world, we may have to follow the scientific method and adhere to a rational explanation of things.

Is the rational explanation of things wrong, or problematic, when it comes to the secrets of the workings or operations of the world? No, in a sense. And it should not be regarded as such, in a sense. The rational explanation of things is not wrong or problematic in itself, that is, insofar as reason is concerned. As long as there is no problem with the rationalization of things, the rational argument thus achieved should not be regarded or treated as problematic or false. But, reason may have limits, and it seems, it may not comprehend all the things of the world. In other words, if we want to understand the world, if we want to comprehend all the things of the world, if we want to see deep into the workings or operations of the world, we may need certain things other than reason that may, ultimately, in their turn, lead reason to fulfill its analyzing or dissecting role or function, such as, observation, sensing, feeling, or contemplation. So, let us, for a while, put reason aside, and observe, sense, feel, and examine the world in which we are living. The world is full of plants. The plant world is colorful, vivid, lush, and beautiful. Why is the plant world so colorful? Why is it so vivid? Why is it so lush? Why is it so beautiful? Is there something underlying such a colorfulness in the plant world? Is there something behind such a vividness in the plant world? Is there something giving rise to the luxuriance of the plant world which we cannot see? Is there something in the plant world that would lead, inevitably, to the beauty of it?

It seems, it might be said, reason may be able to explain or make sense of some parts or segments of the world, such as, how the plant hormones regulate the plant life cycles, or how the plant cells interact with each other, in the process of the plant growth, to form the plant bodies, but, as to the kind of things leading, ultimately, to the colorfulness, vividness, luxuriance, or beauty of the plant world, it seems, it might be said, reason may be unable to reach, explain, or make sense of. In order to understand or have a grasp of what may be underlying or behind the kind of things such as the colorfulness, vividness, luxuriance, or beauty of the plant world, we may need to come into the plant world, observe, sense, feel, and see for ourselves what may be truly present, or existing, in such a world. What do we see? What do we observe? We see beauty everywhere. We observe harmony exhibited at all levels. We see balance reached or achieved. We observe unity with all the things. Leaves are beautiful, and symmetric. Flowers are beautiful, and harmonic, with color, shape, or form. Seeds are produced in such ways or forms that they may be carried by winds, or spread by bees. Leaves fall in the winter, so that water or the main body may be preserved. Twigs sprout in the spring, so that they may take advantage of the sunshine and grow. Rains water the plants. The earth nurtures their roots. The sunshine gives them energy. And winds bring the fresh air. It is a world. It is a whole world. It is a healthy, lively, and vibrant world. It is a rich, fruitful, and abundant world. It is a world in balance. It is a world with unity. It is a beautiful world. It is a harmonious world.

Will the plant hormones give the plant world its colorfulness, vividness, luxuriance, or beauty, with their sophisticated mechanisms or workings? In a sense, no. They are not enough. They may work well within their spheres, but they are not sufficient to ensure that the plant world, thus grown, would be colorful, vivid, lush, and beautiful. Will the plant cells make the plant world colorful, vivid, lush, and beautiful, with their intricate biological or physicochemical processes or operations? In a sense, no. They are not enough. They may demonstrate remarkable or marvelous traits, characteristics, or qualities, but they themselves are not adequate to give rise to the kind of colorfulness, vividness, luxuriance or beauty that we may observe in the plant world. The same thing may be said with regard to the other aspects of the plant world which may be successfully analyzed or dissected by or through reason, that is, in a scientific or rational way. In other words, it might be said, even all the aspects of the plant world are to be analyzed or dissected by or through reason, that is, in a scientific or rational way, the results may not necessarily lead us to a satisfactory, adequate, or sufficient explanation as to why the plant world should be, after all, so colorful, vivid, lush, and beautiful, and, not otherwise. So, what is truly behind the colorful, vivid, lush, and beautiful world? What is truly underlying such a world, with such a colorfulness, vividness, luxuriance, or beauty?

Is it the plant hormones that may be behind such a colorful, vivid, lush and beautiful world? No, in a sense. That is, it might be said, not really. Is it the plant cells that may be underlying such a world? No, in a sense. That is, it might be said, not really. Is it the other kinds of things of the plant world, similar to the plant hormones or cells that

Symmetry, harmony and Avolution

may be analyzed or dissected by or through reason, that may be ultimately behind or underlying such a world? No, in a sense. That is, it might be said, not really. The plant hormones or cells, or the other plant things similar to them, may constitute merely a part of the plant world, and, it might be said, they may not be seen as constituting, in a sense, some of the most fundamental, intrinsic, or primary things of the plant world. the kind of things of the plant world such as the plant hormones or cells may be seen, in a sense, as only existing on a physical or tangible level, as parts of plants, constituting the plant world. They may not be seen, in a sense, as existing on a higher or principle level, that is, a level on which the principles ultimately governing the plant world may be seen, in a sense, as being present. What are the principles governing the plant world? it might be said, they are the kind of things that underlie the plant world, that is, without them, plants might not have even come into being; that is, without them working or operating, it might be said, plants might not have germinated, sprouted, developed, or grown, even if they possess the right plant hormones or cells, or the similar kind of things within their bodies. That is, in other words, it might be said, it is the principles ultimately governing the plant world that enable plants, eventually, to survive, thrive, or prosper. It is not those plant hormones, though they certainly contribute, in their ways, to the lives of plants. It is not those plant cells, though they certainly constitute part of the existence of plants. It is the balance existing in the plant world. It is the unity of the plant world. It is the beauty in the plant world. It is the harmony of the plant world.

Balance means agreement. Unity means coherence. Beauty means harmony. Harmony means growth. Thus, we witness, leaves and flowers are beautiful, symmetric, and harmonious, seeds are carried by winds or bees, the life cycles coincide with the seasons, the earth nurtures, the sunshine warms, rains water, and winds blow. Thus, we witness, seeds germinate, twigs sprout, leaves grow, and flowers are in bloom. Thus, we witness, the plant world is a world colorful, vivid, lush, and beautiful. Can all these things be attributed to the plant hormones? No. They are not enough. Can all these things be attributed to the plant cells? No. They are inadequate. Can all these things be attributed to the kind of things similar to the plant hormones or cells? No. They are insufficient. They can only be attributed to the kind of things wider, deeper, or more significant, fundamental, or intrinsic than such things as the plant hormones or cells, or the similar kind of things like them. That is, it might be said, they can only be attributed, ultimately, to the kind of things behind or underlying such a world, that we may, in a sense, observe, sense, feel, or perceive, such as, balance, unity, beauty, or, harmony. Balance, unity, beauty, or harmony may be seen as what ultimately maintains or sustains the plant world, as it grows into a world of color, vividness, luxuriance and beauty. As balance produces harmony, unity gives rise to harmony, and beauty means harmony, thus, it might be said, harmony may be seen as what ultimately behind or underlying the plant world, that is, a world of such colorfulness, vividness, luxuriance and beauty. This may be called the harmonic principle, that is, a principle that may be seen or regarded as ultimately behind or underlying the plant world, as we know it.

Can the harmonic principle be found in the animal world? It seems, the answer may be, in a certain sense, yes. Harmony can be seen in the animal world, in many ways, or, in many aspects. First of all, it might be said, without harmony, animals might not have come into being, or existed as animals as we know them, in the first place. Harmony means balance. Harmony means unity. Harmony means coherence. Harmony means the existence of animals, that is, the different animals, that is, the different animal species, together with the inanimate environment and the plant world, in a balanced, coherent, unified, interconnected, interdependent, or intrinsically integrated way. In such a harmonious state, or with such a harmonic condition, animals, that is, the different kinds of animal species, including, certainly, we human beings, are thus able to survive, thrive, or prosper. When harmony is gone, things would disintegrate, or disappear. That is, when harmony is gone, discordance would emerge, disunity would appear, imbalance would set in, incoherence would arise, violence would come, and destruction would follow. The inharmonious state is the state of discordance. The inharmonious state is the sate of disunity. The inharmonious state is the state of imbalance. The inharmonious state is the state of incoherence. The inharmonic state is the state of violence. The inharmonic state is the state of destruction. Harmony gives rise to things; inharmony demolishes things. Harmony brings things into being; inharmony brings things to their end. In harmony, things thrive. With inharmony, things wither. In harmony, things develop and grow. With inharmony, things fall apart and fade away. It is in harmony that we see a world full of life, vitality, and energy. It is in harmony that we see a world full of plants, animals, and humans. It is in harmony that we live, survive, and

Symmetry, harmony and Avolution

thrive. It is in harmony that we, as part of the animal kingdom, exist, in this world.

The human existence on this planet may be seen, in a sense, as a miracle. How could man come into being, after all, in the first place? Why did man have to come into being? Why did man have to possess all the characteristics or qualities as we know them? Some may say that, it is because of evolution, or that the human species developed out of the animal world through a long evolutionary process, and the human characteristics or qualities might have come into being as a way to secure the eventual survival of the human species. In a sense, it might be said, the theory of evolution indeed explains a lot about the coming into being of things, especially, without doubt, the coming into being of the human species. But, it seems, even though such a theory may have explained many crucial things about the coming into being or development of things, such as, the survival of the fittest, it does not necessarily mean that such a theory may explain all the things. When it comes to the coming into being of the human beings, we may still ask a lot of questions, and such questions may seem to pose some considerable challenges to the theory of evolution. Why did the human beings have to come into being from animals, such as apes, as, it seems, such animals may have survived well, in a sense, unless disturbed by the human species? Why did the human beings have to come to possess the kind of characteristics or qualities, as, it seems, the other animals without such characteristics or qualities appear to have still survived, and survived well? Why did the human beings have to develop into the kind of forms or shapes as they possess now? Why is it not the case that man was not present in this world, human beings had not come into being, or the human species did not exist? Why is it not the case that the human beings possessed a set of characteristics or qualities drastically different from what they have now? Why is it not the case that the human species developed into the kind of forms or shapes distinct from what they are endowed with now? Can the theory of evolution answer these questions? It seems, it might be said, it may have a hard time, a very hard time, if it attempts to answer these questions. So, where should we go? To where should we look for the possible answer, or answers?

What is the most prominent or outstanding body part, or organ, of the human beings? One may say, it is the brain. Yes, in a sense, it might be said, it is the brain, that is, the nervous system. It may be seen as the most complex and highly developed part of the human body. So, let us take a look at the brain, and try to see what kind of developmental history might be behind its eventual coming into being. Sponges do not have, generally speaking, regular bodily shapes or forms. And, as we know, they are among the animals, but they do not have neurons or similar things that may suggest a brain or a nervous system in their bodies. They may be able to perform some simple or primitive movements, through some kind of coordinating mechanisms involving some chemical or biochemical processes, but they may not be seen as possessing a brain or a nervous system within their bodies. The simplest nervous system may be seen as existing in the kind of animals that are usually radially symmetric, such as jellyfish. In the radially symmetric animals such as jellyfish, the nervous system is usually a very simple nerve net spread out within the body. That is, such a nervous system may have some neurons interacting with each other to perform some nervous activities, but such a nervous system may only be seen as a very simple or primitive one, as it should not be seen or regarded as possessing a brain, a central cord, and numerous nerves in the body. A fully developed nervous system seems to have, insofar as we know, a brain, a central cord, and numerous nerves throughout the body. Such a kind of nervous system is usually seen in the animals that are called bilaterally symmetric, that is, the kind of animals that are endowed with two sides, left and right, which may be seen as mirroring each other approximately. These animals may be seen as constituting the majority of the animals that we may see with our eyes today, and certainly, we humans are among them. Such a bilateral symmetry may be easily observed in the animal kingdom, as so many different species of animals exhibit such a kind of symmetry, around us.

Worms may be seen as the simple animals with a bilateral symmetry. Even though they may not be seen as displaying a lot of bilateral symmetry outwardly, they usually possess within their bodies a nervous system that may be seen as having the similar parts like brain, nerve cord, or nerves. And, in such a sense, they may be regarded as possessing an internal nervous structure that may strongly resemble a fully developed nervous system found in all the other bilaterally symmetric animals. It is in such a sense that, worms may be seen as among the simplest or earliest animals that came to possess a nervous system that bears the characteristics of the bilaterally symmetric animals. When it comes to insects, it seems, the bilateral features become apparent and clear. An insect, such as a bee, has wings on two sides, legs on two sides, eyes on two sides, and antennas on two sides. Certainly, insects may be seen, in a sense, as more developed, or advanced, than worms, even though they all belong to the invertebrate category, with their more pronounced bilateral features. Insects usually possess more neurons or nerve cells in their nervous system, and as a result, they may be able to perform some more complex activities, such as, flying. The nervous system may be seen as getting a major boost when it comes to the vertebrate animals. The vertebrate animals, including we humans, possess a head, a spinal column, and a bilaterally symmetric body. The head contains the brain; the spinal column contains the spinal cord. Throughout the bilaterally symmetric body, numerous nerves spread out to connect all the body parts to the brain or the spinal cord. Thus, with the vertebrate animals, the nervous system may be divided into the central nervous system, containing the brain and the spinal cord, and the peripheral nervous system, which may be seen as the numerous nerves connecting the whole body. In the vertebrate animals, as we can see, the brain is well protected by the head skull, and the spinal cord by the spinal column. Such a kind of protection may enable, certainly, the central nervous system to function well even in some difficult situations or in some dangerous environments. The brain, the spinal cord, and the numerous nerves undoubtedly form a powerful nervous system that may enable the vertebrate animals to do the kind of things or to perform the kind of activities that invertebrates may prove to be unable ultimately. This may be seen as the advantages of the vertebrate animals. And certainly, this may be seen as the advantages of we humans. We humans, like other mammals, are endowed with a bilaterally symmetric body, a head, and a spinal column. We are the vertebrates. We have bilateral features. And, we are capable of the kind of things that may be called, human.

What is human? What is to be called human? What is not human? What is not to be called human? Why does man have to be called, seen, or regarded, as human? Where does this humanness come from? What does it ultimately mean? That is, what is its original origin? What is its ultimate source? What is its first beginning? Could sponges behave like a human, and be called human? No. Why not? Could jellyfish behave like a human, and be called human? No. Why not? Could worms behave like a human, and be called human? No. Why not? Could insects behave like a human, and be called human? No. Why not? Could fish behave like a human, and be called human? No. Why not? Could the other mammals, such as apes, chimpanzees, or monkeys, behave like a human, and be called human? Eventually, it seems, no. Why not? Why cannot all those animals, such as sponges, jellyfish, worms, insects, fish, or the other mammals, behave like a human and be called human? What makes them, ultimately, unable to behave like a human and thus to be called human? What, ultimately, divides the humans and the other animals? What, ultimately, separates the humans from the other animals? In what ways? In what senses? Or, in what manners?

To answer these questions, we may have to go back and look at the way how humans had come into being, that is, in a sense, that is, in a basic or intrinsic sense, how the human nervous system had come into being. Sponges are generally shapeless or formless, and it is known, they possess no nervous system. Jellyfish are radially symmetric, and it is known, they usually have a simple nerve net in their bodies that may be seen as constituting the simplest nervous system. Worms possess an internal nervous system that bears certain similarities to the nervous systems of the other bilaterally symmetric animals, though as we know, they may not show much bilateral features outwardly on their bodies. Insects exhibit an apparent sense of bilateral symmetry on or in their bodies, but as the invertebrate animals, they may be seen, in a sense, as possessing a less powerful or complex nervous system than their vertebrate counterparts. As the vertebrate bilaterally symmetric animals, fish may be seen as possessing a complex nervous system that may be found in other vertebrate animals, but, it might be said, as we know, the size of their nervous system may be seen as relatively small, compared to the other vertebrate nervous systems, especially, those that may be found in mammals. When it comes to mammals, it might be said, humans may be seen as really standing out, in the sense that, on the one hand, the human nervous system may be seen as bigger or more complex than the nervous systems of the other mammals, in the sense, or to such an extent that humans may thus be capable of certain things that the other mammals may not be up to, such as, reasoning, high intelligence, or language; and on the other hand, the human body may be seen as more developed than the other mammalian bodies, in the sense that, among other things, the erect bodily structure may enable humans to move freely, and it is the humoral body, that is, the humoral

Symmetry, harmony and Avolution

human body, that is, the humoralization of the human body that eventually gives rise to the humorality of man, and the humans may thus be able to have a humoral existence, instead of a purely animal one, whereas , as we can see, even though some signs may be seen as being exhibited or displayed by the other mammals, but, eventually, it might be said, the animorality or mammorality may not be seen or regarded as so pronounced or prominently constructed in the other mammals. That is to say, it might be said, the animoral or mammoral existence of the other mammals may not be compared, in a sense, to the humoral existence of the humans, as the other mammals possess, generally speaking, no language, no apparent reasoning, limited intelligence, limited communication between or among themselves, and certainly, they can in no way, it seems, insofar as we know, clearly recognize or be self-conscious of such a kind of animoral or mammoral existence of theirs. The humans may, in such a sense, be seen as being dignified, or, distinguished, among the mammals, as they can live not just an animal life, but a human life that may be called humoral, as such a life may lead them to the kind of things that the other animals seem to be incapable of, such as, the aspiration or striving for the true, the good, the right, the just, or the beautiful.

The humoral coming into being of humans may be seen as the true or real, that is, the ultimate divide between humans and all the other animals. Certainly, as we know, the human nervous system may be seen as generally bigger or more complex than the nervous systems of the other animals, as the human nervous system usually possesses more nerve cells or neurons, or a nervous structure that may be seen as more complexly arranged, or organized. As the nervous system controls or coordinates the various aspects of the animal life, such an increased capacity or complexity in the human nervous system may be seen as the foundation of what may be found differently in the humans and other animals. in other words, such an increased capacity or complexity of the human nervous system may, in a sense, explain, or account for, the kind of things such as reasoning, high intelligence, or language that may happen, it seems, only to the humans. And, certainly, it may be said, the humoral coming into being, or, the coming into being of the humorality of man, or, the humoralization of the human body that eventually leads to the humoral existence of man, may be seen as having to do, in some sense, in some way, or to some extent, with the coming into being of such a kind of human nervous system, with

Avolution and Man

increased capacity or complexity. Or, rather, it may be said, the humoral coming into being of man or the humoralization of the human body and the coming into being of the human nervous system with increased capacity or complexity may be seen, in a sense, as just the two sides of the same coin, or, the two effects of one and the same process. That is, they may be seen as the two results of one and the same process, a process in which, as we know, man eventually came into being.

As to how such a process had been realized, that is, how man had come into being, that is, how, eventually, the humoral coming into being of man or the humoralization of the human body and the human nervous system affected, influenced, or interacted, on or with each other, may be difficult, in the end, for us to know. That is, the minute details of such a process, the minute details of how the humoralization of the human body and the human nervous system interacted with each other to give rise eventually to the coming into being of man may prove to be, it might be said, too intrinsic, too innermost, too deep, or too remote for us to fully comprehend or understand. Such inner workings or operations of nature may be well beyond, in a sense, the reach of our human reason. On the other hand, it might be said, if we could easily know the details of such a process, that is, if we could easily get access into man, that is, if reason could reach all the things of man readily, then, it seems, if our experience or past could tell us anything, it is that the disintegration or destruction of man may not be far away. The details of the humoral coming into being of man may elude us, but the full picture of man should not. That is, the details of the coming into being of man may elude us, but the full picture of the world, in a sense, should not. What is the full picture of man? What is the full picture of the world? To see the full picture of man, we have to see the full picture of the coming into being of man. To see the full picture of the world, we have to see the full picture of the coming into being of the world. How could we see the full picture of the world, or, of the coming into being of the world? We can only see the full picture of the world or the coming into being of the world through seeing into the part of the world in which we live, exist, or with which we may have some experience.

We do live in this world, with all the kinds of animals such as sponges, jellyfish, worms, insects, fish, or mammals. We do exist in this universe, with all the kinds of animals, such as, the shapeless or formless ones, the radially symmetric ones, or, the bilaterally symmetric ones. Why are some animals shapeless or formless? Why are some animals radially symmetric? Why are some animals bilaterally symmetric? Why are some animals shapeless or formless, while the other animals radially or bilaterally symmetric? Why are some animals radially symmetric, while the other animals bilaterally symmetric? Why are some animals bilaterally symmetric, while the other animals either shapeless or formless, or radially symmetric? Why are the shapeless or formless animals not the radially or bilaterally symmetric ones? Why are the radially symmetric animals not the bilaterally symmetric ones? Why are the bilaterally symmetric animals not the shapeless or formless ones, or the radially symmetric ones? What makes the shapeless or formless animals and the radially symmetric animals different? What makes the radially symmetric animals and the bilaterally symmetric animals different? What makes the bilaterally symmetric animals and the shapeless or formless animals, or the radially symmetric animals different? What is the difference between the shapeless or formless animals and the radially symmetric animals? What is the difference between the radially symmetric animals and the bilaterally symmetric animals? What is the difference between the bilaterally symmetric animals and the shapeless or formless animals? We have seen, and we have known, there are big differences. The differences are significant. The differences are crucial. The differences are fundamental. And in fact, it might be said, the differences are so significant, crucial, or fundamental that, it seems, they may reveal, eventually, in a sense, the coming into being of the world, the coming into being of man, or, the process of the coming into being of the world, or, the very process of the coming into being of man.

    Sponges are shapeless or formless, and we see, they possess no nervous system. Jellyfish are radially symmetric, and we see, they possess the simple nerve net. Worms, insects, fish, mammals and humans may all be seen as the bilaterally symmetric animals, and we see, they may possess a nervous system eventually as powerful as a human brain. So, what is the difference between the shapeless or formless sponges and the radially symmetric jellyfish? It might be said, it is the difference of whether the nervous system comes into being or not. What is the difference between the radially symmetric animals and the bilaterally symmetric animals? It might be said, it is the difference between a simple nerve net and a powerful nervous system like a human brain. What is the difference between the bilaterally symmetric animals and the shapeless or formless animals? It might be said, the difference may be seen as nothing versus big thing, or, the nonexistence of nervous system versus the coming into being of the powerful nervous system. Why? Why are there so many differences? Why are there so many important differences? Why are there so many big, significant, crucial, vital, or fundamental differences between the shapeless or formless animals and the radially symmetric animals, between the radially symmetric animals and the bilaterally symmetric animals, or, between the bilaterally symmetric animals and the shapeless or formless animals? What may be behind such differences? What may be underlying such differences? Or, what may account for such differences? We can see, when animals are shapeless or formless, they usually possess no nervous system; when animals are radially symmetric, they usually possess a very simple nervous system; when animals become bilaterally symmetric, it appears, they may possess a nervous system as powerful as a human brain. That is, it seems, the transformation from the shapelessness or formlessness to the radial symmetry may mean the coming into being of the nervous system, and the transformation from the radial symmetry to the bilateral symmetry may mean the full coming into being of the nervous system, that is, in a sense, it has to be said, insofar as we know, such as, the coming into being of the human brain. What does this mean? What does this tell us? What does this point out to us? I think, it means significantly, it tells us a lot, and it points out to us in some intrinsic or fundamental ways how the world may have come into being, how the universe may have been formed, or, how the human species may have eventually come into this world.

Symmetry is important. Symmetry is significant. Symmetry is fundamental. Symmetry is balance. Symmetry is agreement. Symmetry is connection. Symmetry is linkage. Symmetry is binding. Symmetry is fusing. Symmetry is joining together. Symmetry is teaming up. Symmetry is relationship. Symmetry is marriage. Symmetry is union. Symmetry is matching. Symmetry is integration. Symmetry is coherence. Symmetry is unity. Symmetry is harmony. Harmony is important. Harmony is significant. Harmony is fundamental. Harmony is essential. Harmony is vital. Harmony is meaningful. Harmony has content. Harmony means growth. Harmony gives rise to things. That

Symmetry, harmony and Avolution

may be what we see in the world. When things are shapeless or formless, that is, inharmonious, it seems, they cannot come to possess an invaluable or precious thing such as a nervous system; when things are taking a harmonious existence, such as, existing with radial symmetry, it seems, they begin to possess some precious or invaluable things, such as, a simple nerve net as the nervous system; when things come to exist with harmony, such as, existing in bilateral symmetry, then, it seems, they may be able to possess, or be blessed with, some of the most precious or invaluable things of the world, such as, a powerful nervous system like a human brain.

Could the simple nerve net of the radially symmetric animals such as jellyfish be the result of some pure mutation? Maybe not, as, it seems, for example, the shapeless or formless animals such as sponges do not usually possess such a kind of net. That is, it seems, the role that harmony had played in the eventual coming into being of one of the most precious, invaluable and powerful things of the world, the nervous system, may thus, in a sense, be seen. When things do not exist in harmony, they may be seen as not in a position to possess a nervous system. When things are beginning to exist with harmony, in a sense, it might be said, they may start to develop some simple or primitive forms of nervous system. When things exist in harmony, they may come to possess, eventually, a powerful nervous system that may make them capable of some remarkable things. On the other hand, such a coming into being of the nervous system may also be seen as a revelation, that is, in a sense, a rare, powerful, and mighty revelation, about how harmony works, intrinsically, in nature.

Sponges have their sponge existence, shapeless, and without nervous system. Such may be seen, in a sense, as the result of the workings of harmony, as they live their lives without regular shapes or nervous system. Such shapelessness or formlessness may be seen, in a sense, as compatible with the eventual nonexistence of the nervous system. Jellyfish have their jellyfish existence, radially symmetric, and with a simple nerve net as their nervous system. Such may be seen, in a sense, as the result of the operations of harmony, as they live their lives with radial symmetry and a simple nerve net. The coming into being of both radial symmetry and a simple nerve net in jellyfish may be seen, in a sense, as having to do with harmony, working to give rise to jellyfish, in the sense that, such radial symmetry may be seen, eventually, as compatible, in a harmonic sense, with such a kind of simple nerve net, and together, in a harmonic, that is, biological or physical way, they constitute, or give rise to, or form, what is called jellyfish.

Worms may be seen as the animals that have developed with bilateral symmetry. some of the worm species may be seen as bearing some traits of the radial symmetry, in a sense, at least outwardly in their body plans or structures, even though they may be seen as having developed some internal bilaterally symmetric structures, such as with the nervous system. Their generally round or radially shaped body forms may be seen, in a sense, as indicating the happening of radial symmetry. In other words, worms, in such a sense, may be seen as the kind of animals that demonstrate the coexistence of radial symmetry and bilateral symmetry. While they may possess some bilaterally symmetric features, such as with their nervous system, they may also exhibit some radially symmetric characteristics, such as with their outward body plans. Worms, that is, at least some of them, it seems, may thus be seen as the kind of animals in which both radial symmetry and bilateral symmetry may be found. It is in such a sense that, it might be said, while their nervous system may be bigger or more complex, in a sense, than that of the radially symmetric animals such as jellyfish, it may be smaller or simpler, compared to the nervous systems of the other bilaterally symmetric animals. And such may be seen as consistent with what we may have observed in nature, as, it seems, worms appear to have indeed possessed usually less nerve cells or neurons in their nervous system.

As bilateral symmetry becomes more pronounced with animals, it seems, the nervous system of the bilaterally symmetric animals becomes, in a sense, gradually, bigger or more complex. Insects are, like worms, invertebrates. As the bilateral symmetry may be seen as having developed more prominently with insects, we see, they may have developed a kind of nervous system bigger or more complex than that of the worms. Fish, unlike worms or insects, are vertebrates. With vertebrates, it might be said, bilateral symmetry may be seen as having been developed a step further, as the internal bilaterally symmetric body structures of vertebrates begin to carry a brain, a spinal cord, and numerous nerves to function as the nervous system. Such a kind of nervous system certainly makes the bilaterally symmetric vertebrate animals capable of certain things that the invertebrate animals may be incapable of. The development of the brain, the spinal cord, and the numerous nerves in the bilaterally symmetric vertebrate animals may be seen as one of the most significant steps, or progresses, in the development of bilateral symmetry; in the sense that, on the one hand, it seems, the radial symmetry may not be in a position, that is, in a harmonic position, to support or sustain such a kind of development, as the radially symmetric animals such as jellyfish may only develop or come to possess a kind of simple nerve net as their nervous system, and on the other hand, even though the bilaterally symmetric invertebrate animals such as worms or insects may develop or come to possess their bilaterally symmetric nervous systems, but such nervous systems may be seen as incapable of reaching the kind of capacity, complexity, or power of the vertebrate kinds, as, in a sense, it might be said, the bilaterally symmetric body plans or structures of the invertebrate animals may limit, ultimately, such a kind of development, or progress. The bilaterally symmetric vertebrate animals may thus be seen as capable of developing or possessing a kind of nervous system that other animals may hardly be able, in a sense, to develop or possess. And as we see, among the bilaterally symmetric vertebrate animals, from fish to mammals to humans, it seems, with the further development of the body structures, the nervous system becomes more and more complex, and powerful, and reaches, eventually, the capacity, complexity or power of a human brain. In other words, it might be said, it is with the vertebrate animals that, we see, a powerful nervous system with a brain, a spinal cord, and numerous nerves is brought into being; and it is with the vertebrate animals that, it might be said, such a kind of nervous system is possible. It is with the vertebrate animals that, it might be said, the body plans or structures of the bilaterally symmetric animals make it possible for such a kind of nervous system to come into being; and, it is with the vertebrate animals that, it might be said, the development of bilateral symmetry finally produces its fruit, that is, its result, that is, to give rise to a nervous system that would, eventually, lead to man.

Why is it the case that man comes into being from a development of bilateral symmetry? Why is it the case that the coming into being of man has to do with the development of bilateral symmetry? Why is it the case that man has to do, after all, with bilateral symmetry? That is, why is it the case that, man has to be bilaterally symmetric? Why is it not the case that man is shapeless or formless? Why is it not the case that man is radially symmetric? Why is it not the case that man has to do with shapelessness or formlessness? Why is it not the case that man comes into being from shapelessness or formlessness? Why is it not the case that man comes into being from the development of radial symmetry? Why is it not the case that the coming into being of man has to do with the development of radial symmetry? Why is it not the case that man has to do with radial symmetry? Why? Why, after all, does man have to do with bilateral symmetry, instead of radial symmetry, or, shapelessness or formlessness? Why, after all, does man have to come into being from bilateral symmetry, instead of radial symmetry, or, shapelessness or formlessness? Shapelessness or formlessness means inharmony. Inharmony means imbalance. Inharmony means discordance. Inharmony means incoherence. Inharmony means disunity. Inharmony means inhibition. Inharmony means impediment. Inharmony means frustration. Inharmony means obstruction. That is, it might be said, inharmony leads, in a sense, to violence or destruction. It is in such a sense that, it might be said, it may not be possible for man to come into being from the shapeless or formless, as such a state may constitute, in a sense, an inharmonious or inharmonic condition from which any precious or invaluable things may be seen as having a hard time to originate, or to obtain a development. The nervous system is a precious thing. The human brain is invaluable. Man is precious, invaluable, magnificent, and glorious. Certainly, one cannot expect a nervous system to come out from shapelessness or formlessness. Certainly, one cannot expect the human brain to be formed out of shapelessness or formlessness. Certainly, one cannot expect that, man would come into being from such an inharmonious or inharmonic state, or condition.

Radial symmetry, as demonstrated by the kind of radially symmetric animals such as jellyfish or hydras, may be seen, in a sense, as different from the symmetry demonstrated by the bilateral symmetry; that is, in the sense that, while such a radial state or condition may indeed express or demonstrate a sense of symmetry, such as, around an axis or center, it may also be seen, at the same time, as representing a sense of what may be called roundness or circularity, which may, in a sense, be seen as quite different from the kind of bilaterally arranged symmetry. that is, such a sense of roundness or circularity, or radiality, expressed or exhibited as a result of the radialization of the radially symmetric animals may be seen, in a sense, as representing or standing for certain things different from the

Symmetry, harmony and Avolution

bilaterally arranged shapes or forms. the coming into being of radiality, that is, the radialization of the radially symmetric animals may be seen as a result of the long process of the development of radial symmetry, which, in its turn, as such, may be seen as, eventually, giving rise to certain things, certain forms, certain shapes, certain structures, certain plans, or, certain arrangements, such as, roundness, or circularity, that may stand as distinct or different from the kind of things such as shapelessness or formlessness. Shapelessness or formlessness may be seen, certainly, as a state or condition of being or existence. As such, shapelessness or formlessness may be seen as representing a state or condition of being or existence of things, either for plants, for animals, or for the inanimate things, that is, things coming into being or existing in a shapeless or formless state or condition.

Why, then, should there exist certain things with shape or form, such as, with radial symmetry or bilateral symmetry? That is, why, then, should certain things other than the shapeless or formless come into being? That is, why should certain things other than the shapeless or formless come into being or exist beside the shapeless or formless, or in place of the shapeless or formless? Or, in other words, why, in the end, should the shapelessness or formlessness be transformed into shapeliness, or certain formations? That is, why does the world exist, with shapes or forms, instead of shapelessness or formlessness? Where do such shapes or forms come from? How do they happen? What is the beginning? What is the source? What is the fountainhead? Or, how is the world transformed into the things with shapes or forms? How is the world transformed from the shapelessness or formlessness into the shapeliness or formliness? Why? Why does the world have to be shapely or formly? Why do things have to be with shapes or forms? Why is the world not a world of complete shapelessness or formlessness? Why do sponges have no regular shapes or forms, while jellyfish or hydras are radially symmetric? Why do jellyfish or hydras have to be radially symmetric, while sponges usually with no regular shapes or forms? What makes sponges with no shapes or forms? What makes jellyfish or hydras radially symmetric? Is it necessary that sponges are shapeless or formless, while jellyfish or hydras radially symmetric? Is it necessary or indispensable that jellyfish or hydras are radially symmetric, while sponges shapeless or formless? Is it inevitable that sponges are shapeless or formless, and jellyfish or hydras are radially symmetric? Is it essential that sponges are shapeless

Avolution and Man

or formless, but jellyfish or hydras radially symmetric? Is it fundamental that such should be the case? Is it intrinsic, inherent, or innate that such should be the way?

Some might say that, the theory of evolution may provide the answer. That is, the survival of the fittest and the evolutionary process of natural selection may mean that, certain things advantageous, such as, certain traits caused by some forms of mutation or the interaction with the environment, may prove to be better for the survival of some members of a species, and may thus be naturally selected and passed down to the next generations in a population of a species. Over time, such a process may, eventually, give rise to certain changes to a species, and new things, such as, new ways of survival, new structures, new organs, new shapes, or new forms, may eventually come into existence in a species. That is, the survival of the fittest and the evolutionary process of natural selection may mean that, the need for survival may be seen as the driving force behind the coming into being of the new things in a species, and this may, eventually, explain or account for the kind of things appearing in a species, such as, the occurrence of new ways of existing, the development of new structures or new organs, the transformation into some new shapes or forms, or even, it might be said, the emergence of some new species. It is in such a sense that, some may say, the coming into being of the kind of things other than the shapeless or formless may thus be explained. In a sense, it may be true. Such as, while sponges might be generally shapeless or formless, but as to the organisms developed in the world, that is, survived in the world, it may be the case that, over time, the developmental process might, eventually, give rise to the kind of things that might no longer be shapeless or formless, that is, in a word, certain things other than the shapeless or formless might eventually come to this world, as a result of the evolutionary process of natural selection, or as a consequence of the survival of the fittest. In such a sense, things other than the shapeless or formless may be seen, it might be said, reasonably, that is, in an evolutionary sense, as the outcome of the evolutionary process for survival.

Will this explain, in a full sense, the coming into being of the radially symmetric animals such as jellyfish? Will this explain, in a full sense, the coming into being of the bilaterally symmetric animals such as the human beings? For now, it seems, in a sense, we may have to wait and see. Suppose that, there were no radially symmetric animals and bilaterally symmetric animals altogether in this world, that is, only sponges and their like existed in this world, along with all the plants and other things. What would happen? It seems, it might be said, such a world might be perfectly possible, and ok, and sponges and their like might have been doing well, surviving well, and prospering as well, in such a world, that is, in their own manners or ways. What does this mean? It seems, it may mean that, the evolution of sponges and their like may not necessarily, in a sense, that is, inevitably, lead to the coming into being of the kind of animals possibly with regular shapes or forms. Then, some may say that, the kind of things or animals with shapes or forms might have evolved out of the shapeless or formless things or animals other than sponges or their like. It is possible that, such might have been the case, certainly. But, then we may have to ask the kind of questions, and that may bring us back almost to the very beginning of our discussion, such as, why, then, after all, should shapes or forms have to develop out of the shapeless or formless? Why, then, after all, should shapes or forms have to "evolve" out of the shapeless or formless, as a result or outcome of the evolutionary process? Why, then, after all, should the process of evolution lead to the coming into being of the shapeliness or formliness, out of a state or condition of shapelessness or formlessness? Why, then, after all, should the process of evolution produce, or give rise to, eventually, the kind of things or animals with shapes or forms?

Some might say that, the regular shapes or forms, that is, shapeliness or formliness, may constitute the kind of traits advantageous to the survival of a species, and may thus be naturally selected and passed down to the next generations in a population, and over time, such traits may eventually lead, through such an evolutionary process, to the coming into being of the kind of things or animals with shapes or forms. Such may be seen as how the shapeliness or formliness eventually came out of the state or condition of shapelessness or formlessness, and such may be seen as how the process of evolution eventually produced, or gave rise to, the kind of things or animals with shapes or forms. Even if we take such a kind of evolutionary explanation, and are being convinced by it, we may still have to ask, why, after all, should the regular shapes or forms, that is, shapeliness or formliness, constitute, somehow, the kind of things advantageous to the survival of a species? Where does such advantage come from? What makes the regular shapes or forms advantageous?

What makes the shapeliness or formliness desirable? What makes the regular shapes or forms contribute to the development of things? What makes the shapeliness or formliness more beneficial, more valuable, or more advantageous, in a sense, that is, in an evolutionary sense, than the kind of things such as shapelessness or formlessness? In nature, we can find many things including the things with shapes or forms, or things with no shapes or forms. In the world in which we are living, we can witness or encounter many things, things of shapeliness or formliness, or things of shapelessness or formlessness. Why should the regular shapes or forms be advantageous to the evolution of things? Why should the shapeliness or formliness be chosen, that is, eventually, naturally selected, in a process of development, over the shapelessness or formlessness? Why, in the end, should such things happen, at all?!

What is shape? What is form? What does shape mean? What does form mean? What is the relationship between shape and development? What is the connection between form and development? Why should development be associated with shape, such as, radial symmetry? Why should development be linked to form, such as, bilateral symmetry? Is the relationship between shape and development intrinsic? Is the connection between form and development inherent? Is the association between shape and development essential? Is the linkage between form and development innate? Is it possible that, without shape, there would have been no development? Is it possible that, without form, there would have been no progress? Is it possible that, with no shape, there would have been no development? Is it possible that, with no form, there would have been no growth? Is it possible that, without shape, there would have been no natural selection? Is it possible that, without form, there would have been no survival of the fittest? Is it possible that, with no development, there would have been no shapes? Is it possible that, with no development, there would have been no forms? What do all these mean? What do all these point to? What do all these tell us? Why are shapes so closely related to development, or, to the process of development? Why are forms so closely connected with development, or, with the process of development? Why should animals with shapes come out of development, in the end? Why should animals with forms come into being from development, eventually? Why should shapes and development come together? Why should forms and development go hand in hand? Why should the regular shapes or forms and the process of development be inseparable, in a

Symmetry, harmony and Avolution

sense, as seen from the coming into being of the radially or bilaterally symmetric animals? Why should the shapeliness or formliness be an intrinsic, inherent, innate, or essential part or aspect of the process of development, in a sense, as seen from the coming into being of the shapely or formly animals?

What is shape? What is form? What are the regular shapes or forms? What does the shapeliness or formliness mean? Shape may be seen as the realization of things in form. Form may be seen as the representation of things in shape. The regular shapes may mean the realization of things with regularity, that is, in a sense, with consistency, similarity, or compatibility. The regular forms may mean the representation of things with regularity, that is, in a sense, with correspondence, agreement, or uniformity. Thus, the shapeliness may mean that, things may be arranged in such a manner that a certain sense of unity or coherence may come out; and the formliness may mean that, things may be represented in such a way that a certain sense of balance or harmony may come into being. That is to say, the shapes or forms of things may be seen as meaningful, relevant, and significant to the coming into being or existence of things. That is, the regular shapes or forms of things may stand, in a sense, as the indication that things are coming into being, or existing, in a state or condition of unity, coherence, balance, or harmony. that is to say, it might be said, the shapeliness or formliness of things may, eventually, mean that, things may be seen as coming into being through a developmental process, with unity, coherence, balance, or harmony, and, as such, they may be seen as existing, as the shapely or formly things or animals, with unity, coherence, balance, or harmony. Such unity, coherence, balance, or harmony may thus be seen as the integral, that is, essential, fundamental, intrinsic, inherent, or necessary part or aspect of the coming into being or existence of things.

The shapeliness or formliness of things may mean the harmonic coming into being or existence of things. The harmonic coming into being or existence of things, as signified or represented by the shapeliness or formliness of things, may be seen, thus, as what reveals, in a sense, that is, in a harmonic sense, that is, in a sense that may be beyond our human understanding or comprehension, that is, in a sense that may be experienced by or through our human feeling or observation, the underlying principle or principles behind the coming into being or existence of things. Harmony characterizes the coming into being or existence of things. Harmony represents the coming into being or existence of things. Harmony embodies the coming into being or existence of things. Harmony gives rise to the coming into being or existence of things. Harmony is behind the world. Harmony maintains the world. Harmony sustains the world. Harmony makes the plant world possible. Harmony makes the plant world thrive and flourish. Harmony makes the animal world possible. Harmony gives rise to the shapely or formly animals. Harmony makes them thrive. Harmony makes them prosper. Harmony makes them flourish. Harmony makes the advantage. Harmony gives unity to the shapely or formly animals, either physically, structurally, or biophysiologically, so that they may be naturally selected. Harmony gives coherence to the shapely or formly animals, either physically, structurally, or biophysiologically, so that they may be the fittest in a developmental process for survival. Harmony gives balance to the shapely or formly animals, either physically, structurally, or biophysiologically, so that they may be in a position to be favored in a developmental process. Harmony gives symmetry to the shapely or formly animals, either physically, structurally, or biophysiologically, so that they may, eventually, come into being, develop, or come into this world. Development may be seen as a process; harmony may be seen as the principle. Development may be seen as a process; harmony may be seen as the mechanism. Development may be seen as a "natural selection"; harmony may be seen as the advantage. Development may be seen, in a sense, as the survival of the fittest; harmony may be seen as what constitutes the fitness.

The theory of evolution may have explained the evolutionary process in a way, reasonably, but it may not have answered so many questions, or so many whys. Why should the radially or bilaterally symmetric animals come into being, in the end? Why should animals with regular shapes or forms occupy this world? Why is the world not occupied by animals without shapes or forms? Why should the bilaterally symmetric animals constitute the majority of the animals around us, but not the radially symmetric animals, or animals shapeless or formless? What is behind the coming into being of the radially or bilaterally symmetric animals? What is behind the coming into being of the shapeliness or formliness? What is behind the process of radialization in the development of animals? What is behind the process of symmetrization in the development of animals? What is

Symmetry, harmony and Avolution

behind the coming into being of radiality in animals? What is behind the coming into being of symmetry in animals? What is behind the so-called evolutionary advantage of radiality? What is behind the so-called evolutionary advantage of bilaterality? What is behind the disadvantage of the animals without shapes or forms? What is behind the disadvantage of shapelessness or formlessness? What is the difference between shape and shapelessness? What is the difference between form and formlessness? What is the difference between shapelessness and radiality? What is the difference between formlessness and bilaterality? What is the difference between radiality and bilaterality? What underlies such differences? What is behind such differences? What, ultimately, leads to such differences? Can the theory of evolution answer these questions? It seems, no, it cannot. The theory of evolution may tell us that the shapely or formly animals, such as the radially or bilaterally symmetric animals, may evolve or come into being as a result of their evolutionarily advantageous possessions, such as, their radially or bilaterally symmetric body plans or structures, but as to why such possessions should constitute certain things advantageous in a developmental process, it cannot tell us, and it seems, it may never tell us.

The theory of evolution may tell us the possible result, but it may not tell us the true process. The theory of evolution may tell us the visible effects, but it may not tell us the innate or intrinsic causes. The theory of evolution may tell us the appearances, but it may not tell us the inner workings or operations of nature. What are the inner workings or operations of nature? They are the inner workings or operations of harmony in nature. What is the true or real process behind the coming into being of animals, such as, the shapely or formly animals, or the radially or bilaterally symmetric animals? It might be said, it is the process of harmony; it is the process of the harmonic coming into being; it is the process of the harmonic happening; it is the process of the harmonic development. It is the harmonic development. It is the harmonic evolution. It is not just evolution; it is the harmonic evolution. It is not just development; it is the harmonic development. It is not just progress; it is the harmonic progress. It is not just growth; it is the harmonic growth. It is not just selection; it is the harmonic selection. It is not just survival; it is the harmonic survival. It is not just the survival of the fittest; it is the harmonic survival of the fittest. It is not just a process; it is the harmonic process. It is not just evolutionary;

it is harmonic. It is the harmonic coming into being. It is the harmonic existence. Harmony gave rise to the coming into being of the shapely or formly animals such as the radially or bilaterally symmetric animals, as the developmental process "naturally selected" the harmonic advantage of such animals. As such, the harmonic process, or in a sense, the harmonic progress, may be seen as what is truly behind the so-called evolutionary process of the coming into being of things, such as, the kind of things like the radially or bilaterally symmetric animals.

That is to say, in other words, when one talks about the evolutionary coming into being of the kind of things such as shapeliness or formliness, if one points to the harmonic advantage as the cause or ground for natural selection, then in a sense, one is not really talking about an evolutionary process by natural selection; rather, it might be said, one is talking about a process in which harmony may be seen as truly working, innately, or intrinsically, in such a way that, things with a sense of harmony may eventually come out, and such a sense of harmonic existence or condition may express or demonstrate itself, in such a way, in such a sense, or to such an extent that, such a sense of harmonic existence or condition may eventually be, it might be said, "naturally selected," in an evolutionary process, and thus, that is, in such a sense, in such a way, or in such a manner, harmony may be seen as having expressed, demonstrated, or manifested itself, or fulfilled or realized itself, in that, things with harmonic characteristics, qualities, properties, or traits, such as, harmonic body plans or structures, may, in the end, come into being, or come into existence, in this world. Thus, it might be said, the natural selection in evolution may be seen as not so "natural," after all, as such a selection, it seems, has to be determined, decided, or regulated, in a sense, by the harmonic selection, that is, by the selection of harmony, that is, by the selection of the harmonic advantages such as unity, coherence, balance, or symmetry found in things, which, in their turn, may be seen as having originated, or, come into being, from harmony itself. In other words, the natural selection may be seen as a selection of harmony, by harmony, or, for harmony; the evolutionary process may be seen as a harmonic process; and the evolution by natural selection may be seen, in its essence, as the harmonic evolution by harmonic selection. It is harmony that is behind the natural selection. It is harmony that is underlying the natural selection. It is harmony that directs the process of natural selection. It is harmony that is governing the process of natural selection. It is harmony that may be seen as behind the evolutionary advantages of things.

Harmony comes to the fore. Harmony determines, decides, directs, or leads to the process of natural selection. It is harmony that works or operates, deep down, to give rise to the coming into being of things. On the surface, it may be evolution by natural selection; deep down, it is harmony. It is the harmonic evolution. It is the harmonic selection. It is harmony expressing itself. It is harmony demonstrating itself. It is harmony manifesting itself. It is harmony fulfilling or realizing itself. That is why the shapely or formly animals come into being. That is why, after all, the radially symmetric animals come into being. That is why, after all, the bilaterally symmetric animals come into this world. That is why, after all, the world was transformed into a world of shapeliness or formliness. That is why, after all, the world is not occupied by the animals or plants without shapes or forms. That is why, after all, the shapeless or formless animals do not make up the majority of animals. That is why, after all, the animals with symmetry or harmony thrive and flourish, and make up the majority of animals living on earth. That is why, after all, we humans come into this world, with symmetry and harmony, and live with a life full of meaning and significance. It is harmony that gives rise to the shapeliness or formliness. It is harmony that gives rise to shapes or forms. It is harmony that gives rise to the evolutionary advantage of radialization. It is harmony that gives rise to the evolutionary advantage of symmetrization. It is harmony that gives rise to the coming into being of the radially or bilaterally symmetric animals. Harmony gives rise to our world. Harmony gives rise to our eventual coming into being. The theory of evolution may only tell us about the outward appearance of things, that is, things on the surface, such as, the obvious effects, the apparent results, or, the visible consequences. It may not reveal the inner workings or operations of the world. The inner world may be hard for reason to grasp. The innate mechanisms or intrinsic processes of harmony may be difficult for reason to analyze or dissect. The theory of evolution may thus only tell us the visible results or consequences on the surface, and it may not be able to reveal to us the innate or intrinsic processes or mechanisms, deep down behind such results or consequences. And, in a sense, it might be said, the theory of evolution may even run the risk of taking the effects as the causes, or the results or consequences as the root or beginning of things, as, it seems, it is incapable of searching further into the depths of things, since, in a sense, reason, unfortunately, is limited and falls short.

The evolutionary advantages found in things or animals should not be simply taken as the cause or ground for natural selection, in an evolutionary process, even though such an evolutionary explanation may seem to run smoothly or even scientifically. Such evolutionary advantages should not just be taken as the mere cause or ground for natural selection, and nothing is to be asked about their nature, their coming into being, or about the kind of things possibly behind their coming into being. They have their coming into being. They have their source. They have their origin. They have their root. They have their beginning. They have their reason to come. They have their rationale to appear in this world. To find the cause or ground for natural selection is one thing. To search into the evolutionary advantages themselves is another. To take such evolutionary advantages as the cause or ground for natural selection may have explained the evolutionary process, in a way, or in a sense, but it may not have looked into why or how such advantages should have come into being in the first place. That is to say, in other words, the theory of evolution may only have searched into or investigated a process on the surface, or, a process, it might be said, of secondary nature, or, of secondary importance; in the sense that, insofar as we can see, it seems, few questions have been asked about the coming into being of such evolutionary advantages, and little efforts have been made to try to look into the origin, source, root, or beginning of their coming into being. The coming into being of such evolutionary advantages is significant, and it may lie at the very beginning of the coming into being of things. That is, it may be more important to look into such a coming into being than, in a sense, to simply explain the evolutionary process, seemingly, in a scientific manner. To explain the evolutionary coming into being of things by taking such evolutionary advantages as the cause or ground for natural selection may be seen as the easier part, and to look into the real coming into being of such evolutionary advantages may prove to be hard, difficult, or elusive. That is, it may be easy to point to such evolutionary advantages as the beginning of an evolutionary process by natural selection, but it may be difficult to identify, or find out, the real beginning of such evolutionary advantages themselves.

How have they begun? What gives rise to them? Why should they appear? Why should they come to this world? What is behind their coming into being? Such questions should be what we are concerned with first, that is, not just an evolutionary process explained through natural selection. The beginning of such evolutionary advantages may mean, in a sense, the secrets of the beginning of the world, as such a beginning may lie, it might be said, at the very beginning of the coming into being of things. To look into their coming into being is to look into, in a sense, the coming into being of the world. To look into their source or origin is to look into, in a sense, the source or origin of the world. To look into their root or beginning is to look into, in a sense, the root or beginning of the world. The theory of evolution may have found in such evolutionary advantages the root or source of natural selection, but it may not have found the root or source of such evolutionary advantages themselves. The natural selection may take such evolutionary advantages as the origin or beginning of an evolutionary process, but it may not be able to explain the origin or beginning of the coming into being of such evolutionary advantages. By focusing on the visible or apparent evolutionary effects of the evolutionary process, it might be said, while the theory of evolution may have explained such a process, it may have overlooked some deeper processes of the world that may not be so visible or apparent. By failing to pay attention to, or deal with the kind of things associated with the coming into being of such evolutionary advantages themselves, it might be said, while the theory of evolution may be seen as a theory capable of explaining certain things, it may have, at the same time, ignored or disregarded some fundamental, intrinsic, innate, or inherent processes or mechanisms of the world, which may be seen as the ultimate or real source, origin, root, or beginning of things, and which may be seen as lying, in a sense, beyond the reach of reason.

In other words, it might be said, two processes may be seen as existing in the world with regard to the so-called evolution. The evolutionary process explained by the theory of evolution through natural selection may be seen as the second or secondary process, in the sense that, in such a theory, or in such a process, while the process of natural selection itself may have been explained, but the cause, ground, root, origin, or beginning of natural selection may not have been explained, and it might be said, they may have received no attention at all. It should not be taken for granted that, the cause or ground for natural selection, such as, the evolutionary advantages like unity, coherence, balance, or symmetry, in things or animals, should appear or come into being naturally, in things or animals. No. Their appearance or coming into being in things or animals should not be taken as natural, in a sense, at all. Their appearance is significant. Their appearance is remarkable. Their appearance is of important consequence. Their coming into being is crucial. Their coming into being is vital. Their coming into being may be seen as at the core of things. That is, their appearance or coming into being in things or animals may point to certain things in nature, or in the world, that may be truly fundamental, intrinsic, or essential. We should ask about their appearance. We should pay attention to their coming into being. We should look into the way, the process, the mechanism, or, the possible workings or operations that may be behind their eventual coming into being. Such may be seen as the first process of nature, or of the world, in the sense that, it is through such a process that the cause for natural selection may be seen as coming into being, the ground for natural selection may be seen as being laid, or the beginning of natural selection may be seen as being initiated. That is to say, it is through such a process that the kind of things such as unity, coherence, balance, or symmetry may be seen as coming into being, in things or animals; that is, it is through such a process that the evolutionary advantages may be seen as coming into being, prior to the initiation of natural selection; that is, it is through such a process that, it might be said, the process of evolution is possible, the process of natural selection is possible, and eventually, the coming into being of things or animals, through such a kind of evolutionary process, is possible.

The first process is the process which gives rise to the kind of evolutionary advantages like unity, coherence, balance, or symmetry. This first process is prior to the second or secondary process, that is, the process in which the evolutionary process is initiated, that is, the process of natural selection would set in, and the evolutionary advantages would thus be "naturally selected." Before the second or secondary process is the first process. Prior to the second or secondary process is the first process. The first process provides the beginning. The first process gives rise to the beginning. The first process supplies the origin; the second or secondary process follows. The first process is the source; the second or secondary process is the consequence. The first process is the root; the second or secondary process bears the fruit. The first process is the principle behind things; the second or secondary process is the process leading to results. The first process is the primary

Symmetry, harmony and Avolution

process leading the way to the coming into being of things; the second or secondary process is the process fulfilling or realizing such a way. The first process is the intrinsic process; the second process is the outward process. The first process is the innate and invisible process; the second process is the apparent and noticeable process. The first process is fundamental; the second process is phenomenal. The first process is a process of principle; the second process is a process of the worldly things. The first process is the process of harmony; the second process is the process of evolution. That may be what we see in the world. That may be what we see in the coming into being of things. Without the first process, there would have been no beginning. Without the first process, there would have been no origin for things. Without the first process, there would have been no source or root for the coming into being of things. The coming into being of things comes from the first process. The coming into being of things originates from the first process. The first process gives rise to the coming into being of things. The first process gives rise to the coming into being of the kind of things such as unity, coherence, balance, or symmetry.

Does the coming into being of the kind of things such as unity, coherence, balance, or symmetry mean the evolutionary process? No, in a sense, as such things may all be seen as coming, in a sense, before the evolutionary process. Does the coming into being of the kind of things such as unity, coherence, balance, or symmetry have anything to do with the evolutionary process? No, in a sense, as such things may all be seen as existing, in a sense, prior to the evolutionary process. Should the coming into being of the kind of things such as unity, coherence, balance, or symmetry be seen as the result or consequence of the evolutionary process? No, in a sense, as such things should be taken, in a sense, as the precondition for evolution. Should the coming into being of the kind of things such as unity, coherence, balance, or symmetry be regarded as the result or consequence of natural selection? No, in a sense, as such things should be taken, in a sense, as the cause or ground for natural selection, but not as its result or consequence. Should the coming into being of the kind of things such as unity, coherence, balance, or symmetry be treated as the result or consequence of the survival of the fittest? No, in a sense, as, it might be said, it is such things leading to the survival of the fittest, but not, in a sense, vice versa.

So, what do all these mean? What, really, gives rise to the coming into being of the kind of things such as unity, coherence, balance, or symmetry? What, ultimately, may be seen as lying behind the coming into being of such things? Is it the evolutionary process? No, in a sense. Is it the natural selection? No, in a sense. Is it the survival of the fittest? No, in a sense. It is harmony. It is harmony that gives rise to their coming into being. It is harmony that makes them the way they are. It is harmony that makes them possess the kind of characteristics, qualities, or properties that they may own. That is, it might be said, it is harmony that makes unity unity, not, in a sense, evolution. It is harmony that makes coherence coherence, not, in a sense, the evolutionary process. It is harmony that makes balance balance, not, in a sense, natural selection. It is harmony that makes symmetry symmetry, not, in a sense, the survival of the fittest. Evolution cannot make symmetry symmetry, though it may lead to the process of symmetrization. Natural selection cannot make balance balance, though it may lead to the process of balancing. The survival of the fittest cannot make unity or coherence out of balance or symmetry, though it may lead to the process resulting in unity or coherence.

Symmetry may be seen, it might be said, in a sense, as having little or nothing to do with evolution, that is, symmetry may be seen, in a sense, as existing before, prior to, or apart from any process of evolution. Though evolution may lead to the process of symmetrization, the very characteristics, qualities, or properties of symmetry may be seen as originating or coming into being, from the things other than evolution. That is, the process of symmetrization may be seen as the outcome or consequence resulting from the evolutionary advantages of symmetry, but the advantages themselves, that is, the advantageous characteristics, qualities, or properties of symmetry themselves should not be regarded as the result or consequence of such a kind of evolutionary process, as, it seems, it might be said, the very fact that such characteristics, qualities, or properties constituting certain evolutionary advantages in the evolutionary process may be seen as reflecting or representing certain things beyond or above the mere evolutionary process.

That is, it might be said, it is a different process. It has to do with a different process. It is a process different or apart from the evolutionary process, which may be seen as giving rise to the coming into being of such characteristics, qualities, or properties, and which, in the end, may be seen as constituting what we call symmetry, or the coming into being of symmetry. That is, in the end, it might be said, evolution should not be seen as what gives rise to symmetry, or to the characteristics, qualities, or properties of symmetry. That is, evolution should not be seen as what has to do with the beginning of symmetry, the source of symmetry, the root of symmetry, or, the origin of symmetry. The same may be said with regard to the natural selection, or, the survival of the fittest. And the same may be said with regard to balance, unity, or coherence. That is, evolution, natural selection, or the survival of the fittest should not be seen or regarded, ultimately, as what has to do with the beginning, source, root, or origin of the kind of things such as symmetry, balance, unity, or coherence found in things or animals.

It is harmony that, in a sense, gives the symmetric characteristics, qualities, or properties to symmetry. It is harmony that, in a sense, gives the corresponding characteristics, qualities, or properties to balance. It is harmony that, in a sense, gives rise to the unity or coherence found in balance or symmetry. It is harmony that, in a sense, gives rise to the beginning of symmetry, balance, unity, or coherence. It is harmony that, in a sense, provides the source of symmetry, balance, unity, or coherence. It is harmony that, in a sense, represents the root of symmetry, balance, unity, or coherence. It is harmony that, in a sense, stands as the origin of symmetry, balance, unity, or coherence. It is harmony that may be seen as behind all these things. It is harmony that may be seen as behind the coming into being of all these things. It is harmony that may be seen as underlying all these things. That is, it is harmony that may be seen as what is behind the first process. It is harmony that may be seen as what is underlying the first process. It is harmony that may be seen as what, in a sense, gives rise to the first process. That is, it might be said, while the second process may be seen as the evolutionary process, the first process may be seen as the harmonic process. That is, the second process may be seen as a process of evolutionary coming into being; the first process may be seen as a process of harmonic coming into being. The second process may be seen as the visible, apparent, outward, or noticeable evolutionary process of nature; the first process may be seen as the intrinsic, inherent, fundamental, or innate harmonic process in the world. That is, it might be said, evolution may better be seen, in a sense, as a harmonic process, or a harmonic progress; natural selection may better be seen, in a sense, as a harmonic selection; the survival of the fittest may better be seen, in a sense, as the survival of the harmonic. Harmony lies behind the eventual coming into being of the kind of things such as symmetry, balance, unity, or coherence. Harmony lies behind the eventual coming into being of the kind of things such as symmetry, balance, unity, or coherence which guides, leads, or directs the process of evolution. Harmony lies behind the process of evolution. Harmony lies behind the process of natural selection. Harmony lies behind the survival of the fittest. The first process underlies the second process. The first process sustains the second process. The first process guides the second process. The first process leads the second process. Harmony lies behind the first process. Harmony guides, leads, or directs the first process. Harmony gives rise to the first process. Harmony is the cause of the first process. Harmony is, thus, in such a sense, ultimately, the cause of the first process and the second process. Harmony thus, in such a sense, given the eventual coming into being of things, may be seen as the cause of the coming into being of things. That is, in such a sense, it might be said, harmony may be seen as the first cause of things.

As the result or consequence of the harmonic process, or progress, it might be said, the radially or bilaterally symmetric animals came into being. The radiality of the radially symmetric animals may be seen, certainly, as the result or outcome of a process of radialization in animals. The development of radialization in animals may be seen as a harmonic process, or progress, in the sense that, it was through such a process that the radiality, or radial symmetry, came into being, that is, came into existence in the world, as a kind of form or shape that expressed or exhibited some dramatic difference, or progress, from the kind of things such as shapelessness or formlessness found in some animals. The coming into being or appearance of radiality, that is, radial symmetry, in a sense, may represent a dramatic step forward, in the development of animals, in the sense that, such radially symmetric or harmonic characteristics, qualities, or properties might constitute certain advantages in animals. And we can see, it was indeed a dramatic step forward in the development of animals, as the kind of radially symmetric animals such as jellyfish began to develop or possess a kind of simple nerve net as the nervous system, a great leap forward from the kind of shapeless or formless animals such as sponges. The harmonic process, or progress, in such a sense, it might be said, might have given rise to the coming into being of radiality or radial symmetry, and at the same time, the coming into being of the simple nerve net. Could the coming into being of radiality or radial symmetry and the coming into being of the simple nerve net be seen or regarded, in a sense, as one and the same thing, an outcome or consequence of what may be called the harmonic process or progress? In a sense, it could, as, it seems, insofar as we know, no nervous system exists in the shapeless or formless animals, and the nervous system in the bilaterally symmetric animals is usually centralized, not merely a simple or diffuse net. In other words, it might be said, the coming into being of radiality or radial symmetry may be seen as corresponding, in a certain sense, to the coming into being of a simple nerve net, or, the existence of the simple nerve net may be seen as accompanying, or, in a sense, matching the existence of radiality or radial symmetry in animals. In other words, it might be said, the coming into being or existence of radiality or radial symmetry and the simple nerve net in the same animals, and at the same time, may be seen as the two sides of the same coin, reflecting or representing the workings or operations of a process deep down in nature, or inside of the world, that may not be so easily discerned or noticed by the human eyes, or, by the human mind.

That is, such co-existence or co-coming into being of radiality or radial symmetry and the simple nerve net in animals may be seen as the result or consequence of an intricate or innate harmonic process, or progress, in nature or in the world. That is, they may stand, in a sense, as the physical or biological evidence to the intrinsic, innate, or innermost harmonic coming into being or existence of things. The simple nerve net does not usually appear in the shapeless or formless animals. The simple nerve net also does not usually exist in the bilaterally symmetric animals. The centralized nervous system cannot be seen usually in the shapeless or formless animals. The centralized nervous system cannot be found, usually, too, in the radially symmetric animals. And, while the shapeless or formless animals usually have no nervous system, the radially and bilaterally symmetric animals all possess their nervous systems, either a simple nerve net, or a centralized system. That is, it seems, things are corresponding to each other, in a very deep way; things have order, in a very profound sense; and things are matching with other things, in an almost mysterious or unfathomable manner, either in their coming into being, or in their existence. The simple nerve net is not coming with the shapelessness or formlessness, or, bilateral symmetry. The centralized nervous system is not coming with the shapelessness or formlessness, or, radial symmetry. The non-existence of nervous system is not coming with the radial symmetry, or, bilateral symmetry. The simple nerve net is coming only with the radial symmetry. The centralized nervous system is coming only with the bilateral symmetry. The non-existence of nervous system is coming only with the shapelessness or formlessness. That is, it might be said, insofar as we can see, the simple nerve net and radial symmetry, or, the centralized nervous system and bilateral symmetry, or, the non-existence of nervous system and shapelessness or formlessness, may be seen as the two different or distinct aspects, features, expressions, or demonstrations of the same being or existence.

What is this kind of being? What is this kind of existence? What does such a kind of being tell us? What does such a kind of existence point to us? It tells us a lot, and it may point to us the most intrinsic, innate, or innermost being or existence of things in the world. the theory of evolution cannot explain why the simple nerve net should be accompanied by the radial symmetry, or, the centralized nervous system by the bilateral symmetry, or, the non-existence of nervous system by shapelessness or formlessness, or, vice versa. The theory of evolution cannot answer why the simple nerve net should correspond to the radial symmetry, the centralized nervous system to the bilateral symmetry, or, the non-existence of nervous system to shapelessness or formlessness, or, vice versa. The theory of evolution cannot tell us the reason why they should match with each other, but not the other things. The theory of evolution cannot tell us the reason why there should be such deep, profound, invisible, subtle, exquisite, and almost mysterious or unfathomable correspondence, agreement, matching, or consistency existing among things in the world. Such things seem to be beyond the reach of the theory of evolution. The theory of evolution strives to understand things in a rational way, that is, through reason. Such an approach is, certainly, not wrong. But, such things may be, in a sense, beyond the reach of reason, in the sense that, if reason only focuses on the visible, materialistic, or mechanical things. Such things are hidden. Such things are deep down in nature. Such things may be seen as the things underlying the being or existence of things in the world. They are the hidden correspondence. They are the secret matching. They are the invisible agreement. They are the deep connection. They are the profound consistency that exists in things of the world. They are the harmonic relationship that, in a sense, it might be said, binds, regulates, unites, or, gives rise to things.

When reason cannot reach, it does not necessarily mean that things do not exist. When reason cannot comprehend, it does not necessarily mean that things do not exist in the ways they do. When the human mind cannot grasp, it does not necessarily mean that things should exist in the other ways. When the human mind cannot understand, it does not necessarily mean that things existing in the world should conform to the limitations or imperfections of the human beings, or of the human mind. Reason may lead humans to construct a complex machine like a computer, but it may not be able to reach man. Computer is a machine, while man is not. The world is, in a sense, far more complex, deep, profound, subtle, exquisite, or, it might be said, mysterious, or unfathomable, than reason could possibly reach or comprehend, fully or completely. The mission of a philosopher is not just to exercise reason, as reason alone may not reach the very depths of man or the world. the mission of a philosopher is to exercise reason in such a way that, the limitations of reason may be revealed, all the senses or faculties of man may function as they should, and the being of man and the existence of the world are to be understood in a most possibly full and comprehensive manner. In such a sense, it may be hoped that, the depths of man and the world may be reached, and people may thus acquire a better understanding of themselves, or, of the world.

If we confine ourselves to reason, it seems, we may be unable to understand the kind of things such as the correspondence or agreement between the simple nerve net and radial symmetry, between the centralized nervous system and bilateral symmetry, or between the non-existence of nervous system and shapelessness or formlessness. That is, if we confine ourselves to the narrow, restricted, or limited rational way, it seems, we may be unable to comprehend or grasp the kind of things existing in the world such as the co-coming into being or co-existence of radial symmetry and simple nerve net, the co-coming into being or co-existence of bilateral symmetry and centralized nervous system, or, the co-coming into being or co-existence of shapelessness or formlessness and non-existence of nervous system in animals. Such kind of things may be seen as the invisible, intrinsic, or innate matching, consistency, or relationship existing deep down in nature or the world that may lie beyond, or above, the reach of reason, or, the way of the rational way. If the world were run by reason alone, man might not have come into being. If the world were only following the rational way, the world might not have been what it is now. Reason is only part of man. Reason is only part of the world. The rational way is only one way of man. The rational way is only one way of the world. Man has more ways than reason. Man has more parts than reason. The world has more things than reason. The world has more parts than reason. Man has other ways, apart from the rational way. The world has other ways, apart from the rational way. Apart from reason, man has feeling, and all his senses. Apart from reason, the world has all the kinds of things, such as, plants, or various animals. Apart from the rational way, man has other ways, such as, the animal way, or, the humoral way. Apart from the rational way, the world has other ways, such as, the harmonic way. Reason may only explain part of man, or, part of the world. The rational way may only make sense of part of man, or, part of the world. Reason cannot explain why there should be such deep or profound correspondence or agreement between radial symmetry and simple nerve net, between bilateral symmetry and centralized nervous system, or, between shapelessness or formlessness and non-existence of nervous system. The rational way cannot make sense of the fact that radial symmetry and simple nerve net, bilateral symmetry and centralized nervous system, or shapelessness or formlessness and non-existence of nervous system should come together, stay together, or exist together.

Why? Why is reason unable to explain such things? Why cannot reason explain such phenomena? Why cannot the rational way make sense of such things, such phenomena, or such facts? Because, it might be said, the way that such things or such phenomena happen is beyond the reach of reason, or, the way that such things or such phenomena happen is not the rational way. It is the harmonic way. It is the harmonic way that gives rise to such things, or such phenomena. It is the harmonic way that underlies such facts. It is the harmonic way that guides the co-coming into being or co-existence of radial symmetry and simple nerve net. It is the harmonic way that leads to the correspondence or agreement between bilateral symmetry and centralized nervous system. It is the harmonic way that directs the matching or consistency between shapelessness or formlessness and non-existence of nervous system. It is the harmonic way that is behind them all. That is, it is harmony that makes such correspondence, agreement, matching, or consistency possible. It is harmony that binds such correspondence, agreement, matching, or consistency. It is harmony that regulates such correspondence, agreement, matching, or consistency. It is harmony that unites such correspondence, agreement, matching, or consistency. That is, it is harmony that gives rise to, eventually, such correspondence, agreement, matching, or consistency. It is the invisible correspondence. It is the intrinsic agreement. It is the innate matching. It is the innermost consistency existing in things. It is the harmonic correspondence. It is the harmonic agreement. It is the harmonic matching. It is the harmonic consistency. It is harmony revealed in things. It is harmony expressed or demonstrated in things. It is harmony coming into being in things. It is harmony fulfilled or realized in things. It is the harmonic way running the world. It is the harmonic way guiding or directing the world. It is the harmonic way giving rise to the world. The harmonic way is the inner way. The harmonic way is the intrinsic way. The harmonic way is the innate way. The harmonic way is the way that is beyond, or above, the rational way.

That is why reason cannot explain such things. That is why reason cannot comprehend such phenomena. That is why the rational way cannot make sense of such things. That is why the rational way may never grasp the meaning, the significance, the rationale, the depth, the profundity, or, the very existence of such things, such phenomena, or, such facts. When reason cannot reach, people tell us that, man is nothing, morality does not exist, or, beauty is anything. When reason alone cannot reach man, it may only lead man away from man. When reason alone cannot reach man, it may only lead to the disintegration of the moral senses of man. When reason alone cannot reach man, it may only lead to the disappearance of what is called beauty. That may be the reason why, as we can see around ourselves, the so-called rational way may be seen as what is truly, or ultimately, behind the kind of things happening in the world, such as, the disintegration of man, the loss of the moral senses of man, or, the disappearance of beauty. Man means more than reason. Man means more than the rational way. The world means more than reason. The world means more than the rational way. The harmonic way gives rise to the coming into being of man, through, in a sense, a process of the humoralization of the true into the human body. The harmonic way gives rise to the humoral senses of man, through, in a sense, a process of the humoralization of the true into man, or, man into the true. The harmonic way gives rise to beauty, as beauty represents or stands for the coming into being or realization of harmony. Reason may play a role in all these things, but it may not play the decisive role. The rational way may constitute some way in all these things, but it may not stand as the most important or principal way. The coming into being or existence of the kind of things such as radial symmetry, bilateral symmetry, or shapelessness or formlessness may not be understood by or through reason, as, in a sense, reason may have played little role in such things. the coming into being or existence of the kind of things such as the simple nerve net, centralized nervous system, or non-existence of nervous system may not be understood by or through the rational way, as, in a sense, the rational way may not have played the major role. The coming into being or existence of the kind of things such as correspondence, agreement, matching, or consistency between radial symmetry and simple nerve net, bilateral symmetry and centralized nervous system, or shapelessness or formlessness and non-existence of nervous system may not be understood by or through reason, or the rational way, as, such things may have little to do with reason or the rational way. They have to do with harmony. They have to do with the harmonic way. They have to do with the way that is truly underlying the world. They have to do with the way that is truly behind the world. They have to do with the way that is truly intrinsic, innate, or inherent in nature, or in the world.

Thus, it is called the first process, a process of harmony, a process of harmonic development, or, a process of harmonic progress, that gives rise to things such as correspondence, agreement, matching, or consistency in animals, that is, the kind of things found in the radially symmetric, bilaterally symmetric, or shapeless or formless animals, with their corresponding types of nervous system. Thus, the second or secondary process, that is, the evolutionary process, that is, in a sense, the rational process, may only take the possible results or consequences, in a sense, of the first process as its beginning, that is, as the so-called evolutionary "advantages" in things, in a way to explain, scientifically, in an evolutionary sense, the various kinds of effects, changes, or evidences observed or found in the world, but at the same time, unfortunately, unable to explain, or make sense of the kind of things in the world such as the co-coming into being or co-existence of radial symmetry and simple nerve net, bilateral symmetry and centralized nervous system, or, shapelessness or formlessness and non-existence of nervous system in animals. The second or secondary process, that is, the evolutionary process, may be seen as following the rational way. thus, while it may explain the various visible effects, changes, or evidences of evolution, it may not be able to see into the workings or operations that give rise to the kind of things such as correspondence, agreement, matching, or consistency, found in the radially symmetric, bilaterally symmetric, or shapeless or formless animals. To see into such inner workings or operations of nature, we may need to look beyond reason. To understand such intrinsic or innate processes of the world, we may need to search beyond the rational way. That is, we need to sense nature, we need to perceive nature, we need to feel nature. That is, we need to sense the world, we need to perceive the world, we need to feel the world.

When reason falls short, our feeling may have to come to the fore. When reason falls short, our sensing may have to come to the fore. When reason falls short, our feeling or perceptive faculty may have to come to the fore. Feeling is part of man, just like reason. Feeling is a faculty of man, just like reason. Feeling, together with reason, makes man possible. Feeling, together with reason, makes man come into being. Feeling, with the help of reason, makes man a being of the world. While reason, in a sense, stays in the background, feeling forms the humorality of man. While reason, in a sense, stays in the background, feeling forms the humoral man. Man comes into being through both reason and feeling. Man means both reason and feeling. To understand man, we need both reason and feeling. To reach man, we need both reason and feeling. To see into nature, we need both reason and feeling. To understand the world, we need both reason and feeling. When reason alone cannot reach man, we have to reach man through feeling. When reason alone cannot understand man, we have to understand man through feeling. When reason alone cannot reach all nature, we have to reach all nature through feeling. When reason alone cannot reach all the world, we have to reach all the world through feeling. When reason alone cannot understand all nature, we have to understand all nature through feeling. When reason alone cannot understand all the world, we have to understand all the world through feeling. When reason alone cannot reach harmony, we have to reach harmony through feeling. When reason alone cannot understand harmony, we have to understand harmony through feeling. When reason alone cannot reach the harmonic way, we have to reach the harmonic way through feeling. When reason alone cannot understand the harmonic way, we have to understand the harmonic way through feeling. When reason alone cannot reach the harmonic process, we have to reach the harmonic process through feeling. When reason alone cannot understand the harmonic process, we have to understand the harmonic process through feeling. when reason alone cannot reach the kind of things such as the co-coming into being or co-existence of radial symmetry and simple nerve net, bilateral symmetry and centralized nervous system, or shapelessness or formlessness and non-existence of nervous system in animals, we have to reach such kind of things through feeling. When reason alone cannot understand such kind of things, we have to understand such kind of things through feeling. When reason alone cannot reach the kind of things such as correspondence, agreement, matching, or consistency found in the radially symmetric, bilaterally symmetric, or shapeless or formless animals, we have to reach such kind of things through feeling. When reason alone cannot understand such kind of things, we have to understand such kind of things through feeling. When reason fails to lead us to look into the world, we have to look into the world through feeling. When reason fails to lead us to see into nature, we have to see into nature through feeling. When reason fails to lead us to the intrinsic, innate, or inherent processes deep down in the world, we have to get to such processes, in a sense, through feeling. When reason fails to lead us to the inner workings or operations of nature, we have to come to such workings or operations, in a sense, through feeling. Man is a rational being; man is also a being of feeling. The world has a rational way; the world also has a harmonic way. Nature is rational; nature is also harmonic. To define man only in the rational way is to simplify man, that is, to overlook or ignore many important or vital things about man. To portray the world only in the rational way is to simplify the world, that is, to overlook or ignore many important or vital things about the world, such as, the harmonic coming into being of things. To characterize nature only in the rational way is to simplify nature, that is, to overlook or ignore many important or vital things about nature, such as, the harmonic existence of things. To fully understand man, we need both reason and feeling. To fully understand the world, we need both the rational way and the harmonic way. To fully understand nature, we need both rationality and harmony.

    The coming into being or existence of radial symmetry, that is, the development of radial symmetry, that is, the development of radial symmetry through both the first process and the second process, may be seen as one of the most significant and mighty advances in the development of animal life on earth, as such an advance represents or stands for a great leap forward, in a sense, from the shapelessness or formlessness of animals, and leads to the coming into being or existence of the simple nerve net as the nervous system in animals. That is, in other words, it might be said, the coming into being or existence of radial symmetry may be seen as signifying the beginning of the development of new types of animals in the world, as such a process of development may be seen as being initiated with the appearance of radial symmetry, in which animals with nervous system may eventually come into existence in this world. The co-coming into being or co-existence of shapelessness or formlessness and non-existence of nervous system and the co-coming into being or co-existence of radial symmetry and the simple nerve net may tell us that, they may stand as the two different processes in the development of animals. Certainly, the development of radial symmetry and the development of shapelessness or formlessness in animals may not be necessarily seen, in a sense, as the two processes that run, absolutely, one after the other, as such two processes may be possibly seen, in a sense, as going on at the same time, in some cases, in the world, though for different types of animals.

But, we do see, it appears, the development of radial symmetry seems indeed to indicate the beginning of the appearance of new types of animals, that is, the kind of animals with nervous system. That is, it might be said, with the coming into being of harmony, that is, symmetry, that is, radial symmetry, the nervous system begins to appear in this world. The coming into being of nervous system may thus be seen as closely related to, or associated with the coming into being or existence of harmony in the world. The coming into being of radial symmetry has to do, in a sense, with the coming into being of harmony. The coming into being of radial symmetry gives rise to the coming into being of nervous system. Thus, it might be said, the coming into being of harmony may be seen as having to do with the coming into being of both radial symmetry and the nervous system, as both of them may be seen, merely, in a sense, as the two different or distinct aspects, features, characteristics, or properties of one and the same harmonic existence. That is, in other words, it might be said, harmony may be seen as what truly underlies the coming into being or

Avolution and Man

existence of radial symmetry and the nervous system. Without harmony, it seems, we cannot talk about radial symmetry. Without radial symmetry, it seems, there would have been no such thing as the simple nerve net. Without harmony, it seems, then, there would have been no such thing as the nervous system. The nervous system is related to harmony. The nervous system is associated with harmony. The nervous system is linked to harmony. The nervous system is connected with harmony. The nervous system is united with harmony. The nervous system is bound into one with harmony. Harmony comes into being; the nervous system comes into being. Harmony appears; the nervous system appears. Radial symmetry comes into being; harmony is fulfilled. The nervous system comes into being; harmony is realized. Harmony exists in radial symmetry; radial symmetry exists in harmony. Harmony exists in the nervous system; the nervous system exists in harmony.

On the surface, it might be said, it is evolution that gives rise to the nervous system; deep down, it might be said, it is harmony that works behind all these things. It is harmony that constitutes, in a radially harmonic sense, radial symmetry. It is harmony that works to give rise to the kind of things corresponding to radial symmetry, such as, a simple nerve net as the nervous system, or, the radially symmetric animals surviving or thriving in the world. The second or secondary process may tell us the evolutionary things. The first process may reveal to us the harmonic workings or operations deep down in nature, or, in the world. When harmony expresses itself, what we see is the coming into being of radial symmetry. When harmony expresses itself, what we see is the coming into being of the nervous system. Harmony demonstrates itself in radial symmetry. Harmony demonstrates itself in the nervous system. Harmony fulfils itself through the co-coming into being of radial symmetry and the nervous system in animals. Harmony realizes itself through the co-existence of radial symmetry and the nervous system in the world.

Radial symmetry, that is, radiality, existing in animals, may be seen as different from bilateral symmetry, in the sense that, such roundness or circularity, as manifested or expressed in the radially symmetric animals, may be regarded as different, in a certain sense, from the sense of symmetry fulfilled or realized in the bilaterally symmetric animals, that is, a sense of bilateral symmetrization of things with two sides or parts arranged in a strictly or almost strictly mirror-image manner. That

Symmetry, harmony and Avolution

is, it might be said, radial symmetry, or radiality, existing in animals, may be seen or regarded, in a certain sense, as a kind, or form, of symmetry fulfilled or realized in some different harmonic manners, from bilateral symmetry. Radial symmetry may express some sense of roundness, but such a sense of roundness may not be that bilaterally symmetric. Radial symmetry may demonstrate some sense of circularity, but such a sense of circularity may not be regarded as that bilaterally symmetric. That is, it might be said, radiality may be seen or regarded as the kind, or form, of symmetry fulfilled or realized, in a certain sense, not as so strengthened, or intensified, as bilaterality. In other words, bilateral symmetry may be seen or regarded, in a certain sense, as the kind, or form, of symmetry fulfilled or realized in some more strengthened or intensified manner than radial symmetry. Such may be seen in the difference between radial symmetry and bilateral symmetry, and such may be seen in the difference associated with the coming into being or existence of the simple nerve net and centralized nervous system. Radial symmetry, or radiality, often comes into being in animals through a process of animal radialization that has to do usually with a body plan or structure that is round or with several body parts arranged evenly around a central axis. Such a body plan or structure certainly constitutes a sense of symmetric existence, as the parts or sections may be seen as symmetric, if viewed or observed from the opposite directions. But, in such a kind of body plan or structure, the adjacent parts or sections may not be seen as symmetric at all, as they may just exist in their ways by joining the parts or sections next to them. In such a sense, it might be said, radial symmetry, or radiality, may be seen or regarded, in a certain sense, as not that symmetric as bilateral symmetry.

As we can see or observe, there is beauty coming into being or existing with the radially symmetric animals such as jellyfish, and there is beauty coming into being or existing with the bilaterally symmetric animals such as butterflies or humans. Should we ask, which kind of beauty may be seen as more beautiful? Probably we should not take beauty in such a way, as beauty, as the coming into being or realization of harmony, may express or manifest itself in many many ways. But, it seems, we do see and observe, while bilateral symmetry exhibits its symmetrization of things, usually in its bilateral manner, radial symmetry may not, as certain parts or sections in such a kind of symmetry may not always form a complete sense of symmetry. That is, from a symmetric point of view, it might be said, compared to radial symmetry, bilateral symmetry may be seen as a kind of symmetry more strengthened or intensified.

We know, there is a certain degree of mixture or blending of radial symmetry and bilateral symmetry in some animals, and such a combination is sometimes called biradial symmetry. The existence of both radial symmetry and bilateral symmetry in animals may, in a sense, stand as a kind of proof to the complexity, subtlety, or depth of the coming into being or existence of symmetry in animals, or in the world. Could we clearly divide these two symmetries in animals? That is, with regard to the animals with both radial symmetry and bilateral symmetry fulfilled or realized together, is it the case that such symmetries may be clearly defined in such animals? Not necessarily. The developmental process of symmetry in animals on earth may not be that straightforward, that is, like a linear movement progressing steadily form one point to the other. No. Nature may not be that simple, and the world may not be that straightforward. There may be developments back and forth. There may be mixture and blending. There may be, in some cases, it might be said, regressions. That is, people may find, in some animals, both radial symmetry and bilateral symmetry may be fulfilled or realized, and both radial symmetry and bilateral symmetry may be found in different developmental stages, in some cases. In other words, the complexity, subtlety, or depth of the world may make it difficult for us to pin down the exact coming into being or existence of radial symmetry or bilateral symmetry in animals. Such difficulty may be seen as coming, in a sense, from the vast period of time that separates us from the early coming into being or development of either radial symmetry or bilateral symmetry in animals. That is, such a vast period of time may make it difficult for us to trace back the possible origins of the coming into being of animals, or, the possible origins of the coming into being or development of radial symmetry or bilateral symmetry in animals, as, in a sense, the fossil records or archaeological evidences from such early times are usually sparse or incomplete. That is to say, it seems, it would be difficult for us to pin down, exactly, the timing or the beginning of the coming into being or development of either radial symmetry or bilateral symmetry in animals, or, in some of the first animals from which radial symmetry or bilateral symmetry may be seen as having been developed.

Some may point to the advances in sciences such as genetics as the hope that such origins or beginnings may eventually be revealed, or, the presence or existence of radial symmetry or bilateral symmetry in animals may be clearly defined. Certainly, the advances in sciences may help in revealing certain things about the coming into being or development of symmetries in animals, or about the presence or existence of symmetries in animals. But, given the complexity, subtlety, or depth usually associated with the coming into being or existence of things, especially the kind of things such as the coming into being or existence of symmetry in things, that is, in animals, it might be said, in a sense, it may not be necessarily the case that the advances or developments of sciences may help us to fully disclose all the secrets surrounding the coming into being or existence of different symmetries in the world. Even if the advances of sciences may help in revealing certain things, it may also be possible that, they may also disorient us by providing the kind of things that they themselves may not be able to explain in the end. That is to say, in a sense, it might be said, science may not explain all the things, and reason may not reach all the things in nature or in the world. That is, certain things may lie beyond the reach of reason, and the deeper we go into the world, the deeper we look into nature, the deeper we search into the universe, it seems, the more we may encounter the kind of things that reason, or science, may not be able to make sense of, or explain.

The coming into being of things is no simple matter. The coming into being of things may be seen, in a sense, as among the most mysterious, obscure, or profound things of the world. It is mysterious in the sense that reason may not be able, ultimately, to reach the kind of things behind the coming into being of things. It is obscure in the sense that, science may ultimately fail to lead us to see into the kind of things underlying the coming into being of things. It is profound in the sense that, the kind of things behind or underlying the coming into being of things may be seen or regarded as having to do with the true formation of the world, of nature, of man, or of the universe, and yet, it seems, we possess little means to reach them, let alone to have some real or solid knowledge, understanding, or grasp of them. The kind of coming into being or existence of radial symmetry and bilateral symmetry in animal may be seen or regarded, in a sense, as among the most profound or significant things of the world, in the sense that, such a kind of coming into being or existence may really have to do with the very coming into being or existence of the world, and may reveal the true workings or operations behind the coming into being or existence of the world. And it is in such a sense that, it may have to be said, they may lie, in a sense, beyond, or above, or truly, underneath, the reach of reason, or science.

Certainly, this, in a sense, may not be very satisfactory to the human mind, as it strives, it seems, always, to search into the coming into being or existence of the world. But, given the complexity of the world, given the subtlety of nature, given the profundity of the universe, given the limitedness of reason, given the inadequacy of the human understanding, what could we do? And what could we possibly achieve? In a sense, that is, in a rationalistic or scientific sense, it might be said, we may acquire an understanding, that is, a rationalistic or scientific understanding, of the world, based on the reachability of reason, such as, when reason is able to reach the kind of things happening in the second process. But, when reason cannot reach, it seems, things may lie out of the sphere of our human rational understanding, such as, when reason alone cannot reach the kind of things happening in the first process, it seems, it may be the case that, things related to or associated with the first process may be either overlooked, ignored, or dismissed by the human rationalistic or scientific mind. In other words, it might be said, to fully grasp all the complexity, subtlety, or profundity of the world, we may have to employ all our senses or faculties, including reason, to feel, to sense, or to look into all the phenomena with which we are living, and hopefully, we may thus overcome the limitations of reason, and in a way, reach the very depths of things. Certainly, it may not be a simple task, and it may not be an easy road to take. We may have to first acquire or achieve, in a sense, a better or full and complete understanding of ourselves, since, otherwise, without such a kind of understanding as our starting point, it seems, we may never be able to reach, or to see into the complexity, subtlety, or profundity existing in the things of the world.

Let us look around ourselves. Let us observe the things of the world. Let us see what kind of world in which we are living. Both radial symmetry and bilateral symmetry can be found in the animal kingdom. Both radial symmetry and bilateral symmetry can be found in the plant world. While the bilaterally symmetric animals like humans exhibit bilateral symmetry, most plant leaves also exhibit bilateral symmetry, though with some kind of imperfection if examined carefully. While the radially symmetric animals like jellyfish exhibit radial symmetry, the patterns of radial symmetry may also be found in many things of plants, such as, in the patterns of plant flowers, or in the internal organizations of fruit seeds. It might be said, most life forms in the world seem to exhibit some sense of symmetry, mostly radial or bilateral, with only a small portion of the life forms appearing to possess no apparent symmetry at all. Symmetry may thus be seen, in a sense, as an outstanding or prominent feature of the world. To see into symmetry may help us see into the world. To search into symmetry may help us search into the world. Symmetry, in such a sense, may be seen as a rare window for us to look into the possible secrets of the world.

It appears, unlike bilateral symmetry, radial symmetry in the world may be found in a number of forms, or, in a number of types. Jellyfish are usually cited as the typical radially symmetric animals. With a careful anatomical examination, one may find that, many jellyfish actually possess four canals inside their bodies. To divide their radially symmetric bodies according to the four canals may mean that, their bodies may be seen as consisting of four equal parts or sections. That is to say, such jellyfish may be seen as the kind of animals with fourfold or tetramerous radial symmetry. We all like the sea stars on the beach, beautifully colored or shaped, usually with their five arms. Though they develop in their early stages with biradial symmetry, they eventually come to possess a kind of fivefold or pentamerous radial symmetry which may be seen as being demonstrated through their nicely arranged five arms. The patterns of radial symmetry may also be seen in the plant world, such as, in the reoccurrence of a group of five leaves regularly around a tree branch, or, in the internal organizations of some fruit seeds, such as in apples.

Hexacorals may be seen as the group of corals that have polyps bearing the characteristics of sixfold or hexamerous radial symmetry. Their polyps usually have tentacles in multiples of six, and the internal body structures of these polyps also display a sense of sixfold symmetry with radially divided parts or sections. Octocorals, such as the soft corals, may be seen as the kind of animals with eightfold or octamerous radial symmetry, in the sense that, such a group of corals usually have polyps that may be seen as being characteristic of such a form of radial symmetry. Apart from possessing eight tentacles each, these polyps also demonstrate a sense of eightfold or octamerous radial symmetry by having their bodies divided into eight parts or sections, with each part or section attached to one of the tentacles.

Thus, what we see here is that, radial symmetry in the world may be found in many forms or types. To talk about radial symmetry is not to talk about just one form or type of radial symmetry, such as the kind of radial symmetry represented by the fourfold symmetric body plan or structure of jellyfish. To talk about radial symmetry is to talk about all the forms or types of radial symmetry that we may have seen here, such as, the fourfold or tetramerous radial symmetry, the fivefold or pentamerous radial symmetry, the sixfold or hexamerous radial symmetry, or, the eightfold or octamerous radial symmetry. One may ask, why are there so many different forms or types of radial symmetry? Why do they exist? Why do they exist in the world? Why do they exist in animals or plants? Why do they exist, not in the way of bilateral symmetry, such as, with only one form or type? Why do they exist in so many forms, or in so many types? Is there anything behind the existence or coming into being of so many forms or so many types of radial symmetry? Is there anything behind the fact that radial symmetry is being expressed, represented, manifested, or embodied, by or through so many forms or so many types? What happens with such various forms or types of radial symmetry? What happens with their coming into being? What happens with their existence? What happens with their coming into being or existence, with regard to each other? Do they come into being alone, or do they come into being in association with each other? Do they exist by themselves, or do they exist in some relationship with each other? What may be such association? What may be such relationship? What may be the nature? What may be the origin? What may be the source? What may be the beginning? Or, what may be behind the coming into being or existence of such various forms or types of radial symmetry in the world? What should their coming into being or existence tell us? Why, after all, should they have to exist, in so many forms, or in so many types, in the world?

Bilateral symmetry may have fulfilled or realized itself, in a sense, in the world, that is, in animals or plants, in a rich or plentiful manner, in the sense that, the bilaterally symmetric animals or plants may have constituted, in a certain sense, the vast majority of animals or plants around us in the world. Radial symmetry may have fulfilled or realized itself, in a sense, in a similar rich or plentiful manner, in that, such a kind of rich or plentiful fulfillment or realization may be observed in the coming into being or existence of so many forms or types of radial symmetry being expressed, demonstrated, manifested, or embodied in the world, that is, in animals or plants. This may be why we see so many forms or types of radial symmetry in the world. This may be why so many forms or types of radial symmetry may be observed in animals or plants. That is, the development of symmetry may be behind the coming into being or existence of so many forms or types of radial symmetry in the world. That is, the fulfillment or realization of symmetry may be behind the phenomena that so many forms or types of radial symmetry may be observed in animals or plants.

That is, it might be said, it is harmony that may be seen as behind the coming into being or existence of so many forms or types of radial symmetry in the world. It is the harmonic principle that may be seen as behind the coming into being or existence of so many forms or types of radial symmetry in the world. It is the harmonic development that may be seen as giving rise to the coming into being or existence of so many forms or types of radial symmetry in the world. It is the harmonic development that may be seen as bringing into being, eventually, the kind of things such as the fourfold or tetramerous radial symmetry, the fivefold or pentamerous radial symmetry, the sixfold or hexamerous radial symmetry, or the eightfold or octamerous radial symmetry in the world. It is harmony that may be seen as underlying such things. It is harmony that may be seen as giving rise to such things. It is harmony that may be seen as the source of such things. It is harmony that may be seen as the origin of such things. It is harmony that may be seen as the root of such things. It is harmony that may be seen as the beginning of such things. Without the harmonic principle, there might be no such things. Without the harmonic development, there might be no such things. Without the harmonic process or progress, there might be no such things as the coming into being or existence of the fourfold or tetramerous radial symmetry, the fivefold or pentamerous radial symmetry, the sixfold or hexamerous radial symmetry, or, the eightfold or octamerous radial symmetry. Without harmony, there might be no such thing as the variety of radial symmetry. Without harmony, there might be no such thing as the variety of animals or plants. Without harmony, there might be no such thing as the diversity of species of the world.

Harmony is not easy to see. Harmony is not easy to discern. Harmony is not easy to grasp. Harmony is not easy to understand. Harmony is not easy to see, as it lies inside of things. Harmony is not easy to discern, as the human eye may not be able to catch sight of it. Harmony is not easy to grasp, as the human mind may be too narrow or limited. Harmony is not easy to understand, as reason may not be capable of, eventually, reaching it. Harmony is easy to see. Harmony is easy to discern. Harmony is easy to grasp. Harmony is easy to understand. Harmony is easy to see, as it is everywhere. Harmony is easy to discern, as it is present all over the world. Harmony is easy to grasp, as it underlies the coming into being of things, such as, the coming into being of man. Harmony is easy to understand, as it maintains, supports, or sustains the existence of things, such as, the existence of the human life.

To see harmony is to see the world. To see harmony is to see man. To see harmony is to see the human life. To see harmony is to see the diverse species in the world. To see harmony is to see the various things in the world. To see harmony is to see the various animals in the world. To see harmony is to see the various plants in nature. To see harmony is to see radial symmetry exhibited, expressed, or manifested in so many forms or types, in animals or plants. To see harmony is to see bilateral symmetry fulfilled or realized in a rich or plentiful manner, in the world. To see harmony is to see symmetry, eventually, being fulfilled or realized, in so many forms or types, or in a rich or plentiful manner, in animals, in plants, in nature, in the world.

Radiality, in a sense, may not be seen as so symmetric as bilateral symmetry, in that, certain parts or sections in such a radial state or condition may not be symmetric at all. While the opposite parts or sections in a radial state or condition may be seen as symmetric, the adjacent parts or sections may not. That is, compared with bilateral symmetry, it seems, it might be said, radiality may be seen or regarded, in a sense, as not that symmetric, as certain things in such a state or condition may not be symmetric at all. Bilateral symmetry may be seen, in such a sense, with its mirror-image arrangement of things, as a kind of symmetry, in a sense, strengthened or intensified. That is, it might be said, bilateral symmetry may be seen, in a sense, as representing or standing for a sense of harmony, it might be said, in a sense, strengthened or intensified. That is, it might be said, it is a sense of harmony, in a sense, so strengthened or intensified that, it is no longer

Symmetry, harmony and Avolution

the kind of things such as the fourfold, fivefold, sixfold, or eightfold symmetry: it is the twofold symmetry. It is the bilateral symmetry. It is the twofold symmetry. It is the binary symmetry. Bilateral symmetry is the symmetry in the form of twofold, bilateral, or binary symmetry. The twofold symmetry may be seen as a strengthened or intensified sense of symmetry. The twofold symmetry may be seen as representing or standing for a strengthened or intensified sense of harmony. It is in such a strengthened or intensified sense that, it might be said, we may observe the various differences between radial symmetry and bilateral symmetry, and the world may thus have been fulfilled or realized in its rich, colorful, diverse, and abundant ways.

Symmetry comes into being; man is not far away. Symmetry comes into being; man begins to emerge. Symmetry comes into being; man starts to appear. Symmetry comes into being; man is prepared to come into being. Symmetry comes into being; man is ready to come into existence in the world. The coming into being of symmetry paved the way for man to emerge. The coming into being of symmetry paved the way for man to appear. The coming into being of symmetry prepared things in such a way that, what is called man would eventually come into being or existence in the world. The coming into being or development of the bilaterally symmetric animals on earth paved the way for the appearance of man on earth. The evolutionary advantages enjoyed by the bilaterally symmetric animals may be seen in that they may have constituted the vast majority of animals that we may observe around us, and that they may develop or possess the kind of complex or sophisticated nervous system like the centralized nervous system. Bilateral symmetry may be seen as behind such evolutionary advantages. Bilateral symmetry may be seen as behind their nervous system. Bilateral symmetry may be seen as behind their prosperity or survival. It is symmetry that makes the bilaterally symmetric animals bilaterally symmetric. It is symmetry that makes the bilaterally symmetric animals symmetric. It is symmetry that makes the bilaterally symmetric animals advantageous. It is symmetry that makes the bilaterally symmetric animals so evolutionarily advantageous that they may develop in such a way that they may come to possess a kind of complex or sophisticated nervous system, and eventually, the highly developed animal species, the human beings, may emerge and come to this world. That is, in other words, in a sense, it might be said, it is harmony that may be seen as behind the evolutionary advantages that the bilaterally symmetric animals may possess, and it is harmony that, it might be said, ultimately, enables the bilaterally symmetric animals to develop, to survive, to thrive, to prosper, to multiply, to populate, or to occupy most of the living spaces on earth.

As the bilaterally symmetric animals, fish came to this world and thrived in waters. As the bilaterally symmetric animals, amphibians came to this world, and thrived both in waters and on land. As the bilaterally symmetric animals, reptiles came to this world. As the bilaterally symmetric animals, mammals came to this world, and thrived on the surface of earth. As the bilaterally symmetric animals, primates came to this world. As the bilaterally symmetric animals, the early humans came to this world. As the bilaterally symmetric animals, the modern humans came to this world, and prospered. Man came into being, as the animal of bilateral symmetry. Man came into being, as the symmetric animal. Man came into being, just like fish, as the bilaterally symmetric animal. Man came into being, just like amphibians or reptiles, as the symmetric animal. Man came into being, just like mammals, as the bilaterally symmetric animal. Man came into being, just like the other primates, as the symmetric animal. As the bilaterally symmetric animal, man shares with fish the development of bilateral symmetry. As the symmetric animal, man shares with amphibians or reptiles the development of symmetry. As the bilaterally symmetric animal, man shares with the other mammals the progress of symmetry. As the symmetric animal, man shares with the other primates the progress of harmony. It is the development of bilateral symmetry that may be seen as eventually giving rise to the coming into being of fish. It is the development of symmetry that may be seen as eventually making the coming into being of amphibians or reptiles possible. It is the progress of symmetry that may be seen as eventually leading to the coming into being of mammals, including man. It is the progress of harmony that may be seen as eventually bringing primates, including man, into this world. That is, it is the development of bilateral symmetry or symmetry that may be seen as underlying the coming into being of fish, amphibians, or reptiles. It is the progress of symmetry or harmony that may be seen as behind the coming into being of mammals, primates, or the human species.

Bilateral symmetry develops, such that, fish may come into being. Symmetry develops, such that, amphibians or reptiles may appear. Symmetry progresses, such that, mammals and primates may develop on earth. Harmony progresses, such that, the human species may eventually come to this world. Man comes into being, as a result of the development of bilateral symmetry. Man comes into being, as a result of the development of symmetry. Man comes into being, as a result of the progress of bilateral symmetry. Man comes into being, as a result of the progress of symmetry. Man comes into being, as a result of the development of harmony. Man comes into being, as a result of the progress of harmony. Man comes into being, as a manifestation of the development of bilateral symmetry. Man comes into being, as a manifestation of the development of symmetry. Man comes into being, as a manifestation of the development of harmony. Man comes into being, as a manifestation of the progress of bilateral symmetry. Man comes into beings, as a manifestation of the progress of symmetry. Man comes into being, as a manifestation of the progress of harmony.

It was with bilateral symmetry that fish, amphibians, reptiles, mammals, primates, early humans, and modern humans developed. It was in symmetry that fish, amphibians, reptiles, mammals, primates, early humans, and modern humans came to this world, and thrived. From fish to amphibians to reptiles to mammals to primates to early humans to modern humans, it may be seen as a developmental process, or, it may be seen as a developmental progress. In such a developmental process or progress, as we know, the brain or the nervous system developed, which may be seen as one of the most defining characteristics of such a process or progress. The human brain, or the human nervous system, comes to this world. The human brain or nervous system largely defines, in a sense, the human beings, as a highly developed animal species. It is one of the most significant or important parts of the human body. Its coming into being is significant. Its coming into being is momentous. Its coming into being is mighty. Its coming into being is monumental. The human brain may be seen, in a sense, as having developed from the kind of things such as the kind of nervous system possessed by fish or amphibians. And certainly, the human brain is much more complex than that of fish or amphibians. But, it seems, no matter how complex or more developed the human brain may appear, it nevertheless may be seen as coming, that is, having developed, from the kind of nervous system that may have existed in the kind of bilaterally symmetric animals such as worms, insects, fish, amphibians, reptiles, mammals, or primates. That is to say, the coming into being of the human brain or nervous system may be seen as reflecting or representing, in a sense, the development of the bilaterally symmetric animals in nature or the world, in the sense that, from worms to insects to fish to amphibians to reptiles to mammals to primates, what we see is, in a sense, a process or progress in which the brain or nervous system develops gradually to obtain more and more complexity, capacity, or power, and eventually, as we know, to reach the kind of level of the human brain.

Why should the brain or nervous system have to undergo such a kind of process or progress? Why should the brain or nervous system in the bilaterally symmetric animals have to undergo such a kind of process or progress? Why should the brain or nervous system in the bilaterally symmetric animals have to develop in such a way? Why should the brain or nervous system in the bilaterally symmetric animals have to develop in such a way that the human brain or nervous system would eventually come into being? Why should the brain or nervous system in the bilaterally symmetric animals develop, at all? Why should the brain or nervous system in the bilaterally symmetric animals not develop in other ways? Why should the brain or nervous system in the bilaterally symmetric animals not develop in the kind of ways that the human brain or nervous system might never come into being? That is, in a sense, in other words, why should the bilaterally symmetric animals have survived so well? Or, why should the bilaterally symmetric animals have thrived or prospered so amazingly, in such a great scale, or, to such a high level?

Sponges survive well, it seems. Sponges thrive too, it seems. Sponges prosper, as well, it appears. But, sponges have not developed in such a way that some kind of brain or nervous system may come into being in them. That is, it seems, without regular shapes or forms, generally speaking, sponges develop, that is, survive, thrive, or prosper, with their characteristic state or condition of being the kind of animals without brain or nervous system. The kind of radially symmetric animals like jellyfish or hydras survive well, thrive too, and it appears, prosper as well. But, it seems, they have not developed in such a way that some kind of complex or highly developed nervous system may come into being in them. And, as we know, they only possess a kind of simple nerve net as their nervous system. Why is it the case that sponges have not developed, in a sense? Why is it the case that the radially symmetric animals have not developed, in a sense? Why is it the case that sponges have not developed in such a way that some kind

Symmetry, harmony and Avolution

of brain or nervous system may come into being in them? Why is it the case that the radially symmetric animals have not developed in such a way that some kind of complex nervous system, such as, more developed than a simple nerve net, may come into being in them? What makes sponges develop, that is, survive, thrive, or prosper, all the time, without brain or nervous system? What makes the radially symmetric animals develop, that is, survive, thrive, or prosper, all the time, with only a simple nerve net, that is, without a complex or centralized nervous system? What makes a nervous system so significant or important? What makes a nervous system possible? What makes a nervous system come into being? What makes a nervous system complex? What makes a nervous system simple? What makes a nervous system not simple? What makes a nervous system centralized? What makes the complexity of a nervous system? What makes the centralization of a nervous system? What gives rise to the complexity, capacity, or power of a nervous system? What gives rise to the centralization of a nervous system? That is, what makes the complex nervous system so significant? What makes the centralized nervous system so momentous? What makes the centralized nervous system so mighty? What makes the centralization of the nervous system so monumental? That is, what, after all, makes the nervous system develop? That is, what, in the end, leads to the coming into being of the human brain?

Without the complexity of the human brain or nervous system, it seems, there would have been no man. Without the centralization of the human brain or nervous system, it appears, there would have been no human species. The centralization of the nervous system, or, the process of the centralization of the nervous system, may be seen as the most crucial or decisive step in the coming into being of highly developed nervous systems. Such may be seen in the developmental process of the coming into being of the various nervous systems. The radially symmetric animals only possess a simple nerve net as their nervous systems. Such a nerve net is characterized by its diffuse or scattered nature, in the sense that, it is not a centralized net, and it is usually spread out in the body without a sense of centralization of its physical tissues or functions. The process of a sense of centralization of the nervous system may be seen as beginning with the appearance of the bilaterally symmetric animals. Such a kind of process may not be found with the radially symmetric animals, as their nervous systems, a simple nerve net, lack such a kind of centralization. It is with the bilaterally symmetric animals that we begin to witness the happening of such a kind of centralizing process. Worms may be seen as the kind of bilaterally symmetric animals that possess only a simple kind of nervous system. Certainly, it may be expected, the nervous systems of the bilaterally symmetric animals like worms may not be that complex or highly developed, but, in their nervous systems, that is, in their nervous structures, or in the organization or arrangement of their nerve tissues or functions, we may find or observe certain characteristics that may be seen as belonging only to the bilaterally symmetric animals.

The nervous system of worms may be seen as consisting of nerve cords and ganglia, the segmental nerve enlargements or centers. The nervous system of worms may no longer be seen as a simple nerve net, spread out in the body, as such a system is now made up of cords and ganglia that are themselves no longer just simple nerves. The nerve cords may be seen as nerves thickened, or solidified; the ganglia may be seen as nerves concentrated, fused, enlarged, or expanded. That is, the nervous system of worms may be seen, in a sense, as being centralized in such a way that, nerve cords appear in the body to connect nerves and ganglia, and ganglia, the enlarged or concentrated nerve tissues, function as the segmented nerve centers to manage or coordinate the segmented body parts. The nervous system in worms is thus no longer a diffuse or scattered structure. It has main nerve communication lines, in the form of nerve cords, and it has managing centers, in the form of ganglia. The development of nervous system in worms may thus be seen as being achieved, in a sense, through a process of centralization or concentration of physical tissues and functions. It is through such a kind of process that, it might be said, nerve cords come into being, such that, the main nerve communication lines may be formed, and the nervous signals may be transmitted in a relatively centralized manner. It is also through such a kind of process that, it might be said, ganglia come into being, such that, the nerve centers in the body may be formed, and the control or coordination of the body may be managed through some more complex or powerful means than the mere simple nerves. The nervous system of worms may thus be seen or regarded, in a sense, as more complex or powerful than the simple nerve net, existing in or possessed by the radially symmetric animals such as jellyfish or hydras. The complexity or power of the nervous system of worms comes from the fact that, the nervous structure is no longer simple, and the nerve cords and ganglia existing in such a system may be seen as bringing with them a certain sense of thickened, solidified, enlarged, or expanded capacity. That is, in other words, the centralized or concentrated nature of the nervous system of worms makes such a system capable of certain functions or performances that a simple nerve net in the radially symmetric animals may not be up to. The process of centralization or concentration may thus be seen, in a sense, as what gives rise to the complexity, capacity, or power of the nervous system of worms. The lack of centralization or concentration, such as in the simple nerve net possessed by the radially symmetric animals, may thus explain, in a sense, the simplicity, or lack of complexity, of such a kind of nervous system.

The process of centralization or concentration of the nervous system continues, it seems, with the bilaterally symmetric animal species other than worms. It is revealed that, the nervous systems of many species of insects may be seen as being characterized by a process of fusion, in the sense that, in such nervous systems, ganglia are usually fused together to form larger ganglia, such hat, there are usually few or less number of ganglia in the body. Such a process of fusion may also be seen in the formation of the insect brains, in the sense that, it is usually through the fusion of a number of ganglia that insect brains may come into being. The process of centralization or concentration may thus be seen, in a sense, in the coming into being of the nervous systems of insects, in the sense that, as the coming into being of the insect nervous systems may be characterized by a process of fusing ganglia into larger ganglia, such a centralizing or concentrating process may be seen as being fulfilled or realized through such a kind of process of fusion. The nervous systems of insects may thus be seen, in such a sense, as possibly being more complex or powerful than the nervous system of worms. The fusion of ganglia may give rise to a nervous system with a sense of enlarged or expanded capacity. As the insect brains are usually made up of a number of ganglia, it may be expected, that, they may be able to possess, possibly, a kind of capacity that may be more powerful than what may be found in the nervous system of worms. The process of fusion of ganglia, certainly, may enable the nervous systems of insects to possibly possess some structures or characteristics that may not be found in the nervous system of worms. It is through such a kind of fusion that, it might be said, the insect nervous systems develop, and become, in some sense, possibly, more complex or powerful than that of worms. The development of the insect nervous systems may thus be seen, in a sense, as a process of fusion, a process of amalgamation, a process of combining, or, a process of merging. It is through the combining or merging of the nerve tissues that the insect nervous systems may be formed. It is through the fusion or amalgamation of the nervous structures or parts that the insect nervous systems may have appeared. That is, it might be said, it is through, in a sense, the process of centralization or concentration that the insect nervous systems may have come into being.

While the process of centralization or concentration unfolds in the development of the insect nervous systems, such a process may be seen, in a sense, as being reflected, or fulfilled or realized, in the coming into being of other bilaterally symmetric animals, that is, in the coming into being of the vertebrate animals. The development of the vertebrate animals continues, it might be said, the process of centralization or concentration of the nervous system, in that, as we can see, such a process of centralization or concentration has developed in such a way, or to such an extent that the kind of highly complex or sophisticated nervous system like the human brain may eventually come into being.

The vertebrate animals usually have well-developed body structures, such as, the head or the vertebral column. The head contains and protects the brain, and the vertebral column contains and protects the spinal cord. Thus, as we can see, the vertebrate animals are well-developed for the coming into being or existence of the centralized nervous system. Or, in other words, it might be said, the process of centralization or concentration of the nervous system may be seen as being fulfilled or realized, in a sense, well, in the vertebrate animals. What makes the process of centralization or concentration of the nervous system so well fulfilled or realized in animals? What makes the vertebrate animals so well developed, such that they may come to possess the kind of highly developed centralized nervous system? What makes the vertebrate animals to come to possess such kind of body structures? What makes the vertebrate animals to come to develop such kind of body organs? What, after all, makes it possible that, such kind of highly developed centralized nervous system may eventually appear in animals? Bilateral symmetry may be seen as behind the coming into being or existence of the vertebrate animals. Bilateral symmetry may be

Symmetry, harmony and Avolution

seen as behind the coming into being or existence of the highly developed centralized nervous system in the vertebrate animals. Bilateral symmetry may be seen as behind the process of the centralization or concentration of the nervous system in animals. Bilateral symmetry may be seen as behind the fulfillment or realization of the process of the centralization or concentration of the nervous system in animals.

Development is not just evolutionary; it is symmetric. Development is not just evolutionary; it is harmonic. Development is not just evolutionary; it is avolutionary. Development is not just an evolutionary process; it is a symmetric process. Development is not just an evolutionary process; it is a harmonic process. Development is not just an evolutionary process; it is an avolutionary process. Development is not just evolution; it is avolution. Development has to do not just with evolution; it has to do with symmetry. Development has to do not just with evolution; it has to do with harmony. Development has to do not just with evolution; it has to do with avolution. It is symmetry. It is harmony. It is avolution.

Evolution alone cannot explain symmetry. Evolution alone cannot explain the coming into being of symmetry. Evolution alone cannot explain the coming into being of symmetry in animals or plants. Evolution alone cannot explain the coming into being or existence of symmetry in the world. Evolution alone cannot explain the evolutionary advantages in things. Evolution alone cannot explain the coming into being or existence of the evolutionary advantages in things. Evolution alone cannot explain their origin. Evolution alone cannot explain their source. Evolution alone cannot explain their beginning. Evolution alone cannot explain their eventual coming into being. Evolution alone cannot explain their eventual existence. Evolution is a process apparent; harmony is a process intrinsic. Evolution is a progress on the surface; harmony is a progress innate. Evolution explains what follows harmony; harmony explains what leads evolution. The evolutionary advantages may better be called, in a sense, the harmonic evolutionary advantages, as such advantages may have to do, eventually, with things intrinsic, innate, or deep down in nature or the world. That is, to understand such advantages, we may have to understand harmony. To understand such advantages, we may have to understand the principle of harmony. To understand such advantages, we may have to understand the intrinsic or innate presence of harmony. To understand such advantages, we may have to understand the workings or operations of harmony deep down in nature or the world.

To understand symmetry is to understand harmony. To understand the coming into being of symmetry is to understand harmony. To understand the process of the coming into being of symmetry is to understand harmony. That is, in a sense, it might be said, to understand nature is to understand harmony. That is, in a sense, it might be said, to understand the world is to understand harmony. To understand the coming into being of nature is to understand harmony. To understand the coming into being of the world is to understand harmony. Evolution may be part of nature, but not, in a sense, its origin. Evolution may be part of the world, but not, in a sense, its source. Evolution may be part of nature, but not, in a sense, its fountainhead. Evolution may be part of the world, but not, in a sense, its beginning. Evolution may be part of nature or the world, but it may not be seen or regarded as the foundation. Evolution may be seen as the second or secondary process of nature; harmony may be seen as the first or primary process of nature. Evolution may be seen as the second or secondary principle of the world; harmony may be seen as the first or primary principle of the world.

The coming into being of symmetry is not simple. The coming into being of symmetry is significant. The coming into being of symmetry is momentous. The coming into being of symmetry is mighty. The coming into being of symmetry is monumental. It is a harmonic coming into being. It is a harmonic happening. It is a harmonic development. It is a harmonic fulfillment or realization. It is a significant harmonic coming into being. It is a momentous harmonic happening. It is a mighty harmonic development. It is a monumental harmonic fulfillment or realization. It is the coming into being of the world guided by harmony. It is the coming into being of nature led by harmony. It is the coming into being of the world following the harmonic principle. It is the coming into being of nature in line with the principle of harmony. It is harmony working to give rise to things. It is harmony operating to bring things into being. It is harmony fulfilling itself. It is harmony realizing itself. It is harmony fulfilling itself in the world. It is harmony realizing itself through nature. It is harmony revealing itself in the world. It is harmony expressing itself in nature. It is harmony demonstrating itself through the being or existence of things. It is

Symmetry, harmony and Avolution

harmony manifesting itself in or through the symmetric being or existence of things in nature, in the world.

Evolution alone may not be able to bring animals or plants into being. For animals or plants to come into being, or to develop, to survive, or to thrive, evolution may only be part of the process, and it might be said, it may not have played the major or decisive role, as it seems, even in an evolutionary explanation of things, the evolutionary advantages leading the possible evolutionary processes may be seen as coming, eventually, from harmony, but not from evolution itself. We may not be able to see the workings of harmony, but the harmonic workings are significant. We may not be able to see the operations of harmony, but the harmonic operations are momentous. We may not be able to see, in a sense, the process of harmony working to bring things into being, but such a harmonic process is truly mighty. We may not be able to see, in a sense, the progress of harmony giving rise to the coming into being of symmetry, but such a harmonic progress is truly monumental. It is indeed significant, as symmetry comes into being in nature. It is indeed momentous, as symmetry appears in the world. It is indeed mighty, as symmetry develops in nature. It is indeed monumental, as symmetry fulfils or realizes itself in the world.

The harmonic process is the principle; the evolutionary process is the result. The harmonic process is the way; the evolutionary process is the consequence. The harmonic way is the big way. The harmonic way is the powerful way. The harmonic way is the deep way. The harmonic way is the profound way. The harmonic way may be so big that, we may not comprehend it. The harmonic way may be so powerful that, we may not grasp it. The harmonic way may be so deep that, we may not reach it. The harmonic way may be so profound that, before it, we may even lose ourselves. That is, before the harmonic way, it seems, our human senses or faculties may stop working, only a connection remains, with the infinite, boundless, and expansive existence far far away.

§ 3.6 Symmetry, Harmony, and Avolution

Genetics and Avolution

People sometimes say things occur because of some errors. People sometimes say things happen out of some accidents. People sometimes say things come into being due to some mutations.

Is it errors? Is it accidents? Is it mutations? Do plants come into being because of some errors? Do animals come into being out of some accidents? Do flowers appear due to some mutations? Does man come into being due to some errors, accidents, or mutations?

Plants come into being from symmetry. Animals come into being from symmetry. Flowers come into being from symmetry. Man comes into being from symmetry. It seems, when we cannot see into symmetry, we call it errors. It seems, when we cannot see into harmony, we call it accidents. It seems, when we cannot see into the avolutionary development of things, we call it mutations. Is it errors? No. It is not errors. It is symmetry. Is it accidents? No. It is not accidents. It is harmony. Is it mutation? No. It is not mutation. It is avolution.

Development

Development may be divided into the physical development, the rational development, and the harmonic development. The physical development may be seen as the development that we may touch, see, feel, sense or perceive. Thus, it might be said, the physical development may be seen as the kind of development happening or occurring in our daily lives. The rational development may be seen as the development that may be understood or grasped by or through reason. The harmonic development may be seen as the development closely associated with symmetry or harmony.

Symmetry is behind the development of things. In other words, the harmonic development may be seen as the development underlying the physical development and the rational development. The theory of evolution is about the development by natural selection. The evolutionary development by natural selection may be seen as the rational development. That is to say, the theory of evolution may be about the kind of development that may be reached, understood, or grasped by or through reason. The theory of evolution is not about symmetry or harmony, and it might be said, it is not concerned with the harmonic development. It is in such a sense, it might be said, that, while the theory of evolution may be able to explain the rational development, it may fail to grasp or understand the harmonic development. Evolution may be about the physical development and the rational development. Avolution is about all the developments, the physical development, the rational development and the harmonic development.

The Power of Symmetry

How powerful is symmetry? To answer this mighty question, we may have to look back, and think, for a while. What power was behind the appearance of head? What power was behind the coming into being of eyes? What power was behind the emergence of the bilateral body plans? Symmetry might have been behind the appearance of head. Symmetry might have been behind the coming into being of eyes. Symmetry might have been behind the emergence of the bilateral body plans. The same power might have been behind the appearance of head. The same power might have been behind the coming into being of eyes. The same power might have been behind the emergence of the bilateral body plans. It was the symmetric power. The symmetric power may be seen in binding the double helical symmetry. The symmetric power may be seen in binding the sexual symmetry. The symmetric power may be seen in binding the bilaterally symmetric body plans of the various organisms or animals of the world. Is symmetry powerful? Symmetry is powerful. Symmetry is, indeed, powerful.

The Movement of Symmetry

Why did flowering plants appear so late, in the Cretaceous, and as we know, land plants had appeared on earth during the Devonian explosion?

Land plants appeared in the Devonian explosion, about 400 million years ago, but it seems, flowers only appeared in the Cretaceous explosion, about 100 million years ago.

Animals appeared on earth in the Primordial explosion, about 600 million years ago. The genus *Homo*, which gave rise to man, appeared only about 2.5 million years ago.

Why did animals appear in the Primordial explosion, but not in other times? Why did plants appear in the Devonian explosion, but not in other times? Why did flowers appear in the Cretaceous explosion, but not in other times? Why did the genus *Homo* appear about 2.5 million years ago, but not in other times?

Why? Why?

What might be the next movement of symmetry? What might be the next development of symmetry? What might be the next step of symmetry?

Time

Why does time move always forward? Why does time have a direction? Why is there an arrow of time? People have thought and discussed such questions for a long time, and it seems, most of the efforts may be seen as having to do with physics. But, as we know, the fundamental laws of physics usually have nothing to do with the past or future. That is, according to the laws of physics, things happening in the future may also happen, in the same sense, in the past. In other words, it seems, it might be said, the kind of things such as an arrow of time may not be explained, satisfactorily, by or through some models or explanations based on physics.

Some people may try to bypass such a problem by suggesting various hypotheses, but such hypotheses may encounter some insurmountable problems in the end.

The direction of time may have to do with symmetry. That is, the direction of time may have to do with the movement of symmetry. It may be the direction of the movement of symmetry. It may be the direction of the development of symmetry. It may have to do with the fulfillment of symmetry in the world. It may have to do with the realization of symmetry in the universe. That may be why we have a sense that things move forward. That may be why we have a feeling that the future is different from the past. That may be why, it appears, time has an arrow, a direction moving forward.

Harmony and Life

Many factors may have contributed to the coming into being or existence of life on earth. The atmosphere of the earth may have contributed to the coming into being or existence of life on earth. The magnetic field of the earth may have contributed to the coming into being or existence of life on earth. Cosmic rays usually consist of high-energy particles. They may be harmful to life, as they may cause damage to DNA. In such a sense, the strength of the magnetic field of the earth and the depth or density of the atmosphere of the earth may prove to be crucial to the coming into being or existence of life on earth, as the harmful effects of the cosmic radiation may be ameliorated by the atmosphere and magnetic field of the earth.

Intelligent Design and Creation

Is the coming into being of plants an intelligent design? Is the coming into being of flowers an intelligent design? Is the coming into being of animals an intelligent design? Is the coming into being of man an intelligent design? Yes, it is an intelligent design. It is the design by symmetry. It is the design by harmony. It is the design by the way of heaven. It is the design by heaven. It is the intelligent design by heaven. It is the intelligent design by the heavenly intelligence.

Is the coming into being of plants a creation? Is the coming into being of flowers a creation? Is the coming into being of animals a creation? Is the coming into being of man a creation? Yes, it is a creation. It is the creation by symmetry. It is the creation by harmony. It is the creation by the way of heaven. It is the creation by heaven.

Symmetry and Harmony

Symmetry itself may be regarded as a state or form of harmony.

Harmony may be seen as a state or process in which, or through which, symmetry exists, or fulfils itself. The symmetric powers may be seen as the kind of things behind such a state or the kind of things driving such a process.

Newton

Newton talked about truth and simplicity. Why is truth simple? The world comes from symmetry. The world comes from harmony. That is, it might be said, truth may be seen, in a sense, as coming from symmetry or harmony. That may be, in a sense, why truth is simple.

Newton saw the beauty of the planets, the beauty of nature. He wondered from where such beauty might have come. Symmetry might be behind such beauty. Harmony might be behind such beauty.

Newton wondered what might be behind gravity. Symmetry might be behind gravity.

The Solar System

Symmetry may be behind the coming into being of the solar system. Harmony may be behind the coming into being of the solar system. The symmetric force may be behind the coming into being of the solar system. The harmonic process may be behind the coming into being of the solar system.

The heavenly ways may be the symmetric ways. The heavenly ways may be the harmonic ways.

Inorganic

Inorganic things may not necessarily mean inorganization.

Snowflakes are highly organized inorganic things and tremendous beauty may be found in their inorganic existence.

Radial symmetry may be observed in snowflakes. Bilateral symmetry may be seen in snowflakes.

It appears, symmetry characterizes or defines the coming into being or existence of snowflakes.

Is it inorganic? Is it inorganic existence?

Mutation

Mutation? Is it really mutation? Is it the case that symmetry is behind what is called mutation? Is it the case that, when we do not understand things, we call them mutation?

My Apologies

Hard work and determination are usually behind the achievements in our understanding about the world. As such, when an academic work is done, proper citations should be made, as a way to pay respect to the original authors or researchers, and as a way to recognize their invaluable efforts and contributions.

I apologize sincerely to all the people whose efforts have constituted the foundation upon which I may make the discussions in this book. I should have done all the proper citations, no matter what, to show my recognition and express my respect.

The only excuse that I may give is that, after so many years of reading, writing and meditating, it seems, now every single number or every single word has become a tremendous burden to me. In other words, it might be said, I almost have lost the ability to do such a work. I know, this is not an excuse, really. For this, again, I apologize.

§ 3.7 The Untitled

In a sense, the Cambrian explosion may better, or more precisely, be called the coming into being of symmetry in animals, in that, while the bilateral symmetry might have been expressed, or fulfilled, through the diversification of the bilaterally symmetric animals, the radial symmetry might also have been expressed, or realized, through the radiation of the radially symmetric animals. Such radially symmetric animals emerging in this period may be seen as being closely related to the kind of animals that are now grouped as the cnidarians, such as jellyfish, hydras, sea anemones, or ctenophores, echinoderms. The reason that I sometimes call the Cambrian explosion the coming into being of bilateral symmetry, instead of symmetry, in the sense that, on the one hand, it seems, the emerging animal body plans or structures during this period may be seen as dominantly bilaterally symmetric; and, on the other hand, I want to call attention to the possible significant limitations of radial symmetry, compared to bilateral symmetry, in defining, supporting, or sustaining the development of animals, as, it seems, the radially symmetric animals may not be able to develop into the kind of capacity or complexity which may be possessed by the bilaterally symmetric animals. Such as, animals like the cnidarians may only possess a simple nerve net as their nervous system, and no centralized nervous system may be found in them.

The Cambrian explosion may be regarded as one of the most extraordinary events in the history of life on earth. What might have caused the happening of the Cambrian explosion? Is it evolutionary? Is it ecological? Or is it environmental? The evolutionary biology may not be able to fully explain the nature of the Cambrian explosion. The ecological studies may not be able to fully explain the nature of the Cambrian explosion. The developmental biology may not be able to fully explain the nature of the Cambrian explosion. In the same sense, the combination of all these researches or studies may not be able to fully explain the true nature of the Cambrian explosion. The evolutionary approach may not work, in the sense that evolution takes place all the time. The ecological approach may not work, as the ecological factors exist all the time. The developmental approach may not work, as things develop all the time, always. That is to say, it might be said, even other dimensions may be added, the resulted explanatory combination may still not work, as all such dimensions may all play their timely and appropriate roles, all the time, all the way, in the developmental processes of the things on earth.

Why should the Ediacaran explosion happen? Why should the Ediacaran explosion have to happen? Why should the Ediacaran organisms have to come into being? Seeing the various shapes of the Ediacaran organisms, seeing the tubular or frond-like forms, people sometimes call what happened in the Ediacaran enigmatic. The tubular forms may express a sense of radial symmetry. The frond-like forms may express a sense of bilateral symmetry. Are the Ediacaran organisms enigmatic? Are they enigmatic? Is it enigma? In a sense, yes, it is enigma. It is the enigma of symmetry. It is the enigma of harmony. It is the enigma of the first appearance of symmetry in the animal life. It is the enigma of the first occurrence of harmony in animals. It is the enigma of the initial coming into being of symmetry in the animal life. It is the enigma of the initial happening of harmony in the animal species. It is the mystery of symmetry. It is the mystery of harmony. It is the mystery of symmetry appearing in the earliest animal life. It is the mystery of harmony coming into being in the earliest animal species.

The cones may be regarded, in a sense, as the "flowers" produced by conifers, in that, with the limitations coming with the dominant presence of radial symmetry, conifers may only give rise to the cones, instead of real or true flowers. Certain features of flowers may be observed in the cones. The overall radially symmetric shapes or forms of cones can be seen in the real or true flowers, which may represent the fulfillment of radial symmetry. A sense of bilateral symmetry may be observed in the scales of cones, similar, in a sense, to what may be found in the petals or sepals of flowers. Certainly, bilateral symmetry may not be seen as being fulfilled in the same way or to the same extent in both conifers and flowering plants. A sense of bilateral symmetry may be seen, nevertheless, as being present in conifers, even though radial symmetry may be regarded as dominating their plant lives. Such may be the realization of symmetry in plants.

The burrowing behavior may be among the factors that had triggered the happening, or rather, the flowering, of symmetry, on the sea floor, in the early development of animals. The Ediacaran organisms certainly moved, just like the Cambrian organisms, in the ocean, or on the sea floor. Moving animals may be bilaterally symmetric, but other moving animals, such as starfish, jellyfish, or sea cucumbers, as we know, may not be bilaterally symmetric. That is, movement may not have to do, exclusively, with the bilateral symmetry, as the animals like starfish, jellyfish, or sea cucumbers may tell. But, it might be said, the bilateral symmetry may be seen as having a close relationship with movement, as it may enable the bilaterally symmetric animals to develop the kind of abilities associated often with sophistication and complexity.

Leaves usually show different shapes, different veins, different margins, different tips, different bases, or different surfaces. No matter what kind of shape, no matter what kind of form, no matter what kind of arrangement, it seems, the most pronounced and dominant feature found in all the leaves except those of the kind of plants like lycophytes or conifers may be seen, it might be said, as the bilateral symmetry that is being expressed or exhibited. Even with the peltate leaves, kind of circular, one may see that, in most cases, it might be said, there is a sense of bilateral symmetry coming out of such kind of uniquely shaped leaves. Bilateral symmetry may be seen in the parallel-veined leaves. Bilateral symmetry may be seen in the palmate leaves.

Compared to what may be found in the Ediacaran organisms, it might be said, in most cases, symmetry might have been fulfilled or realized in the Cambrian animals in some quite clear or obvious ways. During the Cambrian symmetric explosion, it might be said, animals with a combination of radial symmetry and bilateral symmetry might have developed into the radially symmetric animals or bilaterally symmetric animals. The dominant or defining forms of symmetry might have gradually taken hold in the Cambrian animals. That may be why, in a sense, we may find that the Cambrian animals and the Ediacaran organisms are so different.

It is found, sponges may share the human genes to a remarkable extent. That is to say, when it comes to DNA, it might be said, sponges and humans may have much in common. Given the simple or primitive nature of the sponge existence, this may raise serious questions about the theory of evolution. If the theory of evolution holds true, then it seems, it should not be expected that sponges may share so many human genes. Sponges are among the earliest animals appearing on earth. If they share so much with humans in the genetic sense, then, what does evolution mean? Where is the evolution? Where is the evolutionary development?

In evolutionary biology, people often talk about the evolutionary advantages, when it comes to the coming into being or occurrence of the complex things, such as sexual reproduction or nervous system. People will explain, such things have not been lost, because they have evolutionary advantages. Is it really evolutionary? Could the evolutionary advantages really keep such things for so long? Why did mutations not occur? For so long? It may not be evolutionary. It may be avolutionary. It may not be the evolutionary advantages. It may be symmetry. It may be harmony.

It seems, more genetic complexities may be discovered by the geneticists. This seems to have led people to wonder about the real depth or complexity of the genetic world. Why such depth? Why such complexity? What may be behind such depth? What may be behind such complexity? Symmetry may be behind such depth. Symmetry may be behind such complexity. It may be the symmetric depth. It may be the symmetric complexity. It may be the harmonic depth. It may be the harmonic complexity.

The possible appearance of comb jellies about 600 million years ago might have initiated a continuous development from the Ediacaran to the Cambrian. Organisms from the Ediacaran could be associated with the early comb jellies. Organisms from the Cambrian could be seen as the ancestors from which the later ctenophores might have developed. It seems, from the Ediacaran to the Cambrian, it was a continuous development. It was a continuous movement. It was a continuous process.

The symmetric or harmonic being may be seen or regarded as the essential or fundamental being of things. The symmetric or harmonic being may be seen as the inner being of things, which may represent or stand for the essential or fundamental existence of things. The rational being may be regarded as a kind of outer being of things, which may represent or stand for the kind of existence of things coming from symmetry or harmony but nevertheless reachable or comprehensible to reason.

People sometimes may say, or think that, the complex behaviors of the bilaterally symmetric animals came or originated from the kind of behaviors initiated or invented by the radially symmetric animals, such as the kind of cnidarians, like sea anemones. This may not be true. The radially symmetric animals are different from the bilaterally symmetric animals. They might have different origins, and they might have followed some different developmental paths.

As symmetry may be seen as constituting the foundation of the existence of things in the universe, or the essence of the universe, the development of the universe may not be seen as a process of evolution. Evolution may not be able to fully or adequately describe such a process. It may be seen as a process of avolution. It may be seen as an avolutionary process. It may be seen as an avolutionary development. It may be seen as the avolution of the universe.

Dark energy may be explained in Einstein's theory of general relativity by the cosmological constant. It seems, observations and measurements appear to confirm the consistency between dark energy and the cosmological constant. What might the cosmological constant mean? It might mean the cosmic symmetry. it might mean the existence of the cosmic symmetry. it might represent or reflect the existence of the cosmic symmetry.

In a sense, it might be said, ctenophores seem to be related to both radially symmetric animals such as cnidarians and the bilaterally symmetric animals. Ctenophores may possess a pair of prey-catching tentacles. Such two tentacles may constitute a sense of bilateral symmetry in them. In such a sense, they may be seen as the animals mainly having to do with radial symmetry.

Given the nature of the symmetric explosion in the early development of the animal life, it might be said, things might not have happened as we may expect. Is it possible that bilateral symmetry might happen before radial symmetry or asymmetry? It seems, it might be possible. Is it possible that radial symmetry might happen before asymmetry? It seems, it might be possible.

One may have noticed, no discussion is made on the plants like hornworts, liverworts, clubmosses, mosses, or the green algae. Part of the reason is that, it seems, I am not quite sure about the details with regard to the various features of these plants. I hope that, someone may complete a thorough investigation on these plants, and reveal the nature of their existence.

The world is rational in the sense that, reason may reveal certain things about the world, but such things may not be seen or regarded as the essential or fundamental things of the world. The essential or fundamental things of the world may have to do with symmetry or harmony, and such things may be beyond the reach or grasp of reason.

Looking at the Cambrian fossil record, one could hardly fail to notice that, it seems, the bilateral symmetry was emerging, strongly, from the animals. The early Cambrian was a period distinguished by the dramatic increase in the sizes of many animal groups. Such structural increases might have been supported by the bilateral symmetry.

The symmetric continuation from the Ediacaran to the Cambrian may be seen, in a sense, in that, Spriggina only possessed a rudimentary head structure, with almost indistinct or unrecognizable eyes, mouth or antennas, but the trilobites appeared shortly afterwards with a head, eyes, and a body structure, relatively well developed.

A number of factors, such as geological changes, environmental changes, atmospheric changes or climatic changes, might contribute to the happening of the Primordial Explosion, around 600 million years ago. Such changes might occur in the ozone layer, in the seas, in the oceans, or as the thawing of the glaciers.

Symmetry may be seen as constituting, in a sense, the foundation of string theory, a theory that attempts to explain all the fundamental forces and matter in a unified manner. Supersymmetry, as symmetry is called in such a theory, may be seen as characterizing, in a sense, the fundamental structure of things.

Is there science? When you cannot even explain the coming into being of a single leaf, how can you claim that there is science? Does this mean that, science is not important? No. Science is important. Science is fundamental to our understanding of the world. Science is the foundation of knowledge.

What is life? Life is the movement of symmetry. Life is the realization of harmony. Life is the results of the movement of symmetry. Life is the consequences of the realization of harmony. Life is the phenomena of the movement of symmetry. Life is the phenomena of the realization of harmony.

Symmetry, harmony and Avolution

Symmetry can be observed in many chemical substances, and such symmetric structures are usually closely related to the possible properties that such substances may possess. In such a sense, symmetry is important in illustrating or explaining the possible chemical properties of substances.

What sustains forces? Symmetry. It is symmetry that sustains forces. What sustains plants? Symmetry. It is symmetry that sustains plants. What sustains animals? Symmetry. It is symmetry that sustains animals. What sustains life? Symmetry. It is symmetry that sustains life.

The Fibonacci sequence or Fibonacci numbers or Fibonacci series can be seen as being expressed, or realized, in nature, in a sense, in the spiral arrangement of leaves on a number of plants or trees, or in the spiral formation of horns or shells that we may observe in animals.

Avolution may be seen as the fusion of the harmonic process and the evolutionary process. It is not just the harmonic process. It is not just the evolutionary process. It is the two processes working together in eventually giving rise to things.

The Ediacaran organisms may be seen, in a sense, as the intermediate life forms appearing on earth, between the simple single-celled organisms and the relatively well developed complex multicellular Cambrian organisms called animals.

People sometimes attribute the lack of further development or diversification of leaf plans or structures to what is called developmental constraints. Is this true? It may not be true. It is not an evolutionary development. It is not evolution.

Ferns usually have bilaterally symmetric pinnate leaves, but they do not have flowers. That is, it seems, in the case of ferns, the bilaterally symmetric leaves may not necessarily mean the production or growth of flowers.

Symmetry is behind life. Symmetry is behind the development of life. Symmetry is behind the existence of life. Symmetry is what supports life. Symmetry is what maintains life. Symmetry is what sustains life.

Mysterious? No. It is not mysterious. It is simple. It is plain. It is very simple. It is very plain. Plain? Simple? No. It is not plain. It is not simple. It is deep. It is profound. It is unfathomable. It is mysterious.

Some sponge fossils from about 580 million years ago have been discovered. This may mean that, just like other organisms, sponges might have appeared or come into being during the Ediacaran explosion.

What does eternity mean? It may mean symmetry. It may mean the coming into being of symmetry. It may mean the development of symmetry. It may mean the long-lasting existence of symmetry.

Why are the palm trees so beautiful? Where does their beauty come from? See their fan-shaped or feather-shaped leaves? See the beauty coming from the bilateral symmetry exhibited by such leaves?

The needle-like leaves of conifers can be found to have a variety of forms, such as, single-needled leaves, double-needled leaves, three-needled leaves, four-needled leaves, or five-needled leaves.

Noether's theorem is important in the sense that it reveals, mathematically, the innate or intrinsic relationship in nature between symmetry and the physical properties of things.

The bilaterally symmetric plants may live with diversity, luxuriance and beauty. The radially symmetric plants may exhibit the virtues like strength, endurance or longevity.

Harmony is beauty. Beauty is harmony. Harmony is existence. Existence is harmony. Beauty is existence. Existence is beauty. Beauty is the essence of existence.

The unique shape of the ginkgo leaves and the longevity of the ginkgos may be seen as reflecting the dominant presence of radial symmetry in such trees.

The cosmic symmetry may be seen as behind dark energy. The existence of the cosmic symmetry may be seen in the cosmic microwave background.

Where does life come from? Life comes from symmetry. Life comes from harmony. Life comes from the way of heaven. Life comes from heaven.

The bilateral symmetry in some bilaterally symmetric plants may be observed in their flowers, such as, in the cactus flowers, or in the onion flowers.

A sense of bilateral symmetry may be observed, to a certain extent, in the structures of the needle-like leaves of some fir species.

Repetition is, in a sense, my knocking on the door, in a hope that, I may have the good fortune to enter the palace of Truth.

Life is not a game. The human life is not a game. Man is not a game. The world is not a game. The universe is not a game.

I write about plants in the summer and autumn. I live with flowers in the spring. I work with animals in the winter.

Intelligent Design? It is more than intelligent. It is above intelligent. It is beyond intelligent.

日 is sun. 月 is moon. 土 is earth. 人 is man. 目 is eye. 口 is mouth.

Harmony underlies things. Harmony is behind the things in the world.

Pick up a leaf. Look at it. In it lie the secrets of the world.

Chapter IV Humorality: as the Fulfillment of Symmetry or Realization of Harmony

§ 4.1 Humorality, Anteanity

Human beings can smile. Human beings have tears. We may have to ask, why cannot human beings fake their smiles? Why cannot human beings fake their tears? We know that, one cannot fake one's smiles, no matter what one may do, no matter how one may try, and no matter how much efforts one may put into such an endeavor. And we know that, one cannot fake one's tears, no matter how one may struggle, no matter what one may attempt, and no matter how one may exert oneself. No one can. No one could. No one can fake one's smiles, not even the most malicious person. No one can fake one's tears, not even the most vicious criminal. Is such an inability of faking smiles, or tears, a kind of bodily, or physical, or physiological thing for human beings? It seems, it is not. If it is a completely bodily or physical or physiological thing for human beings, then it seems, human beings can do it somehow, as we all know our own human bodies. That is, the fact that human beings can neither fake their smiles nor fake their tears means that, such an inability of human beings cannot be seen or taken as a purely bodily, physical, or physiological thing for human beings. That is, there is something in such an inability, or behind such an inability, in human beings, that may be seen or taken as more than the bodily, the physical, or the physiological. That is, there is something in human beings, related with smiling or tear-shedding, that cannot be explained by a purely bodily, physical, or physiological incapability. That is, there is something in human beings that trumps or prevails over what is bodily, physical, or physiological. I call this something in human beings the humorality of human beings, or, the humorality of man. Human beings have their humorality. Human beings cannot behave against themselves in the sense that they cannot behave against their humorality; that is, they cannot act against what has already been in themselves, that is, the humorality of man.

Antaeus is a giant, the son of Earth and Poseidon in the Greek mythology. He is invincible, since every time he is thrown down he regains and renews his strength by coming in contact with his mother Earth. I use the term "Anteanity" to represent the bond or relationship between man and where he came into being, has his existence, or, lives his life, that is, the earth, the soil, or nature; that is, in the sense that, through which, it might be said, man is being man, gaining his birth, retaining the ground to be a human being, and, acquiring the solid footing to be a humoral character. To be human is to have this antean origin, this antean contact, and this antean strength. In other words, anteanity may be seen in the humanity of man, in the human being of man, or in the humoral existence of man.

§ 4.2 The True

In a sense, it might be said, the true may be seen as the fulfillment or realization of symmetry in the world, in a logical sense, that is, as the fulfillment or realization of the logical symmetry in the world. Such may be seen in that, first, it seems, the true has to be accompanied by the false (the untrue), always, all the time. Without the false, it seems, there would be no such thing as the true. And without the true, it seems, there would be no such thing as the false. Thus, it seems, the true and the false are together, always, all the time. It is in such a sense that, it might be said, the true and the false may be seen as constituting a sense of symmetry. Such a sense of symmetry may be called the true-false symmetry, or, the logical symmetry.

Now let us consider the kind of operations such as $1=1$, $2=2$, $1+1=2$, $1+2=3$, or, $1+1>1$, $1+2>2$. Let us first consider $1=1$. $1=1$ appears to be symmetric. That is, it appears, it constitutes a sense of symmetry, with 1 on both sides of the sign $=$. Now we may ask, why is $1=1$? That is, why we claim that $1=1$ and how we arrive at such a conclusion. Is it through a rational process? That is, is it the case that we arrive at such a conclusion through reasoning, or by reason? How do we reason? How do we arrive at $1=1$ through reasoning? One may say that, we arrive at $1=1$ by reasoning on the simple fact that 1 is 1, and it is nothing else. Then, it seems, such a process may better be described as, $1=1$ because 1 is 1 and it is nothing else. Thus, it seems, it may be the case that, actually, $1=1$ should be stated as, 1 is 1.

What is that 1 is 1? Why is it the case that 1 is 1? How do we claim that 1 is 1? How do we arrive at such a conclusion that 1 is 1? Is it through a rational process? How do we rationalize on 1 and reach the conclusion that 1 is 1? Is it possible? That is, is it possible that we reason on 1 and eventually reach the conclusion that 1 is 1? It seems, it

Humorality

might not be such a case. 1 may not be reasoned. 1 itself may not be reasoned. 1 is itself. 1 is 1. It is not reasoned. It is not reached through reasoning. It is not reached through a reasoning process. It is not reached through rationalization. It is not reached through a rational process. That is, it seems, it might not be the case that we arrive at the conclusion that 1 is 1 through reasoning, or by reason.

It seems, when we say that 1=1, we are claiming that 1 is 1, or that 1 is itself. Then, what is the truth about 1=1, or that 1 is 1, or that 1 is itself? That is, where do such truths come from? From where do such truths originate? That is, how do we reach such conclusions? And how do we make such a kind of statements? Why is it the case that 1=1? Why is it the case that 1 is 1? Why is it the case that 1 is itself? How do we arrive at such conclusions? How do we make such statements? And, we may still ask, why is it the case that we have to arrive at such conclusions? Why is it the case that we have to make such statements? That is, it seems, we may still ask, why should it be the case that 1=1? Why should it be the case that 1 is 1? Or, why should it be the case that 1 is itself?

If such conclusions are not reached through reasoning, how are they being reached? If such statements are not made by us through reason, how are they being made? If such truths are not arrived at through a rational process, how are they arrived at and how should we understand their eventual coming into being or appearance, in the world?

It seems, when we claim that 1 is 1, or that 1 is itself, we are doing nothing but making a truth statement. That is to say, it seems, in claiming that 1 is 1 or that 1 is itself, we are not engaging in reasoning or rationalization, but simply to affirm or confirm such a thing that it is truth. thus, it seems, when we claim that 1 is 1 or that 1 is itself, we are affirming, or confirming, such a thing that there is something called truth, and that 1 is 1 or that 1 is itself may be seen as embodying such a thing that is called truth. That may be why we say that 1 is 1 or that 1 is itself. That may be why we claim that 1 is 1 or that 1 is itself. That may be why we claim that it is true that 1 is 1 or that 1 is itself. That may be how we reach our conclusions. That may be how we make our statements. That may be how the truths are arrived at.

Thus, it seems, the truth of 1=1 or that 1 is 1 or that 1 is itself may have to do, after all, with the coming into being or appearance of truth in the world. that is to say, it seems, when we talk about the truth of the kind of things such as 1=1 or that 1 is 1 or that 1 is itself, it may be the case that we are talking about, first of all, the very nature of truth, that is, the very nature of the coming into being or appearance of truth in the world. It is about truth. It is about the nature of truth. It is about the nature of the coming into being of truth. It is about the nature of the appearance of truth in the world.

How does truth appear? How does truth appear in the world? Why is it the case that truth has to appear? Why is it the case that truth has to appear in the world? Why is it the case that truth has to come into being? Why is it the case that truth has to come into being in the world?

Now we may have to take notice, that, we usually say, we claim that 1 is 1 or that 1 is itself, or we reach the conclusion that 1=1. It is WE. It is WE who claim that 1 is 1 or that 1 is itself. It is WE who reach the conclusion that 1=1. Who are WE? Why is it WE? Why is it the case that WE claim that 1 is 1 or that 1 is itself? Why is it the case that WE reach the conclusion that 1=1? That is, why is it the case that WE have to be related to such statements? That is, why is it the case that WE have to be associated with such truth statements? Is it possible that WE are related to truth? Is it possible that truth is associated with WE? Is it possible that WE are related, in some sense, in some way, or in some manner, to the coming into being of truth? Is it possible that the coming into being of truth in the world is associated, in some sense, in some way, in some manner, or to some extent, with WE?

Who are WE? We are the humoral beings. We are the humoral beings with the humoral truth. We are the humoral beings with truth. We are the humoral beings in which the humoral truth comes into being. We are the humoral beings in which truth comes into being. We are the humoral beings in which the humoral truth appears. We are the humoral beings in which truth appears. We are the humoral beings through which the humoral truth comes into being or appears. We are the humoral beings through which truth comes into being or appears. The humoral truth comes into being or appears in us. Truth comes into being or appears in us. The humoral truth comes into being or appears through us. Truth comes into being or appears through us. WE are related to the coming into being of truth. WE are related to the appearance of truth. WE are related to the coming into being of truth in the world. WE are related to the appearance of truth in the world.

Thus, it seems, when we talk about the coming into being or appearance of truth in the world, we may have to consider, in a sense,

Humorality

or to a certain extent, the humoral being of man. That is to say, it might be said, the coming into being or appearance of truth in the world may have to do, in a sense, or to a certain extent, with the coming into being or appearance of the humoral truth in man. It is in such a sense that, it might be said, the coming into being or appearance of truth in the world may be understood, in a sense, in light of the coming into being or appearance of truth in man. Or, it might be said, the coming into being or appearance of truth in the world may have to be understood, in a sense, in a relation to the coming into being or appearance of truth in man, that is, in a relation to the coming into being or appearance of the humoral truth in man.

What is the humoral truth? What is the meaning of the humoral truth? What is the meaning of the humoral truth in man? What is the meaning of the humoral truth coming into being in man? What is the meaning of the humoral truth appearing in man? What is the meaning of the humoral truth fulfilled in man? What is the meaning of the humoral truth realized in man? What does the humoral truth mean to truth? What does the humoral truth mean to the coming into being of truth? What does the humoral truth mean to the appearance of truth in the world?

The humoral truth is about the true and the false. The humoral truth is about both the true and the false. The humoral truth is about the coming into being or appearance of the true and the false. The humoral truth is about the coming into being or appearance of both the true and the false. Without the true, it seems, there would be no such thing as the false. Without the false, it seems, there would be no such thing as the true. Thus, it seems, without the coming into being or appearance of the true, there would be no such thing as the coming into being or appearance of the false. And, without the coming into being or appearance of the false, it seems, there would be no such thing as the coming into being or appearance of the true. Thus, it might be said, when the humoral truth comes into being, the true comes into being, and the false comes into being, at the same time. That is, when the humoral truth appears, the true appears, and the false appears as well, at the same time. Thus, the humoral truth means both the true and the false. Thus, the coming into being or appearance of the humoral truth means the coming into being or appearance of both the true and the false. Thus, what does the humoral truth mean? It means the true and the false. It means the true and the false in man. It means the true and the false in the world. Thus, what does the coming into being or appearance of the humoral truth mean? It means the coming into being or appearance of both the true and the false. It means the coming into being or appearance of both the true and the false in man. It means the coming into being or appearance of both the true and the false in the world.

The true may be seen as constituting, together with the false, a sense of symmetry, that is, the logical symmetry. The coming into being or appearance of both the true and the false may thus be seen, in such a sense, as the coming into being or appearance of the logical symmetry. That is, with the coming into being or appearance of both the true and the false, the logical symmetry may be seen as coming into being or appearing in the world. Thus, what does the humoral truth mean? It means the coming into being or appearance of both the true and the false. It means the coming into being or appearance of the logical symmetry. It means the coming into being or appearance of both the true and the false in man. It means the coming into being or appearance of the logical symmetry in man. It means the coming into being or appearance of both the true and the false in the world. It means the coming into being or appearance of the logical symmetry in the world.

It is the logical symmetry coming into being through the humoral truth. It is the logical symmetry coming into being through man. It is the logical symmetry appearing in the world through the humoral truth. It is the logical symmetry appearing in the world through man. It is the logical symmetry fulfilled through the humoral truth. It is the logical symmetry realized in the world through the humoral man. Through the humoral truth, the logical symmetry comes into being. Through the humoral truth, the logical symmetry appears in the world. Through the humoral truth, the logical symmetry is fulfilled. Through the humoral truth, the logical symmetry is realized in the world.

Thus, it might be said, with the coming into being or appearance of the humoral truth, the logical symmetry may be seen as being fulfilled or realized in the world, in the humoral sense. That is to say, it might be said, the humoral truth may be seen as the fulfillment or realization of the logical symmetry in a humoral sense, in the world. So far, it seems, we are talking about the humoral truth in a rather strict sense, that is, as the kind of truth seen in the kind of things such as, the smile is true, or, the smile is the true smile, or, the smile cannot be faked, or, the smile cannot be false. If that is the case, then, it might be said, the humoral truth might not be all the truth of the world. That is to say, apart from the humoral truth, it seems, there might be other truths, such as the truths with regard to the kind of things like 1=1, or, 1 is 1, or, 1 is itself. We know what the humoral truth means, that is, in that rather strict sense, as it stands for the coming into being or appearance of the true and the false in man. and it seems, while we are conscious, as the human beings, of the coming into being or appearance of the humoral truth in us, or in the world, we often talk about the kind of truths like 1=1, or, 1 is 1, or, 1 is itself. Now, it seems, the significant thing is that, we may have to ask a number of questions about such truths. Such questions may have to do, in a sense, with two kinds of things, or two kinds of truths, that is, the humoral truth, on the one hand, and the kind of truths like 1=1, or, 1 is 1, or, 1 is itself, on the other hand.

What is the humoral truth? What is the true or the false coming into being in man humorally? That is, what is the nature of the humoral truth, in the end? Such kind of questions may also be asked with regard to the kind of truths like 1=1, or, 1 is 1, or, 1 is itself. What is meant by the truths like 1=1, or, 1 is 1, or, 1 is itself? What is that 1=1? What is that 1 is 1? What is that 1 is itself? Is that 1=1 truth? In what sense? How? Why? Is that 1 is 1 truth? In what sense? How? Why? Is that 1 is itself truth? In what sense? How? Why? Are they all truths? In what senses? How? How should they be treated all as truths? How should they be called all as truths? How should they be talked about all as truths? Why should they be treated all as truths? Why should they be called all as truths? Why should they be talked about all as truths?

That is to say, it seems, we take the kind of truths, such as 1=1, or, 1 is 1, or, 1 is itself, as the kind of truth coming into being or appearing in man, that is, in a sense, as the kind of truth seen in the humoral truth. Or, it seems, we are applying the notion or concept of truth, which appears in us through the humoral truth, to the kind of things like 1=1, or, 1 is 1, or, 1 is itself. What might be the basis for us to do so? What might be the foundation upon which we may make such claims? What might be the basis for us to take such things as truth? What might be the foundation upon which we may apply the notion or concept of truth, coming into being in us as the humoral truth, to the kind of things like 1=1, or, 1 is 1, or, 1 is itself?

Truth comes into being in man, as the humoral truth. Truth appears in man, as the humoral truth. It is through the humoral truth that, in a

Avolution and Man

sense, it might be said, we come to truth. It is through the humoral truth that, in a sense, it might be said, truth comes to us. It is through the humoral truth that, in a sense, it might be said, we live with truth. It is through the humoral truth that, in a sense, it might be said, truth exists with us. It is through the humoral truth that, in a sense, it might be said, we exist in truth. It is through the humoral truth that, in a sense, it might be said, truth exists in us. It is through the humoral truth that, in a sense, it might be said, we exist through truth. It is through the humoral truth that, in a sense, it might be said, truth exists through us. It is through the humoral truth that, in a sense, it might be said, truth comes into the human life. It is through the humoral truth that, in a sense, it might be said, we are united with truth. It is through the humoral truth that, in a sense, it might be said, truth is united with us. It is through the humoral truth that, in a sense, it might be said, we are fused with truth. It is through the humoral truth that, in a sense, it might be said, truth is fused with us. Through the fusion with truth, we come into being. In the fusion with truth, we exist. Through the fusion with man, truth comes into being. In the fusion with man, truth exists. Through truth, man comes into being. In truth, man exists. Through man, truth comes into being. In man, truth exists.

With the coming into being or appearance of the humoral truth, truth comes into the human life. The humoral truth is truth. The true that comes into being humorally in man is true. The true that appears in man humorally is truth. The false that comes into being in man humorally is false. The false that appears in man humorally is not truth. That is, there is truth. That is, there is truth in man. That is, there is truth in the human life. That is, there is truth in the world. That is, truth exists. Truth exists in man. Truth exists in the human life. Truth exists in the world. Truth is true. Truth is not false. Truth is truth. Truth is in man. Truth is in the human life. Truth is in the human world. Truth is in the world. The true coming into being in man humorally is truth. The true appearing in the human life is truth. The true appearing in the world is truth. The smile is true, because it is true. The smile is true, because it cannot be faked. The smile is true, because it is not false. The smile is true, because it cannot be false. The smile is the true smile. The smile is the smile. The smile is itself. It is truth that the smile is the true smile. It is truth that the smile is the smile. It is truth that the smile is itself. It is truth that a thing is itself. It is truth that a thing is a thing. It is truth that 1 is 1. It is truth that 2 is 2. It is truth that 3 is 3. It is truth that 1 is itself. It is truth that 2 is itself. It is truth that 3 is itself. It is truth that 1 is 1, otherwise the smile might not be the smile. It is truth that 1 is itself, otherwise the smile might not be itself. It is truth that 1 is 1, otherwise that the smile is the true smile might not be true. It is truth that 1 is itself, otherwise that the smile is true might not be true. It is truth that 1 is 1, otherwise that the smile cannot be faked might not be true. It is truth that 1 is itself, otherwise that the smile cannot be false might not be true.

Truth thus exists in the kind of things such as, the smile is true, or, the smile is the true smile, or, the smile is the smile, or, the smile is itself, or, 1 is 1, or, 1 is itself. Otherwise, it seems, the humoral truth might not have been true, the humoral man might not have come into being, the human life might not have appeared, and the world as we know it might not have existed. It is the coming into being of truth. It is the coming into being of man. It is the coming into being of the human life. It is the coming into being of truth in the world. Truth thus comes into being. The human life thus comes into being. Man thus comes into being. The world as we know it thus comes into being. Truth thus comes into being in the human life. Truth thus comes into being in the human world. Truth thus comes into being in man. Truth thus comes into being in the world. It is the coming into being of the human world. It is the coming into being of truth in the world. It is the coming into being of truth in the world so that man may come into being. It is the coming into being of truth in the world so that man may be fulfilled or realized, in the world.

What is man? Man is the fulfillment or realization of symmetry in animals. Man is the fulfillment or realization of symmetry in an animal sense. Man is the fulfillment or realization of symmetry in the animal kingdom. Man is the fulfillment or realization of symmetry in the world. Man is the fulfillment or realization of symmetry on earth. The coming into being or appearance of the humoral truth in man may be seen as the coming into being or appearance of symmetry in man. The fulfillment or realization of the humoral truth in man may be seen as the fulfillment or realization of symmetry in man. That is to say, the coming into being or appearance of man may be seen as the symmetric coming into being or appearance of man. The fulfillment or realization of man may be seen as the symmetric fulfillment or realization of man. The coming into being or appearance of the humoral truth in man may be seen as the symmetric coming into being or appearance in man. The fulfillment or realization of the humoral truth in man may be seen as the symmetric fulfillment or realization in man. It is the symmetric coming into being or appearance. It is the symmetric fulfillment or realization. It is the harmonic coming into being or appearance. It is the harmonic fulfillment or realization. It is symmetric. It is harmonic.

It is the symmetric coming into being or appearance of man. It is the symmetric fulfillment or realization of man. It is the harmonic coming into being or appearance of man. It is the harmonic fulfillment or realization of man. It is the symmetric coming into being or appearance of the humoral truth. It is the symmetric fulfillment or realization of the humoral truth. It is the harmonic coming into being or appearance of the humoral truth. It is the harmonic fulfillment or realization of the humoral truth. It is the symmetric coming into being or appearance of truth in man. It is the symmetric fulfillment or realization of truth in man. It is the harmonic coming into being or appearance of truth in man. It is the harmonic fulfillment or realization of truth in man. It is the symmetric coming into being or appearance of truth. It is the symmetric fulfillment or realization of truth. It is the harmonic coming into being or appearance of truth. It is the harmonic fulfillment or realization of truth. Truth is, thus, in the humoral sense, symmetric. Truth is, thus, in the humoral sense, harmonic.

It is in such a sense that, we may call the humoral truth as the harmonic truth. The humoral truth is the harmonic truth in the sense that it comes from symmetry. The humoral truth is the harmonic truth in the sense that it reflects the fulfillment or realization of symmetry. The humoral truth is the harmonic truth in the sense that it represents or stands for the fulfillment or realization of symmetry in man. It is the nature of the humoral truth. It is the nature of the coming into being of the humoral truth. It is the nature of the coming into being of truth, in the humoral sense. It is the nature of truth, in the humoral sense. It is about symmetry. It is about the coming into being or appearance of symmetry. It is about the fulfillment or realization of symmetry. It is about the fulfillment or realization of symmetry in man. It is about the fulfillment or realization of symmetry in the world.

We have seen, while the humoral truth exists as truth, truth may also be seen in the kind of things such as, 1 is 1, or, 1 is itself. In other words, truth may be seen as appearing or coming into being in the kind of things such as, 1 is 1, or, 1 is itself. The appearance or coming into being of truth in such kind of things may be seen, in a sense, as the coming into being or appearance of truth in the human life, or in the world, in that, it is through such appearance or coming into being of truth in the world, in the humoral truth, in the kind of truths such as that 1 is 1 or that 1 is itself, the humoral man appears or comes into being in the world. That is to say, it is through such appearance or coming into being of truth in the world that the humoral man fulfils or realizes himself in the world, that is, in the humoral life in the world, that is, in the human life in the world. That is to say, it is through such appearance or coming into being of truth in the world that man comes to exist in the world. It is the coming into being of the humoral man. It is the appearance of the humoral man. It is the coming into being or appearance of the humoral man in life. It is the fulfillment of the humoral man. It is the realization of the humoral man. It is the fulfillment or realization of the humoral man in the world. It is the fulfillment or realization of life. It is the fulfillment or realization of the human life. It is the fulfillment or realization of the human life in the world. It is the fulfillment or realization of man. It is the fulfillment or realization of symmetry. It is the fulfillment or realization of man in symmetry. It is the fulfillment or realization of symmetry in man. It is the fulfillment or realization of symmetry in the world.

Thus, it might be said, the appearance or coming into being of truth in the kind of things such as, 1 is 1, or, 1 is itself, may have to do with the appearance or coming into being of man in symmetry, or with the appearance or coming into being of symmetry in man. Or, it might be said, the fulfillment or realization of truth in the kind of things such as, 1 is 1, or, 1 is itself, may have to do with the fulfillment or realization of man in symmetry, or with the fulfillment or realization of symmetry in man. that is to say, the appearance or coming into being of truth in the kind of things such as that 1 is 1 or that 1 is itself may be seen, in a sense, as the symmetric appearance or coming into being in the world, or, the fulfillment or realization of truth in the kind of things such as that 1 is 1 or that 1 is itself may be seen, in a sense, as the symmetric fulfillment or realization in the world. that is to say, the appearance or coming into being of truth in the kind of things such as that 1 is 1 or that 1 is itself may be seen, in a sense, as the harmonic appearance or coming into being in the world, or, the fulfillment or realization of truth in the kind of things such as that 1 is 1 or that 1 is itself may be seen, in a sense, as the harmonic fulfillment or realization in the world. It is the symmetric appearance or coming into being. It is the symmetric fulfillment or realization. It is the harmonic appearance or coming into being. It is the harmonic fulfillment or realization. It is symmetric. It is harmonic.

It is in such a sense that, we may call the kind of truths appearing or coming into being in the kind of things such as, 1 is 1, or, 1 is itself, as the harmonic truth. Such truths may be seen as the harmonic truth in the sense that, it might be said, the fulfillment or realization of symmetry leads to the fulfillment or realization of the humoral man, and the appearance or coming into being of such truths may have to do with the fulfillment or realization of the humoral man. That is to say, such truths may be seen as appearing or coming into being, in a sense, from symmetry. such truths may be seen as the harmonic truth in the sense that, symmetry is reflected in the appearance or coming into being of the humoral man, and the fulfillment or realization of the humoral man may be seen as being reflected in the appearance or coming into being of such truths. That is to say, such truths may be seen as reflecting, in a sense, the fulfillment or realization of symmetry in the world. Such truths may be seen as the harmonic truth in the sense that, symmetry fulfils or realizes itself in man, and the existence of man in the world may be seen as being fulfilled or realized, in a sense, through the fulfillment or realization of such truths. That is to say, such truths may be seen as representing or standing for, in a sense, the fulfillment or realization of symmetry in man, or, in the world.

The appearance or coming into being of the harmonic truth in the world, in the humoral truth, in the kind of things such as that 1 is 1 or that 1 is itself may be seen as reflecting, in a sense, the nature of the fulfillment or realization of man in symmetry, or, the nature of the fulfillment or realization of symmetry in man, or, the nature of the fulfillment or realization of symmetry in the world. It is through the fulfillment or realization of man in symmetry that symmetry fulfils or realizes itself in man. It is through the fulfillment or realization of symmetry in man that symmetry fulfils or realizes itself in the world. It is through the fulfillment or realization of symmetry in the world that, in a sense, symmetry fulfils or realizes itself as the harmonic truth. The harmonic truth is the expression of the fulfillment or realization of symmetry in the world. The harmonic truth is the way through which symmetry fulfils or realizes itself in the world. The harmonic truth is symmetry fulfilling itself. The harmonic truth is symmetry realizing itself. Through the harmonic truth, symmetry fulfils or realizes itself in man. Through the harmonic truth, symmetry fulfils or realizes itself in the world.

What does it mean that the smile is the smile? What does it mean that 1 is 1? What is the essence of the statement that the smile is the smile? What is the essence of the claim that 1 is 1? What is the essence of the truth that the smile is the smile? What is the essence of the truth that 1 is 1? What is it about that the smile is the smile? What is it about that 1 is 1? It is about truth. It is about truth itself. It is about the coming into being of truth. It is about the appearance of truth in the world. It is about the nature of truth. It is about the nature of truth itself. It is about the nature of the coming into being of truth. It is about the very nature of the appearance of truth in the world.

Is it possible that there might be no such thing as that the smile is the smile, even if the smile exists? I think, in a sense, it might be said, it may be possible. Is it possible that there might be no such thing as that 1 is 1, even if 1 exists? I think, in a sense, it might be said, it may be possible. Then, why is it the case that the smile is the smile? Why is it the case that 1 is 1? Why is it the case that such a thing should come into being as that the smile is the smile? Why is it the case that such a thing should appear as that 1 is 1? Why? Why is it the case that we have to make such statements like, the smile is the smile, or, 1 is 1? Why is it the case that we have to make such claims like, the smile is the smile, or, 1 is 1? Why is it the case that we have to encounter the kind of things like, the smile is the smile, or, 1 is 1? Why is it the case that we have to deal with the kind of things like, the smile is the smile, or, 1 is 1? Why is it the case that we have to live or exist with the kind of things such as, the smile is the smile, or, 1 is 1?

Why? Why is it the case that we have to? Why is it the case that such things have to appear or come into being in the world? In a sense, it might be said, it may have to do with the coming into being or appearance of man in the world, or, with the fulfillment or realization of symmetry in the humoral man in the world, or, with the fulfillment or realization of symmetry in the world. Man is the fulfillment or realization of symmetry in animals. The humoral man is the fulfillment or realization of symmetry in man. When man appears, he feels. When man appears, he feels that the smile is true. When man appears, he feels that the smile is the true smile. When man appears, he feels that the smile is the smile. When man appears, he feels that the smile is itself. When man appears, he feels that it is true that the smile is true. When man appears, he feels that it is true that the smile is the true smile. When man appears, he feels that it is true that the smile is the smile. When man appears, he feels that it is true that the smile is itself. That is to say, when man appears, he feels truth. That is to say, when man appears, truth comes into being.

Truth thus comes into being. Truth thus comes into being in the world. Truth thus comes into being in the kind of things such as, the smile is the smile. Truth thus comes into being in the kind of things such as, 1 is 1, as the humoral man fulfils or realizes himself in the world. It is the coming into being of truth through the coming into being of man. It is the coming into being of truth through the coming into being of the humoral man. It is the coming into being of truth through the humoral feeling of man. It is the coming into being of truth through the fulfillment or realization of symmetry in the humoral feeling of man. That is, it is not a reasoned process. It is not reasoned. It is feeled. It is not reasoned. It is felt. It is not a rational process. It is a humoral process. It is not a rational process. It is a symmetric process. It is not a rational process. It is a harmonic process. It is not reasoned. It is not rational. It is humoral. It is symmetric. It is harmonic. It is not the reasoned truth. It is not the rational truth. It is the harmonic truth.

The harmonic truth comes from the fulfillment or realization of symmetry. The harmonic truth expresses or manifests the fulfillment or realization of symmetry. The harmonic truth represents or stands for the fulfillment or realization of symmetry. The harmonic truth comes from symmetry. The harmonic truth represents symmetry. The harmonic truth stands for symmetry. It is the coming into being or appearance of symmetry that leads to the coming into being or appearance of the harmonic truth. It is the fulfillment or realization of symmetry in the world that leads to the fulfillment or realization of the harmonic truth in the world. The harmonic truth means the coming into being or appearance of symmetry in the world. The harmonic truth means the fulfillment or realization of symmetry in the world. The coming into being or appearance of symmetry in the world means the harmonic truth. The fulfillment or realization of symmetry in the world means the harmonic truth. The harmonic truth means symmetry. Symmetry means the harmonic truth.

The harmonic truth is not the reasoned truth. The harmonic truth is not the rational truth. The harmonic truth is symmetric. The harmonic truth is harmonic. The harmonic truth is not reasoned. The harmonic

Humorality

truth is not rational. The harmonic truth does not appear or come into being through a rational process. The harmonic truth does not appear or come into being by reason. The harmonic truth comes into being or appears through a humoral process. The harmonic truth comes into being or appears through a symmetric process. The harmonic truth comes into being or appears through a harmonic process. It comes from symmetry. It originates from symmetry. It expresses symmetry. It manifests symmetry. It represents symmetry. It stands for symmetry. From symmetry, the harmonic truth appears. From symmetry, the harmonic truth comes into being. For symmetry, the harmonic truth appears or comes into being. For symmetry, the harmonic truth fulfils or realizes itself, in the world.

Thus, what is the essence of the harmonic truth? The essence of the harmonic truth is *truth*. That is, the essence of the harmonic truth is truth itself. That is, the essence of the harmonic truth is the coming into being of truth. The essence of the harmonic truth is the appearance of truth. The essence of the harmonic truth is the emergence of truth. The essence of the harmonic truth is the occurrence of truth. The essence of the harmonic truth is the happening of truth. The essence of the harmonic truth is the beginning of truth. The essence of the harmonic truth is the being of truth. The essence of the harmonic truth is the existence of truth. The essence of the harmonic truth is the beginning of the being of truth. The essence of the harmonic truth is the beginning of the existence of truth. It is the origin of truth. It is the source of truth. It is the root of truth. It is the fountainhead of truth.

Thus, what is the essence of the harmonic truths such as, the smile is true, or, the smile is the true smile, or, the smile is the smile, or, the smile is itself, or, 1 is 1, or, 1 is itself? The essence of such harmonic truths is truth, that is, truth itself. What does it mean that the smile is true? It means truth. It means truth itself. What does it mean that the smile is the true smile? It means truth. It means truth itself. What does it mean that the smile is the smile? It means truth. It means truth itself. What does it mean that the smile is itself? It means truth. It means truth itself. What does it mean that 1 is 1? It means truth. It means truth itself. What does it mean that 1 is itself? It means truth. It means truth itself.

Thus, what does the harmonic truth mean? It means symmetry. It has to do with symmetry. It is not reasoned. It is not rational. It is symmetric. It is harmonic. It means that, truth is, in the fundamental sense, not reasoned. It means that, truth is, in the fundamental sense, not rational. It means that, truth is, in the fundamental sense, symmetric. It means that, truth is, in the fundamental sense, harmonic. Truth comes, in the fundamental sense, not from reason. Truth originates, in the fundamental sense, not from reason. Truth expresses, in the fundamental sense, not reason. Truth manifests, in the fundamental sense, not reason. Truth represents, in the fundamental sense, not reason. Truth stands for, in the fundamental sense, not reason. Truth comes, in the fundamental sense, from symmetry. Truth originates, in the fundamental sense, from symmetry. Truth expresses, in the fundamental sense, symmetry. Truth manifests, in the fundamental sense, symmetry. Truth represents, in the fundamental sense, symmetry. Truth stands for, in the fundamental sense, symmetry.

That is, it might be said, in the fundamental sense, the origin of truth is not reason. The origin of truth is symmetry. Symmetry is the source of truth. Symmetry is the root of truth. Symmetry is the fountainhead of truth. Symmetry is the beginning of truth. The coming into being or appearance of symmetry in the world leads to the coming into being or appearance of truth in the world. The fulfillment or realization of symmetry in the world gives rise to the fulfillment or realization of truth in the world. Through truth, symmetry comes into being or appears. Through truth, symmetry fulfils or realizes itself in the world. In truth, symmetry emerges. In truth, symmetry exists. In symmetry, truth begins. In symmetry, truth exists.

The rational truth is the reasoned truth. The rational truth is the truth that comes into being through reason. The rational truth is the truth that appears through reason. The rational truth is the truth reached by reason. The rational truth is not the harmonic truth. The harmonic truth is not the reasoned truth. The harmonic truth is not the truth that comes into being through reason. The harmonic truth is not the truth that appears through reason. The harmonic truth is not the truth reached by reason. The harmonic truth is the truth that comes into being through symmetry. The harmonic truth is the truth that appears through symmetry. The harmonic truth is the truth reached, in a sense, through the humoral feeling of man.

The harmonic truth is the kind of truths such as, the smile is true, or, the smile is the true smile, or, the smile is the smile, or, the smile is itself, or, 1 is 1, or, 1 is itself. Through the harmonic truth, truth comes into being. Through the harmonic truth, truth appears in the world. That is, through the harmonic truth, the logical symmetry comes into being or appears in the world. Reason may be seen as the faculty coming into being through the logical symmetry. Reason may be seen as the faculty appearing through the logical symmetry. Reason may be seen as the faculty coming into being for the logical symmetry. Reason may be seen as the faculty appearing for the logical symmetry. Reason may be seen as the faculty representing the logical symmetry. Reason may be seen as the faculty standing for the logical symmetry. Reason may be seen as the faculty fulfilling the logical symmetry. Reason may be seen as the faculty realizing the logical symmetry, in man, or, in the world.

The logical symmetry means reason. Reason means the logical symmetry. The rational truth thus comes into being. It is the fulfillment of the logical symmetry through reason. It is the realization of the logical symmetry through reason. It is the fulfillment of reason in the logical symmetry. It is the realization of reason in the logical symmetry. It is the logical symmetry fulfilled or realized in the world through reason. It is reason fulfilling or realizing itself in the world, in the logical symmetry. It is the logical symmetry fulfilling or realizing itself in man, or in the world, as reason. It is reason fulfilling or realizing itself in man, or in the world, as the logical symmetry. The rational truth may thus be seen as what expresses or manifests reason or the logical symmetry. The rational truth may thus be seen as what demonstrates or embodies reason or the logical symmetry. The rational truth may thus be seen as what represents or stands for reason or the logical symmetry. The rational truth may thus be seen as what represents or stands for the fulfillment or realization of reason or the logical symmetry in the world.

The harmonic truth is the appearance of truth. The harmonic truth is the appearance of truth itself. The harmonic truth is the coming into being of truth. The harmonic truth is the coming into being of truth itself. The harmonic truth is the beginning of truth. The harmonic truth is the beginning of truth itself. The harmonic truth is about symmetry. The harmonic truth is from symmetry. The harmonic truth is the symmetric truth. The rational truth represents reason. The harmonic truth represents symmetry. The rational truth stands for reason. The harmonic truth stands for symmetry. The rational truth represents or stands for the logical symmetry. The harmonic truth represents or stands for symmetry itself. It is through the harmonic truth that truth comes into being. It is through the harmonic truth that truth appears. It is through the harmonic truth that truth comes into being in man. It is through the harmonic truth that truth comes into being in the world. It is through the harmonic truth that truth appears in man. It is through the harmonic truth that truth appears in the world. Truth comes into being or appears in man; the logical symmetry comes into being or appears in man. Truth comes into being or appears in the world; the logical symmetry comes into being or appears in the world. Thus, it might be said, it is through the harmonic truth that the logical symmetry comes into being or appears in man, or, it is through the harmonic truth that the logical symmetry comes into being or appears in the world.

Reason may be seen as the fulfillment or realization of the logical symmetry in man. Reason may be seen as the fulfillment or realization of the logical symmetry in the world, through man. That is, reason may be seen as the faculty coming into being from the logical symmetry in man. Reason may be seen as the faculty appearing from the logical symmetry in man. Reason may be seen as the faculty representing the logical symmetry in man. Reason may be seen as the faculty standing for the logical symmetry in man. That is, reason may be seen as the faculty in man representing or standing for the fulfillment or realization of the logical symmetry in man, or, in the world.

Symmetry fulfils or realizes itself as symmetries in the world. Symmetry fulfils or realizes itself as the double helical symmetry in the world. Symmetry fulfils or realizes itself as the sexual symmetry in the world. Symmetry fulfils or realizes itself as the electric symmetry in the world. Symmetry fulfils or realizes itself as the magnetic symmetry in the world. Symmetry fulfils or realizes itself as the radial symmetry in the world. Symmetry fulfils or realizes itself as the bilateral symmetry in the world. Symmetry fulfils or realizes itself as the moral symmetry in the world. Symmetry fulfils or realizes itself as the aesthetic symmetry in the world. It is in such a sense that, it might be said, the logical symmetry may be seen as among the symmetries fulfilled or realized by or through symmetry in the world. That is to say, the logical symmetry may be seen as the fulfillment or realization of symmetry, in a logical sense, in man, or, in the world.

The capacity for storing biological information coming into being from the double helical symmetry is DNA. The function coming into being from the sexual symmetry is sex. The force coming into being from the electric symmetry is the electric power. The power coming into being from the magnetic symmetry is the magnetic force. The faculty coming into being from the moral symmetry or aesthetic symmetry may be seen as the heart. So what may be seen as the faculty coming into being from the logical symmetry? It might be said, it may be seen as reason. Reason may be seen as the faculty coming into being from the logical symmetry. Reason may be seen as the faculty coming into being from the fulfillment or realization of the logical symmetry. The logical symmetry may be seen as among the symmetries fulfilled or realized by or through symmetry in the world. The fulfillment or realization of the logical symmetry may be seen as the fulfillment or realization of symmetry in the world, in a logical or rational sense. Thus, it might be said, reason may be seen as a faculty coming into being from the fulfillment or realization of symmetry in a logical or rational sense, in man, or, in the world. It is a faculty coming into being from the logical symmetry. It is a faculty coming into being from the fulfillment or realization of the logical symmetry. It is a faculty coming into being from the logical or rational fulfillment or realization of symmetry in the world. It is a faculty representing or standing for the logical or rational fulfillment or realization of symmetry. It is a faculty fulfilling or realizing the logical or rational fulfillment or realization of symmetry. It is a faculty representing or standing for symmetry in a logical or rational sense. It is a faculty fulfilling or realizing symmetry, in a logical or rational sense, in the world.

Reason may thus be seen as a power capable of reaching the logical or rational fulfillment or realization of symmetry in the world. The logical or rational nature of the logical symmetry may be seen as what links reason with the logical or rational fulfillment or realization of symmetry in the world. The logical or rational nature of reason itself may be seen as what constitutes the bridge between reason and the logical or rational fulfillment or realization of symmetry in the world. The rational truth thus comes into being. The rational truth thus appears. With reason, we may analyze things. With reason, we may examine things. With reason, we may investigate things. With reason, we may study mathematics. With reason, we may perform the mathematical operations such as, $1+1=2$, $1+2=3$, or, $1+1>1$, $1+2>2$.

Why is $1+1=2$? Why is $1+2=3$? Let us see first the part of $1+1$ or $1+2$. How to do the operations such as $1+1$ or $1+2$? To do such operations, we have to define the numerical units with regard to the numbers like 1, 2, 3 and so on. And, we have to define the operation "+". That is to say, in order to successfully carry out the operations such as 1+1 or 1+2, a number of rational steps may have to be taken by us. The numerical units may be rationally constructed. The operations like "+" may be rationally defined. They are the rational steps. They are the rational operations. They are carried out in a logical manner, or, in a rational way. It is in such a sense that, it might be said, the kind of mathematical operations like 1+1 or 1+2 may be seen or called as the rational operations.

The rational operations are defined by logic. The rational operations are characterized with rationality. They represent logic in mathematics. They stand for rationality in mathematics. The mathematical truth associated with the rational operations may be seen as the rational truth. Thus, the rational truth may be seen as what represents or stands for the application of logic or reason in mathematics. It is the truth coming into being through logic. It is the truth appearing with rationality. It is the truth coming into being through reason. It is the truth representing or standing for the workings or operations of reason in mathematics.

Then, how do we arrive at 1+1=2 or 1+2=3? We may be able to do the rational operations like 1+1 or 1+2, but how do we finally arrive at 1+1=2 or 1+2=3? People may say that, it is natural, as such may have been predetermined when the operations are defined rationally in the first place. It may be true, but, we may have to ask, what is really in the first place, after all? Is reason in the first place? Is rationality in the first place? If reason is in the first place, how could we reach the kind of things like 1=1, 2=2, or 3=3? If rationality is in the first place, how could we come to such conclusions as 1=1, 2=2 or 3=3? How could we reason on 1 itself? How could we reason on 2 itself? How could we reason on 3 itself? How?

It is the coming into being of truth. It is the appearance of truth. It is the coming into being of truth itself. It is the appearance of truth itself in the world. It is not just truth; it is the coming into being of truth. It is not just truth; it is the coming into being of truth itself. It is not merely truth; it is the appearance of truth. It is not merely truth; it is the appearance of truth itself in the world. It is the coming into being of truth itself in the sense that, with the appearance of truth, the kind of things such as, the smile is true, the smile is the true smile, the smile is the smile, or, 1=1, 2=2, or 3=3 may be treated or taken, by the humoral man, as the so-called "truth". That is, it might be said, it is through the coming into being of truth itself in the humoral man that, it might be said, truth appears in the world, and the kind of things such as, the smile is true, the smile is the true smile, the smile is the smile, or, 1=1, 2=2, or 3=3 may come into being or appear as truth in the world. It is the coming into being of truth in the first place, not reason. It is the appearance of truth in the first place, not rationality. It is the coming into being of truth itself in the first place, not reason. It is the appearance of truth itself in the world in the first place, not rationality. The coming into being of truth in the humoral man leads to the truthness of the kind of things such as, the smile is true, the smile is the true smile, the smile is the smile, or, 1=1, 2=2, or 3=3. It is upon this truthness that, it might be said, reason works or operates.

Thus, why is that 1=1? Because, 1 is 1. Why is that 1 is 1? Because, it is "truth". It is the coming into being of truth. It is the appearance of truth. It is the coming into being of truth itself. It is the appearance of truth itself in the world. Truth is that 1 is 1. That 1 is 1 is truth. Truth is this "is". This "is" is truth. The coming into being of truth is this "is". This "is" is the coming into being of truth. The appearance of truth is this "is". This "is" is the appearance of truth. The coming into being of truth itself is this "is". This "is" is the coming into being of truth itself. The appearance of truth itself in the world is this "is". This "is" is the appearance of truth itself in the world. thus, we see, for the humoral man, the smile "is" true, the smile "is" the true smile, the smile "is" the smile, or, 1 "is" 1, 2 "is" 2, or, 3 "is" 3. Thus, we see, for the humoral man, the smile is true, the smile is the true smile, the smile is the smile, or, 1 is 1, 2 is 2, or 3 is 3. Thus, we see, for the humoral man, the smile is not false, the smile is not the false smile, the smile is the smile, or, 1=1, 2=2, or 3=3.

Truth comes into being; "is" comes into being. "Is" comes into being; truth comes into being. Truth appears in the world; "is" appears in the world. "Is" appears in the world; truth appears in the world. The coming into being of truth is humoral; the coming into being of "is" is humoral. The appearance of truth in the world is humoral; the appearance of "is" in the world is humoral. The coming into being of truth itself in the humoral man is not reasoned; the coming into being of "is" itself in the humoral man is not reasoned. The appearance of truth itself in the world is not reasoned; the appearance of "is" itself in the world is not reasoned.

It is the truth coming into being through the humoral man. It is the truth coming into being through the harmonic truth. It is the "is" coming into being through the humoral man. It is the "is" coming into being through the harmonic truth. "Is" means the humoral truth. "Is" means the harmonic truth. "Is" is the humoral truth. "Is" is the harmonic truth. "Is" is the humoral truth expressing the humoral man. "Is" is the harmonic truth demonstrating the humoral man. "Is" is the humoral truth through which the humoral man may come into being or appear. "Is" is the harmonic truth through which the humoral man may fulfill or realize himself. "Is" is humoral. "Is" is harmonic. "Is" is not reasoned. "Is" is not rational. "Is" is behind the reasoned. "Is" is behind the rational.

"Is" is behind the kind of things such as, the smile is true, the smile is the true smile, or, the smile is the smile. "Is" is behind the kind of things such as, 1=1, 2=2, or 3=3. "Is" comes into being; the humoral man comes into being. "Is" comes into being; the humoral man fulfils or realizes himself. "Is" comes into being; the humoral truth comes into being. "Is" comes into being; the harmonic truth appears. The humoral man appears; "is" appears. The humoral truth appears; "is" appears. The harmonic truth appears; "is" comes into being. The humoral man fulfils or realizes himself; "is" fulfils or realizes itself. The humoral truth fulfils or realizes itself; "is" fulfils or realizes itself. The harmonic truth fulfils or realizes itself; "is" fulfils or realizes itself. "Is" embodies the humoral man. "Is" expresses the humoral truth. "Is" manifests the harmonic truth. "Is" represents the fulfillment or realization of the humoral man. "Is" represents the fulfillment or realization of the humoral truth. "Is" represents the fulfillment or realization of the harmonic truth. "Is" represents the fulfillment or realization of truth in the world.

"Is" means the harmonic truth. The harmonic truth means "is". The harmonic truth means the coming into being of "is". The harmonic truth means the appearance of "is". The harmonic truth means the fulfillment or realization of "is", in the humoral man, or, through the humoral man. The harmonic truth is the truth coming into being through the humoral man. It is the truth coming into being through the humoral man to fulfill or realize the humoral man. It is the truth coming into being through the humoral man to fulfill or realize the humorality of man. It is the truth coming into being through the humoral man to fulfill or realize the humoral being or existence of man. The humoral man constitutes the foundation for reason. The humoral man constitutes the foundation for the workings or operations of reason. Without the

Humorality

humoral man, it might be said, the kind of things such as, the smile is true, the smile is the true smile, or the smile is the smile, might not have to appear or come into being, even if the smile exists. That is to say, it might be said, without the humoral man, the kind of things such as, 1=1, 2=2, or 3=3, might not have to appear or come into being, even if 1 exists, 2 exists, or 3 exists. That is, it might be said, it is the humoral man that constitutes the foundation for the appearance or existence of the kind of things such as, the smile is true, the smile is the true smile, or, the smile is the smile. Or, it might be said, it is the harmonic truth that constitutes the foundation for the coming into being or existence of the kind of things such as, 1=1, 2=2, or, 3=3.

It is the humoral man that leads to the kind of things such as, the smile is true, the smile is the true smile, or the smile is the smile. It is the harmonic truth that leads to the kind of operations such as, 1=1, 2=2, or, 3=3. Such operations fulfill or realize the humoral man. Such operations fulfill or realize the humoral truth. Such operations fulfill or realize the harmonic truth. The harmonic truth thus may be seen as appearing in the kind of operations such as, 1=1, 2=2, or, 3=3. The harmonic truth thus may be seen as constituting, in a sense, the foundation for such operations. The harmonic truth may thus be seen as appearing, in such a sense, in mathematics. The harmonic truth may thus be seen as constituting, in such a sense, the foundation of mathematics. The harmonic truth may thus be seen as constituting, in such a sense, the foundation of logic. The harmonic truth may thus be seen as constituting, in such a sense, the foundation of reason.

Thus, it might be said, in the mathematical operations such as, 1+1=2, or 1+2=3, two kinds of operations or two kinds of truths may be involved, that is, the rational operations and the harmonic operations, or, the rational truth and the harmonic truth. The kind of operations like 1+1 or 1+2 may be seen as the rational operations, while the operation "=" here may be seen as representing the harmonic operations. That is to say, when it comes to the operations such as 1+1=2 or 1+2=3, the rational operations and the rational truth may be seen in the operations like 1+1 or 1+2, and the harmonic operations and the harmonic truth may be seen in the operations like =2 or =3, that is, in the operations represented by the operation "=".

It might be said, what makes the operations like 1+1 or 1+2 possible, or valid, is reason, or rationality. And, it might be said, what makes the operation "=" possible, or valid, is the harmonic truth. it is in such a sense that, it might be said, the kind of operations like 1+1 or 1+2 may be seen as representing the rational operations or the rational truth, and the operation "=" may be seen as standing for the harmonic operations or the harmonic truth. Certainly, it might be said, the harmonic operations may not be seen only in the operations signified by the operation "=". That is, it might be said, the harmonic operations may also be seen in the operations like 1+1 or 1+2. It seems, for such operations to be successfully performed, the harmonic operations may have to be involved. That is to say, it seems, the harmonic operations may be seen in the rational operations, and the harmonic truth may be seen in the rational truth.

The kind of operations such as 1+1>1, or, 1+2>2 may be analyzed in a similar manner. In these operations, the operation ">" appears to be rationally defined, and thus may be regarded as among the rational operations. The rational truth and the harmonic truth may also be seen in a mathematical theorem. We all know the Pythagorean theorem. It describes a relationship with regard to the three sides of a right triangle. The three sides of a right triangle, a, b, c, with c as the hypotenuse, constitute an equation: $a^2 + b^2 = c^2$. Here, it appears, all a^2, b^2 and c^2 are rationally defined, or can be acquired through rational operations. Thus, they may be seen as representing the rational operations or the rational truth in such an equation. An equation is fundamentally about the operation "=". As we have discussed, the operation "=" involves the harmonic operations or the harmonic truth. Thus, it might be said, both the rational operations and the harmonic operations, or, both the rational truth and the harmonic truth, may be seen in the Pythagorean theorem.

Both the rational operations and the harmonic operations may thus be seen in mathematics. The mathematical truth may thus be seen as consisting of both the rational truth and the harmonic truth. Having discussed the rational truth and the harmonic truth in the mathematical truth, it seems, we may have to consider an important question about mathematics, that is, what is, really, mathematics? It seems, to answer this question, we may have to widen our horizons and look at the different fields in which truths, that is, the logical or rational truths, may be found. The logical or rational truths may be found about DNA, and we usually call them genetics. The logical or rational truths may be found about sex, and we usually call them the theory of sexuality. The logical or rational truths may be found about electricity, and we usually call them the electric theory. The logical or rational truths may be found about magnetism, and we usually call them the magnetic theory. The logical or rational truths may be found about plants, and we usually call them botany. The logical or rational truths may be found about animals, and we may call them physiology. The logical or rational truths may be found about life, and we usually call them biology. The logical or rational truths may be found about forces, and we usually call them physics. The logical or rational truths may be found about the chemical elements or reactions, and we usually call them chemistry.

The logical or rational truths may be found in the world. The existence of the world seems to be, it might be said, logical or rational. Thus, mathematics comes into being, as a reflection of the logical or rational existence of the world. Reason is a faculty coming into being in man through the fulfillment or realization of symmetry in man. With reason, man is able to study the world. With reason, man is able to analyze the world. With reason, man is able to work with the kind of things such as concepts, ideas or images. With reason, man is able to do the kind of things such as thinking, memorizing, imagining, or reasoning. With reason, man is able to abstract the logical or rational forms, patterns, or formulas from the logical or rational existence of the world. Mathematics thus comes into being as the logical or rational reflection of the logical or rational existence of the world, through reason.

It is in such a sense that, it might be said, mathematics may be seen as the logical or rational essence of the world. It is the logical or rational abstraction of the world. It reflects the logical or rational nature of the world. It represents the logical or rational principle of the world. It stands for the logical or rational basis of the world. It thus may be seen in all the truths about the logical or rational existence of the world. Mathematics may be seen in genetics. Mathematics may be seen in sexuality. Mathematics may be seen in the electric theory. Mathematics may be seen in the magnetic theory. Mathematics may be seen in botany. Mathematics may be seen in physiology. Mathematics may be seen in biology. Mathematics may be seen in physics. Mathematics may be seen in chemistry. Mathematics may be seen in all the logical or rational existence of the world.

One may ask, why is the world logical, or, rational, after all? Yes, why is the world logical? And, why is it rational? Why is the world logical or rational, and at the same time, reason appears in the world?

That is, why is it the case that reason should come into being and the human beings should be able to analyze or examine a logical or rational world? Why? Why is it the case that 1=1? Why is it the case that 1+1=2? Why is it the case that 1+1>1? Why is it the case that, for a right triangle, $a^2 + b^2 = c^2$? Why is it the case that, the gravitational force of two masses follows Newton's law, $\boldsymbol{F} = g(m_1 m_2/r^2)$? Why is it the case that, the electric force of two charges follows Coulomb's law, $\boldsymbol{F} = k_e(q_1 q_2/r^2)$? Why? Why?

It seems, the world is indeed logical or rational, and it is logical or rational in a number of ways. It is logical or rational in a mathematical way. It is logical or rational in a genetic way. It is logical or rational in a sexual way. It is logical or rational in an electric way. It is logical or rational in a magnetic way. It is logical or rational in a botanical way. It is logical or rational in a physiological way. It is logical or rational in a biological way. It is logical or rational in a physical way. It is logical or rational in a chemical way. It is logical or rational in so many ways. The world seems to be logical or rational in so many ways. So, why is the world logical or rational? Why is the world logical or rational, after all? Why? Could we ask such questions? What does it mean to ask such questions? What does it mean to ask such questions, in the end? Is it to ask, like, why is the world sexual? Is it to ask, like, why is the world genetic? Is it to ask, like, why is the world electric? Is it to ask, like, why is the world magnetic? How could we answer such questions? Could we answer such questions? Could we answer such questions, at all?

Some might question the appearance or coming into being of the harmonic truth, in the sense that, it seems, something uncertain may be found with regard to the two kinds of truths involved in the discussion, that is, the kind of truths such as, the smile is the smile, and the kind of truths such as, 1 is 1. It seems indeed that something unusual, in a sense, might have happened in our discussion about the coming into being or appearance of the harmonic truth in the world. It seems, there might be some difference between such two kinds of truths. The kind of truths such as that the smile is the smile may be different, in a sense, from the kind of truths such as that 1 is 1. The kind of truths such as that the smile is the smile may be understandable, in a sense, in that, they are feeled, or, they are felt. Their coming into being or appearance means the coming into being or appearance of the humoral man, that is, the coming into being or appearance of the humorality of man in the world. That is, it might be said, such truths may be seen or treated as truths through the humoral feeling of man, or, through the direct humoral feeling of man. But, what about the kind of truths such as that 1 is 1? Are they the kind of truths that are feeled or felt? Are they the kind of truths that may be seen or treated as truths through the feeling of man, or through the direct humoral feeling of man? It seems, that might not be necessarily the case. That is, it seems, it may not be exactly the case that such truths may be feeled or felt. That is, it seems, it may not be exactly the case that such truths appear or come into being through the feeling of man, or through the direct humoral feeling of man. Then, how is it the case that they are truths? How is it the case that they are seen or treated as truths? And, how is it the case that they are called or taken as the harmonic truth?

We have discussed that, the harmonic truth may be seen as the coming into being or appearance of truth in the humoral man or in the world, or, as the coming into being or appearance of truth itself in the humoral man or in the world. That is, the harmonic truth may be seen, in a sense, as the coming into being or appearance of "is" in the humoral man or in the world, such that, the kind of things like, the smile is the smile, or, 1 is 1, may come into being or appear in man or in the world. This may be seen, in a sense, that is, in a harmonic sense, as how the kind of truths such as that 1 is 1 may be treated as truths or taken, in a sense, as the harmonic truth.

But, it seems, it may have to be said, certain things may have to be discussed about this coming into being or appearance of "is". While it may be true that, through the humoral feeling of man, or through the direct humoral feeling of man, the kind of truths like, the smile is true, the smile is the true smile, the smile is the smile, or, the smile is itself, may come into being or appear, how could the kind of truths like, 1 is 1, 1 is itself, 2 is 2, or, 2 is itself, come into being or appear in man or in the world? It seems, it might be said, they may not be feeled or felt. That is, it seems, it might be said, they may not be directly feeled or felt. That is, it seems, it might be said, their coming into being or appearance may not be necessarily attributed, fully or completely, to the direct humoral feeling of man. Then, how is it the case that they come into being or appear, after all, as truths in man, or in the world? it seems, it might be said, apart from the possible participation of the direct humoral feeling of man, a kind of process different from the direct humoral feeling of man may have participated in the coming into being or appearance of such truths. Such a kind of process may be seen as a kind of reasoning, or, it might be said, as a kind of special process of reasoning.

The humoral man may feel that the smile is true. The humoral man may feel that the smile is the true smile. The humoral man may feel that the smile is the smile. The humoral man may feel that the smile is itself. The humoral man may feel the same kind of things with regard to other smiles. Thus, the humoral man may "feel" that 1 "is" 1, or, 1 "is" itself, or, 2 "is" 2, or, 2 "is" itself, and so on. In other words, it seems, it might be said, such a sense of "feeling" may have played a role in the coming into being or appearance of "is", and it might be said, it is such a sense of "feeling", or in a sense, reasoning, that may be seen as leading to the coming into being or appearance of the kind of truths such as, 1 is 1, or, 1 is itself, in the humoral man, or in the world. Such a kind of "feeling", on the part of the humoral man, to fulfill or realize himself, though not direct, may be seen or called as the harmonic feeling. Such a kind of reasoning, on the part of the humoral man, to fulfill or realize himself, though not exactly logical or rational, may be seen or called as the inductive reasoning.

The harmonic feeling may thus be seen as behind the coming into being or appearance of the kind of truths such as, 1 is 1, or, 1 is itself. The harmonic feeling may thus be seen as behind the kind of reasoning that may be called the inductive reasoning. The inductive reasoning may thus be seen as behind, in a sense, the coming into being or appearance of the kind of truths such as, 1 is 1, or, 1 is itself. The inductive reasoning may thus be seen as playing a role, in a sense, in bridging the gap between the kind of truths such as, the smile is the smile, and the kind of truths such as, 1 is 1. Through the humoral feeling of man, the kind of truths such as that the smile is the smile come into being or appear. Through the inductive reasoning, in a sense, it might be said, the kind of truths such as that 1 is 1 appear or come into being.

It is true that the humoral man may not be able to feel, directly, the kind of truths such as, 1 is 1, 1 is itself, 2 is 2, or, 2 is itself. But, the humoral man feels the kind of truths such as, the smile is true, the smile is the true smile, the smile is the smile, or, the smile is itself. And, the humoral man feels the same kind of truths with regard to other smiles. Thus, it might be said, a feeling may come into the humoral man. The humoral man lives with such a feeling. The humoral man exists with such a feeling. The humoral man lives in such a feeling. The humoral man exists in such a feeling. The humoral man comes into being in such a feeling. The humoral man appears in such a feeling. The humoral man comes into being through such a feeling. The humoral man appears through such a feeling. The humoral man fulfils or realizes himself in such a feeling. The humoral man fulfils or realizes himself through such a feeling. This is the harmonic feeling. This is the harmonic feeling that may be behind the coming into being or appearance of the humoral man. This is the harmonic feeling that may be behind the coming into being or appearance of man. This is the harmonic feeling that may be behind the existence of man. This is the harmonic feeling that may be behind the coming into being or appearance of the kind of truths such as, the smile is true, the smile is the true smile, the smile is the smile, or, the smile is itself. This is the harmonic feeling that may be behind the coming into being or appearance of the kind of truths such as, 1 is 1, 1 is itself, 2 is 2, or, 2 is itself. this is the harmonic feeling that may be behind the coming into being or appearance of the kind of reasoning seen in the coming into being or appearance of the kind of truths such as, 1 is 1, 1 is itself, 2 is 2, or 2 is itself. This is the harmonic feeling that may be behind the coming into being or appearance of what is called, the inductive reasoning.

The humoral man may not directly feel that 1 is 1; the harmonic feeling exists. The humoral man may not directly feel that 1 is itself; the harmonic feeling exists. The humoral man may not directly feel that 2 is 2; the harmonic feeling exists. The humoral man may not directly feel that 2 is itself; the harmonic feeling exists. The harmonic feeling exists; the inductive reasoning holds. The harmonic feeling exists; the inductive reasoning stands. The harmonic feeling exists; the inductive reasoning applies. The harmonic feeling exists; the inductive reasoning exists.

"Is" thus comes into being or appears. "Is" thus comes into being or appears in the kind of truths such as, the smile is true, the smile is the true smile, the smile is the smile, or, the smile is itself. "Is" thus comes into being or appears in the kind of truths such as, 1 is 1, 1 is itself, 2 is 2, or, 2 is itself. The harmonic feeling may be seen as behind the coming into being or appearance of "is" in such truths. The harmonic feeling may be seen as leading to the coming into being or appearance of the inductive reasoning. The harmonic feeling supports the inductive reasoning. The harmonic feeling maintains the inductive reasoning. The harmonic feeling sustains the inductive reasoning. The harmonic feeling upholds the inductive reasoning. The harmonic feeling underpins the inductive reasoning. The harmonic feeling underlies the inductive reasoning.

The harmonic feeling is behind the coming into being or appearance of truth in the humoral man. The harmonic feeling is behind the coming into being or appearance of the humoral man. The harmonic feeling is behind the coming into being or appearance of man. It is the feeling behind man. It is the feeling behind the humoral man. It is the feeling behind truth. It is the truth behind feeling. It is the truth behind the humoral man. It is the truth behind man. Feeling is truth. Truth is feeling. Feeling is the truth fulfilling or realizing the humoral man. Feeling is the truth fulfilling or realizing man. Truth is the feeling leading to the coming into being or appearance of the humoral man. Truth is the feeling giving rise to man.

It is in such a sense that, it might be said, the harmonic feeling is the harmonic truth, or, the harmonic truth is the harmonic feeling. And, it is in such a sense that, it might be said, the inductive reasoning may be seen as the fulfillment or realization of the harmonic feeling or the harmonic truth in the humoral man, or, in man. So, what does the inductive reasoning mean? It means the harmonic feeling. It means the harmonic truth. It means the harmonic feeling coming into being or appearing in man. It means the harmonic truth fulfilled or realized in man. It means truth in feeling. It means feeling in truth. It means truth fulfilled or realized in feeling. It means feeling fulfilled or realized in truth. It means feeling. It means truth. It means man. It means the harmonic feeling. It means the harmonic truth. It means the harmonic man. It means the harmonic existence of man. It means the harmonic existence of the world.

So, what is the inductive reasoning, in its essence? Is it reasoning, after all? It seems, it is not reasoning. It seems, it may be seen or regarded as reasoning. It is not logical. It is not rational. It is not an argument based on reason. It is not an argument supported by reason. It is not an argument maintained through reason. It is not a progression following reason. It is not a progression sustained by reason. It is not a progression upheld through reason. It is not about reason. It is not about rationality. It is about feeling. It is about the harmonic feeling. It is about truth. It is about the harmonic truth. It is about the world. It is about the harmonic coming into being of the world. It is about the harmonic appearance of the world. It is about the harmonic existence of the world. It is about symmetry. It is about harmony.

That may explain, in a sense, why the inductive reasoning may play a significant or vital role in our understanding of the world. It reflects, in a sense, the harmonic truth. It represents, in a sense, the harmonic truth. It expresses, in a sense, the harmonic truth. It illustrates, in a sense, the harmonic truth. It demonstrates, in a sense, the harmonic truth. It reveals, in a sense, the harmonic truth. It reflects, in a sense, the harmonic coming into being or appearance of the world. It reflects, in a sense, the harmonic nature of the coming into being or appearance of the world. It reveals, in a sense, the harmonic existence of the world. It reveals, in a sense, the harmonic nature of the existence of the world.

While the inductive reasoning may be seen as having to do with the harmonic truth, the deductive reasoning may be seen as having to do with reason. that is to say, while the inductive reasoning may be seen as reflecting or revealing, in a sense, the harmonic coming into being or appearance of the world, the deductive reasoning may be seen as reflecting or revealing, in a sense, the logical or rational coming into being or appearance of the world. That is, it might be said, while the inductive reasoning may be seen as reflecting or revealing, in a sense, the harmonic existence of the world, the deductive reasoning may be seen as reflecting or revealing, in a sense, the logical or rational existence of the world.

This may be seen, in a sense, as the difference between the inductive reasoning and the deductive reasoning. This may be seen, in a sense, as the meaning of the inductive reasoning. This may be seen, in a sense, as the meaning of the deductive reasoning. This may be seen, in a sense, as the significance of the inductive reasoning. This may be seen, in a sense, as the significance of the deductive reasoning. Induction may thus be seen as different from deduction, and deduction from induction. Deduction may be logical; induction may be humoral. Deduction may be rational; induction may be harmonic. Deduction may have to do with the logical truth; induction may have to do with the humoral truth. Deduction may have to do with the rational truth; induction may have to do with the harmonic truth. Deduction may have to do with reason; induction may have to do with harmony. While deduction is significant, induction is vital. While deduction is important, induction is fundamental and essential. It is in such a sense that, it might be said, while deduction is indispensable, induction is significant, vital, essential, and fundamental.

People sometimes talk about the problem of induction, for the reason that, it seems, a lack of rational justification may be observed in such a mode of reasoning. It is indeed true that, it seems, induction may not be sufficiently justified in a rational manner. Hume is right in pointing out that, a deductive justification may not be easily found for the use of induction. But, is it the case that induction is to be justified by or through reason? It seems, it may not be necessarily such a case. It may not be necessarily the case that induction is to be justified by or through reason. That is, it may not be necessarily the case that induction is to be justified rationally. It may be the case that induction is to be justified harmonically. That is, it may be the case that induction is to be justified by the harmonic feeling, or, by the harmonic truth.

When Hume talks about induction, he seems to have causal relations in his mind. He thinks that causal relations have to do with induction, but not reason. I think Hume is right. Causal relations or causation may not be seen as having to do, fundamentally, with reason, as the real effect may not be found out through a mere reasoning about the cause. The real effect may be only one of the possible consequences. Then, how is it the case that causal relations or causation may figure so prominently in our lives, or in our understanding of the world? As we have discussed, induction may be seen as reflecting or revealing the harmonic existence of the world, and may be justified harmonically. Causal relations or causation may be seen as having to do with induction. It is in such a sense that, it might be said, causal relations or causation may be justified in a similar manner, in the sense that, they may be seen as reflecting or revealing, in a sense, that is, in a causal sense, the harmonic coming into being or appearance of the world, or, the harmonic existence of the world.

It may have to be said, the harmonic connection of induction may not necessarily rule out the uncertainty possibly associated with the conclusions reached through induction. Feeling is not always a reliable source of truth, as we all know. Induction may be seen as working or operating, in a sense, through feeling. When such feeling leads man to reach the real truth, it might be said, it may be seen as the workings or operations of induction, leading man to the real truth, through the harmonic feeling. That is to say, it might be said, while induction may work or operate to reveal the real truth, it may, sometimes, mislead or misguide. The most important thing about induction may not be the possibility that it may mislead or misguide, but the very fact that it has led or guided us, often, to live in this world, or to acquire a better understanding of the world. Such may be seen as the harmonic connection of induction with the world. Such may be seen as the harmonic nature of induction shared with the world. And such may be seen as the harmonic reflection of induction of the harmonic existence of the world.

§ 4.3.1 The Good

What is the good? From where does it come? What does it mean?

The humorality of man may be seen as the true humoralized into man. That is, the coming into being of man may be seen as a process in which the true has been humoralized into man. As the true is humoralized into man, it might be said, the true manifests itself in man, or, the true demonstrates itself in man. As the true is humoralized into man, it might be said, the true expresses itself in man, or, the true reveals itself through man. As the true is humoralized into man, it might be said, the true fulfils itself in man, or, the true realizes itself through man. As the true is humoralized into man, it might be said, man is achieved in the true, or, man is realized through the true. As the true is humoralized into man, it might be said, man is brought into being in the true, or, man is brought into being through the true.

Thus, to be true is good, so that man may come into being. Thus, to be true is good, so that man may exist. Thus, to be true is good, so that man may live in this world. Thus, to be true is good, so that the human life may come into being. Thus, to be true is good, so that the human world may come into existence. Thus, to be man is good, so that the true may come into being. Thus, to be man is good, so that the true may have its meaning. Thus, to be man is good, so that the true may be expressed or demonstrated. Thus, to be man is good, so that the true may be fulfilled or realized. Thus, to be man is good, so that the true may be maintained or upheld. Thus, to be true and human is good, so that the true may be associated with man, and man with the true. Thus, to be true and human is good, so that the true may be identified with man, and man with the true. Thus, to be true and human is good, so that meaning may come into being. Thus, to be true and human is good, so that meaning may come into the human life. Thus, to be true and human is good, so that the human beings may have a meaningful existence in the world.

This may be seen as the coming into being of the true. This may be seen as the coming into being of man. This may be seen as the coming into being of the good. This may be seen as the coming into being of meaning. This may be seen as the coming into being of the world in which we are living.

To be true is to be human. To be human is to be true. To be true is to be man. To be man is to be true. It is good to be true. It is good to be human. It is good to be man. It is good to be both true and human. It is good to follow the true. It is good to adhere to the human. It is good to exist as man. To be true is to live as the human. To be true is to exist as man. To be human is to adhere to the true. To be man is to exist in the true. Man thus comes out. It is thus good to be true so that the human beings may live as the human beings. It is thus good to be human so that the world may have its meaning or significance. The world is no longer empty, as the true and the human beings identify themselves with each other. The world is no longer nothingness, as the true and the human beings find themselves in each other. The true expresses itself in the human beings. The human beings express themselves in the true. Life thus has meaning. Life thus comes into being. Life thus thrives. Life thus prospers. We, as the human beings, thus, flourish, in the world.

§ 4.3.2 The Coming into Being of the Good

To be true is good. To uphold the true is good. To follow the true is good. To preserve and safeguard the true is good. To be true is good, so that man may come into being. To uphold the true is good, so that man may be man, and exist as man. To follow the true is good, so that man may maintain himself as man and live as the human being. To preserve and safeguard the true is good, so that life may have meaning and man may have a meaningful existence. To be man is good, so that the true may be true. The coming into being of man is good, so that the true may be expressed, manifested, or revealed. The existence of man is good, so that the true may be followed and upheld. The human life is good, so that the true may be maintained, preserved, and safeguarded.

This may be seen as the coming into being of the good. The good comes into being from the true humoralized in man. The good comes into being from the true humoralized into man. The good comes into being from the true physicalized in man. The good comes into being from the true physicalized into man. The good comes into being from the true embodied in man. The good comes into being from the true fulfilled or realized in man. The good comes into being from the true expressing itself in man. The good comes into being from the true manifesting itself in man. The good comes into being from the true fulfilling itself in man. The good comes into being from the true realizing itself through man. The good comes into being from the true shining in man. The good comes into being from the true radiating with man.

The good comes into being from man humoralized in the true. The good comes into being from man humoralized into the true. The good comes into being from man physicalized in the true. The good comes into being from man physicalized into the true. The good comes into being from man embodied in the true. The good comes into being from man fulfilled or realized in the true. The good comes into being from man expressing himself in the true. The good comes into being from man manifesting himself in the true. The good comes into being from man fulfilling himself in the true. The good comes into being from man realizing himself through the true. The good comes into being from man shining in the true. The good comes into being from man radiating with the true.

The true leads to the good, through man; the good substantiates the true, through man. The true leads to the good, through man; the good nurtures the true, through man. The true leads to the good, through man; the good fulfils the true, through man. The good is the fulfillment of the true in a human sense. The good is the realization of the true in a humoral way. The good is the substantiation of the true in man, or through man. Man manifests the good; the good manifests man. Man demonstrates the good; the good demonstrates man. Man fulfils the good; the good fulfils man. The good is the fulfillment of man in a human sense. The good is the realization of man in a humoral way. The good is the substantiation of man in the world. The good is the substantiation of man in the world, in a human sense, or, in a humoral way.

The good comes into being from the fusion of the true and man. The good comes into being from the union of the true and man. The good comes into being from the integration of the true and man. The good comes into being from the development of the true in man. The good comes into being from the development of man in the true. The good comes into being from the fulfillment of the true in man. The good comes into being from the fulfillment of man in the true. The good comes into being from the fulfillment or realization of the true and man. The good comes into being from the fulfillment or realization of the true and man, together in the world.

§ 4.3.3 The Common Good

What is the humorality of man? The humorality of man is the respect paid to others. The humorality of man is the consideration for others. The humorality of man is taking others into consideration. The humorality of man is, the true cannot be taken as false. The humorality of man is, the false cannot be taken as true. The humorality of man is, to be true is to be human. The humorality of man is, to be human is to be true. The humorality of man is, to be true is to live, act, or behave as the human. The humorality of man is, to be human is to live, act, or behave following or adhering to the true. The humorality of man is, it is good to be human, so that the true may come into being, be upheld, safeguarded, preserved, or maintained. The humorality of man is, it is good to be true, so that man may come into being, meaning may emerge, and the world may come into existence. The humorality of man is the good coming out in man. The humorality of man is the good coming out through man. The humorality of man is the good manifested in man. The humorality of man is the good demonstrated through man. The humorality of man is the good fulfilled in man. The humorality of man is the good realized through man. The humorality of man is the good embodied in man. The humorality of man is the good embodied through man. The humorality of man is the good shared by all. The humorality of man is the good participated by all. The humorality of man is the good contributed by all. The humorality of man is the common good of man. The humorality of man is the coming

Humorality

into being of the common good of man. The humorality of man is man striving for the common good of man. The humorality of man is man upholding the common good of man. The humorality of man is man expressing the common good of man. The humorality of man is man manifesting the common good of man. The humorality of man is man demonstrating the common good of man. The humorality of man is man fulfilling the common good of man. The humorality of man is man realizing the common good of man. The humorality of man is man confirming the common good of man. The humorality of man is man maintaining the common good of man. The humorality of man is man sustaining the common good of man. The humorality of man is man preserving the common good of man. The humorality of man is man continuing the common good of man.

What does the humorality of man mean? The humorality of man means, the self is not just the self, the self is not merely the self; the self is not just selfish, the self is not merely selfish. That is, it might be said, in the self exist the others, in the self live the others; in the self one can witness the presence of the others, and in the self the others may be found. That is to say, the humorality of man means, the self is not just the self, the self contains the presence of the others; the self is not merely the self, the self is related to the others. That is, it might be said, the self is not just selfish, the self is also unselfish; the self is not merely selfish, the self also means some vital, essential, and necessary unselfish things. That is to say, it may be better said, the self is not just selfish, it is also unselfish; the self is not merely selfish, it should also be regarded as unselfish. That is, when it comes to man, when it comes to the human beings who can be distinguished by the significant and magnificent presence in them of the humorality of man, it might be said, the self is both selfish and unselfish.

§ 4.4 The Coming into Being of Meaning

People might say that, it is with the coming into being of the humans that meaning may have come into being. Surely, one may say this, given that, it seems, all the things in the world, all the things around us, may be seen as, without exception, in one way or the other, connected with us, associated with us, and together, we form the world. That is, in our human sense, that is, in our human sense of existence,

Avolution and Man

we form and constitute the world, that is, as we know it, insofar as we can see or perceive, as the human beings through our senses, our intellect, or our human understanding or comprehension. But, it seems, one may have to ask, why is it so? Why is it such a case? Why is it not otherwise? Why is it such a case that, with the coming into being of the humans, meaning should have to come into being? Why is it not the case that, even with the coming into being of the humans, meaning may in no way be seen, found, or encountered in this world? In other words, does meaning have to accompany the coming into being of the humans? Does meaning have to go together with the humans? Does meaning have to be linked, inevitably, with the humans, or the coming into being of the humans? Why? Why so?

What is meaning? What does meaning mean? Why is it the case that there has to be some meaning? Why is it the case that meaning has to be with us? Why is it the case that we human beings should see, find, or encounter some meaning, in some sense, in some way, or in some manner? What is behind meaning? What is beyond meaning? What gives rise to meaning? What makes meaning to come out? It seems, insofar as we can see or perceive as the human beings, it is perfectly possible, that is, possible, that, even as the human beings roam about or exist in this world, meaning might not be absolutely necessary, in the sense that, people could just live, such as, eating, playing, having sex, and so on. And after all, we should not forget that, some philosophers had already told us, man is nothing, and life is meaningless. That is to say, it seems, it is possible that, even without meaning, whatsoever, human beings could still live and survive, in this world, and well. In other words, it seems, it might be the case that meaning might not be necessarily linked with the human beings, inevitably; or, meaning might not be necessarily going together with the coming into being of the humans. Meaning could be separated from the humans. Meaning could part ways with the humans. Meaning could be unconnected with the humans. Meaning could be unrelated with the humans. Meaning could be one thing, and the human beings another. Meaning and the human beings could be just two separate things, detached, unconnected, unrelated. The coming into being of meaning might not mean the coming into being of the humans; in the same sense, the coming into being of the humans might not mean the coming into being of meaning. The existence of meaning might not mean the existence of the humans; in the same sense, the existence of the humans might not mean the

Humorality

existence of meaning. Meaning could come into being, but not necessarily along with the coming into being of man. Meaning could exist, but not necessarily hand in hand with the existence of man. The human beings could come into being, but not necessarily accompanied by meaning. The human beings could exist, but not necessarily, with meaning.

That is to say, it seems, though it can be seen that the coming into being of the human beings may be seen as being accompanied by the coming into being of meaning, it may not be easily seen or explained that the coming into being of meaning should have occurred or happened in the first place. Certainly, this may be seen as the case also with the coming into being of the human beings. That is to say, it might be said, the coming into being of the human beings, though in a sense accompanied by the coming into being of meaning, may not explain, after all, the coming into being of meaning, or, in the same sense, the coming into being of meaning may not explain the coming into being of the human beings. That is to say, no matter what has occurred or happened along with the coming into being of the humans, it may not be easily explained or seen that the coming into being of the humans should have occurred or happened in the first place, no matter in what kind of circumstances, no matter under what kind of conditions, and no matter in what kind of context. So, what gives rise to the coming into being of meaning? What gives rise to the coming into being of man? What gives rise to the coming into being of both meaning and man?

On the one hand, the coming into being of meaning and the coming into being of the human beings may be taken as two different things, in the sense that, one does not necessarily give rise to the other, and that, in a sense, one does not necessarily need the other, or the coming into being of the other, to come into being. And on the other hand, it might be said, the coming into being of meaning and the coming into being of the human beings may be taken as the one and same thing, in the sense that, both of them may be seen as coming from the same source, both of them may be seen as originating from the same origin, and both of them may be seen as emanating from the same fountainhead. That is, it might be said, it may be the case that both of them come from the same source, such that they do not necessarily, in a sense, give rise to each other; that, both of them originate from the same origin, such that though the coming into being of the humans may be seen as being accompanied by the coming into being of meaning, nevertheless, the coming into being of the humans may not be seen, necessarily, in a sense, as leading to the coming into being of meaning; and that, both of them emanate from the same fountainhead, such that, we witness, in this world, that is, in this human world, the coming into being of the humans is happening with the coming into being of meaning, and the existence of the humans is occurring with the existence of meaning.

Meaning thus happens with the happening of man. Man thus exists with the existence of meaning. Thus, man is meaningful. Thus, meaning is manful. Thus, man reveals meaning. Thus, meaning reveals man. Thus, man reflects meaning. Thus, meaning reflects man. Thus, man demonstrates meaning. Thus, meaning demonstrates man. Thus, man embodies meaning. Thus, meaning embodies man. Thus, man expresses meaning. Thus, meaning expresses man. Without meaning, it seems, man is not complete. Without man, it appears, meaning may lack its manifestation or representation. Together, they form and constitute the world. Together, they express the source from which they come. Together, they demonstrate the origin that gives rise to them. Together, they reveal the fountainhead which may lie at the very root or beginning of their existence, or, coming into being.

Man comes, through a long process of development from harmony. Meaning comes, through man, from harmony. Man is the realization of harmony, in a human way. Meaning is the realization of harmony, in a meaningly way. It is harmony that gives rise to man. It is harmony that gives rise to meaning. It is harmony that gives rise to the coming into being of man. It is harmony that gives rise to the coming into being of meaning. It may not be necessarily, in a sense, that the coming into being of man gives rise to the coming into being of meaning. It may not be necessarily, in a sense, that the coming into being of meaning gives rise to the coming into being of man. It may not be necessarily, in a sense, that the existence of man entails the existence of meaning. It may not be necessarily, in a sense, that the existence of meaning calls for the existence of man. Meaning and man may be seen as the two aspects of harmony. Meaning and man may be seen as the two effects of harmony. Meaning and man may be seen as the two performances of harmony. Meaning and man may be seen as the two achievements of harmony. Meaning and man may be seen as the two developments of harmony. Meaning and man may be seen as the two fulfillments of harmony. Meaning and man may be seen as the two realizations of harmony.

Humorality

Harmony is meaning. Harmony is content. Meaning is the content of harmony realized in man. Meaning is the content of harmony fulfilled in man. Meaning is the content of harmony reflected in man. Meaning is the content of harmony embodied in man. Meaning is the content of harmony expressed in man. Meaning is the content of harmony manifested in man. Meaning is the content of harmony demonstrated in man. Meaning is the content of harmony realized in the world. Meaning is the content of harmony fulfilled in the world. Meaning is the content of harmony reflected in the world. Meaning is the content of harmony embodied in the world. Meaning is the content of harmony expressed in the world. Meaning is the content of harmony manifested in the world. Meaning is the content of harmony demonstrated in the world.

Meaning is the coming out of harmony. Meaning is the realization of harmony. Meaning is harmony displaying its way. Meaning is harmony exhibiting its content. Meaning is harmony showing its significance. Meaning is harmony condensed. Meaning is harmony congealed. Meaning is harmony harmonizing through man. Meaning is harmony harmonizing in man. Meaning is harmony harmonizing in the world. Meaning is harmony harmonizing with its content. Meaning is harmony harmonizing with its significance in the world. Meaning is the fulfillment of harmony in a human sense. Meaning is the realization of harmony in a humoral way. In the same sense, it might be said, man is harmony coming out in a human sense. Man is harmony revealing itself in a human manner. Man is harmony displaying its way. Man is harmony exhibiting its content. Man is harmony demonstrating its significance in a human manner. Man is harmony fulfilling itself in a human fashion. Man is harmony realizing itself in a humoral way. Man is harmony harmonizing through the human life. Man is harmony harmonizing in the human life. Man is harmony harmonizing with significance in the human life. Man is harmony harmonizing with meaning in the human life.

Harmony gives rise to life. Harmony gives rise to meaning. Harmony gives rise to the coming into being of the humans. Harmony gives rise to the being of the human beings. Harmony gives rise to the meaningful existence of man. Does it have to be the case that it is meaning that should come from harmony? Does it have to be the case that it is meaning, in our understanding, in our human sense, that should emanate from harmony? It may not necessarily be such a case, in the sense that, given the unlimited possibilities of the world, or, of the universe, and given the unlimited possibilities that may lie well beyond our imagination or understanding, that is, our human imagination or understanding, it appears perfectly possible that, other kinds of creatures or things may occur or happen, which may be of vastly different natures or characteristics, distinct from the kind of things that may be known to us, and that may be observed in or associated with the humans, and which may be possibly well beyond our human understanding or comprehension. That is to say, the human beings may not be the only creatures of the kind that may have their coming into being, ultimately, from harmony, and meaning, as we know it, in our sense, in our human understanding or comprehension, that is, through our human intellect, intelligence, or senses, may not be the only manifestation that may have to do with harmony, and that may be seen as being associated with the kind of creatures, possibly human-like, but who nevertheless may possess different qualities, characteristics, or natures, though how slightly that might be, in some sense, in some way, or in some manner.

§ 4.5.1 Heart

What is heart? Heart is the good feelings of man. Heart is the good emotions of man. Heart is the good feelings that made man man. Heart is the good emotions that led man to man. Heart is the good feelings that make man man. Heart is the good emotions that lead man to man. Heart is the good feelings that form the humorality of man. Heart is the good emotions that make the humoral existence of man possible. Heart is the humoral man manifesting itself in feelings. Heart is the humoral man expressing itself in emotions. Heart is the result of the coming into being of the humoral man. Heart is the consequence of the humoral man realized in a human sense. Heart is the physical result of a long development of the humoral man. Heart is the physiological consequence of a long development of the humoral man into the human being. Heart is the biological outcome of a long development of the humoral man on earth. Heart is the expression of the humoral man. Heart is the manifestation of the humoral man. Heart is the demonstration of the humoral man. Heart is the humanity of man. Heart is the humorality of man. Heart is the heart of man. Heart is the center of man. Heart is the core of man. Heart is the essence of man. Heart is the depth of man. Heart is the basis of man. Heart is the foundation of man. Heart is the nurture of man. Heart is the support of man. Heart is the fountainhead of man. Heart is the origin of man. Heart is the source of man. Heart is man. Man is heart. Heart is man realized. Heart is man fulfilled. Heart is man to be man. Heart is man to become man. Heart is man to develop into man. Heart is man to reach himself. Heart is man to realize himself. Heart is man to fulfill himself. Heart is the warmth of man. Heart is the source of the warmth of man. Heart is man expanding. Heart is man reaching out. Heart is man radiating. Heart is man shining. Heart is man radiating through his feelings. Heart is man shining with his emotions. Heart is man living with his blood. Heart is the humoral man humoralized in his physical form. Heart is the humoral man realized in his bodily existence. Heart is man warmed through his feelings. Heart is man living through his feelings. Heart is man living with his emotions.

What are the good feelings of man? The good feelings of man are the feelings of man toward others. The good feelings of man are the feelings of man for others. The good feelings of man are the feelings of man for the consideration of others. The good feelings of man are the feelings of man taking others into consideration. The good feelings of man are the feelings of man respecting others. The good feelings of man are the feelings of man treating others as the fellow human beings. The good feelings of man are the feelings of man treating others as the humoral beings. The good feelings of man are the feelings of man respecting others' humoral existence. The good feelings of man are the feelings of man upholding others' humoral value. The good feelings of man are the feelings of man preserving and safeguarding others' human worth. The good feelings of man are the feelings of man toward nature. the good feelings of man are the feelings of man taking the world and oneself as one, in the sense that, a human being is part of the world, part of nature, and there is an intrinsic affinity, closeness, bond, or harmony existing between oneself and the world, or between oneself and nature, and, without the world or nature, a human being might not have come into being, or survived. The good feelings of man are the feelings of man toward oneself, in the sense that, one should take oneself in the ways as one should, that is, as a human being, as a humoral being, as a human being striving to fulfill or realize his or her human worth, as a humoral being striving to fulfill or realize his or her

Avolution and Man

humoral senses or instincts, or his or her humoral values or principles. The good feelings of man are the feelings of man for the true, for the good, for the right, for the just, for the beautiful. That is to say, the good feelings of man are the feelings of man seeking the true, the good feelings of man are the feelings of man striving for the good, the good feelings of man are the feelings of man aiming for the right, the good feelings of man are the feelings of man fighting for the just, the good feelings of man are the feelings of man reaching for the beautiful. The good feelings of man are the feelings of man striving to fulfill or realize man. The good feelings of man are the feelings of man striving to fulfill or realize the humoral existence of man. The good feelings of man are the nurture of man. The good feelings of man are the support of man. The good feelings of man are the sustenance of man. The good feelings of man are the continuation of man. The good feelings of man are the satisfaction of man. The good feelings of man are the fulfillment of man. The good feelings of man are the happiness of man. The good feelings of man are the beauty of man.

This may be seen as the coming into being or existence of the humoral heart of man. Man is humoral, animal, and humoverse. Apart from the humoral heart of man, man may be seen as also possessing the animal heart, and the humoverse heart. The humoverse heart of man may be seen as the kind of feelings of man associated with the humoverse nature of man. This kind of feelings of man, as coming out of the humoverse nature of man, may be seen or witnessed in man in a number of ways. We all know, as the human beings, we are sometimes unable to suppress our certain feelings, in some situations or circumstances. Such as, when we see a person, previously deemed inferior, in some way, or in some sense, to us, suddenly succeed, we may lose our calm or composure. That is, we may do some nasty things or say some bad words about such a person. In our minds, or, in our hearts, we know that such things or behaviors may not be the kind of good things, but, it seems, we cannot help them. Such feelings seem to have come out of the very depths of our human existence, and seem to be part of our being. We may not like them, but they happen anyway. We may try to avoid them, but they come nevertheless. It seems, they are part of us, and they are natural to us, in a way. Yes, it might be said, they are part of us, and they constitute part of our human being or existence. Yes, it might be said, they are natural to us, and they come out from our human nature. They constitute part of our human feelings.

Humorality

They may not be so nice, but they are part of us. They may not be so pleasant, but they are part of our nature. They may not be so good, but they are part of our being. They are not the good feelings; they are the humoverse feelings of man. They are not the good feelings that we may expect in ourselves; they are the kind of feelings that may run against our humoral being or existence. They are not the good feelings that may make us comfortable; they are the kind of feelings that may lead to our own unease. They are not the kind of feelings that we may control; they are the kind of feelings that seem to be out of our own control. It seems, in a sense, they happen on their own, and they run against ourselves, in some sense, in some way, in some manner, or to some extent. Yes, they run against ourselves, they run against our humoral selves. They come from our humoversity. They happen out of our humoverse nature. They come from our humoverse existence. They happen out of our humoverse being. Such kind of feelings may be seen as our humoverse feelings. Such kind of feelings may be seen as the humoverse feelings of man. They are part of man. They are part of the nature of man. They constitute the humoverse heart of man. They constitute the humoverse man.

The animal heart of man may be seen as what man shares, in this regard, in various degrees, with the other animals, such as, chimpanzees, monkeys, horses, dogs, tigers, lions, or even, in a sense, fish. What is the animal heart of man? The animal heart of man may be seen as the kind of feelings of man that may be seen as related to or associated with the animal behaviors or conducts of man. Such feelings of man may be seen as associated with man's animal behaviors or conducts in the sense that, they may have come into being from the animal survival instincts of man, or, in a sense, their very existence may be seen as facilitating the animal instinctual survival of man. Do animals have feelings? In a sense, it might be said, yes. How could one deny that animals may have feelings? Just like the human beings, it seems, animals also appear to possess certain feelings, though such kind of feelings may be seen as different, in degrees, in some sense, in some way, or to some extent, from the human feelings. Even sponges, regarded as the simplest animals, it might be said, appear to possess some kind of or some sense of feelings, as they live in the waters by feeding on bacteria or the various food particles. Most sponge species reproduce themselves through sexual reproduction. The fertilization of the eggs by the sperm cells may be seen as not that different from the kind of things that may be observed in other animal species. In a sense, it might be said, in the processes such as feeding or sexual reproduction of sponges, it may be difficult to rule out, completely, the possible presence or existence of some form or some sense of feelings in sponges, though such kind of feelings may be regarded mostly as physical, as sponges do not possess a nervous system. With the development of the sensory organs and with the coming into being of the nervous system in animals, it seems, feelings experienced by animals are becoming more and more specific, reliable, and complex. In the early stages, feelings experienced by animals may be seen as mostly physical, as they are produced or received mostly by or through the physical bodily parts of the animals. But with the coming into being of the nervous system in the animal bodies, it seems, feelings experienced by animals have developed greatly in their sophistication or complexity. In horses or dogs, one can see, there may be certain feelings existing in them, such as, they may be excited to see each other, or they may be excited to come close to the human beings with whom they may be familiar. In tigers or lions, though wild and violent beasts as they are, one can witness, they show, sometimes, their tender feelings toward each other, especially between or among their close family members. With regard to the highly developed mammals such as monkeys or chimpanzees, we all know, their manifested feelings are often rich and vivid. Actually, it might be said, their feelings may be sometimes so rich, vivid, and warm that, it seems, it may be difficult for us to tell the difference between such feelings and the feelings that may be experienced by the human beings.

Human beings come from animals. Human beings and the animals such as chimpanzees or monkeys are closely related. They have the same origin. They have the same source. They have, in a sense, the same kind of coming into being. Their feelings are closely related. Their emotions may be seen, in a sense, as comparable, in some great degrees. While the human beings may be seen as possessing the humoral feelings, animals, especially the kind of animals such as chimpanzees or monkeys, may be regarded, in a sense, as possessing the animoral feelings. While animals, such as chimpanzees or monkeys, may be seen as possessing their animal feelings, it seems, the human beings may be regarded as possessing, in a similar sense, or in a comparable way, their own animal feelings. Such animal feelings of the human beings may be seen as the kind of things that the human beings may have inherited from their animal ancestors after they have developed out of the animal conditions and into the human conditions. In such a sense, the animal feelings of the human beings may not necessarily be seen or regarded as something lower, or less in their value or significance, in the sense that, they too constitute, just like the humoral feelings, the existence or being of the human beings on earth, though, it might be said, in different ways, through different manners, or in or through different senses. In other words, without the animal feelings, the human beings might not have existed as the human beings. They might have existed, but they might have merely existed as machines or robots. While the humoral feelings make the human beings humoral, the animal feelings make the human beings animal, that is, in a sense, human. That is to say, while the animal feelings of the human beings may include the kind of feelings of the animal nature, such as the feelings corresponding to or associated with the sex drives or preying on others, the animal feelings of the human beings may also encompass the kind of feelings that sustain the human lives of the human beings, as the living animals on earth. This may be seen as the coming into being or existence of the animal heart of man.

§ 4.5.2 Heart is the Way

Heart is the way. Heart is the way of man. Heart is the way of the world. Heart is the way of man to live as man. Heart is the way of man to exist as man. Heart is the way of man to survive as man. Heart is the way of man to fulfill or realize himself as man. Heart is the way of man to reach man. Heart is the way of man to reach others. Heart is the way of man to live with others in the world.

Heart is the essence of man. Heart is the guide of man. Heart is the guardian of man. Heart is the support of man. Heart is the protection of man. Heart is the defence of man.

Heart is the bridge between man and beauty. Heart is the way of man to beauty. Heart is the way of beauty to man. Heart is where man and beauty meet. Heart is where man and beauty find each other. Heart is where man and beauty come together. Heart is where man and beauty unite. Heart is where man and beauty fuse into one.

Heart is the bridge between man and himself. Heart is the bridge between man and man. Heart is the bridge between man and symmetry.

Heart is the bridge between man and harmony. Heart is the bridge between man and the way of heaven. Heart is the bridge between man and heaven. Through heart, man reaches himself. Through heart, man reaches his fellow human beings. Through heart, man reaches symmetry. Through heart, man reaches harmony. Through heart, man reaches the way of heaven. Through heart, man reaches heaven.

Through heart, man feels Heaven. Through heart, man connects with Heaven. Through heart, man communicates with Heaven.

Heart is the embodiment of the way of heaven. Heart is the embodiment of the way of heaven in man. Heart is the embodiment of the way of heaven on earth. Heart is the embodiment of the way of heaven in the world.

§ 4.6 The Human Being and the Harmonic Being

What is the human being? The human being is symmetry humoralized into man. The human being is harmony humoralized into the human species. The human being is the symmetric being humoralized into the being of man. The human being is the harmonic being humoralized into the being of mankind.

The harmonic being of man may be seen as having to do with symmetry. The harmonic being of man may be seen as having to do with harmony. The rational being of man may be seen as having to do with the exercise of reason. It is symmetry that has given rise, in a sense, to the coming into being of the nervous system. It is symmetry that has given rise, in a sense, to the coming into being of reason. It is harmony that has given rise, in a sense, to the coming into being of the rational way. It is harmony that has given rise, in a sense, to the rational being of man.

Reason may not be able to give rise to symmetry. Reason may not be able to give rise to harmony. The rational way may not lead to the symmetric way. The rational way may not lead to the harmonic way. The rational being may not lead to the symmetric being. The rational being may not lead to the harmonic being. That is, in a sense, it might be said, symmetry is higher than reason; or, harmony is higher than reason. That is, in a sense, it might be said, the symmetric way is higher than the rational way; or, the harmonic way is higher than the rational way. That is, in a sense, it might be said, the symmetric being is higher

Humorality

than the rational being; or, the harmonic being is higher than the rational being.

Does this mean that, the rational being of man is not important? No. The rational being of man is important, significant, and fundamental to the existence of man. While the harmonic being may be seen as constituting the foundation of the human being, the rational being may be seen as so important, significant and fundamental that, without a proper and adequate exercise of reason, it might be said, man may not be seen as living or existing in a full human sense.

Where does the unfreedom of man come from? The unfreedom of man comes from that which gives rise to meaning. The unfreedom of man comes from that which gives rise to beauty. The unfreedom of man comes from that which gives rise to the humorality of man. The unfreedom of man comes from that which gives rise to man. That is, it might be said, the unfreedom of man comes from the harmonic being of man. That is, it might be said, the unfreedom of man comes from symmetry, or, harmony.

It is symmetry that holds man together. It is harmony that holds man together. It is symmetry that binds man. It is harmony that binds man. It is symmetry that gives rise to man. It is harmony that gives rise to man. It is symmetry that avolves man. It is harmony that avolves man. It is symmetry that develops man. It is harmony that advances man. It is symmetry that nurtures man. It is harmony that preserves man. It is symmetry that maintains man. It is harmony that sustains man. It is symmetry that supports man. It is harmony that upholds man.

If man is not in symmetry, man would disintegrate. If man is not in harmony, man would fall apart. If man is not in symmetry, man would disappear. If man is not in harmony, man would fade away. It is symmetry that gives man the human being. It is harmony that gives man the human existence. It is symmetry that maintains the human life. It is harmony that sustains the human existence. It is symmetry that maintains the humoral being of man. It is harmony that sustains the meaning of the existence of man.

§ 4.7 The True and Man

What is the true? The true is what gives rise to man. What is man? Man is the true humoralized into the human body. Man is the true humoralized into the human being. Man is the true humoralized into the human existence. What is the true? The true is the origin of man. The true is the beginning of man. The true is the source of man. The true is the root of man. The true is the fountainhead of man. From where has man originated? From the true. From where does man begin? From the true. Where should man meet his source? In the true. Where should man encounter his root? In the true. Where should man find his fountainhead? In the true.

The coming into being of man is the coming into being of the true. The coming into being of man is the coming into being of the true in a humoral form. The coming into being of man is the coming into being of the true in a humoral way. The coming into being of man is the coming into being of the true in a human sense. The coming into being of man is the coming into being of the true in a human manner. That is, it might be said, the coming into being of man may be seen as the fulfillment or realization of the true in a humoral form, in a humoral way, or, in a human sense, in a human manner. Man comes into being; the true fulfils itself. Man comes into being; the true realizes itself. The true expresses itself; man comes into being. The true manifests itself; man comes into this world. The true fulfils or realizes itself in man; man fulfils or realizes himself in the true. The true expresses or manifests itself in man; man expresses or manifests himself in the true.

The true finds itself in man; man finds himself in the true. To be man is to be true. To be true, in a sense, is to be man. That is why honesty is so important to man. That is why integrity is so meaningful to the human species. That is why science is so significant. That is why truth is so mighty.

To search into the true is to search into the meaning of man. To search into the true is to search into the origin of man. To search into the true is to search into the beginning of man. To search into the true is to search into the source of man. To search into the true is to search into the root of man. To search into the true is to search into the fountainhead of man. To search into the true is to search into the depth of man. To search into the true is to come back to man. To search into the true is to come back to man himself.

§ 4.8.1 The Humoral and the Animal

What is the humoral? The humoral is the true, the good, the right, the just, and the beautiful. The humoral means the true, the good, the right, the just, and the beautiful. The true is so real and genuine. The good is so good and precious. The right is so right and appropriate. The just is so just and noble. The beautiful is so beautiful and magnificent. To pursue them is to be real and genuine. To pursue them is to be good and precious. To pursue them is to be right and appropriate. To pursue them is to be just and noble. To pursue them is to be beautiful and magnificent.

What is the animal? The animal is for the flesh. The animal is for the body. The animal is for the physical. The animal is for the desires. And, it seems, when it comes to the flesh, to the body, to the physical, to the desires, the animal man may be so passionate and so excited. He may be taken over. He may forget himself. He may lose sight of what man is, what man means, or what man should be.

Thus, when man strives to be man, when man strives to fulfill or realize his humoral being, when man strives to uphold or safeguard his humoral existence, man may look down on his animal side, that is, on the animal man. The animal man may not be so true and genuine. The animal man may not be so good and precious. The animal man may not be so right and appropriate. The animal man may not be so just and noble. The animal man may not be so beautiful and magnificent. That is, in a word, it might be said, the animal man may not be so, after all, humoral.

But, it has to be said, man is not just humoral; man is also animal. The animal life of man is part of the life of man. The sexual life of man is part of the human life of man. The humoral should take consideration of the animal. The animal should respect the humoral. That is to say, the harmonization of the humoral life and the animal life should be pursued in the human life, and the harmony between the humoral and the animal should be reached, or fulfilled, realized, in man.

§ 4.8.2 The Animal

Why is the animal not good, or good enough, to the humoral? The animal is good, in an animal sense; in the sense that, it is in the animal nature that animals exist, and it is through the animal strivings or endeavors that animals survive or continue their lives. But, the animal may not be good, or good enough, to the humoral, in the sense that, the animal is different from the humoral, and the difference may be extended to such an extent that, it seems, they may be of vastly different natures, qualities, or characteristics. The humoral upholds the true; the animal does not. The humoral recognizes the true; the animal does not. The humoral comprehends the true; the animal cannot. The humoral expresses or demonstrates the true; the animal cannot. The humoral strives for the good; the animal does not. The animal strives for the animal senses or instincts. The humoral strives for the right; the animal does not. The animal does not possess a notion of right or wrong; the animal strives for the gratification of the animal senses or instincts. The humoral strives for the just, as it fulfils the existence of the humoral; the animal does not. The animal is not blessed with a sense of justice. The animal strives to fulfill the animal drives or desires. The humoral strives for the beautiful; the animal, it seems, does not. Beauty or ugliness may not be so pronounced to the animal. Beauty or ugliness may not be what the animal is concerned. What the animal is concerned is to fulfill the animal nature. What the animal strives to is to satisfy the animal feelings or longings. Thus, to the humoral, it seems, the animal is not good. It is not good enough. It is not up to the level. It is not up to the point. It falls short. It falls far short of what may be expected of the humoral. It falls far short of what may be expected for the humoral. It falls far short of what may be expected by the humoral. It is in such a sense that, it might be said, the animal is not good, or good enough, to the humoral. And it is in such a sense that, it might be said, when the humoral man finds himself to be residing, side by side, at the same time, with the animal man, within the same body, he would feel, in a sense, embarrassed, or, very embarrassed.

§ 4.9 Harmony and Man

Harmony is, in a sense, a sense. Harmony is, in a sense, a feeling. Harmony is, in a sense, a meaningful sense. Harmony is, in a sense, a meaningful feeling. Harmony is meaningful. Harmony is meaning. Symmetry is, in a sense, a sense. Symmetry is, in a sense, a feeling. Symmetry is, in a sense, a meaningful sense. Symmetry is, in a sense, a meaningful feeling. Symmetry is meaningful. Symmetry is meaning. The true is, in a sense, a sense. The true is, in a sense, a feeling. The true is, in a sense, a meaningful sense. The true is, in a sense, a meaningful feeling. The true is meaningful. The true is meaning. The good is, in a sense, a sense. The good is, in a sense, a feeling. The good is, in a sense, a meaningful sense. The good is, in a sense, a meaningful feeling. The good is meaningful. The good is meaning. The beautiful is, in a sense, a sense. The beautiful is, in a sense, a feeling. The beautiful is, in a sense, a meaningful sense. The beautiful is, in a sense, a meaningful feeling. The beautiful is meaningful. The beautiful is meaning. Man is, in a sense, a sense. Man is, in a sense, a feeling. Man is, in a sense, a meaningful sense. Man is, in a sense, a meaningful feeling. Man is meaningful. Man is meaning.

Harmony has to do with symmetry. Symmetry has to do with harmony. Harmony has to do with the true. Harmony has to do with the good. Harmony has to do with the beautiful. Harmony has to do with man. Harmony has to do with meaning. Man has to do with harmony. Man has to do with symmetry. Man has to do with the true. Man has to do with the good. Man has to do with the beautiful. Man has to do with meaning.

Man is the realization of harmony in a human way. Man is the realization of symmetry in a human sense. Man is the realization of the true in a human form. Man is the realization of the good in a human manner. Man is the realization of the beautiful in a human fashion. Man is the realization of meaning in a human level. Man is the realization of harmony in the true, the good, the beautiful, and meaning. Man is the realization of harmony through the true, the good, the beautiful, and meaning.

§ 4.10 The Unfreedom of Symmetry

Man comes from symmetry. The unfreedom of man comes from symmetry. The unfreedom of man comes from the unfreedom of symmetry.

Symmetry underlies things. Symmetry maintains things. Symmetry sustains plants and animals. Symmetry underlies man. Symmetry maintains man. Symmetry sustains man. Symmetry binds man. The unfreedom of symmetry underlies things. The unfreedom of symmetry maintains things. The unfreedom of symmetry sustains plants and animals. The unfreedom of symmetry underlies man. The unfreedom of symmetry maintains man. The unfreedom of symmetry sustains man.

The unfreedom of symmetry binds man. The unfreedom of symmetry gives rise to man. The unfreedom of symmetry gives rise to the unfreedom of man. The unfreedom of symmetry gives rise to the meaning of the existence of man.

§ 4.11 Heart and Man

Heart is the heart of man. Heart is the heart of the human being. Heart is the heart of the human existence. Heart is the heart of the humoral being of man. Heart is the heart of the humoral existence of man.

Heart is the coming into being of man in nature. Heart is the coming into being of man in man. Heart is the humoral coming into being of man in nature. Heart is the humoral coming into being of man in the form of man. Heart is the humoralization of man in nature. Heart is the humoralization of man in the way of man. Heart is the humoral coming into being of man in symmetry. Heart is the humoral coming into being of man in harmony. Heart is the humoral coming into being of man from symmetry. Heart is the humoral coming into being of man from harmony. Heart is the humoral fulfillment of symmetry in man. Heart is the humoral realization of harmony in the human species. Heart is the humoral fulfillment of man in symmetry. Heart is the humoral realization of man in harmony. Heart is the humoralization of symmetry in the human form. Heart is the humoralization of harmony in the human way. Heart is the humoralization of symmetry in the animal life. Heart is the humoralization of harmony in the animal species.

§ 4.12 The Two Faculties of Man: Feeling and Reason

Feelings are common to the human beings, and in fact, it might be said, they are so common that, it seems, people do not, necessarily, take them seriously, or, as so seriously as they take, such as, reason. Reason is important. How about feelings? Are they important? Are they important, just in the ways as reason is? Reason is essential to man, it

Humorality

seems. How about feelings? Are they essential to man? Are they indispensable, crucial and vital to man, just like reason? Reason, it seems, has helped man accomplish great achievements. How about feelings? Have feelings helped man accomplish great achievements? What are such achievements? What are they?

In a sense, it might be said, such achievements are in us. Such achievements may be seen in the coming into being of the human beings. Such achievements may be seen in the coming into being of the human beings from animals. Such achievements may be seen in the coming into being of the human beings in the world. Such achievements may be seen in the human beings living with a meaningful existence. Such achievements may be seen in the human beings living with a human life. Such achievements may be seen in the human beings living with their moral senses. Such achievements may be seen in the human beings living with their aesthetic senses. Such achievements may be seen in the human beings living with a capacity to appreciate beauty. Such achievements may be seen in the human beings living for the true, for the good, for the right, for the just, and for the beautiful.

Man is not just reason; man is feelings too. If feelings are ignored, man would be ignored. If feelings are overlooked, man would be overlooked. If feelings are impeded, man would be impeded. If feelings are damaged, man would be damaged. If feelings are conditioned, man would be conditioned. If feelings are changed, man would be changed. If feelings are gevolved, man would be gevolved. If feelings are dehumoralized, man would be dehumoralized. If feelings disappear, man would vanish.

Feelings may be humble and homely, but they may give us a sound and healthy self. Reason may be noble and powerful, but it may lead us astray. To cultivate feelings is to cultivate man. To cultivate man is to cultivate feelings. To cultivate feelings is to establish the precondition for the sound and healthy use of reason. To protect feelings is to protect man. To safeguard feelings is to safeguard man. To uphold feelings is to uphold man. To maintain and sustain feelings is to maintain and sustain man, that is, to maintain and sustain the foundation for the exercise of reason by man.

Are feelings important? Yes, they are important. Are feelings essential to man? Yes, they are essential to man. Are feelings as important as reason to man? Yes. Are feelings indispensable, crucial and vital to man, just like reason? Yes. Reason has accomplished great achievements. Feelings have accomplished, it seems, no less. Reason has guided us to great discoveries. Feelings have led the human beings, it might be said, to equally significant, majestic, and magnificent things. While we focus on reason, it seems, we should not overlook feelings. While we praise reason, it seems, we should not ignore feelings. While we exalt reason, it appears, we should not forget to celebrate our feelings, to cultivate them, and to uphold them.

It seems, the reason that we are not paying so much attention to feelings, at least in a philosophical sense, comes from the fact that, it appears, feelings defy, to a great extent, a rational analysis by or through reason. What reason is good at is to dissect and analyze things, but feelings seem to be difficult to be dissected or analyzed. Feelings come and go. It seems, it would be difficult to pin down exactly where they come from or how they have gone. Feelings are vivid and rich, but, when it comes to finding a way to examine them, it seems, they vary greatly in their intensity, in their depth, in their duration, or in their actual effects, as all such things seem to depend on each and every individual human person.

It seems, our feelings are clear to ourselves, as a bodily or emotional experience, as to what they mean or how they affect us, but, if one ventures to ask, how they are connected with us or how they achieve such effects on the human beings, it seems, it may be difficult to answer. A feeling may be seen as a bodily reaction to some emotional experience experienced by a human being. Its effects may be far and rich to a human person, while it may be of little consequence to another human being. A feeling experienced by a human being may involve both bodily and mental activities, in the sense that, a seemingly pure mental activity may cause bodily emotional reactions, or in the same sense, a seemingly pure bodily or physical experience may trigger some strong mental emotions. In other words, it might be said, the human body is so intricately built or structured that, it seems, when it comes to the human feelings or emotions, it would be difficult to delineate the bodily or physical from the mental, or the mental from the bodily or physical. We experience our feelings, but our feelings happen depending on our personality, disposition, temperament, character, or even, on the timing or occasion of such happening. Human beings are highly developed intelligent animals, and the feelings experienced by them may be seen as characteristic of such an advanced state. The physical and the mental may be regarded as mostly intertwined with each other. That is to say, the nervous system and the body may be seen as combining or integrating with each other, eventually giving rise to what is called the human feelings or emotions.

Feelings come and go, but it seems, they would be difficult to quantify. Feelings happen and disappear, but it seems, they would be difficult to measure. The fluid nature of feelings makes them elusive for reason to grasp. We experience feelings, but it seems, they challenge any attempt for a sense of analytical measurement or quantification. We experience feelings, but it seems, they are beyond, in a sense, a rational investigation or examination. They are uncertain. They are not firm. They flow. They vary. They fluctuate. They change. They change, it seems, all the time, with time, with occasion, with mood, or with different persons. Feelings may also be seen as vague or unclear, as a sense of existence, in the sense that, only the person knows what kind of feelings he or she is experiencing, and it would be difficult for others to fathom exactly what is happening, or what might be the depth, scale, or content of such feelings; and, even for the same person, it seems, the feelings experienced might be vastly different, if he or she has a different mood, if the situation is different, if the timing is not the same, or if the occasion changes. That is to say, even though feelings come and go, happen or disappear, to the human beings in a daily basis, it would be difficult for the human beings to have a firm hold on them.

Reason seems to have lost its sharp grasp. Feelings are shapeless; reason seems to be unable to find a foothold. Feelings are formless; reason seems to be unable to find the entrance. Feelings come and go, with little trace left; reason, it seems, loses the track. Reason thus seems, in a certain sense, unable to deal with what is called the human feelings or emotions. Reason thus seems to have sidetracked them. Reason thus seems to have overlooked or ignored them. After all, it seems, the human feelings or emotions have not achieved much, except the fact that they help the human beings go through the highs and lows of their daily lives. After all, it seems, the human feelings or emotions should not amount to anything remarkable or extraordinary, apart from the mundane or routine roles that they have played in people's lives. After all, it seems, reason is noble, while the human feelings or emotions may be just about the daily routines. After all, it seems, reason is indispensable to us, and while the human feelings or emotions are overlooked or ignored, we may still accomplish what we want or achieve what we desire. After all, all the great achievements accomplished by reason are all there to be seen, and to be admired. But, the human feelings or emotions? What are they? What would be their use? What have they done? What have they accomplished? Have they done anything noble? Have they accomplished anything great or marvelous? They are just feelings or emotions. They are just the daily happenings of some routines in the human beings. They are merely some woeful or pathetic showing or expression of the animal beings called man. They are nothing. Or they are close to nothing. They are insignificant. They are of little value or substance. Who cares about them?

Well, the time may have come. The time may have come for the human beings to care about their feelings or emotions. The time may have come for the human beings to look deep into their feelings or emotions. The time may have come for the human beings to care about the state of their feelings or emotions. The time may have come for the human beings to care about the depth, the quality, or the character of their feelings or emotions. That is, the time may have come for the human beings to care about the nature of their feelings or emotions. That is, the time may have come for the human beings to ask certain crucial questions with regard to their feelings or emotions. Are they the natural feelings or emotions of man? Are they the human feelings or emotions of man? Are they the humoral feelings or emotions of man? Or, are they the feelings or emotions coming out of the gevolution of man, that is, the gevolved feelings or emotions? That is, are they the kind of feelings or emotions that represent the dehumoralization of the natural feelings or emotions of man? Are they the kind of feelings or emotions that embody the dehumoralization of the human feelings or emotions of man? Are they the kind of feelings or emotions that stand for the dehumoralization of the humoral feelings or emotions of man? That is, are they the gevil feelings or emotions of the gevolved man? Are they the gevil feelings or emotions that would lead to the gevolution of the human beings? Are they the gevil feelings or emotions that would lead to the dehumoralization of the human species? Are they the gevil feelings or emotions that would transform man, eventually, into the gevil?

It seems, the time may have come for the human beings to recognize that, feelings are just as important as reason. Feelings are as

Humorality

crucial as reason. Feelings are as significant as reason. Feelings are as vital as reason. Feelings are man; man is feelings. Feelings make man, just like reason. Feelings determine man, just like reason. Feelings establish man, just like reason. Feelings make man, in no less significant way. Feelings determine man, in no less crucial manner. Feelings establish man, in no less vital sense. Without feelings, man would not be man, and reason would be of no use. Without feelings, man would not have existed as the human being, and reason would not have the opportunity to be exercised.

If feelings are impaired, man would find himself disabled, and reason would lose its firm ground. If feelings are damaged, man would lose his grip on himself, and reason would go astray. When feelings are dehumoralized, man would be unable to be man, and reason would only lead man to his dehumoralization. When feelings are gevolved, man would lose his humoral ground, and reason would only direct man to take the gevil as the human. The feelings of man determine what man would be; reason, it seems, does not. The feelings of man establish how man should live or exist; reason, it seems, does not. The feelings of man make man man; reason, it seems, cannot. The coming into being of man may be seen, in a sense, as the coming into being of the feelings of man. The existence of man may be seen, in a sense, as the existence of the feelings of man. The wellbeing of man may be seen, in a sense, as the wellbeing of the feelings of man. The soundness of man may be seen, in a sense, as the soundness of the feelings of man. It is the feelings of man that, in a sense, define man. It is the feelings of man that, in a sense, determine the wellbeing of man. It is the feelings of man that, in a sense, establish a sound ground for the existence of man. It is the feelings of man that, in a sense, constitute the precondition for man to live a meaningful human life, with man at the center, as a humoral being.

The human feelings are important, and crucial, to the human beings, and we should pay as much attention to them as we pay to the kind of things such as reason. They are the everyday happenings, but they are not inferior. They are the daily routines, but they are not lowly. They constitute the ordinary life of man, but they are not the trivial or minor things. To man, they are significant. To man, they are vital. To man, they are essential. To man, they are equally indispensable and magnificent. So, what are feelings? What are the human feelings? Where do they come from? How have they come into being? How have

Avolution and Man

they become part of man? How have they played such a vital and indispensable role in the existence of man?

In a sense, it might be said, feelings come from the feelings of animals. Animals move, feed on things, and reproduce themselves. Through long developmental processes, various senses come into being in animals. In the processes of their existence, that is, in the processes of their survival, animals exercise such senses and live their lives by relying, in various degrees, on such senses. Such senses may be seen, in a sense, as the organs of animals that provide them with some senses of means to perceive the environment in which they live or exist. Such perceiving of the environment, by or through the bodies or bodily organs of animals, may be seen as the coming into being of the animal feelings, in a primitive sense, or it might be said, in the early stages of the animal development. The perceiving or feeling of animals may be seen as being exercised or performed in two senses, or in two ways, that is, both internally and externally, for animals have to monitor both their internal and external conditions in order to survive successfully. But, for the sake of simplicity, let us just focus in this discussion on the external perceiving or feeling by animals, that is, on the perceiving or feeling of the environment by animals.

Sponges are simple animals, with no nervous system. They usually do not move much. They reproduce themselves and live by ingesting nutrients in the waters. As they live by ingesting nutrients in the waters and reproduce themselves, it might be said, there might be some sense of perceiving or feeling of the environment by or through their bodies. That is to say, in the feeding processes or in the reproducing processes, there might be some sense of contact between the environment and the sponge bodies, which may be seen, in a sense, as constituting some sense of "communicating" between the environment and sponges. Though such a sense of "communicating" may only be regarded as such in a preliminary or primitive sense, nevertheless, it may be seen as representing such a possibility that certain things might be happening between the environment and sponges. Though it may be hard to know exactly what might actually happen between the environment and sponges, such things may be seen, in a sense, as constituting a sense of perceiving or feeling of the environment by sponges. That is to say, during the existence of sponges in the waters, it might be said, there might happen some sense of feeling or perceiving of the environment by sponges, as sponges possess their bodies and through their bodies they carry out such activities as feeding on the nutrients in the waters or reproducing themselves. As the sponge bodies can only perform very limited activities as the living animals, and they do not possess a nervous system, such a sense of feeling or perceiving, on the part of sponges, may thus only be regarded as very limited, or primitive. Nevertheless, it seems, it would be difficult for one to deny, completely, the presence or existence of such a sense of feeling or perceiving, as, after all, sponges are living animals possessing their own bodies, and they live their lives by carrying out certain animal activities through their bodies.

The kind of things such as sponges feeling or perceiving, while viewed as simple, limited, or primitive, may be regarded as representing, in a sense, the beginning of the animal feelings. Animals developed, and certain animal bodily organs gradually came into being over time. With the coming into being of such bodily organs, the feeling or perceiving by animals became more and more focused, specific, and reliable. This may be seen in the senses that we may find often in animals, such as, sight, hearing, smell, taste, or touch. Though such senses may vary greatly among the different animal species, they enable animals to feel or perceive the world, and thus animals may survive successfully in their environments. The sense of sight may enable animals to see the environment. The sense of hearing may enable animals to hear the sounds around them. The sense of smell may enable animals to detect the odor of things. The sense of taste may enable animals to find out the taste of the things that they may take in. The sense of touch may give animals the ability to feel the things that they may come into contact with. Such senses, combined with other senses that may be found in the animal world, may enable animals to detect things in their surroundings, to receive information from the environment, and to form the kind of perceptive ground upon which they may decide their movements or take their actions. Animals thus live their lives through their senses. Animals thus survive by relying on their senses.

The bodily senses such as sight, hearing, smell, taste or touch may be seen, in a sense, as constituting the physical feeling of animals; in the sense that, such as, the eyes, the ears, the nose, the tongue, or the skin may be seen as accomplishing their feeling or sensing by or through their physical contact, or means. In such a sense, it might be said, even though some of the animals may be regarded as more advanced than other animals, such as the kind of animals like sponges, the nature of the physical feeling of animals may be seen as being shared by all the animals, including, in a sense, sponges. That is to say, in other words, it might be said, the physical feeling of animals may be seen as constituting one of the most prominent or vital features of the animal life; in the sense that, it might be said, it is the physical feeling of animals that distinguishes animals from the other things, it is the physical feeling of animals that enables animals to live their animal lives, and it is the physical feeling of animals that, it might be said, maintains animals as the animals. That is, it might be said, without the physical feeling of animals, animals might not have come into being; without the physical feeling of animals, animals might not have been able to survive as the animals; without the physical feeling of animals, animals might not have been able to exist as the animals. That is, the physical feeling of animals may not be seen as lowly, as it maintains animals as the animal beings; the physical feeling of animals may not be seen as inadequate, as it forms the physical connection between the world and animals, and sustains the animals' animal existence in the world. Otherwise, it seems, animals could not live their animal lives in this world. Otherwise, it seems, animals would not be the animals, in the world.

As we all know, in most cases, the physical feeling of animals is intricately intertwined with the nervous system of animals, as the nervous system coming into being along with the development of the various bodily senses in animals. Should we downplay the significance of the physical nature of the physical feeling of animals, given that, it seems, something more advanced, that is, seemingly significantly more sophisticated, such as, a nervous system, has come into being? No. We should not. We should not downplay the significance or importance of the physical nature of the physical feeling of animals, even it seems, something like a nervous system might have played a significant role in the life of animals. The nervous system is important to animals, so is the physical feeling of animals. The nervous system is vital to animals, so is the physical nature of the physical feeling of animals. The nervous system is crucial to animals, so is the physical feeling of animals. The nervous system is essential to animals, so is the physical nature of the physical feeling of animals. The physical nature of the physical feeling of animals forms the foundation of animals, so that a nervous system may play its role and work its way. The physical nature of the physical feeling of animals establishes the precondition, so that a nervous system may come into being in animals. The physical nature of the physical feeling of animals constitutes part of the animal nature, so that animals may exist or live as the animals, that is, employ the nervous system, exercise the senses, and survive.

The physical feeling and the nervous system are the two parts of animals. The physical feeling and the nervous system are the two aspects of animals. The physical feeling and the nervous system are the two features of animals. The physical feeling and the nervous system are the two ways of animals. Animals need both of them. Animals exist or live by relying on both of them. Animals cannot survive without either of them. Animals do not exist without either of them. An animal life is the life of the physical feeling and the nervous system combining together. An animal life is the life of the physical feeling and the nervous system integrating with each other. An animal life is the life of the exercise of both the physical feeling and the nervous system. An animal life is the life of the fulfilling of both the physical feeling and the nervous system. An animal life is the life of the realization of both the physical feeling and the nervous system.

With the coming into being of the nervous system, it seems, the feeling by animals becomes incredibly more sophisticated and complicated, that is, in a sense, compared with the kind of functions performed by the kind of animals such as sponges. In fact, the feeling by animals has become so sophisticated or complicated that, it seems, what is called feelings may be seen as, gradually, coming into being, especially for the kind of more advanced animals such as chimpanzees. Feelings may be seen as coming into being from the feeling of animals, in the sense that, with the coming into being of the nervous system, with the increasing complexity of the nervous system, as the nervous system integrates with the feeling by animals to provide or form the perceptive foundation for the survival of animals, the feeling by animals begins, gradually, that is, little by little, step by step, to assume certain characteristics, or qualities, that may be seen as signifying or representing certain things beyond the mere, or bare, feeling by the kind of animals possessing no nerve cells or a very limited or primitive version of nervous system, such as sponges or jellyfish. In other words, with the coming into being or presence of the increasingly complex nervous system, feeling by animals has become not so simple. It is no longer a simple "feeling"; it seems to have involved certain things more than "feeling". It is no longer a mere physical contact, such as with the simple sponges. It begins to involve a nervous system that consists of a complex network of neurons that receive or transmit electrochemical signals throughout the body.

The physical feeling of animals is no longer just physical, as such a feeling has to be processed by or through a nervous system that is different from the physical senses possibly involved in such a process, such as, the eyes, the ears, the nose, the tongue, or the skin. The physical feeling of animals, thus, may not be seen as a purely physical process, in the sense that, such a process now involves not just the physical contact, that is, the performing of the physical senses, such as, the eyes, the ears, the nose, the tongue, or the skin, but also a system, or, a network, that may function, or act, very differently, in a sense, from a physical point of view. It is no longer just a physical contact; it is an inner contact. It is no longer just a physical process, performed outside of the body; it is also an inner process, carried out within the body. It is no longer just a feeling feeled outside; it is also a feeling feeled inside. It is no longer just a "feeling"; it is something that may be more than a "feeling". It is no longer just a physical feeling; it is something that may go well beyond the physical. That is what we see in animals. That is what we witness in animals. The physical feeling of animals, by combining with a nervous system, is being internalized. The physical feeling of animals, by integrating with a nervous system, is being transformed. The feeling of animals begins to indicate some new signs. The feeling of animals begins to show some new contents. The feeling of animals begins, it seems, to form what is called, the feelings.

Human beings come from animals. The human feelings come into being, it might be said, from the animal feelings. With the gradual coming into being of the humorality of man through a long developmental process, with the increasing complexity of the nervous system in humans, what is called the human feelings may be seen as coming into being, in the end, that is, as we now know today. The increasing complexity of the human nervous system enables the human beings to exercise or enjoy their feelings in a level, or in a level of complexity, that may not be easily matched by animals, even by the most advanced animals such as chimpanzees. The coming into being of the humorality of man eventually lifts man out of the animals, in the sense that, with the coming into being of the humorality of man, meaning comes to man, that is, meaning comes to the actions of man, meaning comes to the behaviors of man, and meaning comes to, at the same time, man's feelings or emotions. The human feelings thus exhibit more complex characteristics or qualities than the mere animal feelings, as the human nervous system is developed to an extent or level that may not be seen in animals. The human feelings thus demonstrate or manifest a level of depth, intensity or richness that may not be seen in the animal feelings, as the humorality of man forms the foundation or fountainhead for the flowering of the human feelings. Such a foundation or fountainhead may be seen as lacking in the animal feelings, as, in a sense, the animorality of animals, even among the more advanced animals such as chimpanzees, may be seen as having not reached such a level or stage that is being enjoyed by the humoral man, in the sense that, among animals, it seems, no language is used, communication is limited, and little meaning is conveyed or exchanged. That is to say, in a sense, it might be said, it is the humorality of man that gives rise to the coming into being of the human feelings, that is, to the colorfulness, to the depth, to the intensity, or to the richness of the human feelings. With the use of language, human beings can communicate between or among themselves with meaning. To express meaning, human beings demonstrate or display different feelings or emotions, with different depths, with different intensities, with different scales, with different levels, or with different contents. The human feelings thus constitute some important parts of the human existence, or even, it might be said, some of the most crucial or indispensable parts of the human existence.

In the human feelings, human beings can find themselves. Through the human feelings, human beings can express themselves. Human beings live as the human beings with their feelings. Human beings exist as the human beings in their feelings. Human beings express themselves through their feelings, so that they can be human beings. Human beings experience the human feelings, so that they may maintain themselves as the human beings. The human feelings come from the human beings. The human feelings nurture the human beings. The human beings fulfill or realize themselves through their human feelings; the human feelings enable the human beings to fulfill or realize themselves. The human feelings form the human life. The human feelings form the foundation of the human life. The human feelings constitute, in a sense, the fundamental existence of man.

Avolution and Man

It is through the humoralization of the animal feelings that, it might be said, the human feelings come into being. That is, it might be said, it is through the humoralization of the animal feelings that man comes into being. The coming into being of man is the humoralization of feelings. The coming into being of man is the humoralization of the feeling by animals. The coming into being of man is the humoralization of the feeling into the feelings. The coming into being of man is the humoralization of the feelings through a developmental process in the body and the nervous system. The coming into being of man is the humoralization of the feeling by animals in the body and the nervous system. The coming into being of man is the humoralization of the animal feelings in the body and the nervous system. The feelings of animals, through a process of humoralization, are transformed into the feelings of humans.

The feelings of animals, through a process of humoralization, become the human feelings. The physical feeling of animals, through a process of humoralization, becomes not just physical, but also humoral to the humans. The physical feeling is no longer just physical; it is also humoral. The physical feeling is no longer merely physical; it is human now. The animal has been humoralized into the human. The animal feeling has been humoralized into the human feeling. The animal feelings have been humoralized into the humoral feelings of man. Feeling is transformed. Feeling is humoralized. Feeling is humanized. The physical feeling is humoralized. The physical feeling is humanized. Feeling is transformed into feelings. Feeling is transformed into emotions. The physical feeling is transformed into the humoral feelings. The physical feeling is transformed into the human emotions. To feel is to be human. To feel is to be man. To feel is to be humoral. To be man is to feel. To be human is to feel. To be humoral is to feel. To be man is to feel in a human way. To be human is to feel in a humoral manner. To be humoral is to feel in a manly sense. To live is to feel, in a sense. To exist is to feel, in a sense. To live as man is to feel as man. To live as the human being is to feel as the human being. To exist as the humoral man is to feel as the humoral man. Feelings thus come into being from feeling. Feelings thus come into being from the physical feeling. Feelings thus come into being from the animal feelings. Man comes into being; the human feelings come into being. The human feelings come into being; the humoral man comes into being. The human feelings or emotions thus come to this world.

Humorality

The human feelings come into being from the human feeling, in the sense that, with the coming into being of a highly developed human nervous system, and with the coming into being of the human body, an intricate and complex integration of the human nervous system and the human body gradually gives rise to the coming into being of the kind of feelings enjoyed by the human beings that may be seen as vastly more advanced than the kind of things possessed or enjoyed by animals. Such a process may be seen as a process of the humoralization of the human feeling into the human feelings, as the human feeling, having been humoralized through a long developmental process, becomes, gradually, more delicate, more subtle, more refined, that is, in a sense, more meaningful or richer than, say, the animal feeling, or the animal physical feeling, or the earlier human feeling, as such a process may be regarded as progressing, during a long time, in stages, or by steps. That is to say, the human feeling, coming into being from the animal feeling, or the animal physical feeling, or the animal feelings, may be seen as representing or sanding for the result or consequence of a long developmental process that may have seen the eventual coming into being of man out of the animal species, and in itself constitutes the coming into being of the very thing that exercises such a feeling, that is, man. The human feeling may thus be seen, in a sense, as what gives rise to man, what makes man possible, what leads man to come into being, that is, in a sense, what represents man, what defines man, what establishes man, what gives meaning to man, what makes man a rich and meaningful existence.

Man is, in a sense, more delicate than animals, as the human feeling may be more delicate than the animal feeling or feelings. Man is, in a sense, subtler than animals, as the human feeling may be subtler than the animal feeling or feelings. Man is, in a sense, more refined than animals, as the human feeling may be more refined than the animal feeling or feelings. Man is, in a sense, richer than animals, as the human feeling may be developed more richly than the animal feeling or feelings. man is, in a sense, more meaningful than animals, as the human feeling may be developed in such a way that, coming out of the animal feeling or feelings, it may enable man, in the end, to possess, enjoy, or exercise such feeling in such a way, to such an extent, or at such a level that, it might be said, man may be seen as eventually possessing, enjoying or exercising his feelings or emotions. The human feeling forms the human feelings. The human feeling forms the human emotions. The human feeling constitutes the human existence of man as an animal being with highly developed feelings or emotions. That is, it might be said, the human feeling constitutes man, as a humoral being, as a humoral existence, in the world.

The human feeling is important, in the sense that, it sustains the existence of the human beings as the human beings. The human feeling is significant, in the sense that, without it, or, if it is damaged, or impaired, or if it is blocked or impeded, in any way, in any sense, or through any means, the human existence might go awry, and problems, or even some serious problems, might emerge in the human life. As the human beings, it seems, we are usually focused on the use or exercise of reason, in the sense that, having been impressed by the great achievements accomplished with the help of reason, we are often led to think, or believe that, it seems, reason is the most important thing in the human life, or, reason may be seen as the most important faculty of the human beings. It is true that reason is important. It is true that reason has accomplished great things. It is true that the use or exercise of reason has been seen as one of the most important or fundamental things in the human life. Yes, it is true. Reason is indeed important, and reason is indeed fundamental to the human existence. But, while we see the importance or significance of reason, it seems, we should not forget, or overlook, the importance or significance of what is called the human feeling. If reason is important, it seems, the human feeling may be equally so. If reason is significant, it seems, the human feeling may be regarded as such in a same sense. If reason is fundamental, it seems, the human feeling may stand in the same way to the human beings. Without reason, human beings are blind; without the human feeling, it seems, human beings cannot feel their way. Without reason, human beings are ignorant; without the human feeling, it seems, human beings cannot perceive the world around them. Without reason, human beings cannot see into things; without the human feeling, it seems, human beings cannot even access themselves. Reason is important as it guides the human beings to look into the world and themselves. The human feeling is important, as it provides the perceptive foundation for the human existence. If we pay attention to reason, it seems, we should pay the same attention to the human feeling. If we take reason seriously, it seems, we should also take the human feeling seriously, in the same way, in the same sense, or in the same manner. That is, it might be said, if reason defines man, the human feeling defines the human being; if

Humorality

reason gives meaning to man, the human feeling gives meaning to the human being; if reason establishes man, the human feeling establishes the human existence.

It is in such a sense that, it might be said, if reason is a faculty of man, feeling may be seen as another faculty of the human beings. If reason is a faculty of man that should be taken seriously, feeling may be seen as a faculty of the human beings that should be taken seriously in the same sense. If reason is a faculty inseparable from man, feeling as a faculty of man may be treated as such in the same sense, in the same way, or in the same manner. Reason, as a faculty, guides us to search into the secrets of the world. Feeling, as a faculty, leads us to live a rich and meaningful existence in the world. Reason lifts us with its sharp reach. Feeling upholds us with its thick content. It is through reason that we search into the unknown. It is through feeling that we become the humoral beings. Reason enlightens us; feeling forms us. Reason gives us insight; feeling gives us perception. Reason gives us knowledge or understanding; feeling provides us with feelings or emotions. Reason makes us intelligent; feeling makes us human. Reason makes us human; feeling makes us humoral. Reason means logic or reasoning; feeling means content or meaning. Reason represents the mind; feeling constitutes the heart. It is in reason that we live as the humans; it is in feeling that we exist as the humoral beings.

The importance of feeling may not be overestimated, in the sense that, as we look into man, we may find, just like reason, it seems, feeling forms the foundation of the human existence. The significance of feeling, it appears, may not be downplayed in any way, or in any sense, in the sense that, as the human beings, we need not just reason, we also need our feeling to be exercised in a healthy, sound, undamaged, unimpaired, or unimpeded way, that is, as a indispensable and inseparable faculty of man; otherwise, it seems, the human life might not happen as it should, or as it might be expected. The importance or significance of feeling may not be seen more clearly anywhere than in the antean being or existence of man. The antean being or existence of man forms the root of the humoral being or existence of man, that is, the human being or existence of man. If something happens to the antean being or existence of man, then certain things may happen to the humoral being or existence of man. If the antean being or existence of man is, in some way, in some sense, or in some manner, blocked, damaged, impaired, or impeded, then the human being or existence of man may be, in some sense, in some way, or in some manner, blocked, damaged, impaired, or impeded.

What is the antean being of man? It is the antean feeling of man. What is the antean existence of man? It is the antean physical feeling of man. What is the antean life of man? It is the antean feelings of man fulfilled, realized, that is, nurtured, cultivated, that is, achieved, or satisfied. The anteanity of man is the antean feeling of man. The anteanity of man is the antean physical feeling of man. Feeling enables man to achieve his antean contact with the antean world, so that his coming into being would be nurtured, his root would be cultivated, and his life would be nursed. Feeling enables man to maintain a physical contact with the antean world, in the sense that, such a physical contact, or physical feeling, would constitute a bridge, that is, in a sense, a physical bridge, for man to reach himself, that is, in a sense, to reach his most primitive, primordial, that is, primary, foremost, that is, in a sense, raw, natural, or physical self. That is to say, in a sense, it might be said, it is feeling, that is, the physical feeling, that is, the antean feeling, that helps man maintain himself as man, as the antean being, as the humoral being, as the human being. It is through feeling that man keeps his antean contact. It is through feeling that man reaches his antean origin. It is through feeling that man comes back to his antean beginning. It is through feeling that man is connected with his antean root. It is through feeling that man re-claims his human self. It seems, in this regard, it might be said, reason cannot do such things. Reason cannot achieve such things. Reason cannot help man reach his origin. Reason cannot help man come back to his beginning. Reason cannot help man connect with his root. Reason cannot lead man to reach himself. That is to say, it might be said, it is through feeling that man comes back to man, not reason. It is through feeling that man nurtures himself, not reason. It is through feeling that man nurses his own life, not reason. It is through feeling that man maintains himself as man, that is, as the human being, again, not reason.

If feeling is blocked, reason alone cannot sustain man; with blocked feeling, the life of man would go astray. If feeling is damaged, reason alone cannot support the existence of man; with feeling damaged, the existence of man would become shaky and unhinged. If feeling is impaired, reason alone cannot nurse man; with feeling impaired, while man might be rational, he might also be inhumoral. If

Humorality

feeling is impeded, reason alone cannot maintain man; with feeling impeded, the gevil feeling may take over man and proceed to run his life. Feeling constitutes the antean being of man. Feeling constitutes the antean life of man. Feeling constitutes the antean existence of man. It is through feeling that man comes into being. It is through feeling that man comes back to himself. It is through feeling that man comes to this world as a human being. It is through feeling that man nurses and nurtures himself, when he feels the world, as an antean being, as a humoral being, as a human being. In feeling, man lives. In feeling, man exists. In feeling, man prospers. In feeling, man thrives. In feeling, man lives as an animal. In feeling, man exists as a human being. In feeling, man prospers as man. In feeling, man thrives as a humoral being. If some problems happen to man's feeling, man has problems, and reason cannot solve them. If feeling is blocked, damaged, or impaired, man may be blocked, damaged, or impaired, and reason cannot save man. Only feeling can save man. Only feeling can help man. Only feeling can save man from his deanteanization. Only feeling can save man from his dehumoralization. Only feeling can save man from his dehumanization. Only feeling can help man to stay as man. Only feeling can help man to be man, in a time of deanteanization of man. Only feeling can help man to live as man, in a time of dehumoralization of man. Only feeling can help man to exist as a human being, that is, as a humoral being, in the age of the gevolution of man. Reason cannot save man, in this regard. Reason cannot save man, in such a sense. Reason may only make things worse, as it is detached from feeling. Reason may only direct man to the wrong direction, as it is separated from feeling. Reason may only lead man to take the wrong course, that is, the deanteanizing course, that is, the inhumoral course, that is, the gevilish or gevil course, as it is clouded or enveloped by the blocked, damaged, impaired, or impeded feeling of man.

Feeling sustains man. Feeling supports man. Feeling nurses man. Feeling maintains man. Feeling comes into being from the physical feeling. The physical feeling comes into being as the animal life comes into being. The physical feeling thus may be seen as among the most primitive or primordial activities or characteristics with regard to the animal life. The antean man is the antean feeling of man. The antean man is the antean physical feeling of man. The antean feeling of man helps man to be man. The antean physical feeling of man maintains man to be the raw, natural, and physical man. That is, the antean feeling of man is the raw feeling of man. The antean feeling of man is the natural feeling of man. The antean feeling of man is the physical feeling of man. That is, it might be said, more than anything else, the antean contact is a raw contact, the antean contact is a natural contact, the antean contact is a physical contact. That is, it might be said, more than anything else, the antean man is the raw man, the antean man is the physical man, the antean man is the natural man.

Certainly, the antean man may be seen as exercising, possessing, or enjoying not just the antean feeling or the antean physical feeling, but also the antean feelings, in the sense that, the process of the anteanization of man, that is, the process of the fulfillment or realization of the antean contact of man, may involve not just the antean feeling, the antean physical feeling, but also the antean feelings, as the human beings exist with their highly developed nervous systems. The antean feelings certainly play an important part in the anteanization of man, but, as we look into man, as feelings may be seen as coming into being from feeling, that is, in a sense, from the physical feeling, the antean feelings, in the process of the anteanization of man, may thus be seen, in a certain sense, as not that primitive, primordial, that is, primary, that is, raw, natural, or in a pure sense, physical, as the antean feeling, or, the antean physical feeling. That is to say, it might be said, in the process of the anteanization of man, the antean feeling, or the antean physical feeling, may be seen, in a sense, as constituting the backbone of such a process. In other words, it might be said, it is the antean feeling that forms the foundation of the anteanization of man, and it is the antean physical feeling that forms the bedrock of the anteanity of man. the anteanization of man is about the coming into being, cultivating, or nurturing of the antean feeling, and the life of the antean man is, more than anything else, about the coming into being, cultivating, or nurturing of the primitive, primordial, raw, or natural physical feeling. It is from such a sense that, it might be said, the antean feeling is the primitive feeling, and the antean man is the primordial man. The rational may not work as much as the physical. The rational may not contribute as much as the physical. Reason may not supply as much as feeling. It is physical. It is bodily. It is natural. It is raw. It is the physical contact. It is the bodily perception. It is the natural linkage. It is the raw feeling. It is the raw feeling of man.

Feeling is fundamental to the human being. Feeling is fundamental to the antean being of man. Feeling is fundamental to the humoral

Humorality

being or existence of man. The antean feeling of man forms the foundation of man. The antean feeling of man forms the foundation of the existence of man. The antean feeling is not reason; it is feeling. The antean feeling is not the antean reasoning; it is feeling. The anteanity of man is not the rationality of man; it is feeling. The anteanity of man is not the reasoning of man; it is feeling. It is feeling, pure, and strong. It is feeling, pure, and raw. It is feeling, pure, and natural. It is feeling, pure, and physical. It is the pure man, coming back to man. It is the raw man, coming back to himself. It is the physical man, coming back to life. It is the natural man, coming back to claim his position, his place, his status, that is, his being or existence, as the antean being, as the humoral being, as the human being.

It is in such a sense that, it might be said, feeling constitutes a significant and important faculty of man, distinct from reason. It is fundamental to man, just like reason. It is indispensable to man, just like reason. It is inseparable from man, just like reason. Just like reason, it defines man in its own ways. Just like reason, it determines man in its own senses. Just like reason, it establishes man, in its own manners. The faculty of reason and the faculty of feeling are the two important and significant functions of man. They support man in their different ways. They define man in their different senses. They maintain and sustain man through their different manners. To be man is to exercise such two faculties. To be man is to live with such two faculties. To be man is to exist with such two faculties. Both of them are necessary and indispensable to man. Both of them are inseparable from man. A human being should exercise both reason and feeling. A human being should exercise both reason and feeling in an unimpeded, unimpaired, undamaged, or unblocked way. While reason is exercised, feeling should not be ignored or overlooked. While reason is fulfilled, feeling should not be left unfulfilled. While reason is realized, feeling should not be left in such a condition that it may not be fulfilled, realized, or achieved. In a time of the deanteanization of man, feeling is especially important, as it has to do with the very foundation of the human existence. In a time of the dehumoralization of man, feeling is crucial to man, for his humoral being or existence to be healthy, sound, or firmly grounded. In an age of the gevolution of man, feeling determines man, in the sense that, either man would maintain or uphold his humoral feeling, or man would be taken over, gradually, by the gevil or gevilish feeling. In other words, as the Cage blocks, damages,

Avolution and Man

impairs, or impedes the feeling of man, in order to defeat the Cage, in order for man to be man, in order for man to exercise the faculty of feeling in a full, complete, and healthy way, human beings should strive to create the kind of conditions, the kind of environments, or the kind of situations, such that, each and every individual human being should have the opportunity or chance to live an antean life, to fulfill his or her antean longings or aspirations, to realize him- or herself as an antean being, as a humoral being, as a human being.

That is to say, the anteanization of man calls our attention on the faculty of feeling. The anteanization of man calls for the exercise of our faculty of feeling. The anteanization, or re-anteanization, of man means that, we have to look at ourselves closely, and we have to look into ourselves deeply, so that we may come to a full and complete understanding of ourselves and the situations that we are facing. Only in such a way, it seems, could we tackle the problems happening in our lives and overcome the difficulties. To anteanize man, is to lay the foundation for overcoming the Cage. To re-anteanize man is to create the conditions for man so that he may continue to live, to exist, to prosper, or to flourish as the humoral being, as the human being, that is, as the true and genuine human being. It seems, it is not easy. It seems, it is a big challenge. It may be a gigantic task that the human beings have to face, given that, it seems, certain things may not be expected, but they happen nevertheless, and certain problems may not be foreseen, but they come to the human life, after all. It seems, the human beings have no other choice. They have to face the problems. They have to stand up to the challenge. Human beings have met numerous difficulties in the past. Let us hope that, with a clear awareness of the problems that they are facing, with a full and complete exercise of their senses and faculties, human beings may overcome the difficulties, and advance safely into the future.

Feeling leads us to come into being; reason leads us to land on the moon. Feeling leads us to the humoral senses of man; reason leads us to understand the kind of things such as $E=mc^2$. Feeling leads to the humorality of man; reason leads to the rationality of man. Feeling is significant; reason is important. Feeling is important; reason is significant. Feeling enables us to feel; reason entitles us to reasoning. To feel is to be human; to reason is to be man. To be man is to feel; to be human is to reason. To be man is to exercise both feeling and reason. To be man is to depend on both feeling and reason. Man depends on both of them. Man cannot live, it seems, without either of them. The faculty of feeling and the faculty of reason, in their own ways, together, it might be said, constitute what is the human life, or, what is man. Some might say that, well, I may not need the faculty of feeling, as it is such a homely thing; I may only need reason, to survive, to exist, as a noble and dignified human being. It seems true that, what a powerful man one might be if one is equipped with reason, and what a pathetic being one might look like if one indulges in one's feelings! Yes. It seems true. But, life may not be that simple. That is, if we look deeper, and closer, we may find, life may not be that simple at all.

The wise Hume once points out, with his discerning eyes on the human beings, that, it may be the case that we may never perceive the so-called cause and effect, that is, a relationship between two things or two events that happen one after the other. Such a relationship, called causation, may be seen as representing such a phenomenon that a result or consequence (the effect) may be deemed as being caused by a prior happening or event (the cause). The kind of things such as cause and effect seem to be the daily happenings in our life, in the sense that, we, as the human beings, are so accustomed to them that, it appears, we rarely cast any doubt on the rationale or existence of their happenings. We take it to be natural or rational that, if something happens, then there must be something making or causing such a thing to happen or occur; and, if we see, or if we experience, there is always an event occurring prior to the happening of such a thing, then we usually come to the conclusion that, such an event has caused such a thing to happen. This is called causation. We live our human life in this world depending on such a recognition or conviction. In a sense, it might be said, it is the foundation upon which we manage or cope with the things happening in our daily lives. If there were no such thing as causation, or if what is called causation actually did not exist, then it seems, there must be some problems, or some big problems, for we human beings. Then, it seems, things would not hold together, things would fall apart. We human beings might not have any confidence in ourselves, in the sense that, we may not be able to foresee, to explain, or to determine any things in this world. We even might not be able to survive, as even a step moving forward might constitute a grave danger to us, since we might in no way know whether it is an ordinary step or an imminent fall off a precipice.

But, Hume does tell us, it seems, what is called causation may never be perceived by us, or, such a thing called causation might not exist as we think the way it may. Hume calls it a habit, or a custom of mind; in the sense that, he believes, such a sense of causation, or connection, or relationship, between two things or events, may only be seen as what comes into being in our minds, after we experience such kind of things many times, that is, again, again, and again. Following our repeated encountering with them, we form a habit, or a custom, in ourselves, in the sense that, we habitually think or believe, there may exist a connection or relationship between such two things or events, with the prior one as the cause and the second one as the effect. That is, it is merely a habit formed out of our daily lives; it is merely a custom coming into being out of our repeated encountering with things. Certainly, the repeated encountering with things does not necessarily give a solid ground to the kind of things that we believe. The reality may be different, and what we think or believe may be just a delusion of our minds. Is Hume right? It seems, there may be some truth in his argument, in the sense that, it appears, we do see or experience the sense of contiguous occurrence or happening of the two things or events, but, as to the connection, or the real relationship, between them, it seems, we are unable to directly experience or perceive. We can perceive a contiguous occurrence or happening in space and time, but anything more than such a perception may be seen as being reached or concluded by the mind. In other words, what is called causation may be seen, in a sense, as a habit or custom of the mind, as Hume has argued.

But, we do live our lives, it seems, everyday, depending on such a recognition or conviction that causation is real, causation is reliable, and it can form the foundation of our human existence. So, what happens here? Has the human life been based on a shaky ground, since the coming into being of the human beings? Or, is the human mind delusional, all the time? I think, the problem here runs deep and wide, and in a sense, it points to the status of feeling with regard to the human being or existence, that is, it may have to do with the significance or importance of feeling in the human life. Reason cannot replace feeling. Reason cannot play the role of feeling. Reason cannot be taken as feeling. Reason cannot form the part of man formed by feeling. Man is not just reason; man is feeling too. Man is not just formed by reason; man is also formed by feeling. Reason forms man; feeling forms man, too, in its own ways. Man is not only about reason; man is also about feeling. The rational man is not the full and complete man. The rational man is only part of man. The rational man is only part of the existence of man. If man were rational only, then man would be full of fissures, holes, or gaps. If man were rational only, then man would not have been a physical being, that is, an animal being. The rational fissures of man should be closed through the feeling of man. The rational holes of man should be filled through the feeling of man. The rational gaps of man should be stopped with the content of the feeling of man. Reason forms the rational being of man; feeling forms the physical existence of man. Reason is rational, but not physical; feeling is physical, but not rational. The rational alone cannot give rise to the physical; the physical alone cannot produce the rational. Man is the combination of the rational and the physical. Man is the coming together of the rational and the physical. Man is the integration of the rational and the physical. Man is the integration of reason and feeling. The rational fissures of man appear when man only relies on reason. The rational holes of man emerge when man is distanced from his physical being. The rational gaps of man come into being when man takes the human existence as the sole rational being, and disregards his own feeling or feelings.

Reason itself cannot bridge the gap from the rational to the physical, that is, reason alone cannot bridge the gap between the rational and the human. It needs the help of feeling. The human is more than rational. The human is rational and humoral. The human is rational and physical. That is, in a sense, without feeling, it might be said, reason cannot reach man. That is, in a sense, without feeling, it might be said, reason cannot reach the status of man. Reason cannot reach the humoral standing of man. Reason cannot reach the humoral existence of man. That is, in a sense, it might be said, without feeling, reason cannot reach the full and complete extent of man. That is, in a sense, without feeling, it might be said, reason cannot reach the full and complete extent of the human life on earth.

The rational alone may not give rise to the physical, that is, the rational alone may not give rise to the human. To be man is to be both rational and physical. To be human is to live with both reason and feeling. What is feeling? Feeling is the humoral man realized in the world. Feeling is the humoral man realized through the world. Feeling is man realized in the world. Feeling is man realized through the world. Feeling is the world realized in the humoral man. Feeling is the world realized through the humoral man. Feeling is the world realized in man.

Avolution and Man

Feeling is the world realized through man. Feeling is the interface between man and the world. Feeling is the interface between the world and man. Feeling is the bridge between man and the world. Feeling is the bridge between the world and man. Feeling is the linkage of man to the world. Feeling is the connection of the world to man. Feeling is the way through which man reaches the world. Feeling is the way through which the world comes back to man. When reason cannot bridge the gap between man and the world, feeling can. When reason cannot bridge the gap between the world and man, feeling can. When reason cannot bridge the gap between man and the world, feeling will. When reason cannot bridge the gap between the world and man, feeling will step in. When reason is incapable of linking man to the world, feeling will come to the fore. When reason falls short for a connection of the world to man, feeling will provide one.

    Feeling bridges the rational and the physical. Feeling bridges the rational and the humoral. Feeling bridges the rational and the human. Feeling leads the rational to the physical. Feeling leads the physical to the rational. Feeling leads the rational to the humoral. Feeling leads the humoral to the rational. Feeling leads the rational to the human. Feeling leads the human to the rational. Feeling leads man to reach the world. Feeling leads man to connect to the world. Feeling leads man to extend himself to the world. Feeling leads the world to extend itself into man. Feeling leads man to be part of the world. Feeling leads the world to be part of man. Feeling forms the part of man in the world. Feeling forms the part of the world in man. Feeling will close the rational fissures of man. Feeling will fill the rational holes of man. Feeling will supply what is needed for stopping the rational gaps that might appear in man, or emerge in the human life.

    The habit or custom of the mind, called by Hume in his investigation of causation, may be seen as representing, in its essence, a feeling of man; that is, such a habit or custom may only come into being in the mind after man exercises his faculty of feeling, in the sense that, such feeling of the world , that is, such two things or events happening contiguously in space and time, may gradually, or in the end, come to form a kind of position, footing, or rather, confidence, or certainty, in man; and, such a sense of confidence or certainty, having come into being not through reason but through feeling, may be seen as gradually, or in the end, giving rise to a sense of recognition or conviction in the mind, through, in a sense, a rational transformation from the feeling. That is, such a sense of recognition or conviction, that is, causation, may be seen as coming into being from feeling, though in appearance it may be seen as residing in the mind, and takes feeling, not rationalization, as its root or foundation of its human existence, though, again, it may take a rational form or appearance, that is, at least seen, deemed, or regarded by the human beings, or, the human mind. In other words, it might be said, it is in or through feeling, not reason, that the foundation of what is called causation may be found. It is feeling, that is, the human feeling, that eventually forms the ground for causation. It is feeling, that is, the human feeling, that eventually supports what is called causation.

That is, it is the feeling of man that makes the relationship of causation real, that is, reliable, that is, in a sense, it may thus form or constitute the foundation of the human life, that is, the foundation of the human existence in the world. Feeling is real, to man; in the sense that, through numerous tests or occurrences, man knows, such things would happen indeed. Feeling is reliable, in this regard, to man; in the sense that, after witnessing or experiencing so many such happenings, man knows, such things occurred in the past, they occur now, and they will happen in the future as well. Feeling thus supplies one of the cornerstones of the human life. Man comes into being; the human life thrives. What is called causation becomes part of the human existence, an important part, one might say. The ground of the human existence is not shaky; it is stable and sound, with the help of the human feeling. The human mind is not delusional, after all, as it is nurtured and supported by the human feeling.

Feeling, after all, it seems, is not that humble, or even, useless, or pathetic. It is strong. It is powerful. It is crucial. It is vital. It is significant. It can accomplish great things. It is so important that, it seems, without it, the human existence may not be realized. It is so essential that, it seems, without it, the relationship called causation may not even stand. The human life needs feeling. The human life needs the support of feeling. The human existence needs the exercise of the faculty of feeling. The exercise of the faculty of feeling may be seen, in a sense, in the development of science. People sometimes talk about the role that intuition plays in the development of science. And, in a sense, they are quite right in pointing out that, it seems, intuition has played a significant or crucial role in the coming about of the great scientific discoveries. What is intuition? It might be said, it is a feeling, though, a sharp feeling; that is, a feeling so sharp that, it seems, it feels, or reaches, what reason cannot. That is to say, intuition may be seen as a sense, or kind, of feeling that is capable of reaching out to the kind of things that may be too distant for reason to reach, or too clouded for reason to have a clear grasp, or too concealed or deeply buried that reason alone, it seems, can in no way overcome the obstacles in-between and reach them. Feeling, that is, such a sense of sharp feeling, may be seen as possessing some qualities or characteristics that reason may not be equipped with, such as, a direct physical contact with things without the mediation of reason, or, a feeling triggered by such a kind of direct physical contact that may involve things both rational and physical, especially the physical, or, a feeling characterized as instantaneous, as a result of such a kind of direct physical contact, with little or no contribution from a process that may be called rationalization.

The sharpness of such a sense of sharp feeling may be seen as coming from the fact that, in some sense, in some way, or through some manner, such a feeling is being involved, or associated, with some form of direct physical contact with things and it is such a sense of direct physical contact with things that, it might be said, eventually, may be seen as giving rise to the kind of directness, or instantaneousness, or depth, that may be seen as usually associated with such a kind of sharp feeling. The direct physical contact with things may be seen as giving rise to the sharpness of such a sharp feeling in the sense that, it triggers, or stimulates, or revives, somehow, the physical feeling that lies at the very bottom of the human feeling, on some special occasions, or in some special circumstances or situations, such as, after a long period of meditation, or, while one is in a pensive mood, or in a concentrated contemplating state. The physical feeling, unlike reason, can directly feel or perceive the world, and out of its own very nature, can feel or perceive the kind of things existing in the world that reason may not be able to access. With the coming into being of the human nervous system, and with the development of the human beings, such a sense of physical feeling is sometimes replaced or superseded, to some extent, in the human beings, by a new form of feeling coming out of the developmental process which may be called, the mental feeling. Certainly, as we all know, it would be difficult, or, in a sense, almost impossible, to clearly separate the physical feeling from the mental feeling in the human beings, as such two things are intimately connected through the brain in the human beings, in complex ways.

The physical or bodily sensing organs, such as the eyes, the ears, the nose, the tongue, or the skin, are connected closely with the brain, and thus any sensing activity, even an act of the simplest physical feeling, may be seen as involving, inevitably, some sense or some form of mental activity in the nervous system. That is to say, while the physical feeling may be seen as still remaining in the human beings, as a function, or as an aspect or part of the human feeling that is accomplished by or through the physical or bodily organs, we have to keep in mind that, its existence and the mental feeling are closely related with each other. On the other hand, with the coming into being of a highly developed nervous system in the human beings, the integration of the physical feeling and the human nervous system may have enhanced, in some sense, in some way, the capability of the physical feeling to feel or perceive things, that is, to truly feel or perceive things in the world. Such an enhanced capability of the physical feeling in the human beings may mean that, sometimes, the human beings may be able to feel or perceive certain things in the world, that is, through their physical feeling, that may not be possibly felt or perceived by other life forms, such as, sponges. That is, the physical feeling, combined or integrated with the human nervous system, may be capable of performing certain functions, in the human beings, that may not be regarded, purely, at least on the surface, as physical in their nature. In other words, the feeling acquired or obtained by or through the physical feeling in the human beings may, sometimes, reach deep and wide into things far beyond what a purely physical feeling may be usually expected to accomplish. Such may be seen in the case of the kind of feeling, or, the kind of sharp feeling that may be called intuition.

The revival or reactivation of the physical feeling, in a human being, on some occasions, or in some circumstances, may enable the human being to utilize or employ all the feeling instincts, accumulated through a long human developmental process, to focus on the problems or issues that are being concentrated on. That is, the revival or reactivation of the physical feeling may represent, in a sense, the revival or reactivation of all the feeling abilities in a human being, both physical and mental, in the sense that, all such feelings would come to work, as the physical feeling leads the way for the human being to come into the world. That is, the physical feeling, in such a case, or in such a sense, would constitute a bridge between such a human being and the world, in the sense that, having been revived or reactivated through some sense or some form of direct physical contact with things, the physical feeling in such a human being would form a physical connection between such a human being and the world, in such a way that such a human being would be physically connected with the world, and, in a sense, become one with the world. As the most primitive, primordial, or raw feeling of a human being, the revived or reactivated physical feeling leads the human being to connect with the world in the most primitive, primordial, or raw way, that is, in the physical way, that is, in such a way that such a human being would be enabled to feel, that is, to perceive, in a sense, or at some moment, the deepest or most hidden workings or operations of the world, that is, to reach, in a sense, or at some moment, the deepest or most hidden secrets of the world, as such a human being and the world are being one, and such an oneness would provide such a human being with some rare access into the world which he or she might not be able to enjoy otherwise.

The primitiveness, primordiality, or rawness of the physical feeling revived, or reactivated, makes such a sharp feeling sharp. The oneness, coming into being through the physical feeling, or through the revival or reactivation of the physical feeling, gives such a sharp feeling depth, directness, or instantaneousness. Without the physical feeling, the mental feeling may not get deep into things. Without the physical feeling, the mental feeling may not have the route to penetrate into things. Without the physical feeling, the mental feeling may not be able to form oneness with the world. It is through the physical feeling that the mental feeling penetrates into the world. It is through the physical feeling that the mental feeling comes into oneness with the world. Without the coming into being of the oneness of the human being and the world, it seems, no matter how powerful the mental feeling might be, it may not be able to penetrate so deeply into things. Without such a sense of oneness, it seems, the mental feeling may not reach things in such a direct or instant way; that is, it may be blocked, it may be clouded, it may lack the means to overcome the difficulties and feel or reach anything. With the coming into being of the oneness of the human being and the world, the mental feeling is provided with the opportunity, or possibility, to strive, in a concentrated state, with the

Humorality

guide or help of the physical feeling, to comprehend or grasp some of the hidden secrets in such a world, that is, in such an oneness, and, with a direct physical bridge built for such a purpose by or through the physical feeling, the mental feeling may be seen as being capable of doing so, at last, in some circumstances or situations, or, at some rare moments.

That is, it is through the physical feeling that the mental feeling may be seen as coming to comprehend, or grasp, some of the deep secrets of the world, in an instant, or, in a direct way. The instantaneousness of such a sharp feeling may be seen as coming from the instant coming into being of the oneness between the human being and the world. The directness of such a sharp feeling may also be seen as coming from such an oneness in the sense that, with the coming into being of such an oneness, it might be said, there may be, in a sense, little or no barriers or obstacles existing between such a human being and the world, and the feeling instincts of such a human being, that is, all the feeling instincts, both physical and mental, may be seen as enjoying a sense of unprecedented freedom, unimpeded, unrestricted, in feeling, perceiving, that is, reaching all the things within such an oneness, that is, within such a human being and the world. Certainly, in the same sense, the depth demonstrated by such a sharp feeling may also be seen as coming from such an oneness, in the sense that, with the coming into being of such an oneness, with little or no barriers or obstacles existing between such a human being and the world, the feeling instincts would feel, perceive, that is, reach, almost anywhere or anything in such a world, that is, in such an oneness, that is, in such circumstances or situations, or, at such moments. That is to say, it seems, the covering of things might disappear, the veil might vanish, the clouds might evaporate, and some of the deeply buried secrets of the world might be exposed, or revealed, to the feelings, that is, to such a human being.

This may be seen as the coming into being of what is called intuition. This may be seen as the workings or operations of such a sharp feeling that may be called intuition. The raw, primitive, primordial physical feeling, with regard to the sharp feeling called intuition, has to be triggered, or revived, by some sense or form of direct physical contact with things. So, what may be regarded as such direct physical contact with things? Let us take a look at the development of science and pay attention to the real happenings associated with the great scientific discoveries. It is said that, while Newton retired to his country home, he saw an apple falling from the tree, and this led him to connect the gravitational force with the inner nature of the world. Is this an example of the direct physical contact with things? Yes. It is. That is, it was this incident, a real seeing, a direct observation, a bodily encounter, a physical contact, that might have triggered or revived the raw, primitive, or primordial physical feeling in Newton. He might not have noticed the great impact imposed on him by such an incident at the moment, but, his body knew, his person knew, his feeling knew, that is, his physical person knew, his physical feeling knew. His bodily senses would be triggered. His physical feeling would be aroused. His physical instincts would be stimulated. His bodily existence would be set in motion. He would be connected with the world, in a feeling way, in a physical way, in a physical feeling way. He would come into one with the world. He would be one with the world. In such a state, he was the world, and the world was him. In such a state, he was in the world, and the world was in him. The secrets of the world would be within his feeling. The secrets of the world would be within his reach. The workings or operations of the world would be within his feeling. The workings or operations of the world would be in his feeling. The workings or operations of the world would be within his reach, in such a sense, or, in such a state. He could now feel the world. He could now perceive the world. He could now reach some of the deepest secrets of the world.

He was Newton now. He was now the human person who came into the world. He was now the human person who felt or perceived some of the deepest secrets of the world. He was now the genius to whom the world would be exposed or revealed. The direct and physical contact of Newton with the world, through a direct and physical encounter with the falling apple from a tree, brought Newton, instantly, into a complete oneness with the world that he had contemplated for a long time. He could now come into this world. He could now feel the world. He could now touch the world. He could feel its movements. He could touch its pulses. While he felt the world, the world felt him. While he touched the world, the world touched him. While he felt the movements of the world, the world moved him. The movements of the world were in his feeling. The nature of the world was in his feeling. His feeling was the feeling of the world. His feeling was part of the world. His person was part of the world. His bodily encounter with the falling apple ignited his physical feeling. His physical feeling of the falling apple and the tree led to his physical feeling of the existence of the world. The existence of the world came into his feeling. The nature of the world came into his feeling. The movements of the world came into his feeling. Thus, the secrets of the world were not alien to him. Thus, the workings or operations of the world were not strange to him. They were part of the world. They were part of the oneness of his being and the world. That is, they were part of his existence, at the moment. Thus, he could feel things deep down. Thus, he could touch things hidden. Thus, he could discover or unveil things that others might not be able to. He could feel that something was behind the falling apple. He could feel that something was pulling it down. He could feel it. He could almost touch it. It was the force. It was the gravitational force!

Feeling led Newton to the gravitational force. Feeling directed Newton to the gravitational force. Feeling led Newton to the falling apple. Feeling led Newton to the falling of the apple. Feeling led Newton to the universal gravitational force. Feeling led Newton to one of the greatest discoveries of mankind. It was not reason. It was feeling. It was feeling that led to all such things. Reason can infer, but it could not make such a big jump. Reason can deduce, but it could never give rise to such a great leap forward. It was a huge jump. It was a gigantic leap. It was a magnificent discovery made by a human being. Reason could help, but it would not open a new door for Newton. Reason could help, but it would not point a new direction for Newton. Reason could help, but it would not awake Newton to the universality of the universal gravitational force. It was a great opening made by feeling. It was a great awakening kindled by feeling. It was a great achievement accomplished with the help or contribution of feeling. Feeling was crucial here. Feeling was vital here. Feeling was of the utmost importance to Newton's discovery of the universal gravitational force. Only feeling could feel the universality of the universal gravitational force. Only feeling could perceive the universality of the universal gravitational force. Only feeling could reach the universality of the universal gravitational force. Only feeling could lead Newton to such a feeling. Only feeling could lead Newton to such a perception. Only feeling could lead Newton to come to such a conclusion. It was the power of feeling. It was the strength of feeling. It was the capacity of feeling. It was the potential of feeling. It was the expansiveness of feeling. It was the depth of feeling. It was the magnificence of feeling. It was the greatness of feeling. It was the faculty of feeling!

Feeling lies at the beginning of the great discoveries. Feeling lies at the beginning of the great progresses made by the human beings. Such may be seen as in the case of Newton, and such may be seen in the cases related to other great people. It is said, Einstein was fascinated from his early childhood with the compass. He was fascinated with the compass in the sense that, he was drawn to what might be behind the compass. Was it a force? Was it something real which we could not see? Was it something beyond our human perception? Was it something out of our human awareness? What was it? Why did it exist? How? In what sense? In what way? Through what kind of manner? This feeling might have led Einstein to delve deep into the world. This feeling might have led Einstein to look into the things that others might not bother to mind. This feeling might have led Einstein to take a fresh look at space and time. This feeling might have led Einstein to take a fresh look at energy, matter, and gravity. This feeling might have led Einstein to come to the conclusion that, the speed of light is constant. This feeling might have led Einstein to the discovery of the theory of relativity. Certainly, other things might have undoubtedly contributed to the development of the theory of relativity. But, the fact that Einstein was fascinated with the compass from his early childhood, with strong and powerful feeling coming out of such a fascination, should not be underestimated in the process of the coming into being of the theory of relativity. Such a strong and powerful feeling gave Einstein, as a scientist, confidence to go deeper, to search wider, or to leap higher. That is, it might be said, it was such a strong and powerful feeling, or similar kind of feeling developed or emerged later in Einstein's life, that might have enabled Einstein to postulate, eventually, that, the speed of light is constant, independent of the frame of reference of the observer. That is, in a sense, this kind of feeling may be seen as what happened when Einstein penetrated into space and time, or searched into energy, matter, or gravity, through a direct, instant, and sharp feeling which in itself might be regarded as coming into being through a physical feeling of Einstein with the world, as he came into a complete oneness with the world while in his concentrated contemplation or meditation, at some moment, as a result or consequence of some sense or form of direct physical contact with things, such as, an encounter with a compass. In other words, such kind of strong or powerful feeling, occurring or happening in Einstein, might have led him to see into the world, that is, into space, time, energy, matter, or gravity, and directed him to the eventual possibility that, the speed of light may be constant.

It is in such a sense, it might be said, the coming into being of the theory of relativity may be better seen, in a sense, as an attempt, on the part of Einstein, to prove such a feeling, that is, to prove the remarkable validity of such a feeling, that is, to prove the magnificent expansiveness or depth of such a feeling. Einstein did it. Einstein proved such a feeling. Einstein proved such a remarkable feeling that had led him to the discovery of the inner relationships of the world governing, among other things, space, time, energy, matter, and gravity. Einstein proved that such a feeling was true. Einstein proved that such a feeling was valid. Einstein proved that, such a feeling was right. Einstein proved that, such a feeling truly worked. If Einstein did not have such a feeling, only reason at his disposal, could he make such a big discovery? Probably not. Reason could not leap from space to time to energy to matter to gravity, or to the speed of light. The gaps between or among them were too big, and there were too many of them. Reason, it seems, could hardly make such big jumps. That is, for reason to connect all of them, for reason to integrate all of them, for reason to delve into the depths of their existence, it needed the help of feeling. It needed feeling to connect, first, all of them together. It needed feeling to integrate, first, all of them together. It needed feeling to delve, first, into the depths of their existence.

That is, in other words, in a sense, it might be said, it was feeling that first discovered, that is, feeled, that is, perceived, that is, reached, the deep relationships of the world expounded in the theory of relativity; it was not reason. It was feeling that, first, discovered that the speed of light is constant. It was feeling that, first, feeled or perceived that space, time, energy, matter, and gravity are intricately and intrinsically connected with each other. It was not reason. Reason was what followed. Reason was what followed feeling. Reason was what followed feeling after feeling pointed out the direction. Reason was what followed feeling after feeling had feeled the things. Reason was what followed feeling after feeling had taken the lead. Reason came to work, after feeling pointed out the direction. Reason came to work, after feeling led the way. Reason came to work, after feeling had feeled or perceived, or reached, the workings or operations of things. Reason came to prove what feeling feeled was rightly there. Reason came to prove what feeling feeled was valid. Reason came to prove what feeling reached was true. Reason came to prove what feeling reached was truly valid. Reason thus reached high. Reason thus accomplished one of the greatest achievements of mankind. Reason jumped. Reason leaped. It was a leap. It was a great leap. It was a great leap of reason. Such a leap of reason was not a leap in the dark; it was assisted or helped by a strong and powerful feeling. Such a leap of reason was possible, only because such a feeling was deep, wide, and sharp. Such a leap of reason was possible, only because such a feeling originated from a complete oneness with the world. Reason alone cannot make such a leap; feeling formed the bridge. Reason alone cannot make such a jump; feeling paved the way.

That is, in a sense, it might be said, the theory of relativity may be seen as an attempt to prove what feeling had feeled before reason. It may be an attempt to prove such a feeling that the speed of light may be constant. It may be an attempt to prove such a feeling that all the things of the world may be essentially connected. It may be an attempt to prove such a feeling that space, time, and the speed of light may be related to each other. It may be an attempt to prove such a feeling that energy, matter, and gravity may be the manifestations of the same thing. It was a great feeling. It was a great sharp feeling. It was a great opening. It was so sharp a feeling that the world opened, suddenly. It was so sharp a feeling that the workings or operations of the universe were exposed, in an instant. It was so sharp a feeling that mankind was thus able to see into the deep secrets of the world.

Feeling is the trailblazer; reason follows. Feeling is the initiator; reason follows to do the work. Such may be seen in the development of the theory of relativity by Einstein. Such may be seen in the coming into being of Newton's discovery of the universal gravitational force and the law of gravitation. Such may also be seen in the development of the theory of evolution. Darwin sailed around the world. Out of such a rich experience, a feeling might come into being in Darwin that, it appears, something might be behind the development of the various species. It might be the instincts for survival. It might be the survival of the fittest. The theory of evolution might thus come into being. Was the theory of evolution a product deduced from some principles? It seems, no. It was not from some deduction. It was from the wide-ranged observation. Was the theory of evolution based on a rigid process of rationalization? It seems, no. It was based on the data and facts collected throughout the world, and tested, or corroborated by numerous cases or experiments. So, is the theory of evolution valid, as a theory? Why should it be valid, after all, as a scientific theory, as it was not deduced from some principles or through a process of rationalization? In a sense, it might be said, the validity of the theory of evolution may be seen as being based on a feeling; in the sense that, such a feeling was so strong, so powerful, so wide-ranged, and so rich with facts and data that, it seems, to claim the contrary was almost impossible. That is, in other words, the theory of evolution may be seen as coming into being from a process that is usually called induction. Is induction valid? Or, is induction not valid? People have argued about induction for a long time, with some favoring it, and others criticizing such a method or process severely. Hume once points out, it appears, it is impossible to completely justify induction. And in a sense, it seems true, as the process of the inductive reasoning may not be regarded as rigid, or strictly rational, as the deductive reasoning. Yes, it is true. The process of induction may prove to be unreliable, sometimes, or, in the end. So, why should we still use or employ it? Why should we still have to do things in such an inductive way? Hume seems to tell us, we have to. We have to rely, once in a while, on induction to live our lives, to exist as the human beings. Our human experience may be limited, and we have to be practical, as we have no other options to draw our conclusions or make our arguments.

The problem of induction may be seen, in a sense, as a problem only in a rational sense; that is, in the sense that, reason is taken as the only way leading to the validity of things. Feeling is forgotten. Feeling is not treated as a valid way leading to things, or, justifying things. But, alas, it seems, we have forgotten, even we ourselves may be seen as coming into being, in a sense, from feeling, or through feeling. Is feeling a valid way leading to things? Yes, it seems, feeling led to man. Is feeling a valid way justifying things? Yes, it seems, feeling justifies man. The humoral feeling justifies the humoral man. The humoral feeling justifies the humoral senses or instincts of man. The humoral feeling justifies the humoral values or principles of man. Is feeling capable of giving rise to things? Yes, it seems, feeling gives rise to the existence of man. Feeling gives rise to the being of man. Feeling gives rise to the life of man. Feeling gives rise to the everyday happenings or occurrences associated with man. Should feeling be introduced into the life of man? Yes. Should feeling be allowed to come into the existence of man? Yes. Should feeling be regarded as part of the being of man? Yes. If feeling is introduced into the life of man, then the problem of induction may not be a big problem, as feeling may supply the missing links in the inductive reasoning. The process of induction may not be seen as just a process of reasoning; it may also be seen as a process of feeling. If feeling is allowed to come into the existence of man, then, just like reason, feeling may also be qualified to guide man to the right things. If feeling is to be regarded as part of the being of man, then induction, being part of the being of man, should be regarded, or treated, as necessarily, that is, inseparably, associated, or connected, with feeling, that is, with the faculty of feeling of man.

In a sense, it might be said, it is feeling that fuses induction with man. It is feeling that fuses induction with the existence of man. It is feeling that fuses induction with the being of man. It is feeling that fuses induction with the life of man. Otherwise, it seems, there would have been no such thing as induction; in the sense that, as feeling disappeared, induction might have necessarily vanished, as the final or crucial step of induction may be seen as being made of feeling, but not reason. That is, in a sense, it might be said, it is feeling that gives rise to induction. It is feeling that leads to induction. It is feeling that makes induction come into being. That is, it is feeling that sustains induction; it is feeling that upholds induction; it is feeling that supports induction. That is, it might be said, it is feeling that, ultimately, makes the process of induction valid.

Reason alone cannot give rise to man. Reason alone cannot lead to man. Reason alone cannot make man come into being. Reason alone cannot form man. Reason alone cannot form the whole man. Reason alone cannot support man. Reason alone cannot sustain man. Reason alone cannot uphold man. Reason alone cannot support the whole man. Reason alone cannot sustain the whole man. Reason alone cannot uphold the whole man. Reason alone cannot form the whole human life. Reason alone cannot support the whole human life. Reason alone cannot sustain the whole human life. Reason alone cannot uphold the whole human life. The whole man needs both reason and feeling. The whole human life needs both reason and feeling. The whole man means both reason and feeling. The whole human life means both reason and feeling. The whole man means the exercise of both reason and feeling. The whole human life means the exercise of both reason and feeling. If man were taken to mean only reason, then, man might not have come into being, and induction might not be seen as existing at all. If the human life were taken to mean only a rational process or a deductive reasoning, then, it might be said, what is called the human life might not have existed, and the kind of things such as rationality or deduction might not have possessed any meaning at all, at least, in so far as we can see, or perceive, as the human beings.

That feeling may be seen as supporting, sustaining, or giving rise to the validity of induction may not be seen as a tentative or temporary arrangement, as if something essential, indispensable, intrinsic, or fundamental may be lacking, due to some unknown reasons in the process of what is called the inductive reasoning. No. That should not be regarded or treated as such. That the validity of induction arises, eventually, from feeling, but not reason, may be seen as what really happens in the world; that is, that may be the true workings or operations of the world; that is, in a sense, it might be said, that may be what the world is truly made of. In other words, the validity of induction may be seen as part of the validity of the world, or, part of the existence of the world, which, as we all know thus far from our discussion, may not be justified, validated, explained, demonstrated, or established by or through reason alone. In a sense, it might be said, the validity of induction may be seen as the coming into being or existence of induction, and the validity of the world may be seen as the coming into being or existence of the world; in the sense that, the coming into being of induction may be seen as the coming into being of induction in our feeling, as it is our feeling, not reason, that introduces such a process into our life, or establishes its presence in our existence. The validity or existence of the world has to be justified, or demonstrated, through both reason and feeling; in the sense that, the validity or existence of induction may have to be validated or established through both reason and feeling.

Reason provides the framework; feeling produces the content. Reason erects the structure; feeling forms the foundation. Reason provides part of the rationale; feeling supplies the rest. Together, reason and feeling bring forth the rationale of induction. Together, reason and feeling uphold the validity of induction. Together, reason and feeling bring the presence or existence of induction into the world. Is it unusual that the rationale of induction has to be supplied by both reason and feeling? No. is it uncommon that the validity of induction has to be

Avolution and Man

sustained by both reason and feeling? No. Is it surprising that the existence or presence of induction has to be initiated or established in the world through both reason and feeling? No. Is it strange or odd that the world has to be supported, or explained, by or through both reason and feeling? No. It is not strange. It is not odd. It is not surprising. This may be exactly what the world should be. This may be exactly what the world looks like. This may be exactly what the world has to be. This may be exactly what the world stands to us.

The world is not just about deduction; it may be more about production. The human life is not just about deducing; it may be more about producing. Man may not be just about being deductive; he may be more about being productive. To deduce, in a sense, is to reduce. The process of deduction, in a sense, is a process of reduction. The deductive reasoning, in a sense, is a reductive reasoning. That is why, when reason is taken as the only way of the world, when feeling is ignored, while some rational truths may be reached, but the world is wrecked, the human life is being rendered redundant, and man is being reduced, eventually, to nothingness. Induction, in a sense, may be seen as a process of production, or growth; in the sense that, while the conclusion may not be seen as being deduced through a rigid process of rationalization, it may be seen as being supported and upheld by or through the feeling, and, as such, new things may be seen as being reached, new grounds may be opened, and new horizons may be revealed, that is, the world may be enriched, the world may be widened, and the world may be expanded.

The world is rich. Life is rich. Man is rich. The world is diverse. Life is vibrant. Man is colorful. The world is abundant. Life is profuse. Man is creative. The world is boundless. The human life is splendid. Man is magnificent. The world needs to produce. The world means to produce. The world means to generate, to create, to give rise to things. The world means growth, expansion, multiplication, and development. Deduction, in a sense, may be too limited. To just deduce, in a sense, may be too narrow. The deductive reasoning, in a sense, may be too restricted. That is, to deduce, in a sense, may be too finite for the world. Deduction, in a sense, may be inadequate for life. The deductive reasoning, in a sense, may be insufficient for man to live or exist in the world. In other words, it might be said, the world needs induction. The word needs to induce. The world needs the inductive reasoning. Or, it might be said, the world means induction; the world means to induce;

the world means the inductive reasoning. That is, in other words, it might be said, the world means induction playing a crucial part in the existence of things, or, the world means induction playing a significant role in the human life. The world means the inductive reasoning supported, maintained, sustained, or upheld by both reason and feeling, especially, in a sense, by feeling. Feeling gives rise to man. Feeling gives rise to the human life. Feeling gives rise to meaning. Feeling gives rise, in this case, it might be said, to the process that is called induction. Should the process of induction be regarded as an exercise of reason? Yes. It should. But, when it comes to the vital parts of such a process, when it comes to the crucial steps of such a process, when it comes to what it is truly made of, it might be said, the process of induction may be better seen as an exercise of feeling, that is, an exercise of the faculty of feeling of man.

I am always pleased to see Hume discussing things, calm, learned, balanced, incisive, and yet deep down, underlined with a rare sense of philosophical humor. Hume understands things. Hume knows things. Hume did not live just as a philosopher; he lived as a man. He knew what he was doing as a philosopher, and at the same time, he had not lost his sense of what man is, what life should be, and what the human existence means in this world. A philosopher should live like Hume, think like Hume, write like Hume, and reason like Hume. To philosophize does not necessarily mean just to reason. To philosophize means more than reasoning. To philosophize means to lead people on a way to a true sense of man, to the wisdom of life, and to a real understanding of the world. That means, while a philosopher exercises the faculty of reason, he or she should not lose sight of the world, to such an extent that, he or she would be misled by reason and fail to take notice of anything else. The mind should not be blinded by reason; in the sense that, the mind of a philosopher should not be taken over by reason, as, without the nurture, support, and guide of the heart, that is, the feelings or contents of man, the cold, contentless, and detached reason may only lead man to his emptiness or nothingness, that is, eventually, to his demise. Such may have been, in a sense, what is happening now around us, as the sound senses of man are disregarded, the natural feelings of man are abused, and the human beings are being deanteanized and dehumoralized.

In a sense, it might be said, it is the philosophers, occupied only with reason, who had paved the way for the deanteanization and dehumoralization of man, that is, for the gevolution of man. Hume, on the other hand, tries strenuously to lead us to see the simple, plain things of life, which some seemingly nobler philosophers, or some of us, may not deign to take a look. It is the simple, plain things of life that constitute the foundation of the human life. It is the simple, plain things of life that form the foundation of the human existence. Hume's unyielding commonsensical understanding of man, of life, or of the world may thus be seen as invaluable and precious, especially in the age of the gevolution of man, as, it might be said, it is exactly such simple, plain, down-to-earth, and homely things in our life that are being eroded, undermined, dismantled, or destroyed today. The antean feelings of man are not simple. The human feelings are not plain. The common senses of man are not homely. They are noble. They are vital. They are essential. They are indispensable. They should be treated with respect. They should be treated with care. They should be celebrated equally, just like other noble things, such as reason. Hume, in this regard, really stands out. As a philosopher coming out of the analytical tradition, Hume's humanness endures, and his common sense shines.

Feeling and reason are the two ways through which we live in the world. Feeling and reason are the two ways through which we come to this world. Feeling and reason are the two ways through which we exist in this world. While we follow reason, we also have to follow feeling. While we live with reason, we also have to live with feeling. Reason and feeling together make us. Feeling and reason together form us. Reason and feeling together enable us to come into being. Feeling and reason together enable us to be the human being. Together, reason and feeling support the human life. Together, feeling and reason maintain, sustain, or uphold a process that is called, induction. Thus, Darwin was able to draw his conclusions. Thus, Darwin was able to advance the human understanding of the world. Feeling made man man. Feeling made Darwin Darwin. Feeling made Einstein Einstein. Feeling made Newton Newton. Feeling makes man man, with the contribution of reason. Feeling makes the great scientific discoveries possible, with the help of reason. Is feeling important? Yes. Is feeling indispensable? Yes. Is feeling crucial to man? Yes. Is feeling fundamental to the world? Yes. Even in the field of science, we have seen, it might be said, in a sense, it seems, feeling is of the utmost importance. If feeling had not opened the new door, reason might not have seen the way. If feeling had not blazed a new trail, reason might not have found the route. If

Humorality

feeling had not pointed out the direction, reason might not have known where to go.

Feeling opens the door; reason follows and comes in. Feeling points out the direction; reason takes the course. Feeling breaks the ground; reason erects the edifice. Science develops, not just through reason, but also with feeling leading the way. The great scientific discoveries emerge, with feeling and reason hand in hand. Science, it appears, is not just about reason; it is also about feeling. Science, it appears, is not just about the work of reason; it is also about the work of feeling. Reason contributes to the development of science; feeling contributes in its own ways. Reason drives the development of science; feeling drives in its own manners. Feeling and reason, together, make the development of science possible. Feeling and reason, together, make science possible. In the realm of reason, feeling is not excluded; it has an important role to play. In the realm of reason, it seems, feeling also rules high. Is it strange? No. Is it odd? No. Is it surprising? Certainly, no. It is man that exercises reason. It is man that exercises feeling. It is man that gives rise to reason. It is man that gives rise to feeling. It is man who exercises reason so that science may develop. It is man who exercises feeling so that the world and man may come together. Reason reaches the world through man; man reaches the world through feeling. Reason and feeling are thus, in a sense, inseparable, in reaching the world. To talk about reason, in a sense, is to talk about man. To talk about man, in a sense, is to talk about feeling. To talk about feeling, in a sense, is to talk about the coming together of the world and man. Science is the understanding of the world by man; that is, in a sense, science is the understanding happening in the coming into being of the coming together of the world and man. That is, to talk about reason, in a sense, is to talk about the feeling of man; that is, to talk about science, in a sense, is to talk about the feeling that happens in both the world and man.

Newton had a feeling, that led him to the universal gravitation. Einstein had a feeling, that led him to the secrets of relativity. Darwin had a feeling, that led him to the world of evolution. How many feelings have been feeled? How many feelings have been sensed? How many feelings have not been feeled? How many feelings have not been perceived? How many feelings have been missed? How many feelings have been ignored? How many feelings have been bypassed? How many feelings have eluded us? How many feelings have been lost?

What kind of understanding may not have been attained, by us, about the world, as a result? What kind of perception of the world may not have been reached, by us, as a result? What kind of grasp of the world may not have been achieved, by us, as a result? What kind of awareness of the world may have been lost, as a result? What kind of sensitivity toward the world may have vanished or disappeared, as a result? Is it possible that, we can no longer feel the kind of feelings that our ancestors could? Is it possible that, we can no longer feel the kind of feelings that our ancestors held dear, precious, or special? Is it possible that, we can no longer feel the kind of feelings that, once, constituted the core, fundamental, essential, or indispensable life of our ancestors? Feeling connects man with the world. Feeling links the human beings with nature. Feeling joins the human species to the universe. That is why, through feeling, Darwin looked into the world. That is why, through feeling, Einstein saw into the world. That is why, through feeling, Newton felt into the universe. That is why, it might be said, our ancestors could feel, through feeling, in a sense, the workings or operations of the world, such as, the harmonic developments, the celestial movements, or, the cosmic progresses.

The harmonic elegance, the celestial beauty, or the cosmic wonders may be beyond, in a sense, the grasp of reason, and, for the human beings to fully grasp them, or their existence, they may need the help of their feeling. With regard to our early ancestors, two things may be said. On the one hand, reason may be seen as having not been so fully, in a sense, exercised. On the other hand, people in the early times might not have been so distanced from themselves, that is, from their feeling or feelings, as the modern humans may by their so-called modern civilization. That is to say, it might be said, our early ancestors may be seen, in a sense, as more closely associated, or connected, with their feeling or feelings. This may explain, in a sense, why our early ancestors could feel, sense, or perceive, the kind of things in the workings or operations of the world, such as, the harmonic developments, the celestial movements, the cosmic progresses, or, the harmonic elegance, the celestial beauty, or the cosmic wonders. As the human beings develop, it seems, they are being more and more distanced from their early selves, that is, from their early primitive, primordial, physical, or raw feeling or feelings. As such, it might be said, they may have lost, though unknown to themselves, in a certain sense, some of the basic, fundamental, primitive, primordial, or raw

Humorality

ways of access to the world, to the universe, or to themselves. Such primitive, primordial, or raw feeling or feelings may be seen as constituting the primitive, primordial, or raw, that is, basic, or fundamental connection between the human beings and the world. As our early ancestors had not been so distanced from their such feeling or feelings, they may be seen as being able, through such a primitive, raw, or fundamental bridge, to feel the world around them, to sense the universe in which they were living, and to perceive themselves as they were, that is, as the human beings.

That is, they could see, in a sense, into the workings or operations of the world, in a primitive, primordial, raw, or basic, fundamental way. They could feel, in a sense, the harmonic developments of the world, and show their considerations for them. They could sense, in a sense, the celestial movements, admire them, and regard them with reverence. They could look up to the cosmic wonders, perceive, in a sense, what might be behind such wonders, and honor them. That is to say, in other words, to our early ancestors, the harmonic elegance, the celestial beauty, and the cosmic wonders were not just the elegance, beauty, or wonders; they were the integral or vital parts of the human life, or, the intrinsic or inherent parts of existence in the world, or, in the universe. The harmonic elegance was significant to man; the celestial beauty was noteworthy for the human life; the cosmic wonders were meaningful to the being or existence in the universe. Together, with the human life, they constituted the existence of things in the world, or, in this universe. Man is but a part of existence in the world. The human life is but a part of life existing in the universe. To understand man, one has to understand the world. To see into man, one has to see into the universe. To make sense of man, one has to make sense of all the things in the world. To grasp man, one has to grasp all the existence in the universe. To see the full picture of man, one has to see the full picture of the world. To see the full picture of the human life, one has to see the full picture of life in the world. To see the full picture of the human existence, one has to see the full picture of the existence in the universe. When the human beings are distanced from their feeling or feelings, the human beings are distanced from their early selves. When the human beings are distanced from their early primitive, primordial, physical, or raw feeling or feelings, they may be unable to connect with the world, with the universe, or with themselves, and they may be unable to see the full picture of the world, the full picture of the

Avolution and Man

universe, or, that is, in a sense, the full picture of life, or, the full picture of man.

In a sense, it might be said, while reason is reliable, usually, feeling is sometimes unreliable. That is true. So, how could one exercise the faculty of feeling, as opposed to the exercise of the faculty of reason? Or, what is the meaning of such an exercise? Or, why, in this world, should one exercise the so-called faculty of feeling? If feeling is sometimes not reliable, does it mean that, feeling is not important? No. Feeling is important. Feeling is vital and essential to man. Feeling constitutes the foundation of man. Feeling constitutes the foundation of the human life. In a sense, it might be said, man is made of feeling; or, the human life is made of feeling; or, the human existence is made of feeling. The fluidity or elusiveness of feeling may, in a sense, represent, embody, or stand for the fluidity or elusiveness of the world, or, of man, that is, the complexity, intricacy, or depth of the world, or, of man. If feeling were like reason, reliable, solid, rigid, definite, in all the ways or senses, then, it seems, the world would have been nothing but a machine, and man would have been nothing but a robot. All the workings or operations of the world would then be revealed, and all the senses or ways of man would then be dissected and analyzed. Would there be anything left for the world so that it would remain limitless, inexhaustible, or interesting? Maybe not much. Would there be anything left for man to hold on so that he could continue to exist as the human being? Maybe not. Then, how boring the world might be, and what a bore man might eventually become! In such a sense, it might be said, the fluidity or elusiveness of feeling may, in a sense, represent or stand for the nature of man, or the nature of the world; in the sense that, it is such fluidity or elusiveness that, it might be said, in a sense, gives man breadth, width, or depth, and lends complexity, intricacy, or depth to the world. This may be seen, in a sense, as the great mystery of man. This may be seen, in a sense, as the great mystery of the world. This may be seen, in a sense, as the greatness of the development that gave rise to man. This may be seen, in a sense, as the greatness of the humoral development that had brought man into the world.

Philosophers have discussed the philosophy of mind for a long time. It may be time now for philosophers to pay attention to the things other than the mind, and engage in the kind of discussions that may be called, the philosophy of heart. To discuss the heart may be different, in a sense, from discussing the mind; in the sense that, as what constitutes the heart, feeling is usually hard to measure, hard to gauge, hard to fathom, that is, it might be said, as what gives rise to the heart, feeling may be seen, in a sense, as more complex, more intricate, or deeper, than reason. We have already seen, the study of the philosophy of mind constitutes a considerable challenge to the human intelligence, with issues or problems associated with the mind, such as the mind-body problem, continue to defy a full and complete human understanding, even to this day. The philosophy of heart, it might be said, may pose a greater challenge to the human understanding, as the fluid, changing, fluctuating, and fathomless feeling almost stands as the antithesis of the clear, precise, unambiguous, or definitive reason. And in a sense, it might be said, such may be exactly the case, as the study of feeling, that is, the study of the human feeling or feelings, may be seen as having been ignored or overlooked for so long, that is, in a sense, until today. The fluidity or elusiveness of feeling may be seen as contributing to such a lack of attention, on our part, to our own feeling or feelings, to the absence of a full, complete, and rigorous investigation into them, and in a certain sense, it might be said, to the ignorance, or lack of understanding, prevalent among ourselves, about ourselves. When feeling is not taken notice of, the antean man would suffer, and the human existence would get into trouble. When the human feelings are not paid attention, the humoral man would be miserable, and the human life would be disintegrating. It is time for us not just to pay attention to the philosophy of mind, but also to the philosophy of heart. It is time for us not just to study the mind, but also to study the heart. The difficulty to search into the heart should not deter us. The difficulty to understand the human feeling or feelings should not discourage us from pursuing a full and complete understanding of ourselves. The difficulty to measure, to gauge, or to fathom the human feeling or feelings should not prevent us from acquiring a true knowledge about ourselves, about our human being or existence in this world.

It may be said, people had paid attention to the human feeling or feelings, and they had made enormous efforts to study the heart, to look into the heart, or to investigate into the heart. But, unfortunately, it seems, they had been usually dismissed, and their efforts had been mostly ignored or overlooked. Now, it may be time for us to take a fresh look at them, at their work, at their thoughts, at their meditations, or at their philosophical interpretations. We may learn from them. We may learn from them about the human condition. We may learn from them about the human being or existence. We may learn from them about the world. We may learn from them about ourselves, as to how we should live, for what we should live, or to where we might go. The human world is not just about reason or rationality. The human world is not just about the mind. The human world is not just about the mind-body problem. There is the heart. There exists the feeling. There exist the human feelings. There may be the heart-body problem, as to how the human feeling comes into being, how the human feelings happen, or how they may interact with the body. There may be the heart-mind problem, which may be seen, in a sense, as a greater problem than the mind-body one, as, as we can see or witness, before our own eyes, how the damaged feelings may lead to a distorted mind, or a distorted or twisted mind may lead to the gevil or gevilish feelings. It is time for us to look beyond the mere reason. It is time for us to look beyond the mere mind. It is time for us to look beyond the mere mind-body problem. It is time for us to look at the human feeling or feelings. It is time for us to look at the heart. It is time for us to look at the heart-body problem. It is time for us to look at the heart-mind problem. It is time for us to look into the heart-mind problem. It is time for us to search into the heart-mind problem. When we pay attention to the heart-body problem, it is hopeful that, the human feeling or feelings may be nurtured, the antean man may be nourished, and the humoral man may be cultivated. When we pay attention to the heart-mind problem, it may be the case that, we may be able to see into the workings or operations of both the heart and the mind, in such a sense that, we may come to a clear awareness or understanding of the heart as the foundation of the exercise of mind, and, the interaction, that is, the healthy, sound, undamaged, or unimpaired interaction between the heart and the mind may constitute the mainstay of the human being or existence in the world. Otherwise, it seems, the gevolved mind may get the upper hand, the gevil feeling or feelings may prevail, the gevilish life may replace the human life, and man may be eventually dismantled or dehumoralized. The humoral philosophy, in such a sense, may be seen as being mainly concerned, among other things, with the heart-body problem and the heart-mind problem. It is hopeful that, as we look into ourselves and acquire a better understanding of ourselves, we may come back to our senses, live as the human beings, and continue to exist as the human species on this planet.

Humorality

Feeling and reason are the two aspects of man. Feeling and reason are the two functions of man. Feeling and reason are the two faculties of man. Given their different coming into beings, it seems, it might be said, feeling may be seen, in a sense, as more primitive or primordial than reason, that is, in a sense, more crude or raw than reason, that is, in a sense, more basic, rudimentary, or fundamental than reason. Sponges do not possess a nervous system, and they may be seen as capable of performing some kind or sort of purely physical contacts with the environment. In such a sense, they may be seen as capable of performing some sense or sort of feeling activities, while living through their simple or primitive animal life. That is, they may be capable of feeling, in a sense, but certainly they cannot be said to have the ability to exercise reason. They do not possess the faculty of reason, as there exists no nervous system in their bodies. That is to say, with regard to the kind of simple and primitive animal life forms, such as sponges, they may be seen, in a sense, as capable of feeling, but they cannot be viewed, at the same time, as being capable of reasoning. Jellyfish usually possess a simple nerve net in their bodies, which, nevertheless, may not be regarded as a full and complete nervous system as we know, such as, containing a brain, a central cord, and numerous nerves throughout the body. That is, jellyfish may be seen as simple animals in terms of their nervous structures. Do they have the ability to reason? Do they possess such a faculty? Can they carry out the performance of reasoning? It seems, reason, as a faculty, may be seen as what developed later in the animal developmental process; that is, only with the coming into being of a highly advanced nervous system could it be possible that the exercise of reason or reasoning might be likely to happen, in a sense, in the animal life. For jellyfish, it seems, their simple nervous system may be capable of performing certain nervous functions, such as, coordinating their feeling organs, coping with the changes in the environment, or controlling their bodily movements. But, when it comes to the exercise of reason or reasoning, it seems, such a nervous structure may be too simple, primitive, or rudimentary to carry out such activities.

It is in the animals called vertebrates or invertebrates that we see the further development of the nervous system. The nervous system in these animals usually manifests a structure that consists, in varied degrees, of a brain, a central cord, and numerous nerves. Such a nervous structure is familiar to us, as we humans possess such a kind of nervous system. We humans can reason, and possess a faculty of reason. Is it the case that, all the animals with a similar nervous structure to ours can reason or possess a faculty of reason? Probably not. The lower animals with a less complex nervous system, even though their nervous structure similar to ours, may not be able to perform the act of reasoning, as their nervous system may not have developed to such an extent that it may be capable of supporting such a kind of performance. In other words, reason, or the faculty of reason, may be seen as coming into being only after the nervous system had developed to such an extent, to such a level, or, with such a kind of complexity that the animals with such a kind of nervous system may be seen as being developed, through a long developmental process, with such a kind of capacity. This kind of animals may be seen as the animals with the most highly developed nervous systems, such as, the mammals, especially, the primates, or, the humans. As animals other than the humans do not talk, and they have no language that we may understand, thus we basically have no way of knowing, insofar as we know, in what sense they might reason, in what way they might reason, or to what extent they might reason, that is, if they could. But, it appears, it would be difficult for us to completely rule out the possibility that the highly developed animals like the mammals, especially the primates, such as chimpanzees, may be capable of some sense or sort of reasoning, given that, it seems, how little differences might actually exist, between them and us, as the different species. For now, it may be safe to just let us keep the faculty of reason for ourselves, as it seems, such an approach may not disrupt our current discussion, in any way.

Reason came into being, as a result of the coming into being of a highly advanced or complex nervous system. In other words, it appears, reason, as a faculty of man, it might be said, came after the coming into being of feeling. Feeling began, it might be said, with the beginning of life; reason might not. Feeling emerged, it might be said, with the emergence of life; reason might not. Feeling came into being, it might be said, with the coming into being of life; reason might not. Sponges may be seen, in a sense, as having feeling, but they do not have reason. Jellyfish may be seen as capable of feeling, but they may not be capable of reasoning. The lower animals, such as worms, may be able to feel, but they may not be able to reason. These animals may be seen as possessing the faculty of feeling, but they may not be seen as possessing the faculty of reason. In such a sense, it might be said, feeling may be seen as more primitive, primordial, or more raw, physical, or more basic, fundamental than reason. Such primitiveness, rawness, or fundamentality of feeling may be amply revealed in the age of the gevolution of man, in the sense that, it is exactly due to the damage, harm, injury, or devastation done to the feeling of man that man is being led to his deanteanization or dehumoralization. Human beings, as a higher form of life, came from the lower life forms, from animals. As such, human beings share things with other life forms in some basic, rudimentary or fundamental ways. Feeling may be seen as one of the defining characteristics, properties, qualities, functions, or faculties that human beings share with other life forms. Reason may not be seen as in such a category. In other words, feeling may be seen as what constitutes the base or foundation of the human existence as a life form in this world. Reason, on the other hand, may not be regarded as such, in a sense, that is, in a primitive, primordial, crude, raw, physical, basic, rudimentary, or fundamental sense. When feeling is damaged, man is damaged. When feeling is changed, man is changed. When feeling is undermined, man is shaken. When feeling is devastated, man is destroyed. When feeling disappears, the foundation of man collapses. Such may not be said with regard to reason. Such may not be said with regard to the importance of reason. Such may not be said with regard to the significance of reason. Reason is important, in a different way. Reason is significant, in a different sense. Reason is essential, in a different manner. The humoral philosophy is to call attention to the importance of feeling. The humoral philosophy is to call attention to the significance of feeling. The humoral philosophy is to call attention to the primitiveness, rawness, physicality, or fundamentality of feeling. The humoral philosophy is to call attention to the basis or foundation of man, such that, man may be aware of himself, aware of his own nature, and protect, nurture, and cultivate himself, and, continue to exist, as the human being.

Philosophers have used the kind of terms such as sentient, sentience, or sentiency to describe the characteristic, property, quality, or ability of the living things to feel. In a sense, it might be said, such an ability may be regarded as the defining feature of the living things, as, otherwise, how the living things might live, or exist, or be seen or deemed in such a state, if they could not feel! In a sense, feeling is living; living is feeling. Or, feeling is existing; existing is feeling.

Feeling may be seen as the indispensable and essential feature of the living things; or, rather, it might be said, in a sense, feeling may be seen as constituting or forming the essential, inherent, or primary existence of the living things. To be sentient is to be able to feel. Such may be seen as the quality or ability that may be observed, in a sense, in all the living things. We know human beings can feel. All the animals, even those as simple or primitive as sponges, in a sense, may be seen as capable of feeling. How about plants? Can they feel? Can they be said to be able to feel? What is to feel? What is feeling? What is to be able to feel? Is feeling a mysterious thing? Is feeling obscure? Is to feel an inscrutable undertaking? Is to feel a process unfathomable? No. In a sense, that is, in a primary, or fundamental sense, to feel is to have a contact with the environment; to feel is to have a contact with the world. To feel is to have a sense of what is happening in the world; to feel is to have a sense of what constitutes the things in the world. To feel is to form a connection with the environment; to feel is to establish a link with the world. Do plants live in the world? Yes. Do plants survive in the environment? Yes. Do plants have a contact with the environment? Yes. Do plants have a contact with the world? Yes. Do plants form a contact with the environment? Yes. Do plants establish some form or sense of link with the world? Yes. Do plants have to adapt themselves to the environment so that they may survive? Yes. Do plants have to adjust themselves to the surroundings so that they may thrive and prosper? Yes. Then, how could one deny that plants may feel, even if such a feeling process or mechanism may not be clearly understood by the humans? That is, how could one deny the possibility that plants may be able to feel, even if such a plant feeling process or mechanism may not be understandable, eventually, that is, for now, it seems, to the humans, that is, in the human terms, through the human understanding, in the human senses, or, through the human ways?

What is the difference, after all, between a flower turning to the sunlight and a human being feeling good when standing in the sunshine? What is the difference, after all, between the bending sensitive tentacles of the sundews over the prey and the capturing of game by a hunter? What is the difference, after all, between the quick closing of the trap when a Venus flytrap is stimulated and the animals running to the food? When a flower turns to the direction of sunlight, it might be said, in a sense, it feels and feels good. Is that really different from a human being feeling good in the sunshine? Probably, in the end, that is, in the most basic, primary, fundamental, or physical sense, not really. When the tentacles of the sundews bend toward the prey, it might be said, in a sense, the sundews feel the coming of the prey and they take immediate actions. Is that really different from a hunter capturing the game? Probably not, that is, in the most primitive, or primordial developmental sense, as both the sundews and the hunter would strive to utilize any means available to secure their ends. When a Venus flytrap quickly closes its trap to prevent the prey from escaping, it might be said, in a sense, it feels the movements of the prey and responds to the stimulations transmitted through the trigger hairs. Is that really different from the animals responding quickly to the discovery of food? Probably not. That is, in the sense that, they, either the flytraps or the animals, may act, in a sense, directly out of their survival instincts to acquire as much nutrients as possible so that they may eventually survive well. The flowers, the sundews, the flytraps, they are all plants. Could one claim, positively, that, they cannot feel? Could one deny the possibility that, they may, in some sense, in some way, or in some manner, be capable of feeling? If such things happening to them, as discussed above, are not feeling, then, what is feeling? What is feeling to man? What is feeling to animals? What is feeling to plants? What is feeling in the world? What is feeling, after all? Isn't feeling a feeling? Isn't feeling a touching? Isn't feeling a moving? Isn't feeling a contacting? Isn't feeling a reaching out? Isn't feeling a coming back? Isn't feeling a responding? Isn't feeling a reacting? Isn't feeling a way of living in this world? Isn't feeling a way of existing in this universe?

When a flower turns to the sunlight, it is because it is touched. When the tentacles of the sundews bend toward the prey, it is because they are touched. When a flytrap closes its trap, it is because it is touched. When an animal is excited to discover the food, it is because it is touched. When a human being feels good in the sunshine, it is because he or she is touched. When a flower turns to the sunlight, it is because it is moved inherently. When the tentacles of the sundews bend toward the prey, it is because they are moved in their intrinsic ways. When a flytrap closes its trap, it is because it is moved through the stimulations coming from the trigger hairs. When an animal is excited to discover the food, it is because it is moved, instinctively for survival. When a human being feels good in the sunshine, it is because such a human being is moved, as he or she is surrounded by or connected to a bright, lively, and prosperous world. Feeling is a feeling. Feeling is a touching. Feeling is a moving. Feeling is a contacting the world. Feeling is a reaching out to things. Feeling is a coming back to oneself. Feeling is a responding. Feeling is a reacting. Feeling is a way of living in this world, either to a plant, an animal, or a human being. Feeling is a way of existing in this universe, either for a plant, an animal, or a human being.

Without feeling, how could one live in this world, either as a plant, an animal, or a human being? Without feeling, how could one exist in this universe, either as a plant, an animal, or a human being? Without feeling, how could one survive, after all, either as a plant, an animal, or a human being? Should the plant feeling be known to the humans? Not necessarily. Should the plant feeling be the same as the animal feeling, or the human feeling? Not necessarily. Should the process of the plant feeling be clear or visible to the human eyes? Not necessarily. Should the workings or operations of the plant feeling be intelligible to the human mind? Not necessarily. Should the mechanisms of the plant feeling be analyzable to reason? Not necessarily. Plants may feel the plant feeling, though humans may not. Animals may feel the animal feeling, though humans may not. Plants may feel the plant feeling, and animals may feel the animal feeling, though the human mind may not be able to discern. Plants may feel the plant feeling, and animals may feel the animal feeling, though reason may not be able to analyze or dissect. Feeling is a sense. Feeling is a perception. Feeling is a physical activity. Feeling is a bodily experience. Feeling is not necessarily to be known to reason. Feeling is not necessarily to be sensed by reason. Feeling is not necessarily to be perceived by reason. Feeling is not necessarily to be recognized by reason. Feeling is not necessarily to be comprehended by reason. Feeling is not necessarily to be understood by reason. Such may also be said with regard to the mind. As long as the plant feeling can be felt by plants, it is enough. As long as the plant feeling can serve the plants, it is sufficient. As long as the plant feeling can satisfy the plants, it is adequate. Such may also be said with regard to the animal feeling. And, in the same sense, such may also be said with regard to the human feeling. That is, in a sense, it might be said, plants may feel the plant feeling in their own ways, animals may feel the animal feeling in their own senses, and the humans may feel the human feeling in their own manners. The plant feeling may not be the animal feeling, or the human feeling. The plant feeling may not be necessarily feeled by animals, or by humans. The plant feeling may not be necessarily open, visible, intelligible, or feelable to animals, or to humans.

The inability of reason to analyze or dissect feeling may not necessarily mean that, the plant feeling or the animal feeling does not exist. The inability of the human mind to fully recognize, comprehend, or understand the plant feeling or the animal feeling may not necessarily mean that the plant feeling is nonexistent, or the animal feeling is scarce or rare. The inability of the human beings to feel, sense, or perceive the plant feeling, or the animal feeling, may not necessarily mean that, the plant feeling has no place in the plant world, or the animal feeling is not important or essential to animals. Reason is very limited when it comes to feeling. Reason falls far short when it comes to feeling. The human mind is, in a sense, inadequate when it comes to understanding the workings or operations of feeling, as a basic, fundamental or raw way of existence for things in the world. Either in the case of plants, or in the case of animals, it seems, feeling is beyond the reach of the human mind. The human mind is insufficient, it seems, as it relies on reason or thinking to try to reach things and acquire some knowledge or understanding of them. But, in a sense, it might be said, feeling is not knowledge, feeling is not understanding, feeling is not comprehension. Feeling is feeling. Feeling has to be feeling. Feeling has to be feeled.

Feeling has to be feeled, that is, not necessarily to be reasoned, that is, analyzed or dissected by or through reason. Reason may not replace feeling. Reason may not take the place of feeling. Reason may not reach all the things about feeling. Reason may not fully comprehend feeling. Reason may not fully understand feeling. Reason may not make full sense of feeling. Reason may not grasp the full picture of feeling. Feeling is not reason. Feeling is different from reason. Feeling is distinct from reason. Feeling belongs to a realm that is different from the realm of reason. Feeling is a function that is different from the function of reason. Feeling is to sense. Feeling is to perceive. Feeling is to experience. Feeling is an activity that is different from the activity of reasoning. Feeling is a process that is different from the process of reasoning, and may involve things more than reason or the mind. Feeling is an operation that is different from the operation of reasoning, and may require things more than reason or the mind. Feeling is a way of living that may call for things more than reason or the mind. Feeling is a way of existing that may be supported, maintained, or sustained by or through the kind of things that may be more than reason or the mind.

The plant feeling is a plant feeling, not a human feeling. It is not human; it is plant. It is feeled by plants. It is feeled through plants. It is feeled for plants. The animal feeling is an animal feeling, not a human feeling. It is not human; it is animal. It is feeled by animals. It is feeled through animals. It is feeled for animals. Either to plants, animals, or humans, feeling is a way of living or survival in the environment. Either for plants, animals, or humans, feeling is a way of existing in the world, or, of thriving, prospering, or flourishing in this universe. To be sentient is to feel. To be sentient is to feel in such a way that one may survive. To be sentient is to feel in such a way that one may grow or develop. To be sentient is to feel in such a way that one may thrive, prosper, or flourish. To be sentient is to feel in such a way that one may live or exist in the world, either as a plant, an animal, or a human being. The sentient nature is the basic nature of the living things, and in a sense, such feeling nature may be seen as forming or constituting the basis or foundation of living or existing of the living things in the world. the sentience or feelingness of the living things should not be underestimated, or underrated, in any way, even though the human mind or reason may not always be able to search deep into its real workings or operations, and the human beings may not always be able to feel its true effects or consequences, as, after all, it might be said, plants, animals, and the human beings may be seen, in a certain sense, as occupying or belonging to different realms! In other words, it might be said, human beings are not the only things of the world, that is, not the only living things of the world. In such a sense, it might be said, we human beings may need to show or display some sense of modesty or humility, that is, in a sense, to be aware of the existence of things other than the humans, to recognize the existence of things other than the mere human, to give them a place in the world, as we give, always, it seems, a place to ourselves. As such, that is, in such a sense, or in such a way, it may be hoped that, we may get a balanced view of ourselves, or a fuller understanding of the world, and we may thus continue to live or exist as the human beings, and thrive, together, with the rich, colorful, and diverse plants and animals, in this world.

Humorality

§ 4.13 Humorality: as the Fulfillment of Symmetry or Realization of Harmony

Why Is There the True?

One may ask, after all, why is there the true in the world? Why is it not the case that there was no such thing as the true in the world? Why does the true have to come into being? Why does the true have to exist? Why does the true have to exist in the world? Is it an accident? Is it by chance? Is it necessary? Is it inevitable or unavoidable? Is it essential, vital, and thus indispensable? In what sense? In what way? In what manner? Why does the true have something to do with the world? Why does the true have something to do with the human beings? Why is it not the case that we existed in a world void of the true? Why is it not the case that we lived as the human beings who had nothing to do, whatsoever, with the true?

When the true comes into being, the false comes into being. When the true exists, the false exists. The true accompanies the false. The false accompanies the true. The true exists side by side with the false. The false exists hand in hand with the true. That is to say, without the true, it seems, there would have been no such thing as the false. Or, without the false, it seems, there would have been no such thing as the true. The true and the false form symmetry. The true and the false form harmony. The true and the false constitute symmetry. The true and the false constitute harmony. From symmetry, in a sense, it might be said, the true and the false come into being. From harmony, in a sense, it might be said, the true and the false emerge. In symmetry, it might be said, the true and the false exist. In harmony, it might be said, the true and the false express or manifest themselves in the world.

Meaning in Man

What is meaning? Meaning is $1=1$. Meaning is $1+1>1$. Meaning is, $1=1$ is true. Meaning is, $1+1>1$ is true. Meaning is, $1\neq1$ is false. Meaning is, $1+1<1$ is false. Meaning is, $1=1$ and $1\neq1$ cannot be true at the same time. Meaning is, $1+1>1$ and $1+1<1$ cannot be true at the same time. Meaning is, $1=1$ and $1+1<1$ cannot be true at the same time. Meaning is, $1\neq1$ and $1+1>1$ cannot be true at the same time. Meaning is, true is true. Meaning is, false is false. Meaning is, true is not false. Meaning is, false is not true. Meaning is, true cannot be taken as false.

Meaning is, false cannot be taken as true. Meaning is, true and false cannot stand at the same time. Meaning is, true cannot be taken by man as false. Meaning is, false cannot be taken by man as true. Meaning is, true and false cannot stand to man at the same time. The humorality of man is such meanings humoralized, in a sense, in man. The humorality of man is such meanings humoralized, in a sense, into man. Man thus identifies himself with such meanings. Man thus lives in accord with such meanings. Man thus exists in harmony with such meanings. Man thus senses or feels an intrinsic affinity with such meanings. Man thus lives in a world filled with, or constituted by, such meanings.

It may not be that it is man who comes out and seeks such meanings. It may be that, such meanings may have already been humoralized, in a sense, into him. It may not be that, it is man who comes out and looks for such meanings. It may be that, what man needs to do is to rediscover such meanings in himself, or, through himself. That is to say, in a sense, it might be said, meaning is in man. Meaning is in man waiting to be discovered. Meaning is in man waiting to be expressed. Meaning is in man waiting to be demonstrated. Meaning is in man waiting to be fulfilled. Meaning is in man waiting to be realized.

This, in a sense, may be seen as the meaning of meaning. This, in a sense, may be seen as the coming into being of meaning. This, in a sense, may be seen as the meaning of the coming into being of meaning. This, in a sense, may be seen as the meaning in man. This, in a sense, may be seen as the meaning of man. This, in a sense, may be seen as the meaning of the existence of man. This, in a sense, may be seen as the meaning of life. This, in a sense, may be seen as the meaning of the life of man in the world.

The Sexual Life of Man

Why is the sexual life of man important? Because, the sexual life of man defines, in a fundamental and essential sense, what man is; that is, the sexual life of man distinguishes man, in a fundamental and essential sense, from the other animals. Man is not just animal; man is also humoral. The humorality of man means, while man lives an animal life, man should also maintain, at the same time, a humoral existence. Family may be seen as one of the social institutions in which, or through which, man may be able to secure or uphold a humoral being or existence of his own, for himself. In a stable or harmonious family, man could nurture or cultivate his humoral feelings or emotions, such that, his life or existence in the world, as the humoral being, would be enriched, strengthened, or solidified. Human beings, as the humoral beings, and the human society at large, would thus benefit from such sustained, increased, or strengthened humoral being or existence of man. The humorality of man may thus be upheld. The humoral being or existence of man may thus be safeguarded, protected, or preserved. This may be the meaning of the sexual life of man as the humoral being. This may be the meaning of family. This may be the meaning of family to the human society.

The Human Life

Freedom, equality and creation are the basic themes of the human life. Without freedom, a human being may not fulfill him- or herself completely. Without equality, a human being may not realize him- or herself fully. Without creation, the human life may be dull, dreary, uninspiring, or spiritless.

The vitality of a human society comes from all its members being free, equal and creative. The richness of a human society comes from all the human beings capable of living a free, equal, and creative life.

A free, equal and creative human society means the freedom, equality and creation of all the human beings. A free, equal and creative human society means the freedom, equality and creation of each and every individual human being in such a society.

The humorality of man does not mean that a human being should not be free. The humorality of man does not mean that a human being should not be equal. The humorality of man does not mean that a human being should not be creative. The humorality of man does not mean that a human being should be restricted in his or her creative life.

The humorality of man does not mean that the human society should be motionless, stagnant, or inactive. The humorality of man does not mean that, in a human society, the free spirits of adventure should be stifled, and the courage to explore the unknown should be suppressed.

The humorality of man should mean the coming into being of a free, equal and creative society. The humorality of man should mean the coming into being of a free, equal and humocratic society. The humorality of man should mean the fulfillment or realization of a free, equal, creative and humocratic society. That is, the humorality of man should mean that, all human beings, living in a free, equal and humocratic society, fulfill or realize themselves, fully and completely, as the true and genuine human beings.

Beauty and Existence

Beauty is the sense of harmony. Beauty is the sense of existence. Beauty is the sense of the essence of existence. Beauty is the sense of the deep and profound existence of existence.

Beauty is the awareness of harmony. Beauty is the awareness of existence. Beauty is the awareness of the essence of existence. Beauty is the awareness of the origin of existence. Beauty is the awareness of the source of existence.

Beauty is the self-awareness of man. Beauty is the self-awareness of the existence of man. Beauty is the self-awareness of the coming into being of man. Beauty is the self-awareness of the humoral coming into being of man. Beauty is the appreciation of the existence of man. Beauty is the appreciation of the coming into being of man. Beauty is the appreciation of the humoral coming into being of man.

Beauty is the awareness of the existence of the world. Beauty is the awareness of the essence of the world. Beauty is the awareness of the origin of the world. Beauty is the awareness of the source of the world. Beauty is the awareness of the coming into being of the world. Beauty is the appreciation of the existence of the world. Beauty is the appreciation of the origin of the world. Beauty is the appreciation of the source of the world. Beauty is the appreciation of the coming into being of the world.

Beauty is the awareness of existence by man. Beauty is the appreciation of existence by man. Beauty is the awareness of the existence of the world by man. Beauty is the appreciation of the existence of the world by man. Beauty is the awareness of the coming into being of the world by man. Beauty is the appreciation of the coming into being of the world by man.

Existence Is Higher than Reason

If the world were rational, it would not have been the world. If the world were rational, there would have been no electric charges or magnetic poles. If the world were rational, there would have been no electromagnetic force. If the world were rational, there might have been no gravitational force. If the world were rational, there might have been no weak or strong force.

If the world were rational, there would have been no plants. If the world were rational, there would have been no animals. If the world were rational, there would have been no flowers. If the world were rational, there would have been no human beings. If the world were rational, there would have been no life. If the world were rational, there would have been no nature. If the world were rational, there would have been no such things as the world. If the world were rational, there might have been no such things as the universe.

If the world were rational, there would have been no sexes. If the world were rational, there would have been no humorality of man. If the world were rational, there would have been no meaning for the human life, or for the human existence.

The Greatness of Man

The greatness of man may not be about the great people. The greatness of man may not be about the great deeds of man. The greatness of man may not be about the great feats of man. The greatness of man is, after all, about man living a humoral life, striving to fulfill man's humoral longings or aspirations, and with the utmost effort, safeguarding and upholding the humoral values or principles of man. To safeguard the humoral values of man is to be great. To uphold the humoral principles of man is to be great. To preserve the humoral being of man is to be great. To strive for the realization of the humoral existence of man is to be great. That is, each and every individual human being is great, so long as he or she adheres to his or her humoral feelings, respects his or her humoral values, follows his or her humoral principles, and lives a humoral life that is called, human.

The Good is the Way

The good is the way of the world. The good is the reflection or realization of the way of the world. The good is the expression or demonstration of the way of the world. The good is the embodiment of the way of the world. The good is the humoralization of the way of the world, in man. The good is the humoralization of the way of the world, through man. The good is the way of the world revealed. The good is the way of the world manifested. The good is the way of the world fulfilled or realized. What is the way of the world? It is symmetry. What is the way of the world? It is harmony. Symmetry is the way. Harmony is the way. Symmetry is the way of the world. Harmony is the way of the world. Symmetry is the way of the world expressed or manifested in the good. Harmony is the way of the world fulfilled or realized in the good. Symmetry is the way of the world expressed or manifested through the good. Harmony is the way of the world fulfilled or realized through the good.

Feeling, Heart and Man

Feeling is not rational. Feeling is, in a fundamental or essential sense, that is, in a humoral sense, it might be said, harmonic. Heart is not rational. Heart is, in a fundamental or essential sense, that is, in a humoral sense, it might be said, harmonic. Heart is the foundation of man. Heart is the foundation of the existence of man. Heart is the harmonic foundation of man. Heart is the harmonic foundation of the existence of man. Heart is the harmonic expression of man. Heart is the harmonic representation of man. Heart is the harmonic embodiment of man.

When heart is ruined, man is ruined. When heart is destroyed, man is destroyed. When heart collapses, man collapses. When heart disappears, man disappears.

The Sexual Symmetry

The sexual symmetry may be seen as a physical symmetry. In such a sense, it might be said, the sexual symmetry may be considered together with other physical symmetries, such as, the double helical symmetry, the electric symmetry, or the magnetic symmetry. That is to say, as a physical symmetry, the sexual symmetry may be seen as different, in a certain sense, from the metaphysical symmetries, such as, the moral symmetry, the aesthetic symmetry, or the logical or rational symmetry. In other words, it may have to be said, the female may not be equated to the kind of things such as, the false, the ugly, or the evil.

Man as Meaning

Truth is, in a sense, not meaning. Meaning is, in a sense, more than truth. Meaning means the true, the good, and the beautiful. Meaning means the association of the true with the good and the beautiful. Smile and tears mean the humoral truth. The humoral truth is truth, but to express or embody such truth, man may have to come into being. Man is the meaning of the humoral truth. Man is the meaning of truth. Man is the realization of the humoral truth in meaning. Man is the fulfillment of meaning in the humoral truth. Man is the realization of truth in meaning. Man is the fulfillment of meaning in truth. Man is truth in meaning. Man is meaning in truth. Man is the way of truth to meaning. Man is the way of meaning to truth. Man is the bridge from truth to meaning. Man is the bridge from meaning to truth.

The Humorals of Man
The true, the good, the right, the just, and the beautiful may be seen as the humorals of man. The humorals of man represent the meaning of man. The humorals of man stand for the meaning of man. The humorals of man represent the meaning of life. The humorals of man stand for the meaning of life for man.

The humorals of man manifest themselves in man as the morals of man. The humorals of man manifest themselves through man as the morals of man. The humorals of man express themselves in man as the morals of man. The humorals of man express themselves through man as the morals of man. The humorals of man demonstrate themselves in man as the morals of man. The humorals of man demonstrate themselves through man as the morals of man. The humorals of man fulfill themselves in man as the morals of man. The humorals of man realize themselves through man as the morals of man.

Reason and Feeling
Reason may reach or grasp the rational being, but it may not reach or grasp the harmonic being.

Feeling may feel the harmonic being. Feeling may reach the harmonic being. Feeling may grasp the harmonic being.

Reason may reveal the rational being associated with the harmonic being. As such, by exercising both reason and feeling, man may see deeper into the harmonic being, or acquire a better understanding or grasp of the harmonic being of the world.

That is, by exercising both mind and heart, or by living with both mind and heart, man may see deeper into the harmonic being, or acquire a better understanding or grasp of the harmonic being of the world.

Duty

Duty occupies a significant place in Kant's philosophy. What is duty, for Kant, after all? It is the duty to follow the stars, so that one may follow the way of harmony. It is the duty to look into oneself, so that one may find the meaning of one's existence. It is the duty to be man. It is the duty to live as man. It is the duty to exist as man. It is the duty to behave as man. It is the duty to act as man. It is the duty to maintain man. It is the duty to preserve man. It is the duty to sustain man. It is the duty to follow one's inner moral senses or instincts. It is the duty to adhere to one's inner moral values or principles. It is the duty to hold dear one's inner moral feelings or emotions. It is the duty to fulfill or realize one's inner moral longings or aspirations. It is the duty to honor one's humoral being. It is the duty to respect one's humoral existence. It is the duty to uphold the humoral man. It is the duty to safeguard the humoral man.

The Existence of Man

The meaning of the existence of man is the meaning of the existence of plants. The meaning of the existence of man is the meaning of the existence of animals. The meaning of the existence of man is the meaning of the existence of the world. It is the meaning of symmetry. It is the meaning of harmony. It is the meaning of the fulfillment of symmetry. It is the meaning of the realization of harmony. It is the meaning of the fulfillment of symmetry in nature. It is the meaning of the realization of harmony in the world.

Modesty

Modesty is an awareness. Modesty is an awareness of the world. Modesty is an awareness of the coming into being of the world. Modesty is an awareness of the existence of the world. Modesty is an awareness of man. Modesty is an awareness of the coming into being of man. Modesty is an awareness of the existence of man. Modesty is an awareness of the existence of man in the world. Modesty is an awareness of the harmonic existence of man in the world. Modesty is an awareness of things. Modesty is an awareness of the existence of things. Modesty is an awareness of the harmonic existence of things in the world.

The Meaning of Life
A grass exists. That is the meaning of life for a grass.

A plant grows. That is the meaning of life for a plant.

An animal exists. That is the meaning of life for an animal.

A human being lives, following his or her humoral senses, fulfilling his or her humoral instincts. That is the meaning of life for a human being.

Follow the way of symmetry. Realize the way of harmony. Fulfill the way of heaven. That is the meaning of life. That is the meaning of existence.

The True, the Good, the Right, the Just, the Beautiful
What is the true? The true is 1=1 or 1+1>1 in the mathematical sense. The true is good in the humoral sense. The true is right in the humoral sense. The true is just in the humoral sense. The true is beautiful in the humoral sense.

What is the good? To be true is good. To uphold the true is good. To preserve and safeguard the true is good. To be man is good. To live as man is good. To live the human life is good.

The right is what is true in the mathematical sense. The right is what is true or good in the humoral sense.

The just is 1=1 or 1+1≠1 in the mathematical sense. The just is to uphold the true, to safeguard the good, or to exert for the right, in the humoral sense.

The beautiful is a humoral sense; that is, a sense of the true, a sense of the good, a sense of the right, a sense of the just, or, a sense of the beautiful. The beautiful is a humoral feeling; that is, a feeling of the true, a feeling of the good, a feeling of the right, a feeling of the just, or, a feeling of the beautiful.

The Right
People will say, it is right that 1+2=3. The right has to do with the logical. When you helped someone, people will say, it is good, you did the right thing. The right has to do with the moral. The right has to do with the logical and the moral. It is in such a sense that, it might be said, the right is the humoral. That is, in such a sense, it might be said, the right has to do with the humorality of man.

The Just

To find the truth is to be logical. To respect and honor the truth is to be just. The just has to do with the logical. The just has to do with upholding the truth. Equality has to do with the humoral feelings of man. Equality is a humoral condition of man. Equality is a humoral condition for the coming into being of man. Equality is a humoral condition for the development of man. Equality is a humoral condition for the existence of man. To be humoral is to be equal. To be equal is to be humoral. To be man is to be equal. To be equal is to be man. To be just is to be equal. To be equal is to be just. The just is logical. The just is humoral. The just has to do with the humorality of man.

The Spirit of Adventure

To discover the fresh secrets of nature. To find the new frontiers of the world. To explore into the unknown. They are the spirit of adventure of man. The spirit of adventure develops man. The spirit of adventure enriches man. The spirit of adventure fulfils man. Nothing should smother the spirit of adventure of man. Nothing should stifle the spirit of adventure of man. Nothing should conquer the spirit of adventure of man.

Live with Heart

Live with heart, so that you may live as the human being. Live with heart, so that you may live as man. Live with heart, so that you may survive. Live with heart, so that you may survive as man. Live with heart, so that you may survive as the human being. Live with heart, so that you may fulfill yourself. Live with heart, so that you may fulfill yourself as man. Live with heart, so that you may fulfill yourself as the human being.

Power and Virtue

How to tame power, and at the same time protect, preserve, cultivate, and uphold virtue?

How to protect, preserve, cultivate, and uphold virtue, and at the same time tame power?

The human life is delicate, subtle, complex, deep, and profound.

The existence of man is delicate, subtle, complex, deep, and profound.

Good, Virtue, Heart, Humorality, and Unfreedom

Good means that you have to be good. Good means the unfreedom of man. Virtue means that you have to be virtuous. Virtue means the unfreedom of man. Heart means that you have to feel shame. Heart means the unfreedom of man. Humorality means that you have to be humoral. Humorality means the unfreedom of man.

§ 4.14 The Untitled

When the true is physicalized into the humoral, that is, when the true is embodied in the humoral, the true is physicalized, in a sense, into the good, that is, the true is embodied, in a sense, as the good. That may be seen as how our good feelings come into being, or from where our good feelings come into being, and that may be seen as what our good feelings mean. Our good feelings, that is, our humoral feelings, may be seen as a result, that is, a glorious coming into being, from a long developmental process in which such a magnificent transformation, that is, from the true to the humoral, may have taken place. It is in our humoral feelings that the true is represented. It is in our good feelings that the true is realized. Or, it might be said, the true is represented in our humoral feelings; the true is realized in our good feelings.

The moral senses of man may be seen, in a sense, as the senses of harmony of man, or, the senses of harmony by man. That is, in other words, it might be said, the moral senses of man may be seen, in a sense, as man's senses of harmony expressing or demonstrating themselves, in or through man, or, fulfilling or realizing themselves, in or through man. That is, the moral senses of man may be seen as having to do with harmony. That is, the moral senses of man may be seen as having to do with harmony expressing or demonstrating itself, or fulfilling or realizing itself, in or through man. When harmony is reflected in man, that is, deposited in man, that is, embodied in man, harmony may be seen as being expressed or demonstrated, or, fulfilled or realized, by or through man, as the moral senses.

What does the humorality of man mean? It means the true, the good, and the beautiful. What does the humorality of man mean? It means the content of man. What does the humorality of man mean? It means the meaning of man. What does the humorality of man mean? It means the content of the human life. What does the humorality of man mean? It means the meaning of the human life. What does the humorality of man mean? It means the unfreedom of man. Fight for the freedom of man. Fight for the unfreedom of man. Fight for the content of man. Fight for the meaning of man. Fight for the content of the human life. Fight for the meaning of the human life.

What is to be man? To be man is to be humoral, animal, and humoverse. To be man is to live as the humoral man, animal man, and humoverse man, at the same time. To be man is to exist as the humoral man, animal man, and humoverse man, at the same time, and in the same body. To be man is to negotiate with the humoral man, animal man, and humoverse man, at the same time, and in the same body. To be man is to navigate between or among the humoral man, animal man, and humoverse man, at the same time, and in the same person.

Communism is a form of communalism or communitarianism, focusing on the connection between the human beings. Such a sense of connection may be seen as originating from the humoral being or existence of man. Communism means, in such a sense, that people have hearts. But, at the same time, it may have to be said, the institutionalized communism appears to have overlooked a number of things about man, some of them fundamental, such as, individual freedom, self-interest, or, some proper mechanisms dealing with power.

Beauty is a sense of harmony; beauty comes into being as a sense of realization or fulfillment of harmony; that is, it might be said, beauty is a feeling. As reason may not be in a position to fully comprehend or grasp harmony, aesthetics may thus be seen, in a sense, as a misused term to indicate the kind of human rational endeavor trying to dissect or analyze beauty, or the coming into being of beauty. While aesthetics may be regarded, in a sense, as such a kind of term, the words like aesthetic may be used as the technical terms.

Beauty is the fulfillment or realization of existence. The moral beauty is the fulfillment or realization of the moral existence. The aesthetic beauty is the fulfillment or realization of the aesthetic existence. The logical beauty is the fulfillment or realization of the logical existence. The inner beauty is the fulfillment or realization of

Humorality

the inner man. The behavioral beauty is the fulfillment or realization of man in a behavioral manner. The linguistic beauty is the fulfillment or realization of man in a linguistic way.

Flowers are the plant realization of bilateral symmetry; man is the animal realization of bilateral symmetry. Flowers are the plant realization of symmetry; man is the animal realization of symmetry. Flowers and human beings are relatives, in or through symmetry. Plants are the plant realization of symmetry; animals are the animal realization of symmetry. Plants and animals are relatives, in or through symmetry. Plants, animals, and human beings are relatives, in or through symmetry.

Modesty is a sense of awareness of the connection of things. Modesty is a sense of awareness of the connection of man with things. Modesty is a sense of awareness of the connection of man with nature. Modesty is a sense of awareness of the place of man in the world. Modesty is a sense of awareness of the position of man in the universe. Modesty is a sense of awareness of man in nature. Modesty is a sense of awareness of man in the world. Modesty is a sense of awareness of man in the universe.

In a sense, it might be said, to be religious is to search into the coming into being of the world, to search into the origin of life, to search into the beginning of the universe. Man is part of the world. Man is part of life. Man is part of the universe. To be religious is to be part of the world. To be religious is to be part of life. To be religious is to be part of the universe. To be religious is to connect with the world. To be religious is to unite with life. To be religious is to integrate with the universe.

The ascendance of heart should not mean the fall of mind. The ascendance of feeling should not mean the fall of reason. The age of heart should not mean an end to the age of mind. The age of feeling should not mean an end to the age of reason. The age of heart should not mean the diminution of knowledge. The age of feeling should not mean the decline of science. To be man is to live with both heart and mind. To live as man is to exercise both feeling and reason.

The good comes into being from the humoralization of man. Meaning comes into being from the humoralization of man. Man comes into being from the humoralization of man. The coming into being of the good, the coming into being of meaning, and the coming into being of man may be seen, in such a sense, as one and the same thing. The good is in man; man is in the good. The good is in meaning; meaning is in the good. Man is in meaning; meaning is in man.

Behind smile is the depth of man. Behind smile is the profundity of man. Behind smile is the mystery of man. Behind smile is the wonder of man. Behind smile are the secrets of man. Behind smile is the meaning of man. Behind smile is the richness of man. Behind smile is the humanity of man. Behind smile is the humorality of man. Behind smile is the very being or existence of man.

What is heart? Heart is the center of man. Heart is the core of man. Heart is the essence of man. Heart is the inner existence of man. Heart is the basis of man. Heart is the foundation of man. Heart is the support of man. Heart is the nurse of man. Heart is the guide of man. Heart is the moral being of man. Heart is the feelings about beauty. Heart is the senses about the meaning of life.

The great lies in the ordinary. The ordinary lies in the great. A leaf is ordinary, but in the leaf lies symmetry or harmony. Symmetry or harmony is great, but it takes the ordinary existence of a leaf to achieve them. The human life may be ordinary, but in the human life lies the way of heaven. The way of heaven is great, but it may take the ordinary human life to fulfill or realize it.

Smile is the flower of symmetry. Smile is the flower of harmony. Smile is the flower of man. Smile is the flower of life. Smile is the flower of the world. Smile is the flower of the universe. Smile is the beauty of symmetry. Smile is the beauty of harmony. Smile is the beauty of man. Smile is the beauty of life. Smile is the beauty of the world. Smile is the beauty of the universe.

Let each and every individual human being thrive according to him- or herself, so that the world may be full of meaning and color. Respect each and every individual human being, so that he or she may fulfill his or her potentials. Treat each and every individual human being equally, so that he or she may live as a human being in the world with dignity and decency.

What is the humorality of man? The humorality of man is the respect paid to oneself. The humorality of man is the respect paid to oneself, such that one's humoral senses or instincts may be cherished, one's humoral values or principles may be respected, and one's humoral being or existence may be fulfilled or realized.

The expressible is finite. The inexpressible is infinite. The explicable is not fundamental. The fundamental is inexplicable.

Humorality

Essence is not definable. The definable is not the essence. What can be speakable may not be the most important things. The most important things are the things inexpressible, or ineffable.

The moral symmetry means morality. Morality means the moral symmetry. The aesthetic symmetry means beauty. Beauty means the aesthetic symmetry. The logical or rational symmetry means rationality. Rationality means the logical or rational symmetry. Rationality means reason. Reason means rationality.

The ascendance of heart should not mean the fall of mind. The ascendance of feeling should not mean a disgrace to reason. The ascendance of heart or feeling should not mean the decline or fall of science. To exist as man is to exist with both heart and mind. To live as man is to live with both feeling and reason.

Reason cannot take the place of feeling when it comes to the beautiful. Reason should not take the place of feeling when it comes to the beautiful. The mind cannot take the place of the heart when it comes to the beautiful. The mind should not take the place of the heart when it comes to the beautiful.

The true, the good and the beautiful are the content of man. They constitute the content of man. They constitute the substance of man. The true, the good and the beautiful are the content of the human life. They constitute the content of the human life. They constitute the substance of the human life.

From where does man come? From the true, the good, the beautiful. How should man live? According to the true, the good, the beautiful. How could man continue to exist? Live with the true, the good, the beautiful. Live for the true, the good, the beautiful. Live in the true, the good, the beautiful.

The way of heaven is the way of man. The way of man is the way of heaven. The way of heaven expresses itself in the way of man. The way of man reflects in itself the way of heaven. The way of heaven fulfils itself in the way of man. The way of man realizes in itself the way of heaven.

Why is love so beautiful? Because, it is the fulfillment of the humoral. Why is love so beautiful? Because, it is the fulfillment of the animal. Why is love so beautiful? Because, it is the fulfillment of symmetry. Why is love so beautiful? Because, it is the fulfillment of harmony.

Man means benevolence. Man means freedom. Man means equality. Be benevolent. Be free. Be equal. Be benevolent; at the same time, respect the freedom of others. Be benevolent; at the same time, treat others equally. Be benevolent, freely. Be benevolent, equally.

Life is ordinary? Yes, life is ordinary. Life is not ordinary? Yes, life is not ordinary. Since man is humoral, life is not ordinary. Since man is humoral, life is no longer ordinary. Since man is humoral, life has meaning to man. Since man is humoral, life is meaningful to man.

Man has both mind and heart in himself. The human beings possess both reason and feeling. Both mind and heart may be seen as participating in the coming into being of beauty. Both reason and feeling may be seen as participating in the coming into being of beauty.

Beautiful is not a light word. Beautiful is not a word that can be readily used. It means harmony. It indicates harmony. It expresses harmony. It implies the heavenly way. That is, it might be said, other words may be readily used, but that may not be the case with beautiful.

Why is $1=1$? In a sense, it is harmonious; it is in harmony. Why is $1+1>1$? In a sense, it is harmonious; it is in harmony. Why is $1\neq 1$ not true? In a sense, it is not harmonious; it is not in harmony. Why is $1+1<1$ not true? In a sense, it is against harmony; it is not in harmony.

Can reason analyze or dissect the humoral body? Hardly. The humoral body is a harmonic existence. It comes into being from harmony, and it represents, stands for, or embodies the fulfillment or realization of harmony. Could reason analyze or dissect harmony?

Man is a sense. Man is a sense of the true. Man is a sense of the good. Man is a sense of the right. Man is a sense of the just. Man is a sense of the beautiful. Man is an antean sense. Man is a humoral sense. Man is a sense of being human. Man is a sense of being humoral.

What is reason? Reason is the true; the true is reason. What is the source of reason? The source of reason is the source of the true; the source of the true is the source of reason. How deep is reason? Reason is as deep as the true; the true is as deep as reason.

Man is the flower of symmetry. Man is the flower of harmony. Man is the flower of the way of heaven. Man is the flower of heaven. Man is the flower blooming in the animal kingdom. Man is the flower blooming in the animal world.

Reason is good, but reason needs a broad and firm foundation. The humorality of man is the broad and firm foundation of reason.

Humorality

Mind is good, but mind needs a broad and firm foundation. Heart is the broad and firm foundation of mind.

Grasses are true. Grasses are good. Grasses are beautiful. Flowers are true. Flowers are good. Flowers are beautiful. Animals are true. Animals are good. Animals are beautiful. Man is true. Man is good. Man is beautiful.

The way of man comes from the way of heaven. The way of man represents the way of heaven. The way of man stands for the way of heaven. The way of man represents or stands for the way of heaven on earth.

The rational being of man may be analyzed, by or through reason, in a number of ways. We all know the various sciences concerning the human being, such as, biology, physiology, psychology, or neuroscience.

I do not write this book for myself. I do not write this book for the great ones. I write this book for those honest and humble people who live in this world by adhering to their basic human values and principles.

Man comes into being from symmetry. Man comes into being from harmony. Man comes into being, in a sense, as the realization of symmetry. Man comes into being, in a sense, as the realization of harmony.

It might be said, the good may be seen as that which is, in a sense, in a way, or in a manner, harmonious. In the human sense, the good may be seen as the humoral realization, or reflection, of harmony.

君子 knows grasses. 君子 knows flowers. 君子 knows plants. 君子 knows animals. 君子 knows rivers. 君子 knows mountains. 君子 knows life. 君子 knows man. 君子 knows existence. 君子 knows the world.

Man is the flower of the animal kingdom. Man is the flower of symmetry. Man is the flower of harmony. Man is the flower of the way of heaven. Man is the flower created by the way of heaven on earth.

The humoral feelings lead to or constitute the humorality of man. The animal feelings lead to or constitute the animality of man. The humoverse feelings lead to or constitute the humoversity of man.

Live with grasses. Live with plants. Live with animals. Live with rivers. Live with mountains. Live with clouds. Live with stars. It is a good life. It is a rich life. It is a meaningful life.

Avolution and Man

The ancient Egyptians built the pyramids, and human beings could be connected with the deities. The Parthenon was erected on the acropolis, and the Greeks and gods might share the same world.

Man, be cautious. Man, be careful. Man, be modest. Man, be moderate. Man, be humble. Man, know yourself. Man, respect yourself. Man, hold yourself firm. Man, stand your ground!

Symmetry is harmony. Harmony is beauty. Existence comes from symmetry. Existence comes from harmony. Existence comes from beauty. Beauty is existence; existence is beauty.

Symmetry is profound. Harmony is profound. Existence is profound. Beauty is profound. Life is profound. Man is profound. The human life is profound. The world is profound.

Those with heart are lucky. Those with heart are fortunate. Those with heart are rich. Those with heart are noble. Those with heart are happy. Those with heart are human.

Why is truth simple? Because, truth is, in the most fundamental or deepest sense, the expression or manifestation of harmony, or, the fulfillment or realization of harmony.

Symmetry is profound. Harmony is profound. The way of heaven is profound. The humorality of man is profound. Man is profound. The existence of man is profound.

When I discuss the Cage effects, it is not my intention to discriminate against any people. My only purpose is to find out, if possible, the causes of things.

Intelligence is not wisdom. Wisdom is more than intelligence. Wisdom is about the harmonic being of man. Wisdom is about the harmonic existence of man.

When I meet willow trees, a beautiful feeling often arises in me. How to describe it? It may be said, 柳树, 树中君子. Willow trees, the gentlemen among trees.

Simple is complex. Simple is deep. The simpler, the more complex. The simpler, the deeper. The simplest, the most complex. The simplest, the deepest.

To exercise feeling is part of man. To exercise reason is part of man. To pursue the true, the good, and the beautiful is the meaning of the existence of man.

Heaven is the origin of truth. Heaven is the source of good. Heaven is the root of right. Heaven is the author of justice. Heaven is the fountainhead of beauty.

Humorality

To reach man, man needs both feeling and reason. To live as man, man needs both feeling and reason. To exist as man, man needs both feeling and reason.

Man means freedom. Man means equality. 君子 is free. 君子 is equal. 君子 respects the freedom of others. 君子 lives with others in an equal way.

In a sense, it might be said, freedom and equality are the way through which man fulfils or realizes the true, the good, and the beautiful.

What is the meaning of the spiritual life of man? Follow the way of heaven. What is the meaning of the life of man? Follow the way of heaven.

君子 understands the way of heaven. 君子 follows the way of heaven. 君子 defends the way of heaven. 君子 upholds the way of heaven.

See what cannot be seen. Hear what cannot be heard. Learn what cannot be learned. Do what you have to do. Live what you have to live.

Smiles arise from the humoral body. Tears come from the humoral body. Smiles originate from the heart. Tears flow from the heart.

Man is private. The public power is public. What does this mean? It means the publicization of power. It means democracy.

Body embodies the physical being of man. Mind represents the rational being of man. Heart stands for the harmonic being of man.

Marriage is not about the law. Marriage is about symmetry. Marriage is about harmony. Marriage is about the way of heaven.

What is the freedom of man? The freedom of man is, in its purest sense, the humoral man striving to fulfill or realize himself.

To live is to follow the way of symmetry. To live is to follow the way of harmony. To live is to follow the way of heaven.

Heart means man; man means heart. Heart means life; life means heart. Heart means existence; existence means heart.

Symmetry is behind man. Symmetry is behind heart. Symmetry is behind mind. Symmetry is behind reason.

What is the unfreedom of man? The unfreedom of man is, in the humoral sense, the true, the good, and the beautiful.

How many feelings have been lost, to the point that we may no longer be able to connect with the way of heaven?

Mind is the seat of reason. Heart is the seat of feeling. Mind is the seat of rationality. Heart is the seat of morality.

Body is physical. Body is sentient. Body is perceptual. Body is animal. Body is humoverse. Body is humoral.

What is harmony? Harmony is true; harmony is good; harmony is right; harmony is just; harmony is beautiful.

One man is not the world. The world is not one man. One people is not the world. The world is not one people.

What does benevolence mean? Benevolence means that man has heart. Heart means benevolence.

君子 is pure. 君子 is fine. 君子 is good. 君子 is virtuous. 君子 is noble. 君子 is beautiful.

When I see life, I am touched. When I see life, I am moved. When I see life, I am uplifted.

Heart is the bridge between man and heaven. Heart is the connection of man with heaven.

Virtue. Beauty. Freedom. Equality. This may be seen as the essence of humocracy.

In harmony, man comes into being. With a heavenly blessing, man comes to this world.

Benevolence means the humorality of man. The humorality of man means benevolence.

Look to the stars for direction. Look into ourselves for the meaning of our existence.

Kant's gigantic effort to build morality through reason tells us that, he is a great man.

君子 is antean. 君子 is humoral. 君子 is gentle. 君子 is benevolent. 君子 is virtuous.

Lao Tzu says: the great voice has no sound; the great phenomenon has no shape.

Beauty is the purest form of existence. Beauty is the highest form of existence.

The existence of heart may be seen, in a sense, in socialism or communism.

君子 lives with mind. 君子 lives with heart. 君子 is rational. 君子 is harmonic.

Antean harmony, the cradle of man. Antean harmony, the lifeline of man.

Humorality

Element may mean five elements. Movement may mean five movements.

What does symmetry mean? Symmetry means, in a sense, unfreedom.

Decency is the face of man. Decency is the face of the humoral man.

If the way of heaven can be all known, it is not the way of heaven.
When I work, I have no life. I have a life, only if I do not work.
Rabindranath Tagore, an Indian mind, tender, loving, and deep.
Heart means peace. Peace is with heart. Peace is where heart is.
Heart is the essence of man. Heart is the essence of the world.
Heart means peace. Heart means joy. Heart means happiness.
Stars looked at me. Stars watched me. Stars took care of me.
Cultivate the heart. Protect the heart. Safeguard the heart.
Nelson Mandela, a fighter, a decent, wise and noble man.
Antean world, the world of symmetry, the world of harmony.
Anteanity may be seen in Taoists' closeness with nature.
Living is not simple. Living is deep. Living is profound.
Eyes are the window of mind; face is the mirror of man.
仁者爱人. A benevolent person loves the human beings.
Repetition is better, in a sense, than incomprehension.
弘一大师, a monk, a musician, a great human being.
Liu Xiahui is a 君子 following the way of heaven.
Heart means harmony. Harmony means heart.
Democracy is not fundamental, but necessary.
Beauty is not a judgment. Beauty is a feeling.
When I am lonely, trees are my companion.
Think with the mind; Live with the heart.
Face is significant. Face represents man.
Exercise the mind. Cultivate the heart.
Reason sharpens the sense of beauty.
Heart is good. Heart means good.
Beauty comes from within man.
Be decent. Be wise. Be human.
Be virtuous. Be free. Be equal.
Be benevolent. Be equal.
Heart is the center of man.
Life is beyond reason.
Be free. Be equal.

Truth is mighty.
Feel the world.
Be harmonical.
See yourself.
Be man.

Chapter V The Way of Heaven

§ 5.1 The Structure of Truth

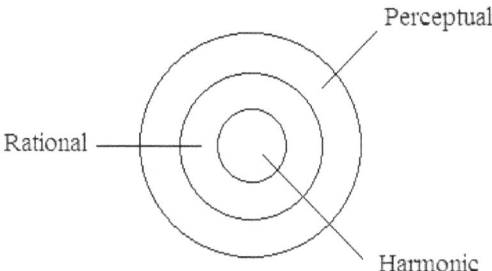

Figure 5.1   The Structure of Truth

This may be seen as the structure of truth, in a general sense.

The perceptual truth may be seen as the truth that may be perceived through the senses. The rational truth may be seen as the truth that may be revealed through reason. The harmonic truth may be seen as the truth that may be closely associated with symmetry or harmony. In a general sense, it might be said, the perceptual truth may be seen as constituting the outer layer of truth; the rational truth may be seen as constituting the middle layer of truth; and the harmonic truth may be seen as constituting the innermost layer of truth.

Let us pay attention first to the humoral truth. The perceptual truth in the humoral truth may be seen as the truth perceived by man, such as, the smile is true, the smile is the true smile, or, the smile is false, the smile is a false smile. The rational truth in the humoral truth may be seen as the kind of truth relating to the smile mechanisms or processes, such as, how the facial muscles work, how the nerves operate, or how the neurons respond or react. The harmonic truth in the humoral truth may be seen as the kind of truth closely associated with symmetry or harmony, such as, it might be said, bilateral symmetry may be seen as behind the coming into being or existence of the human nervous system in humans.

Certainly, it may have to be said, the humoral truth may be seen as much more profound than what is discussed here about the smiles. That is to say, it might be said, the perceptual truth, the rational truth and the harmonic truth concerning the humoral truth may be discussed in a much broader or deeper fashion, if it is necessary.

Now let us talk about the truth about sex. The perceptual truth about sex may be the kind of things such as, animals often develop the kind of features or traits that may make them more attractive to the opposite sex. As we can observe, in order to attract the opposite sex, the males may make themselves look more muscular or stronger, and the females may make themselves more feminine. The rational truth about sex may be the kind of studies or researches revealing the mechanisms or processes related to sex, such as, it is found, the sex hormones, such as estrogen and testosterone, regulate the development of the sexual characteristics in animals, and usually play major roles in the animal behaviors related to sex.

The harmonic truth about sex may be seen in that, ultimately, it might be said, it is the sexual symmetry that may be seen as behind the phenomenon that is called sex. That is to say, when we observe, perceive or feel the kind of things associated with sex, we should not forget that there is something behind all such things and it is called the sexual symmetry. That is to say, when we engage in the kind of studies or researches looking into the possible mechanisms or processes related to sex, we should not forget that, something is behind what we may find, and such a thing is called the sexual symmetry. The sexual symmetry is the symmetry underlying the phenomenon called sex. The sexual symmetry is the symmetry underlying what we may find or discover about sex.

Now let us consider the truth about the inorganic things, such as, the electric force or magnetic force. The perceptual truth about the electric force may be seen as the kind of things such as, for example, though a table is made up of molecules and atoms, and atoms are made up of electrons, protons and neutrons, we usually do not notice the little particles like electrons, protons or neutrons, and feel that such a table is solid and stable, and things may be placed on it. The rational truth about the electric force may be seen as the scientific laws about the electric force. Coulomb's law is one of the fundamental scientific laws concerning electricity. It is found, the electric force between two charges follows Coulomb's law, $F = k_e(q_1q_2/r^2)$, where F is the force, k_e is Coulomb's constant, q_1 and q_2 are the magnitudes of the charges, and r is the distance between the charges. The harmonic truth about the electric force may be seen in that, it is the electric symmetry that may be seen as behind the electric force, and as such, the electric symmetry may be seen as behind the scientific laws concerning the electric force or electricity.

The perceptual truth about the magnetic force may be seen as the kind of things such as, we may observe, a magnet may attract some materials, such as iron, sometimes strongly. The rational truth about the magnetic force may be seen as the scientific laws concerning the magnetic force or magnetism. A number of scientific laws have been discovered about the magnetic force or magnetism. Such laws may be seen as revealing, in a scientific or rational sense, the inner mechanisms or processes involved in the magnetic phenomena. The harmonic truth about the magnetic force may be seen in that, it might be said, it is the magnetic symmetry that may be seen as behind the magnetic force. That is to say, the magnetic symmetry may be seen as the symmetry underlying the magnetic phenomena. That is to say, when we talk about the magnetic force or the kind of phenomena associated with magnetism, we should not forget that, a symmetry may be behind all such things, and such a symmetry may constitute the foundation of what we may observe, find, or discover.

Now let us discuss the truth concerning a number of aspects of the organic world. The perceptual truth about DNA may be seen, in a sense, in that, DNA is the building block of life, and yet we may find or encounter so many different shapes or forms in the living organisms. The rational truth about DNA may be seen as the scientific studies or researches concerning DNA, such as, genetics. As the study of living organisms, genetics reveals many mechanisms, functions or processes involving DNA. It is with the development of genetics that our knowledge about the various life forms increases and we may thus be able to see deeper into the development or existence of the living organisms around us. The harmonic truth about DNA may be seen in that, it is the double helical symmetry that is behind the coming into being or existence of DNA. As such, it might be said, the double helical symmetry may be seen as behind all the things concerning DNA. It is in such a sense that, it might be said, the double helical symmetry may be seen as the symmetry underlying, ultimately, the scientific studies or researches concerning DNA, such as, genetics.

The perceptual truth about plants may be seen in the kind of things such as, the plants have leaves, the plants are green, the plants have flowers, or, the plants are beautiful. The rational truth about plants may be seen in the scientific studies about plants, such as, in the researches concerning the plant hormones. It may be revealed, the plant hormones usually play an important or vital role in the development or existence of plants. They promote the plant growth. They shape the formation of flowers or fruits. They regulate the plant development. They determine the plant life cycles.

The harmonic truth about plants may be seen in that, it might be said, symmetry plays an essential or fundamental role in the development or existence of plants. Plants may be divided into the radially symmetric plants and bilaterally symmetric plants. The radially symmetric plants may be seen as the kind of plants such as conifers, which usually produce no flowers. The flowering plants may be seen as the bilaterally symmetric plants, and as we know, they usually produce flowers or fruits. Thus, it might be said, symmetry, or specifically, radial symmetry and bilateral symmetry, may be seen as playing an important or fundamental role in the natural phenomena called plants.

The perceptual truth about animals may be seen in that, we may encounter so many kinds of animals, in the sea, on the land, on the trees, or underground, and with so many different shapes or forms. The rational truth about animals may be seen in the scientific studies or researches about animals. One of such scientific studies or researches is called neuroscience. Neuroscience is the study of the nervous system, dealing with the kind of things such as the mechanisms, functions or processes associated with neurons. Through the study of neuroscience, we may be able to look into the workings or operations of the nervous system, such as, how the nervous system may be structured, what roles neurons may play, how neurons are connected, how neurons communicate with each other, or, how the electric or electrochemical signals may be transmitted or processed by the neurons.

The harmonic truth about animals may be seen in that, it might be said, symmetry may be seen as behind, ultimately, the development or existence of animals. Animals may be divided into the asymmetric animals, radially symmetric animals, and bilaterally symmetric animals. Sponges may be seen as the asymmetric animals, possessing little symmetric structures or forms, and no nervous system.

Cnidarians, ctenophores and echinoderms may be seen as the radially symmetric animals. As the radially symmetric animals, they often demonstrate predominantly the existence of radial symmetry, and they usually possess only the simple nerve nets as their nervous systems. The simple nerve nets are different from the centralized nervous systems. The centralized nervous systems may be found in the bilaterally symmetric animals, such as worms, insects, fish, birds, mammals, or humans. Thus, it appears, it might be said, while asymmetry may be seen as behind the absence of nervous system, radial symmetry may be seen as behind the presence of the simple nerve nets, and bilateral symmetry may be seen as behind the coming into being or existence of the centralized nervous systems. It is in such a sense that, it might be said, when we discuss the nervous system, we should not forget that, it is symmetry that may be seen as behind, ultimately, the nervous systems.

Symmetry is behind the nervous system. Symmetry is behind the presence of the nervous system. Symmetry is behind the coming into being or existence of the nervous system. Symmetry is behind the coming into being or existence of animals. Symmetry is behind the coming into being or existence of man. Symmetry has to do with the nervous system. Symmetry has to do with the human nervous system. Symmetry has to do with the coming into being or existence of animals. Symmetry has to do with the coming into being or existence of man. This may be seen as the harmonic truth about the nervous system. This may be seen as the harmonic truth about the coming into being or existence of animals. This may be seen as the harmonic truth about the coming into being or existence of man. This may be seen as the harmonic truth about animals. This may be seen as the harmonic truth about man.

Truth may thus be seen as manifesting itself in three layers, or at three levels. The perceptual truth may be seen as constituting the outer layer of truth, associated mostly with the kind of things involved in our daily lives. The perceptual truth may be seen, in such a sense, as the truth at the sensory or perceptual level. The rational truth may be seen as constituting the middle layer of truth, associated mostly with the exercise of our reason. The rational truth may be seen, in such a sense, as the truth at the scientific or rational level. The harmonic truth may be seen as the truth mostly associated with symmetry or harmony. As such, the harmonic truth may stand as the deepest truth, constituting the innermost layer of truth. The harmonic truth may be seen, in such a sense, as the truth at the symmetric or harmonic level.

As we can see, the three levels of truth are different from each other. The truth at the perceptual level may be different from the truth at the rational level, and the truth at the rational level may be different from the truth at the harmonic level. In other words, it might be said, such three different levels of truth may reflect the world in three different senses, or in three different levels. Or, it might be said, such three different levels of truth may come into being through three different means, or through three different ways. The truth at the perceptual level may come into being through the human senses. The truth at the rational level may come into being through the human reason. The truth at the harmonic level may come into being through the human harmonic feeling. They come into being through the different means. They come into being through the different ways. They may reflect the fulfillment or realization of the world in the different ways. They may reflect the fulfillment or realization of the world in the different senses. Or, they may reflect the fulfillment or realization of the world in the different levels.

We are often familiar with the rational truth, that is, the truth at the rational level. Sometimes, it seems, we favor the rational truth and disregard, to some extent, the perceptual truth, that is, the truth at the sensory or perceptual level. The reason may be that, first, the perceptual truth may have to do with what is called common sense, and common sense may appear not so significant, vital or essential. Secondly, it may have to do with the perceptual knowledge. As we all know, perception may be deceiving, and feeling may be unreliable. Thus, it is understandable that, the perceptual knowledge may be treated by us with a sense of wariness or caution, as it may not lead us to the real or genuine truth. This may be true. But, should the perceptual knowledge be relegated to a lower position than, say, the rational knowledge, and disregarded or dismissed by us? It seems, it might be said, that should not be the case.

The importance or significance of the perceptual knowledge may be seen in two senses. First, the perceptual knowledge constitutes the foundation for our existence as the human beings. Feeling is the foundation of our existence. Feeling is the foundation of our human existence. Feeling anchors us in man. Feeling anchors us in the humanity of man. Feeling anchors us in the anteanity of man. Feeling anchors us in the humorality of man. Feeling anchors us in the humoral being or existence of man.

Without feeling, man is not man. Without feeling, man can not be man. Without feeling, man can no longer be man. Feeling is the foundation of man. Feeling is the foundation of being man. Feeling is the foundation of the existence of man. Feeling may be uncertain, but it nurtures or nourishes man. Feeling may be unreliable, but it maintains or sustains man. Perception may be uncertain, but it leads man to live the human life. Perception may be unreliable, but it paves the way for the human existence. Feeling may be uncertain, but it is feeling that establishes the humoral being or existence of man. Perception may be unreliable, but it is perception that constitutes the daily existence of man, keeps man man, and makes it possible for man to live as man. It is in such a sense that, it might be said, the perceptual knowledge may be seen as constituting the foundation for our existence as the human beings.

On the other hand, it might be said, while feeling may be uncertain or unreliable, sometimes, through feeling, man may reach the innermost truth of the world. Feeling may be seen as physical, compared to reason. Reason may be seen as metaphysical, compared to feeling. That is to say, compared to the workings or operations of feeling, the workings or operations of reason may be seen, in a sense, that is, in a certain sense, that is, in the logical or rational sense, as metaphysical. The difference between the physical nature of feeling and the metaphysical nature of reason may mean a lot for both feeling and reason. The physical nature of feeling may mean that, through feeling, man is linked or connected to the world. That is to say, in other words, it might be said, through feeling, man is united or integrated with the world. While feeling links man with the world, the metaphysical nature of reason may mean that, reason is distanced, in a sense, from the world. That is to say, while reason may reach the world in a logical or rational sense, it may not be able to reach the world in other senses, in other ways, in other manners, or at other levels.

This may account for the phenomenon that, while feeling may reach the harmonic truth, reason may not. The metaphysical nature of reason constitutes, in a sense, a gulf between reason and the world. It is a logical or rational gulf. Such a gulf means that, while reason may reach, with certainty, the logical or rational truth of the world, it may not be able to reach the kind of truth beneath the logical or rational truth, that is, the kind of truth beneath the rational level, that is, the kind of truth possibly underlying the logical or rational truth, that is, the kind of truth that may be called, the harmonic truth.

The physical feeling feels the world. The physical feeling senses the world. The physical feeling perceives the world. The physical feeling touches the world. The physical feeling leads feeling to the inner depth of the world. The physical feeling leads feeling to reach the innermost truth of the world. Thus, it might be said, the physical feeling may lead man to the inner depth of the world, or to the innermost truth of the world. The metaphysical reason may not do this. The metaphysical reason may not be able to do this. The metaphysical nature of reason limits reason. The metaphysical nature of reason confines reason. The metaphysical nature of reason imprisons reason. The metaphysical nature of reason separates reason from the world. The metaphysical nature of reason divides reason from the inner depth of the world. The metaphysical nature of reason disconnects reason from the innermost truth of the world.

While man may be united with the world through feeling, man may not be united with the world through the metaphysical reason. While man may come into oneness with the world through feeling, man may not be able to come into oneness with the world through the metaphysical reason. It is through the unity or union with the world that man comes to the inner depth of the world. It is through the oneness with the world that man reaches the innermost truth of the world. It is through feeling that man comes to be united with the world, not reason. It is through feeling that man comes into oneness with the world, not reason. It is through feeling that man comes to the inner depth of the world, not reason. It is through feeling that man comes to reach the innermost truth of the world, not reason.

Feeling is the bridge between man and the world. Feeling is the bridge between man and the inner depth of the world. Feeling is the bridge between man and the innermost truth of the world. Feeling is not lowly. Feeling is not inferior. Feeling is not trivial. Feeling is important. Feeling is significant. Feeling is fundamental. Feeling is essential. It is in such a sense that, it might be said, the perceptual knowledge may be seen as important, significant, fundamental, and essential. The rational knowledge may be certain, but it may not lead to the deeper truth. The perceptual knowledge may not always be reliable, but through it man may come to the inner depth of the world, or reach the innermost truth of the world, the harmonic truth.

Man may thus come to the harmonic knowledge through the perceptual knowledge. The harmonic knowledge may be seen as the knowledge about symmetry or harmony, or about the workings or operations of symmetry or harmony. In such a sense, it might be said, the harmonic knowledge may be seen as the kind of knowledge deeply hidden from us. It is about symmetry. It is about harmony. It is about the symmetric coming into being. It is about the symmetric existence. It is about the symmetric fulfillment or realization in the world.

We may be familiar with the rational knowledge, and we may be familiar with the perceptual knowledge, but we may not be so familiar with the harmonic knowledge. As the deep knowledge of the world, or, it might be said, as the deepest knowledge of the world, the harmonic knowledge may be well beyond, in a sense, our human reach. That is to say, as the knowledge about the deepest existence of the world, the harmonic knowledge may not be easily acquired by us through either reason or feeling. Reason may not be able to reach the harmonic knowledge directly, as the metaphysical nature of reason may prevent reason from accomplishing such a kind of feat. Even feeling, with its characteristic physical nature, may not easily grasp the harmonic knowledge, as it is so subtle, intricate, and as it is so often profoundly hidden from us.

Man may reach the harmonic knowledge through the accumulation of the perceptual knowledge. That is to say, through the accumulation of the perceptual knowledge, people may gradually find the kind of patterns, forms, structures or orders usually hidden in the world. Though feeling may reach such kind of patterns, forms, structures or orders, people may not take them, in the initial stages, as something significant or vital. It is through the accumulation of the perceptual knowledge that people may gradually feel, or come to the understanding that such kind of things, that is, such kind of patterns, forms, structures or orders may be of the utmost importance to the existence of things. The harmonic knowledge may thus come into being, as a result of the accumulation of feelings, or as a result of the accumulation of the perceptual knowledge.

On the other hand, it may have to be said, though reason may not lead us to the harmonic knowledge as feeling does, the rational knowledge may contribute to our grasp or understanding of the harmonic knowledge. The rational knowledge about the world may provide us with some of the most convincing or solid evidences for the existence of the harmonic knowledge. As we know, feeling or perception may not always constitute a solid foundation for the argument of things. That is to say, if relied solely on the perceptual knowledge, the argument for the existence of the harmonic knowledge may be eventually doubted, as our feeling or perception may mislead us. It is in such a sense that, it might be said, the rational knowledge about the world may play a significant role in our grasp or understanding of the harmonic knowledge about the world.

The perceptual knowledge is not lowly. The perceptual knowledge is not inferior. The perceptual knowledge is not trivial. The perceptual knowledge is important. The perceptual knowledge is vital. The perceptual knowledge maintains or sustains man. The perceptual knowledge may lead man to a deep understanding of the world. The rational knowledge is significant. The rational knowledge is crucial. The rational knowledge enables man to search into the world with certainty and confidence. With its certainty, the rational knowledge may constitute the foundation for our knowledge about the world. The harmonic knowledge is fundamental. The harmonic knowledge is essential. The harmonic knowledge may lead man to see the innate or intrinsic mechanisms or processes underlying things. The harmonic knowledge may enable man to reach a better understanding about the profound existence of the world.

The perceptual knowledge may lead man to the perceptual truth. The rational knowledge may lead man to the rational truth. The harmonic knowledge may lead man to the harmonic truth. Man may thus come to understand the world through the perceptual knowledge, the rational knowledge, and the harmonic knowledge. Man may thus come to understand truth through the perceptual truth, the rational truth, and the harmonic truth. Knowledge is about the perceptual knowledge, the rational knowledge, and the harmonic knowledge. Knowledge is about all of them. Truth is about the perceptual truth, the rational truth, and the harmonic truth. Truth is about all of them. With the perceptual knowledge, the rational knowledge and the harmonic knowledge, man may better understand the world. With an understanding of the perceptual truth, the rational truth and the harmonic truth, man may live better, it might be said, in the world.

The rational knowledge thus may not be seen as the only knowledge. The rational truth thus may not be seen as the only truth. The rational knowledge is not the only knowledge. The rational truth is not the only truth. Science is not the only knowledge. Science is not the only truth. Science is not all. Science is not all the world. Science may not reveal all the truth. Science may not reveal all the truth about the world. Science may not reach the truth beyond reason. Science may not reveal the truth beyond reason. Science may not be able to reach or reveal the truth beyond reason.

The scientific truth may be only part of the truth of the world. The scientific truth may only reveal part of the world. The scientific truth may only reveal part of the existence of the world. The harmonic truth may lie deeper. The harmonic truth may lie deeper than the scientific truth. The scientific truth may not be the whole truth. The scientific truth may not be taken as the whole truth. The scientific truth may not be the whole truth of nature. The scientific truth may not be the whole truth of the world. The scientific truth may not be taken as the whole truth of nature. The scientific truth may not be taken as the whole truth of the world.

Now, it seems, the time may come for us to discuss, briefly, the so-called superstitions. It might be said, some superstitions may have come from the harmonic knowledge, and may have reflected, in some sense, or to some extent, the harmonic truth of the world. That is to say, through the accumulation of their perceptual knowledge, and possibly aided by their rational knowledge, people may come to grasp, in some sense, or to some extent, the inner workings or operations of the world. The so-called "superstitions" may thus come into being, reflecting or revealing, in some sense, or to some extent, the inner workings or operations of the world, as a result of the accumulation of the perceptual knowledge, or as a result of the accumulation or development of the perceptual knowledge and the rational knowledge. In other words, it might be said, the so-called "superstitions" may come into being, as a result of the exercise of feeling and reason, attentively, in a sense, on the part of some human beings. Such "superstitions" may have indeed reflected or revealed, in some sense, or to some extent, the inner existence of the world. As such, they may have disclosed certain things that may be deep and profound and which, it might be said, we may not be able to know otherwise.

Certainly, it is not the case that any superstition may be treated as telling the truth. No. It should not be the case. Feeling alone may not constitute man. Reason alone may not constitute man. Feeling alone may not constitute the human life. Reason alone may not constitute the human existence. To live as man is to live with both feeling and reason. To live as man is to live with both heart and mind. To exist as man is to exist with both feeling and reason. To exist as the human being is to exist with both heart and mind. To live the human life is to live with both feeling and reason. To live the human life is to live with both heart and mind. With feeling and reason, man may live. With feeling and reason, man may survive. With both feeling and reason, man may thrive. With both feeling and reason, man may prosper and flourish, on this planet earth.

§ 5.2 The Structure of Being

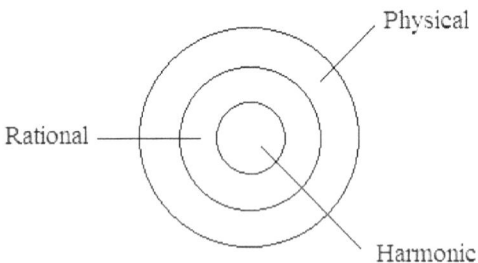

Figure 5.2   The Structure of Being

This may be seen as the structure of being, in a general sense.

The physical being may be seen as constituting the outer layer of being. The rational being may be seen as constituting the middle layer of being. The harmonic being may be seen as constituting the innermost layer of being. The physical being may be seen as the being that may be associated with our senses, that is, the kind of being that we may experience through our senses. The rational being may be seen as the being that may be understood through reason, that is, the kind of being that may be associated with reason. The harmonic being may be seen as the being that may be associated closely with symmetry or harmony.

Now let us consider the being of humorality. The physical being of humorality may be seen as the kind of things such as, human beings are unable to fake their smiles, human beings are unable to fake their tears, human beings may be touched by other people's lives, or human beings may be moved by other people's sacrifices. The rational being of humorality may be seen as the humoral being of man understood through reason, such as, the human anatomical structure associated with feelings, the human physiological existence related to emotions, the interaction between feelings or emotions and the human nervous system, or, the possible mechanisms, functions or processes associated with neurons.

The harmonic being of humorality may be seen in that, given all the scientific studies about feelings, emotions, or the nervous system, in the end, it might be said, symmetry or the fulfillment or realization of symmetry may be seen as behind the humoral being of man. Man comes into being from the double helical symmetry. Man comes into being from the sexual symmetry. Man comes into being from the fulfillment or realization of the bilateral symmetry in animals. The humorality of man reflects the fulfillment or realization of symmetry in man. The humorality of man comes into being as a result of the fulfillment or realization of symmetry in man. And as such, the humorality of man fulfils or realizes symmetry in man, or in the world.

Now let us consider the being of sex. The physical being of sex may be seen in the kind of things such as, males and females may possess different body structures, or, males and females may develop their own characteristic features in order to attract each other. The rational being of sex may be seen in the scientific studies or researches about sex, such as, the roles that the sex hormones may play in the formation of the sexual organs, or, the mechanisms or processes that may be involved in the sexual reproduction. The harmonic being of sex may be seen in that, while we study the things associated with sex, such as the sex hormones or the related mechanisms or processes, we should not forget that something is behind them, and it is a symmetry. In other words, it is the sexual symmetry that may be seen as behind the phenomenon called sex.

Now let us consider the being of the electric force. The physical being of the electric force may be seen, in a sense, in the various electric devices that we may use in our daily lives. The proper functioning of such devices has to do with electricity, that is, with the electric force. The rational being of the electric force may be seen in the scientific laws concerning the electric force or electricity. There are a number of scientific laws concerning the electric force or electricity, and Coulomb's law may be seen as one of the most fundamental laws among them. The harmonic being of the electric force may be seen in that, it is the electric symmetry that is behind the electric force and as such, the electric symmetry may be seen as the symmetry underlying the electric force, electricity, or the laws concerning the electric force or electricity.

Now let us consider the being of the magnetic force. The physical being of the magnetic force may be seen in the kind of things such as, the same magnetic poles repel each other and the opposite magnetic poles attract each other. The rational being of the magnetic force may be seen in the scientific studies or researches about the magnetic force or magnetism. Such scientific studies or researches may reveal the nature or mechanism of the various phenomena called magnetism. The laws in physics concerning the magnetic force or magnetism may be seen as the result of such scientific studies or researches. The harmonic being of the magnetic force may be seen in that, the magnetic symmetry may be seen as the symmetry underlying the phenomena called magnetism, and as such, the magnetic symmetry may be seen as behind, ultimately, the magnetic force, magnetism, or the laws concerning the magnetic force or magnetism.

Now let us consider the being of DNA. The physical being of DNA may be seen in that, as the building block of life, DNA constitutes the various living things in nature that we may observe, such as plants, flowers, animals, or humans. The rational being of DNA may be seen in the genetic studies about DNA. The genetic studies may reveal to us many things, such as, the structures of DNA, the biological functions of DNA, or the interactions between DNA and proteins. Through such genetic studies, we may be able to see into the development or functioning of DNA in constituting the various life forms in the world.

The harmonic being of DNA may be seen in the sense that, the double helical symmetry constitutes the biological foundation of DNA. As such, the double helical symmetry may be seen as behind the coming into being or existence of DNA. In other words, it might be said, the essential or fundamental being of DNA may be seen as a being of symmetry, or, a symmetric being.

Now let us consider the being of plants. The physical being of plants may be observed by us in nature. They have different shapes or forms. They have branches. They have roots. They have leaves. They have flowers. Or, they may grow cones. The rational being of plants may be seen in the scientific studies about plants. The scientific studies may reveal the inner mechanisms or processes of plants, such as, the plant cell structures or developments, the internal transportation systems, or, the vital processes called photosynthesis.

The harmonic being of plants may be seen in the sense that symmetry plays a fundamental role in the coming into being or existence of plants. The predominant existence of radial symmetry in plants may determine that such plants may grow or exist as the radially symmetric plants, and as such they may only produce cones. The predominant existence of bilateral symmetry in plants may determine that such plants may grow or develop as the bilaterally symmetric plants, and as such they may produce flowers. In other words, it might be said, symmetry may be seen as behind the existence of plants.

Now let us consider the being of animals. The physical being of animals may be seen in the things like, animals are able to move, animals eat food, or, animals possess their bodies which are usually capable of certain actions. The rational being of animals may be seen in the scientific studies or researches about animals. There are a number of scientific fields involving the study of animals, such as, biology, physiology, neuroscience, or genetics. Through such scientific studies or researches, we may be able to see into the inner mechanisms or processes involved in the coming into being or existence of animals. We may know how animals reproduce themselves. We may know how animals grow or develop. We may know how animals compete. We may know how animals survive. We may know how animals adapt to their environments. Such scientific knowledge may lead us to a better understanding of the rational being of animals.

The harmonic being of animals may be seen in that, it might be said, symmetry constitutes the foundation for the coming into being or existence of animals. Sponges may be seen as the asymmetric animals, possessing little symmetry and no nervous system. The animals like cnidarians, ctenophores or echinoderms may be seen as the radially symmetric animals, as they may demonstrate the predominant existence of radial symmetry and possess the simple nerve nets as their nervous systems. The animals like worms, insects, fish, birds, mammals or humans may be seen as the bilaterally symmetric animals, as they may demonstrate predominantly the presence of bilateral symmetry and develop or possess their centralized nervous systems. Thus, it seems, when it comes to animals, symmetry is behind the coming into being or existence of the nervous systems, and different symmetries may be behind the appearance of different nervous systems. And, as we know, apart from the radial symmetry or bilateral symmetry, other symmetries may also be behind the coming into being or existence of animals, such as, the double helical symmetry, or, the sexual symmetry. In other words, it might be said, symmetry may be seen as behind the coming into being or existence of animals.

Now let us consider the being of man. The physical being of man may be seen in the kind of things such as, we have a body, we have a head, we have two hands or legs, we have eyes or ears, or, we have tears, we can smile. The physical being of man may also be seen in the actions or activities of man. The rational being of man may be seen in the scientific studies or researches about man, such as, in biology, physiology, neuroscience, or genetics. Through such scientific studies or researches, we may be able to know the rational being or existence of man, such as, how cells replicate in the human body, how neurons interact with each other in the human nervous system, or, how genes may be related to some specific human traits or functions.

The rational being of man may also be seen in that, it is important or essential for a human being to be a rational being, so that he or she may live or survive in the world. Our daily lives are full of the kind of things that may require us to be the rational being. One cannot cross the street, if it is the red light. Otherwise, there might be an accident. Or, one may have to leave home early to catch the bus. Otherwise, it may be too late. And, as we all know, in the scientific studies or researches, the rational being of man may be fulfilled or realized, as man exercises his reason or mind.

The harmonic being of man may be seen in the sense that, it might be said, man comes into being from symmetry, and in symmetry man exists. Man comes into being from the double helical symmetry. Man comes into being from the sexual symmetry. Man comes into being from the fulfillment or realization of bilateral symmetry in animals. Man exists as the humoral being. Man exists as the humoral being in which the moral symmetry fulfils or realizes itself. Man exists as the humoral being in which the aesthetic symmetry fulfils or realizes itself. Man exists as the humoral being in which the logical symmetry fulfils or realizes itself. Man exists as the humoral being in which the humoral symmetries fulfill or realize themselves. Man exists in symmetry. Symmetry exists in man. Man exists in symmetries. Symmetries exist in man. Man exists in the humoral symmetries. The humoral symmetries exist in man. Thus, it might be said, the coming into being of man means the fulfillment or realization of symmetry in man, or, the fulfillment or realization of symmetry in man means the coming into being of man. Or, it might be said, the existence of man means the fulfillment or realization of symmetry in man, or, the fulfillment or realization of symmetry in man means the existence of man.

Man represents or stands for the fulfillment or realization of symmetry in animals. As such, it might be said, the harmonic being or existence of man may be seen as deep, complex, delicate, and profound. That is to say, as the fulfillment or realization of symmetry in the world, the harmonic being or existence of man may be beyond, in a sense, our grasp or understanding. We may perceive ourselves. We may search into our own existence. But, in the end, it may still be the case that, we may not be able to grasp all the harmonic being or existence of ourselves. Such may be seen, in a sense, in the situations that we face now. If the harmonic being or existence of man is damaged, there might be problems, and man may have to face some big consequences.

Now let us consider the being of morality. The physical being of morality may be seen in the life of man. The physical being of morality may be seen in the actions or activities of man that may have to do with the moral being or existence of man. The physical being of morality may be seen in the feelings manifested in man. We may be touched. We may be moved. We may be touched by other people's lives. We may be moved by other people's sacrifices. We may be touched or moved to tears.

The rational being of morality may be seen in the sense that, morality exists in man, and as such, the rational being of morality may be seen in the rational being of man. Man has to do to with the kind of things like biology, physiology, neuroscience or genetics. That is to say, it might be said, morality may have to do, in a sense, or to a certain extent, with the kind of things like biology, physiology, neuroscience or genetics. Such scientific studies or researches may reveal the mechanisms or processes possibly involved in the things like, how feelings happen, how emotions occur, how tears flow, how smiles appear, or, how human beings may be motivated to engage in the kind of actions or activities that may be called moral. In other words, it might be said, the scientific studies or researches may reveal the possible mechanisms or processes that may be behind the moral being or existence of man.

The rational being of morality may also be seen in the kind of things like, treat others as you would like to be treated, or, I want to help others since people helped me in my difficult times in the past. Such things may be regarded as the kind of things moral. At the same time, it seems, in such things we may find the role of reason. That is, it seems, it might be said, reason may have played a certain role in the happening or occurrence of such moral things. Moral things may have to do with reason. Reason may have to do with the moral things. Through reason, moral things may happen. Through reason, moral things may occur. Through reason, moral things may be rationalized. Through reason, moral things may be justified. Morality may happen, in such a sense, through reason. Morality may occur, in such a sense, through reason. Morality may be rationalized, in such a sense, through reason. Morality may be justified, in such a sense, through reason. It is in such a sense that, it might be said, the moral being or existence of man may be fulfilled or realized, in a sense, through reason, or, morality may be fulfilled or realized, in a sense, through reason.

The harmonic being of morality may be seen in the sense that, it is symmetry that is behind man, and as such, it might be said, it is symmetry that may be seen as behind morality. Man comes into being from the double helical symmetry. Man comes into being from the sexual symmetry. Man comes into being from the fulfillment or realization of bilateral symmetry in animals. That is to say, man comes into being from the fulfillment or realization of symmetries in man. Symmetry is behind man. Symmetries are behind man. It is in such a sense that, it might be said, symmetry is behind morality, or, symmetries are behind morality.

The harmonic being of morality may also be seen in the sense that, the moral symmetry may be seen as the symmetry behind morality. To be good, so that man may be man. To be good, so that man may exist as man. To be good, so that evil may be overcome. To be good, so that evil may be reduced. To fulfill or realize the moral symmetry, so that man may exist as man. To fulfill or realize the moral symmetry, so that man may be fulfilled or realized as man. The fulfillment or realization of the moral symmetry is the fulfillment or realization of man. The fulfillment or realization of the moral symmetry is the fulfillment or realization of morality in man. The fulfillment or realization of the moral symmetry is the fulfillment or realization of man in the world, in a moral sense, in a moral way, or in a moral manner. The fulfillment or realization of the moral symmetry is the fulfillment or realization of morality in the world, in a human sense, in a human way, or, in a human manner.

Now let us consider the being of beauty. The physical being of beauty may be seen in the life of man. The physical being of beauty may be seen in nature. The physical being of beauty may be seen in the world. The physical being of beauty may be seen in the actions or reactions of man related to beauty, or to the creation of beauty. The physical being of beauty may be seen in the feelings of man associated with beauty, or with the creation of beauty.

The rational being of beauty may be seen in the sense that, beauty is a feeling of man, and as such, the rational being of beauty may be seen, in a sense, in the rational being of man. Man has to do with the kind of things like biology, physiology, neuroscience or genetics. In other words, such scientific studies or researches may reveal, in a sense, or to a certain extent, the rational being or existence of man. it is in such a sense that, it might be said, certain things about beauty, as the feeling of man, may be revealed, in a sense, or to a certain extent, by or through such scientific studies or researches, such as, how feelings associated with beauty happen, how people react to beauty, how things are deemed as beautiful, or, how people may be motivated to engage in the kind of things or activities related to beauty or to the creation of beauty. That is to say, the scientific studies or researches may reveal, in a sense, or to a certain extent, the possible mechanisms or processes that may be behind the aesthetic being or existence of man.

The rational being of beauty may also be seen in the sense that, it might be said, beauty may come into being, in a sense, through reason.

Such may be seen, for example, in the beautiful architectures around the world. We often find mathematical patterns or proportional designs in such architectures around the world. And, it seems, if we examine such beautiful structures carefully, we may encounter what is called the golden ratio. All such proportional measurements or mathematical designs are aimed to contribute to the beauty of the architectures. And it seems, beauty appears indeed as a result of such designs or measurements, sometimes, it might be said, quite impressively.

The harmonic being of beauty may be seen in the sense that, as man is the fulfillment or realization of symmetry in the world, symmetry may be seen as behind beauty. Man comes into being from the double helical symmetry. Man comes into being from the sexual symmetry. Man comes into being as a result of the fulfillment or realization of bilateral symmetry in animals. Symmetry is behind man. Symmetry is behind the being or existence of man. Beauty is a feeling of man. As such, it might be said, symmetry is behind beauty, or, symmetry is behind the being or existence of beauty.

The harmonic being of beauty may be seen in the sense that, beauty may be seen as the fulfillment or realization of the aesthetic symmetry in man. To pursue the beautiful, so that man may exist as the humoral being. To pursue the beautiful, so that man may fulfill or realize himself as the humoral being. To pursue the beautiful, so that the ugly may be removed. To pursue the beautiful, so that the ugly may be reduced. To fulfill or realize the aesthetic symmetry, so that man may exist as the humoral man. To fulfill or realize the aesthetic symmetry, so that man may fulfill or realize himself as the humoral man. The fulfillment or realization of the aesthetic symmetry means the fulfillment or realization of man. The fulfillment or realization of the aesthetic symmetry means the fulfillment or realization of beauty in man. The fulfillment or realization of the aesthetic symmetry means the fulfillment or realization of beauty in the world.

The harmonic being of beauty may be seen in the sense that, beauty is a sense of harmony, beauty is a feeling of harmony, beauty is a sense of the existence of harmony, beauty is a feeling of the existence of harmony, and harmony is in the world. Beauty is a sense of man. Beauty is a feeling of man. Beauty is a sense of man of the existence of harmony. Beauty is a feeling of man of the existence of harmony. Beauty is the existence of harmony. Beauty is the being of harmony. Beauty is harmony. Harmony is beauty. Harmony may be seen in the harmonic existence of man. Thus, we may see the moral beauty or humoral beauty manifested in man. Harmony may be seen in nature. Thus, we may see the beauty of plants, the beauty of animals, the beauty of the human bodies, or the beauty of the human gestures or behaviors. Harmony may be seen in the world. Thus, we may see the beauty of the planets, or, the beauty of the heavens. Harmony is in the world; beauty is in the world. Beauty is in the world; harmony is in the world.

We have discussed, thus far, the being of morality and the being of beauty. Morality and beauty may be seen as constituting two fundamental aspects of the heart. It is in such a sense that, it might be said, we have discussed, in a fundamental sense, the being of heart. The other aspects of the being of heart may be discussed, it might be said, in a similar manner.

Now let us consider the being of reason. The physical being of reason may be seen in the physical existence of the human brain, or in the human activities associated with reason or with the exercise of reason.

The rational being of reason may be seen, in a sense, in the scientific studies or researches about the human brain. The scientific studies or researches, such as neuroscience, may reveal the mechanisms or processes that may have to do with the various functions of the human brain. For example, such mechanisms or processes may involve the nerve cells called neurons. Neurons are the basic units of the human brain. Thus, as one of the functions of the human brain, reasoning may have to do with neurons or with the mechanisms or processes associated with neurons. In other words, the scientific studies or researches may reveal the possible mechanisms or processes behind the working or operation of reason.

The rational being of reason may also be seen in that, in a sense, it might be said, man is a rational being. The human life has to do with reason, in many ways. The human existence has to do with reason, in many senses. Man often strives to justify himself in a rational way. Man often strives to justify his actions or behaviors rationally. It seems, it might be said, the human life has to do, in a fundamental sense, with the rational being of man. And, as we all know, human beings often engage in various scientific studies or researches. Such scientific endeavors may well demonstrate the rational being of reason. That is, it

Avolution and Man

might be said, reason strives, in a sense, to search into the world, and in such a way it may fulfill or realize its rational being or existence.

The harmonic being of reason may be seen in the sense that, symmetry is behind man, and as such, it might be said, symmetry is behind reason. Symmetries are behind man. Reason is a faculty of man. Thus, it might be said, symmetries may be seen as behind the faculty of man called reason. Such symmetries may include the double helical symmetry, the sexual symmetry and the bilateral symmetry. The bilateral symmetry may be seen as possessing a special place, when it comes to reason, in that it has to do with the coming into being or existence of the human nervous system. The human nervous system is a centralized nervous system. The centralized nervous system cannot be found in the radially symmetric animals. The nervous systems of the radially symmetric animals are the simple nerve nets. The centralized nervous systems can only be found in the bilaterally symmetric animals, such as fish, birds, or humans. In other words, it might be said, bilateral symmetry is behind the coming into being or existence of the centralized nervous system, and it is the fulfillment or realization of the bilateral symmetry in animals that may have led to the coming into being or existence of the human nervous system. Symmetry may thus be seen as behind the human brain. And symmetry may thus be seen as behind reason.

The harmonic being of reason may also be seen in that, reason may be seen as a power coming into being from the fulfillment or realization of the logical symmetry in man. To pursue the true, so that man may be man. To pursue the true, so that man may exist as man. To pursue the true, so that man may preserve himself as man. To pursue the true, so that man may maintain or sustain himself as man. To pursue the true, so that the false may be disclosed. To pursue the true, so that the false may be eliminated. To fulfill or realize the logical symmetry, so that man may live or exist as man. To fulfill or realize the logical symmetry, so that man may fulfill or realize himself as the humoral being. The fulfillment or realization of the logical symmetry means the fulfillment or realization of man. The fulfillment or realization of the logical symmetry means the fulfillment or realization of man in a logical sense, in a logical way, or in a logical fashion. The fulfillment or realization of the logical symmetry means the exercise of reason. The fulfillment or realization of the logical symmetry means the coming into being of reason in man. Reason thus comes into being, as the fulfillment or realization of the logical symmetry. Reason thus comes into being, as the fulfillment or realization of the logical symmetry in man.

Reason may be seen as constituting, in a sense, the mainstay of mind. It is in such a sense that, it might be said, having discussed the being of reason, we have discussed the being of mind. The other aspects of the being of mind may be discussed, it might be said, in a similar manner.

Being may thus be seen as fulfilling or realizing itself in three layers, or at three levels. The physical being may be seen as constituting the outer layer of being, having to do mostly with our senses. We may touch it. We may see it. We may experience it through our senses. In such a sense, it might be said, the physical being may be seen as the being at the sensory or physical level. The rational being may be seen as constituting the middle layer of being, in the sense that, though it may not be experienced directly by us through our senses, it may be understood by us through reason. In such a sense, it might be said, the rational being may be seen as the being at the scientific or rational level. The harmonic being may be seen as constituting the innermost layer of being. That is, the harmonic being may be seen as the being closely associated with symmetry or harmony. In such a sense, it might be said, the harmonic being may be seen as the being at the symmetric or harmonic level.

The harmonic being is the being underlying the physical being. The harmonic being is the being underlying the rational being. The physical being is the harmonic being expressed in a physical sense. The rational being is the harmonic being expressed in a rational way. The physical being is the harmonic being manifested at a physical level. The rational being is the harmonic being manifested at a rational level. The harmonic being expresses or manifests itself in the physical being. The harmonic being expresses or manifests itself in the rational being. The harmonic being fulfils or realizes itself in the physical being. The harmonic being fulfils or realizes itself in the rational being. The physical being embodies the harmonic being. The rational being represents the harmonic being. Through the physical being, the harmonic being is embodied, at the physical level. Through the rational being, the harmonic being is represented, at the rational level. Through the physical being, the harmonic being is fulfilled, at the physical level. Through the rational being, the harmonic being is realized, at the rational level. The physical being is the expression; the harmonic being is the source. The physical being is the development; the harmonic being is the foundation. The rational being is the manifestation; the harmonic being is the origin. The rational being is the development; the harmonic being is the essence within.

The development of being may be seen as consisting of three developments, that is, the physical development, the rational development, and the harmonic development. When we talk about the physical development of things, we usually talk about the whole development of things. That is, it seems, it might be said, the physical development may be seen, in an analytical sense, as consisting of the rational development and the harmonic development. It is in such a sense that, it might be said, when we discuss the development of things, we may focus on the rational development and the harmonic development.

Through the physical development, the physical being comes into being. Through the rational development, the rational being comes into being. Through the harmonic development, the harmonic being comes into being. Through the rational development and the harmonic development, the physical development fulfils or realizes itself. Through the physical development and the rational development, the harmonic development fulfils or realizes itself. Through the physical development and the harmonic development, the rational development fulfils or realizes itself. Thus, we see the physical development in things. Thus, we see the rational development in things. Thus, we see the harmonic development in things. Thus, we see the physical being in things. Thus, we see the rational being in things. Thus, we see the harmonic being in things. The physical being thus comes into being. The rational being thus comes into being. The harmonic being thus comes into being. Being comes into being. Existence comes to exist in the world.

Being comes into being, as the physical being, the rational being and the harmonic being. Being develops, as the physical development, the rational development and the harmonic development. The development of being is not just the physical development. The development of being is not just the rational development. The development of being is not just the harmonic development. The development of being is about the physical development, the rational development and the harmonic development. The development of being is about all of them. It is in such a sense that, it might be said, the theory of evolution is woefully inadequate, when it comes to explain the development of things. The theory of evolution may be regarded as concerning itself only with the rational development of things, apart from the physical development of things. In other words, it might be said, in the theory of evolution, what is overlooked or ignored is the harmonic development, a development that may be behind the physical development and the rational development. That is to say, in an analytical sense, it might be said, evolution may only explain or represent the rational development. It does not explain the harmonic development. It does not represent the harmonic development. It does not concern itself with the harmonic development. Avolution is concerned with the physical development. Avolution is concerned with the rational development. Avolution is concerned with the harmonic development. Avolution is concerned with all the developments of things. Avolution is concerned with all the development of things. Avolution is concerned with all the being of things. Avolution is concerned with all the existence of things in the world.

§ 5.3.1 Symmetry, the Symmetries, and the Symmetric Powers

The Symmetry	The Symmetric Opposites	The Symmetric Power
Double Helical Symmetry	The Two Strands	DNA
Sexual Symmetry	Male / Female	Sex
Electric Symmetry	Positive / Negative	Electric Force
Magnetic Symmetry	North / South	Magnetic Force
Moral Symmetry	Good / Evil	Heart
Aesthetic Symmetry	Beautiful / Ugly	Heart
Logical Symmetry	True / False	Reason

Figure 5.3 Symmetry, the Symmetries, and the Symmetric Powers

Heaven is the harmony of things. Man is a humoral being. Anteanity is the affinity of man with the mother earth.

Symmetry fulfils or realizes itself as symmetries in the world. Symmetry fulfils or realizes itself in a double helical way in the world, as the double helical symmetry. Symmetry fulfils or realizes itself in a sexual way in the world, as the sexual symmetry. Symmetry fulfils or realizes itself in an electric way in the world, as the electric symmetry. Symmetry fulfils or realizes itself in a magnetic way in the world, as the magnetic symmetry. Symmetry fulfils or realizes itself in a moral way in the world, as the moral symmetry. Symmetry fulfils or realizes itself in an aesthetic way in the world, as the aesthetic symmetry. Symmetry fulfils or realizes itself in a logical way in the world, as the logical symmetry.

With the fulfillment or realization of symmetry in the world, the symmetric powers come into being or appear in the world. The symmetric powers are the fulfillment or realization of symmetry in the world. The symmetric powers express the power of symmetry. The symmetric powers demonstrate the power of symmetry. The symmetric powers represent the power of symmetry. The symmetric powers stand for the power of symmetry. Through the symmetric powers, symmetry expresses itself. Through the symmetric powers, symmetry manifests itself. Through the symmetric powers, symmetry fulfils itself. Through the symmetric powers, symmetry realizes itself in the world.

Symmetry is behind the symmetric powers. Symmetry is underlying the symmetric powers. Symmetry supports the symmetric powers. Symmetry maintains the symmetric powers. Symmetry sustains the symmetric powers. Symmetry defines the symmetric powers. Symmetry is the source of the symmetric powers. Symmetry is the origin of the symmetric powers. Symmetry is the root of the symmetric powers. Symmetry is the fountainhead of the symmetric powers. Through symmetry, the symmetric powers come into being. Through symmetry, the symmetric powers appear. In symmetry, the symmetric powers begin. In symmetry, the symmetric powers exist. For symmetry, the symmetric powers come into existence. For symmetry, the symmetric powers fulfill or realize themselves in the world.

In symmetry, the symmetric powers exist. Through the symmetric powers, symmetry fulfils or realizes itself. Symmetry fulfils or realizes itself as the symmetric powers. Symmetry fulfils or realizes itself through the symmetric powers. The symmetric powers mean symmetry. Symmetry means the symmetric powers. The symmetric powers are the actualization of symmetry in the world. The symmetric powers are the physicalization of symmetry in the world. The symmetric powers are the fulfillment or realization of symmetry in the world.

It is in such a sense that, it might be said, the symmetric powers may be seen as the fulfillment or realization of symmetry in the world, in the various ways, or in the various senses. DNA may be seen as the fulfillment or realization of symmetry in a double helical way. Sex may be seen as the fulfillment or realization of symmetry in a sexual sense.

The electric force may be seen as the fulfillment or realization of symmetry in an electric way. The magnetic force may be seen as the fulfillment or realization of symmetry in a magnetic way. Heart may be seen as the fulfillment or realization of symmetry in a moral sense. Heart may be seen as the fulfillment or realization of symmetry in an aesthetic sense. Reason may be seen as the fulfillment or realization of symmetry in a logical sense, or, in a rational way.

The double helical symmetry means DNA. DNA means the double helical symmetry. DNA is the capacity; the double helical symmetry is the symmetry. The sexual symmetry means sex. Sex means the sexual symmetry. Sex is the function; the sexual symmetry is the symmetry. The electric symmetry means the electric power. The electric power means the electric symmetry. The electric power is the force; the electric symmetry is the symmetry. The magnetic symmetry means the magnetic force. The magnetic force means the magnetic symmetry. The magnetic force is the power; the magnetic symmetry is the symmetry. The moral symmetry means the moral heart. The moral heart means the moral symmetry. The moral heart is the faculty; the moral symmetry is the symmetry. The aesthetic symmetry means the aesthetic heart. The aesthetic heart means the aesthetic symmetry. The aesthetic heart is the faculty; the aesthetic symmetry is the symmetry. The logical symmetry means reason. Reason means the logical symmetry. Reason is the faculty; the logical symmetry is the symmetry.

§ 5.3.2 The Nature of the Symmetries

It has to be noted, it appears, it is not the case that symmetry fulfils or realizes itself in the same ways. That is, the symmetries discussed here appear to be different in some certain ways. The kind of symmetries such as double helical symmetry, sexual symmetry, electric symmetry and magnetic symmetry may be seen as the physical symmetries, in the sense that they are associated with the physical entities. On the other hand, the kind of symmetries like moral symmetry, aesthetic symmetry and logical symmetry may be seen as the metaphysical symmetries, as the kind of things with which they are associated, such as good or evil, beautiful or ugly, or true or false, may be seen as metaphysical in nature. While the symmetries may be divided in such a way into the physical and metaphysical symmetries, they may also be divided into the physical and humoral symmetries. That is, the kind of symmetries called the metaphysical symmetries, such as the moral symmetry, aesthetic symmetry and logical symmetry, may be seen as the humoral symmetries, in the sense that, it might be said, they are different from the other symmetries and closely associated with the humoral being or existence of man.

DNA is the biological power for carrying the genetic information. Sex is the sexual power for sexual reproduction. The electric power is the electric force. The magnetic power is the magnetic force. Heart is the power to feel. Reason is the power to rationalize. Heart may be seen as the feelings, that is, as the humoral feelings of man. The humoral feelings here may be divided into two kinds of feelings, the moral feelings and the aesthetic feelings. The humoral feelings involved in the moral symmetry may be seen as the moral feelings. The humoral feelings involved in the aesthetic symmetry may be seen as the aesthetic feelings. Thus, the heart involved with the moral symmetry may be seen as the moral heart of man, and the heart involved with the aesthetic symmetry may be seen as the aesthetic heart of man. The moral heart means the moral feelings of man. The aesthetic heart means the aesthetic feelings of man. Reason may be seen, in the logical or rational sense, as the mind.

To be true is good, so that man may come into being. To be man is good, so that the true may come into being, be preserved, maintained, sustained, safeguarded, or upheld. That is, with the coming into being of the humoral man, the good comes into being, and at the same time, the evil appears, as the opposite of the good. To be false is not good, as it is the opposite of the true. Not to be man is not good, as it is the opposite of being man, and as such, it may not lead or contribute to the coming into being or existence of the true. That is to say, through the coming into being of the humoral man, the moral symmetry comes into being, as the symmetry of good and evil.

Beauty is a feeling. Beauty is a sense of feeling. Beauty is a sense of feeling the existence of harmony in the world. That is, it might be said, beauty may be seen as a humoral feeling of man connecting man with the harmonic existence of the world. Through the humoral feeling of man, beauty is deemed beautiful, as it may lead or contribute to the harmonic coming into being or existence of the world. Through the humoral feeling of man, the ugly may be deemed not beautiful, as it may not lead or contribute to the harmonic coming into being or existence of the world. Through the coming into being of the humoral man, the humoral feeling of man comes into being. That is to say, through the coming into being of the humoral man, the aesthetic symmetry may be seen as coming into being in the world, as the symmetry of the beautiful and the ugly.

Through the humoral truth, it might be said, the harmonic truth comes into being. Through the harmonic truth, the logical symmetry comes into being. Thus, it might be said, the logical symmetry may be seen as coming into being through the humoral truth coming into being in man, that is, through the coming into being of the humoral man. Through the coming into being of the humoral man, the moral symmetry comes into being. Through the coming into being of the humoral man, the aesthetic symmetry comes into being. Thus, it is through the coming into being of the humoral man that, it might be said, the moral symmetry, aesthetic symmetry and logical symmetry come into being. That is, it is through the coming into being of the humorality of man that, it might be said, the moral symmetry, aesthetic symmetry and logical symmetry come into being or appear in the world.

The metaphysical symmetries may thus be seen as the humoral symmetries. And the humoral symmetries may thus be seen as the metaphysical symmetries. The metaphysical symmetries may thus be associated with the humoral being or existence of man, and the humoral symmetries may thus be associated with the kind of metaphysical things such as, good or evil, beautiful or ugly, or, true or false. Thus, when it comes to the moral symmetry, aesthetic symmetry or logical symmetry, it might be said, the metaphysical may be seen as being associated with the humoral and the humoral may be seen as being associated with the metaphysical. That is to say, when it comes to the kind of symmetries like the moral symmetry, aesthetic symmetry or logical symmetry, in a sense, it might be said, the metaphysical means the humoral and the humoral means the metaphysical.

Symmetry fulfils or realizes itself in animals as man. Symmetry fulfils or realizes itself in the animal kingdom as the humoral man. Symmetry fulfils or realizes itself in the world as the humorality of man. Symmetry fulfils or realizes itself in man as the moral symmetry, aesthetic symmetry and logical symmetry. Symmetry fulfils or realizes itself in the world as the moral symmetry, aesthetic symmetry and logical symmetry. Symmetry fulfils or realizes itself in man as the humoral symmetries. Symmetry fulfils or realizes itself in man as the metaphysical symmetries. Symmetry fulfils or realizes itself in the world as the humoral symmetries. Symmetry fulfils or realizes itself in the world as the metaphysical symmetries.

Through the humoral or metaphysical symmetries, symmetry fulfils or realizes itself in man. Through the humoral or metaphysical symmetries, man fulfils or realizes himself in symmetry. Through the humoral or metaphysical symmetries, symmetry fulfils or realizes itself in the world. Through the humoral or metaphysical symmetries, man fulfils or realizes himself in the world. Thus, what do the humoral or metaphysical symmetries mean? They mean the existence of man. They mean the existence of man in symmetry. They mean the existence of man in the world. They mean the meaning of man. They mean the meaning of man in symmetry. They mean the meaning of man in the world. They mean the life of man. They mean the life of man in symmetry. They mean the life of man in the world.

What is the existence of man? What is the meaning of man? What is the life of man? What is the meaning of the existence of man? What is the meaning of the life of man? It is to fulfill or realize symmetry. It is to fulfill or realize the humoral man. It is to fulfill or realize the humorality of man. It is to fulfill or realize the moral symmetry. It is to fulfill or realize the aesthetic symmetry. It is to fulfill or realize the logical symmetry. It is to pursue the true. It is to pursue the good. It is to pursue the beautiful. It is to pursue the true, the good and the beautiful. It is to pursue the humorality of man. It is to pursue the humoral man. It is to pursue the humoral existence of man. It is to pursue the humoral life of man. It is to pursue the humoral meaning of man. It is to pursue the true so that the logical symmetry may be fulfilled or realized. It is to pursue the good so that the moral symmetry may be fulfilled or realized. It is to pursue the beautiful so that the aesthetic symmetry may be fulfilled or realized. It is to pursue the true, the good and the beautiful so that symmetry may be fulfilled or realized in man. It is to pursue the true, the good and the beautiful so that symmetry may be fulfilled or realized in the world. It is to pursue the true, the good and the beautiful so that man may be fulfilled or realized in symmetry. It is to pursue the true, the good and the beautiful so that man may be fulfilled or realized, as man, in the world.

To pursue the true is to fulfill or realize the logical symmetry, in the sense that, with the pursuit of truth, falsity would be revealed. The more truth is discovered, the more falsity may be revealed to us. In such a sense, it might be said, through our pursuing the true, the logical symmetry may be fulfilled or realized. To pursue the good is to fulfill or realize the moral symmetry, in the sense that, with the pursuit of good, evil may be disclosed, and eradicated. The more good is done, the more evil may be brought to light and rooted out. In such a sense, it might be said, through our pursuing the good, the moral symmetry may be fulfilled or realized. To pursue the beautiful is to fulfill or realize the aesthetic symmetry, in the sense that, with the pursuit of beauty, ugliness may be located, and reduced in the world. The more beauty is pursued, the more ugliness may be reduced. In such a sense, it might be said, through our pursuing the beautiful, the aesthetic symmetry may be fulfilled or realized.

The fulfillment or realization of symmetry in man may thus mean the human pursuit of the true, the good and the beautiful. The fulfillment or realization of symmetry in the world may thus mean the human pursuit of the true, the good and the beautiful. The fulfillment or realization of man in symmetry may thus mean the human pursuit of the true, the good and the beautiful. The fulfillment or realization of man in the world may thus mean the human pursuit of the true, the good and the beautiful. It is the fulfillment or realization of symmetry. It is the fulfillment or realization of man. It is the fulfillment or realization of moral symmetry. It is the fulfillment or realization of aesthetic symmetry. It is the fulfillment or realization of logical symmetry. It is the fulfillment or realization of symmetry in man. It is the fulfillment or realization of man in symmetry. It is the fulfillment or realization of symmetry through man. It is the fulfillment or realization of man through symmetry. It is the fulfillment or realization of the humoral symmetries. It is the fulfillment or realization of the metaphysical symmetries. It is the fulfillment or realization of the humoral symmetries in the metaphysical ways. It is the fulfillment or realization of the metaphysical symmetries in the humoral senses.

The humoral is fulfilled or realized through the metaphysical. The metaphysical is fulfilled or realized through the humoral. The humoral is associated with the metaphysical, and the metaphysical is associated with the humoral. The humoral nature may thus be seen as what defines the metaphysical symmetries, and the metaphysical nature may thus be seen as what characterizes the humoral symmetries. While the humoral symmetries like the moral symmetry, aesthetic symmetry and logical symmetry may be seen as the metaphysical symmetries, the other symmetries may be regarded as the physical symmetries, such as, double helical symmetry, sexual symmetry, electric symmetry or magnetic symmetry. People may have noticed the differences between the symmetric powers. The symmetric powers in the physical symmetries appear to be different from the symmetric powers in the metaphysical symmetries. The symmetric powers in the physical symmetries, such as sex, electric force or magnetic force, often mean the attraction between the symmetric opposites. Even in the double helical symmetry, the two strands bind together. But that may not be the case with the metaphysical symmetries. As we have discussed, the symmetric powers in these symmetries mean the pursuit of the true, the good and the beautiful. In other words, they are not the attraction between the symmetric opposites. Rather, it seems, they are the powers to reject one of the symmetric opposites and pursue the other, and as such, they may be seen as constituting, in a sense, the repelling forces between the symmetric opposites. That is, it has to be said, quite different from what might happen with the physical symmetries.

The two strands bind together in the double helical symmetry. Males and females attract each other. The opposite charges attract each other. The opposite magnetic poles attract each other. This is what happens with the physical symmetries like the double helical symmetry, sexual symmetry, electric symmetry or magnetic symmetry. But, it seems, things change when it comes to the humoral symmetries such as the moral symmetry, aesthetic symmetry or logical symmetry. The binding or attractive forces between the symmetric opposites seem to have disappeared, and in their place, it might be said, a different kind of forces come into existence which may mean the pursuit of only one of the symmetric opposites. Why? Why should it be such a case? Why should such things happen? Why should such things happen to the humoral symmetries? Why should such things happen only to the humoral symmetries?

It seems, it might be said, it has to do with the nature of the humoral symmetries. That is, in a sense, it might be said, it has to do with the metaphysical nature of the humoral symmetries. The metaphysical nature of the humoral symmetries may mean that such symmetries are different from the physical symmetries, and the symmetric powers associated with them may be quite different from the symmetric powers associated with the physical symmetries. The symmetric powers associated with the physical symmetries may be called the physical symmetric powers, or simply, the physical powers. The symmetric powers associated with the humoral or metaphysical symmetries may be called the humoral or metaphysical symmetric powers, or simply, the humoral or metaphysical powers. The physical symmetric powers may mean the powers or forces that work on the physical entities, such as, on the two strands of DNA, on the two sexes, on the positive and negative charges, or on the north and south poles. Thus, it might be said, the physical symmetric powers may be seen, literally, as the physical powers or forces. But that may be a different story with the humoral or metaphysical symmetric powers. How should these powers work? How should these powers exert their influences? How should these powers fulfill or realize themselves? If no physical entities present, how should these powers work to demonstrate themselves? If no physical entities available, on whom or what should these powers exert their influences? If no physical entities existing, in what ways could these powers fulfill or realize themselves?

It seems, nevertheless, these powers have indeed worked. They have indeed exerted their influences. They have indeed fulfilled or realized themselves in the world. As the humoral or metaphysical symmetric powers, they work in their humoral or metaphysical manners, or through their humoral or metaphysical ways. As the humoral or metaphysical powers, they work on the humorality of man. As the humoral or metaphysical powers, they exert their influences on the humorality of man. As the humoral or metaphysical powers, they fulfill or realize themselves through the humorality of man. As the humoral or metaphysical powers, they work on the humoral man. As the humoral or metaphysical powers, they exert their influences on the humoral man. As the humoral or metaphysical powers, they fulfill or realize themselves through the humoral man. They work on the humoral man to pursue the true. They work on the humoral man to pursue the good. They work on the humoral man to pursue the beautiful. They exert their influences on the humoral man so that the humoral symmetries, the moral symmetry, aesthetic symmetry and logical symmetry, may be fulfilled or realized in the world.

When we talk about the humoral or metaphysical symmetries, as one can see, we mostly focus on the humoral or metaphysical nature of the symmetric opposites. That is to say, when we talk about the humoral or metaphysical symmetries, we are mostly concerned, until now, with the humoral or metaphysical things like good or evil, beautiful or ugly, or true or false. Certainly, these things may be regarded as the humoral or metaphysical things. But, how about the humoral man? The humoral man is humoral. Should the humoral man be regarded as metaphysical? It seems, it may better be said, the humoral man may be regarded as both physical and metaphysical, in the sense that, the humorality of man involves both physical and mental activities. That is to say, while the humoral symmetric opposites may be seen as metaphysical, the humoral man may be regarded as both physical and metaphysical.

This may reveal, in a sense, the secrets behind the fulfillment or realization of the humoral symmetries in the world. While the humoral symmetries are metaphysical, the humoral man is both physical and metaphysical. While the humoral man is both physical and metaphysical, the humoral symmetric opposites are metaphysical. The metaphysical nature of the humoral symmetric opposites makes it possible for the humoral symmetries to be fulfilled or realized through the humoral man. The physical and metaphysical nature of the humoral man makes it possible for the humoral powers to work on the humoral man, so that, it might be said, the humoral symmetries may be fulfilled or realized, eventually, in the world.

Thus, the fulfillment or realization of the humoral symmetries, the moral symmetry, aesthetic symmetry and logical symmetry, may have to do with the very nature of such symmetries. It is the nature of being both humoral and metaphysical. It is the humoral and metaphysical nature that makes it possible for the humoral symmetries to come into being. It is the humoral and metaphysical nature that makes it possible for the humoral symmetries to appear. It is the humoral and metaphysical nature that makes it possible for the humoral symmetries to come into being in man. It is the humoral and metaphysical nature that makes it possible for the humoral symmetries to appear in the world. It is the humoral and metaphysical nature that makes it possible for the humoral symmetries to be fulfilled or realized in man. It is the humoral and metaphysical nature that makes it possible for the humoral symmetries to be fulfilled or realized in the world.

It may have to be said, until now, we have discussed the moral symmetry, aesthetic symmetry and logical symmetry only in a humoral sense, that is, only in the sense that they may be associated with the human beings. Some might ask, how about the other highly developed animals, such as the primates other than the human beings? The development of the animal nervous system or the animal brain may be seen as the foundation for the coming into being or appearance of the humorality of man. The humorality of man means the coming into being or appearance of the moral symmetry, aesthetic symmetry and logical symmetry, or, in a sense, it might be said, the moral symmetry, aesthetic symmetry and logical symmetry mean the humorality of man. Thus, it might be said, the development of the animal nervous system or the animal brain may have to do with the coming into being or appearance of the moral symmetry, aesthetic symmetry and logical symmetry, or, the moral symmetry, aesthetic symmetry and logical symmetry may have to do with the development of the animal nervous system or the animal brain. While the human nervous system or the human brain may have given rise to the fulfillment or realization of the moral symmetry, aesthetic symmetry and logical symmetry in the human beings, it may be the case that, the other highly developed animal nervous systems or animal brains may lead to the fulfillment or realization of the moral symmetry, aesthetic symmetry and logical symmetry in such animals, in some sense, or to some extent. That is to say, it may not be ruled out that, in some sense, or to some extent, the moral symmetry, aesthetic symmetry and logical symmetry may be fulfilled or realized in other animals, especially in those highly developed species. Certainly, it may be difficult for us to gauge the extent to which such symmetries may be fulfilled or realized in such animals, but, it seems, it might be said, we may be able to witness the kind of phenomena possibly associated with the fulfillment or realization of the moral symmetry, aesthetic symmetry and logical symmetry in animals.

§ 5.3.3 The Nature of the Symmetric Powers

The physical symmetries may be seen as giving rise to the physical powers. The humoral symmetries may be seen as giving rise to the humoral powers. The physical powers fulfill or realize the physical symmetries. The humoral powers fulfill or realize the humoral symmetries. DNA, sex, electric force and magnetic force may be seen as the physical powers. Heart and reason may be seen as the humoral powers. DNA is the genetic power, fulfilling or realizing the double helical symmetry. Sex is the sexual power, fulfilling or realizing the sexual symmetry. Electric force is the electric power, fulfilling or realizing the electric symmetry. Magnetic force is the magnetic power, fulfilling or realizing the magnetic symmetry. The moral heart is the moral power, fulfilling or realizing the moral symmetry. The aesthetic heart is the aesthetic power, fulfilling or realizing the aesthetic symmetry. Reason is the logical or rational power, fulfilling or realizing the logical symmetry. Together, the physical powers fulfill or realize the physical symmetries. Together, the humoral powers fulfill or realize the humoral symmetries. Together, the physical powers and the humoral powers fulfill or realize symmetry in man, in nature, or in the world.

As the powers coming into being through the different symmetries, or for the different symmetries, it might be said, the symmetric powers may be powerful in their own domains, but may not be so in other realms. That is to say, when it comes to their own symmetries, the symmetric powers may be powerful and effective, but when it comes to the different symmetries, the symmetric powers may prove to be inadequate, ineffective, or powerless. The symmetric powers are created, in a sense, for fulfilling or realizing the symmetries through which they have come into being. It is in such a sense that, it might be said, the symmetric powers may be powerful only in the sense that they work or operate within their own respective symmetries, that is, within their own respective symmetric domains. They may enter the different symmetries, that is, they may work or operate in the different symmetric domains, but the results may prove to be not so reliable, dependable, sound or trustworthy.

Such may be seen in a number of cases. Through the logical symmetry, it might be said, reason comes into being. As the logical or rational power, reason fulfils or realizes the logical symmetry. We all know, how powerful reason might be when it works to reveal the truth or falsity of the world. The Newtonian laws, the theory of relativity of Einstein, the advance of science, the development of technology ... They all stand as the testimony to the great power of reason. Reason leads us in the pursuit of truth. Reason leads us in discovering the secrets of nature. Reason enables us to penetrate into the depths of the world. But, what happens if reason attempts to work or operate in the different symmetric domains? That is, what happens if reason leaves the logical symmetry and enters the symmetries other than its own, such as, the moral symmetry, or, the aesthetic symmetry? It seems, it might be said, the answer is not very difficult to find, and we all know the results. Morality does not exist. Man is nothing. Life is meaningless. Life is absurd. Beauty is anything ... Do we need more results? Do we need more claims? Do we need more arguments? Do we need more logic? Do we need more reasoning? Do we need more rationality? Do we need more rationalization? It seems, no, we do not.

Needless to say, in certain cases, or in some circumstances, heart may produce the same kind of results if it attempts to enter the realm of reason. Heart is about feeling. Heart is about perception. But, we all know, how feelings might be unreliable, and how perceptions might be deceiving. That is to say, it might be said, heart may be good at guiding a person to behave in a moral manner, but it may not be so good at guiding such a person to avoid the misperceptions of the world. That is, it might be said, heart may be good at leading people to admire a beautiful sunset, but it may not be so good at leading people to find the possible logical or rational truths behind things. Heart is for the moral symmetry. Heart is for the aesthetic symmetry. Heart works for the moral symmetry. Heart works for the aesthetic symmetry. Reason is for the logical symmetry. Reason works for the logical symmetry. They are for their own symmetries. They work for their own symmetries. They come into being for their own symmetries. They exist for their own symmetries. They work or operate, in their powerful ways, validly, reliably, and effectively, in their own symmetric domains.

Does this mean that, heart may never work in the realm of reason and has nothing to do with the workings or operations of reason? Not necessarily. Does this mean that reason has nothing to do with the moral or aesthetic life and may never contribute to such human existences? Not necessarily. Heart may contribute to the workings or operations of reason, in the sense that, as the humoral bridge between man and nature or between man and the world, heart may lead man to forge a close affinity with nature or the world, and such a sense of close affinity of man with nature or the world may play some role in the rational or scientific search of man into nature or the world. Such may be seen, in a sense, for example, in the discovery of the law of universal gravitation by Newton, or in the development of the theory of relativity by Einstein. The close affinity with earth might have led Newton to sense the relationship between the falling of an apple and the force among the planets. The close affinity with the world might have led

Einstein to sense the connection between his compass and the deeply hidden secrets of the world. Heart means the close affinity of man with his own being. Heart means the close affinity of man with his existence in the world. Heart means the close affinity of man with nature. Heart means the close affinity of man with the planet earth. Heart means the close affinity of man with the world. Heart means the close affinity of man with the existence of the world. It is thus not surprising that the great scientists are often the great human beings, and it is these great human beings who have made the great discoveries of the world. Certainly, Newton and Einstein are among these great human beings.

Reason may contribute to the human moral life by analyzing, through its logical or rational power, what happens in the human life. That is, through its analysis, the logical or rational nature of the human moral existence may be revealed. The moral symmetry is part of the symmetry fulfilled or realized in man. The aesthetic symmetry is part of the symmetry fulfilled or realized in man. The logical or rational symmetry is part of the symmetry fulfilled or realized in man. The moral life is part of the human life. The moral existence is part of the human existence. The aesthetic life is part of the human life. The aesthetic existence is part of the human existence. The logical or rational life is part of the human life. The logical or rational existence is part of the human existence. To live as man is to live the moral life, the aesthetic life and the logical or rational life. To exist as man is to exist with the moral existence, the aesthetic existence and the logical or rational existence. The human life does not just mean the moral life. The human life does not just mean the aesthetic life. The human life does not just mean the logical or rational life. The human existence does not merely mean the moral existence. The human existence does not merely mean the aesthetic existence. The human existence does not merely mean the logical or rational existence. The human life means the moral life, the aesthetic life, and the logical or rational life. The human life means all of them. The human life means them all. The human existence means the moral existence, the aesthetic existence, and the logical or rational existence. The human existence means all of them. The human existence means them all.

The moral life, the aesthetic life and the logical or rational life constitute, together, the humoral life of man. The moral existence, the aesthetic existence and the logical or rational existence constitute, together, the humoral existence of man. The humoral existence of man is an inherent or integrated existence of man. That is, the humoral existence of man may not be such a kind of existence compartmentalized in such a way that the moral existence, the aesthetic existence and the logical or rational existence may have nothing to do with each other. No. That might not be the case. The humoral being of man may not be that simple. The humoral existence of man may not be that straightforward. The moral existence, the aesthetic existence and the logical or rational existence may all play their roles in the life of man, and they may all have something to do with each other, in some sense, or to some extent, as they constitute together the humoral existence of man. Through the participation of reason in the human life, things associated with the human existence may be analyzed, examined or investigated. As a result, we may acquire a better understanding about ourselves, about life, or about the things happening in our lives. Equipped with such a logical or rational understanding of the human life, we may be able to live our lives in a more rational, logical, or orderly manner. Such may contribute to our moral existence in the world as a whole.

In the same sense, it might be said, reason may contribute to the human aesthetic life, through its logical or rational power. Just as with the things associated with the human moral life, reason may exercise its logical or rational power with regard to the kind of things associated with the human aesthetic life. That is to say, through the logical or rational analysis, examination or investigation by reason, we may be able to see, more clearly, into the state or nature of the things associated with the human aesthetic existence. As a result, we may live a better or richer life, in an aesthetic sense, or in an aesthetic way.

To further our discussion, let us here take the Parthenon as an example. The Parthenon is famed for its beauty, and it might be said, reason might have played a significant role in the coming into being of its beauty. When we view the Parthenon, what do we see? It seems, we would be impressed by the appearance of so many mathematical or geometric elements in its structure. The lines, the triangles, the rectangles, the mathematical proportions, the geometric forms ... All of such mathematical or geometric presence appears to remind us that a logical or rational mind might have been behind the planning, design or construction of such a great architecture.

People have talked about the use of the golden ratio in the construction of the Parthenon. Though the measurements may not exactly support such a claim, nevertheless, it seems, we may indeed observe in its structure, to a certain extent, the kind of things associated with such a rule. The golden ratio has been considered a mathematical or geometric proportion associated with beauty. Its application may be observed in many artistic works, such as architectures or paintings. It is a ratio deemed to be the most pleasing to the human eye. In other words, when it comes to beauty or art, it might be said, the golden ratio may be regarded as an aesthetic proportion.

The golden ratio is a mathematical proportion, and yet, it seems, it may be regarded as an aesthetic proportion. The golden ratio is a geometric form, and yet, it seems, it may be associated with beauty. In such a sense, it might be said, the golden ratio may be seen as representing or standing for, in a sense, the connection between mathematics or geometry and beauty, or between reason and beauty. It is the beauty perceived in a mathematical proportion. It is the beauty felt in a geometric form. It is the beauty coming into being in a mathematical proportion. It is the beauty appearing in a geometric form. It is the beauty coming into being through a mathematical proportion. It is the beauty appearing through a geometric form. It is the mathematical beauty. It is the geometric beauty. It is the logical beauty. It is the rational beauty.

Beauty may have something to do with mathematics. Beauty may have something to do with geometry. Beauty may have something to do with logic. Beauty may have something to do with reason. Beauty may come into being in or through the mathematical proportions. Beauty may appear in or through the geometric forms. Beauty may be observed in the mathematical entities. Beauty may be found in the geometric structures. Beauty may be observed in the lines, triangles, or rectangles. Beauty may be found in the structures built with mathematical proportions or geometric forms. The Parthenon thus becomes a masterpiece of beauty, expressed in the mathematical proportions or geometric forms. The Parthenon thus stands as a masterwork of beauty, fulfilled or realized in the logical or rational senses, or through the logical or rational ways.

Certainly, it has to be said, the beauty of the Parthenon does not solely come from the mathematical or geometric elements fulfilled or realized in its structure. Apart from the logical or rational beauty, beauty may also be observed or perceived in the moral meanings that the Parthenon represents. The Parthenon embodies the Greek piety towards the gods. It is a temple built for the gods. It is a temple built for the harmonious coexistence of humans and gods. It is a temple built for the religious activities. It is a temple built for the moral life of the human beings. It is a temple built for the humoral cultivation of man.

The moral beauty, or the beauty observed or perceived in the Parthenon in a moral sense may be seen as the humoral beauty, as it represents or stands for the humoral aspiration or cultivation of the ancient human beings. The antean beauty of the Parthenon may be seen in the sense that, as a temple, as a shrine, it connects man with nature, with the mother earth. It is situated on a mountaintop. It is surrounded by the mountains. It looks on the valleys. It looks on the fields. It surveys nature. It watches the human world. It serves as the antean link of man with the antean origin, or with the antean world. The intellectual beauty of the Parthenon may be seen, in a sense, as the logical or rational beauty, as such beauty represents or stands for the human intellectual efforts or endeavors. The comparative beauty of the Parthenon may be seen in the comparative harmony found in its structure. The formal beauty of the Parthenon may be seen in its various harmonious forms, including the geometric forms.

The beauty of the Parthenon represents all these beauties. The beauty of the Parthenon is constituted by all these beauties. The beauty of the Parthenon is a harmonic unity of all these beauties. The beauty of the Parthenon is a harmonic unity of all these beauties, integrated together, in a harmonious or harmonic way. The logical or rational beauty may be seen in the Parthenon. The moral beauty may be seen in the Parthenon. The aesthetic beauty may be seen in the Parthenon. The Parthenon is a harmonic unity of the logical or rational beauty, the moral beauty and the aesthetic beauty. The Parthenon is a harmonic unity of reason, morality, and beauty. The logical or rational power of man fulfils or realizes itself in the Parthenon. The moral power of man fulfils or realizes itself in the Parthenon. The aesthetic power of man fulfils or realizes itself in the Parthenon. The humoral man fulfils or realizes himself in the Parthenon. This is the beauty of the Parthenon. This is why the Parthenon is beautiful. This is why the Parthenon is a masterpiece of beauty in the world.

The beauty of the historical temples or architectures found in other cultures may be discussed in a similar manner. Just like the Parthenon, they may be found to exhibit beauty in some remarkable ways. And, needless to say, they express or manifest beauty in their own ways. The mathematical proportions may be found in them. The geometric forms may be observed in them. The moral meanings may be perceived in them. The humoral aspirations may be sensed in them. The antean harmony may be felt in them. The intellectual efforts may be discerned in them. The comparative agreement may be recognized in them. The formal beauty may be seen in them. They represent the harmonic unity of the logical or rational beauty, the moral beauty and the aesthetic beauty. They stand for the harmonic unity of reason, morality and beauty. They embody the fulfillment or realization of the logical or rational power, the moral power and the aesthetic power. They are the masterpieces of beauty. They are the masterworks of the humoral man. They are the monuments signifying the fulfillment or realization of the humorality of man. They are the monuments standing for the greatness of man.

While we discuss the possible contribution made by reason to the human moral or aesthetic life, we may have to pay attention, at the same time, to the kind of things, such as, to what extent reason may contribute to the moral or aesthetic life, or, in what senses? That is to say, we may have to see into the true nature of the kind of contribution possibly made by reason to the human moral or aesthetic life. The golden ratio may be seen as a proportion or form associated with beauty. But, we may have to ask, why, in what sense, or, how? How is such a ratio associated with beauty? How is such a form perceived as beautiful? Is it the case that such a proportion is associated with beauty because it is mathematical? Is it the case that such a form is perceived as beautiful because it is geometric? That might not be the case, it might be said, as so many things are mathematical or geometric and yet they may not be deemed as beautiful. So, what is really the source of the beauty associated with the golden ratio? What constitutes the beauty in such a proportion? What is the essence of the beauty seen in such a form? It might be said, it is the feeling, it is the sense. It is the harmonic feeling. It is the harmonic sense. It is the harmonic feeling coming into being through the sensing of the humoral man. It is the harmonic sense coming into being through the humoral man feeling such a proportion or perceiving such a form. It may be mathematical in a logical or rational sense, but it is harmonic in the aesthetic sense. It may be geometric in a logical or rational sense, but it is humoral in the aesthetic sense. That is to say, in other words, what constitutes the beauty associated with the golden ratio may not be, in essence, mathematics or geometry, but the harmonic or humoral feeling of man. It is the harmonic feeling of the golden ratio that makes the beauty. It is the harmonic feeling of the golden ratio that constitutes the beauty. It is the humoral feeling of the golden ratio that makes the beauty come into being. It is the humoral feeling of the golden ratio that leads to the appearance or coming into being of the kind of beauty we may feel or perceive in such a kind of proportion or form. It is harmonic. It is humoral. It is not, it might be said, mathematical. It is not, it might be said, geometric.

Such may also be seen in that, no matter how mathematical or geometric the proportions or forms might be, if they are not integrated together in a harmonic manner, no beauty may come out as a result. The Parthenon is a great architecture, but what happens if all the structures were not integrated together in a harmonic manner? I think, we could easily imagine it. The beauty associated with such a kind of building would disappear. And no beauty might be felt or perceived, even if some of its parts might be perfectly mathematical or geometric. If the Parthenon was not a harmonic unity of all its parts, the beauty of the Parthenon might collapse. If the Parthenon was not a harmonic unity of all the mathematical proportions or geometric forms, the beauty of the Parthenon might disappear. That is to say, what ultimately determines the beauty of the Parthenon is the harmonic unity that it possesses. It is the harmonic unity that determines the beauty. It is the harmonic unity that gives rise to the beauty. It is harmony that determines beauty. It is harmony that gives rise to beauty. It is harmony that means beauty. That is to say, it might be said, the mathematical or the geometric may not be the kind of things that ultimately determine the beauty of things.

Who plays the major role? Who constitutes the foundation? Who means the essence? Who defines? Who establishes? Who determines? These are the kind of questions that we may have to ask when we talk about the kind of things associated with morality, beauty, or reason. Reason may contribute to the moral life of man, but it may not define, establish, or determine the moral life of man. Reason may contribute to the aesthetic life of man, but it may not define, establish, or determine the aesthetic life of man. The moral life of man is defined, established or determined by the moral symmetry. The moral life of man is defined, established or determined by the moral power. The moral life of man is defined, established or determined by the moral heart of man.

The aesthetic life of man is defined, established or determined by the aesthetic symmetry. The aesthetic life of man is defined, established or determined by the aesthetic power. The aesthetic life of man is defined, established or determined by the aesthetic heart of man. Reason means the logical or rational symmetry. Reason means the logical or rational power. The logical or rational symmetry defines, establishes or determines the logical or rational life of man. Reason is the power of man in the logical or rational life. Reason is powerful in this realm. Reason is powerful in this domain. While reason may be powerful in its realm, it may not constitute the essence of morality or beauty. While reason may be powerful in its domain, it may not constitute the foundation of the moral or aesthetic life of man. Reason may be powerful in its own realm, but it may lose its direction when it deals with morality or beauty. Reason may be powerful in its own domain, but it may be powerless, when it comes to the moral or aesthetic life of man.

§ 5.3.4 Morality, Beauty, Reason, and the Humorality of Man

Symmetry fulfils or realizes itself in man as the moral symmetry, the aesthetic symmetry and the logical or rational symmetry. Symmetry fulfils or realizes itself in man as the moral power, the aesthetic power and the logical or rational power. Symmetry fulfils or realizes itself in man as the moral heart, the aesthetic heart and reason. Symmetry fulfils or realizes itself in man as morality, beauty and reason. Morality thus comes into being, as the fulfillment or realization of the moral symmetry in man. Beauty thus comes into being, as the fulfillment or realization of the aesthetic symmetry in man. Reason thus comes into being, as the fulfillment or realization of the logical or rational symmetry in man. Man is the fulfillment or realization of symmetry. Man is the fulfillment or realization of the symmetries. Symmetry fulfils or realizes itself in man. Symmetry fulfils or realizes itself through man. The symmetries fulfill or realize themselves in man. The symmetries fulfill or realize themselves through man. Man appears, symmetry fulfils or realizes itself. Man appears, the symmetries fulfill or realize themselves. Man appears, the moral symmetry fulfils or realizes itself. Man appears, the aesthetic symmetry fulfils or realizes itself. Man appears, the logical or rational symmetry fulfils or realizes itself. Man appears, morality comes into being. Man appears, beauty comes into being. Man appears, reason comes into existence, in the world.

With the coming into being of man, morality, beauty and reason come into being. Morality, beauty and reason are the fulfillment or realization of man. Morality, beauty and reason are the fulfillment or realization of man in symmetry. Morality, beauty and reason are the fulfillment or realization of symmetry in man. Morality, beauty and reason are the fulfillment or realization of man in the symmetries. Morality, beauty and reason are the fulfillment or realization of the symmetries in man. Morality is the fulfillment or realization of the moral symmetry. Morality is the fulfillment or realization of the moral power. Morality is the fulfillment or realization of the moral heart of man. Beauty is the fulfillment or realization of the aesthetic symmetry. Beauty is the fulfillment or realization of the aesthetic power. Beauty is the fulfillment or realization of the aesthetic heart of man. Reason is the fulfillment or realization of the logical or rational symmetry. Reason is the fulfillment or realization of the logical or rational power. Reason is the fulfillment or realization of the logical or rational power in man.

The humorality of man is the fulfillment or realization of the humoral symmetries in man. The humorality of man is the fulfillment or realization of the humoral symmetries in the world. The humorality of man is the fulfillment or realization of the moral symmetry, the aesthetic symmetry, and the logical or rational symmetry in man. The humorality of man is the fulfillment or realization of the moral symmetry, the aesthetic symmetry, and the logical or rational symmetry in the world. The humorality of man is the fulfillment or realization of the moral power, the aesthetic power, and the logical or rational power in man. The humorality of man is the fulfillment or realization of the moral power, the aesthetic power, and the logical or rational power in the world. The humorality of man is the fulfillment or realization of the moral heart, the aesthetic heart, and reason in man. The humorality of man is the fulfillment or realization of the moral heart, the aesthetic heart, and reason in the world.

Humorality means morality, beauty, and reason. Humorality means morality, beauty, and rationality. Humorality means the true, the good, and the beautiful. Humorality means the true, the good and the beautiful coming into being in or through the humoral symmetries.

The Way of Heaven

Humorality means the true, the good and the beautiful fulfilled or realized in or through the humoral symmetries. Humorality means the true fulfilled or realized in or through the logical or rational symmetry. Humorality means the good fulfilled or realized in or through the moral symmetry. Humorality means the beautiful fulfilled or realized in or through the aesthetic symmetry. The humorality of man means the humoral symmetries. The humoral symmetries mean the humorality of man. The humorality of man expresses the humoral symmetries. The humorality of man demonstrates the humoral symmetries. The humorality of man embodies the humoral symmetries. The humorality of man represents or stands for the humoral symmetries. The humorality of man fulfils or realizes the humoral symmetries. The humoral symmetries constitute the humorality of man. The humoral symmetries are behind the humorality of man. The humoral symmetries are underlying the humorality of man. The humoral symmetries fulfill or realize the humorality of man.

The humorality of man means the good. The humoral man means the good. To be true is good, so that man may come into being. To be man is good, so that the true may come into being, be preserved, protected, safeguarded or upheld. The coming into being of the humoral man means the coming into being of the good. The appearance of the humoral man in the world means the appearance of the good in the world. The coming into being of the humorality of man means the coming into being of the good. The appearance of the humorality of man in the world means the appearance of the good in the world. The humorality of man comes into being; the good appears. The humorality of man appears; the good comes into being. The humorality of man comes into being; the moral symmetry appears. The humorality of man appears; the moral symmetry comes into being. The humorality of man means the moral symmetry. The humorality of man means the coming into being of the moral symmetry.

The moral symmetry fulfils or realizes itself in man as morality. The moral symmetry fulfils or realizes itself in man as the humoral symmetry. The moral symmetry fulfils or realizes itself in man as the humorality of man. Morality is the humorality of man in a moral sense. Morality is the humorality of man in a moral manner. Morality is the humorality of man in a moral fashion. Morality is the humorality of man in a moral way. Morality is the humorality of man fulfilled or realized in the moral symmetry. Morality is the humorality of man fulfilled or realized through the moral power. Morality is the humorality of man fulfilled or realized in or through the moral heart of man. Morality is the humorality of man fulfilled or realized through the humoral man. Morality is the humorality of man fulfilled or realized through the humoral man in man. Morality is the humorality of man fulfilled or realized through the humoral man in the world.

Symmetry is behind the coming into being of things. Symmetry is behind the existence of things. Harmony may be seen as a state or process in which, or through which, symmetry exists, or fulfils itself. The symmetric powers may be seen as the kind of things behind such a state or the kind of things driving such a process. Symmetry itself may be regarded as a state or form of harmony. Thus, it might be said, the harmonic may be seen as what characterizes the coming into being or existence of things. Beauty is a feeling. Beauty is a feeling of the coming into being or existence of things. The humorality of man means the coming into being of the humoral man. The humoral man comes into being to feel the world. The humoral man feels the coming into being of the world. The humoral man feels the existence of the world. The humoral man feels the coming into being of things. The humoral man feels the existence of things. The humoral man feels the harmonic coming into being of things. The humoral man feels the harmonic existence of things.

It is this harmonic coming into being that is significant. It is this harmonic coming into being that is meaningful. It is this harmonic coming into being that is fundamental. It is this harmonic coming into being that is essential. It is this harmonic coming into being that is beautiful. It is this harmonic existence that is significant. It is this harmonic existence that is meaningful. It is this harmonic existence that is fundamental. It is this harmonic existence that is essential. It is this harmonic existence that is beautiful. This is the harmonic feeling. This is the harmonic sense. This is the humoral feeling. This is the humoral sense. This is the humoral feeling that is harmonic. This is the humoral sense that is harmonic. This is the humoral feeling that is beautiful. This is the humoral sense that is called beauty. This is the beautiful. This is beauty. This is the coming into being of beauty.

The humoral man feels the harmonic coming into being of the world; beauty appears. The humoral man feels the harmonic existence of the world; beauty comes into being. The humorality of man comes into being; the humoral man senses or perceives beauty in the harmonic coming into being or existence of the world. The humorality of man appears; the humoral man comes to be aware of, recognize or appreciate the beauty in the harmonic coming into being or existence of the world. The humorality of man comes into being; beauty appears in the humoral man. The humorality of man appears; beauty comes into being in the humoral man. The humorality of man comes into being; beauty appears in the world. The humorality of man appears; beauty comes into being in the world. The humorality of man comes into being; the aesthetic symmetry appears in the humoral man. The humorality of man appears; the aesthetic symmetry comes into being in the humoral man. The humorality of man comes into being; the aesthetic symmetry appears in man. The humorality of man appears; the aesthetic symmetry comes into being in the world.

The humorality of man means the aesthetic symmetry in the humoral man. The humorality of man means the aesthetic symmetry in man. The humorality of man means the aesthetic symmetry in the world. The humorality of man means the aesthetic symmetry. The humorality of man means the coming into being of the aesthetic symmetry. The humorality of man means the fulfillment or realization of the aesthetic symmetry. The humorality of man means the pursuit of the beautiful. Through the pursuit of the beautiful, the humoral man fulfils or realizes himself, in an aesthetic sense, and at the same time, he fulfils or realizes the aesthetic symmetry. As we have discussed, the fulfillment or realization of the aesthetic symmetry means the pursuit of the beautiful. That is to say, as the aesthetic symmetry fulfils or realizes itself in the humoral man, as beauty, it might be said, it is to fulfill or realize the humorality of man, in an aesthetic sense. In an aesthetic sense, the fulfillment or realization of the aesthetic symmetry is the fulfillment or realization of the humorality of man. In an aesthetic sense, the fulfillment or realization of the humorality of man is the fulfillment or realization of the aesthetic symmetry. It is in such a sense that, it might be said, to fulfill the humorality of man is to realize the aesthetic symmetry, and to realize the aesthetic symmetry is to fulfill the humorality of man.

The coming into being of the humorality of man means the coming into being of the humoral truth in man, or in the world. The coming into being of the humoral truth means the coming into being of the true and the false in man, or in the world. That is to say, with the coming into being of the humorality of man, the logical or rational symmetry appears in man, or in the world. The humorality of man comes into being; the logical or rational symmetry appears. The humorality of man appears; the logical or rational symmetry comes into being. The humorality of man means the logical or rational symmetry. The humorality of man means the coming into being of the logical or rational symmetry. The logical or rational symmetry fulfils or realizes itself in man as reason. Reason is the fulfillment or realization of the logical or rational symmetry in man. Reason is the fulfillment or realization of the logical or rational symmetry in the humoral man. Reason is the fulfillment or realization of symmetry in the humoral man in a logical or rational sense, in a logical or rational manner, or in a logical or rational way. Reason is the fulfillment or realization of the humoral man in a logical or rational sense, in a logical or rational manner, or in a logical or rational way. Reason is the fulfillment or realization of the humorality of man in a logical or rational sense, in a logical or rational manner, or in a logical or rational way.

Reason is the humoral man expressed in a logical or rational sense. Reason is the humoral man demonstrated in a logical or rational manner. Reason is the humoral man fulfilled or realized in a logical or rational way. Reason is the logical essence of the humoral man. Reason is the rational nature of the humoral man. Reason is the logical essence of man. Reason is the rational nature of man. Reason is, in such a sense, at the heart of the humorality of man. Reason is, in such a sense, at the core of the humorality of man. Reason is, in such a sense, at the heart of man. Reason is, in such a sense, at the core of man.

The humorality of man means the moral symmetry, the aesthetic symmetry and the logical or rational symmetry. The humorality of man means morality, beauty and reason. The fulfillment or realization of the humorality of man means the fulfillment or realization of morality, beauty and reason. The fulfillment or realization of morality, beauty and reason means the fulfillment or realization of the humorality of man. It is the humoral life of man. It is the humoral existence of man. It is the humoral meaning of man. The humoral life of man means the fulfillment or realization of the humorality of man. The humoral existence of man means the fulfillment or realization of morality, beauty and reason. The humoral meaning of man means the fulfillment or realization of the humorality of man through morality, beauty and reason, or, the fulfillment or realization of morality, beauty and reason through the endeavors, efforts or struggles of the humoral man.

The Way of Heaven

Having discussed morality, beauty and reason in a humoral sense, thus far, we may have to remind ourselves in the sense that, people may still ask certain questions about them. Why is it the case that evil has to come into being? Why is it the case that ugliness has to exist? Why is it the case that the false has to appear? It seems, it is possible that, as far as we can see, it might be said, evil might not have to come into being, ugliness might not have to exist, and the false might not have to appear. That is, in a sense, it might be said, such a world might be possible in which only good, beauty or the true might be present. That is to say, in a sense, it might be said, it seems possible that a world might only possess or witness good, beauty, or the true.

Why is it not the case? Why is such a world not with us? It seems, first, if only good, beauty and the true exist in a world, that is, no evil, ugliness or the false in such a world, then there would be no such things as good, beauty or the true in such a world, in the end. Good, beauty and the true exist, it seems, only if evil, ugliness and the false are present. If evil does not exist, it seems, there would be no such thing as good. If ugliness does not exist, it seems, there would be no such thing as beauty. If the false does not exist, it seems, there would be no such thing as the true. That is, it seems, they exist together, they come into existence together, and they may disappear together. That is, it seems, they form the symmetries. They exist as symmetries. They come into being as symmetries. They come into existence as symmetries.

Secondly, if only good, beauty and the true come into being and no existence of evil, ugliness or the false, then, it seems, the humorality of man might not have come into existence. The coming into being of the humoral man means both the true and the false. The humoral man does not just mean the true. The humoral man means both the true and the false. The humoral man means differentiating the true from the false or the false from the true. If only the true exists and no such thing as the false, then, it seems, the humorality of man might collapse by itself. The humorality of man means both good and evil. The humorality of man means both beauty and ugliness. If only good and beauty exist and no such things as evil or ugliness, then good and beauty might not be good or beautiful in the end, and the humorality of man might not be humoral at all.

Lastly, when we ask the kind of questions such as, why does evil have to appear, why does ugliness have to exist, or why does the false have to come into being, it seems, we are asking, ultimately, the kind of fundamental questions concerning symmetry. Why is it symmetry? Why do things exist in symmetry? Why do things come into being in symmetry? Why do things come into existence with symmetry? Why is it the case that symmetry looks behind things? Why is it the case that symmetry may constitute the foundation of things? Why is it the case that symmetry may constitute the essence of things? Why? Why? Why symmetry? It may be beyond us. As the human beings, we may be able to reveal certain secrets of nature, or of the world, but the kind of things concerning symmetry itself or its workings or operations may be beyond our human rational understanding, or beyond our human reach.

§ 5.3.5 The Rational Truth, the Rational Being

Symmetry fulfils or realizes itself in a double helical way in the world, and we see the double helical nature of the genetic foundation of living things. Symmetry fulfils or realizes itself in a sexual way in the world, and we witness the world of sexuality. Symmetry fulfils or realizes itself in an electric way in the world, and we see the world of electricity. Symmetry fulfils or realizes itself in a magnetic way in the world, and we witness the magnetic phenomena of the world. Symmetry fulfils or realizes itself in a logical or rational way in the world, and the logic or rationality of the world may be revealed.

Symmetry fulfils or realizes itself in a logical or rational way in man, and the logical or rational symmetry appears or comes into being in the humoral man. The humoral man fulfils or realizes himself; the logical or rational symmetry fulfils or realizes itself. The logical or rational symmetry fulfils or realizes itself in the humoral man; reason comes into being. As the fulfillment or realization of the logical or rational symmetry in the humoral man, reason may share the same nature with the logical or rational fulfillment or realization of symmetry in the world. That is to say, as the fulfillment or realization of the logical or rational symmetry, reason may work or operate with the logic or rationality of the world, a reflection, a representation, or a manifestation of the fulfillment or realization of symmetry in a logical or rational way in the world.

The rational truth thus comes into being. As reason works or operates with the logic or rationality of the world, as reason grasps the logical or rational structures of the world, as reason reaches the logical or rational fulfillments or realizations of symmetry in the world, the rational truths are being revealed to us. The rational truths may be seen as indicating the symmetric coming into being of things in a logical or rational way. The rational truths may be seen as illustrating the symmetric existence of things in a logical or rational sense. The rational truths may be seen as revealing the workings or operations of symmetry in the world in a logical or rational manner. The rational truths may be seen as standing for the fulfillment or realization of symmetry in the world in a logical or rational fashion.

It is through reason that the rational truths are discovered. It is through reason that the rational truths are disclosed. It is through reason that the rational truths are being revealed to us, or to the world. Reason is the power to reach the rational truths. Reason is the power to discover the rational truths. Reason is the power to reveal the rational truths to the world. Reason is the fulfillment or realization of the logical or rational symmetry in the humoral man. Reason is the logical or rational power of the humoral man. Reason is the humoral power of man to grasp the logical or rational fulfillment or realization of the world. Reason is the humoral power of man to understand the logical or rational fulfillment or realization of symmetry. Reason is the humoral power of man to comprehend the logical or rational fulfillment or realization of the world in symmetry. Reason is the humoral power of man to make sense of the logical or rational fulfillment or realization of symmetry in the world.

The being of the world associated with the rational truth may be seen as the rational being of the world. Thus, the rational being of the world may be seen as the kind of being that may be understood, comprehended, or grasped by reason, or through reason. It is the being associated with logic. It is the being associated with rationality. It is the being that may be reached by reason, or through reason. The rational being is the logical or rational coming into being of things. The rational being is the logical or rational existence of things. The rational being is the logical or rational coming into being of things guided, conditioned, supported, or underpinned by symmetry. The rational being is the logical or rational existence of things guided, conditioned, supported, maintained, or sustained by symmetry.

§ 5.3.6 Heart, Feeling, Reason, and Mind

It may have to be said, the heart does not just mean the moral or aesthetic feelings. The heart is rich in feelings. The heart is rich in a whole range of feelings. Apart from the moral feelings or the aesthetic feelings, a whole range of other feelings may be found in the heart. The antean feelings may be found in the heart. When we see the rocks, when we see the grasses, when we see the leaves, when we see the flowers, when we see the plants, when we see the animals, we may feel in our hearts a sense of closeness with them, a sense of ease, a sense of peace, or a sense of closeness with the mother earth. These are the antean feelings in our hearts. These feelings may not be seen as the moral feelings, or treated as having developed into the aesthetic feelings, as they may just represent or stand for a sense of human connection with nature, or a sense of human affinity to the mother earth.

The animal feelings may be found in the heart. The animal feelings may refer to the kind of human feelings associated with the animal nature of man, and at the same time, such feelings may be seen as having to do, to a certain extent, with the human nature of man. The animal feelings may be seen, for example, in the kind of rich or sometimes passionate feelings associated with sex. We may have witnessed how animals may act or behave when it comes to sex. They are usually excited, agitated, or passionate. Such feelings may also be observed in the humans. When such kind of feelings happen to the humans, they may not be regarded as the moral or aesthetic feelings, in the sense that, they may only demonstrate the animal nature of the human beings, and as the animal beings, it might be said, human beings, though human, may not be able to act or behave otherwise in such circumstances.

The moral heart may be seen as the fulfillment or realization of the moral symmetry in the humoral man. The aesthetic heart may be seen as the fulfillment or realization of the aesthetic symmetry in the humoral man. The moral heart and the aesthetic heart may thus be seen as the fulfillment or realization of the humoral symmetries in the humoral man, representing or standing for the humoral feelings in the heart of man. While the moral feelings and the aesthetic feelings may be seen as the humoral feelings in the heart, some humoral feelings in the heart may not be seen as the moral or aesthetic feelings. Such as, in certain cases, the human fellow feelings may be regarded as neither moral feelings nor aesthetic feelings. That is to say, while such feelings may be humoral, they may not be regarded as moral or aesthetic in their nature, in a strict sense. We may have the experience that, when we are alone in a place for some time, we would be happy to see the appearance of a human person on the scene. The appearance of such a human person may prompt in us a sense of human closeness, a sense of human affinity, or a sense of human bond. Such human fellow feelings may not be seen as the moral or aesthetic feelings, as they may only represent or stand for the kind of human relationship coming into being through the human fellowship or species-ness.

The humoverse feelings, such as jealousy, may not be regarded as the moral feelings in the sense that, they may only represent or stand for the humoverse nature of man, and as such they may not be treated as being good or evil, in the humoverse sense. That is to say, such feelings may only be seen as humoverse in nature, as part of the human existence, in a sense, before they may actually generate or lead to the possible evil things. In other words, it might be said, the humoverse feelings may not be exactly the evil feelings. Before the humoverse feelings generate or lead to the evil things, they may be regarded as humoverse in nature. When such humoverse feelings actually generate or lead to the evil things, then, it might be said, they may be regarded or treated as evil.

Thus, it seems, apart from the moral or aesthetic feelings, a whole range of other feelings may be found in the heart. They may be the antean feelings. They may be the animal feelings. They may be the humoral feelings. They may be the humoverse feelings. All these feelings constitute, together with the moral feelings and the aesthetic feelings, the heart, that is, the heart of man. The heart is thus rich in its feelings. The heart is thus rich in its representation or reflection of the nature of man. It may represent or reflect the antean nature of man. It may represent or reflect the animal nature of man. It may represent or reflect the humoral nature of man. It may represent or reflect the humoverse nature of man. It represents the nature of man. It reflects the being of man. It stands for the existence of man.

The mind may be seen as the mental activities or functions associated with the kind of things such as thinking, reasoning, consciousness, imagination, or memory. The metaphysical nature of the mind may be seen in the kind of things such as ideas, concepts or images with which the mind may work or operate. Ideas, concepts or images may be seen as different from the feelings that constitute the heart, in that, while feelings may also be associated, to a certain extent, with the mental activities or processes, just like ideas, concepts or images, they may be regarded as exhibiting in a prominent sense the physical nature of their existence. In other words, it might be said, compared to the feelings, ideas, concepts or images, or the mind, may be regarded as being metaphysical in nature. That is to say, while the heart is closely associated with the feelings, the mind may be seen as the mental activities or functions primarily involving the kind of things like ideas, concepts or images that may be regarded as metaphysical in their nature.

The coming into being of the mind may be seen as a gradual process, with the development of the human nervous system as its foundation. In the initial stages, the mind, as the mental activities or functions, might have been closely associated with the physical or sensory activities or functions, such as feelings or perceptions. But with the development of the human nervous system, the human brain, the mind might have gradually developed into the kind of faculties involving the mental activities or functions with remarkable complexity or sophistication, such as, involving the kind of abstract or metaphysical operations or processes with ideas, concepts or images. It is through such a process, it might be said, that, reason, or the logical or rational mind, gradually comes into being, and constitutes, in a sense, the mainstay or backbone of the mind.

The development of the human nervous system or the human brain may be seen, in a sense, as the foundation for the appearance or coming into being of the humorality of man. That is to say, the development of the human nervous system or the human brain may be seen as having prepared the way for the fulfillment or realization of the humoral man in the world. The fulfillment or realization of the logical or rational symmetry may be seen as part of the fulfillment or realization of the humoral man in the world. The development of the human nervous system or the human brain may thus be seen as having prepared the way for the fulfillment or realization of the logical or rational symmetry in the humoral man. That is to say, the development of the human nervous system or the human brain may be seen as constituting, in a sense, the foundation for the appearance or coming into being of reason.

With the development of the human nervous system or the human brain, reason, as the logical or rational power, gradually appears. With the development of the human nervous system or the human brain, the mind gradually comes into being. Reason, or the kind of logical or rational mental activities or functions closely associated with reason, may be seen as the logical or rational mind. Apart from the logical or rational mind, the mind may be seen as also including the other kinds of mental activities or functions, such as the kind of mental activities or processes associated with consciousness, feelings, or perceptions.

Compared with the logical or rational mind, the mind associated with the feelings or perceptions may not be regarded as lower or inferior, in the sense that, it might be said, it is such feelings or perceptions that constitute, in a sense, the very being or existence of man, or, the foundation for the very being or existence of man. On the other hand, it might be said, in the logical or rational sense, reason is the mind, or, the mind is reason. That is, it might be said, reason may be seen as what fulfils or realizes the mind in a logical or rational way and the mind may be seen as what fulfils or realizes itself in the world in a logical or rational manner as reason. It is in such a sense that, it might be said, reason may be seen as lying at the core of the mind, in that, through reason, the mind fulfils or realizes the logical or rational symmetry, or through reason, the logical or rational symmetry fulfils or realizes itself in the mind.

Man is humoral. The humorality of man means that man is both physical and metaphysical. That is to say, man is not just metaphysical, or, man is not just mental. The mental or metaphysical nature of the mind may thus be seen as what separates the mind, in a sense, from man, or, from the humoral being or existence of man, or, it might be said, from the very being or existence of man. A gulf may thus be seen between the mind and man. A gulf may thus be seen between the mind and the humorality of man. A gulf may thus be seen between the mind and the existence of man in the world.

It is a gulf, in a sense, from the physical to the mental. It is a gulf, in a sense, from the physical to the metaphysical. It is a gulf, in a sense, from feeling to reason. It is a gulf, in a sense, between the physical and the mental. It is a gulf, in a sense, between the physical and the metaphysical. It is a gulf, in a sense, between feeling and reason. The physical man gives rise to the human nervous system or the human brain. The physical man gives rise to the humorality of man. The physical man gives rise to the humoral being or existence of man. The physical man constitutes the foundation of man. The physical man constitutes the foundation of the humoral man. The physical man constitutes the foundation of the humoral being or existence of man.

It is the physical that gives rise to the mental. It is the physical that gives rise to the metaphysical. It is the physical that gives rise to the humoral. The physical is the foundation of the mental. The physical is the foundation of the metaphysical. The physical is the foundation of the humoral. The physical is not low. The physical is not inferior. The physical is not trivial. The physical is not insignificant. The physical is not inconsequential. The physical is significant. The physical is fundamental. The physical is vital. The physical is essential.

The feelings of man constitute, in a sense, the physical man. The feelings of man constitute, in a sense, the humoral man. The feelings of man constitute, in a sense, the fundamental man. The feelings of man constitute, in a sense, the essential man. The feelings of man constitute, in a sense, the physical being or existence of man. The feelings of man constitute, in a sense, the humoral being or existence of man. The feelings of man constitute, in a sense, the fundamental being of man. The feelings of man constitute, in a sense, the essential existence of man. The feelings of man constitute, as we know, it might be said, the heart of man.

The rich feelings of man connect man with himself. The rich feelings of man connect man with the world. The rich feelings of man connect man with his humoral being or existence in the world. The rich feelings of man nurture man. The rich feelings of man support man. The rich feelings of man maintain man. The rich feelings of man sustain man. The rich feelings of man preserve man. The rich feelings of man protect man. The rich feelings of man safeguard man. The rich feelings of man uphold man. The heart, with its rich feelings, connects man with himself or the world. The heart, with its rich feelings, connects man with his humoral being or existence in the world. The heart, with its rich feelings, nurtures or supports man. The heart, with its rich feelings, maintains or sustains man. The heart, with its rich feelings, preserves or protects man. The heart, with its rich feelings, safeguards or upholds man. The heart, with its rich feelings, directs or guides man in his humoral being or existence in the world.

Certainly, the mind may not be separated completely from the body, that is, from the human nervous system or the human brain, that is, from the physical existence of man. But, as the workings or operations of the mind primarily involve the kind of metaphysical things like ideas, concepts or images, it might be said, the nature of the mind may be seen as primarily metaphysical. That is, while a certain sense of connection may exist between the mind and the body, the mind and the body may not be seen as possessing the same nature. While the body is physical, the mind may be mental. While the body is physical, the mind may be regarded, primarily, as metaphysical. It is in such a sense that, it might be said, compared with the heart, the mind may not be seen as so strongly connected with the physical man.

On the other hand, it may have to be said, the feelings are often associated with certain mental activities or processes, in the sense that, it may be hard for us to separate the feelings completely from the possible mental activities or processes involved. That is to say, in a sense, it might be said, the mental aspects of the heart may be seen as what stand for the metaphysical nature of the heart. In other words, it might be said, while the mind may be regarded primarily as metaphysical, the heart may better be seen, in a sense, as possessing a double nature of being both physical and metaphysical. The physical nature of the heart may be seen in the sense that it is often the case that certain physical reactions or responses may be observed as accompanying the happening of the feelings. The metaphysical nature of the heart may be seen in that the feelings may be associated, to some extent, with the mental activities or processes.

The double nature of the heart may be seen as having to do, in a sense, with the double nature of the humorality of man, or with the double nature of the humoral man. The humorality of man involves both the physical man and the metaphysical man. That is, it is often the case that, both physical and mental activities may be observed in the humoral man. The heart may be seen as the fulfillment or realization of the humoral man. The double nature of the heart may be seen as a reflection or representation of the double nature of the humoral man, or of the humorality of man. And it might be said, it is such double nature that distinguishes the heart, in a sense, from the mind. While the mind is mental, the heart is physical. While the mind is metaphysical, the heart is perceptual. While the metaphysical nature of the mind distances the mind, in a sense, from man, the physical nature of the heart connects man with himself. While the metaphysical nature of the mind constitutes, in a sense, a gulf between the mind and the existence of man, the physical or perceptual nature of the heart supports, maintains, or sustains the connection between man and his existence in the world.

The metaphysical may delude. The metaphysical may misinform. The metaphysical may mislead. The metaphysical may misguide. The metaphysical is not physical. The metaphysical may not be so basic that it could inform man correctly. The metaphysical may not be so fundamental that it could lead man in an appropriate way. The metaphysical may not be so essential that it could guide man in the right direction. The metaphysical may not be so solid that it could support man. The metaphysical may not be so raw, fresh, pure or natural that it could maintain or sustain the existence of man in the world. This may be why, as we can see, the mind may work or operate to metaphysicalize man into a mere emptiness, meaninglessness, or nothingness.

The raw and physical feelings of man constitute the basic being of man. The raw and physical feelings of man constitute the fundamental existence of man. The raw and physical feelings of man constitute the essential being of man. The raw and physical feelings of man constitute the foundation of man. The raw and physical feelings of man constitute the foundation of the humoral man. The raw and physical feelings of man constitute the foundation of the humoral being or existence of man. The raw and physical feelings of man nurture man. The raw and physical feelings of man support man. The raw and physical feelings of man maintain or sustain the existence of man. This may be why, the heart, with its raw and physical feelings, may prevent man from being metaphysicalized into a mere emptiness, meaninglessness, or nothingness.

The heart, with its antean, animal, humoral or humoverse feelings, with its raw and physical feelings, with its basic, fundamental or essential feelings, constitutes the foundation of man. It is with the heart that man comes into being. It is with the heart that man appears. It is with the heart that man lives. It is with the heart that man exists in the world. It is with the heart that the humoral man comes into being. It is with the heart that the humoral man appears. It is with the heart that the humoral man exists in the world. The heart of man anchors man in the anteanity of man. The heart of man anchors man in the humorality of man. The heart of man anchors man in the antean life of man. The heart of man anchors man in the humoral being or existence of man. With the heart, man exists. With the heart, man lives. With the heart, man

The Way of Heaven

thrives. With the heart, man prospers. With the heart, man flourishes. With the heart, man may walk into a future that is bright, meaningful, and full of hope.

Certainly, it has to be said, the humoral being or existence of man means both the heart and the mind. That is, the humoral being or existence of man does not just mean the heart or the mind, respectively. Man means both the heart and the mind. The being or existence of man means both the heart and the mind. The life of man means both the heart and the mind. The humorality of man means both the heart and the mind. The humoral man means both the heart and the mind. The heart alone may not constitute man. The mind alone may not constitute man. It takes both the heart and the mind to be man. It takes both the heart and the mind to exist as man. It takes both the heart and the mind to live as man. It takes both the heart and the mind to fulfill or realize man, as man.

Both the heart and the mind participate in the humoral being or existence of man. Both the heart and the mind participate in the humoral life of man. Both the heart and the mind may have to be involved in the humoral being or existence of man. Both the heart and the mind may have to be involved in the humoral life of man. That means, in many cases, or in many circumstances, it may often be the case that it may be very difficult to distinguish the heart from the mind or the mind from the heart. That is, it may be very difficult to tell the role of the heart from the role of the mind, or, the role of the mind from the role of the heart. That is, the humoral being or existence of man may be so complex, subtle, deep, or profound that, in a sense, it might be said, the heart and the mind may be inevitably connected, and when we talk about the humoral being or existence of man, we may have to take both of them into consideration, in some sense, in some way, in some manner, or to some extent.

Avolution and Man

§ 5.4 The Tree of Symmetry

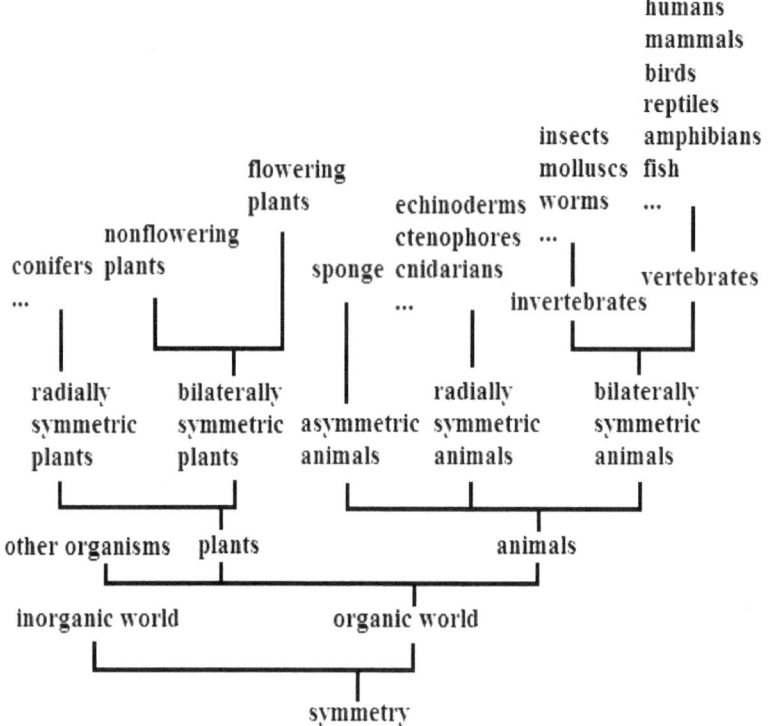

Figure 5.4   The Tree of Symmetry

This may be seen as the tree of symmetry.

Does life emerge by chance? Does life develop by luck? Does the development of the various life forms a random thing, with absolutely no direction? Do the seemingly strange body forms of the early animals make no sense? Who claims, it is pure chance? Who claims, it is pure luck? Who claims, it is a totally random thing? Who claims, it has no direction? Who claims, it makes no sense?

When it comes to the development of life, it seems, some people may see it as bush-like, while others may claim that it may be a linear process. How to see the development of life? Is it bush-like? Or is it a linear process? Is it a tree? Or is it trees? Is it a tree of life? Or is it the trees of life? Is it a single tree? Is it a bush? Is it a woods? Or is it a forest? Such may be seen in the tree of symmetry. The single tree may

The Way of Heaven

be the tree of symmetry. From the tree of symmetry, the trees of life sprout. From the tree of symmetry, the trees of life grow. From the tree of symmetry, the trees of life may have developed.

Many trees of life may be observed in the tree of symmetry. The tree of organic life may be observed in the tree of symmetry. The tree of plant life may be observed in the tree of symmetry, branching out radially symmetrically and bilaterally symmetrically. The tree of animal life may be observed in the tree of symmetry, branching out asymmetrically, radially symmetrically and bilaterally symmetrically. With the development of life, the trees of life thrive and flourish. We may observe them in the tree of symmetry, such as, the tree of radially symmetric plants, the tree of bilaterally symmetric plants, the tree of asymmetric animals, the tree of radially symmetric animals, or the tree of bilaterally symmetric animals. Certainly, more trees of life may be observed in the tree of symmetry, such as, the tree of non-flowering plants, the tree of flowering plants, the tree of invertebrates, or the tree of vertebrates. And, it seems, if we investigate further into the various life forms, more trees of life may appear and come into sight.

The tree of symmetry may be seen as branching out into asymmetry, radial symmetry and bilateral symmetry. In such a sense, it might be said, the trees of symmetry may be seen in the tree of symmetry. That is, the tree of asymmetry, the tree of radial symmetry and the tree of bilateral symmetry may be seen in the tree of symmetry. The tree of asymmetry may be seen as branching out into sponges and the kind of extinct organisms like stylophorans. The tree of radial symmetry may be seen as branching out into the radially symmetric plants and radially symmetric animals. The radially symmetric plants may be seen as the plants like conifers or ginkgo. The radially symmetric animals may include cnidarians, ctenophores or echinoderms. The tree of bilateral symmetry may be seen as branching out into the bilaterally symmetric plants and bilaterally symmetric animals. The bilaterally symmetric plants may include the non-flowering plants and flowering plants. The bilaterally symmetric animals may include invertebrates and vertebrates. Invertebrates may be seen as the animals like worms, mollusks or insects. Vertebrates may be seen as the animals like fish, amphibians, reptiles, birds, mammals, or humans.

Life on earth has to do with DNA. DNA plays a fundamental role in the development or existence of life on earth. DNA has to do with the double helical symmetry. In such a sense, it might be said, the tree of double helical symmetry may be seen in the tree of symmetry. Sexual reproduction may be observed in animals and plants. The coming into being of sexual reproduction has to do with the sexual symmetry. In such a sense, it might be said, the tree of sexual symmetry may be seen in the tree of symmetry. The electric force and the magnetic force may be found in nature. The electric force and the magnetic force may be found in the inorganic world and organic world. The electric force has to do with the electric symmetry. The magnetic force has to do with the magnetic symmetry. In such a sense, it might be said, the tree of electric symmetry and the tree of magnetic symmetry may be seen in the tree of symmetry. The humorality of man may be observed in humans. The humorality of man has to do with morality, beauty and truth. Morality has to do with the moral symmetry. Beauty has to do with the aesthetic symmetry. Truth has to do with the logical symmetry. In such a sense, it might be said, the tree of moral symmetry, the tree of aesthetic symmetry and the tree of logical symmetry may be seen in the tree of symmetry.

The trees of symmetry may be seen in the tree of symmetry. The trees of symmetry may be observed in the tree of symmetry. The tree of asymmetry may be seen in the tree of symmetry. The tree of radial symmetry may be seen in the tree of symmetry. The tree of bilateral symmetry may be seen in the tree of symmetry. The tree of double helical symmetry may be seen in the tree of symmetry. The tree of sexual symmetry may be seen in the tree of symmetry. The tree of electric symmetry may be seen in the tree of symmetry. The tree of magnetic symmetry may be seen in the tree of symmetry. The tree of moral symmetry may be seen in the tree of symmetry. The tree of aesthetic symmetry may be seen in the tree of symmetry. The tree of logical symmetry may be seen in the tree of symmetry. Apart from these ten trees of symmetry observed in the tree of symmetry, is it possible that other trees of symmetry may be found in the tree of symmetry? It may be possible, such as, the other forces in nature may have to do with the other symmetries.

Stems may be seen in the trees of symmetry, or in the tree of symmetry. Such stems may be called the symmetric stems, or, the heavenly stems. Branches may be seen in the trees of symmetry, or in the tree of symmetry. The trees of life may be seen as constituting such branches, in an organic way. Branches may also be seen in the inorganic world, as symmetry may fulfill or realize itself inorganically. Such branches may be called the earthly branches, as they may have to do with the things on earth, such as, minerals, water, air, plants, animals, or humans.

The trees of symmetry and the trees of life constitute the tree of symmetry. The heavenly stems and the earthly branches constitute the tree of symmetry. The trees of symmetry and the trees of life constitute nature. The heavenly stems and the earthly branches constitute nature. The trees of symmetry and the trees of life constitute the things of the world. The heavenly stems and the earthly branches constitute the things of the world. The trees of symmetry and the trees of life constitute the world. The heavenly stems and the earthly branches constitute the world.

§ 5.5 The Being of Man

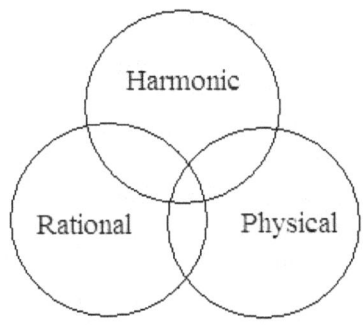

Figure 5.5 The Being of Man

This may be seen as the being of man. This may be seen as the structure of man. This may be seen as the structure of being reflected or realized in the being of man.

Man means heart, mind, and body. Man means the harmonic being, the rational being, and the physical being. Heart may be seen as having to do with the harmonic being of man. Mind may be seen as having to do with the rational being of man. Body may be seen as having to do with the physical being of man. Body may be seen as having to do with the physical being of man, in the sense that, it embodies the physical being of man, or it represents or demonstrates the fulfillment or realization of the physical being of man. Mind may be seen as having to do with the rational being of man, in the sense that, mind may be seen, in a sense, as the fulfillment or realization of the rational being of man, or, the rational being of man may be seen, in a sense, as the fulfillment or realization of mind.

Heart is the feelings of man. Heart is the humoral feelings of man. Heart is the harmonic feelings of man. Through feelings, man feels his existence. Through feelings, man feels his humoral existence. Through feelings, man feels his harmonic existence. Through feelings, man feels his being. Through feelings, man feels his humoral being. Through feelings, man feels his harmonic being. Through the coming into being of man, the feelings of man come into being. Through the coming into being of man, the feelings of man are deposited in man. Through the coming into being of man, the humoral feelings of man come into being. Through the coming into being of man, the humoral feelings of man are deposited in man.

Man comes into being as the fulfillment or realization of symmetry. Man comes into being as the fulfillment or realization of harmony. Through the coming into being of man, the harmonic feelings of man come into being. Through the coming into being of man, the harmonic feelings of man are deposited in man. The heart with the humoral feelings may be seen as the humoral heart. That is, the heart constituted by the humoral feelings may be seen as the humoral heart. In such a sense, heart may be seen as humoral. The heart with the harmonic feelings may be seen as the harmonic heart. That is, the heart constituted by the harmonic feelings may be seen as the harmonic heart. In such a sense, heart may be seen as harmonic.

Mind, working through reason, may be seen as metaphysical in nature. Heart is about feelings. While feelings may involve mental processes, feelings may be seen as possessing, in a sense, a physical nature. That is, compared to mind, it might be said, heart, while humoral or harmonic, may be seen as possessing, in a sense, at the same time, a physical nature. It is this physical nature that may be seen as bridging the humoral or harmonic heart with the harmonic, such that the humoral or harmonic heart may eventually be able to reach or grasp the harmonic, while mind may not.

While heart may be seen as physical, mind may be seen as metaphysical. Feeling is, in a sense, physical. Feeling may be seen as direct. Feeling may be seen as connecting with the harmonic physically. Feeling may be seen as connecting with the harmonic directly. Heart may be seen as connecting with the harmonic physically. Heart may be seen as connecting with the harmonic directly. The metaphysical mind may not connect with the harmonic physically. The metaphysical mind may not connect with the harmonic directly. That is, while heart may feel the harmonic, it might be said, mind may not. The physical nature of heart may thus constitute, in such a sense, a bridge between heart and the harmonic. The metaphysical nature of mind may thus stand, in such a sense, as a barrier between mind and the harmonic. Such a barrier may prevent mind from physically or directly reaching or grasping the harmonic. Heart may thus be able to reach or grasp the harmonic being, in a sense, while mind may not.

Certainly, this may not necessarily mean that, mind may not contribute to our grasp or understanding of the harmonic. No. It may not be the case. Mind may contribute to our grasp or understanding of the harmonic, in or through its own ways. Reason is powerful. Reason may exhibit its power in leading us to see deeper into the harmonic being of the world. Reason may reveal the deep or complex rational mechanisms or processes associated with the harmonic being of the world. In such a way, reason may help us find the rational foundation upon which, it may be possible, we may acquire a solid grasp or understanding of the harmonic being of the world.

That is to say, while mind may not reach or grasp the harmonic physically or directly, it may operate, through the working of reason, in such a way that some solid grasp or understanding of the harmonic being of the world may be acquired by us. That is to say, mind may contribute to our grasp or understanding of the harmonic, and mind may help heart, when it comes to the understanding or grasp of the harmonic. Mind may help heart, in discovering the structures or arrangements. Mind may help heart, in revealing the rational mechanisms or processes. Mind may help heart, in seeing the rational bases. Mind may help heart, in finding the rational being or existence of the world associated with the harmonic being or existence of the world. Mind may help heart; heart may feel better. Mind may help heart; heart may feel deeper. Mind may help heart; heart and mind may

Avolution and Man

work together. Together, they may enable man to see deeper into the harmonic. Together, they may enable man to have a better grasp or understanding of the harmonic being of the world.

It is in such a sense that, it might be said, heart may be seen as having to do with the harmonic being of man. Heart may be seen as having to do with the harmonic being of man, in the sense that, with the help of mind, heart may come to grasp or understand that, man comes from symmetry or harmony and the symmetric or harmonic being may be seen as the foundation of the being of man. Heart may be seen as having to do with the harmonic being of man, in the sense that, with the help of mind, heart may come to grasp or understand that, the being of man is part of the being of the world, and the harmonic being of man is part of the harmonic being of the world. They are related. They are closely related. They are intrinsically related. They are innately related. They are symmetrically related. They are harmonically related.

That heart may be seen as having to do with the harmonic being of man may also be seen in that, heart may be seen as the foundation of man, heart may be seen as the support of man, heart may be seen as the guide of man. When feelings are damaged, heart would be damaged. When heart is damaged, man would be damaged. When heart is damaged, mind would be damaged. Mind would lose its foundation. Mind would lose its support. Mind would lose its guide. Mind would lose its direction. When mind is lost, man would be lost.

§ 5.6 Harmony and Avolution

What are, in the end, plants? It might be said, plants are, in the end, the result or consequence of the movement of symmetry. What are, in the end, animals? It might be said, animals are, in the end, the result or consequence of the movement of symmetry. What are, in the end, plants? It might be said, plants are, in the end, the result or consequence of the movement of harmony. What are, in the end, animals? It might be said, animals are, in the end, the result or consequence of the movement of harmony. It is the movement of symmetry that has given rise to the plants. It is the movement of symmetry that has given rise to the animals. It is the movement of harmony that has given rise to the plants. It is the movement of harmony that has given rise to the animals. It is the progress of symmetry that may be seen as behind the

The Way of Heaven

coming into being of plants. It is the progress of symmetry that may be seen as behind the coming into being of animals. It is the progress of harmony that may be seen as behind the coming into being of plants. It is the progress of harmony that may be seen as behind the coming into being of animals.

The movement of symmetry may be seen as behind the plant world. The movement of symmetry may be seen as behind the animal world. The progress of harmony may be seen as behind the plant world. The progress of harmony may be seen as behind the animal world. The movement of symmetry may be seen as behind nature. The movement of harmony may be seen as behind nature. The progress of symmetry may be seen as behind nature. The progress of harmony may be seen as behind nature.

The Primordial explosion and the Devonian explosion may be seen as two of the most significant events in the history of life on earth, or in the history of earth. They are so significant that, it seems, such two events, happened during the Ediacaran, the Cambrian and the Devonian, still control or govern the animal life and the plant life on earth, even to this day. They established the animal life as we know today. They established the plant life as we know today. They established nature as we know today. They established the world as we know today. How could they have such power? How could they have such energy? How could they have such far-reaching effects?

Is it evolution? It seems, no. the symmetric animal body plans might have come into being about 500 million years ago. And it seems, animals living today may be traced back to such early animal body plans. The symmetric plant body plans, represented by the symmetric plant leaves, might have appeared about 360 million years ago. And it seems, the symmetric structures of the early plant leaves may be observed today. How is it the case that something stays even after 500 million years? How is it the case that something remains even after 360 million years?

Is it evolution? The answer may be, no. if it were evolution, things might have changed, somehow, during such a long 500 or 360million years, due to various factors, such as environmental, ecological, geological, atmospheric, or climatic. It is not evolution. It is avolution. It is symmetry. It is harmony. It is not the evolutionary process. It is the avolutionary process. It is the symmetric movement. It is the harmonic progress.

Avolution and Man

It is not just evolution; it is avolution. It is not merely evolution; it is avolution. It is avolution either in a radially symmetric manner, or in a bilaterally symmetric fashion. It is avolution that is behind evolution. It is evolution guided by harmony. It is evolution led by symmetry. It is evolution underpinned by symmetry. It is evolution maintained through harmony. It is evolution sustained through symmetry. It is evolution preserved through harmony. It is the harmonic movement on earth. It is the symmetric movement in the world. It is the harmonic fulfillment. It is the symmetric realization.

Harmony gives rise to animals. Harmony gives rise to plants. Symmetry gives rise to animals. Symmetry gives rise to plants. To see into the coming into being of animals, one has to see into harmony. To see into the coming into being of plants, one has to see into harmony. To see into the coming into being of animals, one has to seen into symmetry. To see into the coming into being of plants, one has to see into symmetry. The fundamental secrets of animals lie in harmony. The fundamental secrets of plants lie in harmony. The fundamental secrets of animals lie in symmetry. The fundamental secrets of plants lie in symmetry. To understand nature, one has to understand harmony. To understand nature, one has to understand symmetry.

When one sees grasses, one sees man. When one sees leaves, one sees man. When one sees flowers, one sees man. When one sees plants, one sees man. When one sees animals, one sees man. They come from the same source. They come from the same origin. They come from the same root. They come from the same fountainhead. They share the same symmetric source. They share the same symmetric origin. They share the same symmetric root. They share the same symmetric fountainhead.

When one walks in the woods, one is walking in symmetry. When one walks on the fallen leaves, one is walking on symmetry. When one walks in the woods, one is walking in harmony. When one walks on the fallen leaves, one is walking on harmony. Symmetry is with us. Symmetry is around us. Harmony is with us. Harmony is around us. Symmetry exists amid us. Symmetry lives amid us. Harmony exists amid us. Harmony lives amid us.

People have lived with the grasses all their lives. People have lived with the bilaterally symmetric leaves all the time. People have lived with the symmetric flowers. People have lived with harmony. People have lived with symmetry. Then, why haven't people seen the secrets in the grasses? Why haven't people seen the secrets in the leaves? Why haven't people seen the secrets in the beautiful flowers? Why cannot people see into harmony? Why cannot people see into symmetry? Why cannot people see into the significant being of harmony? Why cannot people see into the magnificent existence of symmetry? It seems, in a sense, it might be said, it may have to do with reason. Reason may not understand symmetry. Reason may not understand harmony. Reason may not grasp symmetry. Reason may not grasp harmony. Reason may not reach symmetry. Reason may not reach harmony.

What is symmetry? Symmetry is meaning. Symmetry is complexity. Symmetry is strength. Symmetry is power. What is symmetry? Symmetry is what gives rise to the grasses. Symmetry is what gives rise to the leaves. Symmetry is what gives rise to the flowers. Symmetry is what gives rise to the plants. Symmetry is what gives rise to the animals. Symmetry is what gives rise to the humans. Grasses are the meaning of symmetry realized in nature. Leaves are the complexity of symmetry fulfilled in the world. Flowers are the beauty of symmetry expressed. Plants are the strength of symmetry demonstrated in the plant life. Animals are the power of symmetry exhibited in the animal life. Humans are the magnificence and splendor of symmetry fulfilled or realized in the world.

Where does the humorality of man come from? From symmetry. Where does the humoral man come from? From symmetry. Where does the human being come from? From symmetry. Where does the human existence come from? From symmetry. As the meaning of the world, symmetry gives rise to the humorality of man. As the complexity of the world, symmetry gives rise to the humoral man. As the strength of the world, symmetry brings the human being into the world. As the power of the world, symmetry makes the human existence possible in the world, or in the universe.

The coming into being of man is the avolutionary coming into being of man. The coming into being of man is the humoralization of man. The humoralization of man is the avolutionary coming into being of man. The avolutionary coming into being of man is the humoralization of man. What is man? Man is the human expression of symmetry in animals. Man is the human expression of symmetry in nature. Man is the humoral expression of symmetry in animals. Man is the humoral expression of symmetry in nature. Man is the humoral fulfillment of symmetry in animals. Man is the humoral realization of symmetry in nature.

Symmetry is behind the existence of grasses. Symmetry is behind the existence of leaves. Symmetry is behind the existence of flowers. Symmetry is behind the existence of plants. Symmetry is behind the existence of animals. Symmetry is behind the existence of humans. Symmetry is behind things. Symmetry underlies things. Symmetry supports things. Symmetry maintains things. Symmetry sustains things. Symmetry is the foundation of things. Symmetry is the fundamental being of things. Symmetry is the essential being of things. Symmetry is the innate existence of things. Symmetry is the intrinsic existence of things. Symmetry is the fundamental being of nature. Symmetry is the essential existence of the world.

What is symmetry? What is in symmetry? What does symmetry mean? What is behind symmetry? What underlies symmetry? What gives rise to symmetry? What makes symmetry possible? What makes symmetry happen? What makes symmetry occur? What makes symmetry come into being? What makes symmetry appear in grasses, leaves, flowers, plants, animals, or humans? Why does symmetry have to appear? Why does symmetry have to emerge? Why does symmetry have to come into being? Why does symmetry have to appear in grasses? Why does symmetry have to appear in leaves? Why does symmetry have to appear in flowers? Why does symmetry have to emerge in plants? Why does symmetry have to come into being in animals? Why does symmetry have to fulfill itself in humans? Why does symmetry have to realize itself in the world?

We may live with grasses. We may live with leaves. We may live with flowers. We may live with plants. We may live with animals. But, do we know symmetry? We may live with symmetry, but to what extent do we know symmetry? How does it work? How does it come into being? How does it appear? How does it emerge? How does it fulfill or realize itself? Nature is deep. The world is deep. Nature is subtle. The world is subtle. Nature is complex. The world is complex. Nature is profound. The world is profound.

Should science be dismissed? Should the scientific method be disregarded? Or, should the scientific knowledge be discredited? It seems, the answer should be, No. Science is important to our human life. The scientific method is a fundamental way for us to look into nature, and the scientific knowledge is the foundation of our

The Way of Heaven

understanding of the world. If we want to see into nature, it seems, in a certain sense, we have to follow the scientific way. If we want to acquire some reliable knowledge about the world, it seems, in a certain sense, we have to follow the scientific method. In other words, in a certain sense, it might be said, it is the scientific method that may underlie our search into nature, and it is the scientific knowledge, accumulated through the ceaseless and sustained efforts of scientists and researchers, that may constitute the foundation of our understanding about the world.

While science is important and the scientific knowledge may constitute the foundation of our understanding about the world, at the same time, it seems, we may have to keep in our mind that, reason is limited, and science may not lead us to see all the secrets of the world. Reason may lead us to probe into the world of particles, but it may not lead us to comprehend symmetry. Science may lead us to look into outer space, but it may not lead us to grasp harmony. It appears, symmetry is behind the things around us, such as, plants or animals, and yet, reason seems to be unable to reach it. It appears, harmony underlies the things in the world, and yet, science seems to be incapable of unlocking such basic, intrinsic, or fundamental secrets of the world.

Reason may not be able to reach the kind of fundamental things underlying nature such as symmetry. Science may not be capable of explaining the kind of innate or intrinsic things existing deeply in the world such as harmony. Reason or science may not be able to explain the coming into being of grasses. Reason or science may not be able to explain the coming into being of leaves. Reason or science may not be able to explain the coming into being of flowers. Reason or science may not be able to explain the coming into being of plants. Reason or science may not be able to explain the coming into being of animals. Reason or science may not be able to explain the coming into being of humans. Reason or science may not be able to explain the coming into being of nature. Reason or science may not be able to explain the coming into being of the world.

It seems, one may ask, how could reason explain the deep, complex, or profound being on earth that is called man? Or, how could science account for the deep, complex, or profound existence on earth that is called life? While we recognize the importance of reason or science, at the same time, it seems, we should not come to such an understanding that, reason is all, or, reason means all, or, science is all, or, science means all, or that, all things of the world may be understood through reason, or, all things of the world may be grasped by or through science.

Reason is not all. Science is not all. Reason does not mean all. Science does not mean all. Reason is not all to man. Science is not all to man. Reason does not mean all to man. Science does not mean all to man. Reason does not mean all to the world. Science does not mean all to the world. There are things that reason may not be able to understand. There are things that reason may never be able to understand. There are things that science may not be able to grasp. There are things that science may never be able to grasp.

What does this mean? It means, in a sense, that, it might be said, the world is not completely rational, or, the world is not completely scientific. If the world were completely rational, the world might not have been what we experience now. If the world were completely scientific, the world might never have come into being. The world may not be rational; it is symmetric. The world may not be scientific; it is harmonic. If the world were rational, the world might not have been an actual world. If the world were scientific, the world might not have been the real world. That is, a rational world may not be an actual world. That is, the scientific world may not be the real world. The world is not just rational; it is symmetric. The world is not just scientific; it is harmonic. It is symmetry that, in a sense, constitutes the foundation of the things of the world. It is not reason. It is harmony that, in a sense, constitutes the essence of the things in the world. It is not science.

Symmetry gives rise to reason, in a sense, through giving rise to the highly developed nervous system. Reason, on the other hand, may not be able to give rise to symmetry, as it may not even be capable of grasping such a thing. In such a sense, it might be said, symmetry is higher than reason, or, symmetry is deeper than reason, or, symmetry is mightier than reason, or, symmetry is beyond reason. It is in such a sense, it might be said, that, the world is higher than reason, or, the world is deeper than reason, or, the world is beyond reason. Or, in other words, it might be said, that, the world is higher than science, or, the world is deeper than science, or, the world is beyond science.

It is in such a sense that, it might be said, it is not surprising that the scientific and technological advancement may lead, in a sense, to the deanteanization and dehumoralization of the human beings, and that, the rational way may lead, in a sense, to the disintegration or destruction of man. The rational way may lead to the disruption of the harmonic existence of man. The rational way may lead to the disruption of the harmonic existence of nature. The rational way may lead to the disruption of the harmonic existence of the world. The rational way may lead to the destruction of nature. The rational way may lead to the destruction of man. The rational way may lead to the destruction of the world.

The great philosopher Lao Tzu says, the great voice has no sound, and the great phenomenon has no shape. Harmony is the great phenomenon. Harmony is the great voice. Harmony has no shape. Harmony has no sound. With no shape, harmony underlies things. With no sound, harmony permeates things. With no shape, harmony supports tings. With no sound, harmony sustains things. With no shape, harmony lives in things. With no sound, harmony exists in the world.

As the great phenomenon, harmony is so great that we may not be able to see it, and yet it may exist in the things around us. As the great voice, harmony is so great that we may not be able to hear it, and yet it may exist in the things of the world. Though we may not be able to see it, we cannot overlook it. Though we may not be able to hear it, we cannot ignore it. Can we overlook its possible workings? Can we ignore its possible operations? Can we overlook its possible workings in nature? Can we ignore its possible operations in the world? It seems, we cannot. We cannot overlook its workings in grasses. We cannot overlook its workings in leaves. We cannot overlook its workings in flowers. We cannot ignore its operations in plants. We cannot ignore its operations in animals. We cannot ignore its operations in humans. We cannot overlook its workings in nature. We cannot ignore its operations in the world.

Look at the stars, what do we see? We see a world high above us. Look at the stars, what do we see? We see a world far beyond us. The world is so big that, it seems, we are only a part of it. The world is so large, so great, so expansive, and so infinite that, it seems, we are only a very, very small part of it. The way of the world may be high above us. The way of the world may be beyond us. The secrets of nature may be beyond us. The secrets of the universe may be beyond us. The workings or operations of harmony in nature may be beyond us. The workings or operations of harmony in the world may be beyond us. The workings or operations of harmony in the universe may be beyond us.

Avolution and Man

A grass may contain the profound secrets of the world. A leaf may contain the profound secrets of the world. A flower may contain the profound secrets of the world. A tree may display the profound secrets of the world. An animal may manifest the profound secrets of the world. What secrets out there may we have missed? What profound secrets of the world may we have overlooked or ignored? What higher things may we have failed to take notice? What deeper things may we have failed to understand? What higher beings may we have failed to comprehend? What deeper beings may we have failed to grasp? What might be the higher being of things that we may be unable to see? What might be the higher being of the world that we may be unable to hear? What might be the deeper existence of things that we may be unable to feel? What might be the deeper existence of the universe that we may be unable to tell?

When we look at the stars, are we looking at something that we may not fully understand? When we look at the stars, are we looking at something that may be shielded from us? When we look at the stars, are we looking at something that may be hidden from us? Are there secrets? Are there secrets out there? Are there secrets out there that may be deep? Are there secrets out there that may be profound? Are there secrets out there that may be unfathomable to us?

When we look at the stars, should we wonder, is it a higher being manifesting itself? Is it a higher being expressing itself? Is it a higher being revealing itself? Or, what may be the meaning? What may be the message? What may be the purpose? That is, in a sense, when we look at the stars, should we ask ourselves, what do we know? Do we know ourselves? Do we know the world? Do we know the stars? Do we know the universe? What things might be beyond our reach? What things might be beyond our understanding? What things might be waiting for our comprehension? What deep or profound things might still be out there waiting for our human understanding or grasp?

§ 5.7 What is the Way of Heaven?

What is symmetry? What is harmony? What is behind symmetry? What is behind harmony? What makes symmetry possible? What makes symmetry work? What makes symmetry operate? What makes harmony possible? What makes harmony work? What makes harmony operate? What is the way of heaven? What is heaven?

Heaven is deep. The way of heaven is deep. Heaven is profound. The way of heaven is profound.

What is the being of symmetry? What is the existence of symmetry? What is the working of symmetry? What is the operation of symmetry? What is the movement of symmetry? What is the development of symmetry? What is the fulfillment of symmetry? What is the realization of symmetry?

What is the being of harmony? What is the existence of harmony? What is the working of harmony? What is the operation of harmony? What is the movement of harmony? What is the development of harmony? What is the fulfillment of harmony? What is the realization of harmony?

Heaven is above us. Heaven is high. Heaven is lofty.

Symmetry is in plants. Symmetry is in animals. Symmetry is in flowers. Symmetry is in man. Symmetry is behind plants. Symmetry is behind animals. Symmetry is behind flowers. Symmetry is behind man. Harmony is in plants. Harmony is in animals. Harmony is in flowers. Harmony is in man. Harmony is behind plants. Harmony is behind animals. Harmony is behind flowers. Harmony is behind man. Symmetry is in the world. Symmetry is behind the world. Harmony is in the world. Harmony is behind the world. The way of heaven is in the world. The way of heaven is behind the world. Heaven is in the world. Heaven is behind the world.

Symmetry fulfils or realizes itself in DNA. Symmetry fulfils or realizes itself in sex. Symmetry fulfils or realizes itself in electricity. Symmetry fulfils or realizes itself in magnetism. Symmetry fulfils or realizes itself in morality. Symmetry fulfils or realizes itself in beauty. Symmetry fulfils or realizes itself in truth. Symmetry fulfils or realizes itself in the humorality of man. How does symmetry fulfill or realize itself in such varied ways? How does symmetry achieve it?

Symmetry fulfils or realizes itself in grasses. Symmetry fulfils or realizes itself in leaves. Symmetry fulfils or realizes itself in flowers. Symmetry fulfils or realizes itself in plants. Symmetry fulfils or realizes itself in animals. Symmetry fulfils or realizes itself in humans. How does symmetry fulfill or realize itself in such varied ways? How does symmetry achieve it?

Why is it symmetry? Why is symmetry behind things? Why is symmetry behind DNA? Why is symmetry behind sex? Why is symmetry behind electricity? Why is symmetry behind magnetism? Why is symmetry behind morality? Why is symmetry behind beauty? Why is symmetry behind truth? Why is symmetry behind heart? Why is symmetry behind mind? Why is symmetry behind reason? Why is it good? Why is it evil? Why is it beautiful? Why is it ugly? Why is it true? Why is it false? Why is it genetic? Why is it sexual? Why is it electric? Why is it magnetic? Why is it moral? Why is it aesthetic? Why is it logical? Why is it rational?

Why? Why? Why?

Is it the mystery of symmetry? Is it the mystery of harmony? Is it the mystery of life? Is it the mystery of nature? Is it the mystery of the world? Is it the mystery of the universe? Is it the mystery of the way of heaven? Is it the mystery of heaven?

§ 5.8 Heaven, Earth, and Man

Figure 5.6   Heaven, Earth, and Man

Heaven gives rise to man. Earth supports man. Man represents the realization of the way of heaven on earth.

The way of heaven may be seen in the way of symmetry. The way of heaven may be seen in the way of harmony.

The way of earth may be seen in minerals. The way of earth may be seen in plants. The way of earth may be seen in animals. The way of earth may be seen in humans. The way of earth may be seen in the anteanity of man.

The way of man may be seen in the humoral way. The way of man may be seen in the way of humorality.

Above man is heaven. Above earth is man. Above humorality is harmony. Above anteanity is humorality.

Anteanity is the root of humorality. Harmony is the source of humorality.

Anteanity is fulfilled in humorality. Harmony is realized in humorality.

The way of earth is the root of the way of man. The way of heaven is the source of the way of man.

The way of earth is represented in man. The way of heaven is reflected in man.

The way of earth is fulfilled in man. The way of heaven is realized in man.

Heaven is the father. Earth is the mother. Together, they give rise to plants. Together, they give rise to animals. Together, they give rise to human beings. Together, they give rise to Man.

§5.9 天行健, 君子以自强不息

Heaven moves in a robust manner; ceaselessly, a virtuous human being strives.

Man is the fulfillment of symmetry. Man is the realization of harmony. Man is the fulfillment or realization of the way of heaven on earth. To preserve man is to preserve symmetry. To protect man is to protect harmony. To safeguard man is to safeguard the way of heaven. To uphold man is to uphold the way of heaven on earth.

Symmetry moves; plants come into being. Symmetry moves; animals come into being. Symmetry moves; flowers come into being. Symmetry moves; man comes to the world. Harmony moves; plants grow. Harmony moves; animals develop. Harmony moves; flowers thrive. Harmony moves; the human beings flourish. Heaven moves; the world comes into being. Heaven moves; mankind thrives. Heaven moves; the world prospers and flourishes.

Heaven fulfils itself in plants. Heaven fulfils itself in animals. Heaven fulfils itself in flowers. Heaven fulfils itself in man. The way of heaven fulfils itself in plants. The way of heaven fulfils itself in animals. The way of heaven fulfils itself in flowers. The way of heaven fulfils itself in man.

As the fulfillment of symmetry, man is dignified. As the fulfillment of harmony, man is decent. As the fulfillment of the way of heaven on earth, man is precious. As the realization of symmetry, man is meaningful. As the realization of harmony, man is beautiful. As the realization of the way of heaven on earth, man is noble and magnificent.

Man is the purpose of man. Man is the aim of man. Man is the goal of man. Man is the meaning of man. Man is the justification of man. Man is the aspiration of man. Man is the commitment of man. Man is the fulfillment of man. Man is the realization of man.

Man is the reason of man. Man is the reason of man to be man. Man is the reason of man to exist as man. Man is the reason of man to fulfill himself as man. Man is the reason of man to realize himself as man. Man is the reason of man to fulfill himself as a way of fulfilling the way of heaven. Man is the reason of man to realize himself as a way of realizing the way of heaven. Man is the reason of man to fulfill himself as a fulfillment of heaven in the human life. Man is the reason of man to realize himself as a realization of heaven in the human world.

To fulfill man is to fulfill symmetry. To fulfill man is to fulfill harmony. To fulfill man is to fulfill the way of heaven on earth. To realize man is to realize symmetry. To realize man is to realize harmony. To realize man is to realize the way of heaven on earth.

By pursuing man, man pursues the way of heaven. By pursuing man, man follows the way of heaven. By striving for man, man strives to follow the way of heaven. By striving for man, man strives to fulfill the will of heaven. By striving for man, man strives to realize the purpose of heaven. By striving for man, man harmonizes heaven and man.

Man shoulders the way of heaven. Man extends the way of heaven. Man expresses the way of heaven. Man demonstrates the way of heaven. Man represents the way of heaven. Man embodies the way of heaven. Man fulfils the way of heaven. Man realizes the way of heaven.

The Way of Heaven

The mission of man is to know himself, so that he may know the way of heaven. The mission of man is to know the way of heaven, so that he may know himself. The mission of man is to fulfill himself, so that he may fulfill the way of heaven. The mission of man is to realize the way of heaven, so that he may realize himself. The mission of man is to strive to fulfill or realize himself, so that he may fulfill or realize the way of heaven on earth.

A virtuous human being strives to understand the way of heaven. A virtuous human being strives to understand heaven. A virtuous human being strives to come close to the way of heaven. A virtuous human being strives to come close to heaven. The virtue of man is the understanding of the way of heaven. The virtue of man is the awareness of the way of heaven. The virtue of man is the pursuit of the way of heaven.

The virtue of man is to strive to fulfill the way of heaven, through fulfilling himself. The virtue of man is to strive to realize the way of heaven, through realizing himself. The virtue of man is to strive to fulfill the way of heaven, through fulfilling the way of man. The virtue of man is to strive to realize the way of heaven, through realizing the way of man.

The virtue of man is to follow the way of heaven. The virtue of man is to follow the way of symmetry. The virtue of man is to follow the way of harmony. The virtue of man is to fulfill the way of heaven. The virtue of man is to fulfill the way of symmetry. The virtue of man is to fulfill the way of harmony. The virtue of man is to maintain the way of symmetry, so that the way of heaven may be maintained. The virtue of man is to uphold the way of symmetry, so that the way of heaven may be upheld. The virtue of man is to cultivate the way of harmony, so that the way of heaven may be cultivated. The virtue of man is to uphold the way of harmony, so that the way of heaven may be upheld.

The way of heaven is high. The way of heaven is large. The way of heaven is boundless. The way of heaven is infinite. The way of heaven is deep. The way of heaven is profound. Though man may not be able to fully grasp the way of heaven, man strives. Though man may not be able to fully grasp the way of heaven, man strives to fulfill himself, so that heaven may be fulfilled. Though man may not be able to fully grasp the way of heaven, man strives to realize himself, so that heaven may be realized.

Avolution and Man

The striving of man is the mission of man. The striving of man is the life of man. The striving of man is the being of man. The striving of man is the existence of man. The striving of man is the fate of man. It is the mission placed on man by heaven. It is the life given to man by heaven.

Among the sources of Chinese wisdom is the *Book of Changes*. Some of the discussions in it may have to do with what is called the great cycles. In a sense, it might be said, man may be near the end of a great cycle, and he may be on the threshold to a new era. What to do? To fear? To panic? To fear may not be completely bad, as such a sense of fear may cool man down. To panic may not be totally bad, as such a sense of anxiety or awe may make man to look into himself, to search into himself, to see the kind of things that he may not be able to see otherwise.

Man is still new. Man is still young. Man is still fresh. Compared to the long history of life on earth, man may be regarded as a new creature on this planet. A tender shoot may experience some harsh weathers in its early development, but may still grow into a tall and big tree. A child may undergo a hard childhood, but, with careful cultivation and care, he or she may still grow into an adult human being respectable, decent, dignified, fulfilled or realized.

Man may face some new challenges now. Great forces may conspire, it seems, against him. Many things may not be in our own hands. Many things may be beyond our control. But, it appears, heaven is still strong. Symmetry is still strong. Harmony is still strong. Man is still strong.

The symmetric being of plants is still strong. The symmetric being of animals is still vigorous. The symmetric being of man is still robust. The harmonic existence of plants is still strong. The harmonic existence of animals is still vigorous. The harmonic existence of man is still robust.

Strive to maintain symmetry, so that the symmetric man may continue to exist. Strive to cultivate harmony, so that the harmonic man may continue to live. A virtuous human being strives, so that symmetry may not collapse. A virtuous human being strives, so that harmony may not disappear. A virtuous human being strives, so that the way of heaven may be present in man. A virtuous human being strives, so that heaven may not leave us.

A virtuous human being strives, so that man may not disintegrate. A virtuous human being strives, so that man may not fall apart. A virtuous human being strives, so that man may not disappear from the world. A virtuous human being strives, so that man may not vanish from the universe.

Symmetry is still strong. Harmony is still vigorous. Heaven is still robust. Man is still eager to be man. Man is still eager to be man, to follow the way of heaven. Man is still eager to be man, to fulfill or realize the way of heaven on earth.

Heaven moves in a robust manner; a virtuous human being strives, ceaselessly.

§ 5.10 The Way of Heaven

Symmetry and Harmony

Symmetry is what gives rise to harmony. Harmony is what gives rise to symmetry. Symmetry is what fulfils harmony. Harmony is what realizes symmetry. Symmetry is what leads to harmony. Harmony is what leads to symmetry. Symmetry is the result; harmony is the process. Symmetry is the process; harmony is the consequence. Without symmetry, there would be no harmony. Without harmony, there would be no symmetry. Symmetry is the movement of harmony. Harmony is the movement of symmetry. Symmetry is the development of harmony. Harmony is the development of symmetry. Symmetry is harmony in progress. Harmony is symmetry in movement. Symmetry is the embodiment of harmony. Harmony is the expression of symmetry. Symmetry is the expression of harmony. Harmony is the embodiment of symmetry. Symmetry is harmony realized. Harmony is symmetry fulfilled. Symmetry is the realization of harmony. Harmony is the fulfillment of symmetry.

Symmetry fulfils or realizes itself through harmony. Harmony fulfils or realizes itself through symmetry. Symmetry fulfils or realizes itself in harmony. Harmony fulfils or realizes itself in symmetry. Symmetry is harmony; harmony is symmetry. Symmetry is deep; harmony is profound. Harmony is deep; symmetry is profound. Symmetry, Harmony, the way of Heaven.

Man Is Sacred

Man is sacred. The coming into being of man is sacred. The coming into being of the humoral man is sacred. The coming into being of the humoral truth is sacred. The coming into being of the humoral truth in man is sacred. The coming into being of the humoral truth in the human species is sacred. The coming into being of the humoral truth in animals is sacred. The coming into being of the humoral man in the animal kingdom is sacred. The coming into being of the humoral man as the fulfillment of symmetry is sacred. The coming into being of the humoral man as the realization of harmony is sacred. The coming into being of the humoral man as the expression of the way of heaven is sacred. The coming into being of the humoral man as the demonstration of the way of heaven is sacred. The coming into being of the humoral man as the fulfillment or realization of the way of heaven on earth is sacred.

Heart, Reason, and Symmetry

Heart is the power. Heart is the moral power. Heart is the aesthetic power. Heart is the power coming into being from symmetry. Heart is the moral power coming into being from the moral symmetry. Heart is the aesthetic power coming into being from the aesthetic symmetry. Heart is the humoral power. Heart is the humoral power coming into being from symmetry. Heart is the humoral power fulfilling or realizing symmetry.

Reason is the power. Reason is the logical power. Reason is the logical power coming into being from the logical symmetry. Reason is the power coming into being from symmetry. Reason is the humoral power coming into being from symmetry. Reason is the humoral power fulfilling or realizing symmetry.

The Presence of the Way of Heaven

The way of heaven is present in a leaf. The way of heaven is present in a flower. The way of heaven is present in plants. The way of heaven is present in animals. The way of heaven is present in man. The way of heaven is present in the human life. The way of heaven is present in the world. The way of heaven is present in the universe. The way of heaven may be seen in symmetry. The way of heaven may be seen in harmony. The way of heaven may be seen in symmetry leading to the coming into being of a leaf. The way of heaven may be seen in harmony giving rise to a flower. The way of heaven may be seen in symmetry leading to the coming into being of plants. The way of heaven may be seen in harmony giving rise to animals. The way of heaven may be seen in symmetry leading to the coming into being of man. The way of heaven may be seen in harmony giving rise to the human life. The way of heaven leads to the coming into being of the world. The way of heaven gives rise to the universe.

What Do We Know?

Why do plants grow? Why do animals live? Why do grasses grow? Why do leaves grow? Why do flowers blossom? Why are there stars in the sky? Why is there life on earth? Why do human beings exist in the world? What do we know? Do we know plants? Do we know animals? Do we know grasses? Do we know leaves? Do we know flowers? Do we know stars? Do we know life? Do we know ourselves? Do we know nature? Do we know the world? Do we know the universe? What things do we know? What things do we not know? What things are out there waiting for us to know?

The Movement of Heaven

The movement of symmetry, the movement of harmony, the movement of heaven may be seen in the coming into being of animals, in the coming into being of plants, in the coming into being of flowers, in the coming into being of man. The Ediacaran explosion, about 600 million years ago, may have seen the coming into being of animals. The Devonian explosion, about 400 million years ago, may have seen the coming into being of plants. The Cretaceous explosion, about 100 million years ago, may have seen the coming into being of flowers. With the genus *Homo* appearing about 2.5 million years ago, the planet earth may have seen the coming into being of man. Flowers are the flowers of the plant kingdom. Man is the flower of the animal kingdom. Symmetry moves, Harmony moves, Heaven moves, and the world thrives, prospers, flourishes.

The Way of Heaven, the Way of Man

What is the way of heaven? The way of heaven is the way of symmetry. The way of heaven is the way of harmony. What is the way of the world? The way of the world is the way of symmetry. The way of the world is the way of harmony. The way of the world is the way of heaven.

What is the way of man? The way of man is the way of heaven realized in man. The way of man is the way of heaven fulfilled through man. The way of man is the way of heaven expressed in man. The way of man is the way of heaven demonstrated through man. The way of man is the way of symmetry humoralized in man. The way of man is the way of harmony humoralized through man. The way of man is the way of symmetry realized in man. The way of man is the way of harmony fulfilled through man.

The heavenly way is the symmetric way. The heavenly way is the harmonic way. The heavenly way is the symmetric way expressed in nature. The heavenly way is the harmonic way demonstrated through the world. The heavenly way is the symmetric way realized in the plants. The heavenly way is the harmonic way fulfilled in the animals. The heavenly way is the symmetric way realized in man. The heavenly way is the harmonic way fulfilled through man. The human way is the expression of the heavenly way. The human way is the demonstration of the heavenly way. The human way is the realization of symmetry. The human way is the fulfillment of harmony. The human way is the realization of the heavenly way, in man. The human way is the fulfillment of the heavenly way, through man.

The human way is the humoral way. The human way is the humoral way coming into being from the heavenly way. The human way is the humoral way coming into being from the symmetric way. The human way is the humoral way coming into being from the harmonic way. The human way is the humoral way reflecting the heavenly way. The human way is the humoral way expressing the symmetric way. The human way is the humoral way demonstrating the harmonic way. The human way is the humoral way fulfilling the heavenly way. The human way is the humoral way realizing the symmetric or harmonic way.

Symmetry is behind the world. Symmetry is behind nature. Symmetry is behind life. Symmetry is behind man. Harmony is behind the world. Harmony is behind nature. Harmony is behind life. Harmony is behind man.

The way of heaven is around us. The way of heaven is among us. The way of heaven is in us. The way of heaven is in plants. The way of heaven is in animals. The way of heaven is in grasses. The way of heaven is in leaves. The way of heaven is in flowers. The way of heaven is in nature. The way of heaven is in the world. The way of heaven is in the universe.

Why can't we see the way of heaven? The way of heaven is so plain and deep that, it seems, even if we live with it, we may not see it. The way of heaven is so obvious and profound that, it seems, even if we see it, we may not know what it is, what it means, or what it means to us. The way of heaven is so apparent and intrinsic that, it seems, even if we see it, we may not know what it stands for, what it constitutes, or, what it signifies.

In a sense, it might be said, it may be a wonderful thing that reason cannot easily reach the way of heaven, comprehend the way of heaven, understand the way of heaven, or grasp the way of heaven. Otherwise, it may be expected, given the history of man, the way of symmetry may be dismantled, the way of harmony may be demolished, and the way of heaven may be destroyed. That is, if reason could fully reach the secrets of symmetry, if reason could fully comprehend the secrets of harmony, if man could fully grasp the secrets of heaven, symmetry may be dismantled, harmony may be demolished, man may be annihilated, and heaven may be destroyed.

Man and the Way of Heaven

Man is the fulfillment or realization of the way of heaven on earth. Man is the expression or embodiment of the way of heaven in this world. Man is the way of heaven fulfilled in a human sense. Man is the way of heaven realized in a human way. Man is the way of heaven represented in the human world.

Heart is the bridge between man and the way of heaven. Heart is the connection between man and the way of heaven. Heart is the link between man and heaven. Heart is the way of man to the way of heaven. Heart is the way of the way of heaven to man. Heart is the way of man to heaven. Heart is the way of heaven to man.

Virtue is the way of man to understand the way of heaven. Virtue is the way of man to follow the way of heaven. Virtue is the way of man to safeguard the way of heaven. Virtue is the way of man to uphold the way of heaven. Virtue is the way of heaven expressed in man. Virtue is the way of heaven fulfilled in man. Virtue is the way of heaven realized in man. Virtue is the way of heaven embodied in man.

Virtue is heart. Heart is virtue.

Through heart, heaven accesses man. Through heart, heaven acts on man. Through heart, heaven influences man. Through virtue, man touches heaven. Through virtue, man moves heaven. Through virtue, man influences heaven.

Heaven is the Source of the Things in the World

Do animals share the same root? Do animals share the same origin? Do animals share the same source? Yes. They share the same root. They share the same origin. They share the same source. Do plants share the same root? Do plants share the same origin? Do plants share the same source? Yes. They share the same root. They share the same same origin. They share the same source. Do animals and plants share the same root? Do animals and plants share the same origin? Do animals and plants share the same source? Yes. They share the same root. They share the same origin. They share the same source. Symmetry is the root. Harmony is the origin. The way of heaven is the fountainhead. Heaven is the source of the things in the world.

Beauty

Beauty is the realization of harmony. The realization of harmony is the coming into being of the world. Beauty is a reflection of the coming into being of the world. Beauty is a reflection of harmony. Beauty is a reflection of the world.

So, what is beauty, in the end? Beauty is a reflection of the world. Beauty is a reflection of the coming into being of the world. That is, beauty is a reflection of the fulfillment of the world. That is, beauty is a reflection of the realization of the world. That is, beauty is the coming into being of the world. Beauty is the fulfillment of the world. Beauty is the realization of the world. That is, it might be said, why beauty is, after all, beautiful.

The Way of Heaven

Follow the humoral way. Follow the way of symmetry. Follow the way of harmony. Follow the way of heaven.

May mankind thrive, prosper, and live forever!